GU00992062

CELTIC LINGUISTICS

AMSTERDAM STUDIES IN THE THEORY AND HISTORY OF LINGUISTIC SCIENCE

General Editor
E.F. KONRAD KOERNER
(University of Ottawa)

Series IV - CURRENT ISSUES IN LINGUISTIC THEORY

Volume 68

Martin J. Ball, James Fife, Erich Poppe and Jenny Rowland (eds)

Celtic Linguistics

CELTIC LINGUISTICS
IEITHYDDIAETH GELTAIDD

Readings in the Brythonic Languages
Festschrift for T. Arwyn Watkins

Edited by

Martin J. Ball, James Fife, Erich Poppe and Jenny Rowland

JOHN BENJAMINS PUBLISHING COMPANY
AMSTERDAM/PHILADELPHIA

1990

Library of Congress Cataloging-in-Publication Data

Celtic linguistics = Ieithyddiaeth Geltaidd : readings in the Brythonic languages : festschrift for T. Arwyn Watkins / edited by Martin J. Ball ... [et al.]
p. cm. -- (Amsterdam studies in the theory and history of linguistic science. Series IV, Current issues in linguistic theory, ISSN 0304-0763; v. 68)
Includes bibliographical references.
1. Brythonic languages. 2. Watkins, T. Arwyn. I. Watkins, T. Arwyn. II. Ball, Martin J. III. Title: Ieithyddiaeth Geltaidd. IV. Series.
PB2001.C45 1990
491.6--dc20 90-31745
ISBN 90 272 3565 1 (alk. paper) CIP

CONTENTS

Part 2: Studies in Breton and Cornish Linguistics

Part 3: Studies in Literary Linguistics

Professor T. Arwyn Watkins

INTRODUCTION

This collection of work on the Brythonic languages of the Celtic group has been prepared in honour of Professor T. Arwyn Watkins, to recognise his outstanding work in both linguistics and Celtic studies. To reflect the interests of Professor Watkins, the collection is divided into four parts: Welsh linguistics, Breton and Cornish linguistics, literary linguistics and historical linguistics. This has resulted in a book providing a thorough and comprehensive coverage of this branch of Celtic studies prepared by the leading scholars in their field. Naturally, there are several contributions which overlap the somewhat artificial boundaries just described. In these cases the article has been placed in that section which seemed to the editors to be most appropriate considering the topic covered overall.

The majority of the articles in this volume are written in English. However, the editors felt that his pioneering work in introducing modern linguistics to a Welsh-speaking audience could not be adequately recognised without the inclusion of a study written in Welsh. Furthermore, Professor Watkins' links with European celticists is demonstrated by a number of contributions written by continental scholars.

The preparation of this tribute required an editorial team covering the four main areas of study. Martin J. Ball edited Part 1 on Welsh linguistics, and acted as co-ordinating editor, James Fife edited Part 2 on Breton and Cornish, literary aspects were under the control of Jenny Rowlands, while Erich Poppe had charge of studies in historical linguistics. Each member of this team wished to include their own tribute to Arwyn Watkins in this introduction, and so these initial remarks conclude with some

words from each of them. Apart from the editorial team, especial thanks must go to Gary King for preparing the bibliography of Professor Watkins' published work.
The late Heinrich Wagner had wished to contribute to this collection, but his untimely loss allows us only to include his wishes to Arwyn. The editors would like to express their sorrow at this loss, and take the opportunity to acknowledge the debt of all celticists to the work of this leading scholar.

James Fife writes:

The Welsh title of this collection of articles uses the word *ieithyddiaeth*. Nearly thirty years ago another book appeared having this word in its title, an introduction to modern grammatical analysis by a young scholar named T. Arwyn Watkins. In the years that intervened Professor Watkins has published a wide range of studies of major importance in a number of fields of Celtic language and literature. In compiling a volume to suitably honour one who has been such an active and productive contributor to Celtic scholarship, the editors had their work cut out in covering all the areas to which Professor Watkins has extended his impressive expertise. Nothing better demonstrates the breadth of this expertise than the need to share the work of editing this collection between four other scholars.

In the four-part division of this work it fell to my lot to supervise the section on Breton and Cornish studies. My qualification for this assignment rests more with my great respect for the honouree than any real mastery of the field. All of the small amount of learning I have in this area I owe to Professor Watkins, and I am a fitting editor for this section at least in as far as this is one of the many cases where he has greatly aided, encouraged and enlightened me.

The breadth of Professor Watkin's work is one criterion determining the structure of this anthology, but the inherent latitude of a collection dealing with the Brythonic languages as a whole also demands attention for a number of different fields of study. The part which combines Breton and Cornish studies includes work in historical linguistics, synchronic syntax, phonology, morphology and contrastive studies between languages. If space were unlimited, there are other topics worthy of discussion and colleagues desirous of contributing to a volume in honour of Professor Watkins; for the omission of both, I express regret. But the need to constrain the space devoted to any one field, in this case the south-west Brýthonic languages, is adequately recompensed by the high quality of the studies which are included. I would like to thank all the contributors to this section for their impressive work and their friendly cooperation.

I want to thank also Professor Evans for his essay of appreciation, and my three fellow editors for their hard work and patience. I think I speak for my fellows in extending a special thanks to Martin Ball in his role of managing editor of the volume, an office carrying far more work than glory.

Department of English Philology
Catholic University of Lublin

Jenny Rowland writes:

It is a great pleasure to present the papers of Part 3 to Professor Watkins, a teacher, friend and colleague over the last few years. Although not all the papers deal directly with linguistic matters, they show the directions the study of Welsh literature of the Middle Ages has taken in the last few years. This has in part been based on increased linguistic knowledge, and Professor Watkins has not only contributed to original research, but also helped to interpret it to younger scholars. I myself can attest to this, both as a student in Aberystwyth and a colleague in Dublin. His lively and informative style of lecturing has always assured an extra audience for his courses, and attracted those who might have considered Welsh or Welsh linguistics were outside their field. I first met Professor Watkins by sitting in on his lectures while writing my thesis in Aberystwyth. This tradition has carried on in Dublin, with postgraduates and colleagues from other departments following his courses over the last few years, both in UCD and the Dublin Institute for Advanced Studies.

This enthusiastic contact with his students, official and unofficial, undoubtedly accounts in part for the fact that so many have turned to him for help or comment on their work. (The other factor, of course, is his undoubted mastery of his field.) Professor Watkins has given very freely of himself in this respect, in the official channels of thesis supervision and editorial guidance, as well as casual and friendly casting of a critical linguistic eye over work in progress. I have often benefitted from this kindness, and have seen the time and care the most informal query elicits from him.

It would have been easy to fill this section which is more peripheral to Professor Watkins' own studies many times over, and the limiting of contributors was somewhat arbitrary. Most of us have had personal experience of Arwyn Watkins as a teacher and advisor, and all have reason to honour his pioneering scholarship. Fortunately we can look forward to his continued scholarly activities from new surroundings in Swansea.

Department of Welsh
University College Dublin

Erich Poppe writes:

When I came to University College Dublin as a postgraduate student, T. Arwyn Watkins was one of my teachers, but very soon he became more than just that. He is one of those academics who combine high scholarly standards with an outstanding ability to teach and to impart their own enthusiasm for their subjects to their students. In my own case, Arwyn's classes on Middle Welsh thus became a formative influence on my scholarly inclinations, and my interest in questions of Middle Welsh word-order dates back to his classes on *Branwen*. In the many discussions we had on this and other topics of Welsh linguistics afterwards, Arwyn was more than just a teacher - he became a mentor and a friend whose advice and criticism has always been supportive. *Diolch yn fawr!*

Philipps-Universität Marburg

Martin Ball writes:

I feel the least qualified to write an introduction to Arwyn Watkins' *Festschrift*, never having had the privilege of working with him as a colleague or student. However, I got to know his linguistic work early through his many writings on Celtic linguistics: especially his seminal work *Ieithyddiaeth*. Indeed, I first met Professor Watkins at a meeting of the Welsh Dialectology Circle, when he kindly agreed to sign a copy of *Ieithyddiaeth* proferred by an unknown member of the audience. That copy now has pride of place among my Welsh linguistics collection (which, incidentally, contains three more copies of the work).

Further evidence of the hospitality of both Arwyn and Gwalia came from my visit last year to Dublin when, with very little notice, I was invited to their home in the city. There, not only was there fruitful and friendly discussion, but the finest smoked salmon I have tasted! My regret at not having had the chance to work with Arwyn is mitigated to some extent by the opportunity that I have had with Glyn Jones of cooperating with him on a project on Welsh linguistics that will shortly reach a conclusion. In his work for this project I can not help but be impressed by his depth of knowledge and breadth of vision.

The studies presented to him in the Welsh linguistic section cover dialectology, syntax, morphology, and phonology and include pioneering work on child language. As my colleagues have already noted, we have been able to include only a small number of potential contributors, but we trust those that are included in this section, and the volume as a whole, will bring pleasure to our honouree. The *Tabula Gratulatoria* bears witness to the many scholars who wish to pass on their best compliments to the leading modern linguist that Wales has produced.

At the Eighth International Congress of Celtic Studies in Swansea the four of us were sitting in the coffee lounge one morning when Arwyn came by and asked what we were planning so seriously. We couldn't say then: but now we can, and the following collection is the fruit of that initial meeting.

Department of Behavioural and Communication Studies
Polytechnic of Wales

Publications of T. Arwyn Watkins

1954 The accent in Cwm Tawe Welsh. *ZCP*, **24**, 6-9
Y deuseiniaid *ae*, *ai*, *au*, *oe* ac *wy*. *BBCS*, **15**, 260-67

1955 Linguistic atlas of Welsh dialect. *Orbis*; **4**, 32-42
Archaeology and history and the change from Brittonic to Welsh, Cornish, and Breton. *Archaeologica Cambrensis*, **104**, 166-84.
Review of *Language and History in Early Britain* by Kenneth Jackson. (Edinburgh University Press). *The Scottish Historical Review,* **34**, 147-50.

1956 Y frawddeg enwol amhur. *BBCS*, **17**, 21-30

1957 Yr arddodiad HG, *(h)i*, *in*; CC *y* (=*yn*), *yn*. *BBCS*, **17**, 137-58

1958 *[with P. Mac Cana]* Cystrawennau'r cyplad mewn Hen Gymraeg. *BBCS*, **18**, 1-25

1959 Nodiadau cymysg. Camraniad; *Yg got*. *BBCS*, **18**, 270-74

1960 CC, *y/yn* berfenwol. *BBCS*, **18**, 362-72

1961 *Ieithyddiaeth: Agweddau ar Astudio Iaith.* Caerdydd: Gwasg Prifysgol Cymru

1962 Background to the Welsh dialect survey. *Lochlann*, **2**, 38-49
[with J. R. F. Piette] Ffurfiant a chystrawen y geirynnau adferfol/traethiadol mewn Cymraeg, Cernyweg a Llydaweg. *BBCS*, **19**, 295-315

1963 Language and Linguistics. In Elwyn Davies (ed) *Celtic Studies in Wales. A Survey*. Cardiff: University of Wales Press. Pp 141-82

1964 Cymraeg Abertawe. *Gŵyl*, 40-42.

1965 *[with Alan Conway] Hanes yr Unol Daleithiau*. Llandybie: Llyfrau'r Dryw
Points of similarity between Old Welsh and Old Irish orthography. *BBCS*, **21**, 135-41
Bathu geiriau. Review of *Termau ffiseg a mathemateg*. *Barn*, **35**, 324-25

1966 Review of *A Grammar of Middle Welsh* by D. Simon Evans (Dublin Institute for Advanced Studies). *SC*, **1**, 155-60

1967 Some phonological features of the Welsh dialect of Llansamlet (West Glamorgan). *Beiträge zur Indogermanistik und Keltologie. Julius Pokorny zum 80. Geburtstag gewidmet. Innsbrucker Beiträge zur Kulturwissenschaft*, **13**, 315-22
Cwestiynau Gramadeg. *Barn*, **61**, 23-24.

1968 Dulliau orgraffyddol Cymraeg Canol o ddynodi'r treiglad trwynol. *BBCS*, **23**, 7-13.
Llafar llenyddol Cymraeg. In Jones, T. (ed) *Astudiaethau Amrywiol*. Caerdydd: Gwasg Prifysgol Cymru. Pp 122-36
The contribution of academic research in Welsh and Welsh studies. *Educational Research in Wales*. 66-77
Whither Welsh? *The London Welshman*, May, 4-7.
The odds against Welsh. *The London Welshman*, June, 6-8.

1969 Mynegair i destunau Cymraeg. *BBCS*, **23**, 122-28
Review of *The Gododdin: the oldest Scottish Poem* by K. H. Jackson (Edinburgh University Press). *Archaeologia Cambrensis*, **118**, 157-58
†Henry Lewis (1889-1968) *[obituary]*. *Lochlann*, **4**, 312-14

1971 †Julius Pokorny (1887-1970) *[obituary]*. *SC*, **6**, 195-96

1972 The accent-shift in Old Welsh - its quality and development. *BBCS*, **25**, 1-11
The accent in Old Welsh - its quality and development. *[summary of above.] Études Celtiques*, **13**, 428-29
The Welsh personal pronouns. *Word*, **28**, 146-65
The accent-shift in Old Welsh. *Indo-Celtica: Gedächtnisschrift für Alf Sommerfelt*. München: Max Hueber. Pp 201-05

1975 Common Celtic and Gaulish; Welsh studies (language). *The Year's Work in Modern Language Studies*. **36 (1974)**, 527-31, 532-40

1976 Cyfnewidiadau seinegol sy'n gysylltiedig â'r 'acen' Gymraeg. *BBCS*, **26**, 399-405
Dwyieithedd a chyfnewid systemig yn y Gymraeg. *SC*, **10-11**, 367-82
Common Celtic and Gaulish; Welsh Studies (language). *The Year's Work in Modern Language Studies*. **37 (1975)**, 464-69; 470-78

1977 Litonmaucan. (*BD* 1-16). *BBCS*, **27**, 224
Common Celtic and Gaulish; Welsh Studies (language). *The Year's Work in Modern Language Studies*. **38 (1976)**, 487-92; 493-502
Review of *Iaith Plant Llŷn* by William Ll. Griffith (Gwasg Prifysgol Cymru). *Y Traethodydd*, **132**, 165-67

1978 Y rhagenw ategol. *SC*, **12-13**, 349-66
Trefn yn y frawddeg Gymraeg. *SC*, **12-13**, 367-95
Review of *Iaith Plant Llŷn* by William Ll. Griffith (Gwasg Prifysgol Cymru). *SC*, **12-13**, 477-80
Common Celtic and Gaulish; Welsh Studies (language). *The Year's Work in Modern Language Studies*. **39 (1977)**, 537-39; 540-44

1979 Common Celtic and Gaulish; Welsh Studies (language). *The Year's Work in Modern Language Studies*. **40 (1978)**, 547-48; 549-52

1980 Common Celtic and Gaulish; Welsh Studies (language). *The Year's Work in Modern Language Studies*. **41 (1979)**, 575-76; 577-79

1981 Common Celtic and Gaulish; Welsh Studies (language). *The Year's Work in Modern Language Studies.* **42 (1980)**, 613-15; 616-20

1982 Englynion y Juvencus. In R. Geraint Gruffydd (ed) *Bardos: Penodau ar y traddodiad barddol Cymreig a Cheltaidd. Cyflwynedig i J. E. Caerwyn Williams.* Caerdydd: Gwasg Prifysgol Cymru. Pp 29-43

Welsh Studies (language). *The Year's Work in Modern Language Studies.* **43 (1981)**, 640-45

1983 Welsh Studies (language). *The Year's Work in Modern Language Studies.* **44 (1982)**, 655-661

1984 Trefn y constitwentau yn *Branwen. SC*, **18-19,** 147-57

1985 Welsh Studies (language). *The Year's Work in Modern Language Studies.* **46 (1984)**, 594-602

Review of *Gwaith Owain ap Llywelyn ab y Moel* ed. by Eurys Rolant (Gwasg Prifysgol Cymru). *Celtica,* **17,** 170-71

Review of *Y Mabinogi* addasiad Gwyn Thomas (Gwasg Prifysgol Cymru). *Celtica,* **17,** 171-72

Review of *Welsh Phonology, Selected Readings* ed. by Martin J. Ball and Glyn E. Jones (University of Wales Press). *Celtica,* **17,** 173-77

Review of *Language in the British Isles* ed. by P. Trudgill (Cambridge University Press). *Celtica,* **17,** 177-80

1986 Welsh *-awdd* [-awð], *-odd* [-oð], 3 sg. pret. of the regular verb. *Ériu,* **37,** 127-31

Review of *Cydymaith i Lenyddiaeth Cymru* ed. by Meic Stephens (Gwasg Prifysgol Cymru). *Celtica,* **18,** 202-05

Review of *Aspects of the Poetry of Dafydd ap Gwilym* by Rachel Bromwich (Gwasg Prifysgol Cymru). *Celtica,* **18,** 205-07

Review of *Ysgrifeniadau Byrion Morgan Llwyd* ed. by P. Donovan (Gwasg Prifysgol Cymru). *Celtica,* **18,** 207-08

Review of *Trafod Cerddi* ed. by B. Jarvis (Gwasg Taf). *Celtica,* **18,** 208-09

Review of *Pennod yn Hanes Milwr* by C. Bere (Gwasg yr Ynys Newydd). *Celtica,* **18,** 209-10

1987 Constituent order in the Old Welsh verbal sentence. *BBCS*, **34,** 51-60

1988 Constituent order in the positive declarative sentence in the medieval Welsh tale, 'Kulhwch ac Olwen'. *Innsbrucker Beiträge zur Sprachwissenschaft.* Vorträge und kleinere Schriften, **41**. Innsbruck: Institut für Sprachwissenschaft.

Contributions on 'General Studies', 'Orthography', and 'Old Welsh' in J. E. Caerwyn Williams (gol.) *Llyfryddiaeth yr Iaith Gymraeg*. Caerdydd: Gwasg Prifysgol Cymru.

in press hyt yretilheul *WM* 459.29. *BBCS,* **36.**

Welsh. In Martin J. Ball and Glyn E. Jones (eds) *The Celtic Languages*. London: Routledge

compiled by Gary King

TABULA GRATULATORIA

Bo Almquist	*University College Dublin*
Gwenllian Awbery	*Welsh Folk Museum*
Martin J Ball	*Polytechnic of Wales*
Rolf Baumgarten	*Dublin Institute for Advanced Studies*
P Birt	*University College of North Wales, Bangor*
Ronald Black	*University of Edinburgh*
Robert Borsley	*University College of North Wales, Bangor*
Angela Bourke	*University College Dublin*
D J Bowen	*University College of Wales, Aberystwyth*
Liam Breatnach	*Trinity College Dublin*
Padraig Breatnach	*University College Dublin*
Rachel Bromwich	*Aberystwyth*
Francis John Byrne	*University College Dublin*
Vera Čapková	*University College Dublin*
James Carney	*Dublin Institute for Advanced Studies*
Richard A V Cox	*University of Glasgow*
Sioned Davies	*University of Wales College of Cardiff*
R Delaporte	*University College Cork*
Per Denez	*University of Rennes*
Doris R Edel	*University of Utrecht*
Nancy Edwards	*University College of North Wales, Bangor*
Islwyn Ffowc Elis	*St David's University College, Lampeter*
D Ellis Evans	*Jesus College, Oxford*
D H Evans	*St David's University College, Lampeter*
D Simon Evans	*St David's University College, Lampeter*
Emrys Evans	*University College of Wales, Aberystwyth*
James Fife	*Catholic University of Lublin*
Patrick Ford	*University of California Los Angeles*

Ken George	*Polytechnic South West*
William Gillies	*University of Edinburgh*
James W Gleasure	*University of Glasgow*
James Grant	*University of Aberdeen*
R Geraint Gruffydd	*Centre for Advanced Welsh & Celtic Studies, Aberystwyth*
Eric P Hamp	*University of Chicago*
W G Harries	*University College, Swansea*
Anthony Harvey	*Royal Irish Academy, Dublin*
Marged Haycock	*University College of Wales, Aberystwyth*
Hamish Henderson	*University of Edinburgh*
John Hennessey	*Sacramento, California*
Micheal Herity	*University College Dublin*
Steve Hewitt	*Baghdad, Iraq*
R J Hincks	*University College of Wales, Aberystwyth*
Ian Hughes	*University College of Wales, Aberystwyth*
Tom Jones Hughes	*University College Dublin*
H Ll Humphreys	*St David's University College, Lampeter*
Colin Ireland	*Dublin Institute for Advanced Studies*
A O H Jarman	*Cardiff*
Branwen Jarvis	*University College of North Wales, Bangor*
Diarmuid Johnson	*University College Galway*
David Johnston	*University of Wales College of Cardiff*
Bedwyr Lewis Jones	*University College of North Wales, Bangor*
Dafydd Glyn Jones	*University College of North Wales, Bangor*
Glyn E Jones	*University of Wales College of Cardiff*
J Gwilym Jones	*University College of North Wales, Bangor*
Robert Owen Jones	*University College of Wales, Swansea*
Bob Morris Jones	*University College of Wales, Aberystwyth*
R M 'Bobi' Jones	*University College of Wales, Aberystwyth*
N A Jones	*Centre for Advanced Welsh & Celtic Studies*
Peter Knab	*University of Marburg*
John Koch	*Harvard University*
Katrin Lambertz	*University of Marburg*
Ceri Lewis	*Cardiff*
Fredrik O Lindeman	*Oslo University*
Nesta Lloyd	*University College of Wales, Swansea*
Peredur Lynch	*Centre for Advanced Welsh & Celtic Studies*
Donald MacAulay	*University of Aberdeen*

Proisias Mac Cana	*Dublin Institute for Advanced Studies*
Kim McCone	*Maynooth*
Kenneth MacDonald	*University of Glasgow*
Gearóid Mac Eoin	*University College Galway*
Malachy McKenna	*Dublin Institute for Advanced Studies*
Kenneth MacKinnon	*Hatfield Polytechnic*
Damian McManus	*Trinity College Dublin*
Wolfgang Meid	*University of Innsbruck*
Daniel Melia	*University of California, Berkeley*
Edward G Millward	*University College of Wales, Aberystwyth*
Derec Llwyd Morgan	*University College of Wales, Aberystwyth*
Nicole Müller	*Corpus Christi College, Oxford*
Proinseas Ni Chatháin	*University College Dublin*
Honora Ni Chriogáin	*University College Dublin*
Colm Ó Baoill	*University of Aberdeen*
Brendan Ó Buachalla	*University College Dublin*
Tomás Ó Cathasaigh	*University College Dublin*
Conn Ó Cléirigh	*University College Dublin*
Tomás Ó Concheanainn	*University College Dublin*
Ailbhe Ó Corráin	*University of Uppsala*
Brian Ó Cuív	*Dublin Institute for Advanced Studies*
Brendan O'Hehir	*University of California, Berkeley*
Máirtin Ó Murchú	*Dublin Institute for Advanced Studies*
Cathair Ó Dochartaigh	*Bangor*
A P Owen	*Centre for Advanced Welsh & Celtic Studies*
Morfydd Owen	*University College of Wales, Aberystwyth*
Vincent Phillips	*Welsh Folk Museum*
Herbert Pilch	*University of Freiburg im Breisgau*
Erich Poppe	*University of Marburg*
Huw Pryce	*University College of North Wales, Bangor*
Chris Rees	*University of Wales*
R G Rhys	*University College, Swansea*
Martin Rockel	*University of Berlin*
Hans Rössing	*University of Marburg*
Jenny Rowland	*University College Dublin*
G E Ruddock	*University of Wales College of Cardiff*
Jochem Schindler	*University of Vienna*
Karl Horst Schmidt	*University of Bonn*
Patrick Sims-Williams	*St John's College, Cambridge*
Richard Skerret	*University College of Wales, Aberystwyth*

Elmar Ternes	*University of Hamburg*
Alan R Thomas	*University College of North Wales, Bangor*
Beth Thomas	*Welsh Folk Museum*
Ceinwen Thomas	*Cardiff*
Gwyn Thomas	*University College of North Wales, Bangor*
Peter Thomas	*University of Wales College of Cardiff*
Derick S Thomson	*University of Glasgow*
David Thorne	*St David's University College, Lampeter*
Lenora Timm	*University of California, Davis*
Hildegard Tristram	*University of Freiburg im Breisgau*
Jürgen Uhlich	*Dublin Institute for Advanced Studies*
Heinrich Wagner†	*Dublin Institute for Advanced Studies*
Dafydd Walters	*University of Edinburgh*
Calvert Watkins	*Harvard University*
Bríd Éimear Williams	*University College of North Wales*
G Aled Williams	*University College of North Wales, Bangor*
J E Caerwyn Williams	*Centre for Advanced Welsh & Celtic Studies*
N J A Williams	*University College Dublin*
Rita Williams	*University College of Wales, Aberystwyth*
Stefan Zimmer	*University of Berlin*

Appreciation - Gwerthfawrogiad

Thomas Arwyn Watkins

Professor Arwyn Watkins has been one of Wales's most learned and inspiring linguists in his generation, specializing in the interpretation of his own native language, Welsh, expert also in the analysis of the sister languages, Cornish and Breton, and collaborating with others in important comparative research embracing as well the rich testimony of the Irish language. It is a pleasure to have this special opportunity to pay a short tribute to him as he retires from his teaching duties.

Born on 20 June 1924, and brought up in Llansamlet, near Swansea, in Glamorgan, he became a pupil at Bishop Gore Grammar School in Swansea from 1935 to 1941. He then entered the University College of Swansea. There he studied French and Philosophy before qualifying in 1943 for the B.A. degree of the University of Wales, taking the old Final Examination in Welsh and English. After four years' military service during and after the Second World War he returned to the College for the 1947-48 session to take his Diploma in Education. He was persuaded by Professor Henry Lewis, the distinguished and dynamic Professor of Welsh at Swansea, to continue with his studies in Welsh. During the 1948-49 session he completed the Single Honours course in Welsh and was awarded a First Class in the Honours examination. I can remember clearly both his bright enthusiasm and his evident maturity when, as a young undergraduate, I attended many of the same classes as the ones he would attend in the Department of Welsh (our teachers there were Henry Lewis, Stephen J. Williams,

T. Hugh Bevan and D. Simon Evans).

Arwyn then gained a Postgraduate Studentship which enabled him to undertake research work on the Welsh dialect of his native parish of Llansamlet, for which he was awarded in 1951 the M.A. degree of the University of Wales. Thereafter he was elected to a Fellowship of the University, and in a session crucial for the development of his career as a scholar, he spent one term each at the Universities of Leeds, Zürich and Rennes, all important for greatly extending his knowledge of the study of language, with special reference to dialectology and the Celtic languages (Professor Julius Pokorny and Professor François Falc'hun were among his teachers that year). This led to his appointment in 1952 (in the same year as the one in which Thomas Jones succeeded T. H. Parry-Williams as Professor of Welsh at Aberystwyth) as Assistant Lecturer in the Department of Welsh at the University College of Wales at Aberystwyth where he later became a Lecturer (in 1954), a Senior Lecturer (in 1962), and a Reader (in 1977). He was Acting Head of the Department of Welsh in 1969-70, and for two academic sessions (1976-78) Dean of the Faculty of Arts. The attraction of Ireland had made itself evident during his period of service at Aberystwyth. He was a Visiting Professor at the Dublin Institute for Advanced Studies in 1971 and, once again in Dublin, at University College, in 1980. It was no surprise, albeit a serious loss for his own Department at Aberystwyth, when he was elected to the Chair of Welsh at University College Dublin in 1981, the Chair which he occupied with such great distinction until his retirement. It is unique as the only University Chair in Welsh to have been established outside the University of Wales. During his successful tenure of this Chair Professor Watkins was elected a Member of the Royal Irish Academy and an Honorary Professor attached to the Department of Welsh at the University College of Swansea.

Much could be said of his qualities and achievements as a teacher and researcher and especially as an inspiring and supportive supervisor of postgraduate researchers both at Aberystwyth and at Dublin. His major publication was *Ieithyddiaeth. Agweddau ar Astudio Iaith* (1961), based very largely on the first eight years of his teaching at Aberystwyth - an introduction to a linguistic study of Welsh, dealing concisely with most of the main aspects of the study of the Welsh language and exploiting in particular his own interest in dialectology and his recognition of the continuing importance of comparative studies (reflected here especially by his inclusion in his work of sections dealing directly with the testimony of Breton). As the late Professor David Greene rightly stated, it represented an enormous advance on anything of its kind which had hitherto been available. It became at once a most useful introduction to so many aspects of Welsh linguistics. For all the advances made in the interim, and they are very significant (we have a number of new textbooks and readers and specialist monographs concentrating on Welsh), we have not had so far a comprehensive work entirely devoted to a synchronic study of the modern spoken language. It is the measure of the abiding quality of Professor Watkins's *Ieithyddiaeth* that it is to be one of the first of several scholarly works written in Welsh to be reissued in a German version by Professor Wolfgang Meid of Innsbruck, in order more readily to draw the attention of the international world of learning to some of the best scholarly work produced in Welsh relating both to the Welsh language and to Welsh literature.

Many of his other writings have reflected his special interest in dialectology, not least the need for a Welsh linguistic atlas and dialect survey (*Orbis*, iv. 1955 and *Lochlann*, ii. 1962). He has written on Llansamlet and Cwmtawe Welsh (e.g. his *primitiae* on 'The accent in Cwm Tawe Welsh', *ZCP*, xxiv. 1954; 'Some phonological features of the Welsh dialect of Llansamlet', in the *Pokorny Festschrift* 1967). He has been especially concerned about questions relating to orthography and phonology and mutations, witness, for example, his discussion of the Old Welsh preposition *(h)i*, *in*, Middle Welsh *y* (=yn), *yn* (*BBCS*, xvii/3. 1957), Middle Welsh *y*, *yn* before a verbal noun (*BBCS*, xviii/4. 1960), orthographic conventions observed in Middle Welsh to denote the nasal mutation (*BBCS*, xxiii/1. 1968), and consideration of the morphology and syntax of adverbial-predicative particles in Welsh, Cornish, and Breton (*BBCS*, xix/4. 1962). Following joint supervision of postgraduate research on the topic he wrote on 'Points of similarity between Old Welsh and Old Irish orthography' (*BBCS*, xxi/2. 1965). Later on in his career he returned to questions relating to the accentual patterns of Welsh, especially in Old Welsh (*Sommerfelt Festschrift* 1972; *BBCS*, xxv/1. 1972) and with regard to systemic changes in Welsh related to accentual patterns (*BBCS*, xxvi/4. 1976). He has written on linguistic change in a situation of linguistic contact (*SC*, x-xi. 1975-76) and on various registers in Modern Welsh (as in his essay on 'Llafar Llenyddol Cymraeg' in *Astudiaethau Amrywiol* 1968). He became particularly interested in the political and social background of Welsh and in linguistic interference and the structure of Spoken Welsh. He realized the importance of computer based concordances of Welsh texts (*BBCS*, xxiii/2. 1969). He wrote on the usage of Welsh personal pronouns (*Word*, xxvii/1-2. 1972; *SC*, xii-xiii. 1977-78 - these papers are by and large syntactical studies). He presented a careful analysis of the Old Welsh Juvencus 'englynion' (*Caerwyn Williams Festschrift* 1981) and has considered the vexed question of the origin of the Welsh third singular preterite termination in *-awdd/-odd* (*Ériu*, xxxvii. 1986). Some of his writing reflects his long and critical commitment to acting as an Examiner in Welsh for the Welsh Joint Education Committee. He is a former member of the examination panel of the Schools Council for Wales, of the Ceredigion Education Authority Language Sub-committee and served as secretary of the University of Wales Guild of Graduates Technical Terms Sub-committee.

He has written much on academic research on the Welsh language, as in his important survey of 'Language and Linguistics' in the presentation volume prepared before the Second International Congress of Celtic Studies held in Cardiff in 1963 (*Celtic Studies in Wales* 1963), his contribution to a government report on *Educational Research in Wales* (1968) and contributions to as many as ten volumes of *The Year's Work in Modern Language Studies* (1974-84), chiefly on the Welsh language, but also on Common Celtic and Gaulish. He has reviewed scholarly works in many of the leading Celtic journals, such as *Archaeologica Cambrensis*, *Celtica*, *The Scottish Historical Review*, *Studia Celtica*, and *Y Traethodydd*; his reviews are markedly incisive and uncompromising, but always fair.

Throughout his career he has written on aspects of the syntax of Welsh. This ranges from his well known contribution (in collaboration with Professor Proinsias Mac Cana) on the syntax of the copula in Old Welsh (*BBCS*, xviii/1. 1958 - he had already written on the so-called 'impure nominal sentence' in Welsh in *BBCS*, xvii/1. 1956) to constituent order in the sentence in Welsh (*SC*, xii-xiii. 1977-78). In recent years he has concentrated on analysis of constituent order in particular sources, in the medieval tales *Branwen* (*SC*, xvii-xviii. 1983-84) and *Kulhwch ac Olwen* (vol 14 of the 'Vorträge und kleinere Schriften' series of the *Innsbrucker Beiträge zur Sprachwissenschaft*, 1988), and in Old Welsh sources (*BBCS*, xxxiv. 1987).

Much of his scholarship is reflected in a wide range of dissertations prepared by postgraduate students under his supervision, on Welsh dialects, Welsh onomastics, Old Welsh and Middle Welsh orthography, the syntax and morphology of Middle Welsh texts, Middle Cornish morphology and Middle Cornish and Middle Breton syntax.

Professor Watkins has a most enviable reputation as a generous, warm-hearted, and supportive colleague, a man of great integrity, without flamboyance, without malice. He has served all the institutions of learning with which he has been connected with great distinction. He is not one to compromise when it comes to presenting or defending what he considers to be the right analysis of the evidence available as he sees it and especially to expounding the significance or relevance of that analysis for the well-being of education and society overall. This is a truly rare quality in the academic world of our day.

We greet him most warmly and wish him well as he retires from his labours in Dublin and now returns more permanently to his home in Swansea.

Ni ellid talu teyrnged go iawn i'n cyfaill Arwyn Watkins heb arfer yr iaith a fu'n iaith gyntaf liwgar a bywiog iddo ef ar hyd ei oes. A lliw Llansamlet a Chwmtawe a fu ar y Cymraeg hwnnw ar ei fin erioed, er iddo grwydro o'i fro enedigol am ysbeidiau go hir.

Ef ar lawer cyfrif yw ieithydd Cymraeg mwyaf amryddawn ei genhedlaeth, disgybl teilwng i'w ryfeddu i'r gwŷr dawnus hynny a'i hyfforddodd ac a'i ysbrydolodd gymaint yng Ngholeg y Brifysgol yn Abertawe, gyda'r Athro Henry Lewis yn ei anterth yn arwain yn llawn brwdfrydedd a gofal o blaid ei ddisgyblion yn y Coleg hwnnw.

Afraid, i'r sawl a fydd yn darllen y deyrnged brin hon yn y Gymraeg, yw pwysleisio cryfder Arwyn ei hunan fel athro a chyfarwyddwr ymchwil i fwy nag un genhedlaeth o fyfyrwyr a fu dan ei ofal mewn mwy nag un Brifysgol. Ar ôl gosod seiliau sicr o ran disgyblaeth a dysg yng Ngholeg Abertawe cafodd flwyddyn ryfeddol o ehangu gorwelion ymhellach, yn Lloegr ym Mhrifysgol Leeds, yn y Swistir ym Mhrifysgol Zürich, ac yn Llydaw ym Mhrifysgol Roazhon. Wedyn bu'n dysgu am gyfanrif o 37 o flynyddoedd mewn dwy Brifysgol, ym Mhrifysgol Cymru yn bennaf ac yn gyntaf, yn Adran y Gymraeg yng Ngholeg Prifysgol Cymru yn Aberystwyth, ac yna yn Athro Cymraeg ym Mhrifysgol Genedlaethol Iwerddon yn Adran y Gymraeg yng Ngholeg y Brifysgol yn Nulyn.

Mawr fu ei gyfraniad ym myd dysg ac ymchwil, yn canolbwyntio'n bennaf ar ddeall a dangos teithi'r iaith Gymraeg yn ei hamryfal gyfnodau a'i hamryfal weddau a chyweiriau. Afraid ailadrodd y cyfeirio at rai o fanylion ei gyfraniad tra sylweddol. Ond mae'n iawn inni gofio iddo ddal cannwyll yn gyson a dibetrus i eraill, i'w goleuo ynglŷn â chynifer o bynciau sy'n arwyddocaol ym myd gramadeg hanesyddol a chymharol, tafodieitheg, astudio orgraff hanesyddol a ffurfiant ac yn arbennig gystrawen yr iaith Gymraeg (a'i chwaerieithoedd, Cernyweg a Llydaweg, o bryd i'w gilydd), a phynciau o bwys ym myd ieithyddiaeth ddisgrifiadol neu gyffredinol (megis effaith cyswllt ieithyddol), hanes efrydiau ieithyddol Cymraeg a chyflwr y Gymraeg mewn addysg a chymdeithas ar adeg o encil a cholli safon ac o adwaith cymhleth i hynny ac ymdrech barhaus i ailsafoni.

Bu ei ddylanwad yn helaeth iawn nid yn unig fel athro ac awdur ond hefyd fel cyfarwyddwr ymchwil graddedigion mewn cynifer o feysydd, yn arbennig ym maes tafodieitheg a chystrawen. Cyrhaeddodd ei ddawn fel cyfarwyddwr ymchwil ym myd cystrawen benllanw gogoneddus yn Nulyn lle y bu'n hael a doeth ei gyngor i bawb a ddeuai ato, ac fe ddaethant i Ddulyn o lawer gwlad.

Bu hefyd yn fawr ei ofal a'i arweiniad a'i ymroddiad fel arholwr (a chanolwr hefyd) yn y Gymraeg yn yr ysgolion, yn arholiadau Safon O, O2 ac O3 yr hen drefn ac yn arbennig Safon A y Cyd-Bwyllgor Addysg Cymreig. Bu'n Brif Arholwr Safon A am lawer o flynyddoedd. Ysgwyddodd hefyd nifer o ddyletswyddau gweinyddol digon trwm yn ystod ei yrfa fel athro prifysgol, yn cynnwys Deoniaeth Cyfadran y Celfyddydau yn Aberystwyth.

Cyfarchwn ef, a chydag ef ei briod ofalus Gwalia, wrth iddo roi'r gorau i'w ddyletswyddau yn Nulyn a dychwelyd i'w fro enedigol a'i gartref yn Llwynderw ar lan troad gosgeiddig bae rhyfeddol Abertawe. Bu'n ŵr dysg galluog, gonest, teyrngar a thwymgalon, heb ildio i gyfaddawdu yn unol â chwiw neu ffasiwn munud awr i ddweud yr hyn a fyddai'n boblogaidd a derbyniol, heb wneud cam â'r gwir fel y canfyddai ef y gwir hwnnw. Diolchwn iddo am ei gyfeillgarwch a'i groeso siriol, yn Aberystwyth, yn Nulyn ac yn Abertawe, ei unplygrwydd hynod, ei arweiniad gwerthfawr a'i garedigrwydd i eraill yn y cylchoedd y bu'n gweithio ynddynt ac yn yr aml ddyletswyddau a ddaeth i'w ran.

Boed iddo gael iechyd a hwyl am yn hir eto i arfer y doniau a'r cyneddfau gwiw y cynysgaeddwyd ef â hwy, a chyfle mwy hamddenol i glywed eto, yn hyglyw gobeithio, rywfaint o acenion yr heniaith Gymraeg, Cymraeg byw, iaith lafar frodorol cymoedd Llwchwr a Thawe a'r hen Sir Gaerfyrddin yn siopau ac ar hyd strydoedd a glannau môr dinas helaeth Abertawe.

D. Ellis Evans

PART ONE

Studies in Welsh Linguistics

The Geographical Distribution of Pembrokeshire Negatives

G. M. Awbery

0. Introduction

A comparatively neglected aspect of dialect studies in Wales is the regional variation found in syntax and morphology. A great deal of information is readily available on the lexical and phonological variants which characterise different parts of the country, but there are still quite serious gaps in our knowledge of how syntactic and morphological forms are distributed.

This paper looks at the geographical spread of syntactic variants, the negative forms of *bod*, 'be' found in Pembrokeshire Welsh.[1] These are well known local forms, and are something of a shibboleth as far as the dialect is concerned. However, in spite of their status as a dialectal stereotype, it is not clear whether they are, in fact, found throughout the northern Welsh-speaking part of Pembrokeshire, or whether there is rather a core area where they are dominant and a transition zone where they gradually yield to other, less localised forms.

I shall focus here on those negatives where *bod* co-occurs with a pronoun subject, and in particular on the present and imperfect tenses. The local Pembrokeshire forms are distinguished from those found in other areas primarily in the position of the negative particle *ddim,* 'not'.[2] In Pembrokeshire *ddim* appears immediately following the verb *bod*, with the preposition *o*, 'of' intervening between it and the pronoun subject: *bod – ddim – o* – pronoun subject. In the present tense there are several variants on this basic structure:

sdim ono i'n gwbod

sdim o i'n gwbod
sana i'n gwbod
sa i'n gwbod
'I don't know'

In the imperfect too there is more than variant on this type:

wena i'n gwbod
ana i'n gwbod
'I didn't know'

Dialects found in other parts of south Wales, on the other hand, have the pronoun subject immediately following the verb *bod*, and this is in turn followed by the negative particle: *bod* - pronoun subject - *ddim*. This is true both of the present and the imperfect:

Dw i ddim yn gwbod
'I don't know'
Ôn i ddim yn gwbod
'I didn't know'

In this paper I shall begin with the present tense forms, looking first at the distribution of the Pembrokeshire type as a whole, and then in turn at the distribution of the variant forms. I shall then follow the same approach with the imperfect tense forms, looking first at their overall distribution and then at the individual variants found in the dialect.

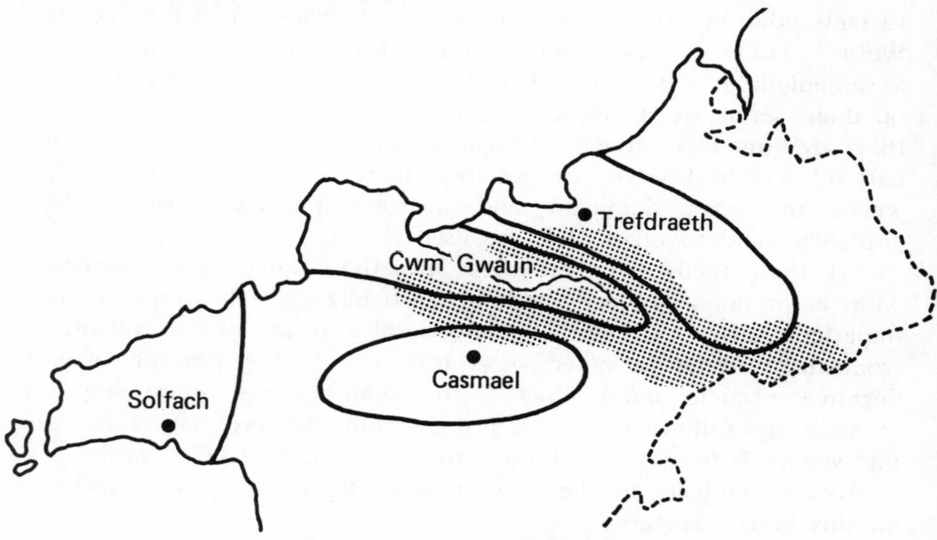

Map 1 North Pembrokeshire

The account presented here is based on taperecordings held in the sound archive of the Welsh Folk Museum. Four districts were chosen within north Pembrokeshire, spaced at intervals across the county, as may be seen from the map below. Five speakers were selected for analysis from three of these districts: Solfach, Cwm Gwaun and Casmael. In the fourth district, Trefdraeth, six speakers were used as one set of tapes consisted of a conversation with two informants together and it was not felt realistic to chose between the two[3].

1. Present Tense

1.1 Distribution

We look first then at the distribution of present tense forms such as the following:

sdim ono i'n gwbod
sdim o i'n gwbod
sana i'n gwbod
sa i'n gwbod

For each speaker the percentage of present tense forms which were of this local type were calculated, and this figure was taken as a score for the individual. These scores, which reflect how closely each speaker adheres to the local negative type in the present tense, are summarised in Figure 1, in the form of a stem and leaf diagram. This is an exploratory technique developed by Tukey, in which the centre column or 'stem' represents the tens, from 0 to 10 (i.e. from 0 to 100), and the units of each score are arranged on the right of the appropriate 'ten' to give the 'leaves' to the right of the stem. The leaves on the left-hand side show the district from which each speaker comes[4].

The majority of the scores cluster together high up on the diagram, revealing a high level of adherence to the local forms throughout the area. A small group of three, however, forms a cluster at a much lower level and here we have a set of speakers whose use of the local present tense negatives forms is much more limited. One of these speakers comes from Fishguard, in the Cwm Gwaun area, the other two from near Trefdraeth.

This may be an indication that the north east is less firmly attached to the local forms than are other districts. The picture, however, is not a simple one in that the scores for the Trefdraeth area range from 100% down to 22%, and those for Cwm Gwaun from 98% down to 39%. All that we can really say is that there is a strong consensus in favour of the local forms in Solfach and Casmael, but that certain individuals have abandoned this consensus in Cwm Gwaun and Trefdraeth.

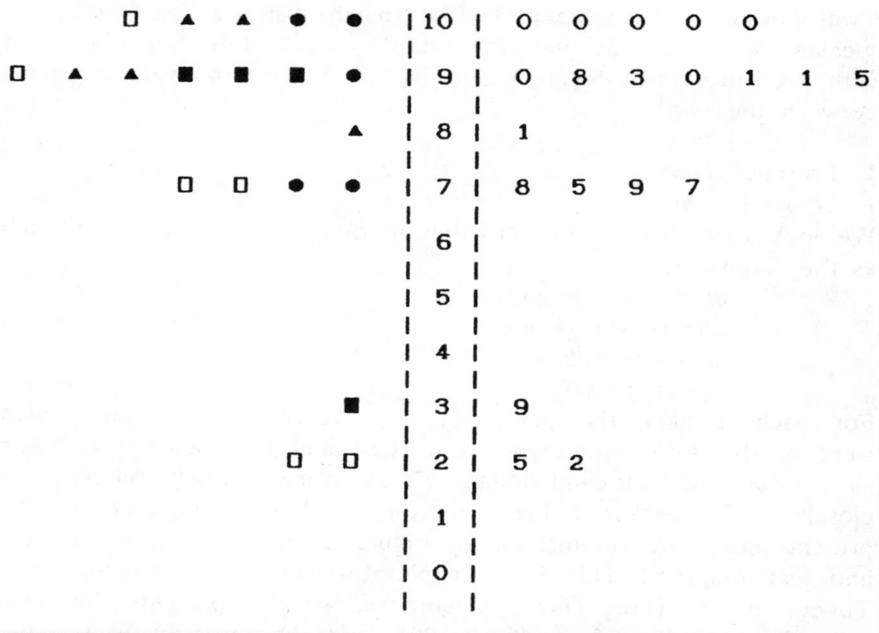

● Solfach ■ Cwm Gwaun ▲ Casmael □ Trefdraeth
stem: tens; leaves: units

Figure 1: Use of Pembrokeshire negative forms in the present tense, by district

1.2 Present Tense: Loss of ddim

The local, Pembrokeshire forms whose overall distribution was shown in Figure 1 fall into two subtypes. In the first of these the negative particle *ddim* is retained throughout the derivation into the surface form:

sdim ono i'n gwbod
sdim o i'n gwbod

In the second set the negative particle is lost in the course of the derivation, and is missing from the surface form of the sentence.

sana i'n gwbod
sa i'n gwbod

For each speaker, accordingly, the percentage of local negatives which were of this latter type was calculated. The scores derived in this way, which reflect how consistently each speaker uses negatives without an overt negative particle *ddim*, are summarised in the stem and leaf diagram shown in Figure 2.

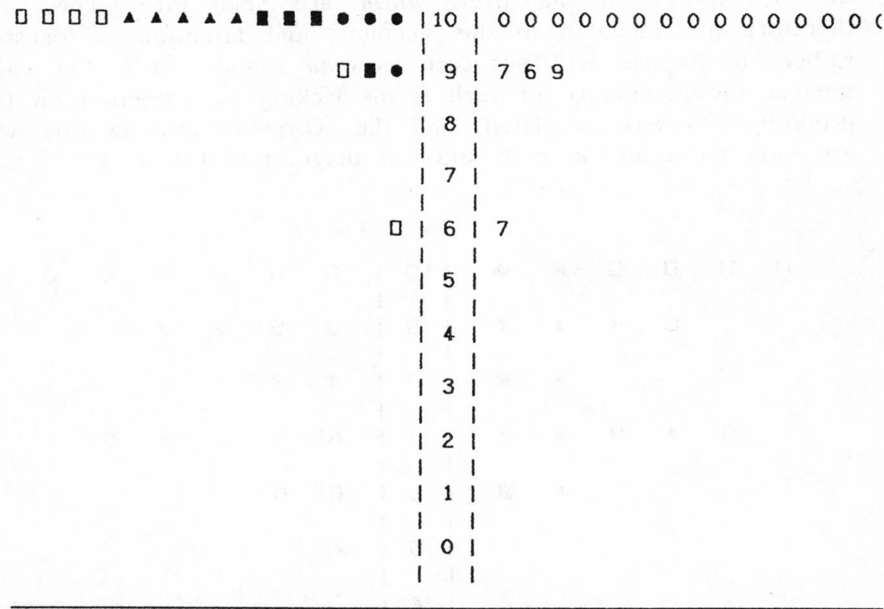

● Solfach ■ Cwm Gwaun ▲ Casmael □ Trefdraeth
stem: tens; leaves: units

Figure 2: Present tense - loss of the negative particle *ddim*, by district

Clearly there is a very high degree of consensus in this case. Only one speaker out of a total of 19 scores below 96%, and 15 of the others have scores of 100%. Negatives without an overt negative particle are the norm throughout north Pembrokeshire.

1.3 Present Tense: Loss of Inflection on o

These local, Pembrokeshire negatives can also be divided into two subtypes in a second way. The preposition *o*, which precedes the pronoun subject may be inflected to agree with it:

sdim ono i'n gwbod
sana i'n gwbod

Or it may appear without an inflection:

sdim o i'n gwbod
sa i'n gwbod

We know already from the scores displayed above in Figure 2 that examples with an overt *ddim* are very rare. They are therefore not included in this account, and attention is focussed rather on the use of forms such as *sana i* and *sa i*. For each speaker the percentage of such forms lacking an inflection on the preposition *o* was calculated, and the scores derived in this way are summarised in the stem and leaf diagram in Figure 3.

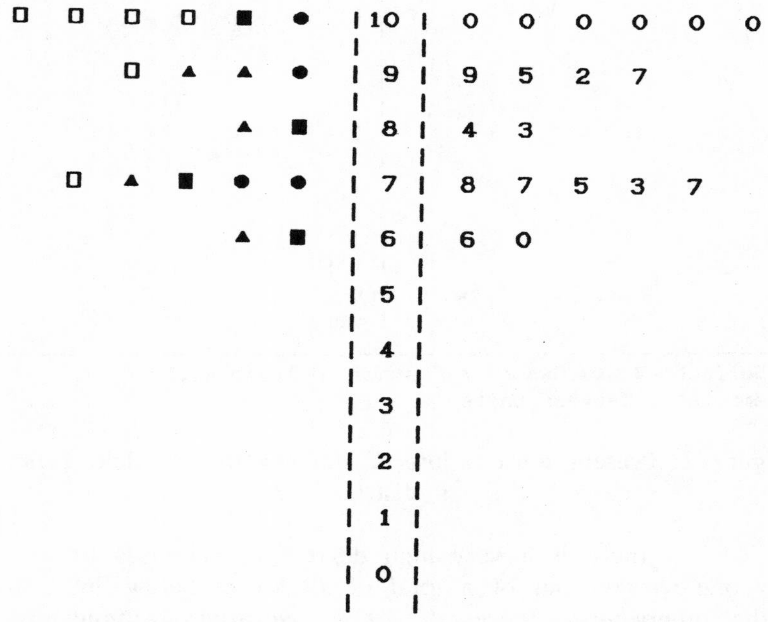

Figure 3: Present tense - loss of inflection on the preposition *o*, by district

The picture here is less clearcut. These scores are all found in the upper part of the diagram, above the 60% level, but there is considerable individual variation within each district. Negatives without an inflection on the preposition *o* are favoured then, but not overwhelmingly.

2. Imperfect Tense

2.1 Distribution

We turn now to the imperfect tense, and look at the distribution of local, Pembrokeshire forms such as the following:

wena i'n gwbod
ana i'n gwbod

For each speaker the percentage of imperfect tense forms which were of this local, Pembrokeshire type was calculated, and the scores derived in this way are shown in the stem and leaf diagram in Figure 4.

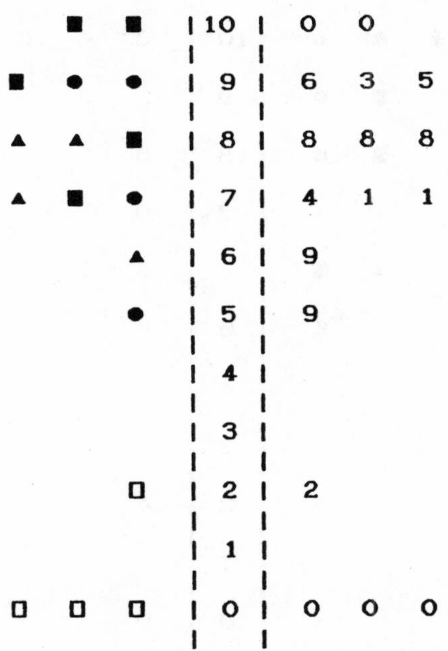

● Solfach ■ Cwm Gwaun ▲ Casmael □ Trefdraeth
stem: tens; leaves: units

Figure 4: Use of Pembrokeshire negative forms in the imperfect tense, by district

The picture here is very clear. Three districts cluster together at the top of the diagram, showing that in Solfach, Cwm Gwaun and Casmael these Pembrokeshire forms are widely used in the imperfect tense. In Trefdraeth, on the other hand, use of the local form in the imperfect tense is very low indeed. Indeed, it has almost disappeared from the spoken Welsh of this district.

2.2 Imperfect Tense: Loss of wê

Loss of the negative particle *ddim* was at least residually an option in the present tense; in the imperfect it is obligatory. Nor is there any choice over the inflection of the preposition *o*, which must be retained. There is, however, a further option in the imperfect tense. The imperfect form of *bod*, that is *wê*, may itself be retained into the surface realisation:

wena i'n gwbod

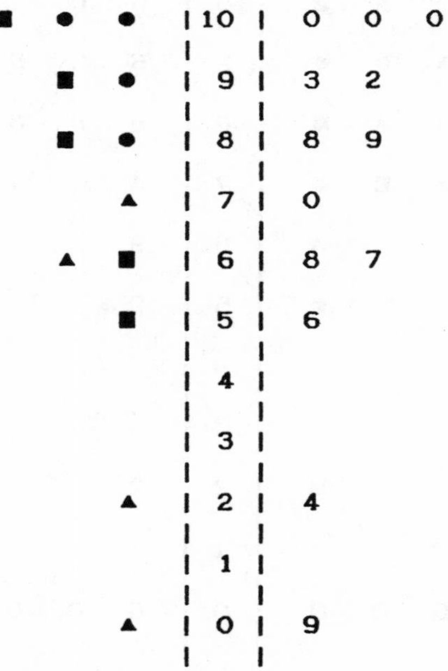

● Solfach ■ Cwm Gwaun ▲ Casmael
stem: tens; leaves: units

Figure 5: Imperfect tense - loss of *wê*, by district

Or it may be dropped, leaving the inflected preposition *o* as effectively the only remaining marker of negation or tense in the sentence:

ana i'n gwbod

For each speaker the percentage of these local imperfect forms which dropped *wê* was calculated, and the scores derived in this way are shown on the stem and leaf diagram in Figure 5.

Not surprisingly, in view of the scores shown above in Figure 4, none of the speakers from Trefdraeth produced sufficient tokens of these local imperfect forms to be included here. The discussion is therefore limited to the other three districts. It appears that two of them, Solfach and Cwm Gwaun, strongly favour forms without *wê*, though there is even so quite a wide range of scores. In Casmael, however, forms without *wê* are less popular. Two speakers fit into the same range as speakers from Solfach and Cwm Gwaun, though appearing in the lower reaches of this range, while the other two speakers reveal very low scores indeed.

3. Conclusions

The local Pembrokeshire negative forms are in widespread use in the present tense throughout the area. In the north-east there are indications that the situation is fluid, with certain speakers abandoning the local dialect forms, but even here four out of the six speakers are strongly dialectal. As to the variant forms of the present tense, there is almost complete unanimity in favour of dropping the negative particle *ddim*, and a rather weaker consensus in favour of dropping the inflection on the preposition *o*. The favoured negative form in the present tense throughout the area then is:

sa i'n gwbod

though this is strongly challenged by:

sana i'n gwbod.

In the imperfect tense the situation is rather different. There is a core area, consisting of the three more westerly districts - Solfach, Cwm Gwaun and Casmael - where the local Pembrokeshire negatives are widely used. The district around Trefdraeth in the north-east, however, rejects these dialectal forms decisively, and uses rather the pattern of negation characteristic of areas further to the east. The imperfect tense is therefore confined to a smaller core area than the present tense, and does not cover the whole of Welsh-speaking north Pembrokeshire. Loss of *wê*, the variant of the imperfect which gives the most 'extreme' dialectal forms, is strong only in the two most westerly districts, Solfach and Cwm Gwaun:

ana i'n gwbod

In Casmael, on the eastern fringe of the relevant core area, speakers vary, some favouring this same variant, others the fuller form of the negative:

wena i'n gwbod

This brief account of the distribution of Pembrokeshire negatives is only a beginning, and inevitably it must be seen as raising questions rather than providing answers. It is tempting, for instance, to assume that what we have here is a stage in the gradual erosion and loss of these dialectal negative forms. On this view, the north-east has already more or less lost the local imperfect forms, and the same process of erosion has now begun in the present tense too. Is this view justified, and if so has this erosion progressed further in the speech of younger age groups?

The pattern of distribution revealed in this material resembles closely that found in studies of phonological transitions[5]. Individual speakers either retain a high level of use of a particular dialectal form, or instead reveal only a very low, residual use of it. No-one appears at the midpoint, undecided as between the two options. Change is, on this view, just beginning in Trefdraeth so far as the present tense forms are concerned, but has been completed in the imperfect tense. In Casmael a similar process has begun with respect to the loss of *wê* in the imperfect tense. Is it indeed the case that phonological and syntactic features pattern regularly in the same way as each other? Are these examples typical of the transition zones found with syntactic variables?

We find here too that not all aspects of the negative paradigm are affected uniformly. The imperfect tense is confined to a narrower area than is the present, and the question arises of why this should be the case. What factors lead to this kind of differentiation between the component parts of a single paradigm? Do we find a similar picture with other syntactic variables, and if so what kind of units must be taken into account in considering the geographical distribution of such syntactic material, and its patterns of change through time?

In the immediate case of Pembrokeshire negatives it would

clearly be useful to carry out a fuller study, including speakers from younger age groups, and looking at a wider range of forms, including other tenses of *bod*, forms with full noun phrase subjects, and inflectional lexical verbs[6]. It would also be useful to extend this study to adjacent areas of Cardiganshire and Carmarthenshire, in order to establish the extent to which these negative forms are found outside Pembrokeshire proper[7]. In more general terms, it would be useful to extend this approach to other syntactic variables, so that detailed individual studies of this kind may begin to lead us to broader based conclusions, whose implications for dialectal variation and language change can be tested in a wider context.

Notes

1. I am grateful to Paul Meara and Beth Thomas for helpful comments and suggestions, which I have tried to incorporate in this paper. They do not of course necessarily agree with the final form it has taken.

2. For a detailed account of the syntax of these Pembrokeshire negatives, see G. M. Awbery (1988).

3. These speakers were all born within the districts to which they are assigned, and have lived locally for most of their lives. Their dates of birth range from 1880 to 1910. With one exception, they have no formal education beyond elementary schooling, and have worked in farming and related occupations. The single exception is one of the speakers from Trefdraeth, who after many years as a school teacher became an Anglican parish priest. He does not however appear to differ in his dialect usage from other members of this group. The English equivalents of the place names used to label the four districts discussed here are as follows: Solva (Solfach), the Gwaun Valley (Cwm Gwaun), Puncheston (Casmael), Newport (Trefdraeth).

4. For a discussion of this technique see Erickson and Nosanchuk (1977, p19-30). Note that syntactic variables do not arise as frequently in the course of a conversation as do phonological variables and it is possible for a speaker to produce only a few tokens of a particular variable. It was therefore decided to include in each section of the analysis only those speakers who had produced a minimum of 10 tokens of the variable under consideration. As a result, the exact number of speakers

taken into account in each section varies slightly.

5. See for instance the discussion in Chambers and Trudgill (1980, p176-80). For a similar example in a Welsh context, see Thomas (1984, p189-94).

6. These forms were not included in the present study as they did not occur in sufficient numbers in the taperecorded material. It would be necessary to scan a great many hours of conversation to be sure of having a minimum of ten tokens of some forms from each speaker, e.g. negatives containing the future tense of *bod*. Or it may prove necessary to develop some more direct elicitation techniques in such cases, though there is then always the problem of ensuring that the informant's judgement is not influenced by having his or her attention drawn to the point at issue, always a difficulty in the case of such shibboleth forms as these.

7. There is some evidence that present tense forms such as *sana i* extend as far as Ceinewydd on the Cardiganshire coast (Davies, 1934, p460), and to Hebron in Carmarthenshire (Thorne, 1977, p391-2). Detailed knowledge of the distribution of these negative forms in south-west Wales generally is, however, lacking.

References

Awbery, G. M. (1988) Pembrokeshire negatives. *Bulletin of the Board of Celtic Studies,* **35**, 37-49.

Chambers, J. K. and Trudgill, P. (1980) *Dialectology*. Cambridge: Cambridge University Press.

Davies, J. J. G. (1934) *Astudiaeth o Gymraeg llafar ardal Ceinewydd*. Doctoral thesis, University of Wales.

Erickson, B. H. and Nosanchuk, T. A. (1979) *Understanding Data*. Milton Keynes: The Open University.

Thomas, B. (1984) Linguistic and non-linguistic boundaries in north-east Wales. In Ball, M. J. and Jones, G. E. (eds), *Welsh Phonology*. Cardiff: University of Wales Press. Pp.189-207.

Thorne, D. A. (1977) Arwyddocâd y rhagenwau personol ail berson unigol yng Nglyn Nedd (Gorllewin Morgannwg), Hebron (Dyfed) a Charnhedryn (Dyfed). *Bulletin of the Board of Celtic Studies*, **27**, 389-98.

Networks, Nuclei and Boundaries in Areal Dialectology*

Alan R. Thomas
University College of North Wales, Bangor

0. Introduction

My aim is to see what kinds of areal features can be deduced from an examination of sameness and difference between enquiry sites in the Welsh language dialect area. The data is taken from 175 enquiry sites and comprises about 1000 regional responses to 390 questions (for which see Thomas, 1973); more detailed discussion of some of the methodologies involved will be found in Thomas (1980).

1. Differences Matrix

We start with a matrix which records the number of instances in which each enquiry site differs from all others: a sort of *lexical* distance chart which resembles conventional mileage distance charts (see Thomas, 1980, Appendix IV). We can then look at individual sites in terms of their degree of difference from others, or their likeness to them.

What I decided to do was to group sites according to degrees of similarity: this had particular interest for me because the data had already been analysed in terms of differentiation between sites, in determining the routes which isoglosses typically followed, drawing lines between sites whenever they differed in their response for a particular word, rather than grouping sites with similar responses together.

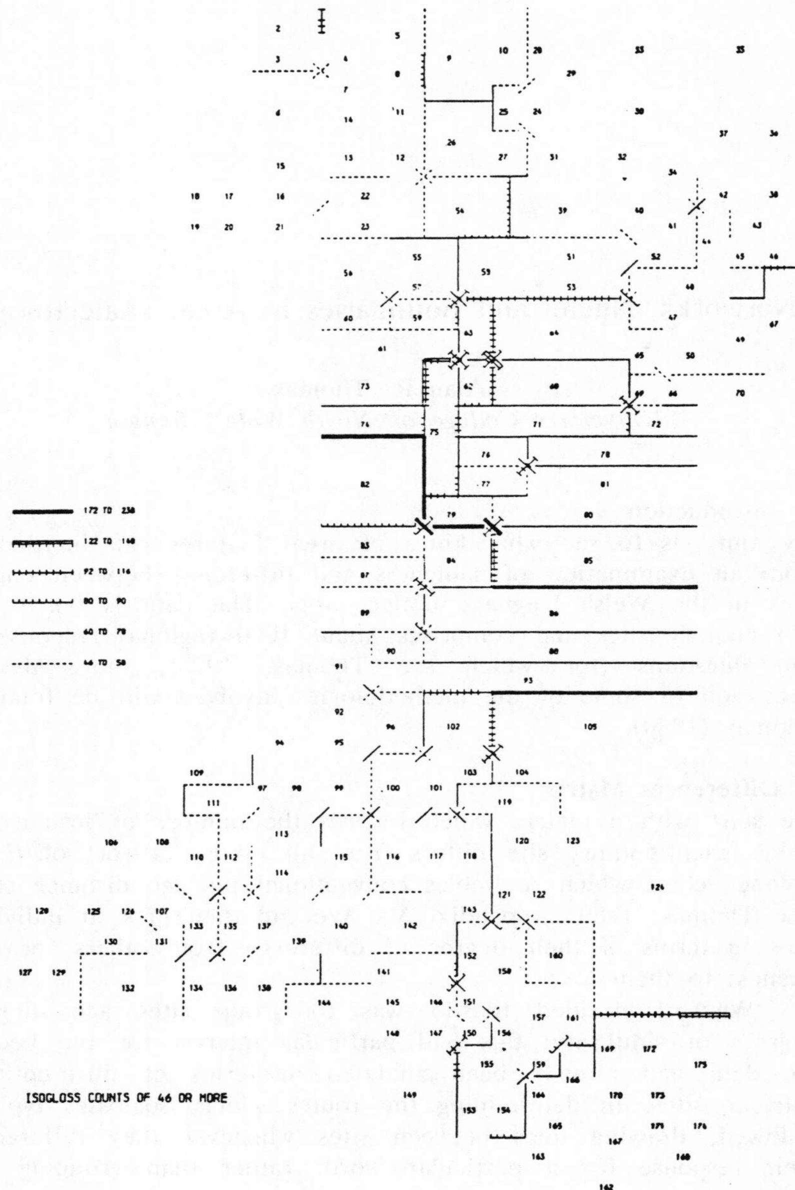
172 TO 238
122 TO 140
92 TO 116
80 TO 90
60 TO 78
46 TO 58
ISOGLOSS COUNTS OF 46 OR MORE

Figure 1

3. Isogloss Layout

The isogloss base map is a grid which provides routes for isoglosses to run along, separating the sites on the basis of their geographical proximity and the layout of communication routes - in this way it was hoped to produce confrontations between sites which were 'meaningful', and avoid any which might be rendered spurious by unreal geographical separation, for example.

The isogloss counts over 45 (see Figure 1) divide the country very plausibly. We have a major north-south divide, and lesser ones running north and south to divide the major north and south dialect areas. The interest of this map for us here is that it provides a basis of knowledge about the areal characteristics of the Welsh dialect area against which to assess the effectiveness of any other technique of analysis we might try.

4. Minimum Spanning Tree

I will compare two ways of grouping sites according to the degree of similarity of their responses - one standard statistical technique, and one developed by myself specifically to meet the needs of the dialectologist.

One interesting procedure which has been applied to some *Survey of English Dialects* (SED) data for the West of England is the Minimum Spanning Tree (MST); this appears in Morgan and Shaw (ms), which develops proposals put forward in Shaw (1974). It is essentially a means of finding the shortest route through the data. The procedure is thus: starting with any site, we link to it the least dissimilar site to it: thus we start to build the tree. We then add to the developing tree (the first pair of sites) the site which is least dissimilar to either of the sites already selected; then we link in the site which is most similar to any of the three, and so on. Each successive site must be new to the tree - it must come from outside those which are already part of the tree - and no closed loops are permitted. Thus at any time during the growth of the tree, we have two sets of sites: those which are part of the tree, and those which wait to be matched. A particular site may have one or many links, and all sites must be absorbed as part of the tree. An important point to note is that where two or more sites, from the unmatched set, have an identical dissimilarity score with a given site within the tree, an arbitrary decision is made as to which match is used; of course, this affects the shape of the overall tree, so that a number of alternative trees may be available for the same data - and, in the case of dialect data, almost certainly will be, due to the inevitable size of the data file.

Figure 2 gives part of the - or, rather, 'a' - MST for the same Welsh data as was analysed for the isogloss grid-map, though in much simplified form: sites are indicated by a filled circle, and site numbers shown only at a few crucial points. We find a continuous tree, with no breaks, linking all sites. We find, too, that sites very considerably in the number of links which they achieve, some achieving as many as four: the hypothesis in relation to these is that they are potential focal sites. That claim, in particular cases, can be verified only from outside the linguistic data of course, by appeal to such factors as known patterns of communication - and I have not yet been able to investigate that for the Welsh data. It must be said, though, that Morgan and Shaw's findings for the West of England look quite promising in this respect. One more point to note is that the tree, as I've drawn it, does not take account of the degree of similarity found between sites in particular cases; clearly, the sites will be more alike in some cases than in others, and the tree should ideally reflect that by varying the distance between points. In practice, however, for the Welsh data, the range of similarity counts appears to be significant only in a small number of instances which I will take up presently, and so I have not incorporated that aspect of the tree's structure.

5. Similarity Networks

The specialised procedure which I want to compare with the MST differs from it in two significant ways:

1. closed loops are permitted, so that we produce networks instead of trees;
2. we work within a *range* of similarity counts, and not with a single one in each case. For each site, we read off, from the difference matrix, the three lowest counts - this pairs each site with at least three others (i.e. the three sites from which it is least differentiated, and hence most similar to) and frequently *more* than three, where there are tied counts.

The procedure is this: we first find the two most similar sites of the whole set, and select one of them as a pivot site; that one in turn selects its partner - and any other sites which meet the matching criteria. The procedure is repeated for every new site selected, until every one of them has been used as a pivot site.

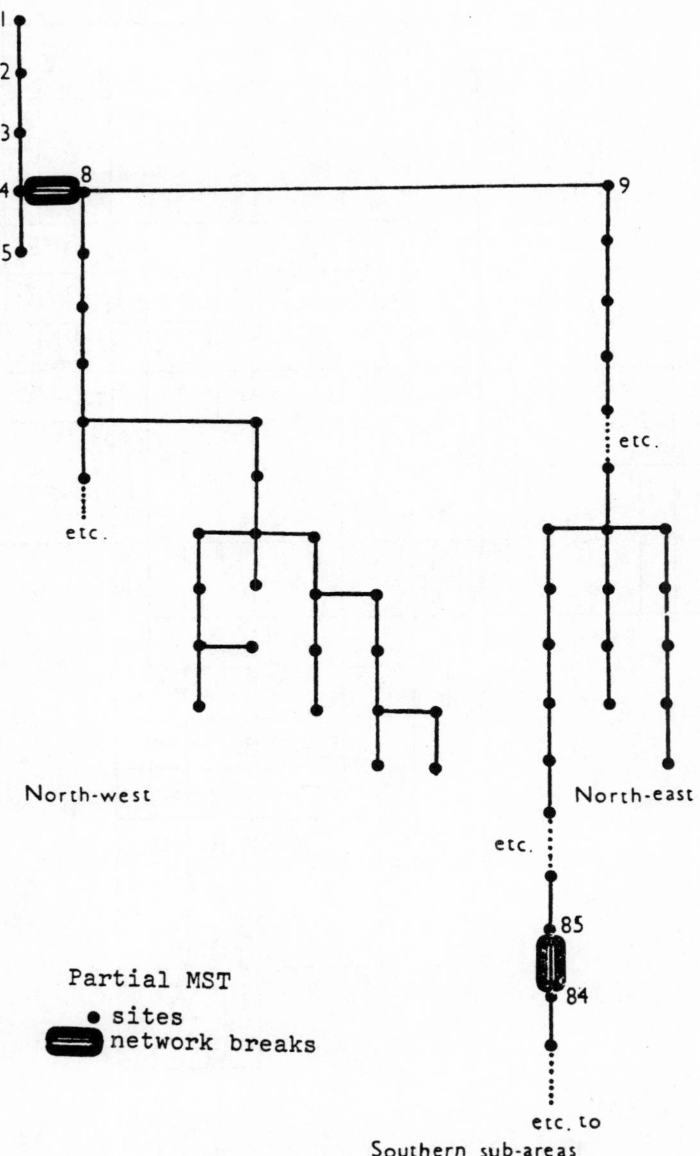

Figure 2

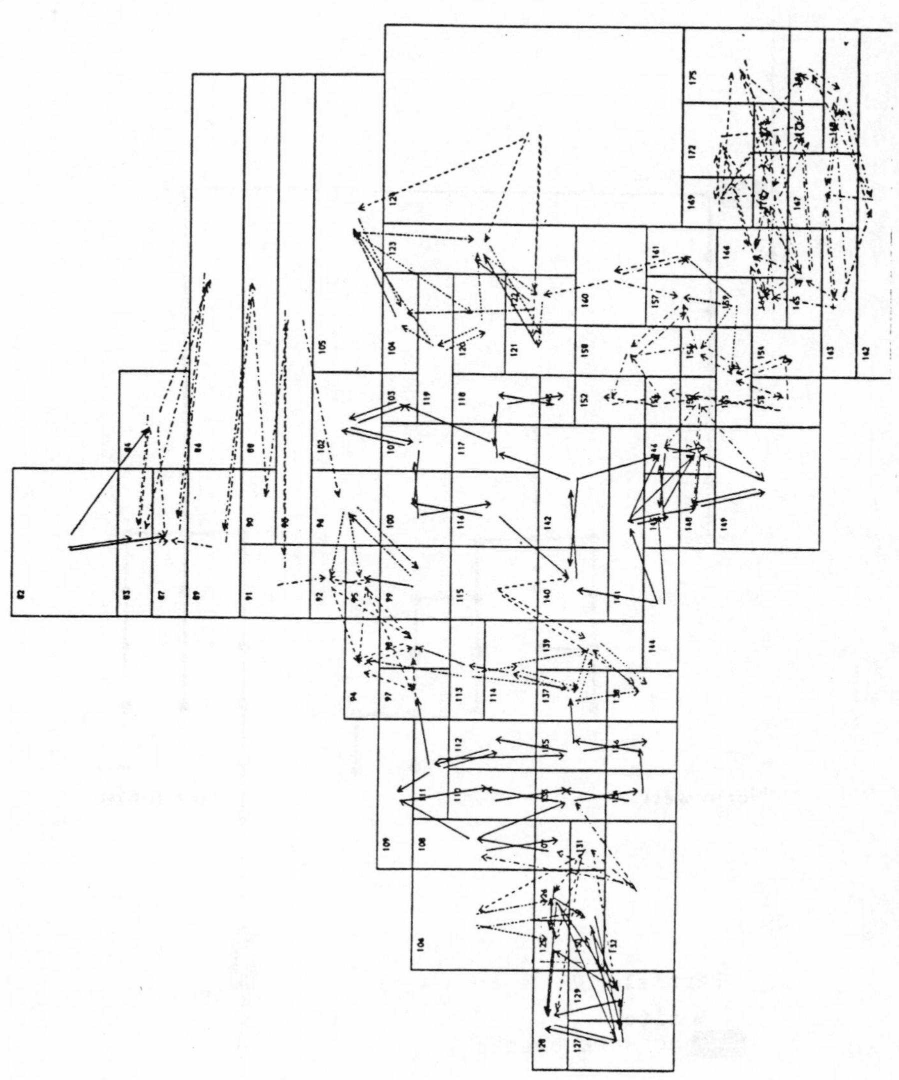

Figure 3. *Similarity networks linked (south)*

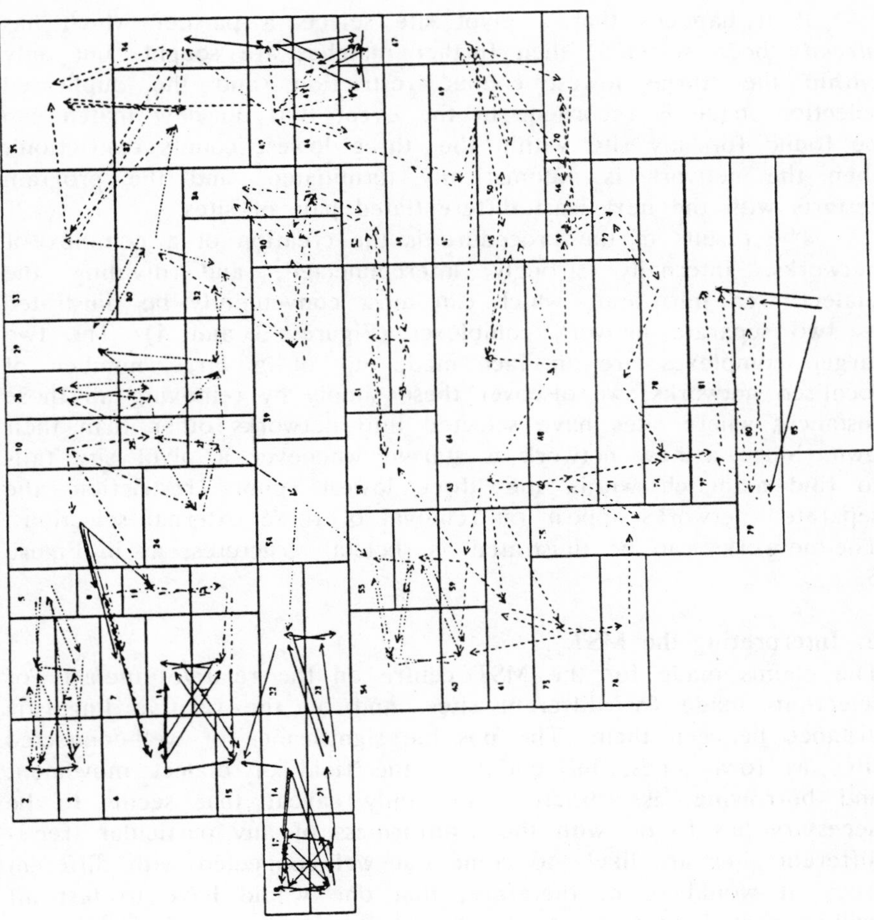

Figure 4. *Similarity networks linked (north)*

If it happens that a pivot site selects a partner which has *already* been selected, then further matches are sought, but only within the 'three lowest counts' restriction, and the duplicated selection made is recorded. In the event that no new match can be found for any site within the 'three lowest counts restriction', then the network is automatically terminated, and the program restarts with the next least differentiated pair of sites.

The results of the procedure is the creation of a complex of networks, internally strongly interconnected, and dividing the dialect area into four, which can most conveniently be illustrated as two separate network complexes (Figures 3 and 4). The two larger complexes are in fact made up of a large number of localised networks; we discover these simply by removing all those instances where sites have selected into networks other than their own. Since a new network is started whenever a pivot site fails to find a match within the 'three lowest counts' restriction, the separated networks appear on removal of these external selections. The networks can be illustrated as skeletal structures, as in Figure 5.

6. Interpreting the MST

The claims made for the MST centre on the relative intensity of selections made for different sites, and on the relative linguistic distance between them. The possible significance of well-connected sites as focal ones, influential in the field of dialect movement and borrowing, is attractive; the only caveat that seems to be necessary has to do with the arbitrariness of any particular tree - different sites are likely to come out well-connected with different trees. it would seem, therefore, that one would have to test *all* well-connected sites, from *all* the possible trees, to find the ones that are supported as focal by independent evidence. Unless, of course, it emerged that the shortest tree threw up the optimum set of focal sites, which I doubt: by definition, the fact that a site is well-connected can only be suggestive of any dominance it could have in sociolinguistic terms.

The role of the relative linguistic distance between sites does seem to be an interesting one. On the whole, distances in this data are relatively small - they range from zero to 18% - but at three points (or, rather, between two sites in three different places) there is a sudden jump, corresponding to the three network breaks: crossing from Anglesey in the extreme north-west into the main northern network, the distance (degree of differentiation) between sites leaps by around 100%, from 2% to 4%; crossing from the main northern network into the main southern one, there is a leap of around 300%, from 6% to 18%; and across the divide between the main southern network and Glamorgan in the south-east, the leap is around 100%, from 4% to 8% (Figure 2 does not show this one).

It seems, then, that although the MST appears as a continuous line or set of them (although it could well be drawn to link sites in geographical dispersion), we can derive information about major dialectal divisions from an examination of its internal structure. We can, however, get even more information from an examination of its physical appearance: the topography of the MST varies in an interesting way - at each end it has a fairly complex, branching structure, while in the middle it merely steps through from site to site, more or less in a straight line. We know from other analyses that the dialect continuum in Wales is made up of two major dialects - north and south - and (broadly speaking) bilateral divisions within each, giving north-east, north-west and south-east and south-west; and there is a broad transition belt linking the two major areas. The branching at each end of the MST, and the relatively direct stepping through its middle correspond closely with those independently arrived at features. And, what is more, the MST can be reorganised in the form of a dendrogram, which resembles a conventional branching-tree diagram, with the intersections of its branches representing decreasing levels of similarity as we move from bottom to top or from tip to root - with the middle section as a relatively level line, and the branches at both ends suspended from it. This gives a very accurate representation of the dialectal situation as we know it to be.

7. Interpreting the Similarity Networks

The network analysis also reflects the fundamental division into north and south, and it additionally - like the MST - sets the extreme northern area of Anglesey and the extreme southern area of Glamorgan apart. It is worth noting that both these areas are significant dialect nuclei, identified as such by independent procedures, though not more significant, and no more distinctive as nuclei than others which these present procedures do *not* pick out.

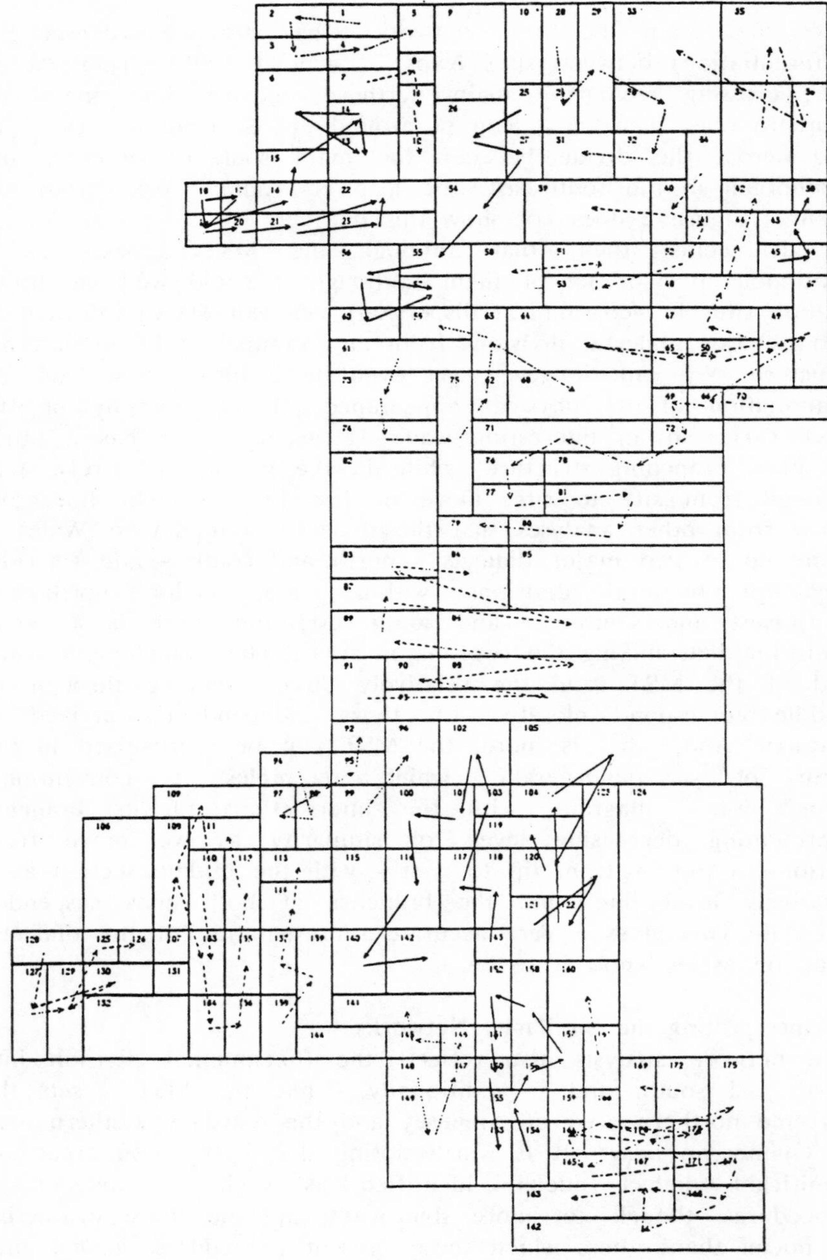

Figure 5. *Similarity networks (seperated)*

The real value of the network analysis lies in the clustering of enquiry sites which it produces: though I will not follow this up here (see further Thomas 1980), the site clusters do correlate closely with known patterns of settlement and community distributions. Additionally, however, we can learn from an examination of the internal structure of the network complex, just as we could from that of the MST. For this we need to take the networks as separated entities, shorn of the interconnections between them. Two characteristics of the networks accurately reflect the overall disposition of the dialect area from other, independent analyses; the degree of internal differentiation within individual networks, and the relative intensity of internal re-selection.

8. Internal Differentiation

Table 1 shows the averaged rate of internal differentiation for individual networks, and the map shows them numbered to correspond with the table. As we would expect, the least differentiated, and hence most cohesive networks are on the peripheries - at or near the dialect nuclei, as is shown in Figure 6. As we get closer to the major network break, the average rate of internal differentiation increases. We have, then, a direct correlation between the rate of differentiation within networks and their positions relative to dialect nuclei and the transition belt.

network	*diff rate*	*network*	*diff rate*
1	16	13	25
2	5	14	14
3	8	15	29
4	4	16	64
5	18	17	23
6	12	18	12
7	14	19	26
8	8	20	15
9	9	21	37
10	16	22	49
11	37	23	51
12	7	overall average	22

Table 1. Average rate of internal differentiation in networks

9. Intensity Rating

I have mentioned the fact that sites frequently select into networks other than those to which they immediately belong - the process by which the network complex is created. At the same time, sites may re-select sites within their own networks, and we can expect such internal re-selection to reflect the cohesion of the site clusters involved. Table 2 gives the percentages of selections, for each network, which were internal. Again, the peripheral networks, close to the dialect nuclei, are distinguished by having the highest ratings, while those closer to the network break make less internal selections (see Figure 6 for location of networks). In this case again, then, the location of the major topographical features - the main dialect areas and the transition belt - can be deduced from an analysis of the internal structure of the networks. We might further expect that the fuller specification of linguistic distance between sites which the networking procedure gives, as compared with the MST, might provide a sound basis for a mapping procedure which reflected these linguistic distances, while still retaining their basic geographical dispositions.

network	intns rate	network	intns rate
1	64%	13	46%
2	66%	14	38%
3	68%	15	44%
4	60%	16	45%
5	62%	17	55%
6	62%	18	20%
7	36%	19	42%
8	68%	20	16%
9	50%	21	37%
10	58%	22	30%
11	50%	23	45%
12	8%	overall average	43%

Table 2 Intensity Rating of Similarity Networks

Finally, in direct relation to the networking procedure, we might expect the more extensive links which are permitted to provide a better basis for predicting which sites are likely to turn out to be focal, since the network is arbitrary only in the sense that we might have chosen to make a more complex one - simply by extending the range of scores for the matching procedure, networks of greater and greater detail can be built up.

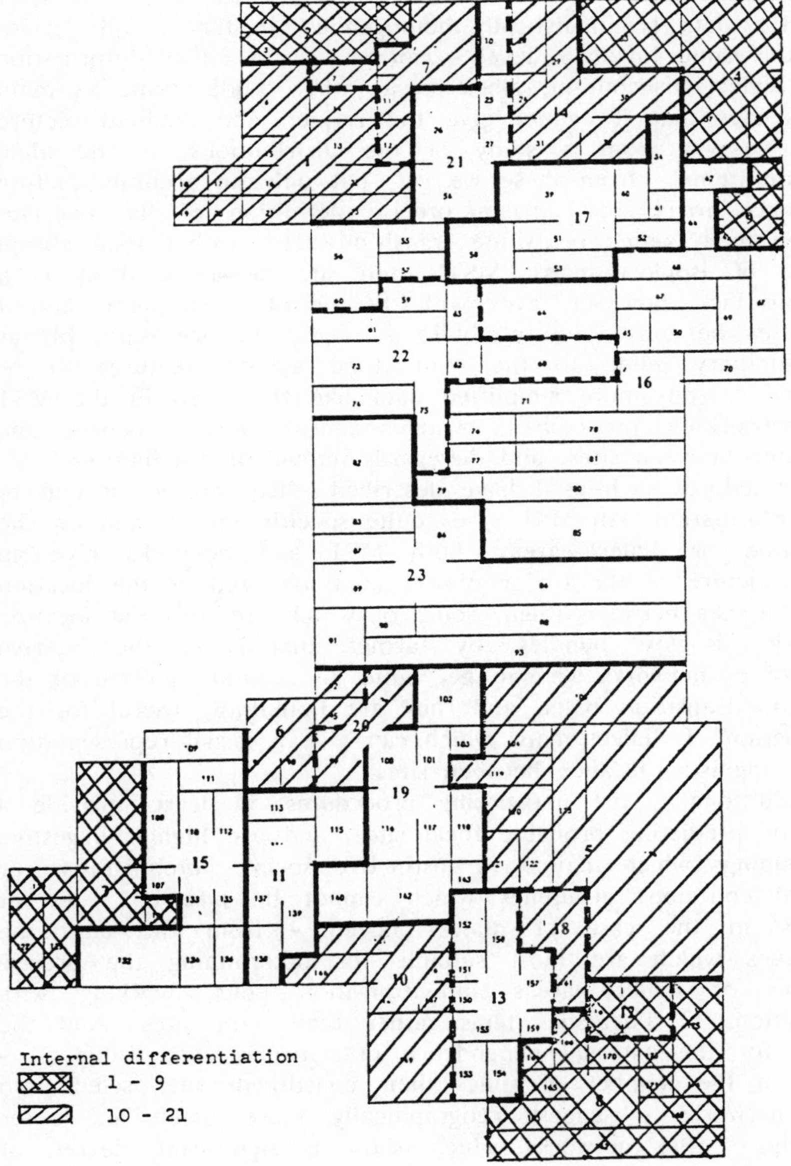

Figure 6

10. Conclusions

It is clear that studies of similarity counts between sites - at least when the data is linguistically homogenous, in that it all derives from the same linguistic level - can give us a lot of information about dialect distribution, albeit in a rather crude form. Its main drawback is that it cannot give the refined and detailed picture which we get from a study of the distributions of individual linguistic items - from these we get, not only an accurate picture of dialect areas, but also a precise definition of the overlaps between them which constitute transition belts, rather than abrupt cut-offs of isogloss maps, MST's and site networks. That is a laborious task, however, even with the aid of a computer, and it may often be convenient to obtain a rougher picture - possibly as a preliminary guide to the main topographical features to be expected - from more simplified data like that used in the MST and networking procedures, which records only sameness and difference between sites, and disregards individual distributions.

Procedures such as I have described, then, are a shortcut to areal information. An MST gives quite specific information on the disposition of dialect areas: both MST and networks give an overall picture of the major dialect continua, and of the location of the breaks between them, some of which are also the location of major isogloss bundles; by further analysis of the internal structure of networks we can get quite an accurate picture of the extent of transition belts, and they are potentially useful for the construction of dialect maps which can give a visual representation of the linguistic distance between sites.

Additionally, the networking procedures, at least, provide a basis for predicting probable focal sites, and are highly suggestive of groupings which may have distinctive social, administrative or political cohesion: groupings which cannot be inferred - except possibly in the case of dialect nuclei - from the clustering techniques which are most suitable for determining the precise locations of dialect areas and transition belts, working with distributions of linguistic items rather than with sites. And the figures for the external dependence of networks (see Table 3) - based on the number of times their constituent sites select into other networks - suggest geographically more extensive, looser groupings - the networks which show a significant degree of interdependence in this respect are separated by dotted lines in Figure 6.

network	ext. depend	network	ext. depend
7	29%	16	12%
9	10%	17	9%
10	5%	18	40%
11	17%	19	5%
12	75%	20	50%
13	18%	21	30%
14	15%	22	35%
15	12%	23	9%
		overall average	17%

Table 3 External Dependence of Similarity Networks

Notes

* This contribution is a modified version of one published in Warkentyne, H. (ed), *Methods IV*, University of Victoria, 1981.

References

Morgan, B. and Shaw, D. (ms) Illustrating data on English dialects.

Shaw, D. (1974) Statistical analysis of dialect boundaries. *Computers and the Humanities*, **8**, iii.

Thomas, A. R. (1973) *The Linguistic Geography of Wales*. Cardiff: University of Wales Press.

Thomas, A. R. (1980) *Areal Analysis of Dialect Data by Computer*. Cardiff: University of Wales Press.

Amrywio Sosioieithyddol yn Nhafodiaith Pont-rhyd-y-fen

Beth Thomas
Amgueddfa Werin Cymru

0. Rhagarweiniad

Un o bentrefi diwydianol cymoedd y De yw Pont-rhyd-y-fen: pentref a dyfodd yn sgîl datblygu'r diwydiant haearn yn Nyffryn Afan, ac a flodeuodd ymhellach oherwydd twf y diwydiant glo. Ardal tra diddorol ydyw i'r sosioieithydd, gan ei bod nid yn unig yn ffiniol yn dafodieithol, ond hefyd yn ymylol o safbwynt y Gymraeg ei hun.

Tan yr Ail Ryfel Byd, ynys o Gymreictod ydoedd mewn ardal a oedd yn prysur Seisnigo, ond oherwydd natur glos ac unffurf y gymuned, llwyddwyd i wrthsefyll dylanwad y Saesneg a pharhau i ddefnyddio'r Gymraeg. Ers y rhyfel, fodd bynnag, bu datblygiadau mawr ym mhob agwedd o fywyd y pentref: lleihaodd y boblogaeth, bu newid ym mhatrymau gwaith y trigolion, ac ail-drefnwyd y gyfundrefn addysg. O ganlyniad, chwalwyd y cysylltiadau rhwng pentrefwyr a'i gilydd, a daeth y gymuned fwyfwy o dan ddylanwad yr ardaloedd Seisnigedig cyfagos. Erbyn heddiw, un rhan o dair yn unig o boblogaeth y pentref sydd yn medru Cymraeg, o'i chymharu â 76% yn 1951.[1] Perthyn y mwyafrif helaeth o'r Cymry Cymraeg i'r genhedlaeth a fagwyd yn y gymuned lofaol glos a fodolai cyn yr Ail Ryfel Byd. Saesneg yw iaith y cenedlaethau a fagwyd ers y rhyfel, mewn cyfnod o newid cymdeithasol a lledu gorwelion.

1. Y Newidynnau Ieithyddol

Mae hanes y Gymraeg ym Mhont-rhyd-y-fen yn ategu dadleuon

Milroy (1980) am allu rhwydweithau cymdeithasol dwys ac amlbleth i gynnal iaith neu dafodiaith warthnodedig. Ateg bellach yw'r modd yr adlewyrchir gwahaniaethau rhwydweithiol y trigolion yn eu Cymraeg llafar. Yn y papur hwn, canolbwyntir ar ddau newidyn ffonolegol a gysylltir yn arbennig â thafodiaith y De-ddwyrain.

Efallai mai'r mwyaf trawiadol o nodweddion y dafodiaith hon yw realeiddio'r orgreffyn "a" a'r ddeugraff "ae" gan lafariad flaen hanner-agored hir mewn unsillafion ac yn y sillaf olaf acennog: [tɛːd] a glywir yn lle [taːd], a [kəmˈrɛːg] yn hytrach na [kəmˈraːg] y De-orllewin. Nodwedd amlwg arall yw calediad, sef dileisio ffrwydrolion lleisiol rhwng y goben a'r sillaf olaf acennog. Gall hyn ddigwydd pan ddaw'r ffrwydrolyn o flaen llafariad neu o flaen cytsain drwynol neu ochrol. Felly ceir [te·pig], [ka·tu] ac [ɛklus] yn lle [te·big], [ka·du] ac [ɛglus].

Er cysylltu'r ddwy nodwedd â thafodiaith y De-ddwyrain, nid ydynt yn ymestyn dros yr un diriogaeth. Clywir calediad trwy Forgannwg gyfan a rhan o ddwyrain Dyfed, tra na cheir yr amrywyn [ɛː] ymhellach i'r gorllewin na Dyffryn Afan. Ffiniol iawn yw Pont-rhyd-y-fen yng nghyswllt yr [ɛː]: ni chlywir yr amrywyn mewn ardaloedd i'r gorllewin o'r pentref, nac ychwaith yng Nghwmafan, y pentref nesaf i lawr y cwm. Ac er i'r sain gael ei huniaethu'n lleol â "iaith Pont-rhyd-y-fen", ni wneir defnydd ohoni ond gan leiafrif o Gymry Cymraeg y pentref. Y mae'r defnydd a wneir o'r amrywyn hwn, a chalediad hefyd, yn amrywio'n gymdeithasol. Nod y papur hwn yw disgrifio union natur yr amrywio hwnnw.

2. Methodoleg

Tua 250 o boblogaeth Pont-rhyd-y-fen oedd yn siarad Cymraeg pan wnaethpwyd y gwaith maes ar gyfer yr astudiaeth.[2] Holwyd a recordiwyd 54 ohonynt yn rhan o sampl tebygolrwydd o Gymry'r pentref. Yn dilyn dull Milroy (1980), rhannwyd y deunydd ieithyddol a gasglwyd yn ddwy arddull, sef arddull cyfweliad a llafar digymell. Oherwydd cyfyngiadau sefyllfa cyfweliad, nid oedd modd casglu deunydd cymharol yn y ddwy arddull gan bob un o'r 54 siaradwr a ffurfiai'r sampl gwreiddiol. Y mae'r deunydd sydd gennyf yma felly'n seiliedig ar sgorau 42 o siaradwyr y llwyddwyd i recordio digon o'u llafar digymell a'u harddull cyfweliad.[3]

Ffig 1: Sgorau ar gyfer yr amrywyn [ɛ:]

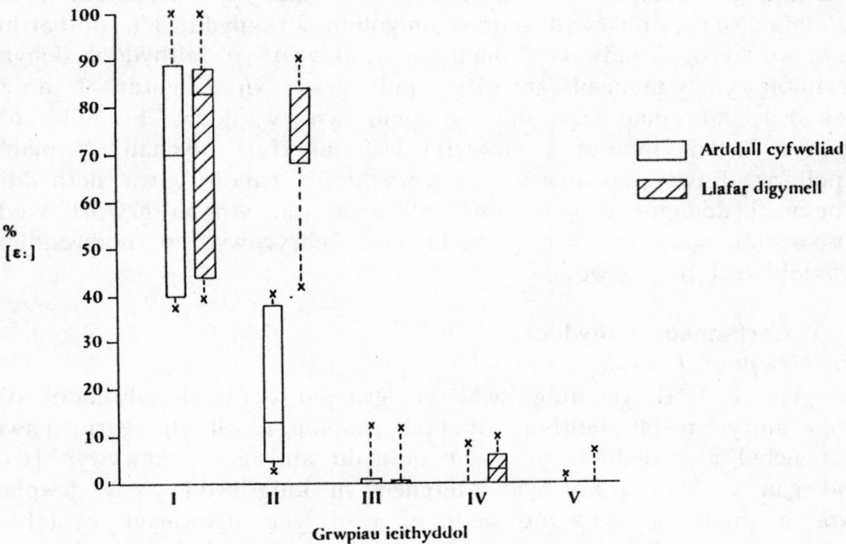

Ffig 2: Sgorau ar gyfer calediad

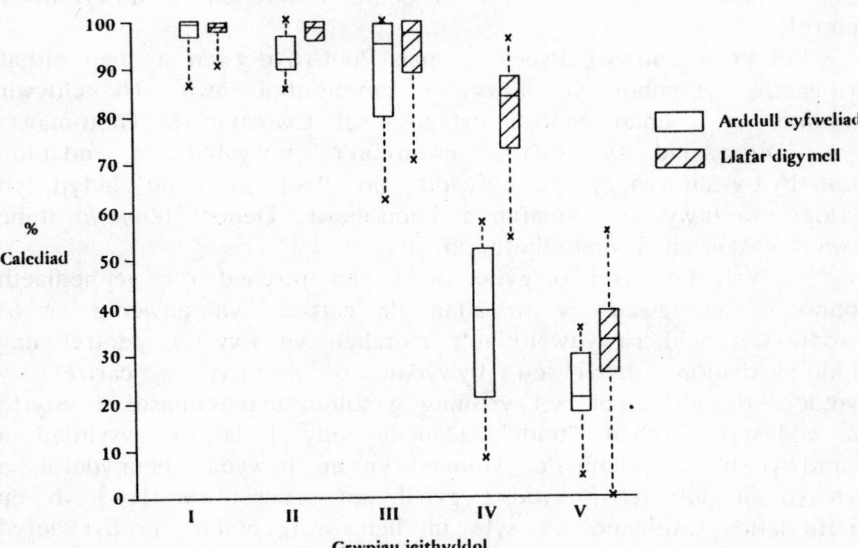

Gyda'r ddau newidyn sgoriwyd pob siaradwr yn ganrannol, yn nhermau presenoldeb neu absenoldeb yr amrywyn tafodieithol yn eu llafar. Yna cymharwyd sgorau unigolion â'i gilydd, a'u dosbarthu yn grwpiau o siaradwyr a oedd yn ymddwyn yn ieithyddol debyg. Crynhoir yr ystadegau ar gyfer pob grŵp yn Ffigurau 1 a 2. Dangosir amrediad sgorau'r grwpiau yn y ddwy arddull, o'r chwartel uchaf hyd at y chwartel isaf, ar ffurf blychau. Y mae'r llinell ar draws pob blwch yn cynrychioli'r canolrif, tra defnyddir croesau i ddangos y sgôr uchaf a'r sgôr isaf ymhob grŵp.[4] Wedi dosbarthu'r siaradwyr yn y modd hwn, edrychwyd ar nodweddion cymdeithasol pob grŵp.

3. Y Carfannau Ieithyddol

3.1 Grwpiau I a II

Grwpiau I a II yn unig sydd yn gwneud defnydd sylweddol o'r *ddau* amrywyn tafodieithol. Er bod grwpiau eraill yn sgorio llawn mor uchel ar galediad, ni wneir defnydd amlwg o'r amrywyn [ɛ:] ond gan y ddau grŵp hyn. Merched yn unig sydd yn y grwpiau hyn, a phob un ohonynt wedi ei geni yng nghwarter cyntaf y ganrif hon, neu'n gynharach. Mae 99% ohonynt hefyd yn hanu o ochr ddwyreiniol y pentref, neu yn mynychu un o'r ddau gapel sydd wedi eu lleoli yno. Rhaid gofyn felly paham y cyfyngir yr [ɛ:] i ferched, ac yn fwyaf arbennig i ferched o ddwyrain y pentref.

Fel yr esboniwyd eisoes, y mae Pont-rhyd-y-fen ar ben eithaf tiriogaeth bresennol yr amrywyn tafodieithol hwn. Ni chlywir mohono yn y ddau bentref cyfagos, sef Cwmafan a Thon-mawr. Cyn Dirwasgiad y 30au, gweithiai'r mwyafrif o ddynion Pont-rhyd-y-fen yn y gweithfeydd glo lleol, a oedd hefyd yn cyflogi gweithwyr o Gwmafan a Thon-mawr. Deuent felly yn ifanc iawn i gysylltiad â thafodiaith ddi-[ɛ:].

Ychydig iawn o gyfle oedd gan ferched o'r genhedlaeth honno i gael gwaith y tu allan i'r cartref, yn enwedig ar ôl priodi. Cyfyngid rhwydweithiau'r merched yn fwy i'r pentref nag eiddo'r dynion: troai eu bywydau o gwmpas y cartref, y gymdogaeth, a'r capel, sef yr unig ganolfan gymdeithasol a ystyrid yn addas i ferched "teidi". Deuent felly i lai o gysylltiad â siaradwyr o'r tu allan i'r gymuned yn eu bywydau beunyddiol, a hyn yn ôl pob tebyg sydd i gyfrif am oroesiad yr [ɛ:] yn eu hiaith lafar. Dadlennol yw sylw un hen wraig bod ei brodyr hefyd yn arfer y sain pan yn blant bach: "On nw'n gweud mæs pan on nw'n rai bæch..ond pan on nw'n tyfu..dethon nw mâs o'r mæs". Gyda chau'r gweithfeydd lleol yn y 30au, a'r newid diwydiannol a chymdeithasol a ddaeth yn sgîl yr Ail Ryfel Byd, ehangwyd rhwydweithiau dynion a merched fel ei gilydd. Y mae'r merched iau felly mor allblyg eu cysylltiadau cymdeithasol â'r dynion, ac o ganlyniad lawn mor ddi-[ɛ:].

Nid yw hyn, fodd bynnag, yn cynnig esboniad am ddiffyg yr [ɛ:] yng ngorllewin y pentref, hyd yn oed yn llafar y gwragedd hŷn. Y mae gan drigolion y pen yma i'r gymuned gysylltiadau cryf ac amlbleth â phentref Ton-mawr - cysylltiadau cryfach, efallai, na'r rhai sydd yn eu clymu â dwyrain Pont-rhyd-y-fen. Yn ysgol Ton-mawr y cafodd nifer o'r siaradwyr eu haddysgu, a bu rhai ohonynt yn gweithio yno yn y glofeydd. Mae rhyngbriodi hefyd yn gyffredin. Un wraig yn unig o'r ochr orllewinol sydd yn arfer yr [ɛ:] yn lled gyson, er nad yw ei defnydd o'r sain mor uchel â'r gwragedd o'r ochr ddwyreiniol. Hon yw'r wraig hynaf yn y sampl, a chredaf fod arwyddocâd i hynny. Y mae'r dystiolaeth yn awgrymu bod yr [ɛ:] ar un adeg yn helaethach ei defnydd trwy'r gymuned, ond i bwysau o'r tu allan - o bentrefi cyfagos a chydweithwyr o ardaloedd eraill - gyfyngu'r amrywyn i'r garfan fwyaf lleol ei rhwydweithiau, sef gwragedd hŷn ochr ddwyreiniol y gymuned.

Nid yw grwpiau I a II yn hollol unffurf yn y modd y defnyddiant yr [ɛ:]. Fel y gwelir wrth ffigur 1, mae merched grŵp I yn defnyddio'r sain yn lled gyson beth bynnag fo'r cyd-destun cymdeithasol, tra gollyngir yr [ɛ:] gan grŵp II mewn cyd-destunau ffurfiol. Gwasanaethir ochr ddwyreiniol y pentref gan ddau gapel: Jerusalem, capel y Methodistiaid, a Bethel, capel y Bedyddwyr. O'r chwe gwraig a berthyn i grŵp I, mae 5 ohonynt yn aelodau yn Jerusalem, tra bo 4 allan o'r 5 yn grŵp II yn mynychu Bethel.

Merched Bethel, felly, sydd yn amrywio yn arddulliol. Yn ôl y dystiolaeth, bu gwragedd Bethel erioed yn fwy cyhoeddus na merched Jerusalem. Mae dwy o'r sampl yn ddiaconesau, a'r lleill yn amlwg yng ngweithgareddau diwylliannol y cylch. Cawsant felly brofiad o ddefnyddio'r Gymraeg mewn cyd-destunau tra chyhoeddus, a thrwy eu gweithgareddau, daethant i gysylltiad achlysurol â Chymry diwylliedig o'r tu allan i'r gymuned. Serch hynny, deil eu cysylltiadau rhwydweithiol beunyddiol yn ddwys a thra lleol.

Pwysig yw nodi felly mai yn eu rhyngweithio â thylwyth a

chymdogion y cofnodwyd y sgorau uchel ar gyfer [ɛ:]. Wrth siarad â mi - neu, yn achos un siaradwraig, â chyfeilles o ardal arall - y mae'r sgorau lawer yn is. Gellir dadlau bod ymddygiad ieithyddol y gwragedd cyhoeddus hyn yn adlewyrchu nid yn unig ffurfioldeb y sefyllfa, ond hefyd y grwpiau cymdeithasol y ceisiant uniaethu â hwy: eu cymdogaeth leol ar y naill llaw, a rhwydwaith ehangach o Gymry diwylliedig ar y llaw arall.[5] Yr hyn sy'n annisgwyl, fodd bynnag, yw diffyg amrywio arddulliol y grŵp hwn yn achos calediad (gw. ffigur 2).

3.2 Grwpiau III a V

Syrthia bron i hanner y sampl, a thrwy ymlygiad y mwyafrif o'r boblogaeth, i grŵp III. Hwn yw'r grŵp mwyaf cyson ei ymddygiad ieithyddol, yn ddi-[ɛ:], ond yn sgorio'n uchel yn y ddwy arddull ar galediad. Digon cymysg, ar yr olwg gyntaf, yw cefndir cymdeithasol y garfan hon o bobl. Dynion a aned cyn blynyddoedd y Dirwasgiad yw 40% ohonynt, rhai yn frodyr neu wŷr i ferched yn grwpiau I a II. Hefyd yn y grŵp cawn ferched o'r un genhedlaeth a fagwyd ar ochr orllewinol y pentref. Magwyd y 40% sydd yn weddill o gyfnod y rhyfel ymlaen, gyda chwech allan o wyth ohonynt yn dechrau eu haddysg gynradd cyn sefydlu Ysgol Gymraeg Pont-rhyd-y-fen yn 1954. Dau o gynnyrch yr Ysgol Gymraeg sydd yn gynwysiedig yn y grŵp hwn.

Mae cryn amrywiaeth ym mhatrymau gwaith a chymdeithasu y gwahanol garfannau a gynhwysir yn grŵp III. Rhwydweithiau lleol iawn sydd gan y gwragedd a'r dynion a aned cyn y Dirwasgiad. Cymraeg oedd iaith yr aelwydydd y magwyd hwy arnynt, a Chymraeg hefyd yw iaith eu hymwneud beunyddiol â'i gilydd. Priododd y mwyafrif ohonynt oddi mewn i'r gymuned. Digon gwahanol yw profiad gweddill grŵp III, a fagwyd yn ystod y Rhyfel, ac a gafodd waith yn y diwydiannau newydd a dyfodd wedi hynny. Gwasgaredig a Seisnig yw eu cysylltiadau rhwydweithiol. Adlewyrchir hyn ym mhatrymau priodi y gwahanol genedlaethau. Tra bo'r mwyafrif o'r sampl a aned cyn y 20au yn briod â Chymro neu Gymraes lleol, ychydig iawn o'r siaradwyr a fagwyd ers y Dirwasgiad sydd wedi priodi'n lleol, a nifer llai fyth a ddewisodd gymar a fedrai'r Gymraeg.[6]

Fodd bynnag, y mae gan y mwyafrif o siaradwyr grŵp III un peth yn gyffredin: ni wnant ddefnydd cyson o'r Gymraeg y tu allan i gyd-destun anffurfiol y cartref a'r gymdogaeth. Er mor eang yw rhwydweithiau cymdeithasol y canol oed o'u cymharu â'r genhedlaeth o'u blaen, nid ydynt yn arfer y Gymraeg ond i siarad â pherthnasau a chymdogion oedrannus. Lleol, felly, yw'r dylanwadau ar eu hiaith lafar. Nid yw hyn, wrth gwrs, yn berffaith wir am y ddau gyn-ddisgybl o'r Ysgol Gymraeg yn grŵp III. Y ffordd orau o esbonio iaith y rhain yw eu cymharu yn gymdeithasol â'u cyfoedion, sydd o ran eu hymddygiad ieithyddol yn perthyn i grŵp V.

Pump siaradwr sydd yn grŵp V: plant y 60au yw tri ohonynt, a'r ddau arall wedi'u magu yn ystod yr Ail Ryfel Byd. Yn achos y newidynnau dan sylw, hwynt-hwy yw'r lleiaf tafodieithol o blith siaradwyr y sampl, gyda'u sgorau yn isel yn y ddwy arddull. Dwy o'r siaradwyr ieuaf sydd wedi cael addysg Gymraeg. Aeth y llall i Ysgol Ton-mawr, gan dderbyn ei Chymraeg ar yr aelwyd gan ei mam. Mewnddyfodiad i'r pentref o ardal fwy gorllewinol oedd ei mam, ac ni siaradai'r ferch Gymraeg â neb o'i chyfoedion. Tafodiaith gymharol ddi-galediad, felly, a etifeddwyd ganddi ac a atgyfnerthwyd gan wersi Cymraeg yn yr ysgol gyfun Saesneg leol. Cafodd y ddwy siaradwraig ifanc arall addysg gynradd ac uwchradd mewn ysgolion Cymraeg. Serch hynny, ni chawsant Gymraeg ar yr aelwyd, ac ni ddefnyddient yr iaith yn eu hymwneud â'u cyd-ddisgyblion o'r pentref. Iaith yr ysgol yn unig oedd y Gymraeg, a'r ysgol honno wedi'i lleoli mewn ardal lle nad oedd calediad yn nodwedd mor amlwg ar y dafodiaith leol.

Yn wahanol i'r bobl ifanc yn grŵp V, magwyd y ddau ifanc yn grŵp III ar aelwydydd Cymraeg eu hiaith. Addysg gynradd Gymraeg yn unig a gafodd un ohonynt. Wedi gadael yr ysgol, bu'n gweithio am gyfnod yn y pentref. Y mae'n awr yn briod, ac yn byw yn ymyl perthnasau Cymraeg eu hiaith. Y dafodiaith leol felly sydd yn ei chlustiau yn feunyddiol. Mae'r siaradwr ifanc arall yn grŵp III yn hanu o'r un teulu. Er mai cyfyngedig erbyn hyn yw ei ddefnydd o'r iaith, yn enwedig wedi gadael yr ysgol, fe'i magwyd yntau ar aelwyd hollol Gymraeg, a deil ei rieni i siarad Cymraeg ag ef. Yn wahanol i'w cyfoedion yn grŵp V, felly, gwrthbwysir effaith addysg Gymraeg ar y ddau hyn gan ddylanwad yr iaith leol.

Os edrychwn ar grŵp V o safbwynt gwrthbwyso dylanwadau allanol a mewnol, gellir cynnig esboniad am ymddygiad ieithyddol aelodau canol oed y grŵp yn ogystal â'r bobl ifanc. Fel eu cyfoedion yn grŵp III, ychydig o ddefnydd a wna'r ddau siaradwr canol oed o'r Gymraeg ar eu haelwydydd yn feunyddiol. Yn wahanol i'w cymheiriaid yn grŵp III, fodd bynnag, y mae ganddynt gysylltiad ag amrywiadau mwy safonol ar yr iaith: un ohonynt yn rhinwedd ei waith fel trefnydd angladdau, a'r llall drwy addysg uwchradd a'i swyddogaeth fel ysgrifennydd i gapel. Felly, yn niffyg pwysau oddi wrth eu rhwydwaith gymdeithasol i gydymffurfio â normau'r dafodiaith leol, daw dylanwad yr iaith safonol arnynt yn fwy amlwg, hyd yn oed yn eu llafar digymell.

3.3 Grŵp IV

Gyda chalediad, yr unig grŵp sydd yn amrywio'n arddulliol i raddau amlwg yw grŵp IV. Y mae eu hymddygiad yn achos calediad yn ddrych o batrwm y gwragedd yn grŵp II o ddefnyddio'r amrywyn [ɛ:]. Tebyg hefyd yw eu nodweddion cymdeithasol, ond mai dynion yw pedwar o'r chwe siaradwr yn y grŵp. Athrawesau yw'r ddwy wraig, wedi'u magu yn y gymuned, a chanddynt hefyd nifer o gysylltiadau rhwydweithiol â Chymry o rannau eraill o'r wlad. Nid yw eu rhwydweithiau lleol mor ddwys â rhwydweithiau merched grŵp II oherwydd eu galwadau gyrfaol. Y mae tri o'r dynion yn y grŵp yn flaenoriaid, ac yn cymryd rhan flaenllaw yn y capel. Patryma rhwydweithiau cymdeithasol y dynion hyn yn ddigon tebyg i eiddo'r merched yn grŵp II: mae'r cysylltiadau lleol yn ddwys ac yn amlbleth, ond oherwydd eu swyddogaeth gyhoeddus, gwnânt ddefnydd cyson o ffurfiau eraill ar yr iaith, yn ogystal â'r dafodiaith leol. Fel merched grŵp II, felly, y mae ganddynt y gallu i amrywio'u hiaith i ateb y cyd-destun cymdeithasol pan fo angen. Yn wahanol i grŵp II, fodd bynnag, ni allant ddefnyddio'r [ɛ:] i arwyddo'r symud oddi wrth iaith y gymuned, gan nad yw'r [ɛ:] yn rhan o'u tafodiaith. Defnyddiant felly newidyn arall at yr un pwrpas, sef calediad.

4. Casgliadau

Hyd y gellir gweld, rheolir y symud oddi wrth y ddau amrywyn tafodieithol hyn ym Mhont-rhyd-y-fen gan ddwy ffactor:

i) Dwysedd rhyngweithio'r unigolyn â Chymry Cymraeg eraill o'r ardal.

ii) Profiad gweithredol o ffurfiau eraill ar y Gymraeg ar wahân i'r dafodiaith leol.

Yn achos grŵp I, y mae rhwydweithiau dwys a thra lleol yr aelodau yn cynnal y dafodiaith ar ei mwyaf ceidwadol. Cyfyngir eu defnydd o'r Gymraeg, fodd bynnag, i feysydd y cartref a'r gymdogaeth, ac o'r herwydd siaradwyr un-arddulliol ydynt. Tebyg yw profiad y siaradwyr hynaf yn grŵp III: lleol ac anffurfiol yw eu defnydd hwythau o'r Gymraeg, ond bod eu rhwydweithiau ar hyd y blynyddoedd wedi ymestyn ychydig ymhellach na grŵp I i bentrefi di-[ɛ:] cyfagos. Er mor wasgaredig yw rhwydweithiau gweddill grŵp III, cyfyngir y defnydd a wnânt o'r Gymraeg bron yn gyfangwbl i'r gymuned, ac i gyd-destunau anffurfiol. Felly, lleol yw'r dylanwadau mwyaf ar iaith grŵp III hefyd, ac nid ydynt yn amrywio'n arddulliol i raddau amlwg.

Grwpiau II, IV a V sydd yn gollwng y ddau amrywyn a gysylltir â'r dafodiaith leol. Y mae aelodau grŵp V, fodd bynnag, fel petaent wedi eu gollwng bron yn llwyr, tra bo siaradwyr grwpiau II a IV yn eu gollwng wrth ffurfioli yn unig. Gellir priodoli'r gwahaniaeth i ddwysedd rhwydweithiol y grwpiau. Er bod grwpiau II, IV, a V fel ei gilydd yn gyfarwydd â ffurfiau safonol ar y Gymraeg, gan grwpiau II a IV yn unig y mae rhwydweithiau cymdeithasol digon dwys a lleol i'w cadw rhag ymwrthod yn llwyr â nodweddion y frodoriaith. Pwysir arnynt yn feunyddiol i gydlynu'n ieithyddol â'u perthnasau a'u cymdogion, beth bynnag fo'u gallu i gynhyrchu Cymraeg mwy safonol mewn cyd-destunau ffurfiol.

Tebyg yw grŵp II i grŵp I o ran natur eu cysylltiadau rhwydweithiol beunyddiol. O ganlyniad, y mae aelodau grŵp II wedi cadw'r [ɛ:] yn eu llafar anffurfiol, yn ogystal â'r calediad sydd hefyd yn arddull ddigymell y bobl gyhoeddus/addysgedig yn grŵp IV. Yr hyn sydd yn annisgwyl, fodd bynnag, yw tuedd grŵp II i ddefnyddio *un* o'r nodweddion tafodieithol hyn yn unig i arwyddo ffurfioldeb, tra byddid yn disgwyl i ffurfioli effeithio ar ddwy. Anodd yw cynnig esboniad am hyn heb astudio ymddygiad y sampl yn achos newidynnau ieithyddol eraill. Rhaid nodi, fodd bynnag, fod yr [ɛ:] yn nodwedd fwy gwarthnodedig na chalediad ym marn y mwyafrif o'r siaradwyr. Gellid dadlau, efallai, fod y siaradwyr yn canolbwyntio ar y nodwedd dafodieithol fwyaf annerbyniol yn eu hiaith lafar wrth ffurfioli. Os felly, teg yw gofyn a ydyw arfer grŵp IV o ollwng calediad wrth ffurfioli yn arwydd fod tynged debyg yn disgwyl y nodwedd honno. Y mae ymddygiad grŵp V eisoes yn awgrymu hyn. Beth bynnag yw'r tueddiadau yn nhafodiaith y gymuned, y mae'n dra thebygol y'u goddiweddir ym Mhont-rhyd-y-fen gan ddiflaniad y Gymraeg ei hun.

Nodiadau

1. Seilir y wybodaeth hon ar ystadegau cyfrifiad 1951 ac 1981 ar gyfer plwyf Llanfihangel Ynys Afan Uchaf, yr uned weinyddol sy'n cyfateb agosaf i bentref Pont-rhyd-y-fen. Am ddadansoddiad manylach o hanes y Gymraeg yn y pentref, gweler Thomas (1987).

2. Gwnaethpwyd y gwaith maes ar gyfer yr astudiaeth ar ddechrau'r 80au. Am fanylion ynglŷn â dulliau a phroblemau samplu a recordio, darllener Thomas (1982).

3. Ar y cyfan, ni ddefnyddiwyd deunydd gan siaradwr a gynhyrchai lai na 10 dangosyn o'r newidyn dan sylw. Cynhyrchwyd llawer mwy na hynny gan y mwyafrif o'r siaradwyr - mwy hyd yn oed na'r 30 dangosyn a argymhellir fel isafswm delfrydol gan Milroy (1987). Mewn nifer fechan o achosion, fodd bynnag, boddlonwyd ar ychydig yn llai na'r 10 dangosyn mewn llafar digymell, pan fo sgorau'r siaradwyr yn gyson â'u defnydd uchel o'r amrywyn tafodieithol yn eu harddull cyfweld.

4. Am ddisgrifiad llawnach o'r dulliau ystadegol a ddefnyddir yma, darllener Erickson a Nosanchuk (1977).

5. Gweler Thomas (yn y wasg) am drafodaeth fanylach ar ddosbarthiad y newidyn |ɛ:| ymhlith merched Pont-rhyd-y-fen, yn defnyddio sampl estynedig o siaradwyr.

6. Gweler Thomas (1987).

Llyfryddiaeth

Erickson, B. H. a Nosanchuk, T. A. (1977) *Understanding Data. Toronto:* McGraw-Hill Ryerson.

Milroy, L. (1980) *Language and Social Networks*. Oxford: Basil Blackwell.

Milroy, L. (1987) *Observing and Analysing Natural Language*. Oxford: Basil Blackwell.

Thomas, B. (1982) Fieldwork problems in a Welsh valley community. *Papurau Gwaith Ieithyddol Cymraeg Caerdydd*, **2**, 53-72.

Thomas, B. (1987) Accounting for language shift in a South Wales mining community. *Papurau Gwaith Ieithyddol Cymraeg Caerdydd,* **5,** 55-100.

Thomas. B. (1989) Differences of sex and sects: linguistic variation and social networks in a Welsh mining community. Yn Cameron, D. a Coates, J. (gol), *Women in their Speech Communities: New Perspectives on Language and Sex.* London: Longmans.

Summary

The industrial village of Pont-rhyd-y-fen in the Afan Valley of south Wales is of particular interest to the sociolinguist, being at a dialect boundary, and at the border between mainly Welsh-speaking and mainly English-speaking areas. This is seen in the fact that the Welsh speakers of the village come mainly from the pre-war generation.

Two linguistic variables were investigated in the study: realization of orthographic "ae" as [ɛ:], and voicing of intervocalic stops (provection). For the first of these the village is just within the area of its general use in south Wales.

54 subjects from a total of 250 Welsh speakers were recorded in two main styles: interview style and casual style. The data presented is based on material collected from 42 of the recorded subjects. Scores for subject groups for the two variables are given in Figures 1 and 2.

Groups I and II scored high in the local forms of both variables: with the use of [ɛ:] varying with style for Group II. Both these groups were of older women with strong Welsh-language social networks. However, most had not had the chance to move outside the area a great deal. Different chapel affiliations seem to correlate with the differences between the groups over [ɛ:].

Group III made little use of [ɛ:], but retained provection. Of different backgrounds, they were characterised by their use of Welsh, which was limited to informal registers. For Group V, the speakers mainly had had Welsh as a school language only, and so show the least use of local (i.e. non-school) forms. Welsh was not their home language.

Group IV is the only one showing style differences for

provection. The majority of the group were older men, and as a whole the group had connections outside of the local community, exposing members to other, more standard, forms of Welsh.

The two most important factors influencing these variables are, then, the closeness of the social network binding the subject to other Welsh speakers and so reinforcing local forms, and the experience of other varieties of Welsh which reinforces alternative forms.

Variation In The Use Of Pronouns In Verbnoun Phrases And Genitive Noun Phrases In Child Language

Bob Morris Jones
University College of Wales, Aberystwyth

0. Introduction

This study is based on a corpus of the spontaneous conversational Welsh of children in the age range of three to seven years old. This data was collected during the 1970's in various schools throughout Wales, and is stored on computer at UCW, Aberystwyth. Unless otherwise indicated, illustrations are taken from the corpus and are presented in colloquial spelling.

The study examines issues of language variation arising from the pronominalisation of certain grammatical elements, particularly the direct object of a verbnoun (i.e. nonfinite verb) and the genitive element in a noun phrase (but see below for further details on the syntactic contexts): that is, this paper is concerned with the Welsh equivalents of examples such as *I'm going to take it* and *the cowboys had gone on* ***his back***.

To begin with, these constructions, which for convenience alone will be referred to as 'pronominal constructions', will be presented in terms of the descriptive facts, starting with the traditional view before moving on to the corpus data. Then, in the light of differences between the traditional patterns and the corpus patterns, sociolinguistic aspects of child pronominalisation will be discussed, supported by statistical analyses where appropriate.

1. The Traditional Account

The writings of John Morris-Jones supply the most comprehensive traditional account particularly (1922:84-90) and also (1913:270-282; 1931:78-86). Valuable critiques of traditional views are given by Arwyn Watkins (1977; 1977/78). In traditional grammars, pronominal constructions are treated within a parts-of-speech analysis of all types of Welsh pronouns. Here, the conventional analysis will be re-cast in syntactic terms using different terminology. Traditional grammars list two patterns for the pronominal constructions which we can label here as *double* and *single* pronominalisation, and instances of both are found in the corpus.

1.1 Double pronominalisation

The following examples illustrate the double pronominalisation of the direct object of a verbnoun and the genitive element in a noun phrase:

dw i am ***'i gymyd o***	I'm going to take it
o'dd y cowbois wedi mynd ar ***'i gefn e***	the cowboys had gone on his back

For the purposes of this paper, an informal generalization can characterize the basic descriptive facts of both verbnoun and noun constructions as follows: a noun or verbnoun occurs as the *head* of the construction; a possessive pronoun occurs as a *prehead*; and a personal pronoun occurs as a *posthead*. (More formal accounts are available in Gwenllian Awbery 1976 and Louisa Sadler 1988; the latter refers to the pronouns as clitics and also uses the term doubling to refer to patterns like the above illustrations). The prehead possessive and the posthead personal pronoun form the pronominal element.

In traditional grammars, the possessive pronouns are referred to as *prefixed pronouns* and the personal pronouns are referred to as *affixed* or *auxiliary pronouns*. Both types of pronouns have different forms reflecting person, number and, in the case of the 3rd singular, gender. Also, the singular possessive pronouns cause various mutations of the following word. This study concentrates on syntactic matters and will not pursue morphological nor mutational issues unless they are of relevance to the main analysis.

To this traditional account, further details can be added about the types of heads which can occur. These additional points all come under either a nominal head or a verbal head.

Firstly, as noted by Arwyn Watkins (1977:156) there are complex prepositions such as *ar ôl* (after), *o flaen* (before) and *ymlaen* (forward, onward) which have nouns as their heads and, when they precede a pronoun, the noun head and the pronoun can form a pronominal construction:

achos oedd dynion drwg yn dod lan ***ar 'i ôl e***

because bad men were coming up after him

Secondly, in certain contexts such as subordinate noun clauses, the finite present and past imperfect tenses of the copula such as *mae* (is) or *oedd* (was) are neutralised and are represented by the verbnoun form *bod* (be). As Awbery (1976:42-43) notes, when a pronoun occurs as a subject, it forms a pronominal construction with the verbnoun *bod*, as in the following devised illustration:

oedd pawb yn meddwl 'i fod o'n mynd yfory

everyone thought he was coming tomorrow

Such patterns satisfy the generalisation that pronominal constructions can have verbnoun heads. But the pronominal element is clearly not an object in the traditional sense and the relationship between these *bod* constructions and transitive verbnoun patterns presents intriguing theoretical issues. This matter does not affect the aims of this paper and will not be pursued here (interested readers might like to consult Awbery 1976 and Sadler 1988).

1.2 Single pronominalisation

Single pronominalisation uses only the prehead possessive pronoun as in the following instances involving noun heads:

coda ***dy lewys*** *i fyny* — pull your sleeves up

na'th o redeg yn ***'i flaen,*** *do* — he ran on, didn't he?

There is a set of contexts with verbnoun heads which, collectively, will be refered to as *x-copy* contexts. Pronominal constructions can be seen in clauses which front the direct object of a verbnoun. In Welsh, in addition to fronting, a copy pronoun can be used to mark the object and thus form a pronominal construction with the verbnoun. Fronted objects are found in *wh*-clauses which are x-interrogatives:

be ma' dad yn ***'i neud?*** — what does dad do?

and in finite and nonfinite *wh-* noun clauses (the nonfinite illustration is devised; although nonfinite *wh-* clauses occur in the corpus, none of them use the form *w* as a copy pronoun - the corpus patterns are discussed below):

chi'n gwbod beth ma'n nhw'n ***'i neud****?*
do you know what they're doing?
ma'n nhw'n gwbod beth i'w ***neud***
they know what to do

Fronted objects are also found in inverted sentences and relative clauses as in the following devised examples:

y beic mae'r dyn yn ***'i ddwyn***
it's the bike that the man is stealing
dyma'r beic oedd y dyn wedi ***'i ddwyn***
here's the bike the man had stolen

Both types occur in the corpus but do not use single pronominalisation in this form (see the corpus variants below).

1.3 The overall traditional system

Thus, combining the two main types of pronominalisation, the traditional account of the syntax of pronominal constructions can be summarised as follows:

prehead	*head*	*posthead*
possessive pronoun	{ noun / verbnoun }	personal pronoun
'i	*gymyd*	*o*
'i	*gefn*	*e*
dy	*lewys*	
'i	*neud*	

John Morris-Jones (1922:85,89-90) gives various rules for the inclusion or exclusion of the personal pronoun, the general suggestion being that the personal pronouns can be added to support or clarify the possessive (hence their traditional labelling as *auxiliary* pronouns). Arwyn Watkins' informative observations (1977:161-162; 1977/78:359-361) show that there are degrees of restrictions on the use of both types of patterns. This current study concentrates on the relationship of the traditional patterns with the corpus patterns (discussed below) and does not aim to discuss the relationships within the traditional system (a separate analysis of the corpus data will be available in Bob Morris Jones in prep. a). But the points made by Arwyn Watkins need to be taken into consideration when the traditional patterns are compared with other patterns found in the corpus, and they will be considered below.

Having sketched the syntactic aspect of the traditional approach, we shall go on to assess its adequacy as an account of the actual data under consideration, bearing in mind that standard Welsh grammars follow the typical traditional practice of describing formal written language with only occasional references to speech. It must be mentioned that the corpus has been analysed with the aid of computer programs and it has not been possible to include relative clauses and fronted clauses in the analysis - the study of x-copy contexts is thus based solely on *wh-* clauses. For similar reasons, constructions labelled by Arwyn Watkins (1977:156) as past participial constructions like *wy wedi'i ferwi* (boiled egg) are also excluded.

2. Variants in Spontaneous Speech

Several studies have compared pronominalisation in formal and informal Welsh, but they have mainly concentrated upon the forms of the possessives (as in Ball 1982, 1984) or the selection of single or double pronominalisation in contexts where a choice is available (as in Arwyn Watkins 1977/78 and Beth Thomas 1980). Arwyn Watkins (1977:154-157) shows that the differences are more extensive than this, and the following description will confirm and add to his observations.

2.1 Mutation as prehead

Certain consonants at the beginning of words are mutated when preceded by the singular possessives, *yn/fy* (my), *dy* (you sing.), *'i* (his/her) - the latter being distinguished by the type of mutation. The plural *yn* and *'i* can produce aspiration before vowels (as can the feminine singular *'i*) but none of the plurals mutate consonants.

In the corpus, it is seen that the possessive prehead can be omitted but its mutational effect remains. Thus, it can be argued that the mutation then acts as the overt indication of the prehead. There are clear instances of syntactic omission of the 3rd singular *'i* and the retention of the soft mutation which it causes. This is seen with double pronominalisation:

*ti sy'n **gal** e, Rhodri.*
it's you that's having it, Rhodri

*o'n i'n meddwl **fod o** isio mynd*
I thought he wanted to go
i mewn 'de.
in, then.

In the first example *gal* is the soft mutated form of *cal* (have, receive) and, as can be seen, there is no prehead possessive; a similar pattern is seen in the second example which has *bod* (be) as its head. It is also found with single pronominalisation in x-copy contexts:

*hei, be dach chdi'n **ddeud?***
hey, what are you saying?

Here *ddeud* is a mutated form of *deud* (say, tell).

However, in terms of empirical analysis, the researcher faces the problem of distinguishing between the omission of a syntactic constituent, on the one hand, and the assimilation and elision of its phonetic realization by surrounding sounds, on the other hand. As is noted by Arwyn Watkins (1977:154), the possessive pronoun *'i* is open to such phonological processes when preceded by another [i] sound, such as occurs finally in the perfect aspect marker *wedi* (after) [wedi] or its shortened form [di]:

*dw i 'di **weld o*** I've seen him

A similar problem occurs with the 1st singular possessive colloquial form *yn* (my) [ən] which can be perceived as being assimilated and elided by a following nasal. Nasals are themselves produced by the mutational effects of this pronoun and they can assimilate the very item that causes them:

*ma' hwn yn mynd i fyny **nhrwsus** i*
this is going up my trousers

The nasals of the initial mutations are either bilabial or alveolar. The possibilties of assimilation and elision can be displayed informally by the following devised illustrations:

**yn mhen i/yn nant i*	:	final [n] before a bilabial is unlikely
ym mhen i	:	[n] > [m] before bilabials
y' mhen i/y' nant i	:	assimilation of final bilabial, leaving schwa
– mhen i/– nant i	:	loss or weakening of schwa

These processes would appear to be long-established in the language and, in respect of the 1st singular in the written language, are referred to by Morris-Jones (1922:86).

There would appear to be checks on the complete loss of

the pronoun - for example, when *yn* occurs between two nasals (although the assimilation of the final nasal can still occur):

*colli sand yn y' **nhrwsus** i*
losing sand in my trousers

We cannot pursue this matter here.

Thus, it might appear reasonable to suggest that in certain phonetic environments the 1st and 3rd singular possessives can be assimilated, and not necessarily omitted. But we cannot discount the fact that the perception of the mutation only may lead speakers to conclude that the mutation alone is sufficient, and phonetic assimilation thus conditions syntactic omission. In contexts which allow assimilation, there would appear to be no way of recognizing in actual data whether an item is not there because of elision or syntactic omission. Consequently, in the statistical analyses offered below, no distinction will be made between prehead as an overt possessive (with or without mutation) and prehead as mutation only.

Before leaving mutation, it must be emphasised that the children also use a possessive pronoun without using the traditional mutation system, as in:

*a gyda chi **'i llygaid** e* and you've got his eyes

As stated earlier, the use of the mutational system will not be considered in this study, except where it is relevant to a discussion of syntax.

2.2 Zero prehead: posthead only

The most striking variant found in the corpus is the rejection of the prehead possessive and the mutation which it might produce. In many contexts, a posthead personal pronoun alone is used:

*ti 'di **colli** o*
you've lost it
*o'dd **gwddwg** e'n symud*
his throat/neck was moving
*a mae o'n rhedeg **ar ôl** fi*
and he's running after me
*ti'n licio **tarten** ti 'de?*
do you like your cake, then?

This variant is scorned by traditionalists. It is specifically rejected by Awbery (1976:15-16), Borsley (1984:285-286) and Sadler (1988:73) all of whom use contemporary linguistic theories but whose data bases continue the tradition of John Morris-Jones.

Jones and Thomas (1977:171-172) explicitly highlight the occurrence of this variant with noun heads but they characterize it as 'certainly sub-standard (though it is one of a number of sub-standard forms which seem to have a disturbingly high frequency in the speech of young children)'. Arwyn Watkins' study (1977:155-161) of the colloquial Welsh of the lower Swansea valley notes this variant in all of the contexts given above. Apparently speaking for the speech community, he suggests that it is regarded as substandard and infantile when occurring with noun heads (in noun phrases and complex prepositions) with the exception of expressions like *Dai ni* (our Dai); but no judgements are offered about nonstandard verbnoun patterns, and these presumably are not considered substandard. A brief reference to nonstandard verbnoun patterns is also found in Beth Thomas (1980:591) but, in an analysis which has other aims, their existence is given little prominence.

There is a problem in identifying zero prehead with: one lexical item; a phonologically-based set of items; and environments where the source of mutation may be ambiguous.

The dictionary entry *GWNEUD* occurs in spontaneous speech either as *gneud* or *neud*, the latter occurring through the loss of the initial [g]. Loss of initial [g] is also a product of soft mutation, so a problem arises as to whether *neud* is a mutated form or a nonmutated variant of *gneud*, as in:

dw i 'di ***neud*** *e* — I've done/made it

It is the impression of this writer, through his use of the corpus, that *neud* occurs mainly as a nonmutated variant of *gneud*. Consequently, instances of *neud* without an overt prehead are treated as zero prehead.

A similar problem occurs with items whose dictionary entries have initial *rh* such as *RHOI*. Soft mutation changes [rh] to [r]. But [r] in spontaneous speech also occurs as a nonmutated variant of [rh] so that *roi* occurs as a nonmutated variant of *rhoi*. In this study, instances of initial [r] without an overt prehead are taken as zero prehead.

A problem also arises where the mutation may either be the remnant of a deleted prehead or the result of other causes of mutation, as in:

... *be nesh i* ***gal*** — ... what I had

... *be i* ***wthio*** *i mewn* — ... what to push in

In the first example, the mutation of *cal* (have, receive) may be the result of its occurrence as the complement to a finite verb and not because of a deleted or assimilated prehead. Similarly, in the second example, the mutation of *gwthio* (push) may be caused by the preposition *i* (to) and not an absent prehead. In this study, in all contexts where there is another source for the mutation, the mutation is attributed to the other source and not to an absent prehead. Consequently, they are analysed as lacking prehead pronominalisation.

2.3 Zero prehead: zero posthead

In the case of pronominalisation in x-copy contexts, neither preheads (including prehead mutation) nor postheads occur:

oo, be ti'n canu? what are you singing?

This context does not allow a posthead and the omission of the prehead results in the absence of any pronominal element i.e. zero pronominalisation.

Note that the remarks above about *GWNEUD* and *RHOI* also apply here.

2.4 The definite article

In this data, another possibility occurs with nominal heads. The prehead is realized by a schwa sound and is thus phonetically identical with the definite article *y*. Indeed, the variants of the article also occur - *yr/'r*. Examples are as follows:

ma' fe'n canu yn ***y stafell canu e***
he sings in his singing room
*ma****'r lori*** *fi'n dod mas, Amanda*
my lorry is coming out, Amanda
yn ***yr ysgol hen ni***
in our old school

As can be seen, the use of *y* (and the other forms) means that the same prehead occurs with a range of person contrasts in the posthead.

2.5 Patterns which retain traditional single pronominalisation

At this point it is interesting to consider some of the contexts highlighted by Arwyn Watkins (1977/78:359-361) which demand compulsory single pronominalisation. In this data, it is found that traditional single pronominalisation is retained in some of these (but not all, as is discussed in Bob Morris Jones in prep. a). These patterns are *passives* as in:

*ma' fe'n cal 'i **daflu*** he's being thrown
ma' fe'n cal **taflu fe / taflu*

the *reflexive pronouns* with *HUN/HUNAN* as their head:
*rhaid ti neud un **dy hunan***
you must do one yourself
rhaid ti neud **hunan ti / hunan*

the *reciprocal pronouns* with *CILYDD* as their head:
*ma' heina efo **'i gilydd***
those are with each other
ma' heina efo **cilydd nhw / cilydd*

and noun phrases which have a *cardinal* as their head:
***ni'n dau** sy'n gneud tywod*
it's us two that's making sand
****dau ni / dau** sy'n gneud tywod*

These would appear to be the only instances where the corpus variants are excluded. Identical results are found in Watkins' study (1977:157) of the vernacular of the lower Swansea valley. In passing, it can be mentioned that NPs with cardinal heads involving the 3rd plural may elide the possessive as in the devised illustration *nhw dau* (them two) and this may then serve as a model to produce *ni dau* (us two) and *chi dau* (you two) - that is zero pronominalisation.

3. The Total System of Pronominalisation: Standard and Nonstandard

The corpus thus demonstrates that there are a total of seven variants in the formation of pronominal constructions:

	prehead	mutation+head	posthead	
1	possess.	mutation+head	personal	*dw i am **'i gymyd o***
2	-	mutation+head	personal	*ti sy'n **gal e**, Rhodri*
3	-	- head	personal	*ti 'di **colli o***
4	possess.	mutation+head	-	*coda **dy lewys** i fyny*
5	-	mutation+head	-	*be ti'n **gal***
6	-	- head	-	*be ti'n **canu***
7	def art	head	personal	*yn **yr hen ysgol ni***

As previously mentioned, the mutation is only available following certain of the possessives. Only patterns 1 and 4 would be regarded as standard by traditional grammars. Numbers 3, 6 and 7 would clearly be regarded as nonstandard. Numbers 2 and 5 are marginal but are saved from disgrace by the retention of the mutation and, in the spoken language at least, they would be regarded as standard. Thus, we can establish standard and nonstandard variants of pronominal constructions as follows:

	standard variants			nonstandard variants
possessive	head personal	-		head personal
mutation	head personal	-		head - (x-copy only)
possessive	head	-	def art	head personal (nominals only)
mutation	head	-		

As previously discussed, some instances of standard single pronominalisation do not allow a nonstandard variant but retain the traditional pattern of single pronominalisation. Consequently, in these circumstances the nonstandard patterns cannot be seen as a variant of the standard pattern. However, no distinction is made in this study between different types of traditional single patterns (further details will be found in Bob Morris Jones in prep. a).

Returning now to a consideration of the different types of patterns, it can be seen that while the standard variants are centred on the prehead possessives with a variable posthead personal pronoun, the nonstandard system is based mainly on the posthead personal pronoun (this becomes very obvious in the light of frequencies given in Table 1). We see here a major repatterning of the structure of pronominal constructions.

Such a difference raises two main questions. Firstly, why have the nonstandard variants arisen and, secondly, are they a change which is taking place in the speech of children at the moment or have they remained unrecognized in colloquial speech generally for some time? The data base of this study only facilitates discussion of the first question. This matter can be approached from two points of view: namely, whether the nonstandard variants arise because of the external influence of English or the internal influences of regularisation. In a study of this scale, the discussion will concentrate upon the influence of English, and it will be approached from a sociolinguistic standpoint. It should be emphasised, however, that this approach is only one aspect of the status of the nonstandard variants and linguistic explanations are discussed in Bob Morris Jones (in prep. b). To begin with, however, we will examine the statistical frequencies of the standard and nonstandard patterns in the corpus.

4. The Frequencies and Proportions of Nonstandard and Standard Variants

Before looking at the basic statistics, two points should be made. Firstly, the children form two separate cohorts of younger children (three to four-year-olds) and older children (five to seven-year-olds), and, although many children were present in all years, gains and losses occurred from one year to the next within these two groups. Secondly, it is convenient to compare the different ages in the form of graphs but any developmental comparisons should bear the first point in mind.

Table 1 emphatically shows that the usage of the children is based primarily on the nonstandard variants and, in particular, on the much-maligned use of a posthead personal pronoun only. The nonstandard variants are particularly high with the three-year-olds, a feature which consistently emerges with all analyses and which is taken up again at various points below.

The percentages are based on the totals for all variants and, in the case of the x-copy nonstandards and the use of *y* as a prehead, this may be misleading as they are variants within subsets and cannot occur as choices in place of all other patterns. A detailed account is not possible within the scale of this study and the approach adopted in Table 1 will serve to indicate the statistical relationships of the patterns in general terms. It should also be remembered that the x-copy contexts are based on *wh*-clauses only and that the percentages of nonstandards would be higher if relative and fronted clauses were included; this point also applies to so-called past participial phrases referred to earlier.

Given the overwhelming preference for nonstandard variants, it must be concluded that the accounts of traditional grammars and their contemporary Chomskyan equivalents are inappropriate for the discussion of child language today (similar misgivings are found in Fife 1986:179-80, although not particularly about child language). It is the custom of traditionalists to respond by saying that conventional grammar is adequate but that users have corrupted the old standards which it codifies. This is an unacceptable response for at least two reasons.

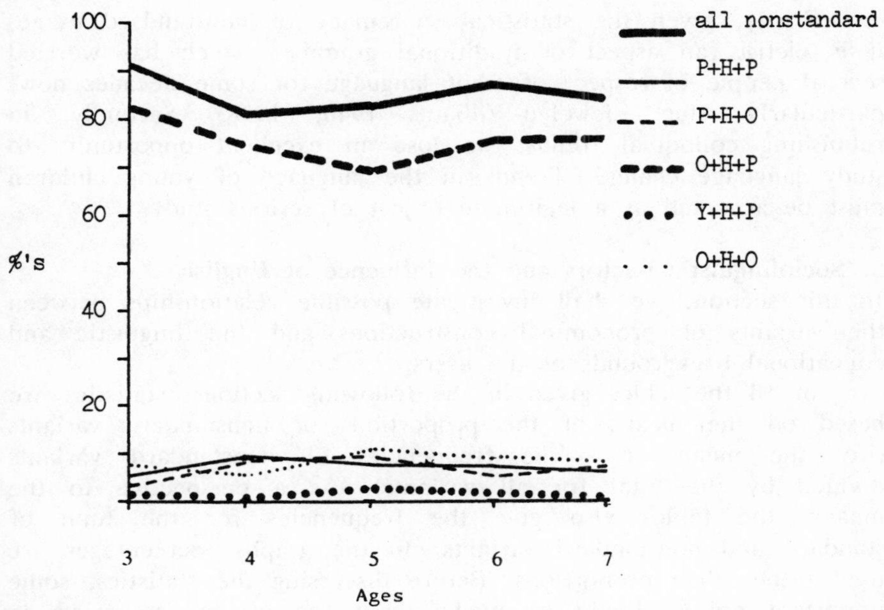

Ages	Total freq's	%'s of individual patterns P+H+P	P+H+0	0+H+P	Y+H+P	0+H+0	Nonstandard %'s
three	441	5.67	2.72	82.09	1.81	7.71	91.61
four	414	9.18	8.94	74.40	0.72	6.76	81.88
five	1210	7.77	9.09	69.50	2.89	10.74	83.14
sixe	1957	7.15	5.37	76.80	1.28	9.40	87.48
seven	2092	6.31	7.89	77.01	0.72	8.08	85.80
all	6114	7.02	7.02	75.65	1.41	8.91	85.97

P+H+P: traditional double pronominalisation (inc mutational prehead)
M+H+0: traditional single pronominalisation (inc mutational prehead)
0+H+P: nonstandard personal pronoun pronominalisation
Y+H+P: nonstandard yas a prehead with a posthead personal pronoun
0+H+0: nonstandard zero pronominalisation in x-copy contexts

Table 1: Percentages of standard and nonstandard pronominal constructions

Firstly, given the statistical supremacy of nonstandard usage, it is eletist (an aspect of traditional grammar which has worried several people in respect of adult language for some decades now, particularly Alun Llewelyn-Williams 1940, 1948). Secondly, in rubbishing colloquial trends, we lose an excellent opportunity to study language change. Trends in the language of young children must be accepted as a legitimate object of serious study.

5. Sociolinguistic Factors and the Influence of English

In this section, we shall investigate possible relationships between the variants of pronominal constructions and the linguistic and educational backgrounds of the users.

In all the tables given in the following sections, statistics are based on the means of the proportions of nonstandard variants (i.e. the mean of - the frequencies of nonstandard variants divided by the total for all variants). As a perspective to the means, the tables also give the frequencies for the total of standard and nonstandard variants. In the graphs, percentages are used rather than proportions. Before discussing the statistics, some important points should be made about the use of a corpus in statistical analyses.

The most important point is that we have individual variance: quite simply, some children talk more than others and produce more examples of pronominal constructions. Means do not indicate the extent of variance, but they are useful in suggesting the general picture. However, in searching for significant differences, t-tests are used which take into account individual variance (the statistical package MINITAB is used for this purpose). Another point arises out of this. Some children have not used any pronominal constructions, particularly amongst the three-year-olds. Non-users are excluded by the t-tests and consequently they are excluded from the calculations of any means.

5.1 Language contact: L1, L2 and school types

The growth of bilingualism in Wales has given greater force to language contact between English and Welsh as a factor in language change. Bilingualism will be discussed here in terms of a broad distinction between L1 and L2 based on language use within the family. No attempt will be made to introduce further classifications in terms of the extent of the use of either English or Welsh as such an approach would be too detailed and unwieldy for the scale of this study. In terms of language contact, bilingualism operates in three ways.

Firstly, L1 Welsh speakers acquire English as an L2 and individual bilingualism brings the two languages into contact within an individual's linguistic repertoire and creates a situation where the L2, English - a major language, can influence the L1, Welsh - a minority language.

Secondly, there are young children in Wales whose L1 is English but who acquire Welsh as an L2 mainly within the educational system. For many L1 English children, the school is the only source for the acquisition of Welsh. The crucial point is that this type of bilingualism promotes the influence of English on L2 Welsh through the well-known process of mother-tongue interference. This process promotes the emergence of L2 Welsh as a distinct variety of Welsh in child and even adolescent language. This is particularly true of Welsh-medium schools in English speaking areas whose intake is mainly English-speaking.

Thirdly, language contact may come about through the interactions of L1 and L2 Welsh speakers. That is, L1 Welsh is influenced by L2 Welsh as L1 Welsh speakers accommodate to the Welsh of L2 speakers. To my knowledge, there have been no formal studies of this type of accommodation, but it is a point which is frequently remarked upon in informal discussions.

Thus, to summarise the above, English influence can arise as follows:

1. In L1 Welsh due to the influence of L2 English
2. In L2 Welsh due to the influence of L1 English
3. In L1 Welsh due to the influence of L2 Welsh

It will be obvious from the above that school types are an important factor in the discussion of child bilingualism and we can now outline these.

In linguistic terms, primary schools in Wales can be classified according to the role of Welsh and English in the curriculum and the L1s of the intake. There are three main types which are relevant to this study.

Firstly, there are schools where Welsh is the *designated* language for the medium of instruction throughout the school, and where skills in written and spoken English are introduced at 7 years of age. In this paper such schools will be referred to as *Welsh* schools (designated bilingual schools is a more official label). Children attend Welsh schools through their parents' choice, and they may be either L1 Welsh or L1 English. In English-speaking areas, the intake may be primarily L1 English children.

Secondly, there are schools where Welsh is not a designated language for the medium of instruction but where the school's intake contains L1 Welsh and L1 English speakers. Such schools can be referred to as *mixed* schools. It is difficult to generalise about the medium of instruction in mixed schools as this will be influenced by the policy of the local education authority and the commitment of the headteacher and staff. There is a spectrum of possibilities ranging through Welsh for everyone, Welsh or English according to the L1 of the children, to English for everyone. In areas where the intake is mainly L1 Welsh, the medium of instruction is predominantly Welsh and in this respect a mixed school compares closely with a designated Welsh school (indeed such schools are sometimes referred to as 'natural' Welsh schools - an unfortunate label if one thinks of its opposite).

Thirdly, there are schools where L1 Welsh and L1 English speakers are taught in different classes and Welsh or English is the medium of instruction according to the L1 of the pupils. Such schools will be referred to as *streamed* schools. In this paper we are exclusively concerned with the Welsh stream.

We can now move on to consider in detail the relationship between these factors and the linguistic variables.

5.2 Standard/nonstandard variables and L1 and L2 Welsh

Table 2 supplies a graph and the details of t-tests which compare the means of nonstandard proportions of native speakers of Welsh and those who speak Welsh as a second language.

Overall, there are more L1 Welsh speakers than L2 speakers and in the case of the three and four-year-olds there are not sufficient numbers for a reliable analysis. The older cohort (five to seven-year-olds) shows that the two groups have different means at five and seven, but both approximate to each other at six. However, only with the seven-year-olds do we have a statistically significant difference. At this age the nonstandard proportions have increased for the L2 group but decreased with the L1 group. Although there is a trend for the L2 group to have higher means there are no consistent statistically significant differences to demonstrate that the L2 group are primarily responsible for the use of the nonstandard variables.

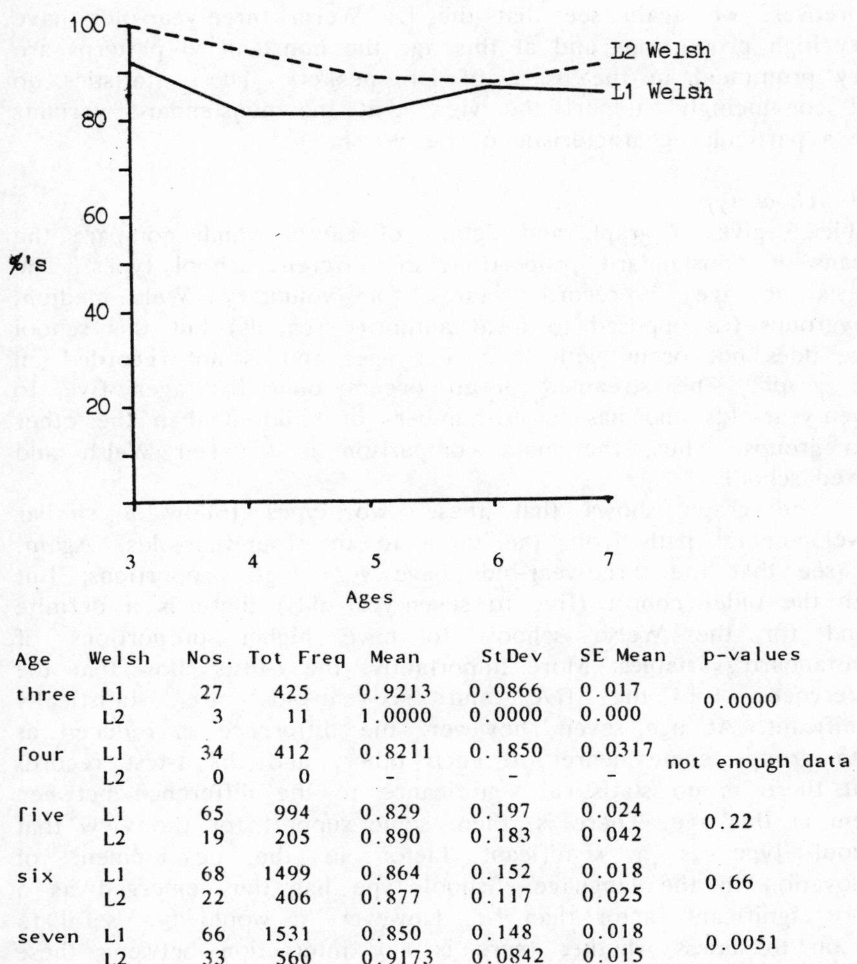

Age	Welsh	Nos.	Tot Freq	Mean	StDev	SE Mean	p-values
three	L1	27	425	0.9213	0.0866	0.017	0.0000
	L2	3	11	1.0000	0.0000	0.000	
four	L1	34	412	0.8211	0.1850	0.0317	not enough data
	L2	0	0	–	–	–	
five	L1	65	994	0.829	0.197	0.024	0.22
	L2	19	205	0.890	0.183	0.042	
six	L1	68	1499	0.864	0.152	0.018	0.66
	L2	22	406	0.877	0.117	0.025	
seven	L1	66	1531	0.850	0.148	0.018	0.0051
	L2	33	560	0.9173	0.0842	0.015	

Table 2: Means of proportions of nonstandard variants and L1 and L2 Welsh

Moreover, we again see that the L1 Welsh three-year-olds have very high proportions and at this age the nonstandard patterns are very prominent in the usage of L1 speakers. These statistics do not convincingly support the view that the nonstandard variants are a particular characteristic of L2 Welsh.

5.3 School types

Table 3 gives a graph and details of t-tests which compare the means of nonstandard proportions of different school types. The t-tests at age 3 record figures for voluntary Welsh-medium playgroups (as opposed to local authority schools) but this school type does not occur with the other ages and is not recorded on the graph. The streamed group occurs only for ages five to seven-year-olds and has lower numbers of children than the other two groups. Thus, the main comparison is between Welsh and mixed schools.

The graph shows that these two types follow a similar developmental path from the three to the four-year-olds. Again, we see that the three-year-olds have very high proportions. But with the older cohort (five to seven-year-olds) there is a definite trend for the Welsh schools to have higher proportions of nonstandard variables. More importantly, the t-tests show that the differences for the five and six-year-olds are statistically significant. At age seven, however, the difference is reduced as both groups come nearer to each other, and the t-test records that there is no statistical significance to the difference between them at this age. There is, then, some support for the view that school type is a significant factor in the development of innovation in the language. School type has thus emerged as a more significant factor than L1. However, it would be useful to go on to assess whether there is any interaction between these two factors.

5.4 Subgroups of combinations of L1/L2 and school types

The framework of L1 categories and school types can be combined to produce 6 subgroups (L1/L2 Welsh x Welsh/mixed/streamed schools). But the numbers in some of these groups are small or nonexistent and only three groups are well represented (at least with the older cohort):

	School Type	
	Welsh	Mixed
L1 Welsh	1	2
L2 Welsh	3	

Group 1 is made up of L1 Welsh speakers in Welsh schools while group 2 is also made up of L1 Welsh speakers but who are in mixed schools. Group 3 is made up of L2 Welsh speakers who attend Welsh schools. Table 4 gives a graph which compares these three groups and also t-tests which check statistical significance. It can be seen from the detailed figures that group 3, L2 speakers in Welsh schools are not adequately represented with the three and four-year-olds. But again we have very high proportions of nonstandard variants at age three.

This analysis is very revealing. With the older cohort (five to seven-year-olds) it shows that the second group, L1 speakers in mixed schools, has consistently lower means of proportions of nonstandard variants and, moreover, that the differences between this group and the other two groups are statistically significant at age five and six. Age seven upsets this trend as we see L1 Welsh speakers in both school types moving in the direction of each other such that the difference between them is no longer statistically significant. But the L2 speakers in the Welsh schools retain higher nonstandard proportions and the difference between them and the L1 speakers of the mixed schools is statistically significant. The most important point is that the L1 speakers in the Welsh schools appear to be a sort of half-way house between the other two groups and it is this group which when combined with the other L1 Welsh speakers prevent any consistent statistical differences between L1 Welsh and L2 Welsh at age five and six (see Table 2).

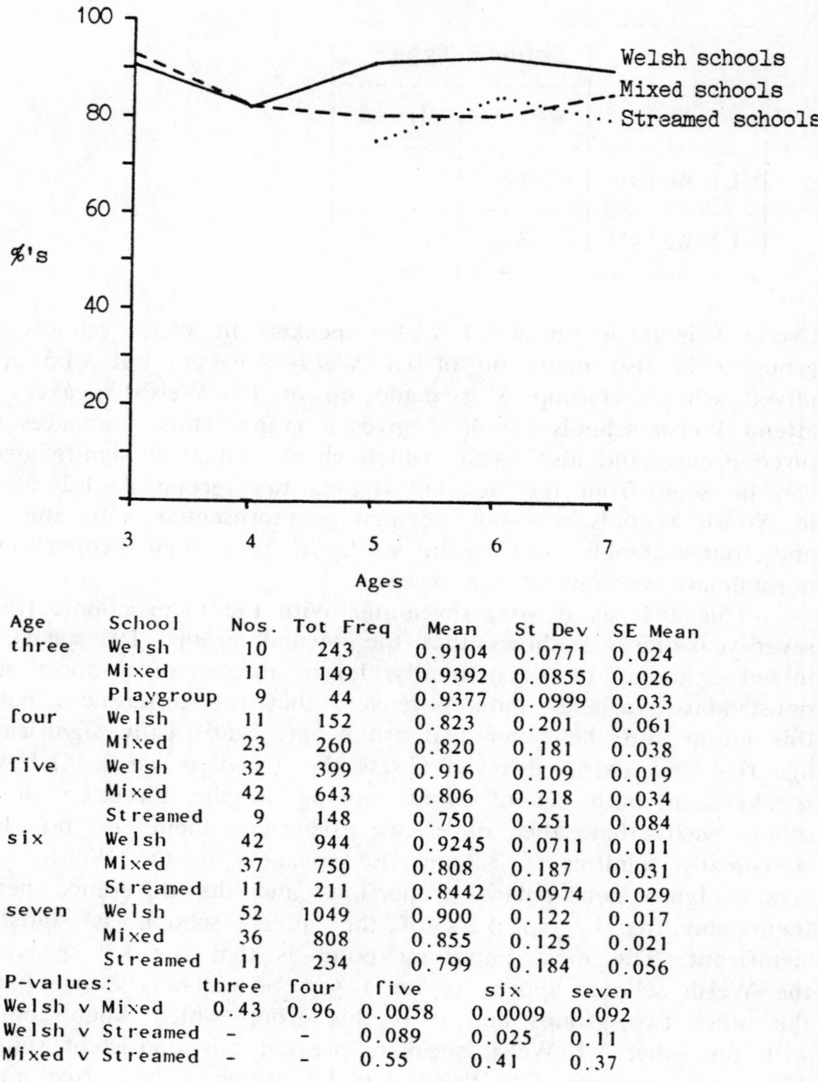

Age	School	Nos.	Tot Freq	Mean	St Dev	SE Mean
three	Welsh	10	243	0.9104	0.0771	0.024
	Mixed	11	149	0.9392	0.0855	0.026
	Playgroup	9	44	0.9377	0.0999	0.033
four	Welsh	11	152	0.823	0.201	0.061
	Mixed	23	260	0.820	0.181	0.038
five	Welsh	32	399	0.916	0.109	0.019
	Mixed	42	643	0.806	0.218	0.034
	Streamed	9	148	0.750	0.251	0.084
six	Welsh	42	944	0.9245	0.0711	0.011
	Mixed	37	750	0.808	0.187	0.031
	Streamed	11	211	0.8442	0.0974	0.029
seven	Welsh	52	1049	0.900	0.122	0.017
	Mixed	36	808	0.855	0.125	0.021
	Streamed	11	234	0.799	0.184	0.056

P-values:	three	four	five	six	seven
Welsh v Mixed	0.43	0.96	0.0058	0.0009	0.092
Welsh v Streamed	–	–	0.089	0.025	0.11
Mixed v Streamed	–	–	0.55	0.41	0.37

Table 3: means of nonstandard proportions and school type

This gives some support to the view that the usage of the L2 Welsh speakers may influence L1 Welsh speakers in Welsh schools: the latter do not use nonstandard patterns to the same extent as the L2 speakers and yet their use of standard patterns is not as great as other L1 speakers in mixed schools. It would appear, therefore, that in respect of pronominal constructions L1 Welsh speakers in Welsh schools may accommodate to L2 Welsh speakers in the same schools.

6. Conclusions

The figures and trends analysed above are tantalizing: they suggest trends of differences in relation to language background and school type but do not show consistent differences overall. However, the most useful approach is one which combines both L1 and school type, for it is here that we can see significant differences between L1 and L2 Welsh, and also the influence of L2 Welsh on L1 Welsh in the Welsh schools, at least until the age of seven. But it should be remembered that the majority of speakers have very high proportions of nonstandard variants and that they are generally characteristic of child language irrespective of background differences. Further, discussion in Bob Morris Jones (in prep. b) shows that there are sound reasons for arguing that the nonstandard variants are the result of internal change and should not be attributed exclusively to the influence of English through bilingualism.

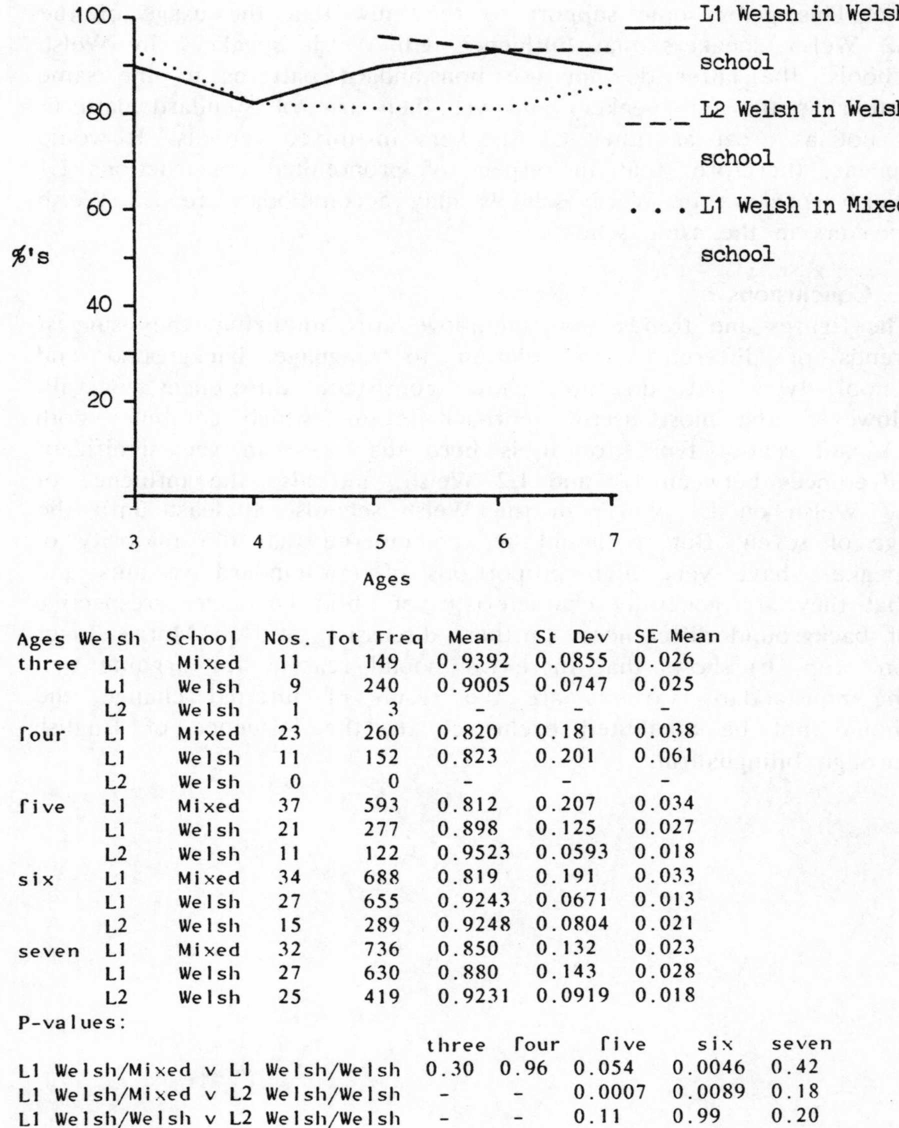

Ages	Welsh	School	Nos.	Tot Freq	Mean	St Dev	SE Mean
three	L1	Mixed	11	149	0.9392	0.0855	0.026
	L1	Welsh	9	240	0.9005	0.0747	0.025
	L2	Welsh	1	3	-	-	-
four	L1	Mixed	23	260	0.820	0.181	0.038
	L1	Welsh	11	152	0.823	0.201	0.061
	L2	Welsh	0	0	-	-	-
five	L1	Mixed	37	593	0.812	0.207	0.034
	L1	Welsh	21	277	0.898	0.125	0.027
	L2	Welsh	11	122	0.9523	0.0593	0.018
six	L1	Mixed	34	688	0.819	0.191	0.033
	L1	Welsh	27	655	0.9243	0.0671	0.013
	L2	Welsh	15	289	0.9248	0.0804	0.021
seven	L1	Mixed	32	736	0.850	0.132	0.023
	L1	Welsh	27	630	0.880	0.143	0.028
	L2	Welsh	25	419	0.9231	0.0919	0.018

P-values:

	three	four	five	six	seven
L1 Welsh/Mixed v L1 Welsh/Welsh	0.30	0.96	0.054	0.0046	0.42
L1 Welsh/Mixed v L2 Welsh/Welsh	-	-	0.0007	0.0089	0.18
L1 Welsh/Welsh v L2 Welsh/Welsh	-	-	0.11	0.99	0.20

Table 4: Means of proportions of nonstandard variants and subgroups combining school types and L1 and L2 Welsh

References

Awbery, G. M. (1976) *The Syntax of Welsh.* Cambridge: Cambridge University Press.

Ball, M. J. (1982) Stylistic Variation in Radio Broadcasts: an Introductory Study. *Cardiff Working Papers in Welsh Linguistics,* **2,** 17-24

Ball, M. J. (1984) Phonological Variation in the Personal Pronouns of Welsh. *Cardiff Working Papers in Welsh Linguistics,* **4,** 25-30

Borsley, R.D. (1984) VP complements: evidence from Welsh. *Journal of Linguistics,* **20,** 277-302

Fife, J. (1986) Additional Facts about Welsh VPs. *Journal of Linguistics,* **22,** 179-186

Jones, Bob Morris (in prep. a) Standard Pronominalisation in Verbnoun Phrases and Genitive Noun Phrases in Child Language

Jones, Bob Morris (in prep. b) Linguistics Causes of Change in Pronominalisation in Child Language

Jones, (Bob) Morris and Thomas, A. R. (1977) *The Welsh Language.* Cardiff: University of Wales Press for the Schools Council.

Llewellyn-Williams, A. (1940) Y Gymraeg ar y Radio. *Y LLenor,* Hydref

Llewellyn-Williams, A. (1948) Arddull Llafar. *Cymmrodorion Society Transactions,* 92-104

Morris-Jones, J. (1913) *A Welsh Grammar.* Oxford: Oxford University Press.

Morris-Jones, J. (1922) *An Elementary Welsh Grammar.* Oxford: The Clarendon Press.

Morris-Jones, J. (1931) *Welsh Syntax: an Unfinished Draft.* Cardiff: The University of Wales Press Board.

Sadler, L. (1988) *Welsh Syntax.* London: Croom Helm

Thomas, Beth (1980) Cymrêg, Cymraeg: Cyweiriau iaith siaradwraig o Ddyffryn Afan, *BBCS*, **28,** 579-92

Watkins, T. Arwyn (1977) The Welsh Personal Pronoun. *Word,* **28,** 146-165

Watkins, T. Arwyn (1977/78) Y Rhagenw Ategol. *Studia Celtica,* **12/13,** 349-366

A Visit to the Galapagos*

James Fife
Catholic University of Lublin

It was during HMS Beagle's visit to the Galapagos Islands in 1835 that Charles Darwin gathered the foundational evidence for his later exposition of the theory of natural selection. As is well known, the evidence which most stimulated his thinking along the lines of gradual evolution was his comparison of species found on the South American continent with the obviously related, but very different, species found in the Galapagos. By contrasting the structural and behavioural differences between the older, original specimens of the continent with the newer, innovative ones of the islands, Darwin was able to posit the how and why mechanism which accounts for the origin and development of the species as a whole.

This paper concerns a feature of Welsh which, in all seriousness, represents a linguistic analog of a divergent speciation which should help us understand a more general problem in historical and descriptive linguistics. The innovative species in Welsh is what I shall call the **perfective passive** and the general issue I believe it illuminates is the relationship between perfective aspect and passive voice. By analyzing the nature and history of the Welsh structures, it is hoped that we will gain new insight into the general issue and into the specific history of the related forms in other Indo-European languages.

It has been known for quite some time that several languages (and not just Indo-European ones) exhibit a definite relation between forms which express perfective aspect and those which express notions of passivity. As a simple example, consider the sentences in item 1.

(1)	a. French:	Il a fermé la porte
		La porte est fermée
	b. Spanish:	El ha cerrado la puerta
		La puerta está cerrada
	c. German:	Er hat die Tür geschlossen
		Die Tür ist geschlossen
	d. English:	He has shut the door
		The door is shut

In these four languages, the construction used to express the present perfect is structurally similar to that expressing passivity. In the corresponding passive forms, the active perfect object is the subject (as is expected in a passive) and an alternate version of the same verb form, here the perfective participle, is used, though with a different auxiliary verb. It has been noted that formal relations of this sort occur in several places in Indo-European. In his textbook on aspect, Bernard Comrie remarked (1976: 84-5) that a special relationship between perfects and passives occurs in many non-Indo-European languages as well, where, for instance, some languages have perfects only in the passive voice or the perfects derive historically from passives. Within the context of Celtic languages, this special relationship has been noted by David Greene and by Heinrich Wagner. The problem of what this relationship is and how it comes about is therefore a widespread one among languages.

As I said, this is well-known in Indo-European studies and in that context, one recent study of the phenomenon is that by Jerzy Kuryłowicz in his *Inflectional Categories of Indo-European*. The precise details of Kuryłowicz's analysis need not concern us. In general terms, his explanation lies in a semantic commonality between the Perfect inflection and the Medio-passive in Proto-Indo-European and this is meant to account for the observed relation in the descendant languages. In essence, Kuryłowicz is stating that this relationship in modern Indo-European languages is an inherited trait stemming from a semantic nexus existing at an earlier stage of these languages. Whatever the adequacy of this scheme for the languages in (1) (and Kuryłowicz himself expresses reservations about it) its adequacy is called seriously into doubt by the existence of a similar relationship of perfective and passive in Indo-European which cannot conceivably share any inherited forms with the continental examples. This is the case with the Welsh perfective passive.

To see this, it is necessary first to survey briefly the nature of the perfective and passive in Welsh. My description here presupposes some elements of the theoretical framework called **cognitive grammar** (see Langacker 1987). This is an evolving grammatical theory whose main tenet is that syntactic behaviour is a reflection of semantic organization. Even a cursory exposition of the framework is far beyond this paper and is dealt with elsewhere (Fife, 1984). For now, it is enough to know that a cognitive grammar analysis looks first to the basic semantic value of a form to account for its grammatical behaviour and that this value provides the basis for other meanings in various extended uses.

It is uncontroversial that the Welsh Perfect construction consists critically of a complex of the verb *bod*, 'be', a verbal noun and the preposition *wedi*, 'after', as in (2).[1]

(2) mae o wedi rhoi syniadau da i mi (052)
be he after giving ideas good to me
'he has given me good ideas'

I am assuming argumentation made in another work that this is indeed the same predicate as the preposition *wedi* and that this same form also turns up in the passive constructions discussed later; see Fife (1984).

As regards the passive in Welsh, the most commonly accepted formation is one using the verb *cael*, 'get', a verbal noun and a subject-referent possessive pronoun, as in (3).

(3) nawr, ymhle gaethoch chi'ch geni? (609)
now where got you-your bearing
'now, where were you born?'

Usually grammarians recognize the form in (4) as a version of the passive in (3).

(4) mi roedd un o'r nofelau wedi cael i chyhoeddi (426)
prt was one of-the novels after getting its publishing
'one of the novels had been published'

Although there are numerous structural differences between (3) and (4), the latter having *cael* occurring as a verbal noun, for example, the net effect is no different from that seen in the actives in (5). Consequently, (4) is to be viewed as no more than a simple Perfect form of the passive in (3).

(5a) mi gawn ni *Sbel Ganol Ddydd* eto Dydd Iau nesa (620)
prt get we again Thursday next
'we'll have *Sbel Ganol Ddydd* again next Thursday'

(5b) 'dan ni ddim wedi cal amser hyd 'n oed i sôn... (617)
are, we neg after getting time even to mention
'we haven't had time even to mention...'

Occasionally grammarians draw attention to another form similar to (4), but without using *cael*, as in (6).

(6) yr un o'r ddau emyn yna sydd wedi eu gwobrwyo (409)
the one of-the two hymn there is after their awarding
'the one of those two hymns which were awarded'

The usual explanation for this is that the verb *cael* can, for some unarticulated reason, delete after *wedi*. I argue elsewhere that this is unsatisfactory and the better analysis is that (6) is another type of passive in Welsh with semantic properties predictably different to those of the *cael* forms; see Fife (1984). Because both the *cael* and the *cael*-less forms partake of an essential co-reference relationship involving the possessive pronoun, I refer to both as **anaphoric passives** in Welsh.

But there is a third construction in Welsh which has passive sense and which does not use anaphoric co-reference, but which otherwise looks very much like the *wedi* construction in (4). Examples of this are given in (7).

(7a) achos wedi colli
cause after losing
'lost cause'

(7b) cig wedi rhewi
meat after freezing
'frozen meat'

(7c) caws wedi pobi
cheese after baking
'baked cheese, rarebit'

(7d) llaeth wedi puro
milk after purifying
'purified milk'

At first sight these may appear to be defective instances of a *wedi* anaphoric passive, and indeed, there are certain forms which suggest such an analysis. Consider (8).

(8) a. mae'r frwydr hon eisoes wedi hennill
be-the battle this already after winning
'this battle is already one'
b. ces i nhemtio'n fawr
got I tempting-in great
'I was greatly tempted'
c. roedd wedi fagu ar ffarm fechan
was after raising on farm small
'he had been raised on a small farm'
d. mae'r ddrama wedi seilio ar...
be-the play after basing on
'the play is based on...'

In these cases, the possessive pronoun is also lacking. However, these are better analysed as dialectal variants of (4). It is to be noted that in some spoken dialects, the standard possessive pronoun complex seen in (9a) is modified to that in (9b) or (9c), where CONF PRO means confirming pronoun and variable elements are enclosed in parentheses.

(9)					
	a.	POSS PRO	N(+mut)	CONF PRO:	*fy nesg i*
	b.		N(+mut)	CONF PRO:	*'nesg i*
	c.		N(+mut)	:	*'nesg*
					'my desk'

The forms in (8a-c) are all of the type in (9c). In (8d) we are faced with a common phonological problem in these dialects. Since /s/ is an immutable consonant, there is no marking on the noun. This form is therefore ambiguous, but this is not a problem confined to the passive forms in these dialects. Accordingly, these are rightfully treated as dialectal variants to the *cael* and *wedi* passives in (3) and (4).

This analysis is not available for the forms in (7), as the required mutations do not appear where possible; there are no descriptions of dialects which have eliminated *both* the pre-nominal pronoun and the mutation behaviour. The forms in (7) must also be distinguished from the forms in (10), where there is passive meaning and no mutations.

(10) a. siop wedi cau
shop after closing
'closed shop'

b. bu farw prifathrawes wedi ymddeol
died headmistress after retiring
'a retired headmistress died'

The verbs in (10) are among those in Welsh which have **variable transitivity**, i.e. they can be either transitive/ergative or intransitive/absolutive. The translations in (10), though natural for English, conceal the fact that these are actual Perfects of intransitive processes (i.e., *has closed, has retired*) and so not passives.

This leaves us with the problem of what the forms in (7) are. My claim is that they are a third passive formation, distinct in form and semantic value from the two anaphoric passives. If this is so, we then have a passive formation in Welsh which bears a striking resemblance to a normal, active perfect structure, as in (2). Consider example (11). We are confronted with another example of the wide-spread tendency for perfective and passive to share similar features. Accordingly, I call the forms in (7) the **perfective passive** in Welsh.

(11) a. llaeth wedi puro
milk after purifying
'purified milk'

b. mae nhw wedi puro'r llaeth
be-they after purifying-the milk
'they have purified the milk'

c. dafad wedi marw
sheep after dying
'dead sheep'

The interesting fact about the Welsh perfective passives vis-à-vis the problem stated at the outset is that, unlike the case of the four languages in (1), the Welsh construction does not use any formative which traces back to the Proto-Indo-European Perfect or Medio-passive. The two critical components of the perfective passive are the preposition *wedi* (which derives from an adverbial form) and the verbal noun (from earlier infinitival forms). Since none of the material constituting the perfective passive can be explained by inheritance, we are faced with an independently developed passive formation which nonetheless mirrors a supposedly inherited relationship of perfective and passive in other languages. Like the divergent species of the Galapagos, an analysis of how the later, transparent Welsh structures are formed should point us toward a general account of the mechanism explaining the origins of the older, more opaque, continental forms.[2]

The solution, I believe, lies in a modified version of the account given in Comrie's study on aspect. Modified, because, like Kuryłowicz, Comrie concentrated too narrowly on a *structural* category, and not on the specific *semantics* of the forms. Comrie assigns the Perfect the meaning of 'a state resulting from a previous action'. Accurate as this may be, it is not the Perfect construction *per se* which accounts for the passive meaning in the related forms. As the examples in (12) show, the passive sense is possible also with structures which are not properly Perfects under Comrie's definition.

(12)	a.	French:	une porte fermée
	b.	Spanish:	una puerta cerrada
	c.	German:	eine geschlossene Tür
	d.	English:	a shut door

If the semantic association of passivity and aspect is narrowly confined to the Perfect construction, then the passive readings in (12) are unexplained. To avoid this, it is important to go behind the specific forms involved and look at a semantic feature having more wide-spread application in language, yet similar to Comrie's analysis.

This feature is the notion of **perfectivity** as defined in cognitive grammar. Very briefly, in cognitive grammar a perfective process is one which predicates change over time. One way a process can express change over time is if it has discernible subphases, 'slices' of the over-all event which, when viewed atemporally, differ from one another. And one minimal way to give a process discernible subphases is to give it definite starting and ending points in the process. Thus, one very common corollary of perfective status is that the process is deemed to be **bounded** in time, since it has distinct termini. Examples of this in Welsh are to be found elsewhere, in Fife (1984). For our purposes it is enough to know that perfectives by their semantic nature allow reference to the endpoints of the process.

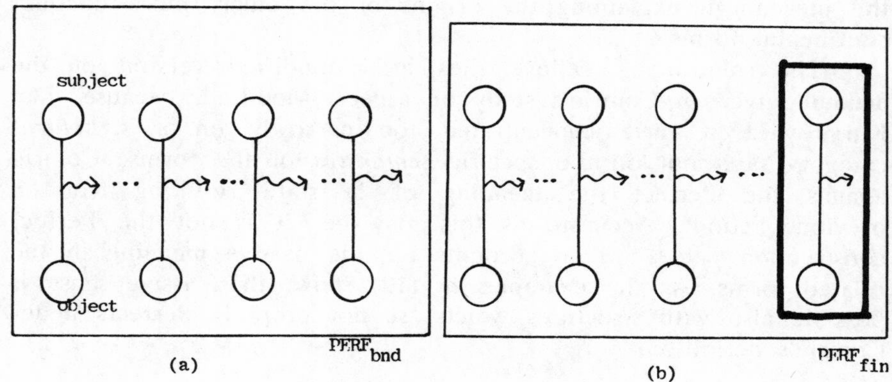

Figure 1

Some uses of the perfectives show a concentration on or highlighting of the initial point in the process. Others, which focus on the final endpoint, are also very common.[3] Translated into cognitive grammar terms, this sort of phenomenon can be illustrated by the diagram in Figure 1. In this diagram, the circles represent abstractly the participants in a relation, represented by the line connecting them. The wavy, horizontal line indicates this relation extends through time (a process). If the diagram labelled (a) stands for a normal, bounded, perfective process, then the diagram labelled (b) represents a common alternate construal of this meaning, namely that where the final state becomes focused, as indicated by the bold outline as the element highlighted. This is a diagrammatic portrayal of Comrie's definition of a 'perfect' meaning: a state resulting from a previous action.

Given that this is a proper description of the 'final state' connotation of perfectives, the link which ties the perfectives in with the passives involves a further 'shift' in meaning from that in Figure 1b. Comrie describes this semantic effect in relation to the example in (13): "With transitive verbs, therefore, the most usual state resulting from an action will be the changed state of the semantic object of the action, in the example given a change in the state of the city" (Comrie, 1976: 86).

(13) the enemy has destroyed the city

In other words, the result of a transitive process is most evident in the object of the process, so when meaning is already focused on the final state of a perfective process, there is a tendency to further confine the meaning, this time focusing on the patient in that final state. This is depicted in Figure 2.

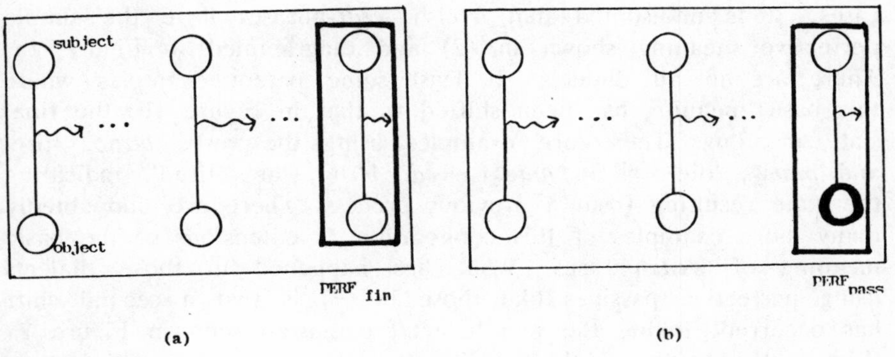

Figure 2

In this figure, we are taking the 'final state' version of the perfective sense as the starting point, so diagram (b) in Figure 1 is now diagram (a) in Figure 2. From this meaning as a base, the extended, passive sense of the perfective involves a shift to the most obvious indicator of the process's effect, the object. In the diagram, this is shown by the fact that the box representing the final state of the process in Figure 2a is in bold, while in 2b the item in bold outline is the participant labelled 'object'.

Comrie's analysis, as revised, involves a two-fold **semantic shift**, a concept having wide currency in cognitive grammar theory. In atheoretical terms, Comrie's analysis concerns what precise subpart of the semantic structure of the whole is most highlighted in a particular use. The cognitive grammar framework merely provides a convenient medium for expressing the idea that the perfective sense of a predicate can be involved in successive shifts of nuance to where it focuses specifically on the patient of a process, which is precisely the role of a passive.

There are numerous examples in language supporting the view that the object is the most prominent item in a perfective semantic image. In a study by Scott DeLancey (1981), a number of examples from languages like Syuwa, Gujurati, Turkish, Thai and Georgian show that speaker viewpoint with perfectives most naturally resides with the object of the process, leading him to comment, "Thus a unitary account of split ergativity requires a principled association between terminal (patient) viewpoint and perfective aspect" (p646).

All well and good, but how does this apply to our Welsh cases? It is undisputed that Welsh *wedi*-phrases have the simple perfective meaning shown in (2) and diagrammed in Figure 1a. There are in all dialects, at least some patent examples where this basic meaning has been shifted to that in Figure 1b, the final state meaning. These are examples using the verbs *blino*, 'tire' and *marw*, 'die', as in *mae e wedi blino*, 'he's tired', indicating the state resulting from a previous process. There are undoubtedly many more examples of this connotation as extensions of the basic meaning of *wedi*-phrases. What has happened in those dialects using perfective passives like those in (7) is that a second shift has occurred, taking the pan-dialectal extension seen in Figure 2a (Figure 1b) a step further to its natural, semantic corollary seen in Figure 2b, where the most prominant element of the structure is the patient of the process. In (7b), this prominent patient is in the entire phrase explicitly stated to be 'milk' and so the whole has the meaning of a passive.

By this argument I hope to have shown that the Welsh perfective passives follow in the footsteps of a general semantic shift found in numerous languages. It is the inherent nature of perfectives that allows them to have additional, extended meanings like 'final state' and 'most affected entity' and these extended meanings account for the by-versions of perfectives in language.

The Welsh perfective passives are therefore a further example of this common semantic nexus. What is so interesting about the Welsh forms, as I have said, is their transparency in being derived from the regular Perfect structure and the impossibility to treat this as a mere inheritance. The Welsh forms show that the semantic dynamic which accounted for the ancient, inherited perfective-passive pairs in other Indo-European languages need not be considered dead and buried, but is a general semantic principle which can be exploited by any language having the appropriate forms. In that sense, the Welsh perfective passives are indeed particularly enlightening in understanding the mechanism which underlies the inherited traits of perfective-passive relationships in other branches of Indo-European. And in that sense too, an understanding of the Welsh forms is like a visit to the Galapagos.

Notes

* This paper was originally presented at the Eighth International Congress of Celtic Studies, Swansea on July 23rd 1987. It has benefitted from the comments and suggestions of the audience.

1. The numbers following an example indicate it is drawn from the files of the Department of Linguistics at the University College of North Wales, Bangor and the number indicates the relevant file card.

2. Indeed, a more broad-based account is evidently needed in any case, as Comrie's examples of perfective-passive correlation extend beyond Indo-European. This argues a general semantic feature of the two categories must be used to explain this.

3. This is probably what accounts for the common connotation of perfectives as indicating completion, though, as Comrie points out, this is not a defining characteristic of perfectivity or Perfects.

References

Comrie, B. (1976) *Aspect*. Cambridge: Cambridge University Press.

DeLancey, S. (1981) An interpretation of split-ergativity. *Language*, **57**, 626-57.

Fife, J. (1984) *Semantic Structure of the Verb in Modern Welsh.* Doctoral thesis, University of Wales.

Greene, D. (1979) Perfect and passive in Eastern and Western Gaelic. *Studia Celtica,* **14/15**, 87-95.

Kuryłowicz, J. (1964) *The Inflectional Categories of Indo-European*. Heidelberg: Carl Winter Verlag.

Langacker, R. (1987) *Foundations of Cognitive Grammar*. Palo Alto: Stanford University Press.

Wagner, H. (1959) *Das Verbum in den Sprachen der britischen Inseln*. Heidelberg: Carl Winter Verlag.

Welsh Passives*

Robert D. Borsley
University College of North Wales, Bangor

0. Introduction

Welsh has received very little attention within modern syntactic theory. Welsh passives, however, have been discussed at length in Awbery (1976). Awbery develops a detailed analysis within the standard theory of transformational grammar of Chomsky (1965). In this analysis, the surface structures of passive sentences are derived from abstract underlying structures by a complex sequence of transformational operations. Until the late 70's, it was generally accepted that only such transformational analyses could capture the generalizations that are characteristic of natural languages. Since the late 70's, this view has been widely questioned and a number of non-transformational approaches have been developed. In this paper, I will argue that the approach known as Head-driven Phrase Structure Grammar (HPSG) can provide a simple and elegant analysis of Welsh passives.

The paper is organized as follows. In section 1, I will summarize the basic data and indicate what is required of a satisfactory analysis. In section 2, I will outline the theoretical framework. In section 3, I will show how Welsh passives can be accommodated within this framework. Finally, in section 4, I will summarize my proposals.

1. The Basic Data

We can summarize the basic facts quite briefly. The following are typical passives:[1]

(1) Cafodd Megan ei tharo (gan Emrys).
got Megan 3SGF hit by Emrys
'Megan was hit (by Emrys).'

(2) Mae Megan wedi cael ei tharo (gan Emrys).
is Megan after get 3SGF hit by Emrys
'Megan has been hit (by Emrys).'

(1) is a simple passive, and (2) is what is known as a 'periphrastic' passive. Both involve a form of the verb *cael*, 'get', a non-finite verb preceded by a pronominal element agreeing with the subject and an optional prepositional phrase headed by *gan*, 'by'. For reasons that are outlined in Borsley (1987a), I will call the pronominal element in these examples a clitic.[2] Clitics also appear with a non-finite verb followed by a pronominal object, and with a noun followed by a pronoun denoting a possessor. The following illustrate:[3]

(3) Mae Emrys wedi ei tharo hi.
is Emrys after 3SGF hit she
'Emrys has hit her.'

(4) ei thŷ hi
3SGF house she
'her house'

Having summarized the basic facts, we can now consider what is required of a satisfactory analysis. The first requirement for any grammatical analysis is that it should get the facts right, or, in Chomsky's terminology, that it should achieve observational adequacy. In the present context, this means among other things ensuring that there is an appropriate form of *cael*, allowing an optional *gan*-phrase, and ensuring agreement between the clitic and the subject.

A second requirement for any grammatical analysis is that it should capture whatever generalizations are apparent, or, in Chomsky's terminology, that it should attain descriptive adequacy. In the present context, the most important generalization concerns the complements that passive verbs take. It emerges when we compare passive sentences with related active sentences. (1) and (2) are related to the following examples:

(5) Tarodd Emrys Megan.
hit Emrys Megan
'Emrys hit Megan.'

(6) Mae Emrys wedi taro Megan.
is Emrys after hit Megan
'Emrys has hit Megan.'

In the following, we have four more passives together with their active counterparts.

(7) a. Cafodd y llyfr ei roi i Megan (gan Gwyn).
got the book 3SGM give to Megan by Gwyn
'The book was given to Megan (by Gwyn).'
b. Rhoddodd Gwyn y llyfr i Megan.
gave Gwyn the book to Megan
'Gwyn gave the book to Megan.'

(8) a. Mae'r llyfr wedi cael ei roi i Megan (gan Emrys)
is the book after get 3SGM give to Megan by E.
'The book has been given to Megan (by Emrys).'
b. Mae Gwyn wedi rhoi 'r llyfr i Megan.
is Gwyn after give the book to Megan
'Gwyn has given the book to Mary.'

(9) a. Cafodd Megan ei pherswadio (gan Gwyn) i fynd adref
got Megan 3SGF persuade by Gwyn to go home
'Megan was persuaded (by Gwyn) to go home.'
b. Perswadiodd Gwyn Megan i fynd adref.
persuaded Gwyn Megan to go home
'Gwyn persuaded Megan to go home.'

(10) a. Mae Megan wedi cael ei pherswadio (gan Gwyn) i fynd adref
is Megan after get 3SGF persuade by Gwyn to go home
'Megan has been persuaded (by Gwyn) to go home.'
b. Mae Gwyn wedi perswadio Megan i fynd adref
is Gwyn after persuade Megan to go home
'Gwyn has persuaded Megan to go home.'

This data shows that passive verbs take no object but otherwise take whatever complements related active verbs take. Any analysis must capture this generalization.

2. The Theoretical Background

We can now look at HPSG. This is a framework developed over the last few years by Carl Pollard, Ivan Sag, and others. (See Pollard, 1985, 1988, Sag and Pollard, 1987 and Pollard and Sag, 1988.) At its heart is the idea that grammars can be simplified quite radically if heads incorporate information about the categories with which they combine. In Borsley (1987b), I argue for a particular version of HPSG, and in Borsley (forthcoming), I consider how Welsh might be accommodated within this version of HPSG.

In Borsley (1987b), I argue that heads should incorporate a feature SUBCAT, which indicates what complements they take and a feature SUBJ, which indicates what kind of subject they require. Both features take as their value a list categories. In the case of SUBJ, this list never has more than one member. In both cases, the list can be empty. Within this framework, a simple intransitive verb, e.g. sleeps, will have the following category:

(11) V[+FIN;SUBCAT< >;SUBJ<NP[3SG]>]

For a simple transitive verb, e.g. *admires*, we will have the following category:

(12) V[+FIN;SUBCAT<NP>;SUBJ<NP[3SG]>]

Finally, for a ditransitive verb, e.g. *puts*, we will have the following category:

(13) V[+FIN;SUBCAT<PP[+LOC],NP>;SUBJ<NP[3SG]>]

Where a verb takes more than one complement, the complements appear in the SUBCAT list in the order most oblique to least oblique. Thus, an object follows any other complement.

The main proposal of Borsley (forthcoming) is that post-head subjects such as *Emrys* in (14) and NP's denoting possessors such as *Gwyn* in (15) should be analysed as additional complements.

(14) Darllenodd Emrys y llyfr.
read Emrys the book
'Emrys read the book.'

(15) darlun Gwyn o Megan
picture Gwyn of Megan
'Gwyn's picture of Megan'

This means that *darllenodd* will have the category in (16), and *darlun* the category in (17).[4]

(16) V[+FIN;SUBCAT<NP,NP[-PRO]>;SUBJ< >]

(17) N[SUBCAT<PP[o],NP[-PRO]>;SUBJ< >]

I use PP[o] here to mean a PP headed by the preposition *o*. Within this framework, SUBJ is relevant to pre-head subjects and understood subjects or controllers. In (18), *darllen* has a pre-head NP subject, *Gwyn*, and in (19), it has an NP controller, *Emrys*. (Here and subsequently, I use the unmutated form when referring to a lexical item in the text.)

(18) Disgwyliodd Emrys i Gwyn ddarllen y llyfr.
expected Emrys to Gwyn read the book
'Emrys expected Gwyn to read the book.'

(19) Mae Emrys wedi darllen y llyfr.
is Emrys after read the book
'Emrys has read the book.'

In both cases, *darllen* takes a non-pronominal NP complement. Here, then, we will have the following category:

(20) V[-FIN;SUBCAT<NP[-PRO]>;SUBJ<NP>]

Two of the very few rules that are needed in this version of HPSG are the following:

(21) a. [SUBCAT< >] ---> H[SUBCAT<...,Y_n>], C*
b. [SUBJ< >] ---> H[SUBCAT< >;SUBJ<Y>], C

I will call (21)a. the head-complement rule and (21)b. the subject-predicate rule. Both are immediate dominance rules. Hence, the order of elements on the right hand side is of no significance. H is a head, C is a subject or complement, and Y is an arbitrary category. A number of universal principles interact with these rules. One is the Head Feature Principle, which can be formulated as follows:

(22) A head and its mother are identical unless some rule allows them to differ.

This ensures that a verbal head has a verbal mother, that a nominal head has a nominal mother, and so on. Another general principle is the Subcategorization Principle, which we can formulate as follows:

(23) A category that is on the SUBCAT list of a head and not on the SUBCAT list of its mother or on the SUBJ list of a head and not on the SUBJ list of its mother must be matched by a sister of the head.

The categories in (16) and (17) will interact with the head-complement rule and these principles to allow the following trees:

(24)

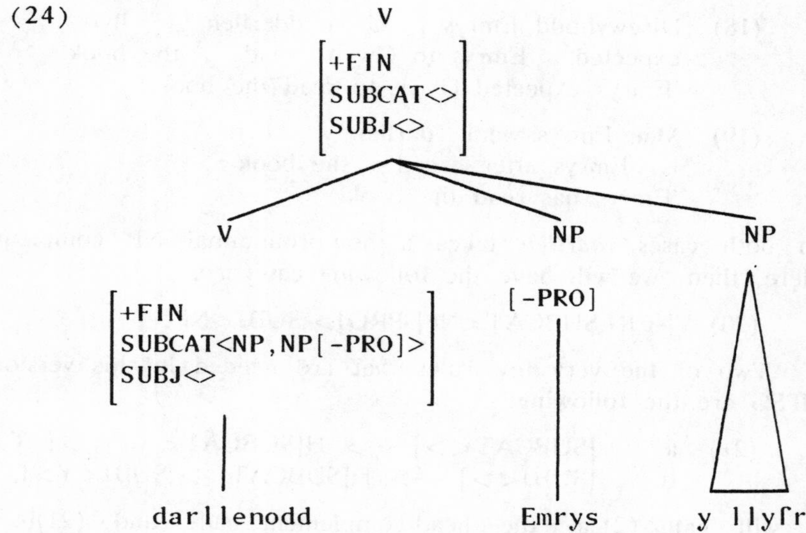

(25)

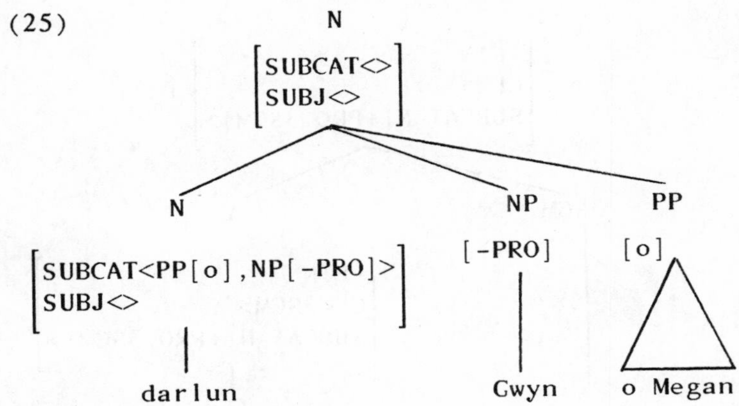

In both trees, the mothers are identical to the heads except that they have the feature SUBCAT< >. Thus, they conform to the Head Feature Principle. And in both cases, the categories that are on the SUBCAT list of the head and not on the SUBCAT list of the mother are matched by sisters of the head. Hence, they also conform to the Subcategorization Principle. The subject-predicate rule will play a limited role in Welsh, but it will be responsible for the subordinate clause in (19).

A second proposal in Borsley (forthcoming) is that Welsh has a feature CL (clitic) which indicates what kind of clitic a head requires. Assuming this feature, we can assign *darllen* in (26) (which is very similar to (3)) to the category in (27).

(26) Mae Emrys wedi ei ddarllen ef.
is Emrys after 3SGM read he
'Emrys has read it.'

(27) V[-FIN;CL<α>;SUBCAT<NP[+PRO,α]>;SUBJ<NP>]

α here is a variable ranging over sets of person, number and gender features. To utilize such categories, we need the following rule:

(28) [CL<>] ---> α, H[CL<α>]

(27) will interact with this rule and the Head Feature Principle to allow the following tree:

(29)

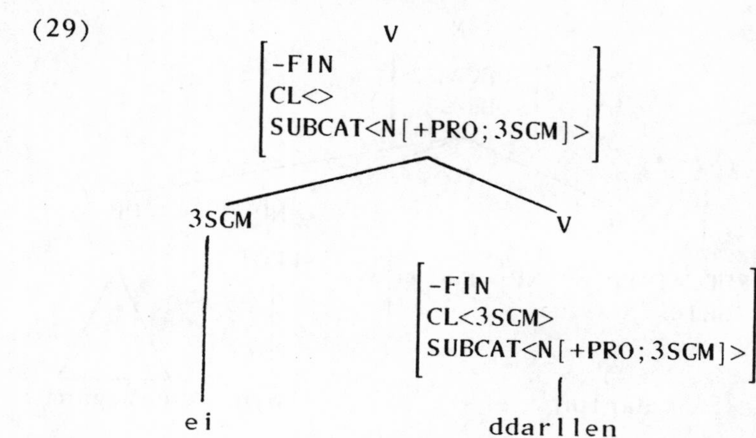

This will combine with a third person singular masculine pronoun.[5]

3. The Analysis

Having outlined the general framework that I will assume, we can now return to passives.

Firstly, we must ask what the basic structure of passives looks like. For Awbery, the superficial structure of (1) would be essentially as follows:

(30)

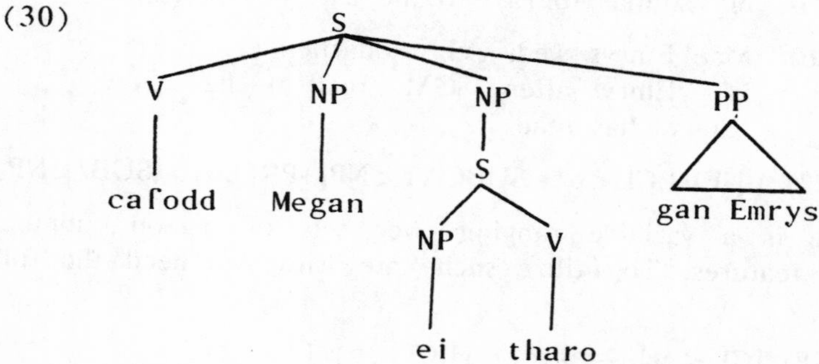

I want to argue that the correct structure is in fact the following:

(31)

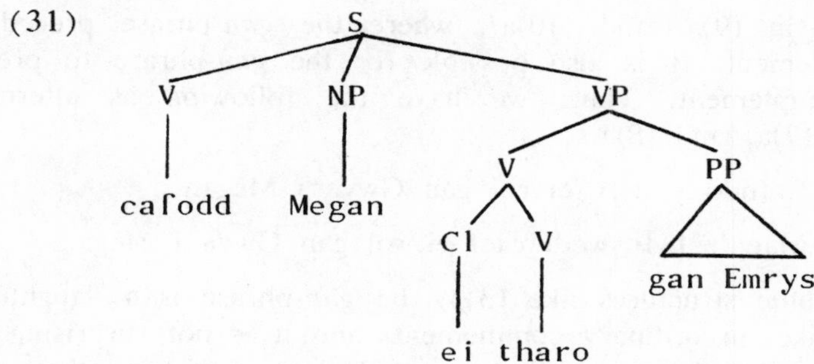

One difference between the two structures is that in (30) the constituent containing the non-finite verb is an NP, whereas in (31) it is a VP. Awbery offers no real argument for the assumption that this constituent is an NP. Moreover, as Borsley (1983) points out, constituents containing non-finite verbs do not in general have the distribution of NP's. Hence, there is a good reason not to analyze them as NP's.

A second difference between the structures is that the *gan*-phrase is outside the constituent containing the non-finite verb in (30), whereas in (31), it is inside. Awbery argues that the combin: tion of clitic, non-finite verb and *gan*-phrase is not a constituent because it cannot be preposed. She illustrates with the following example:

(32) *Ei rybuddio gan ferch a gafodd y dyn.
3SGM warn by woman PCL got the man
'The man was warned by the woman.'

One point that undermines this argument is that not all VP's can be preposed in English. Whereas, (33) is grammatical, both (34) and (35) are ungrammatical. (The preposed VP's are bracketed.)

(33) They said he would do it and [do it] he would

(34) *They said he would be going and [be going] he would

(35) *They said he would have left and [have left] he would

Hence, we cannot conclude from the fact that the combination of clitic, non-finite verb and *gan*-phrase cannot be fronted that it is not a constituent.

One thing that argues against Awbery's analysis is the fact the *gan*-phrase can precede a complement of the verb. This is illustrated in (9)a. and (10)a., where the *gan*-phrase precedes a VP complement. It is also possible for the *gan*-phrase to precede a PP complement. Thus, we have the following as alternative forms of (7)a. and (8)a.:

(36) Cafodd y llyfr ei roi gan Gwyn i Megan.

(37) Mae 'r llyfr wedi cael ei roi gan Gwyn i Megan.

If we assume structures like (31), the *gan*-phrase is a daughter of VP just like an ordinary complement, and it is not surprising if it sometimes precedes an ordinary complement. On the other hand, if we assume structures like (30), the *gan*-phrase is a daughter of the matrix S, whereas an ordinary complement will be a daughter of the embedded S, and it is not at all clear how the *gan*-phrase can precede an ordinary complement.

A further difference between the two structures is that Awbery does not analyze the pre-verbal pronominal element as a clitic. Given the reasons noted in Borsley (1987a) for analyzing these elements as clitics, the structure in (31) seems preferable to Awbery's.

Assuming that passives have structures like (31), we can ask how such structures can be provided for within the framework that I am assuming here. Firstly, we need appropriate categories. From now on I will omit features with the empty list as their value and I will use 'VP' as an abbreviation for V[SUBCAT< >;SUBJ<Y>] and 'PP' as an abbreviation for P[SUBCAT<>]. Assuming these conventions, we can assign *taro* to the category in (38), and *cafodd* to the category in (39).[6]

(38) V[+PAS;CL<α>;SUBCAT<PP[gan]>;SUBJ<NP[α]>]

(39) V[+FIN;SUBCAT<VP[+PAS],NP>]

Given these categories, the clitic rule and the head-complement rule will allow the following tree:

(40)

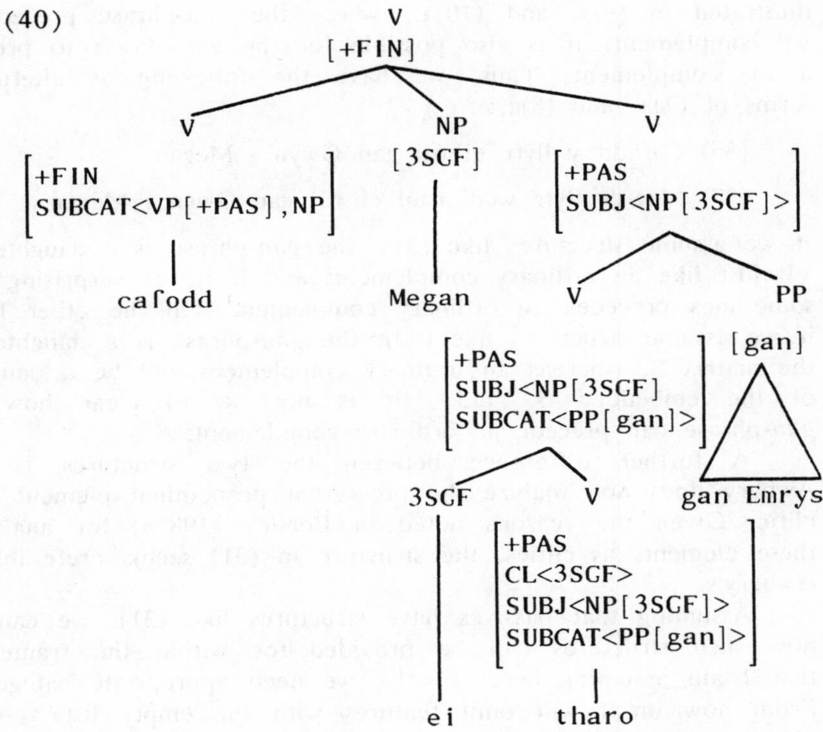

Here, then, we have the basis of an analysis of Welsh passives. We still, however, need some way to ensure that the subject of *cafodd* matches the value of SUBJ on the VP complement. We can do this with another general condition, the Control Agreement Principle (CAP). If we define a predicative complement as a complement with a non-empty value for SUBJ, we can formulate the CAP as follows:

(41) The value of SUBJ on a predicative complement in the SUBCAT list of some item must be identical to the next item on the SUBCAT list.

In (40), this will affect the category of *cafodd*, requiring the value of SUBJ on the predicative complement abbreviated as VP[+PAS] to be identical to the NP which is the next item on the SUBCAT list. Thus, we will have the following category:

illustrated in (9)a. and (10)a., where the *gan*-phrase precedes a VP complement. It is also possible for the *gan*-phrase to precede a PP complement. Thus, we have the following as alternative forms of (7)a. and (8)a.:

(36) Cafodd y llyfr ei roi gan Gwyn i Megan.

(37) Mae 'r llyfr wedi cael ei roi gan Gwyn i Megan.

If we assume structures like (31), the *gan*-phrase is a daughter of VP just like an ordinary complement, and it is not surprising if it sometimes precedes an ordinary complement. On the other hand, if we assume structures like (30), the *gan*-phrase is a daughter of the matrix S, whereas an ordinary complement will be a daughter of the embedded S, and it is not at all clear how the *gan*-phrase can precede an ordinary complement.

A further difference between the two structures is that Awbery does not analyze the pre-verbal pronominal element as a clitic. Given the reasons noted in Borsley (1987a) for analyzing these elements as clitics, the structure in (31) seems preferable to Awbery's.

Assuming that passives have structures like (31), we can ask how such structures can be provided for within the framework that I am assuming here. Firstly, we need appropriate categories. From now on I will omit features with the empty list as their value and I will use 'VP' as an abbreviation for V[SUBCAT<>;SUBJ<Y>] and 'PP' as an abbreviation for P[SUBCAT<>]. Assuming these conventions, we can assign *taro* to the category in (38), and *cafodd* to the category in (39).[6]

(38) V[+PAS;CL<α>;SUBCAT<PP[gan]>;SUBJ<NP[α]>]

(39) V[+FIN;SUBCAT<VP[+PAS],NP>]

Given these categories, the clitic rule and the head-complement rule will allow the following tree:

will have rather different categories in the following examples. ((46)a. is identical to (3).)

(46) a. Mae Emrys wedi ei tharo hi.
is Emrys after 3SGF hit she
'Emrys has hit her.'
b. Mae Gwyn wedi ei roi ef i Megan.
is Gwyn after 3SGM give he to Megan
'Gwyn has given it to Mary.'
c. Mae Gwyn wedi ei pherswadio hi i fynd adref.
is Gwyn after 3SGF persuade she to go home
'Gwyn has persuaded her to go home.'

Here, we have pronominal objects and pre-verbal clitics. The necessary categories are the following:

(47) a. V[-FIN;CL<α>;SUBCAT<NP[+PRO;α]>;
SUBJ<NP>]
b. V[-FIN;CL<α>;SUBCAT<PP[i],NP[+PRO;α]>;
SUBJ<NP>]
c. V[-FIN;CL<α>;SUBCAT<VP[+INF],
NP[+PRO;α]>;SUBJ<NP>]

We can derive these categories from those in (45) with the following lexical rule:

(48) V[-FIN;SUBCAT<...NP[-PRO]>] ===>
V[-FIN;CL<α>;SUBCAT<...NP[+PRO;α]>]

We can now return to passives. For *taro* in passives like (1) and (2), we need the following categories:[7]

(49) a. V[+PAS;CL<α>;SUBCAT< >;SUBJ<NP[α]>]
b. V[+PAS;CL<α>;SUBCAT<PP[gan]>;SUBJ<NP[α]>]

PP[gan] here means a PP headed by *gan*. For *rhoi* in passives like (7)a. and (8)a., we need the categories in (50):

(50) a. V[+PAS;CL<α>;SUBCAT<PP[i]>;
SUBJ<NP[α]>]
b. V[+PAS;CL<α>;SUBCAT<PP[gan],PP[i]>;
SUBJ<NP[α]>]

Finally, for *perswadio* in passives like (9)a. and (10)a., we need the categories in (51).

(51) a. V[+PAS;CL<α>;SUBCAT<VP[+INF]>;
SUBJ<NP[α]>]
b. V[+PAS;CL<α>;SUBCAT<PP[gan],VP[+INF]>;
SUBJ<NP[α]>]

We can derive these categories from the categories in (47) with the following lexical rule:

(52) V[-FIN;CL<α>;SUBCAT<...NP[+PRO;α]>;
SUBJ<NP>] ===>
V[+PAS;CL<α>;SUBCAT<(PP[gan])...>;
SUBJ<NP[α]>]

This rule embodies the generalization about passive complements that we have highlighted. Given this rule, we can claim that we have an analysis which achieves descriptive adequacy.

We must now consider periphrastic passives. Here, I will assume with Harlow (1983) that *wedi* and other items that occupy the same position are items that combine with a VP to form a larger VP. Unlike Harlow, however, I will assume that these items are heads. I will also assume that they are verbs, though nothing really hangs on this. Given these assumptions, we will have the following category for *wedi*:

(53) V[+PART;SUBCAT<VP[+INF]>;SUBJ<NP>]

We can assign *cael* to the category in (54) and *mae* to the category in (55).

(54) V[+INF;SUBCAT<VP[+PAS]>;SUBJ<NP>]
(55) V[+FIN;SUBCAT<VP[+PART],NP>]

Given these categories, the clitic rule and the head-complement rule will allow the following tree:

(56)

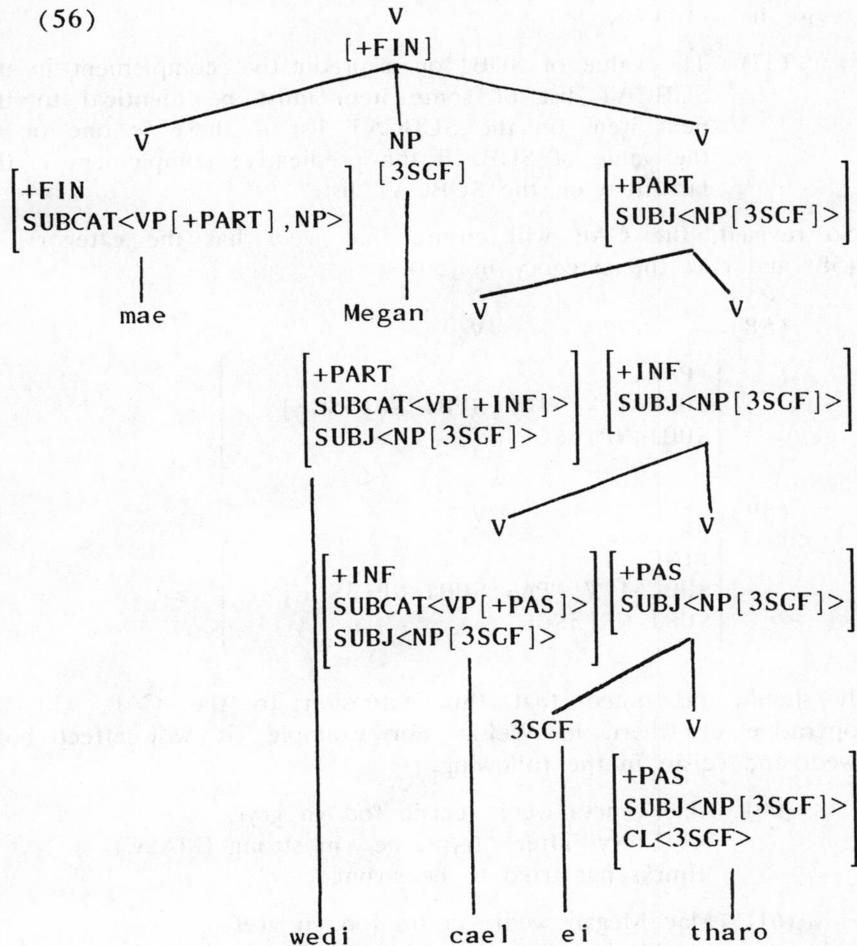

The CAP will ensure that the value of SUBJ on the VP complement of *mae* is identical to subject of *mae*. At present, however, we have no way to ensure that the value of SUBJ on *wedi* matches the value of SUBJ on its complement and that the value of SUBJ on *cael* matches the value of SUBJ on its complement. We can ensure this with an extension of the CAP. In the category of *wedi*, the predicative complement is the last item on the SUBCAT list. Hence, the basic CAP is inapplicable.

We can bring this category within the scope of the CAP if we revise it as follows:

(57) The value of SUBJ on a predicative complement in the SUBCAT list of some item must be identical to the next item on the SUBCAT list if there is one or to the value of SUBJ if the predicative complement is the last item on the SUBCAT list.

So revised, the CAP will ensure that *wedi* has the category in (58) and *cael* the category in (59).

(58) V

[+PART
SUBCAT<V[+INF;SUBJ<NP[3SGF]>]>
SUBJ<NP[3SGF]>]

(59) V

[+INF
SUBCAT<V[+PAS;SUBJ<NP[3SGF]>]>
SUBJ<NP[3SGF]>]

It should be noted that this extension to the CAP will be operative elsewhere in Welsh. For example, it will affect both wedi and ceisio in the following:

(60) Mae Emrys wedi ceisio fod yn gryf.
is Emrys after try be in strong (MASC)
'Emrys has tried to be strong.'

(61) Mae Megan wedi ceisio fod yn gref.
is Megan after try be in strong (FEM)
'Megan has tried to be strong.'

Thus, we need no special devices to accommodate periphrastic passives.

4. Summary

I have now developed an analysis of both simple and periphrastic passives, which I think can claim to achieve both observational and descriptive adequacy. The analysis employs quite complex categories but is essentially rather simple. The examples that I have considered involve just two syntactic rules - the head-complement rule and the clitic rule - and three general principles - the Head Feature Principle, the Subcategorization Principle, and the Control Agreement Principle. All the distinctive features of passive sentences are a consequence of the categorial makeup of passive verbs, which is a consequence of the passive lexical rule. I think, then, that we can conclude that the HPSG framework permits a very satisfactory analysis of Welsh passives and hence that there is no need here for a transformational analysis.

Footnotes

* I am grateful to Ewa Jaworska and Andrew Radford for helpful comments on an earlier version of this paper, and to Marion Williams for assistance with the data. The analysis that I outline has been incorporated into a computational grammar of Welsh developed during a visit to the IBM UK Scientific Centre, Winchester. I am grateful to IBM UK for the opportunity to do this work and to Richard Sharman for his assistance.

1. Throughout the paper, I follow Awbery in citing data from standard literary Welsh. Welsh also has impersonal passives, exemplified by the following:

   (i) Gwelwyd Megan gan Emrys.
   saw-IMPS Megan by Emrys
   'Megan was seen by Emrys.'

   I will not offer an analysis of such sentences.

2. Non-finite verbs are traditionally referred to as verbal nouns. Awbery assumes that they are in fact verbs. A number of arguments for this assumption are advanced in Sproat (1985).

3. The pronouns are superficially optional in these examples. Hence, both the following are possible:

   (i) Mae Emrys wedi ei tharo.

   (ii) ei thŷ

   I assume that these examples involve phonologically empty pronouns.

4. I assume that third person singular verb forms are members of two separate categories, one taking a third person singular pronominal subject

and having the feature SUBJ<NP|+PRO;3SG|> and one taking a non-pronominal subject and having the feature SUBJ<NP|-PRO|>.

5. To ensure that an item combines with a clitic that it requires before it combines with a complement it requires, it is necessary to add CL<> to the head in the head-complement rule, i.e. to reformulate it as follows:
(i) |SUBCAT<>| —> H|CL<>;SUBCAT<...,Y_n>|, C*

6. From now on, I will simplify things by ignoring the restrictions that finite verbs impose on their subjects.

7. Instead of having two separate categories, one might have a single category with PP|gan| in brackets to indicate that it is optional. The same point applies to the categories in (50) and (51).

References

Awbery, G.M. (1976) *The Syntax of Welsh: A Transformational Approach to the Passive*. Cambridge: Cambridge University Press.

Borsley, R.D. (1983) A Welsh agreement process and the status of VP and S. In Gazdar, G., Klein, E. and Pullum, G. K. (eds.), *Order, Concord and Constituency*. Dordrecht: Foris.

Borsley, R.D. (1987a) A note on "traditional treatments" of Welsh. *Journal of Linguistics*, **23**, 185-90.

Borsley, R.D. (1987b) Subjects and complements in HPSG. *CSLI Report*, No. **107**.

Borsley, R.D. (forthcoming) An HPSG approach to Welsh. *Journal of Linguistics*.

Chomsky, N.A. (1965) *Aspects of the Theory of Syntax*. Cambridge, Mass.: MIT Press.

Harlow, S. (1983) Celtic relatives. *York Papers in Linguistics*, **10**, 77-121.

Pollard, C.J. (1985) Phrase structure grammar without metarules. *WCCFL*, **4**.

Pollard, C.J. (1988) Categorial grammar and phrase structure grammar: An excursion on the syntax-semantics frontier. In Oehrle, R., Bach, E. and Wheeler, D. (eds.), *Categorial Grammars and Natural language Structures*. Dordrecht: D. Reidel.

Pollard, C.J. and Sag, I. A. (1988) *Information-Based Syntax and Semantics. Vol.1: Fundamentals*. CSLI Lecture Notes, **13**.

Sag, I.A. and Pollard, C. J. (1987) HPSG: An informal synopsis. *CSLI Report*, **No 79.**

Sproat, R. (1985) Welsh syntax and VSO structure. *Natural Language and Linguistic Theory*, **3**, 173-216.

The Lateral Fricative: lateral or fricative?

Martin J. Ball
Polytechnic of Wales

0. Introduction

The lateral fricative phoneme of Welsh, /ɬ/, presents a problem to the phonologist as to whether it should be classed with the other lateral, /l/ as a liquid sonorant, or with the other fricatives as an obstruent. This problem has implications for phonological rule formulation in at least one area of the phonology of Welsh: initial mutation. Soft mutation is a phonological change affecting a range of word-initial consonants when in certain lexical/syntactic environments. However, in this mutation (and indeed in the aspirate as well, see Tables 1 and 2 below) although different phonological features may be involved, by and large major class features are preserved.

p	→	b	b	→	v
t	→	d	d	→	ð
k	→	g	g	→	Ø
		m	→	v	
ɬ	→	l	r̥ʰ	→	r

Table 1 The Soft Mutation

p	→	f
t	→	θ
k	→	χ

Table 2 The Aspirate Mutation

There are certain apparent exceptions to this general principle that can now be considered. Firstly, we find in the case of the voiced velar plosive that SM (soft mutation) gives the change /g/ → Ø. As argued elsewhere (e.g. Awbery, 1975, Ball, forthcoming, a) this change is perhaps best considered as part of a general rule, [-cont] → [+cont], giving /g/ → *[ɣ]. If this is accepted, then /g/ → *[ɣ] still preserves major class features, in that both are obstruents.

A second problem is /m/ → /v/. This is quite as complex change involving alterations to the features [cont] and [nasal], and resulting in a major class change from sonorant to obstruent. The presumed historical process of /m/ → *[ṽ] → /v/ does not offer an alternative explanation, though it may help a simplification of the basic phonological rule (see Awbery, 1975).

However, this change is isolated in that it is the only nasal consonant to be affected by soft mutation (or indeed by any of the mutations). Also, nasal stops (which are are sonorants) are phonetically similar to oral stops (which are obstruents). This means that a [-cont] → [+cont] change with oral stops results in fricatives (i.e. obstruents → obstruents), and the same rule applied to nasal stops gives us fricatives, but this time we see sonorant → obstruent. It must be admitted, however, that the application of SM to /m/ does result in what is apparently a major class change. We will return later to the nasal mutation (NM).

Let us now turn our attention to /ɬ/. /ɬ/ is one of a group of sounds affected by the phonological rule [-voice] → [+voice]. The others are the oral stops /p, t, k/ and the trill /r̥ʰ/. In the case of the first three we have /p, t, k/ → /b, d, g/, which involves the retention of the major class of obstruent, while with the last we find /r̥ʰ/ → /r/ with the class sonorant unaffected.

The change with /ɬ/ gives us /ɬ/ → /l/, and the question that faces us here is this: does this change also involve a change from obstruent to sonorant, as well as the altered value to the voice feature?[1] If /ɬ/ is included with the sonorants due to its shared features with other liquids (such as /l/), then no such extra change is involved. If, however, it is classed as an obstruent because of its similarity to other fricatives, then such a change has to be accounted for.

1. Descriptions in the literature

Most traditional, and indeed modern, descriptions of Welsh

phonetics and phonology have not considered in detail the problem noted above. Nevertheless, reference to a selection of these will show that different authors have considered /ɬ/ to be either a liquid or alternatively a fricative.

For example, Morris-Jones (1913) classes /ɬ/ as a voiceless liquid. He recognises, of course, the 'his' element of the sound, but his main description is that it "is a voiceless l pronounced on one side" (p19). This description is also very much what occurs in Williams (1980: 2). Evans (1909) is not very helpful in his description of /ɬ/. He does not attempt to assign it to any consonant category, simply giving an account of its articulation:

> Ll represents a peculiar sound. If the vocal organs be in readiness to pronounce tl as in English antler, the sound ll can be arrived at by attending to two particulars -
> (i.) Emit the breath more freely than for tl, and
> (ii.) Let the emission of the breath be continuous, without the sudden explosive sound of t at the beginning. (p64)

With Jones (1926) we are on firmer ground. He clearly classes /ɬ/ with the fricatives, stating "a strong current of air is forced through the narrow aperture, giving the ear the impression of a strong fricative" (p14). He concludes that "the ɬ is therefore best described as a voiceless lateral-fricative" (p14).

Sommerfelt's (1925) study of Cyfeiliog Welsh also attempts a classification of the vowel and consonant system. In his classification he appears to recognise the problem found with /ɬ/, for he does not class it either with the spirants (fricatives) or the liquids, but in a separate class he calls 'spirant-liquids' along with /rʰ/. This dual nature is stressed in his description of the sound: "the tip of the tongue is in the same position as for l ... L̥ [i.e. ɬ] is energetically blown and followed by strong aspiration.

A more recent approach to Welsh phonology is found in the collection edited by Ball and Jones (1984). In Jones' chapter on the distinctive vowels and consonants of Welsh, /ɬ/ is classed as a fricative (p46). In Awbery's chapter on Welsh phonotactics, the author notes the importance of the sonorant-obstruent distinction in her discussion of consonant clusters in Welsh. Unfortunately, she does not specify to which group /ɬ/ is assumed to belong; at one point it is termed a "voiceless lateral" (p71), but soon after it is included in an example of a fricative+stop cluster (p72). The table for consonants (p81) suggests, however, that the classification of /ɬ/ as a fricative is the one intended by the author.

Interestingly, the discussion by Awbery on consonant clusters reveals that the classification of /ɬ/ as a (liquid) sonorant or as an obstruent would not affect the constraints she describes for consonant cluster phonotactics. /ɬ/ in clusters only occurs in word-medial and word-final positions, and only with a following obstruent (or preceding sonorant). Considering word-final position (Awbery notes that medially all four obstruent/sonorant combinations are permissible), this would produce an obstruent-obstruent cluster if /ɬ/ is a fricative, or a sonorant-obstruent cluster if it is a liquid. Both these types are phontactically possible in Welsh (Awbery, 1984: 87). Words like *iarll*, 'earl', will be characterised as either sonorant-sonorant, or sonorant-obstruent; again both of these are phonotactically allowed.

Some experimental data on /ɬ/ (and other Welsh consonants) will be available in Ball (forthcoming, b), and Ball and Williams (forthcoming) but this evidence will be looked at in §2 below.

2. Phonetic evidence

As in any phonological question, evidence from phonetics may be fruitfully brought to bear. In this case what we require is evidence concerning the acoustic characteristics of [ɬ] as compared to fricatives and liquids, both in general and in the specific case of Welsh.

In his major survey of the sounds of languages based on the UPSID corpus (= UCLA Phonological Segment Inventory Database), Maddieson (1980, 1984) includes under the heading 'liquid' "all lateral segments except lateral clicks and all sounds that are included in the somewhat heterogeneous class of r-sounds" (1980: 93). Within the lateral class he notes four main types: "lateral approximants, taps/flaps, fricatives and affricates" (p94).

In this same discussion on laterals, Maddieson brings up the important point for us in this discussion of whether there is a real distinction between voiceless approximants and voiceless fricative laterals. If there is not, then the classification of [ɬ] as the same as [l̥] allows us to place it in the sonorant class of consonants.

In terms of phonological systems, Maddieson feels that such a distinction may be an important one to maintain. "Unlike voiceless approximants, voiceless lateral fricatives are reported in inventories that contain no voiced lateral approximant ... so there may be an important distributional difference between the two types of sounds (p95).

Further phonological evidence is proferred by Lass (1984). Referring to the distinction between sonorants and obstruents he notes that voicing preference can play a part: "this might be a cross-linguistic definition of the feature [±obs]: segment types showing a clear statistical preference for voicelessness are obstruents, those with a preference for voice are sonorants" (p155-6). This would lead him to classify [ɬ] as an obstruent, as with lateral fricatives the voiceless variety is much commoner than the voiced (as shown in Maddieson, 1980, 1984).

However, this view is relaxed when Lass describes the liquid sonorants. He notes that the term 'liquid'

> covers a disparate set of segments, primarily lateral approximants and 'r', i.e. alveolar and post-alveolar trills, taps, and approximants, and occasionally fricatives, and some uvular and velar trills, fricatives and approximants. (p157).

The important point to note here is that fricatives can be 'liquids', and in this respect Lass states, "whether a fricative 'counts as' an obstruent or a liquid is a matter of phonological analysis ..." (p157). Of course, this conclusion would suit us well in the attempt to regularise the status of the soft mutation in terms of the feature changes involved.

However, this is still *phonological* not *phonetic* evidence, and we must turn elsewhere to find information on any [l̥ - ɬ] distinction. Maddieson and Emmorey (1984) examined this distinction instrumentally to see whether it was a valid one. They point out that many phoneticians have viewed the term 'voiceless lateral' as synonymous with 'lateral fricative', while for others "voiceless lateral fricatives and voiceless lateral approximants are distinct types of sounds" (p181).

Maddieson and Emmorey address the question of whether these two labels actually refer to different sounds rather than a terminological/transcriptional difference. They point to the fact that phoneticians working on languages of Africa, the Americas and Europe tend to utilise the description of lateral-fricative, and those working on Asian languages prefer the term voiceless lateral. The investigation they undertake includes languages from both categories in an attempt not only to establish phonetic differences, if any, but to look at the areal consequences of any such differences.

In an instrumental analysis of five languages (unfortunately not including Welsh) the authors came to the conclusion that on several parameters [ɬ] and [l̥] are clearly distinguishable phonetically. They note in their summary that the lateral fricatives "tend to have later onset of voicing, relatively greater noise amplitude and greater energy at high frequency than the approximants" (p187). They add that, as with many phonetic features, these differences are not absolutes, and that languages differ from each other in this respect by degree[2]. The question for us must be, then, whether Welsh [ɬ] is most like Maddieson and Emmorey's fricative lateral or voiceless lateral approximant.

The only experimental phonetic data on Welsh /ɬ/ known to the author is that in Ball (forthcoming, b) and Ball and Williams (forthcoming). The spectrographic data available there does not completely reproduce the analysis of Maddieson and Emmorey, but the information given on the noise component in Welsh /ɬ/ clearly aligns it with the [ɬ] category of those authors.

From a phonetic viewpoint, then, it would appear that /ɬ/ in Welsh is a fricative (and therefore an obstruent) rather than an approximant (and so a sonorant). It should be noted, however, that the analysis in Ball (forthcoming, b) does show that /ɬ/ in Welsh shares to some extent the same formant structure as the sonorant /l/, though this does appear to be a less prominent feature.

Phonology does not, however, need to be a simple copying of phonetics, but can be thought of as an interpretation of phonetic facts. In §4 below we will explore a possible phonological account in terms of generative phonological rules that does attempt to avoid the problem outlined in §0 above. Before this we must confron the problem of Welsh [l̥].

3. [l̥] in Welsh

This attempt to address the phonological nature of Welsh /ɬ/ is complicated by the fact that a voiceless alveolar lateral approximant, [l̥], also occurs in Welsh. This sound is generally classified as an allophone of /l/, and is described by Jones (1984) as follows:

> Except where it is devoiced by a preceding voiceless consonant as in, e.g. [kl̥ɪsd] 'ear', [pl̥ɒiv] 'parish', the lateral is generally voiced. (p48-9).

In word-initial position the only preceding voiceless consonants occurring in native words are /p-, t-, k-/ and /f-, s-/, with these last two being much less common and usually deriving from loan words, albeit well-integrated and long-standing loans in most cases. The combination of /l/ following a fortis obstruent can also occur word-medially across a syllable boundary, e.g. *machlud* [maχlɪd], 'sunset', but it is unclear whether in these environments we get a devoiced allophone, and if so whether it is as devoiced as in word-initial position.

No acoustic evidence is available for [l̥] in Welsh, though it would appear to be a partially devoiced approximant, thereby fitting many of the acoustic characteristics noted by Maddieson and Emmorey as regards [l̥] in their study.

It is worth noting here that although Welsh [l̥] is usually classed as an allophone of /l/ in terms of complementary distribution, there is perhaps an equally strong argument for considering it part of an /ɬ/ phoneme (I will not go into the argument here as tto whether the /l/ - /ɬ/ distinction is truly phonemic). [l] occurs after fortis obstruents pre-vocalically, whereas [ɬ] occurs pre- (and post-) vocalically, but never after fortis obstruents word-initially. Indeed, apart from in loans and after mutation, word-initial [l] is not permitted phontactically. (Apparent exceptions, like *lan* [lan], 'up', can be explained as being derived, at least in formal registers of Welsh, via SM.)

Nevertheless, whatever phonemic analysis is proposed, it appears we still have two voiceless laterals to account for: a sonorant [l̥] and an obstruent [ɬ].

4. A Generative Phonological account

As we noted earlier, phonology is an interpretation of phonetics. It is no place here to re-enter the debate on abstractness in generative phonology, but a proposal can be advanced that accounts for both [l̥] and [ɬ] in Welsh, and which results in a soft mutation change of /ɬ/ → /l/ without invoking a major class change. In order to examine this proposal we first need to look at the distinctive feature matrices for liquids. In fact, for the rule schema suggested below, we need only to give a full matrix for the voiceless lateral approximant - [l̥].

Therefore, in this proposal we have an underlying segment [l̥] only, with the following feature matrix:

(1)
$$\begin{bmatrix} \text{+voc} \\ \text{+cons} \\ \text{-high} \\ \text{-back} \\ \text{-low} \\ \text{+ant} \\ \text{+cor} \\ \text{-voice} \\ \text{+cont} \\ \text{+son} \\ \text{+lat} \\ \text{-nasal} \\ \text{-strid} \end{bmatrix}$$

This would differ by only one feature from the specification for /l/ - in terms of voice. Therefore, the soft mutation rule shown in §0: [-voice] → [+voice], can equally well apply here.

A later specification rule can be applied to remaining unmutated examples of [l̥], changing the features necessary to derive the surface form /ɬ/, this being shown in the two related rules (2a) and (2b) where the first changes the major class features and the second the manner feature of [strident]:

(2a)
$$\begin{bmatrix} \text{+cons} \\ \text{+voc} \\ \text{+son} \end{bmatrix} \rightarrow \begin{bmatrix} \text{+cons} \\ \text{-voc} \\ \text{-son} \end{bmatrix}$$

(2b) [-strident] → [+strident]

To account for the remaining [l̥] in post-fortis consonant position, two strategies are available, reflecting the problem of whether [l̥] is to be considered an allophone of /l/ or of /ɬ/. In the former case we need a rule (3) to be applied *after* (2):

(3)
$$\begin{bmatrix} +\text{cons} \\ +\text{voc} \\ \overline{} \\ +\text{lat} \\ +\text{voice} \end{bmatrix} \rightarrow [-\text{voice}] / \ \# \begin{bmatrix} +\text{cons} \\ -\text{voice} \end{bmatrix} \_\_\_$$

In the latter, we need only to specify that rule (2) must not apply after a fortis consonant. This can be shown as in (4), where the rule is specified according to just those phonological environments where it *can occur:*

(4)
$$\begin{bmatrix} +\text{lat} \\ -\text{strid} \end{bmatrix} \rightarrow [+\text{strid}] / \begin{Bmatrix} \#\_\_\_ \\ \begin{bmatrix} +\text{voc} \\ -\text{cons} \end{bmatrix} \_\_\_ \begin{Bmatrix} \begin{bmatrix} -\text{voc} \\ -\text{cons} \end{bmatrix} \\ \begin{bmatrix} +\text{voc} \\ -\text{cons} \end{bmatrix} \end{Bmatrix} \\ \_\_\_ \ \# \end{Bmatrix}$$

5. The Nasals and Mutation

We must now return to the problem of the nasals and mutation. As noted in §0, another reflex of SM involves a major class change: /m/ → /v/. Coupled to this is the Nasal Mutation (NM) which changes fortis and lenis plosives to homorganic fortis and lenis nasals (see Table 3).

p	→	m̥	b	→	m
t	→	n̥	d	→	n
k	→	ŋ̊	g	→	ŋ

Table 3 The Nasal Mutation

Using historical evidence, and the same kind of abstract phonology proposed in §4, we can posit for the first of these changes (i.e. /m/ → /v/) an abstract underlying segment *[ṽ]: the SM reflex of /m/. If this can be classed as a sonorant (admittedly debatable), then major class change is avoided, and in the same way as with [l̥] → /ɬ/ can be subject to a later phonetic specification rule converting it to surface /v/.

However, such an analysis is not possible with the NM, whose changes have to be seen as being of a different type to those of the other two mutations: as involving not just a segment change, but a change from obstruents to sonorants. Any other solution would surely be pushing abstractness too far.

The attempts to provide an account of the lateral fricative in traditional generative phonological terms has created problems. We have had to resort to strategies that are not supported by phonetic evidence, and that are in reality devices that postpone the change sonorant to obstruent to a later stage in the description. Nevertheless, there is nothing in Welsh phonology that suggests that NM is viewed as somehow a more salient change than AM or SM, or indeed that within SM the change involving lateral fricatives is itself more salient than the other consonant changes[3]. Perhaps it would be more fruitful to scrutinise the adequacy of the traditional feature analysis in this particular case.

Why should a change of [ɬ] → [l] be counted as greater than [b] → [v]; and why should [b] → [m] be likewise counted as greater than [b] → [v] or [p] → [b]?

Alternative feature systems, such as the multivalued system of Ladefoged (1971), do not offer a solution, as the sonorant-obstruent distinction is maintained. It might be necessary, therefore, to look outside generative phonology to other theoretical accounts.

6. Dependency Phonology

Recently there has been a growth in interest in phonology, and various novel approaches have been developed. It is likely that several of these (in particular non-segmental theories) could help to resolve the problem outlined in §0 above. However, we have space only to examine one of these, though without claiming it as the 'correct' approach, or even the best one. In particular, we could note that Natural Phonology could fruitfully apply to mutations, but in this section we will examine the contribution of Dependency Phonology.

It is not our intention to defend or promote any one phonological theory *in toto*, rather to explore how Dependency Phonology (DP) can provide a satisfactory account for just that one area of the phonology of Welsh described in earlier sections of this contribution.

As its name suggests, DP as a theory of phonology is concerned with describing the dependency relationships that hold between syllables, segments, segment features and so on, in particular the relative strengths or importance of these factors. What is of immediate interest to us, however, is that binary, or multivalued features (and divisions into 'major' and 'minor' features) are absent from DP. Instead we have a set of unary 'gestures'. These gestures may be individually absent, present, or in combinations of various dependency types (see Anderson and Durand, 1986: 24f, Anderson and Ewen, 1987: 151f).

There is as yet no complete agreement as to how these gestures are organised (Anderson and Durand, 1986: 21f), but one account divides them into three groupings: categorial (consonantality, voice, continuancy and sonorance in traditional parlance), articulatory (place, height, rounding, backness, nasality), and initiatory (glottal stricture, glottalicness, velar suction).

Of particular relevance to us is the Categorial Gesture. Two components are suggested for this gesture: "|V|, a component which can be defined as 'relatively periodic', and |C|, a component of 'periodic energy reduction'" (ibid :34). Combining these via various dependency relations gives us an inventory of category types:

(5)							
	V	V	V	V,C	V:C	C	C
		|	|	|		|	
		V,C	C	V		V	
	vowls	liqs	nasls	vcd frcs	vls frcs	vcd pls	vls pls

These configurations can also be shown in a simpler notation (from Anderson and Durand, 1986; a slightly different version is used in Lass, 1984, and Anderson and Ewen, 1987):

(6) {|V|}, {|V;V,C|}, {|V;C|}, {|V,C;V|}, {|V:C|}, {|C;V|}, {|C|}

These notations are explained by Anderson and Durand (1986: 24) as follows:

> a notation employing unary components which may individually be absent, present, in simple combinations, or, if in combinations, either of equal or unequal strength.

And further (p25):

> Unary components may either be absent or present. If two components - a and b - are part of a gesture..., they may enter into a simple combination (symbolised by a comma)... But they may enter into contrastive dependency relations

> whereby a governs b..., or b governs a..., or a and b mutually govern each other... government in the case of components is often symbolised in the DP literature by semi-colon for unilateral government... and by colon for mutual government...

Looking at (5) and (6) above, we can see that vowels are characterised by the component |V| ("relatively periodic") alone, whereas liquids are characterised by the component |V| governing the simple combination of |V| and |C| ("periodic energy reduction"). In other words, liquids are governed by sonorancy, with continuancy represented by the combination of |V| and |C|. (Other accounts suggest {|V;V:C|} is a better motivated characterisation of liquids, see Anderson and Ewen, 1987, but this difference does not materially affect the argument below.)

If we consider the soft mutation data from §0, we will see that all the changes involve a move from one type of sound to another, with no one such change being classed as major or minor in the sense utilised in generative phonology.

For example, the soft mutation change of /p, t, k/ → /b, d, g/ involves a change from |C| → |C;V| (an increase in sonorisation), whereas /b, d, g/ → /v, ð, *ɣ[4]/ is a change from |C;V| → |V,C;V| (an increase in opening).

There are clearly some sound types not included in (5) and (6), for example voiceless approximants which have been of particular interest in this paper. To cope with these sounds DP utilises the Initiatory Gesture, and in particular the component |O| ('glottal opening') (see Lass, 1984: 290; Anderson and Durand, 1986: 40). There is, unfortunately, no precise agreement yet as to how this component should be utilised to show different phonation types, but we will follow Anderson and Durand (1986) who show the use of the Initiatory Gesture along with the Categorial Gesture in, for example, vowels and nasals:

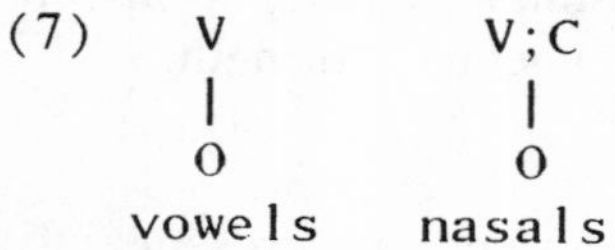

Normally, however, the inclusion of |O| is redundant. As Anderson and Ewen (1987: 192) state, "while both voiced and voiceless sonorants will display |O| phonetically,... one member of the opposition lacks the component in phonological representations". This member for sonorants is the voiced one, capturing the difference in naturalness between voiced and voiceless sonorants.

Obstruents can, of course, occur as both voiced and voiceless: but here the distinction is well captured via the |V| and |C| components, so here too |O| is usually redundant (though it can, of course, be utilised for full phonetic specifications). It is needed, however, to show aspirated stops and /h/ (see below; Lass, 1984: 289f; Anderson and Ewen, 1987: 193).

Adapting Lass (1984: 292), we can draw up a diagram demonstrating a hierarchy of lenition. This shows the various routes and stages that different languages go through in consonant softening, and it will be seen that Welsh soft mutation of the stops is captured here (incidentally, it also captures Gaelic lenition which takes a slightly different route than that of Welsh):

```
(8a) o   C   →    O    →   V:C   →   O
     p   ↓        |         ↓        |       ↘
     e            C                  V
     n   ↓        ↓         ↓        ↓    →      Ø
     i   C   →   V,C   →    V    →   V
     n   |        |         |
     g   V        V        V,C
          sonorisation

(8b)     k   →   kʰ    →    x    →    h      ↘
         ↓       ↓          ↓         ↓           Ø
         g   →   γ     →   liq   →   vowel   ↗
```

((8b) illustrates (8a) with velar consonants)

This diagram shows that at each step on either axis there is a re-arrangement of the dependency relations generally involving minor adjustments (e.g. |C| → |C;V| and |C| → |O;C| etc), which demonstrates the gradual increase of strength of the |V| component and decrease of strength of the |C| component.

However, (8a) does not include the changes /ɬ/ → /l/ or /r̥^{h}/ → /r/. For these changes we do need to include the component |O| to specify /ɬ/ and /r^{h}/. As voiceless liquids (or approximants) we can show them in the following notation:

(9)
```
      O
      |
   V;V,C⁵
```

The process of lenition whereby the voiceless approximants become voiced can therefore be seen in (10) below:

(10a)
```
   O            V
   |     →      |
 V;V,C         V,C
```

Or with full specification of |O|:

(10b)
```
   O          V;V,C
   |     →      |
 V;V,C          O
```

This change is therefore no more major than, for example, the weakening of voiceless plosives to aspirated voiceless plosives[6] (see (8)).

Dealing with nasals, Anderson and Durand (1986: 40) suggest that voiceless nasals can be shown as:

(11)
```
   O
   |
  V;C
```

We can therefore construct a 'nasal' section to the lenition hierarchy to deal with both /m/ → /v/, and nasal mutation (see Table 3). This is shown in (12):

(12a)
```
   C    →    C
   ↓         |      ↘
             V
   ↓         ↓           V,C
   O    →   V;C   →       |
   |                      V
  V;C
```

(12b)
```
   p    →    b    ↘
   ↓         ↓         v
   m    →    m    ↗
```

((12b) illustrates (12a) with labial consonants).

The change represented by {|O|;|V;C|} to {|V;C|} (e.g. m̥ → m) is not part of soft mutation, but is reflected in those (mainly southern) dialects of Welsh, where all voiceless nasals are replaced by voiced (see G. Jones, 1984, and Ball and Williams, forthcoming).

Again, it is seen from (12) that changes from obstruent to nasal sonorant or vice versa are of the same type as other Welsh mutation changes, and we have avoided the problems raised by the major/minor classes of generative phonology.

7. Conclusion

The DP approach clearly avoids the undesirability of the traditional phonological analysis of SM, whereby one process involves changes of differing magnitudes, and answers the question posed in the title: from a phonological viewpoint it no longer matters whether /ɬ/ is more a lateral than a fricative.

There may, however, be other approaches to solve this problem. One such might be to move mutations out of the phonological component altogether, and treat radical and mutated forms of lexemes as morphological alternants (Fife, personal communication).

We do not have space to pursue this or other alternatives, but it is clear that as a linguistic issue, the celtic mutations "will run and run"!

Acknowledgement

I would like to thank James Fife for his very helpful comments on an earlier version of this paper. It is purely my fault if I was not perceptive enough to act on all of them.

Notes

1. Of course, this class change also involves changes to the major feature |vocalic|, and to the feature strident.

2. The final section of Maddieson and Emmorey (1984) discusses the phonological implications of maintaining this distinction. These are not of great relevance to the discussion here, though it is noted that cross-linguistically |ɬ| has a greater distribution phontactically than |l̥| which coincides with the Welsh data.

3. Indeed, sociolinguistic evidence reported in Ball (1988) suggests that the

aspirate mutation is the least salient in terms of likelihood to be dropped. Soft mutation is the most resilient to this change, with the nasal mutation somewhere between the two. Within soft mutation, there is no marked distinction between usage with /ɬ/ and other consonants, though for historical reasons /ɬ/ and /r̥ʰ/ are excluded from the operation of the mutation in the case of a couple of the triggering environments (see, for example, Williams, 1980).

4. For a discussion of */ɣ/ see §0.

5. It is, of course, no longer necessary at this level of description to distinguish between /ɬ/ and |l̥|, as we have now removed the major/minor class distinction. DP can capture this difference, however, as representations are available to show the strident ~ non-strident contrast (see Anderson and Ewen, 1987: 165). This would be incorporated into the phonetic description, where all voiceless laterals are realised as /ɬ/ except when following voiceless plosives in a cluster.
It is also not necessary here to distinguish /ɬ/ from /r̥ʰ/, although again representations are available to distinguish laterals from non-laterals (Anderson and Ewen, 1987: 164).

6. The inclusion of the dependency relations to show stridency (and indeed laterality) would of course produce more complicated diagrams. However, a complexity of notation does not imply necessarily that these sound classes differ from others in a 'major' way.

References

Anderson, J. and Durand, J. (1986) Dependency Phonology. In Durand, J. (ed.), *Dependency and Non-linear Phonology*. London: Croom Helm. Pp 1-54.

Anderson, J. and Ewen, C. (1987) *Principles of Dependency Phonology*. Cambridge: Cambridge University Press.

Awbery, G. (1975) Welsh mutations: syntax or phonology? *Archivum Linguisticum (New Series)*, 6, 14-25.

Awbery, G. (1984) Phonotactic constraints in Welsh. In M. J. Ball, and G. E. Jones (eds.)

Ball, M. J. (1988) *The Use of Welsh*. Clevedon: Multilingual Matters.

Ball, M. J. (forthcoming a) The soft mutation of /g/ and its implications for phonological rule ordering in Welsh. *Studia Celtica*, **24/25**.

Ball, M. J. (forthcoming b) Voicing and Welsh fricatives. *Cardiff Working Papers in Welsh Linguistics*, **6**.

Ball, M. J. and Jones, G. E. (eds.) (1984) *Welsh Phonology. Selected Readings*. Cardiff: University of Wales Press.

Ball, M. J. and Williams, B. (forthcoming) *Welsh Phonetics*. Amsterdam: John Benjamins.

Evans, S. J. (1909) *Studies in Welsh Phonology*. London: David Nutt; Newport: John E. Southall.

Jones, G. E. (1984) The distinctive vowels and consonants of Welsh. In M. J. Ball and G. E. Jones (eds.)

Jones, S. (1926) *A Welsh Phonetic Reader*. London: University of London Press.

Ladefoged, P. (1971) *Preliminaries to Linguistic Phonetics*. Chicago: University of Chicago Press.

Lass, R. (1984) *Phonology. An introduction to basic concepts*. Cambridge: Cambridge University Press.

Maddieson, I. (1980) A survey of liquids. *UCLA Working Papers in Phonetics*, **50**, 93-112.

Maddieson, I. (1984) *Patterns of Sounds*. Cambridge: Cambridge University Press.

Maddieson, I. and Emmorey, K. (1984) Is there a valid distinction between voiceless lateral approximants and fricatives? *Phonetica*, **41**, 181-90.

Sommerfelt, A. (1925) *Studies in Cyfeiliog Welsh. A Contribution to Welsh Dialectology*. Oslo: I Kommission Hos Jacob Dybwald.

Williams, S. (1980) *A Welsh Grammar*. Cardiff: University of Wales Press.

PART TWO

Studies in Breton and Cornish Linguistics

Traditional Morphological Processes and their Vitality in Modern Welsh and Breton

Humphrey Lloyd Humphreys
St. David's University College, Lampeter

1. Introduction

The appearance, in 1961, of Professor Arwyn Watkins' *Ieithyddiaeth* was an important milestone in Welsh linguistic scholarship, partly because it extended the domain of the Welsh language, but even more, and more specifically, because it constituted the first sustained, systematic, contrastive presentation of traditional literary Welsh and current colloquial Welsh. It may be added that comparisons with Breton (and Cornish) play a subsidiary, but by no means negligible, role and that these have played their part in stimulating the present article.

The aim is to provide a concise and convenient survey of the main morphological categories in the two languages and lies more in the direction of useful generalisation than the production of irrefutable theoretical constructs. The co-ordinated presentation ought to provide insights into the structures of both languages, both synchronic and diachronic. The questions raised certainly identify lines for further investigation.

Established spellings (*orthographe universitaire* in Breton; both traditional and *Cymraeg Byw* spellings in Welsh) are generally used and examples of very localised forms have only been sparingly given.

It is relevant, I think, to state that I am a habitual user of both languages, being a native-speaker of Welsh and having integrated through marriage into the traditional Breton-speaking society, my home language now being the Breton of Plounévézel in the immediate vicinity of the central town of Carhaix.

2. Preliminaries

Suffixation is easily the most important morphological process, followed by apophony or vowel modification. Prefixation, infixation (but not in as literal a sense as in Tagalog) and consonant modification also occur on a smaller scale, the last two with a purely auxiliary role.

The syllabic suffixes impose prosodic modifications which impinge too much on morphology to be ignored, so the dominant characteristics of the accentual systems occurring are summarised in Table 1 below. In Breton, the diversity imposes a subdivision into five zones, working from northwest to southeast as follows: Ia - northwest and all western extremities (mainly Léon); Ib - neighbouring western fringes of the Median Zone (western Cornouaille) and most of its northern portion (Trégor); Ic - the centre and southwest of the Median Zone (central Cornouaille). II lies to the east of the Median Zone (eastern Cornouaille, western Vannetais, southeastern Trégor and Goëlo) separating it from III (eastern Vannetais) to the southeast.

		intensity	position	pitch	centr^{n}	neutr^{n}	delet^{n}
Breton	Ia	++	2	2	(1)	–	–
	Ib	+++	2	2	1	1	–
	Ic	++++	2 (1)	2	–	1	1
	II	+(++)	12345	1	–	–	2
	III	–	1 (2)	1	2	2	–
Welsh		+	2	1	–	3	3

Table 1 Word Prosody in Breton and Welsh: a Summary

In Breton, variations in intensity and position of stress (numbering of syllables starting with the final) are considerable. It is not certain to what extent stress is found in III, where, furthermore, the word is not necessarily a prosodic unit everywhere. II has the most complex system, with main stress a variable lexical feature which is not displaced by most suffixes. Ic is in a state of transition, with the historical penult becoming final, either sporadically or definitively, owing to the erosion of the original final. It is in this zone that diachronically secondary changes associated with stress movement may be found assuming the main, or even the entire, burden of differentiation: around the central town of Carhaix, the forms written *protestant*, pl. *protestanted* are generally realised [prot ˈɛsn̩, protɛst ˈɑ̃nt]. In Welsh, areal variation is much slighter, though the erosion of the antepenultimate syllable is particularly marked in the north, where, for instance, the normal spoken singular of *pysgod* 'fish' is *sgodyn*.

I have deliberately broken with the traditional diocesan labels of Breton dialects with their overall efficiency little exceeding 50% and their undue suggestion of discreteness. They seem particularly inappropriate as viewed from Carhaix, at the centre of the broad Median Zone which crosses the country from sea to sea on the northeast-southwest Tréguier-Quimper axis and whose diversities are overshadowed by a unity readily noted by naive native-speakers (Falc'hun, 1963).

3. Nouns

These are only inflected for number, with a basic opposition between singular and plural - to which such categories as singulative and collective are normally assimilated. Table 2 provides a schematisation intermediate between the valid enough, but rather abstract statement that imparisyllabicity (Gagnepain, 1960) is the normal mark of number in Breton (true of 97% of cases in Bothoa) and the meticulous labelling of all possible subdivisions (Welsh plural formation involves, either separately or in combination, 18 suffixes and 26 vowel changes). Consonant modification includes the activation of latent consonants deleted in the singular (spoken Welsh *ffenest/ff(e)nestri* 'window/s') and intercalated consonants (Breton *timp/timpchou* 'stamp/s') as well as the substitution of one consonant for another. The table makes no provision however for the accumulation of suffixes (Welsh *cân/caneuon* 'song/s') or the intercalation of adjectival (Welsh *Cristion/Crist(io)nogion* 'Christian/s') or feminine suffixes (Breton *yar/yarezed* 'hen/s').

	I				II				III				IV	V	VI
	a	b	c	d	a	b	c	d	a	b	c	d			
* V	0	+	+	0	0	+	+	0	0	+	+	0	+	0	0
* C	0	0	+	+	0	0	+	+	0	0	+	+	0	0	0
Suffix	+	+	+	+	–	–	–	–	±	±	±	±	0	0	0
Prefix	0	0	0	0	0	0	0	0	0	0	0	0	0	–	+

**Modification*

Table 2 Noun Morphology: a summary table of the traditional processes of plural formation in Breton and Welsh

A selection of examples will suffice to relate the table to the concrete realities:

> Ia - Br *mamm/mammou*, W *mam/mamau* 'mothers'; Ib - Br *mab/mibien* W *mab/meibion* 'son/s'; Ic - Br *pred/prejou* 'meal/s', W *dant/dannedd* 'tooth/teeth'; Id - Br *roh/reier* 'rock/s', W *rhaw/rhofion* 'shovel/s'; II - (a) Br *pérenn/pér* 'pear/s', (b) W *plentyn/plant* 'child/ren'; III - (a) Br *kartenn/kartou* 'card/s', (b) W *cerdyn/cardiau* 'card/s'; IV - Br *dant/dent* 'tooth/teeth', W *brân/brain* 'crow/s'. In Breton alone: V - *penn-yér/yér* 'fowl/s'; VI - *lagad/daoulagad* 'eye/s' - this last class is problematic in so far as these forms preserve the etymological dual meaning, in which case there is a ternary opposition embracing *daoulagadou* 'eyes (of several people)'.

The processes summarised are by no means equal in their functional importance, their precise status varying within as well as between both languages. Apophony as the sole mark of plurality is no longer productive: in written Welsh it concerns a maximum of some eighty simple lexemes of which perhaps 50 are found in the spoken language, more perhaps in the north than in the south, where *geifr* 'goats' is only found as a place-name element, having been supplanted in speech by *gafrod*. The process has gone rather further in Breton with a maximum of about 50, of which 25-30 are in current use in northern and western areas; Bothoa has reduced them to five. Consonant modification is most important in Breton (affecting 10% of nouns in Bothoa), largely because of the wide-spread palatisation of dentals (*-d*, *-z* > *-j-* etc.) everywhere except in the southeast.

There are inequalities, too, between the various suffixes of which not more than five remain productive in either language, while Welsh *-en* is only found in one word: *ychen* 'oxen'. Watkins (1961: 154) estimated that *-(i)au* (NE, C, SW *-(i)e*, NW, SE *-(i)a*) accounts for 40-45% of Welsh plurals. Its Breton cognate *-ou* (with its variants, diphthongal still in the eastern and southeastern third of its territory) appears to be distinctly more dominant everywhere and accounts for 70% of Bothoa plurals, including /mˈa:bə́w/ 'sons'.

3.1 External Interference

Such plurals as *des majorettes* may be heard in spoken Breton and it is tempting to interpret them as containing a new prefix of number, syntactically if not semantically similar to *penn-*. In fact, the /de-/ marks indefiniteness as well as plurality and if a definite plural is required, the choice is between *les majorettes* and *ar majoretou*, between morphological non-integration and integration; a definite plural */ən de-maʒorɛt/, if it existed, would of course prove the borrowing of a morpheme. These forms occur in particular with new and unfamiliar French words and involve a brief code-switch; it is difficult to say to what extent they establish themselves as a permanent feature of particular idiolects.

In colloquial Welsh, the traditional processes have all but ceased to be productive - although the schools have undoubtedly done a little to counter this trend, their greatest successes, ironically enough, being among those who learn Welsh as a second language. The English //-s// has been added to its inventory in all its allomorphic variety, except in the northwest, where [z] has not yet become naturalised. The normal spellings are *-ys/-us* (which, being syllabic, does not alter the existing pattern unduly) and *-s* (with its potential to increase very considerably the number of final consonant clusters). Herein may lie the explanation of such plurals as *rwmsys* (from *rŵm* 'room') and *jobsys* (from *job*).

As might be expected, recent loanwords are particularly well represented: hippies became a prominent feature of the Welsh rural scene in the 60's and the set *hipi/hipis* was brought into the language - I do not recall having heard or seen any other plural form used in any register. The more modest arrival of the same phenomenon in Brittany spontaneously generated the plural *hipied* in all areas - and that without any institutional backing. The naturalisation of this suffix is so complete that it has supplanted the traditional process in *-wr/-wyr* words (*gweithiwr* has, besides the traditional plural *gweithwyr* a colloquial plural *gweithiwrs*) while I have heard in Ceredigion both *llewz* and *tarwz* used in addressing small children instead of *llewod*, *teirw* (*tarwod*), the normal plurals of *llew* 'lion' and *tarw* 'bull'. *-s* may sporadically attach itself to forms which are already plural - especially forms in which the mark of plural is not segmentally apparent: *sêrs* for *sêr* 'stars', *heyrns* for *heyrn* 'irons', *milgwns* for *milgwn* 'greyhounds', the singulars being respectively *seren*, *haearn*, *milgi*.

4. Adjectives

4.1 Gender and Number

feminine	*plural*		
apophony	apophony	apophony + suffix	suffix
Ø	Ø - 1	N	N
12 -42 +	2 -13	2 -17	5 -21

Table 3a Adjective Morphology: gender and number

As Table 3a shows, Breton does not mark these categories except in the case of *keiz*, plural of *kaez* 'poor, wretched' which is current in the northwest; other adjectives may have a plural when used nominally. Welsh can, but does not always, mark them in a small number of adjectives: *gwyn* m., *gwen* f., *gwynion* pl. 'white'. Marking gender is restricted with few exceptions to monosyllabic adjectives containing the vowels *y* and *w* (which become *e*, *o*). The vestigial nature of the two subsystems is evident from the figures given in the table, the lower one, probably not the minimum, representing my own spontaneous usage, the second the most archaising literary usage (Morris-Jones, 1921). The vitality of individual items varies considerably, *gwen* apparently surviving everywhere, sometimes as the only stable feminine (Watkins, 1961: 158), while many show considerable collocational restrictions: *poteli gweigion* 'empty bottles', but *tai gwag* 'empty houses' in my own usage, for example.

4.2 Comparison

	suffixes			synthetic comparison	
*	(*-ad*)	*-oh*	*-a(ñ)*	+	(+)
*	exclam^{ive}	compar^{ive}	super^{ive}	short native	long borrowed
†	equative				
†	*-ed*	*-ach*	*-a(f)*	+	Ø

* *Breton*, † *Welsh*

Table 3b Adjective Morphology: comparison

Table 3b shows that both languages have similar sets of provecting suffixes, though the Breton *-ad* (mainly southeastern) is exclusively exclamative, a meaning sparingly found in literary Welsh:

Br	*gleb*	'wet'	[*glepad*]	*glepoh*	*glepa(ñ)*
W	*gwlyb*	'wet'	*gwlyped*	*gwlypach*	*gwlypa(f)*

Breton has only two irregularly compared adjectives, Welsh fourteen. Beside synthetic comparisons, both languages use analytic means, as exemplified here in words meaning 'interesting':

	comparative	superlative
Br literary	*muioh dedennuz*	*muia(ñ) dedennuz*
Br colloquial	*muioh interesant*	*muia(ñ) interesant*
W lit + coll	*mwy diddorol*	*mwya(f) diddorol*
W colloquial	*mwy interesting*	*mwya(f) interesting*

The role of the two systems is easiest to describe for Welsh, the situation being similar to that found in English: analytic forms are used with polysyllables. Synthetic comparison is probably no longer productive in any variety of the language and **diddorolach* is not used even in the most archaising literary usage while **interestingach* is even more unthinkable - the very grotesqueness of such forms might conceivably offer them a modest future in burlesque! Areal variations are little documented and may not be great; I have nevertheless been struck by the not infrequent use of such forms as *mwy byr* 'more short' even by elderly traditional speakers in central Ceredigion. These I instinctively classify as 'childish'; in my own usage, such a form has a very marginal status and would signal hesitation or a last-minute switch from a longer adjective. They may, however, be consistent with a general analytic trend and occur occasionally in serious, indeed solemn, literature: *yr Enw mwyaf mawr* 'the greatest Name' in an eighteenth-century hymn and *mwy trist na thristwch* 'sadder than sadness' in a First World War elegy - both examples admittedly subject to constraints of versification.

In Breton, the Median Zone has a similar pattern, which has been quantified for Plougrescant in the extreme northeast, where out of 116 synthetically compared adjectives, 85 were monosyllabic. Elsewhere, synthetic comparison may well dominate - although the conventions of synchronic description unfortunately inhibit observations on absent forms. Analytic comparison is certainly rejected in Bothoa in the east (where I noted such forms as /interes˙ɑ̃ntɑ̆/ 'most interesting', /hrəspõs˙a:póh/ 'more responsible') and in Querrien in the south and it is apparently not used in the northwest in Cléder.

5. Person

There are three persons in both singular and plural, 3sg further distinguishing masculine and feminine in preposition morphology. There is in addition an impersonal, in Welsh limited to the verb. It should be noted that the southeastern-central third of Breton's territory lacks 2sg, and 2pl forms function as a single, neutral second person as in English.

5.1 Prepositions

The functioning of personal suffixes can be presented most clearly in the morphology of the prepositions, of which 14 inflect in

Welsh, 25 in Breton (including compounds and mutually exclusive geolexical variants). The suffixes may be segmented as follows:

a) The person-specifying finals highlighted in Table 4, which are consonantal in 1st and 2nd persons (except in 1sg of many varieties of Breton (-Ṽ) and all spoken Welsh. They are vocalic in the 3rd persons (except in the Welsh 3pl).

b) Consonantal finals are preceded by a vowel which varies according to preposition, person and locality - the constancy of *y* in the Welsh 3pl no doubt reflecting the comparatively late accretion of *-nt* (Evans, 1964: 59).

c) The vowel of the suffix may be preceded by a consonant not present in the uninflected preposition, particularly in the 3rd persons.

1sg	2sg	3sgm	3sgf	1pl	2pl	3pl	impers[1]
-n /-n,Ṽ/	*-t* *-s* esp SE	*-añ* *-oñ* SE	*-i*	*-m(p)*	*-h*	*-e* E *-o* W *-n* SE	*-r* NW

Breton

	1sg	2sg	3sgm	3sgf	1pl	2pl	3pl	impers
a	*-f*	*-t*	*-o*	*-i*	*-m*	*-ch*	*-nt*	Ø
b	*-f i*	*-t ti*	*-o ef*	*-i hi*	*-m ni*	*-ch chwi*	*-nt hwy*	Ø
c	/-j/	/ti/	/-ovɛ/S /-ɒvɒ/N	/-ihi/N /-iði/S	/-ni/	/-xi/	/-nʊ/	Ø
d	*'i*	*-t ti*	*-o fe* *-o fo*	*-i hi*	*-n ni*	*-ch chi*	*-n nhw*	Ø

Welsh:
a) traditional spelling; b) traditional spelling with enclitic pronoun; c) usual colloquial forms; d) Cymraeg Byw *spellings*

Table 4 Morphology of the preposition: the mark of person

5.2 Verbs

The mark of person is not as easily isolated in the case of the verb, whose finite suffixes can often only be interpreted as an amalgam: in Breton *kani*, Welsh *cani* 'you (fam.) will sing', *-i* simultaneously marks futurity and 2sg. Tables 5 (a, b, c) provide convenient tabulations for the systems most frequently met with in print, of which literary Welsh is the only one to depart substantially from spoken usage. The Breton forms are specific to the northwest but the areal variations are matters of detail - if sometimes numerous - rather than differences of fundamental system. Points are used to indicate potential points of segmentation: where the same consonant is consistently used for a particular person, as in Breton 1pl and both Breton and Welsh 3pl, the argument for pin-pointing the final as a mark of person is strong, but the case of the Welsh 2sg in particular, with its four different finals, shows that this is far from being globally true of the paradigm as a whole. Some dialects have gone further than others in making the final fully characteristic of person: Bothoa only has consonantal variation in 2pl (/-d, -h/), the other persons invariably having a single characteristic mark throughout the paradigm - 1sg /-n/, 3sg /-V/, 1pl /-m(p)/, 3pl /-ɲ or ṅ(č)/. The elimination of 2sg, the impersonal and the preterite have clearly contributed in no small measure to this rationalisation.

The synthetic forms - which cannot be used sentence-initially - are, as a general rule, obligatory in the negative, in subordinate clauses and whenever preceded by an element other than the subject. A fully analytic conjugation is used on the other hand when the affirmative verb is preceded by its subject and whatever that subject is, the verb remains in the 3sg form:

me (a) gan	*c'hwi (a) gan*	*al lapoused (a) gan*
'I sing'	'you sing'	'the birds sing'

This construction topicalises the subject, without giving it the heavy emphasis that is found in Welsh (*fi (a) ganodd* 'I am the person who sang'). 'I sing' is more neutrally expressed in Breton with a *'do'* auxiliary: *kan(a) a ran*. The analytic and synthetic forms co-exist in a stable complementary distribution in the Breton of habitual traditional speakers. Any increase of the use of analytic forms under the influence of French SV word-order is purely statistical in most areas and restricted to permitted contexts. Only the extreme southwest seems to have gone as far as allowing analytic forms in non-traditional contexts such as subordinate clauses.

person / *tense*	1sg	2sg	3sg	1pl	2pl	3pl	impers	diff. V's
imperative	–	*-Ø.Ø*	*-e.d*	*-o.m(p)*	*-i.t*	*-e.nt*	-	4
preterite	*-i.s*	*-j.ou.t*	*-a.s*	*-j.o.m(p)*	*-j.o.h*	*-j.o.nt*	*-j.o.d*	4
future	*-i.n*	*-i.Ø*	*-o.Ø*	*-i.m(p)*	*-o.h*	*-i.nt*	*-o.r*	2
present hab.	*-a.n*	*-e.z*	*-Ø.Ø*	*-o.m(p)*	*-i.t*	*-o.nt*	*-e.r*	5
past hab.	*-e.n*	*-e.s*	*-e.Ø*	*-e.m(p)*	*-e.h*	*-e.nt*	*-e.d*	1
	The conditionals have the same suffixes preceded by the infixes .f. or .ch.							
diff. C's	2	3	3	1	2	1	2	

Table 5a Finite suffix paradigms of the regular verb in the Breton of Léon (NW), which has traditionally received fairly wide acceptance as the basis for a common written language.

5.3 Enclitic Resumptive Pronouns

Most varieties of Breton only follow personal forms of the verb and preposition with stressed pronouns where contrastive emphasis is required. *ALBB* (106-110 *da* 'to', 208-214 *gand* 'with') shows unstressed enclitic pronouns as being usual in a large northwestern area and in much smaller areas in the south and southeast; they are almost completely absent in a large northeastern and smaller southern and southeastern areas. It should be noted that these enclitics seem to be confined to 1st and 2nd person forms whose suffix happens to be stressed: *ALBB* 159 (*hebdon* 'without me') only notes four points with an unstressed enclitic - one in each corner. *ALBB* shows no verbal forms with enclitic pronouns.

person *tense*	1sg	2sg	3sg	1pl	2pl	3pl	impersonal	df Vs
imperative	-	*-Ø.Ø*	*-e.d*	*-w.n*	* *-w.ch*	*-e.nt*	-	3
preterite	* *-ai.s* *i*	* *-ai.st* *ti*	*-o.dd* *ef/hi*	*-(a)s.o.m* *ni*	*-(a)s.o.ch* *chwi*	*-(a)s.a.nt* *hwy*	*-wy.d*	4
subj. pres.	*-wy.f* *i*	* *-y.ch* *di*	*-o.Ø* *ef/hi*	*-o.m* *ni*	*-o.ch* *chwi*	*-o.nt* *hwy*	*-e.r*	4
future pres.	*-a.f* *i*	* *-i.Ø* *di*	† *-Ø.Ø* *ef/hi*	*-w.n* *ni*	* *-w.ch* *chwi*	*-a.nt* *hwy*	* *-i.r*	4
condit imperf	*-w.n* *i*	*-i.t* *ti*	*-ai.Ø* *ef/hi*	*-e.m* *ni*	*-e.ch* *chwi*	*-e.nt* *hwy*	* *i.d*	4
	The pluperfect has the same suffixes preceded by the infix .(a)s.							
diff. C's	3	4	3	2	1	1	2	

* *a>e,* † *apophony (13 possible modifications)*

Table 5b Finite suffix paradigms of the regular verb in traditional written Welsh

person / tense	1sg	2sg	3sg	1pl	2pl	3pl	imper-sonal	df V's
imper-ative	-	-a.Ø	(-e.d)	(-w.n)	-w.ch	?	?	2
pret-erite	-e.s +i	-e.st +ti	-o.dd +e/hi	-(s).o.n +ni	-(s).o.ch +chi	-(s).o.n $+n^hw$	-w.d -wy.d	3
future	-a.Ø +i	-i.Ø +di	-i.th +e/hi	-w.n +ni	-w.ch +chi	-a.n $+n^hw$	(-i.r)	3
condit	-w.n +i	-e.t +ti	-e.Ø +fe/hi	-e.n +ni	-e.ch +chi	-e.n $+n^hw$	?	2
diff. C's	3	3	3	1	1	1	2	

Table 5c Finite suffix paradigm of the regular verb in spelling fairly close to the now commonly written *Cymraeg Byw*, which is modelled on 20th century vernacular usage rather than on the very conservative literary model

The bare personal forms of both the verb and preposition can be freely used in all contexts in formal literary Welsh - though, oddly, the Bible (1588, 1620) makes such extensive use of postposed pronouns that they cannot all have been emphatic. In spoken Welsh the enclitic is obligatory in most contexts as described by Watkins (1978: 349-366) and Rolant (1986: 192-198). This makes for rather striking prosodic contrasts between what could be termed classical and demotic Welsh

classical:	*gwaeddodd*	*arni*	
			'he shouted at her'
demotic:	*waeddodd-o*	*arni-hi*	

A trend towards the 'oralisation' (*llafareiddio* 'to bring closer to the spoken language') of written Welsh - *Cymraeg Byw* in its institutionalised form - quite often brings over-generalisation of the enclitic pronouns.

5.4 Impersonal Forms

Breton shows considerable areal variation in its use of the synthetic impersonal forms. In the whole of the northern quarter of its territory, their vitality seems to continue unimpaired despite the presence of broadly synonymous analytic alternatives: in Le Vieux-Marché in the northeast their active presence is dependably reported for a speaker born as late as 1956, while in the northwest they occur for prepositions as well as for verbs. In contrast, *ALBB* (353-355) noted no such forms in a continuous area the shape of an inverted Y fringeing the Median Zone to the southeast and the central part of the Breton-French divide. In the remaining half of Breton territory, various transitional stages may be found with the *-r* forms resisting most strongly: in Plougrescant, which has a full paradigm - albeit with syncretism of the present habitual and future /-ɛr/ - the conditionals now end in /-fɔr, -ʒɔr/, leaving /-d/ only in the past habitual /-ɛd/; in the northwest central Breton of Berrien only the present habitual and future are found, in the island of Groix, only the present. Lexical restriction is the final stage in the process of obsolescence. Of a number of analytic constructions which assume the functions of the impersonal, the commonest are (a) the pronoun *an den* 'one' (but entirely free of affectation!) and generally pronounced *an nen*, nasalisation marking its semantic divergence from the noun *den* 'person'; and (b) the 3sg (*beza* + past participle) passive construction, used at least as frequently as the English passive and even with intransitive verbs.

In literary Welsh, the synthetic impersonal, though entirely limited to verbs, is entirely productive. Most speakers regard it as an elegant equivalent of the *cael* passive (Awbery, 1976: 146) and it can in fact collocate with an agent as well as an intransitive verb. These forms are not common in any variety of spoken Welsh, although full sets have been recorded from aged speakers, especially in the south (Phillips, 1955). The only form free of lexical or connotational restrictions anywhere is the preterite, which is in reasonably common use in the south, rather more unusual in the north. The future-present is much rarer; in the northwest it seems restricted to a single expression *faint fynnir* 'any amount' (literally 'the number/amount that is desired') and it is doubtful whether it is synchronically verbal here, for it has lost the capacity to align to the tense of the main verb.

6. Tense

In Table 6 only simple tenses are tabulated and this answers the purpose of an article on morphology. It must be remembered, however, that both languages have an elaborate inventory of compound and periphrastic tenses whose emphatically non-optional role has been neglected with a blithe blatancy by grammatical traditions with an excessively morphological orientation (see Hewitt 1986 on the Breton progressive). This is the reason for the inclusion of the key auxiliaries Breton *beza* (*boud*) 'be' (along with its derivative *a-m-eus* 'I have') and Welsh *bod* 'be', whose more elaborate tense systems are collated with those of the regular verb.

6.1 Core Systems of the Regular Verb

Most Breton dialects, having eliminated the preterite and one of the conditionals, have four simple tenses (+ imperative) although the extreme southeast (Plouharnel: Hammer, 1969), with the loss of *-h-*, no longer distinguishes the conditional from the past habitual. Allegedly normative written Breton - under the influence of French - makes extensive use of of the preterite, over-uses the conditional and under-uses the progressive.

Conservative literary Welsh can use all the simple tenses with the meanings implied by the traditional labels, although such use of the pluperfect and present subjunctive is probably losing ground. In the spoken language, three simple tenses (+ imperative) are normally found. The system is generally stable in the south, but in the north all synthetic forms are under threat from periphrastic alternatives:

a) gwneud 'do' + verbal noun is common in the future and preterite:

(w)neith-o redeg
will do-he run
'he will run'

(w)naeth-o redeg
did-he run
'he ran'

NB: Where the verbal noun precedes *gwneud*, the meaning is different:

rhedeg (w)neith-o 'run he certainly will'

b) *bod* + *yn* + verbal noun, i.e. the progressive construction, is common in the conditional:

fase-fo'n rhedeg
would be-he running
'he would run'

c) *(dd)aru* + lenited verbal noun (literary *darfu* 'it finished') is common in the preterite:

(dd)aru -o redeg
it finished (to-)him running
'he ran'

The (a) construction may be heard, not infrequently, from southern speakers aiming at enhancing the formality of their Welsh: a curious by-product of their perception of northern Welsh as being qualitatively superior.

6.2 Breton beza *and Welsh* bod

These have additional tenses in both languages - too often identified as the habitual past and present. In Breton, the situative tenses are localised, being virtually autonomous only in the northwest, where personal forms are found in both present and past. In the east, only 3rd person forms of the present are found and they never occur in the negative. Their opposition to the descriptive tenses is in fact never total, for with SV word order, they share common forms (*zo*, *oa*). The opposition between descriptive and habitual tenses, on the other hand, except in the southeastern fringe, always has a sharp clarity.

In Welsh, the descriptive tenses have expanded into the

functions of the habitual tenses, particularly in the south, where the *bydd* and *byddai* forms have generally become restricted to future and conditional sense respectively. In the north, the opposition has been rather better maintained, *bydd* retaining its habitual present, side-by-side with its future meaning, while *byddai* is seldom conditional.

6.3 The Mark of Tense

This is even more difficult to isolate than the mark of person (Tables 5a, b, c): only the past habitual and the conditionals, in Breton, have generalised a single vowel throughout. A similar generalisation has been achieved in most varieties of spoken southern Welsh, though at the expense of syncretism of 1sg and 1pl; forms that are generally written *-en i*, *-en ni*, in a 'realistic' representation are, in fact, homophonous. From Table 5a, the infix *-f-* would appear to be a unique mark of the conditional in Breton, but in an area larger than that represented by the table, occupying the west central, and in particular the northern parts of the Median Zone, *-f-* also appears as an infix in the plural forms of the future.

7. Non-finite Verbal Forms

7.1 Verbal Noun

In many varieties of Breton 'infinitive' would be a perfectly suitable term for this form whose morphology - in both languages - is strikingly less unified than that of the finite verb: each has some fifteen different suffixes, including -Ø. Productive suffixes, as might be expected, seldom exceed three or four, and there is areal variation, particularly in Breton. For Welsh Watkins (1961: 96) gives lexical frequencies of 14% for Ø, 32% for *-(i)o*, 30% for *-u* and 16% for *-i* (the last two being orally undifferentiated in the south). In view of the commonness of suffixless verbal nouns, it is surprising that recent English loans are invariably provided with a suffix - almost always *-(i)o*, but sometimes *-i* in the south. In Breton, *-a(ñ)* and *-i(ñ)* are both found in similar percentages (Plougrescant, 30% and 35% respectively), elsewhere only a single vocalic suffix is found (*-eiñ* in the southeast, *-o* in a belt bordering it (Bothoa, 54%)) or has disappeared as in much of the centre; *-i* seems to be ousting *-a* in the southwest.

simple tenses restricted to *be* & derivatives					
Br *beza*		Br *beza*, *a-m-eus*; W *bod*			
present situative		present decriptive		present habitual	
ema (SV *zo*)	Ø	*eo* (SV *zo*)	Ø	*bez*	*kan(a)*
pers & neg in W only					
		present descriptive		future (trad. present)	
Ø	Ø	*(yd)yw mae* (SV *sydd*)	Ø	*bydd*	*cân* *canith*
past situative		past descriptive		past habitual	
edo (SV *oa*) NW only	Ø	*oa*	Ø	*beze*	*kane*
		past descriptive		conditional (trad imperfect)	
Ø	Ø	*oedd*	Ø	*byddai*	*canai*

Table 6 Synoptic table of the simple tenses of Breton and Welsh

The top half of each box is devoted to Breton, the bottom half to Welsh; the right-hand half to the verbs *to be*, the left-hand half to the regular verb.

The table is organised on a diachronic basis in that Breton and Welsh tenses appearing in the same box are the reflexes of one and the same Brittonic tense (though individual forms may diverge as in the case of the preterite).

Forms: imperative - 2sg; otherwise 3sg which, except for certain tenses specific to *beza*, *bod*, are those which follow any subject in affirmative sentences.

The vitality tables (6a, 6b) suggest the tense structure, pecked lines indicating threatened or vestigial oppositions, five +'s a fully operational set. Both languages, of course, have in addition a wide range of mainly non-optional compound or periphrastic tenses.

simple tenses common to all verbs					
preterite		future			
(b)oe	*kanas*	*b(ez)o*	*kano*		
preterite		present subjunctive		imperative	
bu buo(dd)	canodd	b(ydd)o	cano	*bez*	*kan*
(past) conditional		(present) conditional		imperative	
	{ch}		{f}		
bije	*kan(e){j}e*	*be(fe)*	*kan(e){h}e*	bydd	cân cana
	{z}				
(past) conditional (trad pluperfect)		past subjunctive			
b(u)asai	canasai	b(ydd)ai	canai		

+		+		+	+	–	+	+	+		
+		+		+	+			+	+		
+	Ø	+	Ø	+	+			+	+		
		+		+	+			+	+		
		+		+	+			+	+	+	+
											+
+		+		+	+	+	+	+	+		+
		+		+	+	+	+	+	+		
	Ø	+	Ø	+	+	+	+	+	+		
		+		+	+	+	+	+	+		
		+		+	+						

Table 6a Vitality of simple tenses in Breton

		+		+	+	+	+	+	+		
		+		+	+	+	+	+			
Ø	Ø	+	Ø	+	+	+	+				
		+		+	+	+	+				
		+		+	+					+	+
										+	+
		+		+	+	+	+	+	+	+	+
		+		+	+	+					
Ø	Ø	+	Ø	+	+						
		+		+	+						
		+		+	+						

Table 6b Vitality of simple tenses in Welsh

7.2 Past Participle

Breton has a past participle in *-et* whose uses are very similar to those of English: adjectivally (with synthetic comparison in the southeast and northwest) and verbally (in full sets of perfective and passive tenses). The *a-m-eus* 'have' perfectives are generally accepted as being due to French influence, although the existence of objectively synonymous constructions involving *beza* + *gand* 'with, by', a construction also occurring in Irish, suggests further investigation. 'Have you combed your hair?' may be translated:

> *Kribet (ho-)peus ho pleo?*
> combed have-you your hair

> *Kribet eo ho pleo ganeoh?*
> combed is your hair with-you

Welsh alone among the Celtic languages has lost the past participle even as a pure adjective, although some traces of the formation survive: *agored* 'open'. An analytic formation, *wedi* + verbal noun, replaces it in many functions: *ŵy wedi'i ferwi* 'a boiled egg' (literally 'an egg after its boiling').

8. Conclusion

It is difficult not to conclude that Breton has maintained the traditional morphological processes in better working order than Welsh - and the Breton that I have taken as a norm is that of traditional habitual speakers, not that of an archaising literary tradition. This makes it all the more surprising to find the late Léon Fleuriot (1984) claiming that any Breton spoken since 1900 has not been worthy of scientific attention, a rather extravagant position no doubt coloured by his idealisation of Old Breton, a stage of the language to which he brought great illumination. Celtic studies - in both countries - would benefit if scholars, and others, ceased to assume that Welsh is the norm from which Breton has to varying degrees deviated.

Note on sources

I have been a direct observer of practically all the phenomena referred to, either in the field or on radio or cassette. I have also had particularly stimulating discussions on the material with Jean Le Dû (Plougrescant), Steve

Hewitt (Le Vieux-Marché), François Le Provost (Bothoa) and Albert Boché (Ploërdut and Baud) for Breton and D. Simon Evans, Islwyn Ffowc Elis and David Thorne for Welsh.

There is a mass of material in unpublished local monographs submitted for higher degrees, whose contents I have extensively perused but not fully collated. There are over twenty of these on Welsh which are listed in Awbery (1982). For Breton, there are, from UHB (Rennes): Douarnenez (P. Denis), Poullaouen (F. Favereau), Saint-Servais and Langonnet (J.-Y. Plourin) and Lanvénégen (E. Evenou); and from UBO (Brest): Plougrescant (J. Le Dû), Saint-Yvi (G. German) and Bothoa (H. Ll. Humphreys).

References

Awbery, G. M. (1976) *The Syntax of Welsh*. Cambridge: Cambridge University Press.

Awbery, G. M. (1982) A bibliography of research on Welsh dialects since 1934. *Cardiff Working Papers in Welsh Linguistics*, **2**, 103-19.

Evans, D. S. (1970) *A Grammar of Middle Welsh*. Dublin: Dublin Institute for Advanced Studies.

Falc'hun, F. (1963) *L'histoire de la language bretonne d'après la géographie linguistique*. Paris: PUF.

Fleuriot, L. (1984) Les réformes du breton. In I. Fodor and C. Hagège (eds.) *Language Reform, vol 2*. Hamburg: Buske. Pp 27-47.

Gagnepain, J. (1960) Pour une description structurale du breton. *Annales de Bretagne*, **67**, 377-388.

Gros, J. (1976) *Le trésor du breton parlé: 3 – Le style populaire*. Lannion: Barr-Heol.

Guillevic, A. and Le Goff, P. (1902) *Grammaire bretonne du dialecte de Vannes*. Vannes: Galles.

Hammer, F. (1969) *Der bretonische Dialekt von Plouharnel*. Karlsrühe: O. Berencz.

Hemon, R. (1975) *A Historical Morphology and Syntax of Breton*. Dublin: Dublin Institute for Advanced Studies.

Hewitt, S. (1986) Le progressif en breton à la lumière du progressif anglais. *La Bretagne linguistique,* **2,** 132-148.

Humphreys, H. Ll. (1979/80) *La langue galloise: une prèsentation. Studi* vols. 13-14. Brest: UBO.

Jackson, K. H. (1967) *A Historical Phonology of Breton.* Dublin: Dublin Institute for Advanced Studies.

Kervella, F. (1947) *Yezhadur Bras ar Brezhoneg.* La Baule: Skridoù Breizh.

Le Clerc, L. (1908) *Grammaire bretonne du dialecte de Trèguier.* Saint-Brieuc: Prud'homme.

Le Roux, P. (1924-1963) *Atlas linguistique de la Basse-Bretagne (ALBB),* vols. 1-6. Rennes: Plihon.

Le Roux, P. (1957) *Le verbe breton.* Rennes: Plihon.

Morris-Jones, J. (1921) *An Elementary Welsh Grammar.* Oxford: Oxford University Press.

Phillips, V. (1955) *Astudiaeth o Gymraeg llafar Dyffryn Elái a'r cyffiniau.* Cardiff: University of Wales M.A. dissertation.

Plonéis, J.-M. (1983) *Au carrefour des dialectes bretons: le parler de Berrien, essai de description phonématique et morphologique.* Paris: SELAF.

Rolant, E. (1985) Rhagenwau personol cyfosodiadol: y pwysleisiol a'r ategol. *Studia Celtica,* **20/21,** 192-198.

Ternes, E. (1970) *Grammaire structurale du breton de l'île de Groix.* Heidelberg: Carl Winter.

Trépos, P. (1957) *Le pluriel breton.* Brest: Emgleo Breiz.

Trépos, P. [1962] *Grammaire bretonne.* Rennes: Simon.

Watkins, T. A. (1961) *Ieithyddiaeth.* Caerdydd: Gwasg Prifysgol Cymru.

Watkins, T. A. (1976) Cyfnewidiadau seinegol sy'n gysylltiedig â'r 'acen' Gymraeg. *BBCS,* **26,** 399-405.

Watkins, T. A. (1977) Y rhagenw ategol. *Studia Celtica,* **12/13,** 347-366.

Non-finite Clauses in Breton

Janig Stephens
South Glamorgan Institute of Higher Education

0. Introduction

This paper examines the order of constituents in infinitival clauses which occur both as embedded clauses and independent clauses. Although Breton is a VSO language (Stephens, 1982; Borsley and Stephens, 1989), the paper will show that the order of constituents in infinitival clauses is SVO.

I shall argue, as Sproat (1985) does for Welsh, that the Government and Binding theory (hence GB) of Chomsky (1981) provides a natural explanation for the difference in surface word order in finite and non-finite clauses.

The paper is organised as follows. The aspects of GB relevant to the analysis are presented in section 1, followed by a presentation of the data in section 2. In section 3, I shall examine the order of constituents in three types of embedded clauses:

i) complement clauses introduced by a prepositional complementiser,

ii) clauses complement to control verbs, and

iii) complement clauses with exceptional case-marking.

Section 4 deals with the analysis of non-finite independent clauses, those introduced by *da* and those introduced by *ha*. Section 5 is a summary of the discussion and concludes that, in Breton, finite and non-finite clauses have a different word order: VSO and SVO respectively.

1. The Framework

The aspects of GB relevant to the present analysis are:

i) Following the Extended Projection Principle every clause contains a subject.

ii) Apparently subjectless clauses have a subject position which is filled either by a trace 't' after a movement rule, a phonologically null pronominal anaphor 'PRO', or the phonologically null pronoun: 'pro'. Unlike lexical subjects, 'pro' and 'trace', PRO cannot be governed and do not receive case.

iii) Within the GB framework the contrast between subjects and objects is attributed to the structural configuration: the NP object is within the VP whereas the subject is outside.

iv) The subject gets nominative case from the AGR element which carries person and number in INFL and the object receives its case from the verb. It thus follows that Verb-initial languages must be analyzed in terms of a Verb-fronting rule to ensure that case assignment takes place.

Arguing for a GB analysis for Welsh Sproat (1985) claims that the dictinction between VSO and SVO languages is to be attributed to a difference in case assignment and not to a difference in deep-structure.

In SVO languages case is assigned both to the left and to the right, but in VSO languages it is restricted to one direction, to the right only. Verb-fronting which is illustated in (1) becomes obligatory because:

(1)

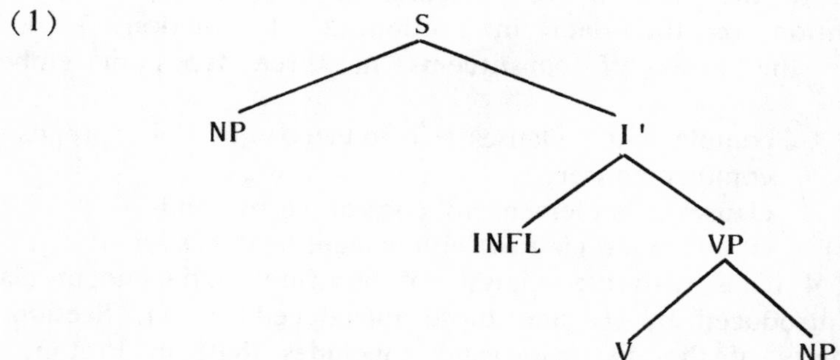

a) AGR in INFL can only assign case to the right and INFL must precede the subject: (2a).
b) INFL must be lexically supported; in other words the verb must move to INFL: (2b).

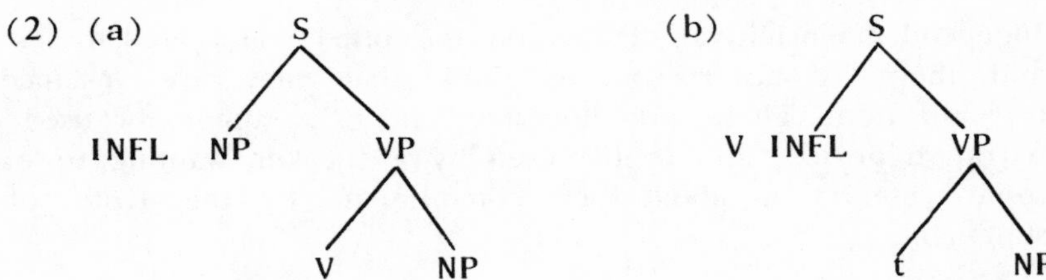

Whereas in finite clauses the subject is assigned case to the right by INFL, in non-finite clauses INFL does not contain AGR and therefore cannot assign case to the subject. It thus remains in sentence-initial position in order to be able to receive case from either a prepositional complementiser or from a higher verb in exceptional case marking context.

2. Data

Finite clauses in Breton show three different constituent orders.

a) Embedded clauses are VSO as in (3)

(3) Gouzout a ra Lenaig [e lennas Yann al lizher]
know PART does Lenaig PART read+past Yann the letter
'Lenaig knows that Yann read the letter.'

b) Independent and topicalised clauses have the structure: XP V (S) (O). The lexical subject is always postverbal unless it is topicalized as in (4). These SVO structures have been shown to be instances of topicalisation (Borsley and Stephens, 1989).

(4) Yann a lennas al lizher
Yann PART read+past the letter
'Yann read the letter.'

c) Independent and non-topicalised : V[-finite] Aux (S) (O); (Stephens, 1983), (Borsley, 1989).

(5) Lenn a ra Lenaig ul levr.
Read PART does Lenaig a book
'Lenaig reads a book.'

d) Negated clauses are VSO.

(6) Ne lenn ket Lenaig al lizher.
NEG read NEG Lenaig the letter
'Lenaig does not read the letter.'

Independent infinitival clauses on the other hand are always SVO and there is no reason to think that they are instances of topicalization. These are illustrated in (7), commonly used as a narrative device, and in (8) used by a speaker wanting to express some reservation about her commitment to the truth of her statement.

(7) Ha Yann da lenn al lizher.
Yann to read the letter

(8) Da Yann da welout e oant holl aze.
to Yann to see were+3P all there
'As far as Yann could see they were all there.'

The contrast between embedded non-finite (9) to (12) and finite clauses shows up not only in the tense and subject inflection but in the absence of a subject NP in post-verbal position in non-finite clauses. The present analysis supports Sproat's claim that embedded infinitival clauses have the same structure, which for Breton is: [NP da V NP]

(9) Kavet ez eus un tu [dezhañ da vont e-barzh]
found PART is a way for+3SM to go in
'He has found a way to get in.'

(10) Pedin a reas Lenaig ar vugale [da zebrin krampouezh]
invite PART did Lenaig the children to eat pancakes
'Lenaig invited the children to eat pancakes.'

(11) Lakaat a ra Yann [ar baotred da lenn al lizher]
make PART does Yann the boys to read the letter
'Yann makes the boys read the letter.'

(12) Lezel a ra Lenaig [ar vugale da lenn al lizher]
allow PART does Lenaig the children to read the letter
'Lenaig allows the children to read the letter.'

The *da* immediately preceding the verb resembles English infinitival "to" which has been shown by Pullum (1982) to be neither a preposition nor a complementiser.

3. Infinitival Embedded Clause

3.1 Clauses Introduced by a Prepositional Complementiser.

I shall examine embedded infinitival clauses first and then the independent clauses. Subordinate clauses in Breton can be introduced by various complementisers, some of which are formally identical to prepositions and which can therefore be called prepositional complementisers. The complement clause may be finite or non-finite. In the infinitival subordinate clauses either an overt subject precedes the verb (as in (13) and (14)) or (as in (15) and (16)) prepositional complementiser is inflected. Here the subject is the phonologically null pronoun 'pro' which determines the inflection of the prepositional complementiser.

(13) Krenv awalc'h eo Lomm [evit Yann da spontan dirazañ]
strong enough is Lomm for Yann to frighthen before+3SM
'Lomm is sufficiently strong to frighten Yann.'

(14) Sonet e vije ar c'hloc'h [d'an dud da zont da verenn]
rung PRT was the bell to-the people to come to dinner
'The bell was rung to call the people to dinner.'

(15) Kavet ez eus un tu [dezhañ da vont e-barzh]
found PART is a way for+3SM to go in
'Someone found him a way to get in.'

(16) Kavet am eus ur bluenn vat [din da skrivañ gwelloc'h]
found have+1S a quilt good for+1S to write better
'I have found a good pen so that I can write better.'

The subordinate clause in (13) is an adjectival adjunct, in (14) and (15) it is a nominal adjunct and in (16) it is adverbial. It can be noted that the preposition *evit* can also be followed by a finite clause, in which case the verb precedes the subject.

(17) Kavet ez eus un tu [evit e teufe Yann e-barzh]
found PART is a way for PART come+Cond Yann inside
'A way was found for him to come in.'

In the first instance we can show that the prepositional complementiser and the following elements form a constituent using the cleft test: only a constituent can occur in the focus position of a cleft construction. These are in the focus position preceding *eo* or the focus particle *'ni* in examples (18) to (21).

(18) [Dezhañ da vont e-barzh] eo ez eus kavet un tu.
for+3SM to go in PART is found a way

(19) [Din da skrivañ gwelloc'h] eo am eus kavet ur bluenn vat
for+1S to write better I-have found a pen good

(20) [Evit Yann da spontañ dirakañ] 'ni eo Lomm krenv awalc'h
for Yann to bend before+3SM is Lomm strong enough

(21) [D'an dud da vont da verenn] 'ni e vije sonet ar c'hloc'h
for-the people to go to dinner PART was rung the bell

By contrast ungrammatical sentences result from the fronting of two elements which do not form one constituent, as in (22) and (23):

(22) *Un tu dezhañ eo a zo bet kavet da vont e-barzh.

(23) *Ur bluenn vat din eo am eus kavet da skrivañ.

Thus the prepositional complementiser and the following elements form a constituent. The Case-marking requirement is respected in these non-finite clauses as the subject receives Case from the prepositional complementiser similar to the situation in English where 'for' assigns case to the following NP

(24) It is dangerous for John to name the officer.

3.2 Clauses Complement to Control Verbs

A number of verbs such as *pedin* (to invite), *galvout* (to call), *klask* (to look for) take an object NP followed by a non-finite clause.

In sentence (25) the NP immediately to the left of the non-finite verb could be an object in the main clause or a pre-verbal subject in the subordinate clause.

(25) Pedin a reas Lenaig ar vugale da zebrin krampouezh.
invite PART did Lenaig the children to eat pancakes
'Lenaig invited the children to eat pancakes.'

(26) V1 NP1 NP2 V2

There is however clear evidence that the subordinate clause contains a subject: (27), which is introduced by an inflected prepositional complementiser is an alternative to (25) reflecting only greater emphasis but no change of meaning.

(27) Pedin a reas Lenaig ar vugale [dezho da zebrin krampouezh]
invite PART did Lenaig the children for+3P to eat pancakes
'Lenaig invited the children to eat pancakes.'

Sentence (27) contains an inflected prepositional complementiser and hence, like (15) and (16), contains also a 'pro' subject. In (27), NP2 is clearly the object of the main clause and it is thus natural to assume that this is also the case in (25). The difference between (25) and (27) is due to the fact that in (25) the complement clause has an empty COMP and consequently an ungoverned subject, whereas (27) has a prepositional complementiser and hence a governed subject.

Evidence for the presence of a PRO subject in the subordinate clause is supported by the reflexives and agreement arguments. Anaphors such as reflexives are bound in their governing category and must have either an antecedent within the same clause or in the next clause up in the case of a reflexive in the subject position of an exceptional case-marking clauses or a small clause. Pronouns on the other hand are free in their governing category. Sentence (29) is ungrammatical because the pronoun and the antecedent are in the same clause and (30) by contrast is ungrammatical because its antecedent is not in the same clause.

(28) Pedin a reas Yann Lenaig [PRO da respont anezhañ]
invite PART did Yann Lenaig to answer him
'Yann invited Lenaig to answer him.'

(29) *Pedin a reas Yann Lenaig [PRO da respont anezhil]
invite PART did Yann Lenaig to answer her
'Yann invited Lenaig to answer her.'

(30) *Pedin a reas Yann Lenaig [PRO da respont e-unan]
invite PART did Yann Lenaig to answer himself
'Yann invited Lenaig to answer himself.

(31) Pedin a reas Yann Lenaig [PRO da respont he-unan]
invite PART did Yann Lenaig to answer herself
'Yann invited Lenaig to answer herself.'

Some further evidence for this position comes from agreement. Attributive complements agree with the subject of their own clause. This agreement feature is shown in (32) by the mutation of the initial consonant of the adjective *kentañ*: K → G when the subject is feminine as in (32). In (33) the correct form is *gentañ* and not *kentañ*.

(32) Breman eo Lenaig an hini gentañ.
now is Lenaig the one first
'Lenaig is the first one now.'

The same rule applies in the embedded clause (33).

(33) Pedet e oa Lenaig da vezañ an hini gentañ/*kentañ
invited PART was Lenaig to be the first one+F *one+M
'Lenaig was invited to be the first one.'

Thus it is fairly clear that control verbs like *pedin* have a sentential complement with a subject. The subject is either PRO when there is no sentence initial governor or 'pro' when a governor in the form of a prepositional complementiser is present.

3.3 Clauses with Exceptional Case-marking

Two verbs take non-finite complement clauses which contain a full subject NP and *da* before the verb: *lakaat* (make) and *lezel* (allow). *Lezel* corresponds to English "allow" and can similarly mean "give permission" or "do nothing to prevent". Sentence (34) can have either one of the interpretations depending on the speaker/listener's judgement and context, although the "do nothing to prevent" is the most natural one.

(34) Lezel a reas ar gouarnamant ar vugale da ren ar skolioù
allow PART did the government the children to rule the schools
'The government allowed the children to rule the schools.'

Schmerling (1978) has argued that speakers' choice between

the two interpretations is determined not by structural differences, but by interpretive strategies and that English "allow" has only one lexical entry: as a verb taking S complement.

Lakaat corresponds to the French causative "faire" which, according to Rouveret and Vergnaud (1980), takes S complement with a full subject.

(35) Lakaat a reas Lenaig Yann da dewezhaat ar re vihan.
make PART did Lenaig Yann to look-after the one little
'Lenaig made Yann look after the little ones.'

Both verbs differ from control verbs. Unlike *pedin* their complement clause cannot contain a 'pro' subject:

(36) *Lezel a reas ar gouarnamant ar vugale dezho da ren ar skolioù.

(37) *Lakaat a reas Lenaig Yann dezhan da dewezhaat ar re vihan.

It seems therefore reasonable to analyse *lakaat* and *lezel* as verbs taking a non-finite complement clause with NP2 as a subject.

Since there is no governor inside the subordinate clause, the only possible way it can be assigned case is by the verb in the higher clause: the exceptional case-marking process.

NP2 in (34) and (35) can be replaced by a pronoun which is the *a*+inflection pronoun occuring with transitive verbs.

Although it is derived from the inflected partitive preposition, it has now gained full pronominal status, but, unlike the strong pronouns which occur in topic position, this is restricted to a post-verbal position (Urien and Denez, 1977).

(38) Lakaat a ra Yann anezho da lenn al lizher.
make PART does Yann them to read the letter
'Yann makes the boys read the letter.'

(39) Lezel a ra Lenaig ar anezho da lenn al lizher.
allow PART does Lenaig the them to read the letter
'Lenaig allows them to read the letter.'

In this context however this is not due to the pronoun being the object of the higher clause, but to it being the subject of the lower clause and receiving case from the higher verb.

The *a*+inflection pronominal form of NP2 which is the

subject of the subordinate clause is due to exceptional case-marking by the verb in the higher clause. This can be demonstrated using the expletive subject argument.

Expletive pronouns found with weather and time expressions are semantically empty and have a syntactic function only:

(40) Il pleut.

(41) It is raining.

(42) Il est deux heures.

(43) It's two o'clock.

Expletive subjects in Breton are not realized in the strong form (Denez 1983). Nonetheless weather verbs show tense and 3S inflection.

(44) Glav a ra
Rain PART does
'It rains.'

(45) *Hi a ra glav
she PART does rain

(46) *En a ra glav.
he PART does rain

Expletive subjects of weather and time expressions occur in the *a*+inflection form.

(47) Ober a ra glav anezhi.
do PART do rain her
'It's raining.'

(48) *Ober a ra glav hi

(49) Abenn e vije eizh eur anezhi.
at-when PART be+past eight hour her
'When it would be eight o'clock.'

(50) *Abenn ma vije eizh eur hi.

Weather expressions can be embedded as complement to *lezel* and to *lakaat* and their subjects turn to be to the left of the verb:

(51) Fall an amzer! Netra d'ober met lezel anezhi/anezhañ d'ober.
Bad the weather nothing to-do but allow it to-do
'The weather is bad but what can you do!'

(52) Sec'h an amzer, ezhomm a zo ur bannac'h glav!
dry the weather need PART is a little rain
Laka anezhi/anezhañ d'ober ta neuze!
make it do so then
'The weather is dry, we need some rain. Make it rain then if you can !'

Control verbs like *pedin* or *galvout* do not take a complement with expletive subjects

(53) *Pedin/galvout a reas anezhi d'ober glav.
invite/call PART did her to-do rain

The subject of infinitival verbs complement to *lakaat* and *lezel* is in the *a*+inflection form. As in English they derive their case from exceptional case-marking by the verb in the higher clause.

The analysis of embedded non-finite clauses has shown that the subject precedes the verb and that, unlike finite clauses, which are VSO, non-finite clauses are SVO.

This is to be expected as Case is assigned to the right. The subject NP in the infinitive cannot receive Case from INFL; it does get Case marked by either a prepositional complementiser or via the higher verb (exceptional Case marking). When there is no Case assigning category present, the subject is PRO (Control verbs).

4. Independent Non-finite Clauses

There are two kinds of independent infinitival clauses in Breton: one which has a preposition in initial position, as in the complement clauses introduced by a prepositional complementiser shown in (54) and (55), and the other introduced by *ha* as in (7), repeated in (62).

(54) Da Yann da welout e oa ar baotred aze.
to Yann to see PART was the boys there
'As far as Yann could see the boys were there.'

(55) Din da c'houzout ez eo evel zo dleet.
to+1S to know PART is like is ought
'As far as I know it is alright.'

Although the translation appears to suggest that the main clauses are adjuncts, there is evidence that they are not. The non-finite clause is the main clause and not an adjunct. Sentence initial adjuncts can be postposed, as in (56) and (57):

(56) Dezhañ da vezañ kozh e oa serzh bepred.
to+3SM to be old PART was fit still
'Although he was old, he was sitll fit.'

(57) Serzh eo bepred dezhañ bezañ kozh.
Fit is still to+3SM be old
'He is still fit although he is old.'

Postposing the P NP in (54) and (55) gives ungrammatical results in (58) and (59)

(58) *Aze e oa ar baotred da Yann da welout
there PART was the boys for Yann to see
'The boys were there for Yann to see.'

(59) *Evel zo dleet eo din da c'houzout.
like is ought is to+1S to know
'It is alright as far as I know'

In this respect the initial infinitival clause behaves like main clauses which cannot be postposed either:

(60) Gouzout a ran emañ Yann er ger.
know PART do+1S be Yann in+the home
'I know that Yann is home.'

(61) *Emañ Yann er ger a c'houzon.
is Yann in+the home know+1S

These independent infinitive clauses have the same structure as the complement clauses introduced by a prepositional complementiser and the subject is case-marked by the preposition.

Sentence (7), given here as (62), is somewhat different, as it is not clear how the subject receives case.

(62) Ha Yann da lenn al lizher.
Yann to read the letter

This type of independent infinitive clause is found in narrative discourse as a stylistic device and is commonly used.

Only strong pronoun forms are allowed; (64) and (65) are ungrammatical:

(63) Hag en da lenn al lizher.

(64) *Hag anezhan da lenn al lizher.

(65) *Hag anezhi d'ober glav.

This can be explained by the fact that *a*+inflection forms are restricted to post-verbal positions (Urien and Denez, 1977). One explanation as regards the status of the obligatory initial *ha* is that it fills the COMP position, thus allowing the subject of the infinitival clause which lacks a case marker to stay in the initial position.

There are at least two *ha* in Breton (traditionally *ha* has been regarded as a coordinating conjunction; however Timm (1986) and Urien (1987) note that it also functions as a complementiser). One *ha* is the coordinative conjunction and the other is used as a question marker for indirect questions and yes/no questions, especially in written Breton.

(66) Goulenn a reas Maia ha brav e vije an amzer
ask PART did Maia if nice PART be+Cond the weather
'Maia asked if the weather would be good.'

(67) Ha dont a raio da ger?
come PART do+fut to home
'Will he come home?'

It also used as an exclamative marker:

(68) Hag a lizheroù a lenne Lenaig!
of letters PART read Lenaig
'How many letters was Lenaig reading!'

(69) Sell hag a evned a zo aze!
look of birds is there
'Look how many birds are there!'

Whereas *ha* can be omitted in questions and exclamatives in spoken form, it cannot however be omitted in the independent infinitive used as a statement:

(70) *Yann da lenn al lizher.

In other words, *ha* inserted under COMP allows the subject to be case-marked when INFL and Preposition are lacking.

It seems clear that Breton has a special case-marking device operating when neither INFL or P are present. If *ha* is interpreted as being in COMP and enabling case-marking of the following NP, we are able to say that the lexical subjects of non-finite clauses are all assigned case.

5. Conclusion

The analysis of Breton infinitival clauses within the GB framework has shown that Breton clauses have two different word orders: VSO in finite clauses and SVO in infinitival clauses. The present analysis also falls in line with Sproat's argument that the difference between finite and non-finite clauses can be explained by the direction of case-assignment, which in VSO languages is always to the right. The correct word order in finite clauses is obtained by fronting INFL and the verb, whereas in the infinitival clauses, the subject remains in sentence initial position, where it can be assigned case either by a prepositonal complementiser or the higher verb, where exceptional case-marking takes place.

The distribution of non-finite clauses in Breton is extended to independent clauses and is thus wider than in English. This is not unique to Breton. Chung and MacCloskey (1987) have shown that in Irish the distribution of non-finite clauses includes independent clauses as well as embedded clauses. In Irish, however, the special case-marking device has no phonological realisation. It is case marking by default. In Breton non-finite clauses are allowed in independent position because there is a Case-marking element in COMP.

Acknowledgement

I wish to thank Bob Borsley for his encouragement and enlightening discussions . All errors and shortcomings are mine.

References

Borsley, R. (1989) A GPSG approach to Breton word order. In R. Hendrick (ed.), *Syntax and Semantics, 23. The Syntax of the Modern Celtic Languages*. New York: Academic Press.

Borsley, R. and Stephens, J. (1989) Agreement and the position of subject in Breton. *Natural Language and Linguistic Theory,* **7.**

Chomsky, N. (1981) *Government and Binding*. Dordrecht: Foris.

Chung, S. and McCloskey, J. (1987) Government, barriers, and small clauses in Modern Irish. *Linguistic Inquiry,* **18,** 173-237.

Denez, D. (1983) An dibersonel. *Hor Yezh,* **151,** 5-31.

Pullum, G. (1982) Syncategorematicity and English infinitival TO. *Glossa,* **16,** 181-213.

Rouveret, A. and Vergnaud, J. R. (1980) Specifying reference to the subject: French causatives and conditions on representations. *Linguistic Inquiry,* **11,** 97-202.

Schmerling, S. F. (1976) Synonymy judgements as syntactic evidence. In P.Cole and J. Sadock (eds.) *Syntax and Semantics,* **9,** 299-313.

Sproat, R. (1985) Welsh syntax and VSO structure. *Natural Language and Linguistic Theory,* **3,** 289-348.

Stephens, J. (1982) *Word order in Breton*. Doctoral thesis, University of London.

Stephens, J. (1983) Neutral word order in Breton. Paper presented at the 7th International Congress of Celtic Studies.

Timm, L. A. (1986) *Relative-clause formation in Breton*. Doctoral thesis, University of California, Davis.

Urien, J. Y. (1987) *La Trame d'une Langue: Le Breton*. Lesneven: Hor Yezh.

Urien, J. Y. and Denez, P. (1977) Essai d'analyse sémiologique du mot verbal et du syntagme verbal en Breton contemporain. *Studia Celtica,* **14/15,** 259-290.

The Progressive in Breton in the Light of the English Progressive[1]

Steve Hewitt

Speakers of major European languages such as French, German, Scandinavian and Slavic languages, etc. usually associate the progressive with English. Nevertheless progressive constructions are quite widespread. The progressive form is typically a periphrastic construction composed of the verb 'to be' (locative if separate forms exist) and either a present participle of the verb or the verb in a locative construction ('in', 'at', etc.):

English	John is singing
Breton	Yann zo a kana
Welsh	Mae Ioan yn canu
Irish	Tá Seán ag canadh
Dutch	Jan is ann het zingen
Icelandic	Jón er að syngja
Italian	Gianni sta cantando
Spanish	Juan está cantando
Portuguese	João está cantando

Languages as varied as Chinese (Mandarin), Georgian, Yoruba, Shona, Igbo, Kpelle and other Niger-Congo languages, Hindi-Urdu, Punjabi and North American Indian languages all have analogous constructions (Comrie, 1976: 100-102). The locative construction of the verb sometimes differs from the normal locative construction (loss of nasal mutation in Welsh; development of the mixed mutation in Breton; comparable differences of detail in Yoruba, Igbo, etc.). Comrie (1976: 103) suggests that the association of locative with progressive might be explained by a spatial conceptualisation of time; hence it is natural to be 'in' or 'at' a process, cf. English 'to be in the process of doing s.t., to be in progress', or French être en train de faire qqch.'

The use of the progressive is not identical across languages. For instance in the Italian, Spanish and Portuguese examples the progressive *stá/está cantando* could always be correctly replaced by a simple *canta*, since in those languages the progressive is never obligatory, and in French the specifically progressive phrase *Jean est en train de chanter* is even more marginal (Comrie: 33).

> Juan sabia [S]/*estaba sabiendo [P] que hablaba [S]/estaba hablando [P] demasiado de prisa
> John knew [S]/*was knowing [P] that he *spoke [S]/was speaking [P] too quickly
> Yann a ouie [S]/*oa o c'hoûd [P] e *komze [S]/oa o komz [P] re vûan

All three languages above exclude the progressive with a verb like 'to know'; Spanish admits either simple or progressive for 'was speaking' while both English and Breton require the progressive if the meaning is 'at that particular moment', cf. Comrie (p34). In Welsh and Scots Gaelic, the progressive *form* has spread to cover the entire domain of the imperfective, thus losing any specific progressive *meaning* (apparently less completely so for Scots Gaelic, but details are difficult to obtain), whereas their sister languages, Breton and Irish, make an obligatory semantic distinction between the simple tenses and the progressive, cf. Comrie (p99-100).

The first attestation of a progressive form in English dates from the 9th century (Strang, 1970: 350). In Old English, the present participle was in *-ende* with variants in *-ung*, *-ing* (Crépin, 1978: 97; Mossé, 1958: 62). From the 14th century *-ing* becomes established as the general form (Mossé: 62; Strang: 280). In Middle English, the progressive with the present participle is at first restricted to a few verbs such as 'go, come, live, fight, last, think, work', reinforced by, and eventually confused with, locative expressions of the type *this church was in building*, *he was on hunting*, *a-hunting* (Mossé: 64,77). The progressive, used in Old English first essentially in the past, then in the present *was doing*, *is doing*, spreads in the 15th-16th centuries to a whole range of other combinations (perfect, future), at the same time as it gains noticeably in frequency (Strang: 207; Mossé: 112). Even so, Polonius can still ask Hamlet *What do you read [S], my lord,* impossible today (Strang: 150). *Be going to* for the future of present intention or cause appears around 1650 (Mossé: 131). The perfect progressive *have been doing*, attested as early as Chaucer at the end of the 14th century, only becomes common during the 18th century (Strang: 207), and it is only towards the end of the 18th century that the progressive passive *the book is being printed* starts ousting *the book is printing*, not without some resistance (Strang: 99; Mossé: 131). Other more specific extensions continue over the 19th and 20th centuries.

In Breton, the progressive as such, and all the more so its history, are far less well-known than in English. Fleuriot (1964: 330) finds a pseudo-example in Old Breton, *is cumal gurth,* (Welsh *wrth*, M., Mod.B. *ouz*, *o*) *guarthuar adec Dionisi est hic* "c'est une proposition se morquant (à moquer) de la période de Dionysius qui se trouve ici", presumably a gerund rather than a true progressive. However, the absence of the progressive may be more apparent than real, given the 'pauvret des sources en véritables phrases'. Le Roux (1957: 377-378) and Hemon (1975: 268-269) give several examples in Middle Breton, where it seems already well-established. Its present extension seems to correspond roughly to the situation in English around the early 18th century, for as we shall see, it is found in all the primary tenses and the progressive 'go' may be used with future tense, but the perfect of 'be' plus progressive verb does not make a perfect progressive; there is normally no progressive passive and most of the more recent specialisations of English have not taken place.

The Breton progressive is formed by the verb 'to be', (with separate locative or more properly situative forms available for 3rd person present in the east, all persons present in the west, and all persons present and imperfect in the northwest) plus the infinitive of the verb preceded by the Middle Breton preposition *ouz*, *oz* 'at, against', which is the origin of the Modern Breton progressive particle *o*, with a variant *é*, both of which cause the mixed mutation. The particle is often not realised phonetically, even though the mutations it causes remain. For this reason it will not always appear in examples heard in spontaneous speech, nor will other verbal particles (direct, indirect, negative). For an explanation of other aspects of the orthography used, cf. Hewitt

(1987a).

Most analyses of English agree in describing 'to be' as an auxiliary in the progressive construction. In Hewitt (1987b, c, 1988a, b), three types of auxiliary were distinguished for Breton, according to their syntactic behaviour. The following is a summary of some of the arguments presented there. For pragmatic reasons some of the sentences below would not occur very frequently, but are given better to illustrate the paradigm. Presentation types are non-fronted: P 'initial tensed predicate constituent', and fronted: S 'initial subject' and X 'any other initial constituent'; S and X presentation types are distinguished mainly because S triggers subject-agreement in the negative; for more information on subject-agreement, see Hewitt (1985). Verbal structures are V 'simple lexical verb', A 'true auxiliary', and D 'dynamic'. There is a 'tense non-initial constraint' in Breton which prevents verbs from appearing in tensed form sentence-initially, with the notable exception of *emañ* 'to be-situative'. The following may be glossed *a* 'direct tense particle (after subject, object, infinitive)', *e* 'indirect tense particle (after other elements)', *ne* 'negative tense particle', *o* 'progressive infinitival particle'.

(1) skriva a ra Yann lizeroù
write *a* do Yann letters
'Yann writes letters.'

(2) skrived neus Yann lizeroù
written has Yann letters
'Yann has written letters.'

(3) skrived e veẑ lizeroù
written *e* be-habit. letters
'Letters are written.'

(4) hîr ê ar lizer
long be the letter
'The letter is long.'

(5) ne neus ked skrived Yann lizeroù
ne has not written Yann letters
'Yann has not written letters.'

(6) lizeroù neus skrived Yann
letters has written Yann
'Yann has written letters.'

(7) emañ Yann en tî
be-sit. Yann in-the house
'Yann is in the house.'

(8) emañ Yann o skriva lizeroù
be-sit. Yann *o* write letters
'Yann is writing letters.'

(9) lizeroù emañ Yann o skriva
letters be-sit. Yann *o* write
'Yann is writing letters.'

(10) *o skriva emañ Yann lizeroù
o write be-sit. Yann letters
'Yann is writing letters.'

(11) o skriva lizeroù emañ Yann
o write letters be-sit. Yann
'Yann is writing letters.'

(12) skriva lizeroù a ra Yann
write letters *a* do Yann
'Yann writes letters.'

(13) *skrived lizeroù neus Yann
written letters has Yann
'Yann has written letters.'

(14) skriva lizeroù neus gwrêd Yann
write letters has done Yann
'Yann has written letters.'

(15) skriva lizeroù e hê red ober
write letters *e* be necessary do
'It is necessary to write letters/some letter-writing must be done.'

(16) goûd a ra an istoar
know *a* he-does the story
'He knows the story.'

(17) *o c'hoûd an istoar emañ
o know the story he-is-sit.
'*He is knowing the story.'

(18) *?goûd an istoar a ra
know the story *a* he-does
'He knows the story.'

The first type of auxiliary or 'dummy-auxiliary' arises in (1) solely to satisfy the tense non-initial constraint in V-structures with P-presentation in the affirmative. The second type or 'true auxiliary' includes the perfect tenses (2), passive (3) and copula (4). They satisfy the tense non-initial constraint in affirmative P-presentation by 'predicate-fronting' (2)-(4), not necessary in the negative (5). Common to all true auxiliary or A-structures is adjacency between the auxiliary and predicate, with the subject following (preceding in S-presentation) the auxiliary-predicate (predicate-auxiliary with predicate fronting) constituent (2)-(6).

The third type or D-structure (7) includes the situative verb 'to be' plus a situative complement (typically prepositional or adverbial), a construction which cannot be described as auxiliary, and (8) the situative verb 'to be' plus a progressive dynamic infintival VP constituent (historically a prepositional phrase PP). Syntactically neither is auxiliary because there is no adjacency between the situative verb and its complement: the subject intervenes (7)-(9), unlike in A-structures. There is no A-structure predicate-fronting (*10), however it is possible to front the whole progressive VP in initial focus (11). This is also possible with non-progressive VPs (12), a construction usually considered by Breton grammarians to be a simple variant of (1), however that cannot be so: 'to do' does not arise here simply to get round the tense non-initial constraint. The VP-fronted equivalent of (2) is not (*13) but (14), where 'to do' remains, as it does in (15). What we have then is 'activity-do', which like the situative 'to be', enters into collocation only with non-stative or dynamic verbs: (16), with a stative verb, may appear neither in the progressive (*17) nor in practice in the VP-fronted activity-do construction (*?18) (it is difficult to get informants to reject (*?18) outright, probably because of the apparent similarity with the extremely common (12) type, but sentences like (*?18) with stative verbs are never heard in spontaneous speech).

It could be argued that the progressive construction is semantically auxiliary because situative 'to be' enters into collocation with a lexical verb (progressive infinitive) to define the progressive aspect, just as 'to be' and 'to have' enter into collocation with a lexical verb (past participle) to form the perfect tense series or the passive voice. However, syntactically the progressive is not an auxiliary structure like the perfect, passive or copular constructions because of the lack of adjacency between auxiliary and predicate and the non-application of the predicate-fronting rule, both of which define a clear syntactic class of construction. From this point of view, Breton is fundamentally different from English and this may provide a partial explanation of why there is no perfect progressive and usually no progressive passive in Breton: could it be that only true A-structures may combine, e.g. perfect passive, perfect copula?

Trépos (1962: 198-199) describes the progressive construction in Breton, noting that it is equivalent to the French tre en train de'. Kervella (1947: 185, 189-190) calls it *ar stumm ober* 'the doing form', but says nothing about its use. According to Le Roux (1957: 377) the progressive "consiste à marquer que l'action indiquée se développe, dure; il exprime l'aspect de durée." Jules Gros (1974: 169) is the most detailed: *"l'aspect progressif*, indiquant une action en cours, qui dure, se continue, progresse, qui n'est pas tèrminée" and although he calls *beža*, 'to be' an auxiliary, he adds with fine intuition "ce n'est pas *bezañ* qui définit ici l'aspect progressif, mais l'association de ce verbe avec un participe présent". That is just about all in the literature on the progressive in Breton, apart from examples.

The English progressive has been described abundantly. In addition to Comrie's theoretical considerations (1976: 32-40 and passim), what follows is based mainly on three simple presentations: Swann (1980: 502-503, 256, 468, 496-498); Thomson and Martinet (1980: 139-144); Leech and Svartik (1975: 63-75 passim), which will suffice to initiate a comparison with Breton.

The basic function of the progressive in English and Breton is to signify an action or process that is in progress, developing, unfolding, whose internal temporal constituency is explicit (Comrie 1976: 4-5), that is of momentary or temporary duration and not necessarily finished: *o skriva ur lizer emañ [P]*, 'He is writing a letter (at this moment)'. It is used in all the tenses of the simple verb: *o skriva ur lizer emañ [P]*, 'He was/will be/would be writing a letter', etc. with restrictions for the perfect and passive in Breton. A progressive process may provide a frame that contains another process perceived as punctual: *o tibri e oa [P] pa ho-on antred* 'He was eating when I came in'. This is why in narratives the context or background is often given in the progressive while successive events are presented in simple tenses. The progressive is used for changing, evolving situations: *an amzer zo o tond e-barz [P]* 'The weather is getting better', and for repeated actions (iterative): *da barâ 'mañ tenna [P] war ar pichoned?* 'What's he shooting at the pigeons for?'

In both languages a fairly well defined group of so-called stative verbs are not used progressively. They have been studied in detail for English. Below is given a representative, if not exhaustive, list of stative verbs for Treger Breton (northeast of the Breton-speaking area) arranged more or less according to semantic class. The list seems to correspond quite closely to English.

Emotions

karoud	love
plijoud dežañ	like
displijoud dežañ	dislike
en em interessi deuz/da	be interested in
euzi	be horrified
heugi	be disgusted
sponta	take fright
fromi	be thrilled, shaken
soûeza	be astonished, surprised

Causative Emotions

plijoud da	please
displijoud da	displease
soûeza	astonish. surprise
estoni	amaze
sourpren	surprise
interessi	interest

Non-directed Mental States, Impressions

goûd	know (knowledge)
anvežoud	know (acquaintance)
jonjal	think (opinion)
kompren	understand
ankoaz	forget
kredi	believe
jonjal dežañ	think, seem to
kaoud dežañ	think, seem to, find

ffelloud deẑañ	want
ffota deẑañ	want
mankoud deẑañ	want, have to
c'houantâd	desire
ffiẑioud e	trust
disfiẑioud deuz	distrust
en em renta kont deuz	realise
en em c'houll	wonder
soûeti	wish
divinoud	guess
douti	doubt, suspect
esperoud	hope
Non-directed Perception	
gweled	see
klewed	hear
santoud	feel
santoud c'hwéz	smell
santoud blâs	taste
Inherent Qualities, Appearance	
diskoueẑ (beẑa)	seem
pouesa	weigh
musuri	measure
General Relationships, States	
beẑa	be
kaoud	have
chom	stay, remain
galloud	be able
renkoud	'must'
kléa	'must'
gléoud	owe
existoud	exist
mankoud	lack
kompren	include
depantoud	depend
selled	concern
meritoud	deserve
siniffîoud	mean
mond e	fit (in)
mond da	fit suit

koustoud	cost
talveẑoud	be worth
tapoud gantañ	be lucky

Several verbs of emotion may be progressive when causative: *Yann a oa o sponta [P] aneẑi* 'John was frightening her'. Verbs of non-directed mental states or impressions sometimes have homonyms with directed or performative meaning, which may then be used progressively: *me zo o chonjal [P] bah ar ffilm-se* 'I am thinking about that film', *me a oa o ssoûeti [P] Bloawez Mâd dezañ* 'I was wishing him Happy New Year'.

Similarly, directed perception may be progressive: *selled deuz, jilaou, tastornad, tañvä, c'hwézza* 'look at, listen to, feel, taste, smell'. Breton has separate verbs for each pair of directed and non-directed perception, whereas in English there are homonyms in some cases: 'feel, taste, smell'. The inherent qualities *pouesa, musuri* 'weigh, measure' also have transitive homonyms which may be progressive. This principle of progressive potential for verbs whose subject exercises control of the action should be kept in mind--it will be seen to be of more general importance for Breton. Impersonal or subjectless verbs of the type *kaoud deẑañ: me a gav din* 'me (it) find to-me, methinks, I think, I find', where there is no grammatical subject that could exercise control, seem to be stative by definition in Breton.

One is struck in Breton by the considerable proportion of stative loanwords with infinitives in *-oud*, otherwise a fairly uncommon ending. It is thought to derive from *boud* 'to be', cf. Welsh *bod* 'to be', *adnabod* 'to know (acquaintance)', Middle Breton *bout* 'to be', *aznauout* 'to know (acquaintance)', Modern Breton *boud/beẑa, anaoud/anveẑoud.* It would seem that this ending has become, in Treger Breton at least, almost a productive mark of stativity.

Many English stative verbs are rendered in Breton by expressions containing *kaoud* 'have' or *beẑa* 'be':

kaoud plijiadur gant	enjoy, appreciate
kaoud aoun deuz	be afraid of, fear
kaoud kâs deuz	hate, detest
kaoud c'houant	want
kaoud jonj deuz	remember
kaoud hast da	look forward to
kaoud fiẑians e	trust

kaoud disfiẑ deuz	distrust
kaoud keuñ da	regret, miss
kaoud un êr	look, seem
kaoud blâs	taste
kaoud c'hwéz	smell
kaoud poân	hurt, ache
kaoud eẑomm	need
beẑa welloc'h deẑañ/gantañ	prefer
beẑa fae gantañ	disdain, can't stand, be fed up with
beẑa kerse gantañ	regret, be sorry
beẑa...da weled	look, seem
beẑa...da glewed	sound
beẑa kad, barreg	be able
beẑa moyen deẑañ	be able
beẑa da	belong to
beẑa gantañ	have (on one's person)

English and Breton thus agree on the basic function of the progressive, which is to denote the unfolding or development of the action or process, and to a large extent on the class of stative verbs which do not normally occur in the progressive. They also share a special expressive use of the progressive which serves to characterise a habit as surprising, excessive, even annoying: *hennez zo ordinal o c'houlenn [P] arc'hant ganin ha ne neveẑ ked jonj [S] james da renta anê din* 'He is always asking me for money and he never remembers to pay me back'. As this example shows, the expressive function of the progressive occurs only in the affirmative. However, Breton goes further than English: thanks to habitual forms of 'to be' in the present and imperfect, it also has a true neutral habitual progressive (HP): *"beb sadorn e vez o werzañ [HP] legumaj e Douarnenez"* (Trépos 1962: 198) 'Every Saturday he sells vegetables in Douarnenez (can [habitually] be found selling...)'. Other examples are *"ma breur a vez o kousked [HP] e-pad an deiz"* 'mon frère est habituellement en train de domir pendant toute la journée'" (Gros 1974: 169) 'My brother sleeps (can be found sleeping) all day long'; *"ma mamm a veze e-pad an deiz o kanañ [HP]"* (Gros: 181) 'My mother used to sing (could be found singing) all day long'; *"honnez a vez o tevezia [HP] eno pa vez ezomm aneẑi"* (ibid.) 'She works days there when she's needed'. The latter may be explained in part by the fact that *dewezia* 'to do day-labour' is only used in infinitive form.

While the progressive in English spread, starting in the late 18th century, to the passive (*The house is building* becomes *the house is being built*), that has not really happened in Breton, where it is still normal to say *ma montr zo o tréssa [P]* 'My watch is fixing (=being fixed)'. Nevertheless, Jules Gros has noted at least one progressive passive: *"evel pa vefe unan bennag o veza lazet* 'comme si quelqu'un était en train d'être tué (comme si on était en train de tuer quelqu'n)'" (Gros 1970a: 207) 'As if someone were being killed', which may be due to the selectional restrictions of 'kill': 'someone' could equally be the logical subject or object. Thus the construction is apparently possible, yet it seems extremely rare in practice.

Another domain which the progressive invades massively in English during the 18th century is the perfect tenses. The English perfect progressive has two distinct uses, the second of which is fairly difficult to render in most European languages, including Breton. The first is for an activity or process that has been going on since a particular moment or for a certain period of time up to the present (or other point of reference). In this case, Breton, like most European languages, does not use the perfect distinction; the progressive however is maintained if it would otherwise be used: *me zo o c'hortoz [P] abaoe dég eur* 'I am waiting since ten o'clock (= I have been waiting...)'; *"pell zo ema oc'h evañ [P]* 'y a-t-il longtemps qu'il boit'" (Gros 1974:180) 'Is he drinking long (= has he been drinking long)'; cf. Irish usage. The second use concerns an activity or process whose quantative result or logical accomplishment is not the main point, but rather the consequences or what that activity or process may explain at the point of reference. In this case Breton is forced to choose between a perfect simple tense (*ne oa ked gléed dežañ kondûi; eved neus [S]* 'he shouldn't drive, he has drunk (= he has been drinking)') or an imperfect (durative past) progressive (*me a oa o skriva [P] ur lizer* 'I was writing a letter (= I have been writing...)').

Why can Breton, with both its well-developed progressive and perfect tenses, not combine them with the same semantics as English? Once again, Jules Gros (1974: 181) provides the fullest answer: "avec le p.p. *bet* 'été (= allé)', l'aspect progressif s'atténue fortement pour insister d'avantage sur la notion du passé", with one of several examples: *"Jakez a oa bet o freuzañ an embannou* 'Jacques avait été déchirer les publications de marriage'" 'Jacques went and tore up the marriage banns.' In other words, *bed* 'been (= gone and come back)' takes VP complements preceded by the progressive infinitival particle, just as certain verbs in English require complements in *-ing*, without there necessarily being any progressive meaning; certainly there is no restriction on using stative verbs here: *me zo bed o weled* 'I have been seeing (= I have been to have a look/went and had a look)'. Another use of *bed* 'been' plus progressive complement is *"bet eo o vond e-unan"* 'il a été (un moment) à marcher seul (il fut un moment où il marchait seul - mais plus maintenant'" (Gros 1974: 181) 'He used to (be able to) walk by himself.'

The present progressive is also used in English to express plans for the future. The Breton equivalent is usually in the simple present: *piw a deu [S] ganeomp?* 'Who is coming with us?'; *pa vo ffin ar barti-mañ me h-a [S] d'ar gêr* 'When this game is over I am going home'. However progressives are sometimes possible: *honz zo timî [P] 'benn dissadorn* 'She is getting married on Saturday'; *Brest zo c'houari [P] 'eneb da St. Etienne 'benn ar sûn all* 'Brest is playing St. Etienne next week'; but for some reason *??me zo o c'hoari [P] gant Jean-Yves 'benn ar sûn all* 'I am playing with Jean-Yves next week' seems less acceptable. In this case *me meus d'ôr c'hoari* or *me zo ssansed da c'houari* 'I am supposed to play...' is preferred. Why? Could it be that the present progressive for future plans is reserved for major staged events in Breton? What is certain is that it is definitely marginal compared to English.

Breton shares with English and French the use of the verb 'to go' as an auxiliary to express a future intention or cause. In the west of the Breton-speaking area it is usually progressive as in English: *emon o vond [P] da lared did* 'I am going to tell you'. In the east it is more typically simple in the present: *e h-an [S] da lared did*, with the future auxiliary 'go' exceptionally not subject to the tense non-initial constraint, rather as the English 'going to' may have special pronunciation /gënë/ when used as a future marker. In the imperfect the progressive is normally used everywhere: *e oann o vond [P] da lared did* 'I was going to tell you.'

Breton does not have the attenuating, polite use of the English future progressive for events which should take place as a matter of course and whereby the intentions of the subject are not questioned too directly: *pegoulz e tilojïd [S]?* 'When will you be moving?' Nor does Breton have the imaginary or make-believe use of the progressive, which extends even to stative verbs in English: 'I've only had six whiskies and already I'm seeing pink elephants' (Comrie, 1976: 37), *ne meus ked eved 'med c'hwec'h bannac'h whisky ha dijâ e welan [S] elephanted ros*.

Being in progress implies that a process is momentary, temporary, of limited duration. English has verbs of position or posture which, although they describe a state, may be freely used in the progressive to underline the temporary nature of the state. The corresponding verbs in Breton are usually dynamic-inchoative, thus for states, whether permanent or momentary, past participles or prepositional phrases are used: *asežed ê [S]/en e goasež emañ [S] bah ar c'houign* 'He is seated/in his sitting in the corner (= he is sitting...)'; *gourvežed [S]/en e c'hourvez emañ [S] war an doûar* 'He is laid/in his lying on the ground (= is lying...)'; strangely enough and contrary to all documented Breton usage, I once heard from an extremely competent and dependable speaker *ar genaoueg brâs zo ssevel [P] deuz ar c'hontoûar* '...the big idiot who's standing at the counter.'

English is making increasing use of the momentary function of the progressive, using it even with some stative verbs to mark contingent state: 'wishing, hoping, forgetting, needing, remembering, wondering, etc.' In Breton ankoaz may be used progressively when framing a punctual event: *(pa laran sé) me zo o h-ankoûaz [P] ar réoù all* '(When I say that) I am forgetting the others'. Two stative verbs may have an expressive progressive use, but mainly in the negative imperfect: *ne oann ked o kompren [P] sé* 'I wasn't understanding that (= that's hardly what I understood)'; *oann ked chonzal [P] oa aï bah ar poent-se honz* 'I wasn't thinking she was that far gone (= I hardly thought...)'.

The progressive can be used for temporary habits in English: 'I'm getting up early these days.' In Breton it cannot; one can only mark the inception of a temporary period by *beža krog* 'to be hooked, attached = have begun/be beginning': *me zo krog da sevel abréd en déižioù-mañ*. English can also use the progressive for temporarily repeated states: 'We're hearing a lot about pregnant fathers', *krog omp da glewed ur bern komz deuz an tadoù lourd*, or recently developing states 'People are knowing more about nuclear waste'. Once again Breton cannot, but in Treger at least it is possible, indeed common, to underline the change in state with a resultative particle *aï* < *arri* 'arrive, happen': *an dud zo aï da c'hoûd muioc'h diwar-benn ar restachoù nukléair*.

In English several normally stative verbs may be used in the progressive with secondary meanings 'see (socially, professionally); see about; see to; be = behave; expect[S] = suppose, [P] = wait for arrival; like[S] = cherish, appreciate, [P] = find, be pleased with, enjoy.' In Breton too one can find semantic differences linked to the use of the progressive: *bez̃a* 'to be', but *"pa oa ar moh bihan o vez̃a [P]"* 'quand les porcelets étaient en train de naître'" (Gros, 1970b: 48) 'When piglets were being born'; *chom [S]* 'stay, remain', *[P]* 'live somwhere (temporary or permanent)': *hennez zo o chom [P] e Lannûon* 'He lives/is living in Lannion'; *hennez zo o labourad [P] e Plouared* 'He works/is working in Plouaret'; *hennez zo o terc'hel [P] ostaleri* 'He runs/is running a café.' Since certain vital activities are always considered to be progressive in Breton, the distinction cannot be used to differentiate the permanent from the temporary as in English. *Labourad a ra [S]* 'he works' means more properly 'he works well, he is a good worker'. Similarly expressions for 'to take care of, look after, deal with' *ober deuz*, *ober war-dro*, *en em okupi deuz*, *soursîal deuz* have a strong tendency to be used in the progressive, which may easily be interpreted as habitual for the non-specific instances.

Ober 'to do' may have secondary meanings when progressive: 'pretend to be, play at': *"honnez a vez oh ober [HP] he braz* 'elle fait la grande dame, elle est prétentieuse, vaniteuse'" (Gros, 1970b: 384) 'She puts on airs'; 'be, be used for': *"hennez a oa oh ober [P] pod-koavenn ganin-me* 'celui-là me servait de pot de crème'" (Gros, 1970b: 383) 'I was using that as a cream pot'; '*object* made of *subject*': *er Frans amañ n-eus ked tôl kén h-ober [P] an autoioù* 'Here in France cars aren't made with (decent) metal plate any more'; *"mad! ne gomprenan ked petore danvez a zo oh ober [P] da vab-te!"* (Gros, 1970a: 87) 'Well, I don't understand what stuff your son is made of!' Could it be for Bretons that the substance that enters into the makeup of a particular object must retain its characteristics if that object is not to decompose or disintegrate; hence 'make' meaning 'make up' or 'constitute' is often progressive to underline the additional effort or energy input one may imagine is required to maintain the constituent state (cf. Comrie, 1976: 49).

In at least one case in Breton the use of a simple tense instead of the expected progressive would seem to assimilate the dynamic verb to another with stative meaning: *n-onn ked pehini a leres [S]* 'I don't know which one you are talking about (= you mean)'.

The simple tense in Breton may signify a capacity, whether momentary or general, while the progressive is kept for factual instances: *mond a ra en-dro [S]* 'It's working/it works'; *emañ o vond en-dro [P]* 'It's running, it's on'. Allied to this notion of capacity there is a certain type of utterance in which Breton has a marked preference for simple tenses where English requires a progressive because the context is momentary or temporary. These are (limited or specific) instances of a manifestation of a potential, where the subject does not really control the process: *kreski ra [S]* 'He's growing', *Brug a divlew [S]* 'Brug [dog's name] is shedding', *amañ verw [S] ked an dour c'houaz?* 'Isn't the water boiling yet?', *diskorn [S] ked an hent?* 'Isn't the road thawing?' In each case the progressive could have been used, but the momentariness of the process would have been more explicitly emphasised than in English, where it is the only form possible, given the the context. This is probably why weather-related verbs are more often in simple tenses even when referring to momentary processes: *glaw a ra [S]* 'it's raining' than the progressive: *glaw zo o h-ober [P]*. The difference is not always clear, and both are possible; the following were heard within a couple of seconds of each other in the context 'it's getting hot': *an tréoù a labour [S]* 'Things are growing' and *ar maïs zo labourad [P]* 'The maize is growing'.

Where the subject could exercise control over the action, the choice of whether or not to use the progressive in Breton says something about the intentionality of the action, simple tenses being easily used for momentary actions or processes that are less subject to direct will: *c'hwerzin ra [S]* 'He's smiling' (something's made him smile); *me glewe toud péz a larent [S]* 'I could hear everything they were saying' (the words emerging, not what they were trying to say); *en Télé-Bretagne déc'h da nós h-annonsent [S] erc'h c'houaz* 'On Télé-Bretagne last night they were predicting snow again' (it's their normal job to predict the weather); *parâ sell [S] ar gouaier-se deuz ar chass?* 'What's that guy looking at the dogs for?' (what's the matter with him?); *déc'h da nós heñ ffleuke [S] bah ar loch* 'Last night he [a dog] was rummaging around in the shed.'

Related to the principle of weak intention in Breton there is an exclamatory use of simple tenses for exaggerated momentary actions: *gopal rént [S] 'had!* 'They sure are shouting!'; *c'houari rént lass [S]!* 'They are (really) whooping it up!'; *karza rént [S]* 'They are (really) tearing along!'; *poania réd [S]!* 'You're working hard, you're hard at it' (common greeting in Treger, often proffered to groups of drinkers!). In each case it's 'more than they can help'.

If simple tenses may imply an absence of particular will, conversely the progressive may be used to suggest strong intention: *kamma a ra [S]* 'He limps/He's limping', *o kamma emañ [P]* 'He's limping (on purpose)', and may even take on conative meaning: *n-onn ked tifenn parâ 'mañ [P] henz ahe* 'I don't know what he's fighting for there (trying to fight for)'. An interesting case is *honz zo sseparì [P] Ar C'houerc'had deuz Plounewez̃* 'It [a stream] separates Vieux-Marché from Plounevez', a general truth, which accounts for the simple tense in English, but which is nevertheless the result of sustained human determination to define administrative boundaries, which may explain the progressive in Breton. However this speculation should perhaps not be pushed too far, as one can also hear *honz a ra [S] ar sseparation 'tre ar C'hot-du-Nor hag ar Ffinistèr* 'It forms the boundary [makes the separation] between the Côtes-du-Nord and Finistère.'

In any case, in reference to a specific issue of town politics (*me gav din lar gewier [S] ar mair* 'I think the mayor is lying'), a simple tense in Breton suggests simply that the mayor is not right, what he is saying is not true; a progressive *'mañ lared gewier [P]* would have constituted a far more serious accusation: the mayor would be intentionally trying to fool people. Of all the examples noted, the one which best illustrates this correlation between control and progressivity in Breton is this one, about a seemingly endless truck journey: *roula oamp [P], med chench plass raemp ked [S]* 'We were driving along, but we weren't getting anywhere' - we were in control of the action of driving, indeed we were doing our best to drive along (hence the progressive), but to no avail, we didn't seem to be moving, which was quite beyond our control (and thus the simple tense is chosen).

Conclusion

After noting the existence of progressive forms in many languages, whether they are marginal (French), optional (Italian, Spanish, Portuguese), obligatory (English, Breton, Irish) or so prevalent as to lose all progressive meaning (Welsh, Scots Gaelic), the Breton progressive was described as resulting from the conjunction of a lexical infinitive VP preceded by a progressive particle (not always realised phonetically) and situative forms of *beẑa* 'to be', which judging by its syntax, and contrary to English, is not an auxiliary, but the main syntactic verb. This construction is analogous to one with 'activity-do' which also gives rise to continuous VPs which seem to be limited to the same class of non-stative verbs as the progressive.

Both languages agree in the basic use of the progressive to indicate an action or a process as it unfolds; it may provide a framework that contains punctual events; it describes changing or developing situations and repeated actions or events (iterative). The class of stative verbs normally excluded from the progressive is essentially the same in both languages and semantic sub-classes of stative verbs can be distinguished (the otherwise infrequent infinitive ending *-oud* is found commonly in stative loanwords and may be a productive semantic marker of stativity). Many Breton equivalents of English stative verbs are either 'impersonal' subjectless verbs (stative by definition) or expressions formed with the statives *beẑa* 'to be' or *kaoud* 'to have'. Finally both languages have an expressive use of the progressive (in the affirmative only) to denote surprising, excessive or annoying habits.

Then we reviewed the discrepancies between the two languages. Breton, unlike English, also has a neutral habitual progressive, formed with specifically habitual forms of 'to be'. On the other hand, it lacks almost totally (a single example noted) a progressive passive and a perfect progressive (what appears to be formally so has quite a different meaning, since the past participle *bed* 'been' can also denote, as in English, 'gone (and come back)' and takes a progressive VP complement). It is known that the English progressive passive and perfect progressive developed essentially as recently as the 18th century; it may be that in other areas of divergence the English development is also recent.

Breton does not often use the present progressive for planned future events; it prefers the simple present or some sort of modal modification. 'To go' can be used progressively as in English for a future of present intention or cause, but in the east mainly in the imperfect (past intentional or cause); in the present 'to go' is usually in the simple tense. Breton does not have the English 'imaginary' use of the progressive. Nor does it use the future progressive in an attenuated, polite manner, to speak of future events which should take place as a matter of course, while carefully avoiding to impute any intentionality to the subject. Indeed intentionality seems to be a major component of the Breton progressive.

In English several normally stative verbs like 'see, like, be, expect' etc. may be used progressively with secondary meanings. In Breton we noted *beẑa* 'be, [P] be born', *chom* 'stay, [P] live', *labourad* '[P] work (even permanently), [S] capacity for work', *ober* 'do, [P] pretend to be; be used as; make up, compose'; in general, vital activities like 'live, work, take care of, look after, run (business)' etc. are progressive, even when considered as permanent. Comrie (1976: 49) motivates the progressive for dynamic situations claiming that they require a continuous input of energy to remain dynamic and suggests (footnote, pp. 49-50) that this principle might in part explain the spread of the English progressive to new uses: a contingent state is not normal, therefore more difficult to maintain.

Indeed Comrie notes (pp.38-39) that the English progressive has extended far beyond its original definition as 'continuous, non-stative' to include temporary (contingent) states and contingent habitual situations; it thus seems to be developing towards 'contingent' use, although the transformation is not yet complete. In Breton momentariness is of course implicit in the definition 'continuous, no-stative', but rather than narrow down the momentary, contingent/permanent, general cleavage, the Breton progressive seems to be furthering the distinction of control by the subject. Many momentary processes and actions were noted in simple tenses where the subject exercised little or no control. Conversely, the progressive may convey strong intention, even in a stable situation which results from human will.

Thus we have used English as a heuristic to elucidate the use of the progressive in Treger Breton. A syntactic difference was found: 'to be' an auxiliary in English, a main syntactic verb in Breton; a similar basic use for the progressive, but developing in different directions: [progressive → contingent] in English; [→ control of subject] in Breton.

It could be objected that some of the Breton examples seem to betray French influence. Apart from typical examples that can be heard dozens of times a day, care was taken to note only utterances produced by speakers for whom Breton is plainly the dominant language. So if French influence is apparent there, it must be everywhere. Even the few remaining monoglots must be exposed to it through contact with the great mass of more bilingual speakers. But rather than clear French influence, which would manifest itself in a gradual blurring of the progressive distinction, we found a surprisingly intact and coherent system, which revealed little-suspected and hitherto undescribed nuances.

Ne oann ked o chonjal [P] e viche bed kemend-all da lared diwar-benn ar progressif en brezoneg! 'I hardly thought there would be as much to say about the progressive in Breton!'

Note

1. The present article is a slightly revised and adapted translation of Hewitt 1986. The syntactic framework and definition of auxiliary have been made clearer in the light of Hewitt 1987b, c, 1988a, b. I would like to pay homage here to Professor Watkins for kindling my initial interest in problems of Breton word order, which led to those articles and talks. Thanks also go to Bernard Comrie for several valuable, last-minute comments. The Breton of examples invented here and not actually noted from spontaneous speech has been made more standard. Otherwise the main conclusions remain unchanged. In the examples [P] stands for progressive, [HP] for habitual progressive and [S] for simple tense constructions.

References

Comrie, B. (1976) *Aspect*. Cambridge: Cambridge University Press.

Crépin, A. (1978) *Grammaire historique de l'anglais*. Paris: Presses Universitaires de France.

Fleuriot, L. (1964) *Le vieux breton: éléments d'une grammaire*. Paris: Klincksieck.

Gros, J. (1970a) *Le trésor du breton parlé: le langage figuré*. Saint-Brieuc: Les Presses Bretonnes.

Gros, J. (1970b) *Le trésor du breton parlé: dictionnaire breton-français des expressions figurées*. Saint-Brieuc: Les Presses Bretonnes.

Gros, J. (1974) *Le trésor du breton parlé: le style populaire*. Barr-Heol, Lannion: Giraudon.

Hemon, R. (1975) *A Historical Morphology and Syntax of Breton*. Dublin: Dublin Institute for Advanced Studies.

Hewitt, S. (1985) Quelques ressemblances structurales entre le breton et l'arabe: conséquence d'une typologie commune? *La Bretagne Linguistique*, **1**, 223-62.

Hewitt, S. (1986) Le progressif en breton à la lumière du progressif anglais. *La Bretagne Linguistique*, **2**, 132-48.

Hewitt, S. (1987a) Réflexions et propositions sur l'orthographe du breton. *La Bretagne Linguistique*, **3** (forthcoming).

Hewitt, S. (1987b) The different types of auxiliary in Breton. In *La question de l'auxiliaire/l'auxiliarie en question*, **1** (1986-87). Pp183-191. Rennes: CERLICO.

Hewitt, S. (1987c) The pragmatics of Breton word order. Paper given at the Eighth International Congress of Celtic Studies, Swansea.

Hewitt, S. (1988a) Being in Breton: the auxiliarity of beẑa/boud. In *La question de l'auxiliaire/l'auxiliaire en question*, **2** (1987-88) (forthcoming). Rennes: CERLICO.

Hewitt, S. (1988b) Ur framm ewid diskriva syntax ar verb brezoneg. *La Bretagne Linguistique*, **4** (forthcoming).

Kervella, F. (1947) *Yezhadur bras ar brezhoneg*. La Baule: Skridoù Breizh.

La Bretagne Linguistique: travaux du groupe de recherche sur l'économie linguistique de la Bretagne (GRELB), Centre de recherche bretonne et celtique (CRBC), Université de

Bretagne Occidentale, B.P.814, 29285 Brest Cédex.

Leech, G. and Svartvik, J. (1975) *A Communicative Grammar of English*. London: Longman.

Le Roux, P. (1957) *Le verbe breton*. Paris: Champion.

Mossé, F. (1958) *Esquisse d'une histoire de la langue anglaise* (2e. édition). Paris: IAC.

Strang, B. (1970) *A History of English*. London: Methuen.

Swann, M. (1980) *Practical English Usage*. Oxford: Oxford University Press.

TBP: see Gros, J.

Thompson, A. and Martinet, A. (1980) *A Practical English Grammar*. Oxford: Oxford University Press.

Trépos, P. [n.d.1962]. *Grammaire breton*. Rennes: Simon.

Some Observations on the Syntax of the Breton Verbal Noun

Lenora A. Timm
University of California, Davis

1. Introduction

The Celtic verbal noun (VN) is well known for its chameleon characteristics: behaving in one syntactic environment as a noun and in another as, decidedly, a verb, its categorial status has been debated by linguists, notably in recent theoretical work on three of the Celtic languages - i.e. Anderson (1981) for Breton, McCloskey (1983) for Irish, and Sproat (1985) for Welsh. Anderson argues for nominal status of the Breton VN (phrase), whereas McCloskey and Sproat argue for their respective languages that the VN (phrase) is a verb (phrase). It is of interest that a verbal interpretation of the VN has been used to support the postulation of a VP in Irish and Welsh, traditionally assumed not to exist in these VSO languages; I shall return to this point later. Anderson, on the other hand, denies the existence of a VP in Breton (also a VSO language), a position he sees strengthened by the claim that the VN is nominal.

In this paper I extend Anderson's analysis of the Breton VN by examining some of its "verbier" manifestations not included in his analysis. The question guiding this investigation will be: where does evidence from contemporary Breton texts lead in the attempt to determine the categorial status of the Breton VN?[1]

Traditionally, Breton linguists such as Hemon (1975) and Kervella (1976) have interpreted the VN as a noun, while recognizing its possibilities to be deployed as a verb. The most ample treatment of the VN is provided by Le Roux (1957), who calls the Breton VN, and the Celtic VN in general, an "infinitif", which is "essentiellement un substantif verbal" (p. 44). Yet he goes on to say that "ce caractère substantif est resté très net dans les trois langues brittoniques, mais de bonne heure l'infinitif a eu une tendance à prendre les fonctions d'un verbe" (ibid.); this will be evident in section 3 below.

2. Nominal Features of the VN

The following characteristics of Breton VNs are commonly cited as demonstrating their nominal status; there are features both of phrase-level structure and of external distribution in the sentence:[2]

a. The VN may be preceded by an article (almost always definite) and is usually interpreted as masculine in gender; however, my perusal of modern Breton texts has shown them to be relatively sparse.

(1) ar rannañ war ar feurm
the divide on the farm
'the dividing up of the farm' (Duval, 1980: 59)

(2) an troha-baro pe an troha-bleo
the cut beard or the cut hair
'beard-cutting or hair-cutting' (Medar, 1981: 129)

b. It may be in a possessive relation with another N; this, too, is not of frequent occurrence in modern Breton, though some examples may be found:[3]

(3) Goude merenn e veze ar c'hoari domino pe gartoù
after dinner prt. was(hab.) the play dominos or cards
'After dinner there was domino or card playing' (Jacq, 1977: 81)

(4) c'hoari brezel eo ar hoari a blij deom
play war is the play prt. likes to-us
'Playing war is the game we like' (Medar, 1981: 87)

c. It is occasionally the subject or object of a verb, but it is found far less frequently in this use than as the object of a preposition (as shown in d.):

(5) Bezañ 'zo pennaouiñ ha pennaouiñ
be is pilfer and pilfer
'There is pilfering and pilfering' (Gerven, 1986b: 30)

(6) e veze d'ober paeañ al lojeiz
prt. was(hab.) to make pay the lodging
'he was to pay for the lodging' (Duval, 1980: 136)

d. It may be the object of a preposition:[4]

(7) araok kimiadiñ
before say-goodbye
'before saying goodbye' (Gerven, 1986a: 335)

(8) hep marc'hata
without bargain
'without bargaining' (Drezen, 1972: 14)

(9) evit lavarout ar wirionez
for say the truth
'to tell the truth' (Herri, 1982: 96)

(10) lezet e peuriñ
left in graze
'left in grazing [land]' (Jacq, 1977: 36)

e. It may serve as the head of a relative clause; Anderson gives an example of this, shown in (11); the latter strikes me as a fairly unusual usage, for I have found no additional ones in any texts that I have examined.

(11) Staotad a rae ar gigerez
piss prt. did (3sg. imf.) the butcher (f.)
en he dilhad gand *ar choarzin a rae*
in her clothes with the laugh prt. did (3sg.imf.)
'The butcher-woman pissed in her clothes with the laughing that she did' (Anderson, 1981: 33)

The foregoing seems a considerable list of nominal uses of the VN, but it must be remembered that several of them are of low frequency. Anderson 1981 adds to the list of nominal features by examining the VN in the *ober* periphrastic construction of Breton, whose constituent structure is shown in (12):

(12) $_{\text{peri}}$[VN-a-ober$_{\text{infl.}}$]

The vowel *a* is a preverbal particle that appears between the VN head and an inflected form of the verb *ober* 'to do/make':

(13) Selaou a reas ar vamm
listen prt. did (3sg. pret.) the mother
'the mother listened' (Herri, 1982: 194).

(14) Anavezout a ran al lezenn
know prt. I-do the law
'I know the law' (Miossec, 1987: 34)

It is argued by Anderson that inasmuch as the preverbal particle *a* is elsewhere found following a regular NP, as in

(15) Un sell du a reas Seza ouzh he gwaz
a look black prt made (3sg pret) Seza at her husband
'Seza cast a dark look at her husband' (Abeozen, 1986: 52)

(16) Yec'hed ha joa a souetan dit
Health and joy prt. I-wish to-you
'I wish you health and joy' (Malmanche, 1973: 36)

whereas the preverbal particle *e* (*ez* or *eec'h* before vowels) is used when any other sort of constituent precedes the verb, as in

(17) En em gavet **e** oant e Brest
reflx. found prt. they-were in Brest
'They found themselves in Brest' (Huon, 1971: 14)

(18) Betek neuze **e** oa bet sae ganin
Until then prt. was been skirt with-me
'Until then I had been in skirts' (ar Gow, 1978: 70)

this then constitutes indirect evidence for classifying the VN as an NP. He concludes that the VN (and any complements it may have) in the periphrastic construction shown in (12) is a verbal NP, thereby rejecting his earlier interpretation (with S. Chung, 1977) of the VN and its complements in the *ober* periphrastic as some sort of VP.

The appearance of the VN in the *ober* periphrastic is one of its more interesting uses. On the basis of sentences such as (13) and (14), especially when compared with fully nominal counterparts, as in (15) and (16), it is tempting to say that the VN is clearly serving in these instances as a noun, and specifically as the direct object of the verb *ober*. But matters become less clear when the VN within the *ober* construction itself takes a verbal complement such as a personal pronoun as direct or indirect object, or an adverbial adjunct. Cf. (19) to (26):

(19) Trugarekaat ac'hanon a reas c'hoaz
thank of-me prt. did (3sg. pret.) again
'He thanked me again' (Herri, 1982: 181)

(20) rak he c'harout a ra kalz
for her love prt. did (3sg. imf.) much
'for he loved her greatly' (ar Gow, 1978: 41)

(21) komz outo a ra ar hoarierien war-eeun
speak to-them prt. does the players directly
'the actors speak to them directly' (F.B., 1987: 25)

(22) ober a reas din ur mousc'hoarzh
do prt. did(3sg. pret.) to-me a smile
'She gave me a smile' (Drezen, 1972a: 15)

(23) deraouiñ boudinelliñ a reas e benn
begin throb prt. did (3sg. pret.) his head
'his head began to throb' (Konan 1980:65)

(24) rentañ servij d'an holl a rae
render service to the all prt. did (3sg. imf.)
'He rendered service to everyone' (Gerven, 1986a: 339)

(25) kompren mat a ran
understand good prt. I-do
'I understand well' (Duval, 1980: 148)

(26) anavezout a-walc'h a ran ac'hanout
know enough prt. I-do of-you (sg.)
'I know you well enough' (ibid.: 35)

It is difficult to maintain the case for the VN as NP in these strongly verbal environments within the periphrastic construction; the VN appears in such contexts to be functioning much more as a verb than a noun, paralleling some of the structures in which it is found incontestably as the only verb in the clause (see section 3).[5] The basic constitutent structure of *ober* clauses as shown in (12) has many variations due to the permissible insertion of verbal complements and modifiers, as suggested by (19)-(26) - a full analysis of these possibilities is underway. In any event, the argument developed by Anderson that because the particle in this construction is always *a* therefore the VN is an NP is weakened by at least two further facts: (a) the preverbal particle may, in other types of sentences, sometimes be *e*, even when an NP precedes it;[6] (b) the preverbal particle may be *a* even when something other than an NP precedes it. Cf. sentences (27) to (30):

(27) Ur pennad e chomas evel-se
a moment prt. remained (3sg. pret.) like-that
'He remained like that for a moment' (Konan, 1980: 110)

(28) evit gouzout piv e oa ar paotr
for know who prt. was the man
'in order to know who the man was' (Herri, 1982: 169)

(29) Ha setu a anavezas mouezh Yann ar Rouz
and there prt recognized (3sg pret) voice Y ar R
'And then she recognized the voice of Yann ar Rouz' (Duval, 1980:67)

(30) Leun kouch a oa ar sal
full inclined prt. was the room
'The room was filled to overflowing' (Treger, 1988: 12)

As examples (29)-(30) show with, respectively, an adverb and and adjective phrase preceding the particle *a*, the distribution of the preverbal particles does not lend unqualified support to the claim that the VN in the *ober* construction must be an NP because it is followed by *a*. In addition, there are several distinctly verbal characteristics and uses of the VN which need to be considered.

3. Verbal Features of the VN

a. It may be modified by adverbs:[7]

(31) da choarziñ kenañ, kenañ
to laugh greatly greatly
'to laugh heartily, heartily' (Riou, 1944: 14)

(32) hep morse klemm na fallgaloniñ
without never complain nor become discouraged
'without ever complaining or becoming discouraged'
(Kervella, 1986a: 102)

(33) gouzout a raent lenn mat-tre
know prt. did (3pl. imf.) read good-very
ha skrivañ difazi a-walc'h
and write faultless enough
'they knew how to read very well and write sufficiently without error' (ar Gow, 1978: 20)

b. It can follow an independent subject to indicate past action; this is an especially common construction in narrative and storytelling, and is always introduced by the conjunction *ha(g)* 'and'; VNs in this construction may be coordinated across clauses, as in (36):

(34) Ha me skrivañ kement-se war va c'haier
and I write all-that on my notebook
'And I wrote all of that in my notebook' (Kervella, 1986b: 354)

(35) hag eñ ha mond war-du an antant
and he and go toward the farm
'and he went toward the farm' (Miossec, 1987: 36)

(36) Hag ar mevel bras ha lezel e gorn-butun
and the servant big and leave his pipe
war an daol ha mont da heul ar paotr-saout
on the table and go to pursuit the lad-cows
'And the big servant left his pipe on the table and went after the cowherd' (Abeozen, 1986: 70).

c. It may be preceded by the preposition *da* in a construction having an initiative aspect; the sequence, as in b., always begins with *ha(g)* 'and', followed by a subject (typically pronominal):

(37) ha me da asantiñ
and I to agree
'so I agreed' (Gerven, 1986a: 353)

(38) Ha hemañ da bêo eur litrad deze
and that-one to pay a litre to-them

'And he paid for a litre [of wine] for them' (Rolland, 1985: 12)

(39) Hag hi da zigeriñ an nor gant evezh
and she to open the door with care
'And she went to open the door carefully' (Konan, 1981: 50)

d. It may be used as an imperative:

(40) Tennañ ho potoù diouzhtu hag o reiñ din
pull your(pl) boots immediately and them give to-me
'Pull off your boots at once and give them to me' (Konan, 1981:42)

(41) Bevañ evel a-raok, en em douezіañ gant an dud
live like before reflx. mingle with the people
'Live as before, mix with people' (Kervella, 1986a: 106)

e. It may be used as a nonfinite verbal complement of a main verb; this is an extremely frequent use of the VN (and its immediate complements).

(42) raktal e fell dezhi *dimeziñ*
immediately prt. is-necessary to-her marry
'She must get married at once' (Priel, 1950: 53).

(43) Gallout a ra *dont da ziv eur*
be able prt. does come to two hour
'He can come at two o'clock' (Herri, 1982: 176).

(44) ret eo *skeiñ war an houarn* e-pad m'eo tomm
necessary is knock on the iron while is hot
'It's necessary to strike while the iron is hot' (ibid: 179).

(45) Ne zeue kammed den *da c'houlenn tra pe dra digantañ*
neg. came never person to ask thing or thing from-him
'No one ever came to ask a single thing of him' (Huon, 1971: 36)

f. It may be used as a verbal complement after such interrogatives as *penaos* 'how?', *pelec'h* 'where?', and *petra* 'what?'

(46) Penaos ober bremañ?
How do now
'How to act now?' (Desbordes, 1986: 37)

(47) Pelec'h mont?
where go?
'Where to go?' (Herri, 1982: 176)

(48) Petra debriñ neuze?
what eat then
'What to eat then?' (Mouton, 1986: 206)

Cf. (49) - (51), which are unacceptable with a following NP in a direct question:

(49) *Penaos (al) levr?
how (the) book

(50) *Pelec'h (an) ti?
where (the) house

(51) *Petra (ar) boued
what (the) food?

g. It may take direct objects, including those that may be adjuncts only of verbs, such as *kement-se*.

(52) koll amzer e rafen
lose time prt. I-would-do
'I would lose time (Herri, 1982: 175)

(53) evit kompren ano ar parkoù
for understand name the fields
'to understand the names of the fields' (Miossec, 1987: 26)

(54) ha me skrivañ kement-se
and I write all-that
'and I wrote all that' (Kervella, 1986b: 354)

Regarding (54), note that a sequence of two nouns, such as *levrioù brezhoneg* is grammatical, but that *kement-se*, itself a NP may not follow another noun; thus **levrioù kement-se* is ungrammatical and must be reworked as a PP: *kement-se a levrioù* ('so many books').

h. It may be used as a head verb on which another clause is dependent:

(55) hep soñjal [pa vez an tan pe an brezel
without think [if is (hab.) the fire or the war
war dreuz an nor]
on threshhold the door]
'without thinking if it is fire or war on the threshold of the door' (Kidna, 1985: 346)

(56) da hortoz [ma teufe ar re all en-dro
to wait [conj would-come (3sg) the those other returned
'to wait until the others would come back' (Skaouidig, 1987: 5)

(57) O welout ['oa antreet en he zremenvan] n'em lakaas
progprt see [was entered in her agony] reflx put(3sg pret)
Mère Saint Lucien da lâret ... pedennoù
Mother Saint Lucien to say prayers
'Seeing that she was at the point of death, Mother Saint Lucien set about saying...prayers' (Duval, 1980: 111)

i. It may be the (only) verb in a tenseless clause, typically introduced by a preposition; a very popular structure is the one shown in (60), introduced by the preposition *hep* 'without', having the constituent structure [hep-VN-$Prep_{conj.}$].

(58) *Evit tennañ peoc'h eus va genoù*, ec'h aotreas
for extract peace from my mouth prt ordered (3sgpret)
din va goulenn
to-me my request
'In order to keep me quiet, he ordered my request for me' (Duval, 1986: 67).

(59) *goude ober ur c'hwesadenn bennak a-gleiz hag*
after do a sniffing some left and
a-zehou ez eas er chapel
right prt. went (3sg. pret.) in-the chapel
'after giving a sniff to the left and to the right, he entered the chapel (Konan, 1980: 125)

(60) *Hep gouzout dezhañ zoken* e oa en em lakaet
without know to-him even prt. was reflx. put (ppl.)
da sutellat
to whistle
'Without his even knowing it, he had started to whistle' (Kervella, 1986a: 104)

j. In another type of untensed clause containing a VN as the only verbal element, a conjugated form of the preposition *da* 'to' is placed at or near the beginning of the clause in the sequence [da_{conj}-(Prep)-VN-X]; this is a turn of phrase very typically Breton, with a range of translations possible in English, depending upon the larger discourse context:

(61) din da c'houzout!
to-me to believe
'I should know' (Priel, 1950: 26)

(62) Deomp da dapout anezhi en he c'hlud!
to-us to take of-her in her perch
'Let's take her in her perch!' (Drezen, 1972b: 57)

(63) Dit lakaat evezh mar kerez
to-you (sg.) put attention if you(sg.)-want
'It's for you to pay attention if you want' (Malmanche, 1973: 49)

(64) kent dezhañ va c'hrafignat an disterañ
before to-him me scratch the least
'before he can scratch me in the least' (Konan, 1980: 122)

4. Discussion

In comparing sections 2 and 3, it can be seen that the verbal traits and uses of the VN documented in examples (21)-(64) push just as much, or more, toward a verbal classification of this element as do its nominal characteristics adduced earlier (and leaned on by Anderson). Finally, lending further support to its categorial status as a verb is the VN's appearance in the progressive construction of Breton. This, in its simple or basic form, has the structure:

(65) [bezañ-progprt-VN-(X)][8]

as in (66):

(66) Emaon o lenn (ar gazetenn)
I-am-sit. progprt. read (the newspaper)
'I am reading (the newspaper)'

There are analogous constructions in Irish and Welsh which have lately been drawn on to demonstrate the existence of a VP of the traditional sort (a maximal projection in X-bar terms) in these two languages. In a work in progress I examine the scope of this construction in Breton and assess its implications for the claim that a VP can exist in a VSO language. Though the data have not yet been fully worked through, I anticipate that the Breton progressive construction will not pass all of the tests that are said to establish its status as a VP (or V2) in the work of McCloskey (1983) and Sproat (1985), for Irish and Welsh, respectively. Yet, undeniably, the Breton progressive construction is verbal and not nominal in its syntactic function, and is certainly so in semantic force. The substructure of the progressive (that portion excluding a form of the verb *bezañ* 'be')

(67) [progprtVN-(X)]

is quite clearly a nonfinite complement of the copula and may be transitive or intransitive. While it is true that in intransitive sentences certain NPs can be substituted for the progressive substructure shown in (67), such substitution cannot take place in transitive structures. Cf. (68a-b) with (69a-b) and (70a-b):

(68a) Emañ [o tont en ti]
is (sit.) [progprt. come in-the house]
'She is coming into the house'

(68b) Emañ [Janig en ti]
'Janig is in the house'

(69a) Edo [o klask ho ti]
was (sit.) [progprt. look-for your (pl.) house]
'She was looking for your house'

(69b) *Edo [Janig ho ti]
*Was Janig your house

(70a) Me 'oa [o troc'hañ ed du]
I was [progprt. cut wheat black]
'I was cutting buckwheat' (Duval, 1980: 112)

(70b) *Me 'oa [kontell ed du]
*I was knife wheat black

The degree of syntactic/semantic bonding between the VN and its complement in the progressive construction is great, and points to their perception as some sort of coherent unit. E.g., the progressive substructure shown in (67) may readily be shifted to the left of *bezañ* in matrix clauses:

(71a) [O klask h ti] edon
[progprt. look-for your (pl.) house] I-was
'I was looking for your house' (Priel, 1950: 31)

(71b) [Oc'h ober goap ouzhin] emaout
[progprt make mockery at-me] you-(sg)-are (sit.)
'You are making fun of me' (Herri, 1982: 33)

The evidence I have suggests that that a direct object of the [prog. prt-VN] sequence may only be fronted when the it is an interrogative, as shown by the following:

(72) Peseurt emaout oc'h ober?
what are-you (sgsit.) progprt. do/make
'What are you doing?' (ar Gow, 1978: 64)

(73) Nezue peseurt emaout o kanañ?
so what are-you (sgsit.) progprt. sing
'So what are you singing?' (Malmanche, 1973: 89)

(74) Petra emaoc'h o soñjal?
what are-you (plsit.) progprt. think
'What are you thinking?' (ibid.: 98)

Texts examined show no evidence of the fronting of only the direct object in declarative sentences, though they *may* prove acceptable, or marginally so, if presented to native speakers - e.g., sentences (71') and (75):

(71') ?Ho ti edon o klask
your (pl.) house I-was (sit.) progprt. look-for
'I was looking for your house'

(75) ?Skeul ar c'hrignol emañ o tiskenn
ladder the granary is (sit.) progprt. descend
'The granary ladder he is taking down'
(permutation of Priel, 1950:16)

My own intuition is that sentences (71') and (75) would be acceptable if the fronted and topicalized direct object were repeated with a resumptive pronoun: i.e., *ho ti, edon o klask anezhañ* and *skeul ar c'hrignol, emañ o tiskenn anezhañ.* If correct, this further underscores the uninterruptibility of such transitive VNs with their (non-interrogative) direct object complements.[9] The segment therefore does look like some sort of verb phrase; but it cannot be so construed in the traditional sense of VP = [V_{main} (O)] since the progressive substructure of (67) is always dependent on the presence of an inflected form of the verb *bezañ* or another tensed verb.[10] The tensed verb supports the semantic realization of the VN, and its absence leaves the progressive substructure as a post nominal modifier (still verbal in semantic effect and perhaps interpretible as a truncated relative clause) - cf. (76)-(77); or as an adverbial modifiying another verb (78)-(79):[11]

(76) Bretoned *o chom er c'harter-se*
Bretons progprt. live in-the quarter-that
'Bretons living in that quarter' (Duval, 1980: 156)

(77) ar medisin *o tont d'he gwelout bemdez*
the doctor progprt. come to-her see everyday
'the doctor coming to see her everyday' (ibid.: 139)

(78) Skrijal a rae Loeiz *o tistagañ* ar ger
scream prt did (3sg imf) L progprt pronounce the word
'Louis screamed in pronouncing the word' (Kervella, 1986b: 350)

(79) hag aner e vefe din terriñ va dent
and vain prt. would-be (sg.) to-me break my teeth
o krignat va chadennoù
progprt. gnaw my chains
'and it would be useless for me to break my teeth by gnawing my chains' (Priel, 1950: 198)

On balance, then, the substructure of the progressive construction shown in (67) would seem to be most plausibly analyzed as a nonfinite verb phrase that necessarily complements another verb, or a noun (phrase).

5. Conclusion

Though space has not permitted a comprehensive investigation of the distribution and functions of the Breton VN, the data presented lead to the following conclusions: the Breton VN does indeed manifest some of the syntactic "schizophrenia" (McCloskey, 1983; cf. also Stenson, 1981) associated with the VNs in Irish and Welsh, capable of serving as either a noun or verb in Breton clauses; however, in the majority of its appearances, the syntactic distribution and the semantic role of the VN call for its interpretation as a (nonfinite) verb. This interpretation does not oblige one to conclude that there is a VP of the traditional sort in Breton: two of the salient verbal constructions in which the VN is the principal element - the *ober* periphrastic and progressive constructions - are always complements of an auxiliary; moreover, a pronominal direct object in these structures may precede the VN, yielding the constitutent order [D.O.-VN-Aux], which scarcely resembles a VP in the usual sense - cf. (80) and (81):

(80) E drugarekaat a reas Garan
him thank prt. did (3sg. pret.) Garan
'Garan thanked him' (Konan, 1981: 62)

(81) Emaom ouzh e c'hortoz da zonet er-maez
we-are (sit.) progprt. him wait to come outside
'We are waiting for him to come out' (ibid.: 62)

In sentences in which the VN is the sole verbal element (as shown in examples in paragraphs 3b-d), there are some sequences of constituents that do more closely resemble a VP (as in (40) *tennañ ho potoù* 'take off your boots'), but these are special modal or aspectual uses of the VN and as such are not representative of basic word order of the language, which, as I have documented elsewhere (Timm, 1986), is strongly VSO in nature. In sum, the Breton VN is unquestionably a highly versatile syntactic constituent, and is one of the distinctive and ingenious components of the verbal system of the language.

Notes

1. The data drawn on for this study come from 22 writers of twentieth-century Breton (one, Rolland, is actually a well-known storyteller); their material consists chiefly of fiction and memoirs, but included also are a few essays from literary journals. Although dialect variation is apparent in some of the works, the examples cited throughout this paper represent widespread usages.

   There are currently two popular orthographies in use for writing Breton; the reader should therefore not be alarmed at seeing such orthographical doublets as *ur/eur* 'a', *da hortoz/da c'hortoz* 'to wait', *gwelout/gweled* 'see', etc.

   Abbreviations used in the glosses to the examples or elsewhere in the text as as are follows: conj. = conjugated; hab. = habitual (form of the verb); infl. = inflected (form of the verb); imf. = imperfect; imp. = imperative; neg. = negative (marker); peri. = periphrastic construction (with *ober*); pl. = plural; ppl. = (past) participle; poss. = possessive; prep. = preposition; pret. = preterite; prog. = progressive (aspect); prn. = pronoun; prt. = (preverbal) particle; reflx. = reflexive (marker); sg. = singular; sit. = situational (form of the verb); VN = verbal noun.

2. The Breton VN is far less predictable in form than, say, the infinitive of the Romance languages. Kervella (1976: 110-111) lists 13 different endings that the VN may carry (*-añ, -iñ, -at, -out, -et, -al, el, -en, -in, -ezh, -er, -ek, -a*), and cites over 90 VNs that bear no ending at all. Many of these variants will be evident in the examples cited in this paper.

3. Note that a sequence of |(prep.)-poss. prn.-VN| is not usually interpretible as a possessive construction in Mod. Breton. E.g., *d'he direnkañ* is 'to disturb her' (and not *'her disturbing (someone)'; *unan bennak o tont d'e gerc'hat pe d'e welout* is 'someone coming to find him or to see him' (and not *'someone coming for his finding or his seeing'). However, a possessive interpretation of this construction is encountered more in Middle and Early Modern Breton: Hemon (1975: 88) cites examples, with variants of the VN 'be', as *dre he bout parfet* 'through her being perfect' and *evit ma besan ampereur* 'in spite of my being emperor' from, respectively, the seventeenth and eighteenth centuries. Willis (1986) uses the possessive interpretation of the analogous construction in Welsh as a piece of evidence in favor of the nominal status of the Welsh VN. Anderson (1981) similarly points to the putatively possessive meaning of such a sequence as *sevel an ti* 'building |of| the house'

(structurally analogous to *doriou an ti* 'doors of the house') as evidence for the nominal status of the Breton VN. I do not agree that *sevel an ti* has, necessarily or uniquely, a possessive meaning, and would argue that a larger syntactic context must be available in order to deduce the appropriate semantic interpretation. Standing on its own, the sequence *sevel an ti* would most likely be interpreted as an imperative 'build the house' (with *an ti* as a direct object). Embedded in larger constructions, *an ti* would still most likely be interpreted as the direct object of the VN, as in

(i) Sevel an ti a raent
build the house prt. they-did (imf.)
'They built the house'

(ii) O sevel a ti emaint
progprt. build the house they-are (sit.)
'they are building the house'

(iii) Pelec'h sevel an ti?
where build the house
'Where to build the house?'

The clearest example of a possessive interpretation would have the definite article preceding the VN, as in

(iv) Gwelet 'm eus ar sevel an ti
seen I-have the build the house
'I've seen the building of the house'

However, as noted in the text (section 2a), such definite article + VN occurs fairly rarely in Mod. Breton, and I offer ex. (iv) only dubiously, to illustrate the possibility of a possessive meaning.

4. This is an extremely common construction, one that often serves as the basis for untensed clauses, typically best translated into English with the *-ing* participle.

5. Another linguist who has written on the Breton *ober* periphrastic, Wojcik (1976), does not seem to question the verbal status of the Breton VN, and argues that the periphrastic construciton results from a rule of Verb Fronting that places the verb (=VN) in clause-initial position; by his analysis, this then gives rise to the auxiliary *ober* as support for the main verb.

6. It is true that the NP in such cases is usually semantically an adverbial

or in a copular construction in which the NP preceding the *e* is the predicate nominal. As Anderson points out (1981: 38, n. 4), predicative nominatives may have different syntactic properties than referential nominatives. Nevertheless, the rules underlying the distribution of *a* and *e* are not simply stated, forming part of a larger complex system of anaphora recently explored in a fine study by Urien (1987).

7. This is often ambiguous in Breton, since many adverbs are homophonous with the semantically related adjective - e.g., *prim* may mean either 'quick' or 'quickly'; however, there is a large class of adverbs that have no adjectival twin - e.g., *morse*, 'never', *a-walc'h* 'enough, sufficiently', *a-grenn* 'completely', etc.

8. *Bezañ* is the verb 'be', which has a special form beginning in *em-* to indicate location in space or time; this form is often found in the progressive construction, though ordinary or habitual forms of *bezañ* may also occur in the construction. The progressive particle has the basic form *o*, with written variants *oc'h* before vowels and *ouzh* before personal pronouns (whatever their phonological shape) found as direct objects of the VN.

9. Their cleftability also remains to be tested - e.g.,

   ? |ho ti | eo |edon o klask|
   |your (pl.) house| is |I-was (sit.) progprt look for|
   'It's your house I was looking for'

   I have found virtually no examples of this sort of structure in texts. (See Timm (1987) for a discussion of Breton clefts.)

10. Verbs of perception often take the progressive substructure as a complement type.

11. This is an oversimplification, though it will suffice here, of the other functions of the progressive construction-minus-copula, which are investigated more fully in a work in progress.

References

Abeozen (1986) *Pirc'hirin kala-goañv*. Brest: Al Liamm.

Anderson, S. R. (1981) Topicalization in Breton. *Proceedings of the Berkeley Linguistics Society*, 7, 27-39.

Anderson, S. R. and Chung, S. (1977) Grammatical relations and clause structure in verb-initial languages. In P. Cole and J. Saddock (eds.) *Grammatical Relations (=Syntax and Semantics, 8)*. New York: Academic Press. Pp1-25.

ar Gow, Y. (1978) *E skeud tour bras Sant Jermen*. Brest: Al Liamm.

Desbordes, Y. (1986) Pet skrivagner? *Al Liamm*, **234**, 34-40.

Drezen, Y. (1972a) *An dour en-dro dan inizi*. Brest: Al Liamm.

Drezen, Y. (1972b) *Skol-louarn veig trebern (lodenn gentañ)*. Brest: Al Liamm.

Duval, A. (1980) *Tad-kozh Roperz-Huon (1822-1902)*. Lesneven: Hor Yezh.

F.B. (1987) Eun anti-Bro-Bagan?. *Brud Nevez*, **108**, 23-27.

Gerven, Y. (1986a) Aldebaran. *Al Liamm*, **239**, 330-345.

Gerven, Y. (1986b) *Brestiz o vreskenn*. Brest: Al Liamm.

Hemon, R. (1975) *A historical morphology and syntax of Breton*. Dublin: Dublin Institute for Advanced Studies.

Herri, H. (1982) *Evel-se e oamp*. Brest: Al Liamm.

Huon, R. (1971) *An irin glas*. Brest: Al Liamm.

Jacq, G. (1977) *Pinvidigezh ar paour*. Brest: Al Liamm.

Kervella, F. (1976) *Yezhadur bras ar brezhoneg*. Brest: Al Liamm.

Kervella, G. (1986a) Ar saout. *Al Liamm*, **235**, 96-109.

Kervella, G. (1986b) Charretour-Doue. *Al Liamm*, **239**, 346-358.

Kidna, S. (1985) Aze an dour a oa sklaer ha klouar. *Al Liamm*, **233**, 346-359.

Konan, R. (1980) *Lannevern e kañv*. Brest: Al Liamm.

Konan, R. (1981) *Ur marchadour a vontroulez*. Brest: Al Liamm.

Le Roux, P. (1957) *Le verbe breton (morphologie, syntaxe)*. Rennes: Plihon.

Malmanche, T. (1973) *An intanvez arzhur*. Brest: Al Liamm.

McCloskey, James. (1983) A VP in a VSO language? In G. Gazdar, E. Klein and G. Pullum, (eds.) *Order, Concord and Constituency*. Dordrecht: Foris. Pp9-55.

Medar, T. (1981) *An tri aotrou*. Guingamp: Couvent des capucins.

Miossec, J-C. (1987) *Enezenn ar razed ha kontadennou all*. Brest: Brud Nevez.

Mouton, J. E. (1986) Progress is beautiful. *Al Liamm,* **236-237,** 206-208.

Priel, J. (1950) *Ar spontailh*. La Baule: Al Liamm - Tir na N-og.

Riou, J. (1944) *An ti satanazet*. La Baule: Skridoù Breizh.

Rolland, J-L. (1985) Ar voualh aour. *Brud Nevez,* **83,** 9-25.

Skaouidig, M. (1987) Marhig glaz Yann ar hovel. *Brud Nevez,* **110,** 5-9.

Sproat, R. (1985) Welsh syntax and VSO structure. *Natural Language and Linguistic Theory,* **3,** 176-216.

Stenson, N. (1981) *Studies in Irish syntax*. Tübingen: Gunter Narr Verlag.

Timm, L. (1986) Word order in 20th-century Breton. *ERIC Document* 274199.

Timm, L. (1987) Cleft structures in Breton. *Word,* **38,** 127-42.

Treger, F. (1988) Seizh avel. *Le peuple breton,* **293,** 12.

Urien, J-Y. (1987) *La trame d'une langue. Le breton*. Lesneven: Mouladurioù Hor Yezh.

Willis, P. (1986) Is the Welsh verbal noun a verb or a noun?. Unpublished manuscript.

Wojcik, Richard. (1976) Verb fronting and auxiliary *do* in Breton. *Recherches linguistiques à Montréal,* **6,** 259-278.

Spirantization to Lenition in Breton: Interpretation of Morphophonological Variability*

John S. Hennessey Jr.

1. Introduction

Language death may be defined as the final shift within a speech community from the use of one language to the use of another, for all members and in all contexts. Phenomena surrounding such communal shifts in language choice have been the focus of increasing interest by social scientists and linguists. Research has been directed toward the social and economic correlates of language shift, the ethnography of speaking and contextual determinants of code choice, and most recently the possible structural ramifications for the dying language of shifting language dominance. Recent studies of terminal speech communities, notably Dorian on the Gaelic of East Sutherland (Dorian, 1973 and subsequent) and Schmidt on Dyirbal, a language of northeastern Australia (Schmidt, 1985) have uncovered sometimes striking differences in syntax, morphology and morphophonology between the production in the dying language of its oldest and youngest speakers.

Such findings have led researchers to hypothesize that there may be distinct characteristics of languages in the death process, reflecting shifting language dominance and competence in the communities in which they are used. In the final stages of communal language shift, terminal speakers may be expected to display clear evidence of reduced competence in the dying language and interference from the competing language, including in the most extreme cases destabilization of linguistic structures, loss of complex and/or rare features, overgeneralization of common features, large scale loss of "native" lexicon, and relexification by borrowing. Particularly likely to suffer are features without parallels in the dominant language.

Dorian (1973, 1981) has suggested that loss of the types just mentioned characterizes the collective competence in the losing language of any bilingual community. The effects will be more pronounced temporally and generationally as shift proceeds and the dominance of the replacing language increases, but even fully proficient bilinguals will necessarily have some reduced competence in the non-dominant language and some characteristic forms will be lost.

This paper will examine one proposed example of a language death grammatical phenomenon in contemporary Breton, the waning of spirant mutation (Dressler 1972, 1981; Favereau 1984; Le Dû 1986), and will adduce evidence that it should not be understood in those terms. Historical and contemporary dialect data will be brought to bear to show that the current situation everywhere reflects a normal stage in a pattern of long-term and widespread innovation in the mutational system having its roots many generations back in monolingual speech communities.

2. The claims

In his 1972 paper "On the phonology of language death" Wolfgang Dressler describes ongoing mutational innovation in the Breton of Buhulien (Lannion, Côtes-du-Nord) in terms of primary independent rule loss" in Breton, specifically the simplification and loss by terminal Breton speakers of the rules that generate the initial consonant mutations. While the paper contains a number of general claims regarding the mutations at Buhulien and in contemporary Breton as a whole, the primary grammatical facts treated concern generationally marked variability relating to the practice of the spirant mutation. The key facts presented are:

> ... teenagers use lenition or no mutation at all after the spirantizing numerals '3, 4' 9', and also increasingly after the spirantizing possessives *ma*, 'my', *i*, 'her', *o*, 'their', so *ma benn*, 'my head' etc., is heard more often than *ma fenn/venn/ ˇfenn* from *penn*. (1972: 450).

and

> ... the older generation uses lenition instead of the inherited

spirantization after the numeral [n(ao)] '9', but only optionally - the teenagers never use a mutation after '9'; the older generation uses either the standard spirantization or lenition after the numerals '3' and '4' - the teenagers use lenition only. (1972: 452).

That is to say that older speakers variably replace spirant mutation by lenition after the numerals but preserve it after possessives, while younger speakers regularize the use of lenition after numerals and extend the innovation to possessives as well.

Dressler's older speakers appear to be members of the pre-First World War generation, while his younger speakers were persons born around 1955. Thus the changes described occur over a span of three generations.

Dressler interprets the usage of the younger members of the community as unmotivated grammatical simplification by overgeneralization of most common rules, resulting in functional loss in the dialect through what he calls the confounding of the possessive pronoun inflections (Dressler, 1981), specifically characteristic of declining linguistic competence in the terminal generation of a dying speech community.

Favereau (1984) reports a highly similar set of phenomena in his thesis on the Breton of Poullaouen (Finistère). At Poullaouen lenition after the numerals is general in the speech of all living speakers. The oldest generation, roughly comparable in age to Dressler's older speakers, use only spirant mutation after the spirantizing possessives. The next generation, however, persons born between 1920 and 1940, show a distinct tendency toward innovative use of lenition in these environments, particularly after the third singular feminine *hi* and the first singular *ma*. By the third generation, persons born between 1940 and 1960, this tendency is generalized with innovative lenition also occurring third plural *o* and becoming the predominant mutation pattern in these environments.

While no theoretical claims are put forward, the data are presented in the context of a more general discussion of generational language differences evidencing decline in the Breton of Poullaouen.

But is there, in fact, anything about these innovations other than the circumstances in which they are being carried out, to suggest that language decay is involved? Are they in some way incompatible with processes of change in healthy languages or with general evolutionary trends in modern Breton? I believe the answer to be no. Innovative lenition in environments where spirant mutation historically occurred is quite common in modern Breton, and has been a feature of the language for some time.

3. History of the innovation

The earliest stage of the innovative replacement of spirant mutation by lenition dates back at least to the beginning of the eighteenth century. In the early modern period, when initial mutations are first generally marked in the written sources, spirant mutation is usually found in the environments of the numerals 3, 4 and 9, as well as with the possessives and enclitic object pronouns 'my/me', 'her', 'their/them', and to a varying extent 'our/us'. However, almost from the beginning instances of lenition can be found. Hemon (1975) cites such examples as *teir Bater*, 'three Our Fathers' and *pevar dra*, 'four things' from early Leonard texts, the *Heriou Brezonec ha Latin* of 1710, and the *Reflexionou Profitabl var an Finvezou diveza* of about 1718. Examples continue to be found in texts from later in the century, becoming more common toward and into the nineteenth century. Le Fèvre, in his *Grammaire celto-bretonne* of 1818 notes both spirant mutation and lenition as common with the numerals in Trégor.

By the second half of the nineteenth century the innovation is well advanced, as evidenced by the *Atlas linguistique de la Basse-Bretagne* (ALBB, Le Roux, 1924). The relevant maps, no. 372 "3, 4 tailors", no. 384 "3, 4, 9 dogs", no. 385 "3, 4 bitches", no. 509 "3 boys", and no. 578 "3, 4 tables" show that lenition in place of spirant mutation is to be found after the numerals over a wide area, including all of western and northern Cornouaille, eastern and south central Léon, Goélo, and adjacent areas of eastern, southern and western Trégor, as well as peripheral points in northern and southern Vannetais. Spirant mutation is still found after the numerals in three areas: in western Léon in an area centered on points 1 through 3 (Ouessant-Plourin-Landéda) and often including points 4 and 8 (St. Frégant, Trébabu); in north central Trégor in an area centered on points 16, 17 and 19 (Pleubian-Prat-Plouzelambre); and in the south in a large area including generally the southern part of Haute-Cornuaille and all of Bas-Vannetais, extending regularly as far west as points 43 and 53 (Edern, Clohars-Fouesnant), north as far as points 44 (Roudouallec) and 61-2 (Cleguerec, Ploerdut), and east and south regularly to points 64 (Bubry) and 84 (Languidic) and sometimes beyond.

All this early evidence for lenition in spirant mutation environments relates to the numerals. But the most recent innovation at Buhulien and Poullaouen go beyond these environments to involve the possessives as well. Evidence concerning lenition after spirantizing possessives is slim, and it can be said with some certainty that this innovation has nowhere near the age of that with the numerals. Hemon (1975) cites no examples of lenition after spirantizing possessives, nor do the relevant ALBB maps, no. 41 "my brother", no. 172 "my hand", no. 174 "her hand", no. 175 "their hands", no. 383 "my/our dogs", and no. 572 "my father", show anywhere anything other than spirant mutation of voiceless stops and non-mutation of other consonants. Nor do major twentieth century grammars such as Le Clerc, Kervella and Trépos, which admit without necessarily approving the commonplace of lenition after the numerals, make any mention of lenition after possessives.

There is, however, some evidence to support a claim that the innovation had begun to spread to possessives already in the nineteenth century. At the same time that spirant mutation of voiceless stops is being replaced by lenition after the numerals, there is some extension of lenition in the same environments to other lenitable initials not affected by spirant mutation. Thus Hemon cites *tri c'her*, 'three words', *teir c'hreunnen*, 'three grains', again from the beginning of the eighteenth century. Later examples also show lenition of radical *b* and *m* in nineteenth century sources. ALBB also shows sporadic lenition of voiced stops after numerals.

Le Roux (1896) in discussing this phenomenon after the numerals at Pleubian mentions that such mutations are also noted by Loth after *ma*, 'my' and *o*, 'their' in his field notes from Plougonven, east of Morlaix, and Glomel, near Carhaix. The presence of these mutations can be considered evidence for lenition of voiceless stops as well in these areas.

At the same time Le Moal, in his 1890 supplement to Troude's dictionary, notes that after numerals *and possessives* voiceless stops may be either spirantized or lenited.

Timm (1985) notes that at Plounevezel, adjacent to Carhaix, the oldest speakers in her sample, born before the First World

War, already have absolutely normative lenition after the numerals and nearly normative lenition after the possessives as well. This suggests strongly a starting date for local innovation with the possessives not later than the 1870s and possibly a good bit earlier.

4. The Pattern of Innovation

There is repeated evidence in contemporary descriptions of Breton dialects that the innovative substitution of lenition for spirant mutation follows a regular pattern of development. We have already seen that lenition after the numerals appears to be quite a bit older than lenition after the spirantizing possessives. But lenition after the numerals was not adopted everywhere at the same time. In many areas it was still not found in the late nineteenth century (cf. Le Roux, 1924) and indeed is not found in the late twentieth century, as in many parts of the south. Spirant mutation is preserved after 3, 4 and 9 at St Ivy (German, 1984), at Lanvenegen (Evenou, 1987), at Langonnet (Plourin, 1982), at Querrien and at Arzano (Derrien, 1975).

The temporal relationship between lenition after numerals and after possessives is not only general; the phenomena are linked in specific sequence everywhere they occur. Where lenition after possessives is found at all, it is normative or nearly so after numerals. This is the pattern found at Kerauzern, at Groix (Ternes, 1970), Bothoa (Humphreys, 1985), Plounevezel (Timm, 1985), Berrien (Plonéis, 1975), St Servais (Plourin, 1982), Plougrescant (Le Dû, 1978), Bourg Blanc (Falc'hun, 1951), St-Pol-de-Léon (Sommerfelt, 1978), and Pleubian (Le Roux, 1896). It is also the pattern found at Buhulien and Poullaouen.

There is also evidence of an innovational hierarchy with regard to the possessives themselves. Wherever there is indication of innovation with only a single possessive, that possessive is the first person singular (Plonéis 1975; Le Dû 1978; Plourin 1982; Humphreys 1985). On occasion there is indication of a single possessive relatively resistant to the innovation: the third person feminine singular (Falc'hun 1951). Thus an implicational model of sorts can be developed:

3, 4, 9, < my < their, our < her

In the relatively few instances where information is available there are suggestions of temporal differences in the progress of innovation that correlate reasonably well with a pattern of geographic spread from innovating centres. We have noted already that the earliest evidence for lenition after the possessives points to the western part of the Cornouaille panhandle, roughly between Carhaix-Plouguer and Mael-Carhaix. It is probably more than coincidental that at Plounevezel, abutting Carhaix-Plouguer, lenition after possessives is general (Timm, 1985); that at Poullaouen, immediately to the north, such lenition is not used by the oldest generation but is found already in the speech of the next generation and is fairly general in the speech of a third generation (Favereau, 1984); and that at Berrien (Plonéis, 1975) and St Servais (Plourin, 1982), two communes to the northwest and northeast respectively, lenition after possessives is considered incorrect but may nevertheless be heard sporadically after 'my'.

Similarly, the extension of innovative lenition by younger speakers at Buhulien can be set against a background of innovation in preceding generations. The ALBB shows the area in north Trégor roughly from Plouzelambre to Pleubian to be conservative regarding lenition after 3, 4 and 9. But at Buhulien, at Kerauzern, and at Plougrescant, all within this area, the pre-First World War generation, perhaps the grandchildren of Le Roux' informants, show extensive lenition (at Buhulien) or near normative lenition (Kerauzern and Plougrescant) in these environments. At Plougrescant, this generation also shows already sporadic lenition after 'my' and 'our'.

5. Sources of Innovation

With the history and structure of the innovation reasonably established, it is also possible to identify analogical motivations fostering the changes. Firstly, a precise analogical model for lenition after 3, 4 and 9 apparently existed. While these numerals, as adjectives, spirantized the initial of a following noun, the same numerals used as substantives lenited the initial of a following adjective. Thus, beside *tri c'hi*, *tri faotr*, *tri mab*, 'three dogs, three boys, three sons', were *tri gozh, tri bounner, tri vad,* 'three old ones, three heavy ones, three good ones', and so on. The construction in question is described by Kervella and Trépos, and for modern dialects by Le Dû and Favereau.

Secondly, there was some pre-existing lenition of noun initials after spirantizing numerals. Already in 1659 Maunoir (reproduced in Lambert, 1979) noted lenition of *m* and *b* after the feminine *teir*, 'three'. Gregoire de Rostrenen, in his grammar of 1738, notes lenition of *m* and *t* after the feminine *teir* and *peder*, 'three, four'.

Finally, the correspondences shown in the ALBB between the areas where innovative lenition after the numerals is found and those where initial new lenition occurred suggest a contributory role. The temporal correspondence between the beginning of initial new lenition in eastern Léon, around 1700 (Jackson, 1967; Fleuriot, 1983a), and the early examples of innovative lenition with all spirantizing numerals, the first quarter of the eighteenth century, even permits speculation that this may have been the direct trigger for the initial innovation.

Innovative lenition after the possessives is a later and secondary phenomenon, modelled on observed variation in spirantizing environments in the speech of older generations, as possibly at Buhulien, on observed differences in more innovative neighboring dialects, as apparently at Poullaouen, or in some areas presumably both.

6. Functional Loss

From the functional perspective, the potential loss from these innovations is not great, and it is not clear that functional loss is in fact occurring where the potential does exist. As noted already by Falc'hun (1951), whether the spriantizing numerals are in fact followed by spirant mutation or by lenition is of no consequence for the efficiency of the linguistic signals, since no potential homonyms exist with which the numerals might be confused in context. The same is true for the first person possessives *ma/va*, 'my' and *hon/hor/omp*, 'our'. Although there is homonymy (in most areas) between *ho*, 'your' and *o*, 'their', the innovation does not present a potential for functional loss. The second person plural provokes provection, unvoicing voiced stops; the third person plural provokes spirant mutation or innovatively lenition, either spirantizing or voicing unvoiced stops. Either way, the number of distinctive signals provided by the mutational alternations is the same.

The only real potential for functional loss exists with the third person singular possessives, masculine and feminine. These have widely fallen together in /i/ and are distinguished only by the mutations following. Since the masculine causes lenition already, innovative lenition after the feminine would result in confusion of the two pronouns. This possibilitv is avoided in two ways. First, since innovative lenition is frequently limited to the voiceless stops a partial contrast is maintained, between radical voiced stops and their lenition products. Second, and potentially more imprtantly, there is evidence of recourse to a disambiguating periphrastic construction.

Most if not all Breton dialects make use of a possessive construction based on the conjugated forms of *da*, 'to' following a noun, used alternatively with the possessive pronouns, or together with them for reinforcement. With the third person singular possessives these can also be used to distinguish masculine and feminine where a noun initial is subject neither to spirant mutation nor lenition, e.g. *e loa dezhañ*, 'his spoon' versus *hi loa dezhi*, 'her spoon' in dialects where the first part of both utterances is /i ˈlwa:/. Bothorel (1982) indicates that at Argol (Finistère), where the mutational distinctions have been lost, *da* constructions are in regular use with the possessives. Favereau (1984) indicates by text examples that the same pattern is present at Poullaouen, at least to some extent. Other relevant dialect descriptions, notably Dressler and Timm, do not provide information on this usage, but provide no counterexamples either. It is quite within the realm of possibility that mutational conflation of the third person singular possessives results in no functional ambiguity at all, anywhere.

7. The Pace of Innovation

It has been suggested that even if the observable innovations follow a regular course, the pace of change itself at such places as Buhulien or Poullaouen is indicative of a weakening of communal constraints on language use and thus an indicator of decay. But it is not established that the pace of change in these speech communities is in fact abnormal. Favereau indicates roughly a span of three generations for the change from spirant mutation to lenition after possessives. Dressler indicates probably the same for the complete generalization of lenition after spirantizing numerals and extension of the innovation to possessives.

Over the last twenty years, numerous sociolinguistic studies of urban speech communities have demonstrated that a span of three generations is more than ample time for fairly extensive innovations to take hold. While the Breton speaking areas of Brittany are not urban by any standard, they do share characteristics of population mobility, contact between competing speech forms, and supra-dialectal influences which make them comparable in important respects.

Members of very localized Breton language speech communities commonly have a well-formulated notion of 'their' Breton as opposed to 'other' Bretons. Still one of the often striking features of contemporary local speech forms is their relative non-discreteness, materially or ideologically. At Kerauzern, the area in which the same Breton is recognized as being spoken can vary with context between the southern part of the commune of Ploubezre and an area extending from Plestin to Guingamp and from the channel coast at least to Belle-Isle-en-Terre. Perhaps not surprisingly, characteristic 'pure' forms of local dialects cannot readily be identified and contrasted as one moves from community to community. Differences often involve relative frequencies more than the presence or absence of features, with tendential differences among speakers in a community often as great as overall differences between adjacent communities. Each community is a dynamic network, liable to variation within and change through time, and intricately bound into its larger region, as are the speakers who comprise it.

The admixture of 'outside' (by narrowest definitions) Breton to be heard in a community can be quite large, representing the usage of as many as half the adult speakers. This situation has been variously documented by e.g. Hewitt (1976) who reports that among Breton-speaking adult residents of Sept-Saints (Vieux-Marché) half were born outside the commune; Favereau (1984) who provides figures showing that more than 60% of all marriages performed at Poullaouen between 1900 and 1920 involved one conjoint from outside the commune; Humphreys (1985) who reports that more than half of all marriages at St-Nicolas-du-Pelem between 1861 and 1910 involved a conjoint from outside the commune; and Segalen (1985) who shows that in a group of south Bigouden parishes a high percentage of marriages among consanguines were commune exogamous.

The construction of the ALBB itself betrays this pattern of population mobility. Among seven inquiry points in Trégor for which information is given, Le Roux notes for three that his informant had a parent originally from a different commune, in one case both parents. He further notes that four of his seven informants had a spouse from a different commune. This state of affairs is echoed by Humphreys, who notes that at Bothoa he first intended to make use of informants all of whose grandparents had been born in the commune, but was eventually unable to secure any suitable persons meeting the criterion. At Bothoa, to paraphrase Humphreys, the confrontation between speech forms slightly or even quite noticeably different is a daily occurrence.

There is also specific evidence to indicate that the rates of morpho- phonological innovation found at Buhulien and Poullaouen are comparable to those obtaining in the second half of the nineteenth century and the beginning of the twentieth. The time and generation spans indicated by Le Roux (1896) for innovation with the numerals at Pleubian are about the same for those for the innovations at Buhulien and Poullaouen. The comparative data suggest approximately the same spans for innovation after the numerals at Plougrescant, Kerauzern, and Buhulien itself, occurring at the same time or perhaps a generation later. Lastly, the absence of any indication of innovation with the possessives in the ALBB, together with its presence in fully generalized form in the speech of the oldest living generation at Plouneyezel (ALBB point 39) and nearby areas suggest that this, too, was accomplished in the space of a few generations.

8. Conclusion

There is no question but that the practice of Breton as a medium of daily communication is declining, and has declined drastically over at least the last fifty to seventy-five years. There is also no question but that the decline in language use has been accompanied in many places by an attrition in Breton-specific language skills and by large-scale interference from French in the speech of the numerically much reduced youngest generations, evidenced in limited vocabularies with sometimes surprising lacunae, ad hoc borrowing of words and whole phrases from French, apparent calquing on French syntactic structures, etc. There has accordingly been some tendency to treat all notable innovations in the contemporary language as presumptive evidence of further decline (as Dressler, 1972, 1977, 1981; Favereau, 1984; Fleuriot, 1981, 1983b; Le Dû, 1986). It would appear that the presumption is sometimes faulty.

Language death theory is as yet in its infancy. We have a corpus of instances of language innovations in dying speech communities which appear to be characterizable in terms of simplification and loss, and which are unexpected in terms of known evolutionary trends in the affected languages. But no general interpretive structure yet exists. Each proposed instance must be carefully evaluated in its own context.

In considering the shift in modern Breton from spirant mutation to lenition we have uncovered a fairly extensive set of facts that argue consistently against a language decay/decline/death interpretation. They suggest instead an unexceptional pattern of linguistic innovation which in some contemporary dialects has an incidental connection to decay in local speech communities.

The history of spoken forms of Breton of the last two to three hundred years, as opposed to that of the written language, has been relatively little studied, and for that matter relatively little documented. Such research is essential to a proper understanding of contemporary language dynamics. Unlike the classic examples in the language death literature, such as East Sutherland Gaelic and Dyirbal, local Breton speech communities have not been, and generally are not now, isolates. The sound interpretation of dialect specific variable data will require consideration of current language use and recent language history on a regional basis.

In considering variable dialect phenomena in contemporay Breton, what is often striking in the descriptions is in fact not the evidence of decline in the language, but the extent to which observations appear to be accountable on the basis of features in other dialects, without reference to the social circumstances of the language and their presumed ramifications, i.e. the extent to which bilingualism, shifting dominance and decline have quite failed to interrupt the internal dynamics of the language even among the youngest and demonstrably least competent speakers. Innovations have recently occurred and are continuing to occur in a living language, the practice of which continues to show the response of speakers to regional trends.

It is possible and even likely that many of the 'terminal' innovations noted in the recent literature: loss of impersonals, loss of the past definite, regularization of nominal inflection, will, like the supplanting of spiraant mutation, be shown to be the contemporary stages of long-term change processes, founded in the monolingual speech communities of preceding centuries. While it may be that a generalized decline in the language competence of terminal speakers of Breton plays some role in the course of grammatical innovation in contemporary dialects, that role has yet to be described.

Note

* An earlier version of this contribution was presented at the Eighth International Congress of Celtic Studies, University College Swansea, July 1987.

References

Bothorel, A. (1982) *Etude phonétique et phonologique du breton à Argol (Finistère-Sud)*. Lille/Spezed: Université de Lille III/Diffusion Breizh.

Derrien, R. (1975) *Isolation as a major determinant in the study of natural languages*. Master's thesis, University of Brest.

Dorian, N. (1973) Grammatical change in a dying dialect. *Language,* **49**, 413-38.

Dorian, N. (1976a) A hierarchy of morphophonemic decay in Scottish Gaelic language death: the differential failure of lenition. *Word,* **28**, 96-109.

Dorian, N. (1976b) Gender in a terminal Gaelic dialect. *Scottish Gaelic Studies,* **12**, 279-82.

Dorian, N. (1977) The problem of the semi-speaker in language death. *International Journal of the Sociology of Language,* **12**, 23-32.

Dorian, N. (1978) The fate of morphological complexity in language death. *Language,* **54**, 590-609.

Dorian, N. (1980) Language shift in community and individual: the phenomenon of the laggard semi-speaker. *International Journal of the Sociology of Language,* **25**, 85-94.

Dorian, N. (1981) *Language Death: the life cycle of a Scottish Gaelic dialect*. Philadelphia: University of Pennsylvania Press.

Dressler, W. (1972) On the phonology of language death. In *Papers from the Eighth Regional Meeting, Chicago Linguistic Society*. Chicago: Chicago University Press.

Dressler, W. (1977) Wortbildung bei Sprachverfall. In Brekle, H. and Kostovsky, D. (eds), *Perspektiven der Wortbildungsforschung*. Bonn: Bouvier.

Dressler, W. (1981) Language shift and language death - a protean challenge for the linguist. *Folia Linguistica,* **15,** 5-28.

Evenou, Y. (1987) *Studi fonologel brezhoneg Lanijen (Kanton ar Faoued, Kernev)*. Doctoral thesis, University of Rennes.

Falc'hun, F. (1951) *La système consonantique du breton*. Rennes: Plihon.

Favereau, F. (1984) *Langue quotidienne, langue technique et langue litteraire dans le parler et la tradition orale de Poullaouen*. Doctoral thesis, University of Rennes.

Fleuriot, L. (1981) Review of Brekle, H. and Kostovsky, D. (eds) (1977). *Études Celtiques,* **18,** 363-4.

Fleuriot, L. (1983a) Edward Lhuyd et l'histoire du breton. *Études Celtiques,* **20,** 104-8.

Fleuriot, L. (1983b) Les réformes du breton. In Fodor, I. and Hagege, C. (eds), *Language Reform II: history and future*. Hamburg: Buske.

German, G. (1984) *Une étude linguistique sur le breton de St Yvi*. Doctoral thesis, University of Brest.

Gregoire de Rostrenen, P. (1738) *Grammaire françoise-celtique ou françoise- bretonne*. Rennes: Julien Vator.

Hemon, R. (1975) *A Historical Morphology and Syntax of Breton*. Dublin: Institute for Advanced Studies.

Hewitt, S. (1976) *The morphology of the Breton verb in ar Seizhsant*. Master's thesis, University of Wales, Aberystwyth.

Humphreys, H. Ll. (1985) *Phonologie, morphosyntaxe et lexique du parler breton de Bothoa en Saint-Nicolas-de-Pelem (Côtes-du-Nord)*. Doctoral thesis, University of Brest.

Jackson, K. (1967) *A Historical Phonology of Breton*. Dublin: Institute for Advanced Studies.

Kervella, F. (1947) *Yezhadur bras as brezhoneg*. La Baule: Skridoù Breizh.

Lambert, P-Y. (1979) Les grammaires bretonnes, additions au tome XV, fascicule 1. *Études Celtiques*, **16**, 233-36.

Le Clerc, L. (1908) *Grammaire bretonne du dialect de Tréguier*. Saint Brieuc: Prud'homme.

Le Dû, J. (1978) *Le parler breton de la presqu'île de Plougrescant (Côtes-du-Nord)*. Doctoral thesis, University of Brest.

Le Dû, J. (1986) A sandhi survey of the Breton language. In Andersen, H. (ed), *Sandhi Phenomena in the Languages of Europe*. Berlin: Mouton de Gruyter.

Le Fèvre, G. (1818) *Grammaire celto-bretonne*. Morlaix: Guilmer.

Le Roux, P. (1896) Mutations et assimilations de consonnes dans le dialecte armoricain de Pleubian (Côtes-du-Nord). *Annales de Bretagne*, **12**, 3-31.

Le Roux, P. (1924) *Atlas linguistique de la Basse Bretagne*. Rennes/Paris: Plihon et Hommay.

Moal, J. (1890) *Supplément lexico-grammatical au dictionnaire pratique français-breton du colonel A. Troude en dialecte de Léon*. Landerneau: Desmoulins.

Plonéis, J-M. (1975) *Description phonologique et morphologique du parler de Berrien*. Doctoral thesis, University of Brest.

Plourin, J-Y. (1982) *Description phonologique et morphologique comparés des perlers bretons de Langonnet (Morbihan) et de Saint-Servais (Côtes-du-Nord)*. Doctoral thesis, University of Rennes.

Schmidt, A. (1985) *Young People's Dyirbal: an example of language death from Australia*. New York: Cambridge University Press.

Segalen, M. (1985) *Quinze générations de bas-bretons*. Paris: Presses Universitaires de France.

Sommerfelt, A. (1978) *Le breton parlé à Saint-Pol-de-Léon*. Nouvelle édition. Oslo: Universitetsforlaget.

Ternes, E. (1970) *Grammaire structurale du breton de l'île de Groix*. Heidelberg: Carl Winter Universitätsverlag.

Timm, L. (1985) Breton mutations: literary vs vernacular usages. *Word*, **35**, 95-107.

Trépos, P. (1980) *Grammaire bretonne*. Rennes: Imprimerie Simon.

A Comparison of Word-Order in Middle Breton and Middle Cornish

Ken George
Polytechnic South West

0. Introduction

In this article, word-order in the Middle Breton play *Buhez Santez Nonn (BN.)*, written *circa* 1500 A.D., is compared with the contemporary Middle Cornish play *Beunans Meriasek (BM.)*. The editions used are Ernault (1887) and Combellack-Harris (1985) respectively.

0.1 General comparisons between the two plays

These two mystery plays have several superficial similarities. Although *BM.* is more than twice as long as *BN.*, both plays are redolent of mediaeval Catholicism, *BN.* perhaps more than *BM.*: the saints are so perfect as to be unbelievable. Similar character-types are found in both: saints and professional people; characters named REX, PRIMUS MAGUS, SECUNDUS MAGUS and TIRANNUS occur in both cast-lists. Certain scenes are similar: Meriasek at school and Dewi at school; a king hunting in a forest; the miraculous healing of the sick.

These similarities are perhaps not so surprising if we remember that the lives of saints usually had a Latin source, and that characters and even scenes were borrowed from one play into another. The Latin origin of the plays makes one wonder whether the word-order was not in fact influenced by that of mediaeval Latin.

The metrics of *BN.* are different from those of *BM.*:

(a) internal rhymes occur in *BN.* but not in *BM.*;
(b) in *BM.*, almost every line is of either seven or four syllables, whereas most of those in *BN.* are octosyllabic.

0.2 Notation

Every clause in the two plays was examined, but in the interests of brevity, only the following are considered in this article: statements as main clause (both affirmative and negative) and affirmative imperative clauses, all containing a finite verb; i.e. excluded are subordinate clauses, questions, answers, and clauses containing the verb 'to be'. Full series of word-orders are tabulated for clauses with main verbs rather than auxiliary verbs.

Every clause contains a verbal group ***V***, and may also contain one or more of the following primary groups:

S Subject
O Object
A Auxiliary verb

These four categories constitute a "broad description" of the syntax. A "narrow description" requires sub-dividing the primary groups, using the notation in Table 1.

In order to reduce all the examples to a common basis, each has been related to one of several type-clauses, whose semantic elements are shown in Table 1. These type-clauses have been written in Modern Breton using *ordinary italics*, and in the case of Cornish in the new orthographic system known as *Kernewek Kemmyn* (George, 1986), using ***bold italics***.

A more detailed examination of word-order in *BM.* is to be found in George (1988), where it is shown that, contrary to what one might expect, the normal order of words in clauses is recoverable from verse. Orders may be perturbed by rhymes if a significant element is placed at the end of a line, but need not be otherwise. Provided that the corpus is large enough, the "signal" of the normal word-orders will be evident above the "noise" of the rhymes, i.e. a statistical argument is brought into play.

TYPE	*SUB-TYPE*	*EXAMPLE*
SYNTACTIC (S) SUBJECT	Noun subject (S_n)	*ar vugale* the children ***an fleghes***
	Pronoun subject (S_p)	*me* I ***my***
SEMANTIC (\$) SUBJECT	Noun subj (\$$_n$)	*ar vugale* ***an fleghes***
	Pronoun subject (\$$_p$)	*me* ***my***
MAIN VERB (V)	Invariant form (V_3)	*wel* see(s) ***wel***
	Verbal noun (V_n)	*gwelout* to see ***gweles***
	Conjugated form (V_s)	*welan* I see ***welav***
AUXILIARY (A) VERB	Invariant form (A_3)	*ra* does ***wra***
	Conjugated form (A_s)	*ran* I do ***wrav***
VERBAL (p) PARTICLE	Positive particle (p_+) *a*	***a***
	Negative particle (p_-)	*ne ...{ket}* not ***ny***
SYNTACTIC (O) OBJECT	Noun object (O_n)	*ar c'hazh* the cat ***an gath***
	Pronoun object (O_p)	*en* it ***'n***

{ } optional item

Table 1 Notation

1. Grammatical Analysis

The clauses considered in the two plays may be divided according to:

(a) the structure of the verbal group - nominal or verbal

(Desbordes, 1983, p.53);
(b) the type of verb - main or auxiliary.

In the nominal clauses, the verb (either main or auxiliary) is not conjugated, but takes the form of the third person singular, denoted by V_3 or A_3. The verb is invariably preceded (though not necessarily immediately preceded) by the syntactic subject. This construction is restricted to affirmative statements.

In the verbal clauses, the verb is conjugated, and if the subject is a pronoun, it is contained within the verb. The verb is preceded by a leading element I, and optionally followed by an enclitic pronoun, which emphasizes the subject.

Clauses containing an auxiliary verb may be:
either nominal, with an auxiliary verb in the form p_+A_3;
or verbal, with an auxiliary verb in the form $I\ A\ \{\Sigma\}$.
It is sometimes useful to divide the auxiliary verbs between, on the one hand, 'to do' (*ober* in Breton and ***gul*** in Cornish), which makes little difference to the sense of the clause; and on the other hand, all the other auxiliaries, since they change the sense. For example, *gwelout a ran* is a translation into Breton of the phrase 'I see'; but in the phrase *gwelout a c'hellan*, the sense is changed to 'I can see'. In clauses containing an auxiliary verb, the main verb V takes the form of a verbal noun, denoted by V_n.

NUMBER OF CLAUSES	*BN*	*BM*
Total number analysed	1104	1450
- in the normal series with an auxiliary verb	70 (6%)	185 (13%)
- with an enclitic	28 (2.5%)	57 (3.9%)
Number of verbal clauses	817 (74%)	987 (68%)
- with an impersonal ending	28 (3.4%)	3 (0.3%)
Number of nominal clauses	287 (26%)	463 (32%)

Table 2 General Statistical Analysis of Clauses

Table 2 shows that:

(a) The relative frequency of nominal and verbal clauses is not significantly different in the two plays.
(b) Clauses containing auxiliary verbs are rarer in *BN*. than in *BM*.
(c) Clauses containing enclitics are rarer in *BN*.
(d) The impersonal ending of the verb (e.g. *tud a weler* 'one sees people') is fairly common in *BN*., but very rare in *BM*.

2. Word-order in Nominal Clauses

Table 4 shows the number of examples of each type found in each play. There is a notable difference between Middle Breton and Middle Cornish in clauses with a pronoun subject. In Breton, the verbal particle *a* is found only in the first and second persons singular; otherwise it is omitted: whereas in Cornish it is always present. This explains why in Breton, orders like $S_pO_pV_3$ are commoner than those like $S_pp_+O_pV_3$. Middle Breton had reduced forms like *moz* for *me hoz*, which had no exact counterparts in Cornish (see Table 3). One occasionally finds in Cornish the form ***my as gwel*** as an abbreviation of ***my a'gas gwel*** 'I see you', but this risks confusion with ***my a's gwel*** 'I see her, I see them'.

	MIDDLE BRETON		*MIDDLE CORNISH*	
Form	full	reduced	full	
S1	*te am gwel*		***ty a'm gwel***	thou seest me
2	*me az gwel*	*mez gwel*	***my a'th gwel***	I see thee
3m	*me en gwel*	*men gwel*	***my a'n gwel***	I see him
3f	*me he gwel*		***my a's gwel***	I see her
P1	*te hon gwel*		***ty a'gan gwel***	thou seest us
2	*me hoz gwel*	*moz gwel*	***my a'gas gwel***	I see you
3	*me ho gwel*	*mo gwel*	***my a'ga gwel***	I see them

Table 3 Infixed Pronouns

Note that in *BM*. an order existed which was unknown in *BN*., $O_nS_pp_+V_3$, represented by ***an gath my a wel***. Here we have a fronted noun object (emphasized) with a pronoun subject in a nominal clause; it shows how the group $S_pp_+V_3$ was perceived as a unit in Middle Cornish, and must be regarded as an innovation.

SUBJECT	OBJECT	ORDER	TYPE-CLAUSE	Nº OF EXAMPLES BN.	BM.
Normal series with a main verb					
Pronoun	(none)	$S_p p_+ V_3$	*me a wel* ***my a wel***	29	63
		$S_p V_3$	*me wel* I see	29	0
Pronoun	Pronoun	$S_p p_+ O_p V_3$	*me az gwel* ***my a'th gwel***	14	85
		$S_p O_p V_3$	*mez gwel* I see thee	73	0
Pronoun	Noun	$S_p p_+ V_3 O_n$	*me a wel ar c'hazh* ***my a wel an gath***	28	101
		$S_p V_3 O_n$	*me wel ar c'hazh* I see the cat	50	0
Noun	(none)	$S_n p_+ V_3$	*an den a wel* ***an den a wel***	3	36
		$S_n V_3$	*an den wel* the man sees	1	0
Noun	Pronoun	$S_n p_+ O_p V_3$	*an den az gwel* ***an den a'th wel***	7	5
		$S_n O_p V_3$	*an den 'z gwel* the man sees thee	1	0
Noun	Noun	$S_n p_+ V_3 O_n$	*an den a wel ar c'hazh* ***an den a wel an gath***	8	17
		$S_p V_3 O_n$	**an den wel ar c'hazh* the man sees the cat	0	0
Emphatic order with a main verb					
Pronoun	Noun	$O_n S_p p_+ V_3$	***an gath my a wel*** I see the cat	0	29

Table 4 Word-Order in Nominal Clauses

In order to emphasize a noun object, Middle Breton preferred $O_n p_+ V_p$, the order represented by *ar c'hazh a welan*.

3. Word-order in Verbal Clauses

3.1 Affirmative statements (main clauses)

The series of "normal" orders in clauses with a main verb are given in Table 5. In both languages, it is extremely rare to find a verbal particle fronting a main clause which is an affirmative statement. (There are only eleven examples of this in the entire corpus of extant traditional Cornish). There must normally be an element preceding the particle, usually either an adverb, or the object, but the conjunction *hag* 'and' may suffice.

3.2 Negative clauses

The commonest word-orders with a pronoun subject are the normal orders (see Table 6). For a noun subject, the "normal" orders tend to become ambiguous or clumsy, and as a result, orders where the subject precedes the verb are just as common. In *BM*., though not in *BN*., clauses are found in which a emphasized semantic pronoun subject precedes a negative verb.

The main difference between Breton and Cornish is the presence of the word *ket* in *BN*. No analysis has been made of the frequency of this word, which appears to be optional in *BN*. It was purely emphatic, the negative sense being given by the particle *ne*, *ned* or *na*. In Modern Breton, however, the negative sense has been transferred to *ket*, because (as in spoken French), one may omit the particle *ne* (Desbordes, 1983, p.56).

3.3 Affirmative imperative clauses

For the sake of consistency, the same words are used for the type-clauses in Table 7 as in the other tables, even if the resulting examples are rather artificial. The distribution of the forms in *BN*. and *BM*. are broadly similar, but there are two important differences. Firstly the order $O_p V_n$ is unknown in Cornish; secondly, the orders with an auxiliary verb are rarer in Breton.

Thus, in order to translate 'see me!', there are three possible alternatives:

	MODERN BRETON	REVIVED CORNISH	ORDER	Nº EGS BN	BM
(i)	*gwel me!*	*gwel vy!*	V_sO_p	13	25
(ii)	*gra va gwelout!*	*gwra ow gweles!*	$A_sO_pV_n$	2	9
(iii)	*va gwelout!*	**ow gweles!*	O_pV_n	16	0

It seems that (i) is the original, and that (iii) is an innovation in Breton; (ii) might be an intermediate step in the evolution. In modern spoken Breton, the usual construction is another innovation, that using the pronominal preposition from *a*, e.g. *lez ac'hanon!* 'leave me!'.

4. Statements in Main Clauses

4.1 Which were the commonest word-orders used?

It is of interest to consider these in more detail. In affirmative statements, the nominal word-orders in Table 4 are in competition with the verbal word-orders in Table 5. In negative statements (Table 6), the normal word-orders are in competition with those having a fronted semantic subject.

In Table 8, the commonest word-orders in *BM*. are presented. A very clear conclusion may be drawn from these figures, since in every case the commonest word-order has an absolute majority over all other word-orders. It is as follows:

The usual word-order in main clauses in Middle Cornish was:

(a) **In affirmative statements, the normal series of nominal clauses with main verb** (Table 5);

(b) **In negative statements, the normal series of verbal clauses with main verb** (Table 6).

A similar layout for *BN*. is given in Table 9. The "normal" orders are still the commonest, but they have no absolute majority, as in the case of *BM*. Affirmative verbal clauses seem to be commoner in *BN*.: Middle Cornish preferred the nominal conjugation.

SUBJECT	*OBJECT*	*SYNTAX*	*TYPE CLAUSE*	*Nº OF EXAMPLES BN.*	*BM.*
Normal affirmative orders with a main verb					
Pronoun	(none)	*a* $p_{+}V_{s}$	*amañ e welan* ***omma y hwelav*** here I see	36	8
Pronoun	Pronoun	*a* $p_{+}O_{p}V_{s}$	*amañ en gwelan* ***omma y'n gwelav*** here I see it	27	2
Pronoun	Noun	*a* $p_{+}V_{s}O_{n}$	*amañ e welan ar c'hazh* ***omma y hwelav an gath*** here I see tha cat	32	5
Noun	(none)	*a* $p_{+}V_{3}S_{n}$	*amañ e wel an den* ***omma y hwel an den*** here the man sees	3	2
Noun	Pronoun	*a* $p_{+}O_{p}V_{3}S_{n}$	*amañ en gwel an den* ***omma y'n gwel an den*** here the man sees it	1	0
Noun	Noun	*a* $p_{+}V_{3}S_{n}O_{n}$	**amañ e wel an den ar c'hazh* ***omma y hwel an den an gath*** here the man sees the cat	0	0
Affirmative order with fronted subject					
Pronoun	Noun	$O_{n}p_{+}V_{s}$	*ar c'hazh a welan* ***an gath a welav*** I see the cat	59	18
Really abnormal affirmative order					
Noun	Noun	*a* $V_{3}O_{n}S_{n}$	*amañ e wel ar c'hazh an den* ****omma y hwel an gath an den*** here the man sees the cat [sic!]	1	0

Table 5 Word-order in Verbal Clauses

SUBJECT	*OBJECT*	*SYNTAX*	*TYPE-CLAUSE*	*N^o^ OF EXAMPLES* *BN.*	*BM.*
Normal negative orders with a main verb					
Pronoun	(none)	$p\text{-}V_s$	*ne welan {ket}* ***ny welav*** I do not see	18	13
Pronoun	Pronoun	$p\text{-}O_pV_s$	*nen gwelan {ket}* ***ny'n gwelav*** I do not see him	10	3
Pronoun	Noun	$p\text{-}V_sO_n$	*ne welan {ket} ar c'hazh* ***ny welav an gath*** I do not see the cat	26	40
Noun	(none)	$p\text{-}V_3S_n$	*ne wel {ket} an den* ***ny wel an den*** the man does not see	3	13
Noun	Pronoun	$p\text{-}O_pV_3S_n$	*nen gwel {ket} an den* ***ny'n gwel an den*** the man does not see it	2	2
Noun	Noun	$p\text{-}V_3S_nO_n$	*ne wel {ket} an den ar c'hazh* ***ny wel an den an gath*** the man does not see the cat	0	2
Orders having a fronted syntactic noun subject					
Noun	(none)	$\$_np\text{-}V_s$	*an den ne wel {ket}* ***an den ny wel*** the man, he does not see	1	7
Noun	Pronoun	$\$_np\text{-}O_pV_s$	*an den nen gwel {ket}* ***an den ny'n gwel*** the man, he does not see it	2	0
Noun	Noun	$\$_np\text{-}V_sO_n$	*an den ne wel {ket} ar c'hazh* ***an den ny wel an gath*** the man, he does see the cat	3	1

Table 6 Word-order in Verbal Clauses (continued)

SUBJECT	*OBJECT*	*ORDER*	*TYPE-CLAUSE*	*Nº OF EXAMPLES BN.*	*BM.*
Normal series with a main verb					
Pronoun	(none)	V_s	*gwel!* ***gwel!*** see!	128	215
Pronoun	Pronoun	O_pV_n	*va gwelout!*	16	0
		V_sO_p	*gwel me!* ***gwel vy!*** see me!	13	25
Pronoun	Noun	V_sO_n	*gwel ar c'hazh!* ***gwel an gath!*** see the cat!	104	127
Noun	(none)	V_3S_n	*gwelet an den!* ***gweles an den!*** may the man see!	2	6
Noun	Pronoun	(no examples in either play)			
Noun	Noun	$V_3S_nO_n$	*gwelet an den ar c'hazh!* ***gweles an den an gath!*** may the man see the cat!	0	1
Series with an auxiliary verb					
Pronoun	(none)	A_sV_n	*gra gwelout!* ***gwra gweles!*** do thou see!	0	2
Pronoun	Pronoun	$A_sO_pV_n$	*gra va gwelout!* ***gwra ow gweles!*** see me!	2	9
Series with a fronted object					
Pronoun	Noun	O_nV_s	*ar c'hazh gwel!* ***an gath gwel!*** see the cat!	8	13
Pronoun	Noun	$O_nA_sV_n$	*ar c'hazh gra gwelout!* ***an gath gwra gweles!*** see the cat!	0	3

Table 7 Word-order in Affirmative Imperative Clauses

OBJECT	SUBJECT → *PRONOUN*	*NOUN*
(NONE)	*my a wel* I see (69%) *ny welav* I do not see (68%)	*an den a wel* the man sees (90%) *ny wel an den* the man does not see (65%)
PRONOUN	*my a's gwel* I see it (85%) *ny's gwelav* I do not see it (60%)	*an den a's gwel* the man sees it (63%) *ny's gwel an den* the man does not see it (100%)
NOUN	*my a wel an gath* I see the cat (57%) *ny welav an gath* I do not see the cat (56%)	*an den a wel an gath* the man sees the cat (100%) *ny wel an den an gath* the man does not see the cat (68%)

The percentages refer to the proportion of occurrences of the given word-order relative to the total number of occurrences of all word-orders.

Table 8 Commonest Word-orders in statements in Main Clauses in *BM*.

OBJECT \ SUBJECT →	*PRONOUN*	*NOUN*
(NONE)	*me wel/me a wel* I see (55%) *ne welan {ket}* I do not see (100%)	*an den a wel/an den wel* the man sees (57%) *ne wel {ket} an den* the man does not see (75%)
PRONOUN	*men gwel/me an gwel* I see it (71%) *nen gwelan {ket}* I do not see it (100%)	*an den an gwel* the man sees it (89%) *nen gwel {ket} an den* the man does not see it (50%) *an den nen gwel {ket}* (50%)
NOUN	*me wel ar c'hazh* *me a wel ar c'hazh* I see the cat (45%) *ar c'hazh a welan* (34%) *ne welan {ket}* *ar c'hazh* I do not see the cat (68%)	*an den a wel ar c'hazh* the man sees the cat (80%) *an den ne wel {ket}* *ar c'hazh* the man does not see the cat (100%)

Table 9 Commonest Word-orders in Statements in Main Clauses in *BN*.

It is interesting to note that the commonest word-order in Modern Breton, $V_n p_+ A_p$, (e.g. *gwelout a ran* for 'I see') hardly appears at all in *BN*. When and how did this series of orders, originally emphasizing the verb, become the commonest, and in the process losing the emphasis? When we add the other major change in Modern Breton, the replacement of the infixed pronoun object by the pronominal preposition based on *a*, a syntactic gulf opens up between the Breton of the twentieth century and that of the fifteenth. Thus, the trisyllabic phrase *me az kar* 'I love thee' (Cornish **my a'th kar**) has been replaced in Modern Breton by *karout a ran ac'hanout*, which with its seven syllables, is much more awkward.

4.2 The choice of word-orders to express a given idea
As a more detailed example, Table 10 examines the various ways of translating the clause 'I see the cat', with the top half of the table demonstrating how this would have been done in *BN*. and the lower half as it would have been done in *BM*.

BUHEZ SANTEZ NONN
ORDER

$S_p V_3 O_n$	*me wel ar c'hazh*	29%
$S_p p_+ V_3 O_n$	*me a wel ar c'hazh*	16%
$O_n p_+ V_s$	*ar c'hazh a welan*	34%
$a\ p_+ V_s O_n$	av + *e welan ar c'hazh*	18%
$V_s O_n$	---------------	0%
$O_n S_p p_+ V_3$	---------------	0%
	(several other minor orders)	
$V_n p_+ A_s O_n$	*gwelout a ran ar c'hazh*	1%

BEUNANS MERIASEK		
ORDER		
$S_pV_3O_n$	———————————	0%
$S_pp_+V_3O_n$	***my a wel an gath***	57%
$O_np_+V_s$	***an gath a welav***	10%
$a\ p_+V_sO_n$	av + ***y hwelav an gath***	3%
V_sO_n	***gwelav an gath***	5%
$O_nS_pp_+V_3$	***an gath my a wel***	16%
	(several other minor orders)	
$V_np_+A_sO_n$	***gweles a wrav an gath***	1%

Table 10 How to Translate 'I See the Cat'

Again, it is remarkable that the form $V_np_+A_sO_n$, represented in Breton by *gwelout a ran ar c'hazh*, should account for only 1% of the cases.

5. Conclusions

The following forms are not found in the Middle Cornish of *Beunans Meriasek*, and they are taken to be innovations in Breton:

(a) compound tenses using the verb *kaout* 'to have' and the past participle of the main verb, e.g. *gwelet am eus* 'I have seen';

(b) the possessive pronoun used as a direct object in imperative clauses, e.g. *va sikourit!* 'help me!'

(c) the loss of the verbal particle *a* after the subject, e.g. *me wel* instead of *me a wel* for 'I see'; (this loss did occur at times in Late Cornish);

(d) the particle *a* before questions beginning with the subject, e.g. *a te a wel?* 'seest thou?'

(e) the **frequent** use of a word like *ket* in negative expressions (as opposed to the **occasional** use of an emphatic word).

The emphatic word-order $O_nS_pp_+V_3$, represented by ***an gath*** *my a wel*, appears to be an innovation in Cornish. Negative clauses with an emphasized semantic pronoun subject are found in *BM*. but not in *BN*.

The imperative using the auxiliary verb 'to do' (e.g. *gra e lazhañ* for 'kill him!' is much less common in *BN*., and seems to be obsolescent at that stage of Middle Breton. In general, Middle Breton made less use of nominal clauses, of the auxiliary 'to do', and of enclitics than did Middle Cornish.

The impersonal ending of the verb (e.g. *tud a weler* 'one sees people') is ten times as common in *BN*.

References

Combellack-Harris, M. M. (1985) *A critical study of BEUNANS MERIASEK*. Unpublished Ph.D. thesis, University of Exeter.

Desbordes, Y. (1983) *Petite grammaire du breton moderne*. Mouladurioù Hor Yezh, Lesneven.

Ernault, E. (1887) La vie de Sainte Nonne. *Revue Celtique,* 8, 230-301, 406-491.

George, K.J. (1986) *The pronunciation and spelling of Revived Cornish*. Cornish Language Board, Saltash, Cornwall.

George, K.J. (1988) Word-order in the Middle Cornish play *Beunans Meriasek*. Paper presented to the Seventh Forum of the Centre for Advanced Welsh and Celtic Studies, Aberystwyth, Wales.

A Problem in Cornish Phonology

N.J.A. Williams
University College, Dublin

1. Introduction

Cornish is unique among the insular Celtic languages, in that the last native speakers died before their speech could be recorded and described by modern methods. This presents scholars and revivalists alike with a serious problem. All understanding of Cornish pronunciation has to be inferential. It has to be deduced from the spelling of our existing literary remains and from the pronunciation of place-names and of survivals in English dialect.

Since the 1920's the Cornish revival has been using a phonology and orthography devised largely by R. Morton Nance and his collaborator A.S.D. Smith. This system, known as Unified Cornish,[1] has little scientific basis. The quickening pace of the Cornish revival in recent years has brought about a gradual disillusionment with Morton Nance's system, or *Mordonnek*, as it is sometimes called.

In a recent work, *The Pronunciation and Spelling of Revived Cornish* (George, 1986), Dr. Ken George has succeeded in producing a new phonemic orthography for revived Cornish that represents as closely as possible the pronunciation of Middle Cornish, in particular the phonological system of the early sixteenth-century play, *Beunans Meriasek*. PSRC is an outstanding work of linguistic reclamation. Although its main purpose is practical, that is, to provide the Cornish language movement with a sound orthographic base, it also provides the best scholarly description of Middle Cornish phonology to date.

Dr. George's method is simple. He systematically analyses the phonology of Middle Cornish in the light of Breton and Welsh cognates. He then devises a phonemic spelling based for the most part on the MC texts themselves, but bearing in mind where the traditional orthography fails to indicate phonemic distinctions. Over all Dr. George's method is sound and his enterprise is highly successful. There can be no doubt that most of his proposed orthography will replace both *Mordonnek* and the other systems that have been advanced by *Mordonnek*'s disillusioned users.[2]

There are, unfortunately, parts of the phonological system of MC where the comparative method is of little use. Where Cornish, Welsh and Breton develop in parallel, there is no difficulty. Similarly, where Breton and Cornish or Welsh and Cornish agree, the comparative method can be applied. Where Cornish has undergone a development unique to Cornish, comparisons do not exist and Welsh and Breton cannot be used as controls.

2. The Problem of British D and T in Cornish

The most striking series of sound-changes that are unique to Cornish are those involving the reflexes of Brit. *t* and *d* in medial and final position. In Welsh and Breton these sounds remain stops. In Cornish they ultimately become sibilants of some kind. The position can briefly be stated as follows:

1.1 Brit. *-nt*, *-lt* had already become sibilants in the late OC period (c. 1050-1100) and were written <ns, ls>. Thus OC *dans* 'tooth' corresponds to WB *dant*, and OC *als* 'shore' to W *allt*, B *aod* (Jackson, 1953: 507-508).

1.2 Brit. *d* in final position had become a sibilant by the MC period and was written <s>. Thus MC *tas* 'father' corresponds to WB *tad*. In LC *tas* appears as *taz* with final *z*.

1.3 Medially before a front vowel and *w*, *d* is similarly shifted in MC and appears as *s* or *g*/*i*. Thus MC *wose*, *woge* 'after' corresponds to W *wedi*, B *goude*; MC *peswar* 'four' corresponds to W *pedwar*, OB *petguar* > MB *pevar*; MC *crysy*, *crygy* 'believe' corresponds to MB *kredin*. In LC this sound is frequently written <g> or <dg>. Lhuyd (1707:231, col 1) spells it <dzh>.

1.4 Internally *nt* had been shifted by the MC period and was written <ns> or <ng>. Thus MC *kerense*, *kerenge* 'love' corresponds to MB *karantez*, *karanté*; and MC *ganso* 'with him' to MB *gantan, gantaff*.

It is to be noted, however, that *nt*, *lt* and *d* are unaffected medially before the back vowels *a* and *o*, e.g. *caradow* 'loveable', *ledan* 'wide', and also if followed in the next syllable by *l*, *n* or *r*, e.g. *padel* 'pan', *fenten* 'well', *peder* 'four (fem.)'.

3. The Loth-George Hypothesis

There is general agreement that *tas* in MC probably meant [ta:s] or [ta:z]. Similarly MC *dans*, *als* probably represent [dans] and [als] respectively. The problem is to decide what was meant by such variant MC spellings as *wose/woge*, *kerense/kerenge*, *crysys/crygy* and MC *peswar* but LC *padzhar*. In his solution Dr. George has followed J. Loth (1897).

Loth noticed that in *wose/woge*, *crysy/crygy*, *s* and *g* appear to be in free variation. He assumes therefore that the graphs <s>, <g> and occasionally <i/j>, represent a sound that is neither [s/z] nor [dʒ]. Had either [s/z] or [dʒ] been the sound in these words, <s> or <g> would have been written consistently. *Wose/woge*, *crys/crygy* must accordingly contain a sound not easily represented by the orthography. In LC moreover we find *bohodzhak* 'poor' for MC *bohosek*, and *padzhar* for MC *peswar*. Loth assumes therefore that the sound lying behind the MC graphs <s> and <g> was sufficiently close to [dʒ] to develop into [dʒ] in the LC period. Loth thus takes <s>, <g> and <i/j> to represent a palatalised *d*. This sound Loth writes as <dj>. Moreover, since the *s* in MC *ganso* 'with him' and the *s* or *g* in *kerense*, *kerenge* 'love' correspond to *t* in B *gantan*, *karanté*, Loth assumes that the sound in these MC words is the voiceless equivalent of *dj*, i.e. a palatalised *t*, which he writes <tj>.[3]

George adopts most of Loth's hypothesis as the basis on which to construct this part of his orthography. He thus, with Loth, takes <s>, <g> to represent a palatalised *d* in *wose/woge*, *bohosek*, *peswar*, *aswon* 'know', etc., and he recommends spelling these as <wodja>, <boghodjek>, <pedjwar> and <adjwon> respectively (PSRC: 81-83, 164-67). Similarly he takes *kerense* and *ganso* to contain a voiceless palatalised stop and he recommends the spellings <kerentja> and <gantjo> (PSRC: 81-83, 157-59).

4. Theoretical Objections to the Loth-George Hypothesis

The solution to the question of *s/g* in MC proposed by Loth and adopted by George is both elegant and consistent. Unfortunately, it is based, I believe, on two quite mistaken assumptions. Firstly, it is not true that <s> and <g> in MC are in free variation. The distributions of the two graphs overlap considerably, but they are nonetheless different, as I hope to demonstrate below. Secondly, MC *bohosek*, *peswar*, *aswon*, etc. are not the immediate ancestors of LC *bohodzhak*, *padzhar*, *adzhan*, etc. The latter are dialectal variants. As I hope will become clearer later on, the evidence indicates that there were two separate MC developments of Brit. medial *d*: (i) [z] written <s> and (ii) [dʒ] written <g> or <i/j>.

Although it is less important to the general argument, it should also be noted here that Loth is mistaken about the final consonantal segment in *ganso* and *kerense*. The evidence indicates that <s> here in MC represents a voiced, not a voiceless, consonant.

Palatalised *d* and *t* are immediately familiar to anyone who has an acquaintance with Irish. These two sounds, to judge by George's descriptions of them, are to be understood as a voiced alveolo-palatal plosive and its unvoiced equivalent. Loth writes them as <dj>, <tj>, while George in his phonetic notation represents them by the signs [δ] and [τ]. I, following the conventions of Gaelic phonologists, will write them [d´] and [t´].

The Gaelic languages are distinguished by having two series of consonants, palatalised and velarised. The Brythonic languages are without such an overall distinction. The consonantal inventory of Cornish, at least as far as points of articulation are concerned, seems like that of Breton and Welsh, not to be particularly varied. MC had both [tʃ] and [dʒ] in ME borrowings, for example, *chambour* 'chamber', *tuchya* 'touch' and *gentyl* 'gentle, noble', *page* 'page'. Now, if the Loth-George hypothesis were correct, MC would have contained the following threefold oppositions: /t:t´:tʃ/ and /d:d´:dʒ/. These two series are in themselves highly unstable. If they had ever existed in MC, a language lacking the overall opposition palatalised:velarised, they would have simplified very quickly to /t:tʃ/ and /d:dʒ/. This simplification did indeed take place, according to Dr. George, but not fully until c. 1625,[4] i.e. not for about 500 years or so after the two series had arisen, and not in the MC period.

There is a further serious theoretical objection to the suggested phonemes /t´/ and /d´/ in MC. The change of *d* > *s* in words like *tas* 'father', *bos* 'to be', etc. is a movement away from stopped articulation towards greater continuance, i.e. towards a fricative pronunciation. Yet according to the Loth-George hypothesis the related sound-change *d* > *s* seen, for example, in OC *bochodoc* 'poor' > MC *bohosek*, does not involve movement towards greater continuance, but only towards a different point of articulation, from dental/dental-alveolar stop to alveolo-palatal stop. Not only would the shift of *d* > *d'* be quite unlike the simultaneous shift of *d* > *s* in final position, but it would also seem to be without phonetic motivation. If a final dental stop has become assibilated, by how much the more should an intervocalic dental stop experience the same change. After all, the intervocalic environment in *bochodoc* would be more conducive to the movement obstruence → continuance than would the final position in *tad*.

5. Orthographical Objections

There are a number of orthographical objections to the supposed shift *d* > *d'* and *t* > *t'* in MC. In the first place, it is curious that MC scribes did not attempt to devise some sort of graph for /d´/ and /t´/. For /d´/ they could have used *di*, *dy*, *ds*, *dg*,[5] or perhaps some other combination. If the Loth-George hypothesis were true, then /d´/ was by no means a marginal phoneme. It occurred widely in all positions. The failure of the scribes even to attempt to devise separate graphs for /d´/ and /t´/ would *a priori* make one think that such phonemes never existed in the language.

In Middle English [dʒ] is usually written <i> (later <j>) before back vowels, e.g. *ioye*, *iudge*, but <g> before front vowels including *y*, e.g. *gentil*, *gyst*, *giterne*. The same rule applies in MC with English loanwords, e.g. *iolyf* RD 2013, *ioy* OM 154, but *gentyl* OM 1566, *geyler* PC 1865. The same rule also obtains, however, in the case of the reflexes of OC *d* in MC. Thus *crygyans*, *cregyans* 'faith' PC 1994, BM 1161, 1208, 1319, *a'n geffo* 'may have (subj.)' OM 422, *an geffa* 'id.' BM 20, but *pyiadow* 'prayer' PC 24, 334, *peyadow* (*y* for *i*) 'id.' BM 128, 1443, *peiadow* 'id.' BM 132, 3624, *peiadov* 'id.' BM 2189, 4015. MC orthography, then, spells ME [dʒ] as <g> or <i> according to position. It also spells the reflex of OC *d* as either

<g> or <i> according to the same criteria. It seems reasonable to assume, therefore, that ME [dʒ] in loanwords in MC and native <g/i> < OC *d* are identical in pronunciation. <g/i>, then, in MC cannot represent [d´].

The OC word for 'house' was *ti* (Norris 1859a :425). In the MC texts, however, the form is almost invariably *chy*, or in its lenited form, *gy*. *Chy* seems to have arisen because the assibilation of *nt* could take place across a word boundary. It appears that MC **ty* was so frequently used with the proclitic article *an* that the whole phrase was taken as one unit and thus became *an chy*.[6] According to Dr. George, *chy* represents [t´i:], which he recommends spelling <tji>. *Ch*, then, in the word *chy*, George believes, represents the same sound as is indicated by <s> or <g> in *kerense/kerenge*. If this were really so, however, one would expect *chy* (unlenited) occasionally to be written **sy* or **gy*, which it never is. Or one would perhaps more probably expect that *kerense* and *ganso* might on occasion be spelt **kerenche* and **gancho*. MC, after all, has no aversion to the group <nch>; cf. *wrynch* 'stratagem'. **Kerenche*, **gancho* are, however, unattested anywhere.

The absence of forms like **kerenche* in the texts brings us face to face with one of the most unsatisfactory aspects of the Loth-George hypothesis. According to Loth and George, <ns>, <ng> in, for example, *nyns yw*, *nyng yw* 'is not' represent [nd´], but in *kerense/kerenge* <ns>, <ng> represent [nt´]. Or to put it another way, we must convince ourselves that Cornish scribes frequently wrote [t´], a voiceless alveolo-palatal stop, as <g>.

According to Dr. George MC /d´/ < Brit. *d* became /dʒ/ c. 1625. If this were so, then the text of *The Creation of the World* (see Stokes 1864) written in 1611 should still show clear evidence of unchanged /d´/. CW is unique in Cornish texts in using the graph <dg> before *y*. Given that the orthography of CW is late and heavily influenced by that of English, it seems reasonable to assume that <dg> in CW is based on English spellings like *bridge*, *judgment*, etc., and represent [dʒ]. Yet the graph <dg> in CW occurs where one would expect [d´] by the Loth-George hypothesis, e.g. *devidgyow* 'sheep' CW 1070, *ny bydgyaf* 'I do not pray' CW 1364, 1670, *marodgyan* 'wonders' CW 1804, 1898, *marrudgyan* 'id.' CW 2124, *grydgyan[s]* 'faith' CW 2317.

The MC word for 'after' has various spellings in the texts, *wose*, *woge*, *wosa*. Loth and George believe that <s> alternating with <g> in these forms are variant graphs for [d´]. In CW, however, 'after' is only ever spelt *wo3a* (CW 1295, 1412, 1427, 1856, 1942, 2144, 2499). In CW the symbol <ȝ̣> is used as a graph for two quite separate sounds: [ð] initially, e.g. *3a* 'thy' CW 156, 233, *3a* 'to' CW 201, 236, *3om* 'to my' CW 239, *3a warta* 'from him' CW 266, and [z] between vowels, e.g. *y vo3a* (i.e. *y vos e*) 'his being' CW 672, *y fo3a* 'id.' CW 1249, *the3o* 'to thee' CW 739, 1279, 2253, 2379, *a gow3as* 'spoke' CW 2422. Quite clearly <3> in *wo3a* cannot represent [ð]. It can only then stand for [z]. In CW therefore the word 'after' must be pronounced [wo·zə] or something similar, not [wo·d´ə].[7]

The position is similar in CW with regard to the long forms of *bos* 'be'. In CW the spellings are as follows: 1st person sg. present *esaf* CW 130, 327, 424, 1540, 1667, 1696; 3rd person sg. imperf. *ega* CW 827, *esa* CW 1905, 1908, *essa* CW 2429, *e3a* CW 2426, 2456. The 3rd sg. imperfect clearly has two forms, [e·zə] and [e·dʒə]. These are a continuation of the two forms in the *Ordinalia*, e.g. *ese* RD 514, *ege* RD 1095. Neither represents [ed´ə].

As has been noted, Dr. George, following Loth, believes that the word for 'with him', *ganso*, was pronounced in MC [gant´o]. This he spells <gantjo>. He also believes that [nt´] had become [ndʒ] by c. 1575. If this were so, then the spellings in CW (written 1611) should reflect the pronunciation [gandʒo]. We might then expect to find some spellings of the kind *<gango>, *<ganga>, *<gandgyo>. Such forms do not occur. What we do find in CW are the following: *gansa* CW 160, *ganso* CW 310, 492, 1203, *gousa* (leg, *gonsa*) CW 604, *gon3a* CW 324, *gan̈3a* CW 734, 1566. In view of the spellings with <3>, it seems virtually certain that the scribe of CW pronounced the word for 'with him' as [ganzo] or [gonzə], but certainly not [gandʒo].[8]

6. Phonological Objections

The difference between [d] and [d´] is a difference in point of articulation. Before [s], a tip-alveolar fricative, one would expect the contrast between [d] and [d´] to be neutralised.[9] The tongue, in anticipation of the following tip-alveolar consonant [s], while articulating either [d] or [d´] would move to the same alveolar position in readiness for the next segment. Since [s] is voiceless, both [d] and [d´] would be devoiced immediately before it. The 2nd person sg. preterite of *redya* 'read' thus gives *retsys* 'thou didst read' < *red + sys*. According to George, 'leave' in MC, written *gasa*, is pronounced [ga·d´ə]. The 2nd sg, preterite with i-affection should then give **ged' + sys*, **gyd' + sys* > **getsys*, **gytsys*. It does not, of course. The attested form is *gyssys*, the regular development of *gys + sys*.[10]

As is well-known, in LC (*yth*)*esa* 'was' becomes (*th*)*era*. Similarly, *gasa*, 'leave' becomes *gara*. Dr. George believes that in these two words intervocalic [d´] was rhotacised to [r]. He says "the realization of /δ/ [i.e. /d´/] must have been close to [r]." (PSRC:165). Presumably he means that [d´] was sufficiently close to [r] as to be able to change into it. Yet elsewhere [d´] does not, according to George, become [r] but [dʒ]. The sound [d´], then, is apparently quite unlike [r] except in *esa* and *gasa* only.

I can think of no other instance in any European language where [d´] is rhotacised. The usual candidate for rhoticisation is [z]. Compare, for example, English *rise* < PG **rīsan-*, but *rear* < PG **raizjan-*, or Lat. *flōs*, *flōrem*.[11] If we assume that *esa* and *gasa* were [e·zə] and [ga·zə] respectively, there is no difficulty. It should be noticed here that Loth inconsistently took *gara* 'leave' to derive from [ga·zə]. He appears to have believed that [z] was the normal outcome of [d´] in some cases (Loth, 1897: 416).

7. Further Orthographical Objections

The chief reason that Loth and George have for taking <s> and <g> or <i/j> to represent the single sound [d´] is that the graphs seem to be in free variation. I have already pointed out although they both represent the same sound - in my view [dʒ] - <g> and <i/j> are in complementary, but not free, distribution. The position with respect to <s> on the one hand and <g/i> on the other is much more complicated. Although there is some apparently free variation, much of it can be explained by reference to the phonetic environment. Furthermore, paradigmatic pressure has regularised variation in many cases. In those instances in the surviving texts where neither phonetic environment nor paradigmatic pressure can be invoked, there is no variation, or hardly any.

In BM the hero of the play, St. Meriasek (B *Meriadec*, Lat. *Meriadocus*) is mentioned no fewer than 114 times. His name is variously spelt: *meryasek* x 94, *veryasek* x 9, *meriasek* x 8, *mereasek* x 1, *varyasek* x 1, *vryasek* x 1. There are no instances with <g>. Notice further that at BM 2851-52 *meryasek* rhymes with *tasek* 'paternal'. This I take to be a full rhyme, yet *tasek* can only be for [ta·zek], since *g*-forms of the word *tas* 'father' are unknown.[12]

We can, I believe, be certain that the scribe of BM pronounced his hero's name as [merja·zek] and not [merja·d΄ek]. In fact, a variant [merja·dʒek] was known, but it is a dialectal form, alien to BM, and indeed to classical MC. It is certainly not a mere orthographical alternative.

The word *gallosek* 'powerful' (B *galloudek*) is variously spelt in MC: *gallosek*, *galosek*, *galosak*, *gollousacke* (CW 13). I have counted 40 instances of the word from PA, OM, PC, RD, BM, TH, SA and CW. Only once is it spelt with a <g> as *gallogek* (RC 2376). Elsewhere in RC it is spelt with an <s> eight times.

The word *bohosek* 'poor' is much less frequent than *gallosek*. I have counted 25 examples from PA, PC, BM, and TH. In all cases it is spelt with an <s>, except one instance in BM where the plural form is written *bohogogyon* (BM 4204). I ascribe the presence of <g> = [dʒ] here to the position of the accent.

If we look at spellings with <g> rather than <s>, we find the same pattern of invariance. I have, for example, noted 32 examples of the word *crygyans*, *cregyans*, 'faith, belief' from the texts. It is always spelt with a <g> (<dg> in CW). It is never spelt **crysyans*. The only example with an <s> is the curious mixed spelling *crisgians*, which occurs once in TH.

If the Loth-George hypothesis were correct, the <s> in *Meryasek*, *gallosek* and *bohosek* on the one hand and <g> in *crygyans* on the other were both pronounced [d΄]. Yet the scribal practice in all our texts makes it abundantly clear that this is not so. The surviving texts range in date from the fourteenth to the seventeenth century, but in this matter they all show a striking uniformity. The inescapable conclusion from the evidence of the texts is that *Meryasek*, *gallosek*, *bohosek* are to be pronounced with a [z], while *crygyans* has a [dʒ]. The forms [galo·dʒek] and [boxodʒogjon] do occur in the texts. One is a dialect variant (see below), the other is phonetically determined. There is no evidence whatever for the free variation of <s> and <g> in any of these four lexical items.

John Tregear's Homilies afford us a most instructive insight into the alternation of <s> and <g>. TH spell the word for 'love' as *kerensa, gerensa* (lenited) no fewer than 28 times. Twice it is spelt *carenga*. On the other hand, the adjective **kerensedhek* 'loving' is variously spelt *kerengyek*, *kerengeak*, etc., with a <g> six times. Only once does it occur as *kerensyak* with an <s>. for the most part, then, TH distinguish *kerensa* 'love' from *kerengyek* 'loving'. As is the case with *bohogogyon* mentioned above, the presence of [dʒ] in *kerengyek* is, I believe, to be explained by the position of the accent (see below). *Carenga* x 2 and *kerensyak* x 1 are analogical in origin.

8. Toponymic Objections to the Loth-George Hypothesis

When a people abandons its ancestral tongue, the transference of place-names from the old language to the new takes place within the community itself as part of the general language shift. The change of language typically occurs across three generations. The first is monoglot in the retreating language, the second bilingual in both, the third can speak the advancing language only. The first generation use the retreating language for everything, including local place-names. The second generation pronounce local place-names in the 'old' way even while using the 'new' language. The third generation is unable to pronounce the local names in the 'old' way. Members of this generation pronounce local place-names in accordance with the phonetic system of the 'new' language. The transmission of place-names from one language to another, then, is entirely an oral matter. It has nothing to do with writing or orthographical systems.

According to Dr. George, OC medial *d* became [d´] in MC and then fell together with [dʒ] from other sources c. 1625. If this were so, then place-names in Cornwall containing the reflex of OC medial *d* might be expected to show two separate developments. In those places where Cornish had been spoken in the MC period, but had become extinct before c. 1625, place-names pronounced by English-speakers should show the nearest English equivalent of [d´]. In those places where Cornish survived beyond c. 1625, place-names with OC medial *d* should display [dʒ], spelt <dg>, <g>, <dj> or <j>.

The nearest English equivalent of [d´] is *d*. Palatalised *d* in Irish place-names almost invariably appear in English as *d*, e.g. *Deargail* > *Dargle*, *Spidéal* > *Spiddle*, *Cúil na gCuiridín* >

Killygordon, etc. In that area of Mid-Cornwall where Cornish was spoken in the Middle Ages, but not after c. 1530, one might expect OC medial *d* to appear in place-names as *d*. It does not, of course. In this area such forms with *d* do not occur. It might then be argued that MC [d′] was so strongly palatalised that English-speakers were unable to distinguish it from [dʒ]. If so, then everywhere in Mid-Cornwall OC medial *d* should appear in place-names as [dʒ] and as [dʒ] only. This is not the case.

The reflex of OC medial *d* in place-names is not infrequently [dʒ], particularly in the west of Cornwall, e.g. *Adjaporth*, *Cadgwith*, *Kenidjack* (cf. B *keuneudek* 'abondant en bois à brûler'). As common a reflex of OC medial *d* in place-names, however, in West- and Mid-Cornwall is *s* or *ss*. Here are some examples: *Trelogossick* (Veryan) < *tre* + OC **logodec*, 'place full of mice'; *Trelissick* (St. Erth, Sithney) < *tre* + OC **guledic*, 'leader'; *Rissick* (Perranarworthal) < OC **ridec*, 'race farm'; *Tregassack* (earlier *Tregarasek*) (Ludgvan) < *tre* + OC **Caradec* (PN, cf. W *Caradog*); *Nanphysick* (St. Mewan) < *nans* + OC *fodic* 'fortunate'; *Carnsew* (Mabe) < *carn* + OC *deviov*, 'gods, fairies'.[13]

If, as Dr. George claims, OC medial *d* gave first [d′] and then [dʒ], these place-names and others like them are quite inexplicable. It is impossible to explain the medial sibilant from OC *d* in these names by the Loth-George hypothesis. The above place-names are in my view quite sufficient to refute the supposed shift [d] > [d′] in Cornish, even if no other evidence were forthcoming.

9. A Suggested Solution: Schema

In the preceding pages I have attempted to show why the supposed development of OC *d*, *t* > MC *d′*, *t′* is illusory. It would perhaps be right for me at this point to set out exactly how I believe Brit. and OC medial and final *d*, *t* developed in MC. This I will now do.

2.1 In medial and final position the second segment in *lt*, *nt* was affricated to *ts* already in the OC period, i.e. before c. 1100. Thus Primitive Cornish *[alt], *[nant], *[kerenteθ] became *[alts], *[nants], *[kerentseθ].

2.2 Probably at the same period *t* in *ti* 'house' became *[tsi] after the article, thus *[an tsi] 'the house'.

2.3 Intervocalic *t* < *d* + *h* was affricated to *ts* in some words: *[pɪsketa] > [pɪsketsa] 'to fish'.

2.4 Probably slightly later, i.e. c. 1100, *d* was affricated to *dz* finally, medially before certain vowels and *w*: *[ta:dz] 'father', *[marxadz] 'market', *[boxo·dzek] 'poor', *[pedzwar] 'four', *[adzwo:n] 'know'.

2.5 Similarly before a stressed front vowel or yod followed by a stressed vowel initial *d* was affricated to *dz* in some common words, when immediately preceded by a proclitic with final *n*: *[an dzɪ:ð] 'the day', *[an dze·van] (< Lat. *daemonem*) 'the demon', *[an dzjawl] 'the devil', *[an dze·ves] 'he has', *[an dze·vɪθ] 'he will have'.

2.6 Medially after *l* and *n* *ts* was voiced to *dz*: *[kerentseθ] > *[kerendze], *[gweltsek] 'grassy' > [gweldzek].

2.7 In certain condition, notably before stressed front vowels and yod + vowel, [dz] was palatalised to [dʒ]: *[an dzɪ:ð] > [an dʒɪ:ð], *[krɪdzjans] > [krɪdʒjans], *[an dze·ves] > [an dʒe·ves].[14] Similarly *[an tsi:] became [an tʃi:].

2.8 Some varieties of Cornish applied the rule of palatalisation more consistently than others. This gave rise to forms like [pɪdʒi] 'to pray' as against *[pɪdzi], [krɪdʒi] 'to believe' as against *[krɪdzi], [kerendʒe] as against *[kerendze], [logo·dʒen] as against *[logo·dzen].

2.9 These varieties of Cornish also had a tendency to palatalise *dz* where there was no following high front vowel to motivate such palatalisation. Thus *[go:dz] 'blood' became [go:dʒ], *[adzwo:n] became [adʒwo:n] and *[pedzwar] became [pedʒwar].

2.10 The palatalising varieties of Cornish also palatalised [ts] > [tʃ]: *[pɪsketsa] > [pɪsketʃa].

2.11 [dz] was simplified to [z] and fell together with [z] from intervocalic *s*, e.g. [gwezjon] 'servants', written <gwesyon> and with [z] in English loanwords, e.g. [prajzja] 'to praise', written <praysya>.

2.12 [ts] was simplified to [s] and fell together with [s] in initial position and [s] from earlier *ss*, e.g. [nesa] 'second', written <nessa>.

2.13 In some dialects intervocalic [z < dz] was rhotacised sporadically to [r]: *era* 'was', *gara* 'to leave'.

10. Discussion of Above Schema

All stages except 2.13 were complete before the MC period. 2.13

was never general. It appears to have occurred early in the sixteenth century.

If the above schema is in outline correct - as I believe it is - then Cornish never possessed either [tʹ] or [dʹ]. In fact the dental/alveolar inventory of MC is both simple and stable: (voiceless) /t:θ:s:tʃ:ʃ/; (voiced) /d:ð:z:dʒ:(ʒ)/. This persisted, albeit with the sporadic change [z > r] (and possibly also [dʒ > ʒ] in some words; see note 19 below) until the death of Cornish in the eighteenth/nineteenth centuries.

2.4 That [d] became [dz] before simplifying to [z] seems guaranteed by the Cornish name for *Market Jew*. This place-name, which means 'Thursday Market', was originally OC [marxad jow]. spelt *Marchadyou, Marcadyow*. It then became [marxadz jow]; compare the spelling *Marghasdiow* (1359). The final [dz] in [marxadz] was then palatalised before the yod in [jow] to give [marxadʒ jow/ow]. This latter is the form given by Lhuyd as (lenited) *Varha Dzhu*.[15] Spellings like *Marghas yow* (PC 2668), *Markasiou* (AD 1261) and *Margasiou* (AD 1277), etc. are etymological.[16]

2.6 The voicing of *nts* > *ndz* seems to be guaranteed by the common spelling *kerenge* 'love' and the absolutely universal spelling of *bolungeth* 'wish', later *blonogath* with <g>. Loth was led astray here by Breton. The MB equivalent of *kerense/kerenge* and *bolungeth* both contain *nt*: *caranté*, *carantez* and *bolunté*, *boluntez*. If *nts* had not already become **ndz* in these words in Cornish, it could not have palatalised to [dʒ], spelt <g>. Dr George follows Loth here and takes *kerenge*, *bolunge* to stand for *[kerentʹe] and *[boluntʹe]. One might conceivably take the spelling <kerense> to mean the final consonant was voiceless, but not <kerenge>. As *bolungeth*, *blonogath* are never spelt with an <s>, we can, I believe, be certain that the group <ng> was voiced in this word and others like it.

2.8 This whole question of palatalisation before *i* is discussed below. Palatalisation before *e* is less common than before *i*. The difference between, for example, *gallosek* and *gallogek* may have something to do with the unrounding of the vowel in the final syllable. Where *ö* in **gallodzök* unrounded to *e* early, *dz* palatalised to [dʒ]. Where **gallodzök* persisted, [dz] had already simplified to [z] before the *e* could palatalise it.

2.9 Lhuyd writes *gûdzh* 'blood' and *lûdzh* 'grey', but elsewhere in LC the word for 'grey' is *looez*. Note also the spelling *oydge* 'age' CW 2101. In MC the words for 'blood', 'grey' and 'age' are not infrequently written with the vowel *oi* or *oy*. This presumably reflects the OC forms *guit* (Norris, 1859a: 379), **luit* and **uit*, with yod before the final consonant. It is presumably this yod that has triggered palatalisation in these words in some dialects.

2.11 I say that [dz] simplified to [z]. In fact *d*, **dz* and *z* are all probably partially voiced lenes. English-speakers would have heard the half-voiced lenis *z* as either [s] or [z]. This would account for the occurrence of *s*(*s*) in place-names. Notice also, incidentally, that the stage *dz* is written *ts* in the thirteenth-century place-name *Retsic* (AD 1244; Pool 1973:66), modern *Rissick*.

11. Dialect Variation in Late Cornish

Late Cornish no longer uses the spelling system of the MC literary language, but rather follows the orthographical conventions of English. Moreover, Edward Lhuyd uses his own 'universal alphabet', i.e. an early system of phonetic transcription. If the above schema from 2.1 to 2.12 is correct, then we would expect to see in LC a series of words where [z] alternates dialectally with [dʒ]. This is precisely what we do find. Note the following doublets from Late Cornish (I give the forms with [dʒ] after the diagonal stroke):[17] *pazuera* 'fourth' Lhuyd, *peswarra* Pryce, *bozvevah* (leg. *bozverah*) Gwavas MS, *bizwau·dhu* (Newlyn 1875; see Trans. Phil. Soc. (1876), 539) / *padgurra* 'fourth' J. Boson, *padzhuera* Pryce, *pagwera* T. Boson; *karensa* 'love' Pryce, *grensa* T. Boson / *karendzha* Pryce, Lhuyd, *crenga* N. Boson, *crenjah* Kerew; *uoze* 'after' Lhuyd, *guozna* 'after that' Lhuyd, *guozma* 'after this' Lhuyd / *udzhe* 'after' Lhuyd, *ugge* N. Boson, *vge* T. Boson, *udzhna* 'after that' Lhuyd, *udzhma* 'after this' Lhuyd; *azuan* 'know' Lhuyd / *adzhuan* 'know' Lhuyd; *nawnzack* 'nineteen' Pryce / *nowndzhak*[18] 'nineteen'; *genzynz* 'with them' Lhuyd / *gyndzhanz*, *gynzhanz* 'with them' Lhuyd.

Notice also the LC alternation in the long forms of the verb *bos*: *idzha* 'is' Lhuyd (AB 242, col. 1, for example), *igge* (e.g. Boson's *iggeva*; Padel 1975:9) / *eravi*, *eram* 'am' (e.g. AB 250, col. 2), (*th*)*era* 'was' (e.g. Padel 1975:15), etc. *Eram*, *era*, etc. are from **e·za + m*, **e·za*, with [z], while *idzha*, *igge* < MC *ugy* [y·dʒi], with reduced final [i] before the enclitic pronoun.

Alongside the above [z/d] alternation in LC one can also set the similar alternations in place-names, for example (forms with [dʒ] appear after the diagonal stroke): OC **melin-di* > *Mellinsey / Mellingey*; OC **hen-di* > *Hensy-wassa / Hengy-yghall*; OC **adwy* (**adwe* ?) > *Assa-wine / Adja-porth*; OC **cadwith* > *Tre-gaswith / Tre-gadgwith*; OC **gueltec* 'grassy' > *Car-walsick / Illis-wilgig*.

A similar and quite remarkable alternation between [s/z] and [dʒ] survives in the English dialect of Cornwall. People who washed in St. Meriasek's well in Camborne were known as *Merrasicks* (Jago, 1882: 216) or *Merrasickers* (BM, introduction p xii) by the local inhabitants. They were also known as *Moragicks*, *Mearagaks* (Jago, ibid.). Moreover, *Merry-geeks* or *Mera-jacks* (Ellis, 1974: 40) was a general nickname for Camborne people themselves. These various survivals clearly continue two separate reflexes of the name of St. Meriasek, [merja·zek] and [merja·dʒek].[19]

The question remains how to explain the distribution of forms in [z] and [dʒ]. As for the reflexes of OC *d* before unstressed *i* and *y*, it would seem from place-name evidence that, curiously enough, palatalisation could occur or fail to occur anywhere in the Cornish-speaking area. I discuss some of the evidence from the texts for this kind of palatalisation below. As far as less motivated palatalisation is concerned, i.e. before *w*, *e*, etc. (in *caswyth*, *gallosek*, etc.), it seems from place-names that Cornish-speaking Cornwall falls into two separate regions. Before examining them, however, something will have to be said about the extent of the Cornish-speaking area itself and the origins of the standard language.

12. Celtophone Cornwall in The Middle Ages

OC *rid* 'ford' and *bod* 'dwelling-place' became *res* and *bos* in MC. According to Jackson, the change *-d* to *-s* was already beginning c. 1100.[20] In the area of east Cornwall between the Tamar to the east and the Camel and Fowey rivers to the west, place-names exhibit forms of these two etyma with *d* rather than *s*. It has been suggested, therefore, that Cornish was extinct in this area before *-d* > *-s*, i.e. before c. 1100.

This argument is based on a false assumption. Certainly English settlement before the Norman Conquest had been more widespread in this far eastern part of Cornwall than further to the west. It is also very likely that English was spoken by many in this area before the advent of the Normans. The appearance of place-names in English with original *d* rather than shifted *s* does not, however, mean that Cornish was extinct in this part of Cornwall by c. 1100. It means only that the English had been familiar with names of settlements in the area since before the change *-d* > *-s* began.

Let us look at an Irish parallel. There are many place-names in Ireland that contain the element *áth* 'ford', *Athy*, *Athlone*, *Athboy*, *Athenry*, for example. The <th> in these names in English is pronounced as [θ], even though [θ] in Irish had become [h] by the end of the twelfth century (Thurneysen, 1946: 76). Yet Irish continued to be spoken in the area of Athy and Athlone until the nineteenth century. In the district around Athboy and around Athenry it continued well into the twentieth.

The place-name *Redruth* in western Cornwall contains the pre-1100 form of *rid*, yet Cornish continued to be spoken in the surrounding district well into the seventeenth century.

There is direct evidence that Cornish was spoken east of the Camel-Fowey line at least until the middle of the fourteenth century. In 1349 the prior of Minster near Boscastle and many of his community and tenants died of the Black Death. A chaplain could not be found for the parish, since none of the surviving friars spoke Cornish (Wakelin, 1975: 88-9). Obviously in Minster c. 1350 many of the laity were monoglot Cornish-speakers. This could hardly have been the only district east of the Camel-Fowey line that spoke Cornish. We can, I think, be fairly confident that Cornish was widely spoken in this most easterly region of Cornwall into the fourteenth century and beyond.

There is certainly good evidence that Cornish was spoken in Bodmin and the Bodmin district in the fourteenth century. In 1354/5 Brother John, a member of the Franciscan house in Bodmin, was appointed penitentiary to hear the confessions of both those who knew Cornish and those who knew English (Wakelin, 89). Moreover we read in the same fourteenth-century source of a certain priest, Ralph de Tremur, from Lanivet just west of Bodmin, who spoke Cornish and English fluently.[21]

The Norman invasion was obviously of the utmost significance for Cornish. The use of new language, French, in administration and law could only mean the weakening of English in Cornwall - at least initially. Moreover, many Bretons were given land in Cornwall and presumably brought with them Celtic-speaking servants and retainers.[22] The renewed links with Brittany clearly affected Cornish literature greatly. It is significant that all surviving MC literature (except for TH) owes more to Breton and French models than to Middle English.[23]

It is very likely that the survival of Cornish in Minster, and presumably elsewhere in the far east of Cornwall, was a direct result of the Norman invasion. The presence of Breton-speakers and the weakening of English probably produced something of a revival in the fortunes of Cornish in those districts where, judging by the place-names, it had been in decline. I would even suggest that Bodmin, as a result of the Norman Conquest, became strongly Cornish in speech, whereas before the coming of the Normans it had probably been largely Anglophone.[24]

13. The Origin of Standard Middle Cornish

The MC texts are remarkable for the uniformity of their spelling and grammar. Apart from CW, all our surviving literary remains exhibit essentially the same orthography and accidence. We are obviously dealing with a highly cultivated and standardised form of language.

The orthography of the OC *Vocabularium Cornicum* is clearly that inherited by Cornish from the Common British period (see LHEB 67-75). The *Vocabularium*, however, shows some admixture of Old English spelling habits.[25] The orthography of MC continues this spelling system but with a number of Anglo-Norman features, e.g. <gh> for [x] and <th> for [θ]. Clearly MC spelling has been influenced by the presence of the Normans in Cornwall. MC orthography also exhibits the assibilation of OC *d*, *t* (the subject of this article), that started sometime in the late 11th century. I would suggest that standard literary MC arose in the hundred or so years after the Norman Conquest, probably in the period 1150-1175.

Standard languages do not emerge in a vacuum. They are usually the speech of a high prestige group in a place where power is exercised. Now it is clear from the Domesday Survey and other sources that the centre of power in Cornwall at this period was Bodmin.[26] I assume, therefore, that literary MC was developed from the earlier OC standard by educated clerics and others in and around Bodmin in the latter half of the twelfth century.

14. The Eastern and Western Dialects of Cornish

Exactly where the linguistic frontier between Cornish and English was in the twelfth century it is now impossible to say. There is evidence that Cornish was widely spoken in or near Padstow c. 1540.[27] It was spoken by the older generation in St. Ewe near St. Austell in 1595.[28] Two generations previously, i.e. c. 1535, it was presumably spoken by everyone in the district. It seems probable, therefore, that the Cornish-English linguistic frontier in the first half of the sixteenth century was at least as far to the east as Padstow and St. Austell. I assume that until the Reformation, Cornish was spoken everywhere west of the Camel and Fowey rivers, if not further to the east.

As has been suggested above, Cornwall as far east as the Camel-Fowey line appears to fall into two separate dialect regions. In the eastern area, to judge from place-name evidence, the reflex of OC medial and final *d* is always *s* (except before *i* or yod). In the western area OC medial and final *d* sometimes appears as [dʒ].

To exemplify the dialectal variation between [s/z] and [dʒ], I list below the place-names containing reflexes of five different OC etyma: (i) **adwy* 'gap'; (ii) **cadwith* 'thicket'; (iii) *logoden* 'mice', **logodec* 'place of mice'; (iv) **gueltec* 'grassy'; (v) **Cadoc* PN, cf. **Madoc*. The forms containing [dʒ] are given after the diagonal stroke:

(i) *Assa Govrankowe* (Gwennap 1580); *Assawine* (Illogan? 1582) / *Adga Bullocke* (Lelant); *Adgewella* (Camborne); *Adgyan Frank* (Constantine 1649); *Adgaporth* (Madron 1614); *Adjawinjack* (Ruan Major); *Agahave* (Ruan Major); *Aja-Bullocke* (Perranuthnoe); *Aga-Gai* (Sennen); *Agareeth* (St. Hilary 1665); *Nangidnall* (< *Goone Agga Idniall* 1670) (Madron).

(ii) *Tregaswith* (St Columb Major); *Rosecassa* (St. Just in Roseland) / *Cadgwith* (Grade); *Trecadgwith* (St. Buryan).

(iii) *Trelogossick* (Veryan); *Legossick* (St. Issey) / *Parken Legagen* (St. Keverne 1710).

(iv) *Carwalsick* (St. Stephen in Brannel) / *Illiswilgig* (Scilly)

(v) *Ventongassick* (St. Just in Roseland); *Roscarrack* (< **Ros Casek*) (Budock); cf. *Polmassick* (< *pons* + **Madoc*) (St. Ewe) / *Porth-cadjack Cove* (Illogan).[29]

Several things must be noted about the above list. Firstly, I have had access only to O.J. Padel's magnificent work on place-name elements while compiling it. I am therefore unaware for the most part of earlier forms for any of the names given.[30] It is more than likely that further information would mean revising the list.[31]

The second point to notice is the remarkable consistency of the distribution. This is particularly apparent from the accompanying map.

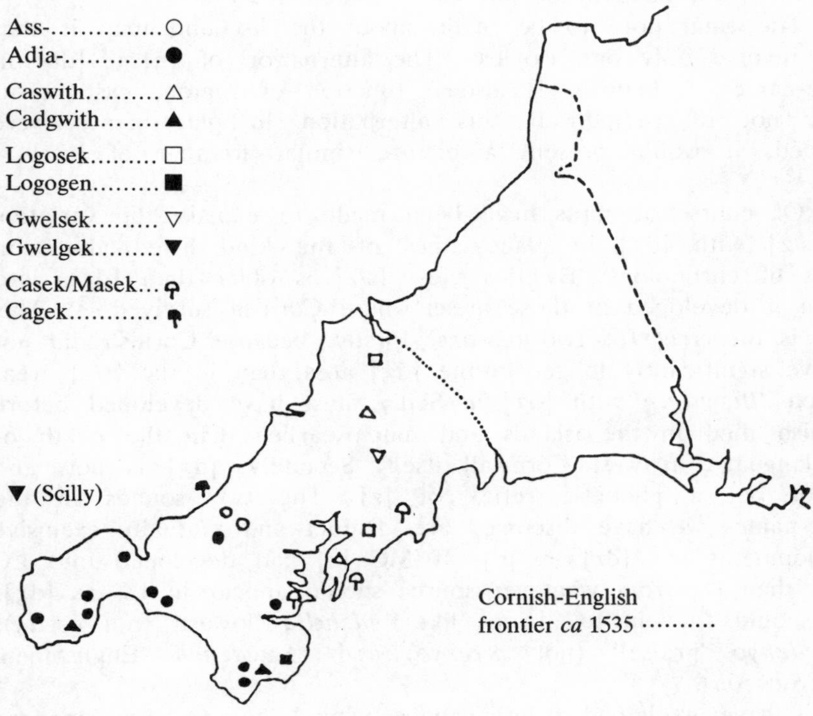

Map 1. The alternation <S>~<G/J> in place-names

Thirdly, it is to be observed that the two dialects seem to overlap in the Camborne-Illogan area. This is exactly what one would expect, given the two forms *Meriasek* and **Meriagek* associated with Camborne.

The fourth point to notice is the following. The distribution of forms shown in the above list and map could no doubt be refined by examining the distribution of *Boj-* forms in place-names as against the case of *Bos-*. Unfortunately, the picture is complicated in the case of *Boj-* by the presence of eastern forms with initial yod in the second element, e.g. *Bogee* (St. Ervan), *Bojea* (St. Austell) < *bod* + **yuf* 'lord' (Padell, 1975: 140). This and other difficulties mean that the question of *Bos-/Boj-* will have to be left for the moment.

The final note to be made about the list and map is that they involve only one isogloss. The alternation of [n] ~ [dn] in place-names, I believe, is also a function of region, east versus west, not of period. If this alternation in place-names were mapped, it would present a picture similar to that of [s/z] ~ [dʒ].[32]

Of course attempts have been made to explain the variation of [s/z] with [dʒ] in place-names of the kind listed above in terms of chronology. By this view [s/z] is older than [dʒ], into which it developed in those areas where Cornish survived.[33] This view is incorrect for two reasons. Firstly, because Cornish did not survive significantly longer in the [dʒ] area than in the [s/z] area. Indeed *Illiswilgig* with [dʒ] in Scilly must have developed before Cornish died in the islands and much earlier than the death of the language in west Cornwall itself. Secondly, [dʒ] is not, and cannot be, a phonetic reflex of [z]. The two sounds in the place-names we have discussed are distinct and mutually exclusive developments of *[dz] < [d]. If MC [z] had developed into LC [dʒ], then [z] from whatever source should appear in LC as [dʒ]. We should find in LC forms like **edzhella* 'lowest' (not *ezella*), **preedzhyo* 'praise!' (not *preezyo*) and **Sawdzhon* 'Englishmen' (not *Sawzon*).

I have explained briefly above why I believe that standard MC emerged in Bodmin. Bodmin is at the far eastern end of our eastern area in which the 'unmotivated' palatalisation of [dz > dʒ] was unknown. This is the reason, I would suggest, that standard MC consistently writes <peswar>, <bohosek>, <gallosek>, etc. Only rarely in the MC texts does one encounter forms with [dʒ], *gallogek*, for example. Such forms reflect the scribe's more westerly dialect. Even though literary MC could tolerate *gallogek*, forms like [go:dʒ] 'blood' and [o:dʒ] 'age' seem to have been quite inadmissible and are not attested until CW.

Literary MC was obviously cultivated at a number of centres. The *Ordinalia* are associated with Glasney, near Penrhyn.[34] BM was almost certainly written in Camborne.[35] We have a dramatic fragment that may have been written in St. Stephen in Brannel (see Fudge, 1982). A life of St. Columba in Cornish, now lost, was in all probability written in St. Columb Major (see Ellis, 1974: 69). CW was written in Helston, while TH were probably written in Newlyn East. Clearly the influence of literary MC was widespread and of considerable importance at least until the dissolution of the monasteries. Even CW, written some 80 or 90 years after the Reformation, though modern in spelling in some ways, is very much in the MC literary standard and tradition.

When we come to LC we find that the literary standard has almost been forgotten. The language is now confined to the western extremities of Cornwall; here forms in [dʒ] are normal in speech. The only spelling known to the Bosons, to Gwavas, Kerew, etc., was that of English. The only dialect of Cornish known to them was the moribund speech of the west. Edward Lhuyd, though he uses his own phonetic alphabet, again has only the dialect of the far west as evidence for the pronunciation of Cornish. Indeed he tells us that most of his oral material was gathered in St. Just in Penwith.[36] It is not astonishing, then, that LC should abound in forms containing [dʒ], where *s* only had been the rule in the MC period.[37]

If western Cornish dialects were so given to forms in [dʒ], it may be legitimately asked why forms like *pezwara*, *kerenza*, etc. survive in Late, and therefore written, Cornish. There are two reasons. As has been noted above, 'unmotivated' palatalisation was not universal and invariable in western dialects. For example CW, written in Helston in 1611, always writes <woʒa>, [wo·zə], never [wo·dʒə]. Similarly the place-name *Trelissick* in Sithney and St. Erth (< *tre* + OC **guledic* 'leader') shows *s* not [dʒ]. Even in the far west, then, dialects may have been mixed. The second reason is that even where the dialect was prone to palatalisation, in former times at any rate, speakers would have been in regular maritime and other contact with dialects further east. Such dialects would have been of higher social standing than that of the westerners. Even if the western dialects had not been spontaneously mixed, constant contact with speakers from further east would have tended to make them so.

15. Palatalisation in the Texts

Having discussed the origin and significance of the alternation *s* ~ *g*, I should like to finish this article by examining in some depth the alternation as it is to be observed in our surviving MC texts.

The palatalisation in 2.7 is clearly the most universal. *An geyth*, 'the day' and forms of *a'm bus* after *y'n*, *a'n* are invariably spelt with <g/i> in the texts. Similarly, words containing OC *d* followed by yod + vowel are always palatalised, e.g. *brygyon* 'boil', *esgygyow* 'shoes', *crygyans/cregyans* 'faith' (see below). The position is similar in place-names. Note, for example, *Rees*, *Rice* < OC *rid*, but *Ridgeo* < pl. **ridiou* (Padel, 1985: 198 A).

Palatalisation before a high front but unstressed vowel is much less consistent. This is obvious from place-names, where one finds doublets of the kind *Melinsey/Mellingey* (Padel, 1985: 161), *St. Issey/St. Jidgey* (ibid., 204, 304; cf. also *Mevagissey*), etc. If we compare the spelling of the three forms *crysaf* (*cresaf*) 'I believe', *crysy/crygy* 'to believe' and *crygyans* 'belief, faith' in the MC texts, we obtain the following picture (the *g*-forms are given after the diagonal stroke):

	crysaf	*crysy/crygy*	*crygyans*
PA	-/-	-/-	0/1
OM	2/0	6/0	0/1
PC	-/-	0/3	0/4
RD	3/0	2/24	0/7
BM	7/0	4/0	0/6
TH	-/-	17/1	0/10
SA	-/-	0/2	0/1
CW	-/-	0/4	0/2

Table 1.

The first point to notice here is that *crysaf* always has *s*, *crygyans* always *g* (the spelling *crisgians* in TH has not been included). This is compelling evidence that <s> and <g> are not in free variation. The second point to notice is that the hesitation *St. Issey/St. Jidgey* is reflected in *crysy/crygy*. We appear to have two separate groups among the texts. OM, BM and TH prefer *crysy*, while PC, RD, SA and CW prefer *crygy*. The position is similar, though not identical, in the case of *pysaf* 'I pray', *pysy* 'to pray'. I tabulate the instances with those of *pysadow/peiadow* 'prayer' in Table 2. Again forms in *g/i* are given after the diagonal stroke.

	pysaf	*pysy/pygy*	*pysadow/peiadow*
PA	-/-	7/0	1/0
OM	2/0	5/0	1/0
PC	2/0	1/6	0/3
RD	4/0	0/6	-/-
BM	10/0	31/0	0/7
TH	-/-	1/0	2/0
SA	-/-	0/1	1/1
CW	0/2	0/1	-/-

Table 2.

Here *pysaf* is spelt universally with an *s* except in CW. Presumably the 1st person sg. in CW, *pydgyaf* (CW 1364, 1670) has been reshaped on the basis of the verbal noun. It can hardly be from a dialectal 3rd sg. *[pɪ:dʒ] (cf. *oydge* 'age' CW 2101), since the 3rd sg. in CW ends in [z]: *my ath pyese* CW 617, *ath pys* CW 172.[38] As far as the verbal noun in Table 2 is concerned, it is obvious that the texts hesitate in their spelling in precisely the same way as with *crysy*. PA clearly falls into the *s*-group (there was no evidence for *crysy* in PA), as do OM, BM and TH. On the other hand, PC, RD, SA and CW prefer *g*. The sample is small, but its aggreement with the pattern vis-à-vis *crysy* gives it the appearance of versimilitude. Notice incidentally that both *pysy* and *pygy* survive in LC. Lhuyd gives both *pizi* and *pidzhi* (AB 250, col.2 and AB 223).

As far as both *crysy* and *pysy* are concerned, BM is the text least likely to palatalise. This does not mean, however, that BM never palatalises before a high front vowel. Note, for example, the quite remarkable alternation: *dewosa*, *dewose* 'bleed' BM 1575, 1584, 1619, but *dewogys* 'bled' BM 1556.

A further isogloss cuts across the *pysy/pygy* division. PC and BM regularly have [dʒ] in the word for 'prayer', while *pysadow* occurs elsewhere (though there are no examples from either RD or CW), and SA has one example of each. The basic form *[pɪdza·dow] is analogical anyway, since *d* would not assibilate before *a*. The reason that *dz* in *[pɪdza·dow] was palatalised in some dialects is probably to be sought in the position of the accent. It would appear that *dz* had a tendency to become [dʒ] before back vowels, if such back vowels bore the accent. This would explain such forms as *bohogogneth* 'poverty' BM 2010, *bohogogyon* 'poor people' BM 4204. For the alternation of *kerensa* with *kerengeak* [kerendze·ðek] in TH see 2.7 above.

If we look at the reflexes of OC **ni*(*n*)*d* 'not' before forms of the verb *bos* 'to be', we obtain the following interesting picture (again *g*-forms are given after the diagonal stroke):

	nyns yw	*nyns eus*	*nyn usy*	*nyns o*	*nyns esa*
PA	0/3	0/4	0/1	0/8	0/3
OM	3/0	17/0	1/0	–/–	–/–
PC	7/0	4/0	–/–	–/–	–/–
RD	12/0	2/0	1/0	–/–	1/1
BM	16/0	14/0	1/0	2/0	1/0
TH	19/3	15/5	8/3	10/2	4/1
SA	0/9	0/2	0/2	0/4	0/2
CW	1/6	0/11	–/–	–/–	0/2

Table 3.

It is apparent from this table that all MC texts favour either the *s*-forms (OM, PC, RD, BM) or the *g*-forms (PA, SA, CW). There is no variation except in TH. Clearly the writer's dialect was a mixed one. At all events, there is little support in the above table for the contention that <s> and <g> are in free variation. The origin of *nyng* rather than *nyns* is not difficult to explain. *Nyng* < *[nɪnd] arose spontaneously in some dialects before the high front vowel in *yw* 'is'. This was then generalised. *Nyns* on the other hand represents the normal development of **nind* before *eus* [œːs] and *usy*/*ugy* [y·zi, y·dʒi].

I have already alluded to the different treatment of OC *-d-* in *esof*, *esa*, etc., on the one hand, and *usy*, *ugy* on the other. The following table gives the spelling of the three forms of *esof* 'I am', *esa*, *ega* 'was' and *usy*, *ugy* 'is'.

Here again the picture is as one would expect. With *esof* there is no variation; <s> is universal. With *esa* <s> is much commoner than <g>. On the other hand, *ugy* is slightly commoner overall than *usy*. *Ege* in RD and *ega* in TH are presumably the result of palatalisation before the original *-e* of the ending: *[e·dze] > [e·dʒe].

	esof	*esa*	*usy*
PA	-/-	44/0	0/2
OM	-/-	1/0	1/3
PC	1/0	-/-	0/1
RD	-/-	3/1	1/3
BM	3/0	3/0	4/0
TH	2/0	44/1	37/36
SA	-/-	5/0	0/13
CW	6/0	-/-	6/1

Table 4.

Ege has yielded to paradigmatic pressure from *esof*, *esos*, etc. and *esa* is the usual form. Only with the high front ending in *usy*, *ugy* is palatalisation at all common. Notice incidentally that SA not only exhibits 5 examples of *esa* and none of *ega*, but also has a number of instances of *era* < *[e·za].

16. Wosa 'after'

I have already discussed the word 'after' in CW. The distribution of *s*- and *g*-forms in the texts as a whole is as follows (*g*-forms are given after the diagonal stroke): PA -/-; OM 0/2; PC 1/5; RD 0/3; BM 7/0; TH 31/0; SA -/-; CW 7/0. Clearly [wo·zə] is the only form in BM, TH and CW. There is no 'free variation'. The three plays of the *Ordinalia* prefer [wo·dʒə]. Reflexes of both [wo·zə] and [wo·dʒə] occur in LA, as has been noted above.

One of the two instances in OM is not *woge* but *wege* (OM 2828). This is probably not a mistake, but a historic variant. The British form was **wodi3*; with *i*-affection this gave OW *guetig*, W *wedi*, MC *wege*. An unaffected **wodi3* persisted side-by-side with **wedi3*, however, giving B *goude* and MC *wose*, *wosa* (Lewis and Pedersen, 1961: 109). It is possible that MC *woge* is a conflation of **wedi3* > *wege* and **wodi3* > *wose*.

17. Tressa, tryge 'third'

The Proto-British word for 'third' was **tritiyo–*, giving W *trydydd*, B *trede*. The regular MC development would have been *tryge*, *trege* if [d > dz > dʒ], and **tryse* if [dz] became [z]. *Tryge*, *trege* occurs five times in RD (339, 452, 681, 691, 2605), but nowhere else in MC. Elsewhere the form is *tresse*, *tressa*, *tryssa*, *trissa*. This form in PA, OM, BM, TH and CW occurs in all 32 times. **Tryse* is nowhere attested. Loth (1897: 416) takes *tryssa*, *tressa* as an orthographic variant of *trege*, with <ss> as yet another graph for [dʹ]. He cannot be right. Firstly, because [dʹ] does not exist, and secondly, because <ss> is used regularly in MC as a graph for [s] between vowels from a variety of sources, e.g. *brassa* 'greater', *ressys* 'thou gavest', *grassa* 'to thank', *Massen* < Lat. *Maximus*.

In *tryssa*, *tressa* the medial consonant is by analogy with the preceding ordinal, *nessa* 'second'. The series *kensa*, *nessa*, **tryse* has quite understandably become *kensa*, *nessa*, *tryssa*. Although *tryssa* is the customary form in standard MC, the (western?) dialect of RD prefers *tryge*. So also does LC, for John Boson writes *tridga*, *tridgia* (Padel, 1975: 52, 55).

18. Back-spellings, etc.

The alternation of [z] and [dʒ] in speech obviously led to a certain amount of confusion in spelling. If, as seems probable, [z] was considered preferable to [dʒ] in some words, one might expect scribes to substitute <s> for <g>, even where <g> was the correct graph. This indeed has happened in a few cases. Note, for example, *ow hobersen* 'my habergeon' for *ow hobergen* at RD 2536 and *nynsevith* (TH 40), *nynsevas* (TH 49) for *nyngevith* and *nyngevas* respectively.

More important than such purely graphemic slips are the cases of back-formation in speech itself. BM is the text least likely to write <g> when it is possible to write <s>. I take this to mean that the scribe was particularly careful to adhere to standard norms. Camborne was in all probability, however, in an area where *s*-forms and *g*-forms were somewhat confused. This factor appears to have led the scribe of BM to adopt spellings in which *g* is unetymological, e.g. *martegen* 'perhaps' (B *marteze*)) at BM 61. *Martegen* was probably the form in the Camborne dialect.

One could also perhaps explain *falge* (< English *false*) at BM 777, 987, 1161, etc. and *calge* (B *cals*) at BM 2046 in this way. It may be, however, that these two forms are analogical in origin. Compare also LC *algia* [aldʒə] instead of the expected *alsa* (W *(g)allasai*). *Falge*, *calge* and *algia* have in all probability been influenced by the frequency of forms in *-ld-* from OC *-lt-*, e.g. **gwelgek* 'grassy' (*Illiswilgig*), **algyow* 'shores', etc.

A similar analogical formation is probably the explanation for certain place-names. The word *lesyow* 'herbs' (W *llysiau*) occurs in the place-names *Lidgiow*, *Bithen Lidgeo* and possibly *Ponslego* and *Carn Lodgia* (Padel, 1985: 142 (s.v. *les* 'plant')). Here *lesyow* has become **lejyow* under the influence of forms like **rejyow* 'fords' (< OC **ridiou*) and LC *lidzhiw* (< **ludeu*) 'ashes'.

Before leaving the topic of how the texts spell the reflexes of OC *d*, the following point should be made. Judging by the distribution of *s*- and *g*-forms, it is apparent that the dialect of OM differs considerably from that of PC and RD. Whatever the original authorship of the three plays, it seems likely that the scribal exemplar of the *Ordinalia* in the Bodleian manuscript was written by two different hands. Moreover, the original scribe of OM was probably from further east in Cornwall than the scribe of PC and RD.

19. Conclusion

Neither /t´/ nor /d´/ ever existed in Cornish. Where OC *t*, *d* were assibilated, they became in standard MC either [tʃ], e.g. *chy*, [s], e.g. *pyskessa*, [z], e.g. *bohosek*, or [dʒ], e.g. *bolungeth*, *an geyth*, *crygyans*. Some more western dialects, where standard Cornish had [z], written <s>, frequently preferred [dʒ]. [dʒ] for standard [z] is not common in the MC texts, but is abundant in our fragmentary remains of LC, which are exclusively western in provenance.

Since neither /t´/ nor /d´/ ever existed in Cornish, there is no reason to introduce them into the revived language. Indeed there is every reason to resist their introduction. A historically accurate orthography can perfectly well indicate the phonemic reflexes of OC *t*, *d* in MC with <t>, <d>, <ss>, <s>, <ch> and <j>, i.e. as is the case already in *Mordonnek*. Whatever new orthography is devised for revived Cornish, it ought not contain the unnecessary and unhistorical graphs <tj> and <dj>. My advice to the linguistic planners of the Cornish revival would be that of John Chyanhor's master to him after three years' labour (Padel, 1985: 17): *Bethez gueskez duath, ken gueskel eneth, rag edda eu an guella point a skeeans oll*, 'Do nothing without second thoughts, for that is the best advice of all'.

Abbreviations

AB	*Archaeologia Britannica* |Lhuyd 1707|
B	Breton
BM	*Beunans Meriasek* |Stokes 1872|
Brit.	British
CW	*The Creation of the World* |Stokes 1864|
Lat.	Latin
LC	Late Cornish
LHEB	*Language and History in Early Britain* |Jackson 1953|
MB	Middle Breton
MC	Middle Cornish
ME	Middle English
OC	Old Cornish
OM	*Origo Mundi* |Norris 1859a:2-219|
OW	Old Welsh
PA	*Pascon agan Arluth* |Stokes 1860|
PC	*Passio Domini Nostri Jhesu Christi* |Norris 1859a:223-479|
PG	Proto-Germanic
PN	Personal name
PSRC	*The Pronunciation and Spelling of Revised Cornish* |George 1986|
RC	*Revue Celtique*
RD	*Resurrexio Domini Nostri Jhesu Christi* |Norris 1859b:1-201|
SA	'The Sacrament of the Altar' |13th homily in TH|
TH	*The Tregear Manuscript* |Bice n.d.|

Notes

1. See, for example, Nance (1949). The best grammar of Unified Cornish (though it contains much reconstruction) is Brown (1984).

2. Other systems include Tim Saunder's etymological spelling and *Carnoack Tithiack*, favoured by Rod Lyon. See PSRC 32-4. For a compromise between Unified Cornish and LC, see Lyon (1984).

3. Loth (op. cit., 404-6) also believed that *s* in *tas* represented |s| < |t|. This is an erroneous view, as the OC spelling *tat*, 'father', was phonetically |ta : d|.

4. George dates |nd´| > |ndʒ| c. 1575 and |Vd´V| > |VdʒV| c. 1625;

see PSRC 165.

5. The graph <dg> occurs in CW, but it is based on English <dg>; see below.

6. The form *ty* survives in some place-names, e.g. *Tywardreath*, *Tywarnhayle*, *Tybesta*. Notice also *ow thy a piyadow* 'my house of prayer' PD 334, with *ty* spirantised to *thy* after *ow* 'my'.

7. Loth (op. cit., 416) claims that in *woʒa* in CW *ʒ* has the value *dj*, i.e. |d´|. This is special pleading and the principle of Occam's razor disposes of it.

8. A LC form of *ganso* |gondʒə|, variously spelt, is attested. It does not occur in MC.

9. George believes MC *d* and *t* were alveolar not dental; PSRC 156, 163. This makes his two threefold series /t̪:t´:tʃ/, /d̪:d´:dʒ/, even less credible, since the articulatory distances are so small.

10. If *esos* 'thou art' were *|ed´os|, then the form with enclitic pronoun *-ta*, **ed'os* + *ta* > **ed´sta* should give **etta*. The attested form is, of course, *esta* < *esosta*.

11. Nance suggested understanding *gyr tero* in *John of Chyanhor* as 2nd pl. imperative, *gortero*, 'tarry' < **gortoseugh*. If this were correct, it would be a further example of *s* |z| > *r*. See Padel (1975: 23).

12. Curiously George believes that OC *tadou*, 'fathers' would have developed normally to *|tad´ow| in MC (PSRC 81). *-adow* remained unshifted in MC, cf. *caradow*, *casadow*, *piyadow*, etc.

13. The place-names in this section and their etymologies are from Padel (1985).

14. Lewis & Pedersen (1961: 155) believe that 'palatalisation' > |dʒ| occurs before front vowels, but they accept Loth's view that |d´| is the starting point; see also LHEB 397.

15. AB 253, §7, Cf. also the place-names *Bogee*, *Bojea* both from *bod* + **yuf*; see Padel (1985: 140).

16. These and the other early instances of the name *Market Jew* are quoted in Fowler (1961).

17. Unless otherwise stated these examples are taken from AB, Pryce (1790), Loth (1900) and Padel (1975).

18. Quoted by Jackson (1967: 793). Note further that MC *bohosek*, 'poor' and MC *ollgallosek* 'omnipotent' are recorded in LC as *bohodzhak* (Lhuyd) and *agallasack* (Norris, 1859b: 466). i.e. with |dʒ| and |s/z| respectively.

19. Lhuyd (AB 224) gives the name as *Meriazhek*. This is apparently a weakened form of *Meriadzhek*. The weakening of |dʒ| > |ʒ| is noticeable in CW, where enclitic *ge* 'thee' is devoiced after *s* to *sche* (not **che*); e.g. CW 216, 268.

20. LHEB 396-8. This dating may be slightly too late, given that phonetic processes occur sooner than they appear in orthography.

21. Ellis (1974: 33). De Tremur also knew French and Latin. He was instituted to the rectory of Warleggan. John de Grandisson, Bishop of Exeter 1327-69, to whom we owe the reference to de Tremur, presumably mentions that de Tremur could speak Cornish because it was of use to him in his parish. He was excommunicated for heresy, however. At all events it is likely that Cornish was spoken at Warleggan in the mid-fourteenth century.

22. Some observers refer to the Norman Conquest as the Amorican Return, so important do they regard the presence of Bretons in Cornwall and the renewed contacts with Brittany. Cf. the observations of Tim Saunders: "Linguistically, Cornwall remained fairly stable from the Amorican Return until the rise of the centralizing Tudor state, approximately four hundred years. Cornu-Breton...formed the medium of daily intercourse over the most of the territory, except in the East which it shared with Western English"; Ó Luain (1983: 253).

23. For the relationship of the *Ordinalia* to French and Breton models, see Longsworth (1967: 1-2) and Bakere (1980: 1). Note that PA and OM contain traditions uncommon in England but common in France; Bakere (1980: 105). BM deals with a Breton saint and is largely set in Brittany.

24. George believes that Cornish was spoken widely in east Cornwall after the Norman Conquest. He says "After the Norman invasion, Cornish was less under threat from English, for English itself was threatened by French. Cornish was spoken by the vast majority of the populace except in the far north-east which had been settled by English-speakers." Commission (1986: 194).

25. OC uses three Anglo-Saxon letters, þ, ð and ƿ that are virtually

unknown in W and completely so in B; LHEB 67-75.

26. See Wakelin (1975: 69-70). Notice also that the gospel-book containing the records of manumitted slaves was written in Bodmin in the period 940-1040.

27. John Leland visiting Cornwall at some time during the years 1535-43 noted that Padstow was called *Lodenek* in Cornish. This implies, I think, that Cornish was widely spoken in the Padstow area at the time. See Ellis (1974: 58).

28. In a deposition of the Bishop's Consistory Court a girl at St. Ewe in 1595 said she heard two of the witnesses talking together in Cornish and English; Wakelin (1975: 89). This can only mean that a girl heard two people older than herself talking Cornish with a large admixture of English words and phrases. Even when a language is dying, truly bilingual conversations are not normal.

29. Note also that Tregassack in Ludgvan was called *Tregaragek* in 1326; Pool (1973: 71). The name is obviously from *tre* + **Carasek*, the Cornish equivalent of W *Caradog*. In West Penwith the form in *-agek* would be the expected one.

30. Early forms of some place-names in West Penwith often show *s* as well as *g*, e.g. *Lanscoisek* 1302, *Lanscoegek* 1327, modern *Lescudjack*; see Pool (1973: 57). The *s*-forms reflect standard spelling; see also note 29 above. I do not agree, however, with Padel's etymology of *Bosoljack* (Gulval) < *bod* + **houliek*, 'sunny'. The early forms given by Pool are *Bossulsek* 1334, *Bossolsak* 1478, *Bossulsack* 1575. I would understand the second element as **solsek* < *sols* 'shilling, money', with the transferred sense 'wealth, cattle', cf. B *saout*, 'bétail'.

31. I suspect that if they had survived, the names *Assawine* and *Assa Govrankowe* might conceivably have shown <dg> as well as <ss>. This would mean the loss of one item from our list, but it would not invalidate the general argument, since the two names in *Assa-* are at the far western limit of the *s*-area.

32. For the distribution of *-dn* in place-names, see Wakelin (1975: 79). The explanation given there for them is incorrect, I believe. Since *-dn* occurs in BM, it is probably older than the early sixteenth century. I would place it at least as early as the mid-fifteenth century. It appeared late in spelling because it was considered substandard. Note, however, that it is attested in Scilly.

33. See Wakelin (1975: 75-6) and cf. the rather naive statement of Rod Lyon: "Del ve leverys kens, yth esa trelyans a'n son 'd' dhe'n son 's' ha wosa dhe 'j'. Mes...yth esa trelyans a ogas dhe bup lytheren 's' dhe 'j', kens oll pan esa an 's' ynter deu vogalen." |As has been mentioned, there was a mutation of the sound 'd' to 's' and afterwards to 'j'. But...there was a mutation of almost every letter (sic) 's' to 'j', in particular when the 's' was between vowels.| in Ó Luain (1983: 236). Nance also believed that *s* gave *j* in place-names; see, for example, Nance (1967: 4).

34. See Fowler (1961) and Fudge (1982) for references.

35. Fudge (1982: 22-4). Note that at the end of part one of BM the Duke invokes the blessing of Christ, Meriasek, patron of Camborne and of Mary of Camborne upon the audience: *wy agis beth gor ha gruek/banneth crist has meryasek/banneth maria cambron* BM 2508-10.

36. "An fòr' a 'rykemeraz vi dho deska an nebaz skîanz-ma a'n Tavazeth Kernûak, ô enrâdn dre skrefyanz dhort genauo an bôbl en Gorleuen *Kernou* enuedzhek en pleu *Yst*." |The method I adopted to learn this little knowledge of the Cornish dialect was in part through writing down from the mouths of the people in the west of Cornwall, in particular in St. Just in Penwith|, AB 222.

37. Richard Angwyn of St. Just in Penwith, who died c. 1671-75, was a scholar of Cornish who could read and write the language. All his papers were destroyed after his death. See Ellis (1974: 88). It is likely that Angwyn when speaking Cornish said |bohoˑdʒək|, |adʒwoˑn|, |goːdʒ|, but he probably wrote them with an *s*, at least some of the time.

38. Notice, however, Pryce under "Mottoes and Sentences" cites *me a pidge thu Deew*, 'I pray to God'.

References

Bakere, J. (1980) *The Cornish Ordinalia*. Cardiff: University of Wales Press.

Bice, C. (n.d.) *The Tregear Manuscript: Homilies in Cornish*. [Multigraphed typescript].

Brown, W. (1984) *A Grammar of Modern Cornish*. Saltash.

Commission of the European Communities. (1986) *Linguistic Minorities in Countries Belonging to the European Community*. Luxembourg.

Ellis, P. (1974) *The Cornish Language and its Literature*. London: Routledge and Kegan Paul.

Fowler, D. (1961) *Mediaeval Studies* **23**. Toronto.

Fudge, C. (1982) *The Life of Cornish*. Redruth.

George, K. (1986) *The Pronunciation and Spelling of Revived Cornish*. Cornish Language Board.

Jackson, K. (1953) *Language and History in Early Britain*. Edinburgh: Edinburgh University Press.

Jackson, K. (1967) *Historical Phonology of Breton*. Dublin: Dublin Institute for Advanced Studies.

Jago, F. (1882) *The Ancient Language and Dialect of Cornwall*. Truro.

Lewis, H. & Pedersen, H. (1961) *A Concise Comparative Celtic Grammar*. Göttingen: Gunter Narr.

Lhuyd, E. (1707) *Archaeologia Britannica*. Oxford.

Longsworth, R. (1967) *The Cornish Ordinalia*. Cambridge.

Loth, J. (1897) Études corniques i. *Revue Celtique,* **18,** 410-24.

Loth, J. (1900) Études corniques ii. *Revue Celtique,* **23,** 173-200.

Lyon, R. (1984) *Everyday Cornish*. Redruth.

Nance, R. (1949) *Cornish for All: A Guide to Unified Cornish*. St. Ives: James Lanham.

Nance, R. (1967) *A Guide to Cornish Place-names*. Marazion.

Norris, E. (1859a) *Ancient Cornish Drama,* vol.i. London.

Norris, E. (1859b) *Ancient Cornish Drama,* vol. ii. London.

Ó Luain, C. (ed.) (1983) *For a Celtic Future*. Dublin.

Padel, O. (1975) *The Cornish Writings of the Boson Family*. Redruth: Institute of Cornish Studies.

Padel, O. (1985) *Cornish Place-name Elements*. Nottingham.

Pool, P. (1973) *The Place-names of West Penwith*. Federation of Old Cornwall Societies.

Pryce, W. (1790) *Archaeologia Cornu-Britannica*. Sherborne.

Stokes, W. (1860) Poem of Mount Calvary: Pascon agan Arluth. *Transactions of the Philological Society,* **1860-61**, Appendix, 1-100.

Stokes, W. (ed.) (1864) *Gwreans an Bys: The Creation of the World*. London and Edinburgh.

Stokes, W. (ed.) (1872) *Beunans Meriasek: The Life of St. Meriasek, Bishop and Confessor*. London.

Thurneysen, R. (1946) *Old Irish Grammar*. Dublin: Dublin Institute for Advanced Studies.

Wakelin, M. (1975) *Language and History in Cornwall*. Leicester: Leicester University Press.

PART THREE

Studies in Literary Linguistics

Irish Elements in Late Medieval Welsh Literature: The Problem of Cuhelyn and *Nyf

Patrick Sims-Williams
St John's College, Cambridge

The dearth of evidence for early medieval Welsh knowledge of vernacular Irish literature[1] could conceivably be explained by the loss of relevant material. Such an explanation would be less plausible for the later Middle Ages, from which so much Welsh literature survives, including a large corpus of highly allusive poetry. The poets prided themselves on their learning, and alluded copiously to the legends of Wales and the 'Old North', of the Bible, of the Ancient world, of France and Norman England. Yet, significantly, their allusions to Irish literature are extremely scarce.[2] These allusions provide a more objective yardstick of Irish influence than the subjective inferences that T. Gwynn Jones and others drew from comparisons of the themes and metrics of Irish and Welsh poetry.[3] This point was already made by Ifor Williams in 1910. Arguing against the late tradition that the Welsh court-poetry of the Gogynfeirdd was inspired by Irish influences brought in by Gruffudd ap Cynan in the early twelfth century, he observed:

> Y ddadl gryfaf, fodd bynnag, yn erbyn olrhain y mudiad i Iwerddon yw hyn: nid oes olion dim cydnabyddiaeth â llên nac â hanes y Gwyddel yng ngwaith y Gogynfeirdd. Cyfeiriant yn ddibaid at arwyr Cymru Fu, enwogion Mabinogi a chwedl, - ond ni sonir [*sic*] gair am Gocholyn a Chonchobar. Yn wir, trwy holl lenyddiaeth Gymraeg y Canol

> Oesoedd, nid oes ond rhyw brin hanner dwsin o gyfeiriadau pendant diamwys at chwedlau Gwyddelig.[4]

It might be objected that the Welsh bards knew Irish stories but deliberately avoided mentioning them, rather as their Irish counterparts tended to ignore Arthurian tales.[5] Such a hypothesis would be difficult to square with the fact that three Irish characters (and only three), Fionn, Deirdre, and Cú Chulainn *are* referred to, on six or seven occasions, by four or five poets.[6] Moreover, if Irish stories were known but despised, we would expect to find references to them in satirical poetry; but, again, only *Derdri* is mentioned (twice) in such contexts, whereas satirical allusions to the Irish and Irishmen are all too common in Welsh poetry from the days of Gruffudd ap Cynan onwards.[7]

When Sir Ifor referred in 1910 to 'a bare half-dozen definite, unambiguous allusions to Irish tales' he was probably thinking of *Corröi* and *Cocholyn* (Cú Roi and Cú Chulainn) and *kaer sidi* (cf. Irish *sidhe*) in the Book of Taliesin, the Irish names in *Culhwch and Olwen*, and the allusion to *Ffin* (Fionn) in *Araith Iolo Goch*; these had been discovered and discussed in the previous twenty years by John Rhys, Kuno Meyer, and Ludwig Stern.[8] After the First World war, native Welsh scholars became more interested in Irish literature and the number of such references was swelled, notably by T. Gwynn Jones, who emphasized the fourteenth- and fifteenth-century allusions to *Derdri*, and by J. Lloyd-Jones, who discovered one (or possibly two) further allusion(s) to *Ffin(n)* in fourteenth-century poetry.[9] These allusions to Fionn and Deirdre are certainly important. They are a hero and heroine who had appeared neither in extant early Welsh poetry, nor in the long list of heroes and heroines in *Culhwch and Olwen*, so Welsh knowledge of them is probably due to fourteenth-century contacts with Ireland rather than to a long literary tradition in Wales; they differ, then, from the fossilized late medieval references to *sidi*, which simply derive from the earlier Book of Taliesin poems.[10] Moreover, the poems which allude to them are not deliberately esoteric like the Book of Taliesin boasting poems, so we may presume the names *Ffin(n)* and *Derdri* evoked some narrative - however minimal and however different from any told in Ireland - unlike some native heroic names, which the poets kept alive for the sake of their traditional 'aura' long after their stories were forgotten.[11]

Nevertheless, one or two swallows should not be allowed to make an Indian summer of Irish influence: T. Gwynn Jones greatly exaggerated the strength of the late medieval evidence in trying to maintain both that the allusion to Deirdre in Gruffudd ap Maredudd (fourteenth century) reflects an 'old' Welsh narrative tradition, and that the one in Lewys Glyn Cothi (fifteenth century) is 'interesting evidence of the character of Welsh culture shortly before its suppression'.[12]

Ifor Williams seems to me to have been basically correct in 1910 in minimizing the Irish element. After the First World War, however, the pendulum swung and even the sceptics[13] Morris-Jones and Ifor Williams detected two new 'Irish' names in the Welsh sources: *Cuhelyn* representing *Cú Chulainn* and **Nyf* representing *Niamh*. I hope to show that both these identifications, now generally accepted, were almost certainly mistaken.

1. Cuhelyn

In his 1895 paper on 'The Goidels in Wales', Sir John Rhys popularized the view that the many early Welsh names which would now be analysed as containing **kuno-* 'hound', **kom-* 'co-', and **koimo-* 'dear' were really the names of such 'Goidels'.[14] Rhys did not mention *Cuhelyn*, but his paper presumably lies behind Morris-Jones's mistaken identification of a number of personal names in the Old Welsh 'Surexit' memorandum as Irish, including *Cinhilinn*:

> *Cinhilinn* is the Irish name *Cūchulainn*, with the stem *Con-* instead of the nominative *Cū-* of the first element. The name usually occurs in Welsh as *Cuhelyn*.[15]

No comparative philologist would now equate these three names.[16] *Cuhelyn*, which is already well attested in Welsh by the twelfth century,[17] is surely a native name, perhaps compounded from *cu* 'dear',[18] *hel-* (< **selg-*) 'hunt', and the suffix *-yn*.[19]

Admittedly, *Cuhelyn* might conceivably be used in Welsh as the nearest available native substitute for the Irish name *Cú Chulainn*, despite the great phonetic difference. On the other hand, the Welsh representations of *Cú Chulainn* which are in fact attested are *Cocholyn* in the early *Marwnat Corroi* in the Book of Taliesin (MS fourteenth-century), *Cocholyn* (var. *Cocholyñ*) in the name of a landholding (*gafael*) in the early-fifteenth-century *Extent of Merioneth*, *Cychwlynn* in a fifteenth-century autograph poem by Lewys Glyn Cothi, and *Cochwlyn* (varr. *Cycholyn*, *Cychôlyn*, *Kachwlyn*) in the name of an (?Irish) tune (*caniad* *ar gainc Cochwlyn*) in the sixteenth-century lists of traditional Welsh music.[20] Nevertheless, in 1952 Thomas Parry, in a note on three thirteenth- and fourteenth-century references to *ysgwyd Guhelyn* ('Cuhelyn's shield'), in the poetry of Prydydd y Moch, Iolo Goch, and Dafydd ap Gwilym, quoted Morris-Jones' identification of *Cuhelyn* and *Cú Chulainn* and the equation has been accepted by more recent scholars.[21] A problem with the identification is that Dafydd ap Gwilym's other allusion to Cuhelyn - describing a singing nightingale (*eos*) as 'Cuhelyn's sister' (*chwaer Guhelyn*) - makes no apparent sense in relation to the Irish warrior Cú Chulainn, but could well refer to Dafydd's twelfth-century ancestor, Cuhelyn Fardd, whose epithet shows him have been a poet.[22] The nightingale is naturally compared to a poet, and still more to a musician: one thinks here of the epithet of the fifteenth-century harpist Siôn Eos,[23] and Dafydd ap Gwilym's comparison of himself, singing a *cainc* ('melody', etc.), with a nightingale singing 'as taught by Hildr'; the latter was a traditional master-musician (and father of another, Adda ap Hildr), according to the sixteenth-century lists.[24] Indeed, this raises the possibility that Dafydd ap Gwilym's allusion is to the master-musician Cuhelyn to whom various *ceinciau* were attributed (rightly or wrongly) in the sixteenth-century lists: interestingly one *cainc* of these was entitled *Eos Werful* ('Gwerful's nightingale').[25] Is it possible that this Cuhelyn could indeed be the one and the same person as the twelfth-century Cuhelyn Fardd of Dyfed? The floruit of the master-musicians is unclear, but Gwgon seems to be placed in the twelfth century in *Araith Wgon*.[26] While some names of *ceinciau*, such as *Awen oleudhydh* (attributed variously to Cuhelyn, Cadwgan, and Gwgon),[27] suggest the late Middle Ages (the celebrated Goleuddydd was the mistress of Gruffudd Gryg),[28] the sixteenth-century tract *Llyma henwav yr athrawon* <*tyleinorion*>[29] *kerdd dant* in National Library of Wales, MS 17116 (Gwysaney 28), 61v, locates Cadwgan and Cuhelyn in Uwch Gwyrfai and Is Gwyrfai respectively (commotes in Arfon), which would rule out any identification with the Dyfed Cuhelyn; yet this may not be reliable, for the tract goes on to say that 'but really Cadwgan dwelt in *Ymwythig* (Shrewsbury) and built the chapel which is today called Capel Cadwgan'.

While nightingales do not consort easily with Cú Chulainn, shields do, and naturally enough his shield is described in the *Táin*. Moreover, in the sixteenth-century Irish law manuscript, Dublin, Trinity College, 1336 (H. 3. 17), col. 664, there is a story, to which Dr Bromwich drew attention, about how the design of Cú Chulainn's shield was originally drawn in ashes (*luaith*) by supernatural intervention. The story purports to explain the expression *luathrinne lūth* ('*luathrind(e)*'s vigour'), which perhaps occurred in some poetico-legal work (to judge by the poetic inversion of the genitive).[30] Macalister suggested that this story was invented to explain the existence of some remarkable shield of La Tène type.[31] A more immediate possibility is that it was invented as part of the etymology of the term *luathrind(e)* ('swift-point'?), which seems to describe some type of decoration[32] or decorative technique or instrument.[33] According to the Triads, *lúd lúathrinna*, 'vigour/swiftness with regard to *luathrind(e)*', was essential for a craftsman (*sáer*).[34] The story of Cú Chulainn's shield may, then, be a craft-legend, comparable to the Welsh craft-legend in the *Four Branches of the Mabinogi* which etymologizes the name of the foreign saddle- and shield-decoration known as *calch lassar* ('enamel/chalk of lapis lazuli/azure') by attributing it to the legendary Irish settler Llassar, who was also credited with importing a remarkable cauldron to Wales.[35] Conceivably such an Irish craft-legend about Cú Chulainn's shield might become known in Wales, perhaps in connection with some fashion or technological innovation, and the Welsh name *Cuhelyn* might then be substituted for *Cú Chulainn*.

On the other hand, both the name of Cú Chulainn's shield, *Dubán* (cf. *dub* 'black') and that of its supernatural designer, *Dubdethba* ('wohl *Dub debtha* "der Schwarze des Streites", der Teufel', according to Thurneysen),[36] suggest a dark shield, and this is also what Cú Chulainn carries in the *Táin*, where his 'dark shield' (*dondsciath*) is 'dark-red' (*dubderg*, *dondderg*, *dondchorcra*), albeit 'with five circles of gold' and a rim of either *findruine* or silver;[37] Cuhelyn's shield, on the contrary, would seem to have been bright. Iolo Goch, thanking his patron for a dagger flashing like lightening, describes it as *heulo ysgwyd Guhelyn*, 'gleaming (cf. *heul* 'sun') like Cuhelyn's shield', and Dafydd ap Gwilym addresses a gleaming (*gloyw*) sword as *ysgwyd Guhelyn*.[38] In the light of these two fourteenth-century references, the reference by Prydydd y Moch, in the previous century, to

Cuhelyn's *ysgwyd ball* is best understood as containing *pall* (< Latin *palla*), either referring to the cloth facing of the shield (probably heraldically decorated), or else referring to the shield as a metaphorical 'tent' (presumably brightly decorated) protecting Llywelyn's host:

> yth ysgwyd tebygwyd toryf wŷn.
> ysgwyd ball güall guhelyn.[39]

> To your shield was likened, O army-hurter, the cloth-faced/tent-like shield of swift Cuhelyn.

This would take up the metaphor of the previous stanza where Llywelyn is called *kyndlid kynuelyn* 'of the cloth [i.e. worth] of Cynfelyn'.[40]

If, as seems likely, the three Welsh poets are referring to a Welsh Cuhelyn, no identification can be proved since the name is not unusual.[41] Cuhelyn Fardd, however, is again an attractive possibility, since he is known to have been the subject of folktales in the sixteenth century.[42] Moreover, George William Griffith, an early-seventeenth-century writer, states that

> his coate of Armes is to be seene on the window of Nevarne church, in the auncient house of Pentre Jevan, in the cathedrall of St Davids, & in dyvers other gent houses in Pembr & knowen by the name of Kyhylyn's coat.[43]

Perhaps the brilliant heraldry of this Cuhelyn's shield - '*azure* a lion rampant *or* within an orle of eight roses *or*'[44] - caught the eye and imagination of the thirteenth- and fourteenth-century poets. According to the Laws, shields coloured gold, silver, or blue were double the value of ordinary shields.[45]

2. *Nyf

It is widely believed that *Niamh*, under the name *Nyf*, was a byword for beauty in late medieval Wales; which Irish heroine of the name this would be is unclear, though Myrddin Lloyd's candidate, Cú Chulainn's mistress, Niamh (or Niabh) daughter of Celtchar, is suitable, since she is quite prominent in the fifteenth-century version of *Aided Con Culainn*.[46] Yet it is decidedly doubtful that Welsh *Nyf* is a borrowing of Irish *Niamh*. In the first place, the form *Nyf* is unexpected; one would expect **Niaf* in Middle Welsh - compare a 'Dafydd ap Jack ap *Diarmed*' in Anglesey in 1406[47] - or perhaps **Nief* - compare *Brien* and *Diermit* for *Brian* and *Diarmaid* in *Historia Gruffud vab Kenan*.[48]

In any case, it is by no means clear that **Nyf* does occur as a personal name in Welsh. The first to say that it does was Dr John Davies in his *Dictionarium Duplex* of 1632:

> Nŷf, *Pl. a* Nef. *Coeli, orum. Est & nomen proprium mulierum apud antiquos. Et vid. an Niuem significet,* gwynbryd nŷf cyn dattawdd. *Ior.G.*

Of these three interpretations, the last is in fact the most certain: *nyf* is quite well attested in the fourteenth and fifteenth centuries as a common noun meaning 'snow', perhaps a borrowing from Latin *nix, nivis*, rather than a native cognate of Irish *snigid*.[49] The earliest examples seem to be early-fourteenth-century, in a penitential poem by Casnodyn, *goreu oed uadeu orneu oernyf*[50] ('it were best to forgive faults cold [as] snow'), and in a love poem by Sefnyn:

> Prif degwch dilwch eiry dolyd   kynn glaw.
> praw nwyf gyryf anaw ny[f] gorvynyd.[51]

> surpassing beauty of the unsullied snow of meadows before rain, test of the stalwarts of passion, [one who has] the riches of upland snow.

Dr Davies's first interpretation of *nyf*, as a plural of *nef* 'heaven' (instead of the normal and etymologically regular plural *nefoedd* < **nemesa*), probably derives from Wiliam Llŷn (d. 1580), who gives 'nyf nef' in his bardic glossary in NLW, Peniarth 230, 54v.[52] This unhistorical plural form is in fact very rare. A possible instance occurs in *gwas nym* 'land of the ?heavens' in line 233 of the *Gododdin*, although this is usually taken as fossilized (and historically irregular) gen. sg. from **nemī* rather than as an undeclined pl.[53] In a poem by Casnodyn in the Red Book of Hergest God is *creawdyr nyf* 'creator of the heavens', but the latter word has been retraced in the manuscript and may originally have been *naf* 'lord'.[54] Again, *nyf* in a late-sixteenth-century manuscript of the *Seven Sages*[55] looks like a marginal addition (date?) filling a lacuna where earlier manuscripts read *ser* 'stars'.[56]

One or other of these common nouns may be meant in all

alleged instances of the proper name. The supposed attestations of Nyf are very ambiguous. For example, Nyf has been regarded as a pseudonym for Dafydd ap Gwilym's girl, in the following passage:

> Neithiwyr y bûm mewn uthr bwyll,
> Nyf gain, gyda nef gannwyll,
> Yn mynnu tâl am anun,
> Yn aml barch yn ymyl bun.[57]

> Last night I was in strange doubt, *nyf gain*, with heaven's candle (i.e. the girl), wanting recompense for [my] sleeplessness, dancing attendance on a girl.

It may, however, be an elliptical expression, '[one as] fair [as] snow', for a girl (since women were frequently likened to snow),[58] or it may conceivably mean 'fair one of the heavens', addressing or referring to Christ, the girl, or the poet himself. Again, when Dafydd ap Gwilym describes his beloved as *pryd nyf/Nyf*[59] and *Nyf hoen*,[60] the collocations may be comparable with his *pryd eiry* 'of the beauty of snow'[61] rather than with his *pryd Fflur* 'of the beauty of [the legendary heroine] Fflur'.[62] Similarly *pryt nyf* in *areil bryt nyf* ('watching over [one of the] beauty of snow') in Gruffudd ap Maredudd's elegy for Gwenhwyfar has been taken as a reference to 'one as fair as Nyf',[63] but some lines earlier *lliw nyf gorthir* 'colour of upland snow' must refer to snow, as does *pryt eiry kelli* 'beauty of snow in a grove'.[64] Similarly *nyf* definitely means 'snow' in the line of Iorwerth ab y Cyriog cited by Dr Davies, *gwynnbryt nyf kynn dattawd* 'white beauty of snow before it dissolves',[65] just as in the same poet's *eiry nawnyf oerhin Ionawr* 'snow of nine snows of the cold weather of January'.[66]

It has been argued[67] that *Nyf* definitely appears twice as a personal name in the poetry of Lewys Glyn Cothi (*fl.* 1447-89). The better example is:

> Pryt ada a seth priodod Johñ.
> pryt *nyf* a selyf a roet i Johñ.
> pryt deu o sandeu i Johñ. bryt angel.
> pryt assa a sel paradwys i Johñ.[68]

> Siôn joined together the beauty of Adam and Seth, the beauty of *nyf* and Solomon was given to Siôn, the beauty of

> two Sandde Angel-faces [was given] to Siôn, the beauty of Asaph and the seal of Paradise [was given] to Siôn.

Given the many proper names here, the poet may appear to intend *nyf* to be taken as a personal name; on the other hand, *sel paradwys* is not a personal name, and comparison with a woman, rather than 'snow' or 'the heavens', would be odd praising a man. Lewys Glyn Cothi's other reputed reference is in an elegy on a woman, so the epithet *llaw Nyv* might naturally be understood as '[one with] the hand of *Nyf*';[69] on the other hand, the same expression occurs earlier in an elegy on a man by Rhys Goch Eryri,[70] where *llaw Nyf* is more easily understood as '[one with a] hand [the colour of] snow', whiteness being admired in the Middle Ages.[71] Yet, if Lewys Glyn Cothi did indeed use *Nyf* as a personal name, this might have been as a result of misinterpreting the obsolescent noun *nyf* 'snow' in collocations like *pryd nyf*; we might compare how he and later poets, followed by Dr Davies, misinterpreted the phrase *anap y lleian* 'the nun's misfortune' (that is, Merlin) as a personal name An ap y lleian ('An son of the nun').[72]

In stating, or conjecturing, that *Nyf* was formerly a female name, Dr Davies says nothing about an Irish connection, so even if he were right the name should not necessarily be derived from *Niamh*.[73] For instance, **Nyf* could be a native Welsh name based on *nyf* 'snow'; or it might be derived from the same root as *nef* 'heaven' (e.g. from **nemiā* or **nemī-*), or from the weak grades of the root seen in Old Irish *niam* 'beauty' (< **nei- mā*) or of that in *niab* 'passion' (: Welsh *nwyf*) and *noib* 'sacred' (< **nei- bho-*/**noi- bho-*).[74] An unpublished seventeenth-century manuscript list of 'Some words omitted in Dr Davies Welch and Latin Dictionary' (NLW, Llanstephan 86, 66^{v}) identifies Dr Davies' Nyf as Peredur's mistress:

> Nyf. n.pr f. cariad Peredur ap Efrog

and the same explanation was given by eighteenth- and nineteenth-century scholars, such as Lewis Morris and William Owen[-Pughe].[75] The identification with Peredur's nameless beloved, whose white skin that hero compared to the snow (*eira*),[76] is surely no more than an intelligent guess. In 1914 Ifor Williams, who accepted the existence of a personal name Nyf, was content simply to repeat it.[77] Seven years later, however, he queried whether Nyf was the Irish heroine Niamh ('onid *Niamh* y Gwyddyl?'),[78] the suggestion since widely accepted. It is surely significant that in the interim the Welsh public had been captivated by the character of Oisin's beloved, Niamh Chinn Óir, appearing under the name Nia Ben Aur in T. Gwynn Jones's music-drama *Tír na n-Óg*, published in 1916.[79]

In his preface to *Tír na n-Óg*, T. Gwynn Jones declared:

> Mawr yw fy nyled i, o leiaf, i gymaint âg a wn am lenyddiaeth Wyddeleg, a byddai'n hyfryd tros ben gennyf pe gwasanaethai hyn o gais ar fydru chwedl Wyddeleg yn y Gymraeg i ddenu rhai o'm cydwladwyr at hen iaith ardderchog a llenyddiaeth ryfeddol Iwerddon.[80]

Possibly he, and those who followed his lead, tended to project their own debt to Irish literature back onto their medieval precedessors? Certainly, Ifor Williams' earlier, more negative view of 1910, quoted at the beginning of this paper, squares better with the evidence: very little Irish literature was known in late medieval Wales.

Nevertheless, it is difficult not to sympathize with T. Gwynn Jones at the present time, when the future of Celtic studies (as opposed to Irish or Welsh) is so uncertain in both Ireland and Wales. At the moment only four scholars in Ireland appear to be actively studying Welsh literature (Arwyn Watkins, Jenny Rowland, Rhian Andrews, and Proinsias Mac Cana), while in Wales the position is even more dire: since the days of T. Gwynn Jones only J. E. Caerwyn Williams and the Rees brothers have published significant studies of Irish language and literature. Is there any consolation in the thought that interest was equally low in the late Middle Ages?[81]

Notes

1. Patrick Sims-Williams, 'The Evidence for Vernacular Irish Literary Influence on Early Mediaeval Welsh Literature', in *Ireland in Early Mediaeval Europe*, ed. Dorothy Whitelock et al. (Cambridge, 1982), pp. 235-57.

2. Cf. Rachel Bromwich, *Trioedd Ynys Prydein*, 2nd edn (Cardiff, 1978), p.

lxxxii, n. 1; D. Myrddin Lloyd, *Rhai Agweddau ar Ddysg y Gogfynfeirdd* (Cardiff, 1977), pp. 14-15; D. Geraint Lewis, 'Mynegai i'r Enwau Priod Storïol yng Ngwaith Cyhoeddedig y Cywyddwyr' (unpublished M.A. diss., University of Wales, Aberystwyth, 1968), pp. 3-4.

A summary of some of these comparisons is given by Cecile O'Rahilly, *Ireland and Wales* (London, 1924), pp. 122-34. For a critique see D. Simon Evans, *Historia Gruffud vab Kenan* (Cardiff, 1977), pp. xcix-civ.

Arthur Hughes and Ifor Williams, *Gemau'r Gogynfeirdd* (Pwllheli, 1910), p. xvii ['The strongest argument against tracing this movement to Ireland is this: there are no traces of any familiarity with Irish literature and history in the work of the Gogynfeirdd. They refer incessantly to the past heroes of Wales, the famous characters of *mabinogi* and myth, but there is no mention of Cú Chulainn and Conchobar. Indeed, throughout medieval Welsh literature there are only a bare half-dozen definite, unambiguous allusions to Irish tales.']. Cf. R. Geraint Gruffudd, 'The Early Court Poetry of South West Wales', *Studia Celtica*, 14/15 (1979-80), 103: 'All the evidence suggests that any reform brought about by Gruffudd ap Cynan had more to do with music than with poetry.

Cf. William Gillies, 'Arthur in Gaelic Tradition, Part II', *Cambridge Medieval Celtic Studies*, 3 (Summer 1982), 66.

Patrick Sims-Williams, 'Fionn and Deirdre in Late Medieval Wales', *Éigse*, 23 (1989), 1-15; 'Cú Chulainn in Wales', *Celtica* (forthcoming).

See references in Patrick Sims-Williams, 'The Significance of the Irish Personal Names in *Culhwch ac Olwen*', *Bull. Board of Celtic Studies*, 29 (1980-82), 616, n. 1; Evans, *Historia Gruffud vab Kenan*, p. cix, n. 296; Lloyd, *Rhai Agweddau*, p. 15. Prof. D. J. Bowen points out to me the symptomatic reference to 'Gwyddel, neu gi o Iddew,/ Neu gi Sais' in *Lewys Glyn Cothi (Detholiad)*, ed. E. D. Jones (Cardiff, 1984), p. 75.

For references see Sims-Williams, 'Evidence'; 'Significance'; and 'Fionn and Deirdre'.

See Sims-Williams, 'Fionn and Deirdre'.

Patrick Sims-Williams, 'Some Celtic Otherworld Terms' (forthcoming in a *Festschrift* for Eric P. Hamp).

Bromwich, *Trioedd*, pp. lxxiv-lxxviii.

T. Gwynn Jones, *Gwaith Tudur Aled* (Cardiff, 1926), I, xxxv (on the evidence mentioned in his n. 10 see David Greene, 'The Irish Numerals of Cardiganshire', *SC*, 10/11 (1975-76), 305-11); 'The Welsh Bardic Vocabulary', *BBCS*, 1 (1921-23), 313.

13. Cf. John Morris-Jones, 'Taliesin', *Y Cymmrodor*, 28 (1918), 239: 'why all this assumption of borowing? It rests on the perfectly gratuitous supposition that the British had no traditional lore of their own'; Ifor Williams, 'Dafydd ap Gwilym a'r Glêr', *Trans. Hon. Soc. Cymmrodorion*, 1913-14, p. 182: 'rhaid cofio fod y Cymro hefyd weithiau wedi "meddwl" drosto'i hun wrth greu mesur'.

14. *Archaeologia Cambrensis*, 5th ser., 12 (1895), 29-36.

15. 'Taliesin', p. 273.

16. cf. Dafydd Jenkins and Morfydd E. Owen, 'The Welsh Marginalia in the Lichfield Gospels, Part II', *CMCS*, 7 (Summer 1984), 108.

17. For references see J. Lloyd-Jones, *Geirfa Barddoniaeth Gynnar Gymraeg* (Cardiff, 1931-63), s.n.; P. C. Bartrum, *Early Welsh Genealogical Tracts* (Cardiff, 1966), p. 179, s.n.; Ifor Williams, *Canu Aneirin* (Cardiff, 1938), p. 361; *The Description of Penbrokshire by George Owen of Henllys*, ed. Henry Owen (London, 1892-1936), IV, 428; *The Text of the Book of Llan Dâv*, ed. J. Gwenogvryn Evans (Oxford, 1893), pp. xlvi, 76, 162, and 279; Francis Jones, 'Family Tales from Dyfed', *THSC*, 1953, p. 67; *Materials for the History of Thomas Becket*, ed. James Craigie Robertson, Rolls Ser. (London, 1875-85), III, 528.

18. For this element see Lloyd-Jones, *Geirfa*, s.v.; Kenneth Jackson, *Language and History in Early Britain* (Edinburgh, 1953), p. 417, and *A Historical Phonology of Breton* (Dublin, 1967), pp. 141, 591-92, and 610; cf. OIr *Caém*, discussed by Brian Ó Cuív, 'Aspects of Irish Personal Names', *Celtica*, 18 (1986), 179. For the loss of the lenited *-m-* cf. the compounds listed by Lloyd-Jones, and compare the case of OW *luird*, discussed by Jackson, *Language and History*, pp. 416 and 437, and *Phonology of Breton*, p. 610.

19. This suffix would absorb the preceding lenited *-g*; cf. OW *colginn* > *colyn* (Jackson, *Language and History*, p. 466). The element **selg-* probably occurs in the tribal name *Selgovae* (ibid., p. 467), and conceivably in Welsh *Selyf*, 'whose derivation from *Salamo(n)* has never been satisfactorily explained' according to David Dumville, 'Late-Seventh- or Eighth-Century Evidence for the British Transmission of Pelagius', *CMCS*, 10 (Winter 1985), 46 (the usual view is that the biblical Latin name was treated as an *n*-stem **Salamō*); cf. Léon

Fleuriot, 'Les Rois Héliseus et Salamon et le rôle de la Bretagne armoricaine dans la transmission du texte de Pélage', *Études celtiques*, 24 (1987), 281.

20. Sims-Williams, 'Evidence', p. 250 and n. 72; 'Significance', p. 608, n. 8; and 'Cú Chulainn in Wales'.

21. *Gwaith Dafydd ap Gwilym*, ed. Thomas Parry, 2nd edn (Cardiff, 1963), p. 547; Rachel Bromwich, 'Cyfeiriadau Dafydd ap Gwilym at Chwedl a Rhamant', *Ysgrifau Beirniadol*, 12 (1982), 65-66 = *Aspects of the Poetry of Dafydd ap Gwilym* (Cardiff, 1986), pp. 140-41; *Gwaith Iolo Goch*, ed. D. R. Johnston (Cardiff, 1988), p. 243.

22. *Gwaith Dafydd ap Gwilym*, ed. Parry, no. 25.41; cf. Bromwich, *Aspects*, p. 140.

23. See Dafydd ap Edmwnd's elegy on him, ed. Thomas Parry, *The Oxford Book of Welsh Verse* (Oxford, 1962), no. 75.

24. *Gwaith Dafydd ap Gwilym*, ed. Parry, no. 142.24-25 and n. on p. 545.

25. In the list printed by T. Gwynn Jones, 'Cerdd Dant', *BBCS* 1 (1921-23), 149, this is attributed to Cadwgan, while in the version in the Book of Taliesin (printed by Marged Haycock, 'Llyfr Taliesin', *National Library of Wales Jnl*, 25 (1988), 359) it is anonymous; it is, however, ascribed to Cuhelyn more often than to Cadwgan in the manuscripts collated by Bethan E. Miles, 'Swyddogaeth a Chelfyddyd y Crythor' (unpublished M.A. diss., University of Wales, Aberystwyth, 1983), I, 102, n. 359, II, 612 and 616.

26. *Yr Areithiau Pros*, ed. D. Gwenallt Jones (Cardiff, 1934), pp. 3 and 77. J. Lumley Davies, 'The Contribution of Welshmen to Music', *THSC*, 1919-20, pp. 46-47, refers to 'Caius' testimony regarding Cyhelyn ab Gwrgant who flourished about 348 B.C.' as 'a Roman's testimony'. This farrago probably derives ultimately from John Caius, *De Antiquitate Cantabrigiensis Academiae* (London, 1568), pp. 20-21, on Gurguntius, fl. 375 B.C., the predecessor of King Guithelinus (= *Kuelyn* in the *Brut*) according to Geoffrey of Monmouth's *Historia Regum Britanniae*! On Caius as an authority on mythical bards see G. J. Williams, 'Leland a Bale a'r Traddodiad Derwyddol', *Llên Cymru*, 4 (1956-57), 20-21.

27. *Areithiau Pros*, ed. Jones, p. 78; 'Cerdd Dant', ed. Jones, p. 148; Miles, 'Swyddogaeth', II, 612 and 616.

28. She is mentioned by Dafydd ap Gwilym, *Gwaith*, ed. Parry, no. 20.20.

29. This word is inserted above the line. The tract is edited by Miles, 'Swyddogaeth', II, 704.

30. *Corpus Iuris Hibernici*, ed. D. A. Binchy (Dublin, 1978), VI, 2114; also edited (without translation) by R. I. Best, 'Cuchulainn's Shield', *Ériu*, 5 (1911), 72, and trans. by Myles Dillon, 'Stories from the Law-Tracts', *Ériu*, 11 (1930-32), 54-55. A summary is given by Bromwich, 'Cyfeiriadau', pp. 65-66 = *Aspects*, pp. 140-41.

31. R. A. S. Macalister, *The Archaeology of Ireland*, 1st edn (London, 1928), p. 146; cf. William Ridgeway, 'The Date of the First Shaping of the Cuchulainn Saga', *Proc. Brit. Acad.*, 2 (1905-6), 153 and 160-61.

32. *luathrinda* glosses *plectas* in 3 [= 1] Kings VII 26; see *Dictionary of the Irish Language*, s.v. *lúathrinde*.

33. 'a moulding pair of compasses used by iron or brass-founders' according to O'Donovan: see *Sanas Chormaic: Cormac's Glossary*, trans. John O'Donovan, ed. Whitley Stokes (Calcutta, 1868), p. 41. According to this text three seas forming a whirlpool 'are whirled round in the manner of *luathrind(e)*' (*Foscerd īarom imonsech fo c[h]osmailess l̄uathrinde*: *Anecdota from Irish Manuscripts*, IV, ed. O. J. Bergin et al. (Halle, 1912), p. 27, §323).

34. *The Triads of Ireland*, ed. and trans. Kuno Meyer, Todd Lecture Ser. 13 (Dublin, 1906), pp. 16-17, §118.

35. *Pedeir Keinc y Mabinogi*, ed. Ifor Williams, 2nd edn (Cardiff, 1951), pp. 35, 52-54, 179, and 233-34. On the importance of crafts in Celtic societies see W. Gillies, 'The Craftsman in Early Celtic Literature', *Scottish Archaeological Forum*, 11 (1981), 70-85.

36. Rudolf Thurneysen, *Die irische Helden- und Königsage* (Halle, 1921), p. 672.

37. *Táin Bó Cúailnge: Recension I*, ed. and trans. Cecile O'Rahilly (Dublin, 1976), lines 2233 and 2360-61; *Táin Bó Cúalnge from the Book of Leinster*, ed. and trans. Cecile O'Rahilly (Dublin, 1967), lines 2251 and 2364-65. Cf. the echo in 'Beir mo sciath, sceo fri úath', ed. and trans. Máirín O Daly, *Ériu*, 20 (1966), 191-201, §4. See also J. P. Mallory, 'Silver in the Ulster Cycle of Tales', in *Proceedings of the Seventh International Congress of Celtic Studies*, ed. D. Ellis Evans et al. (Oxford, 1986), pp. 45-46.

38. *Gwaith Iolo Goch*, ed. Johnston, no. XI.94; *Gwaith Dafydd ap Gwilym*,

ed. Parry, no. 143.39.

Llawysgrif Hendregadredd, ed. John Morris-Jones and T. H. Parry-Williams (Cardiff, 1933), p. 281 (my accents). For *pall* see Williams, *Pedeir Keinc*, pp. 167-68. Elen M. Jones, 'Gwaith Prydydd y Moch' (unpublished Ph.D. diss., University of Wales, Aberystwyth, 1985), II, 548-50, interprets the lines differently as 'I'th ysgwyd tebygwyd (gan) torf arteithiol, ysgwyd farwolaeth/fethedig gyflym Guhelyn', and equates Cuhelyn with Cú Chulainn.

cf. Ifor Williams and J. E. Caerwyn Williams, *The Poems of Taliesin* (Dublin, 1968), p. 59.

Fifteenth-century poets refer to people called Cuhelyn in various parts of Wales. Lewys Glyn Cothi calls Caio (north-east Carmarthenshire) *Y cae chelaeth cylch Tŵr Cuhelyn* 'The extensive field around Cuhelyn's tower' (*Gwaith Lewis Glyn Cothi* (Oxford, 1837), p. 312.21), and, asking a patron in Oswestry for a sword, calls him *un edn Cuhelyn*, apparently meaning 'a descendant of Cuhelyn' and alluding to an ancestor from Llansilin in Denbighshire (ibid., p. 376.7; cf. p. 373 and E. D. Jones, *Detholiad*, no.35.7; cf. p. 172). See also *Gwaith Guto's Glyn*, ed. John Llywelyn Williams and Ifor Williams (Cardiff, 1939), no. LXXII.8 and p. 348. Tudur Aled seems to refer to an ancestor figure in Dyffryn Iâl called Cuhelyn (*Gwaith Tudur Aled*, ed. Jones, nos XXVIII.12 and LII.29).

See A. O. H. Jarman, *Llyfr Du Caerfyrddin* (Cardiff, 1982), p. xli; Jones, 'Family Tales', pp. 66-68, 71-73, and 78-80.

ibid., p. 67.

ibid., p. 67, n. 12 (source not cited); but cf. p. 80 for a different heraldry: 'Arfae keheylyn fardd oedd, ben baedd gwyn mywn maes o wyrdd a llew aur a cheiliog coch ai adanedd ar lled.'

Llyfr Blegywryd, ed. Stephen J. Williams and J. Enoch Powell (Cardiff, 1942), p. 98.

Lloyd, *Rhai Agweddau*, p. 15. See *Compert Con Culainn and Other Stories*, ed. A. G. Van Hamel (Dublin, 1933), p. 84; *A Celtic Miscellany*, trans. Kenneth Hurlstone Jackson, 2nd edn (Harmondsworth, 1971), p. 43, no. 6. *Niab* is mentioned in the earlier fragment in *The Book of Leinster*, ed. R. I. Best et al. (Dublin, 1954-83), II, 443, line 13792, but her amour with Cú Chulainn is not clear there. Cf. Thurneysen, *Heldensage*, pp. 550 and 560-61.

47. A. D. Carr, *Medieval Anglesey* (Llangefni, 1982), p. 164. Cf. the argumentation in favour of emending *Grednel*, in a Welsh poem of 1394-98 referring to Niall Mór Ó Néill, to *Gred Nïal*: E. I. Rowlands, 'Iolo Goch', in *Celtic Studies*, ed. James Carney and David Greene (London, 1968), p. 128; David Johnston, 'Rhai Sylwadau Testunol ar Waith Iolo Goch', *YB*, 13 (1985), 162; Johnston, *Gwaith Iolo Goch*, no. XX.131 and p. 302. Here the MS forms with *-e-* may be compared with forms such as *Dermod* in *The Song of Dermot and the Earl* (cf. T. F. O'Rahilly, 'Notes on Middle-Irish Pronunciation', *Hermathena*, 20 (1926-30), 162), and there are also the possibilities of anglicization and influence from the genitive (Ó) *Néill*; cf. J. Lloyd-Jones, 'Cyfeiriadau at Iwerddon yng Nghanu Iolo Goch', *BBCS*, 11 (1941-44), 118.

48. Evans, *Historia Gruffud vab Kenan*, p. cxiv. The Connacht examples of *ia* > *ī* cited by Thomas F. O'Rahilly, *Irish Dialects Past and Present*, 2nd edn (Dublin, 1972), pp. 193-94, are unfortunately too late (c. 1700) to be relevant to Welsh **Nyf*.

49. Cf. Patrick Sims-Williams, 'The Development of the Indo-European Voiced Labiovelars in Celtic', *BBCS*, 29 (1980-82), 218-19 and references; to which add: Liam Mac Mathúna, '"Snow" and "It is snowing" in Irish and Welsh: A Semantic Study', *BBCS*, 29 (1980-82), 68-69 and 77; Karl Horst Schmidt, 'The Celtic Languages in their European Context', *Proceedings of the Seventh International Congress of Celtic Studies*, ed. D. Ellis Evans et al. (Oxford, 1986), p. 203.

50. *The Poetry in the Red Book of Hergest*, ed. J. Gwenogvryn Evans (Llanbedrog, 1911), col. 1236.35-36.

51. ibid., 1262.40-41 (MS *nyt*!); cf. Lloyd-Jones, *Geirfa*, s.v. *goruynyd*.

52. This manuscript was formerly ascribed to Gruffudd Hiraethog (d. 1564), whose work it may indeed incorporate, but see now Roy Stephens, 'Geirfâu Wiliam Llŷn', *LlC*, 15 (1984-88), 308. (My n. 33 to 'Fionn and Deirdre' needs to be corrected accordingly.) See also 'nŷf nef' in the *Geirlyfr Wm Llŷn* printed in *Barddoniaeth Wiliam Llŷn*, ed. J. C. Morrice (Bangor, 1908), p. 282; on this work see Stephens, 'Geirfâu', p. 313. *Nyf* is one of the words which William Salesbury included without translation in his *Dictionary in Englyshe and Welshe* of 1547.

53. cf. John T. Koch, 'The Loss of Final Syllables and the Loss of Declension in Brittonic', *BBCS*, 30 (1982-83), 227 and 229-30.

54. *Poetry in the Red Book*, ed. Evans, col. 1247.16; idem, *Poetry by*

Medieval Welsh Bards, II |= 'a second part to the *Poetry* from the *Red Book of Hergest*'| (Llanbedrog, 1926), p. 368.

55. NLW 13075 (Llanover B.17), 85^{v}, ed. Henry Lewis, 'Modern Welsh Versions of the Seven Wise Men of Rome', *Revue celtique*, 46 (1929), 55. I owe this reference to the unpublished Geiriadur Prifysgol Cymru slips, consulted when writing 'Voiced Labiovelars'.

56. Cardiff MS 6 (2.83) of *c.* 1550 (ibid., pp. 53 and 83) and NLW Llanstephan 171, p. 79 (of 1574) (on which cf. Patrick K. Ford, 'A Fragment of the Hanes Taliesin by Llywelyn Siôn', *ÉC*, 14 (1974-75), 451, n. 2.

57. *Gwaith Dafydd ap Gwilym*, ed. Parry, no. 129.7 10. Rachel Bromwich translates line 8 '|with| fair Nia, with heaven's candle' (*Dafydd ap Gwilym: A Selection of Poems*, 2nd edn (Harmondsworth, 1985), p. 146, and Richard Morgan Loomis has '(A fine Nyf) with heaven's candle' (*Dafydd ap Gwilym: The Poems* (Binghamton, 1982), p. 238. On the other hand, Melville Richards translated 'Snow white fair, with a heavenly candle' ('Welsh', in *Eos: An Enquiry into the Theme of Lovers' Metings and Partings at Dawn in Poetry*, ed. Arthur T. Hatto (The Hague, 1965), p. 572). Cf. 'lliw'r ôd' in the apocryphal imitation of Dafydd's poem, printed ibid., p. 573.

58. T. Gwynn Jones, *Rhieingerddi'r Gogynfeirdd* (Denbigh, 1915), pp. 28-29 and 42.

59. *Gwaith*, ed. Parry, nos 71.24 ('Nia's beauty', Bromwich, p. 114, 'she of Nyf's beauty', Loomis, p. 160), and 84.69 ('with snow-like beauty', Bromwich, p. 38, 'a face of snow', Loomis, p. 180).

60. *Gwaith*, ed. Parry, no. 98.56 ('Nia's loveliness', Bromwich, p. 46, 'Nyf's color', Loomis, p. 199).

61. *Gwaith*, ed. Parry, no.97.3, etc.

62. ibid., no. 111.8.

63. Bromwich, *Trioedd*, p. lxxxii; *The Earliest Welsh Poetry*, trans. Joseph P. Clancy (London, 1970), p. 188.

64. *Poetry in the Red Book*, ed. Evans, cols 1320.21-22 and 1321.29 and 32.

65. ibid., col. 1287.8.

66. *Cywyddau Iolo Goch ac Eraill*, ed. Henry Lewis et al., 2nd edn (Cardiff, 1937), p. 219.13. There may be some word-play with the

common idea of *naw nef* 'nine heavens'. For further probable examples of 'snow' see ibid., p. 336.19-20: 'Am roi tydwedd ar gleddyf/ Noeth cyn ddisgleiried â nyf'; *Gwaith Iolo Goch*, ed. Johnston, no. XXXIV.9-10: 'Ti a gwynaist, teg ener, / Wrthyf am liw nyf, fy nêr'; *Gwaith Dafydd ab Edmwnd*, ed. Thomas Roberts (Bangor, 1914), p. 32, no. XVIII: 'dycked hyn a fo dickia/ deuliw nyf i dal a wnaf'; *Cywyddau Dafydd ap Gwilym a'i Gyfoeswyr*, ed. Ifor Williams and Thomas Roberts, 2nd edn (Cardiff, 1935), no. XXV.11: 'Deuliw Nyf, peth nis dlâi neb'; ibid., no. XXXIV.45: 'Degle'n nes, dwg i liw Nyf'. The last two poems are not by Dafydd.

67. Lewis et al., *Cywyddau Iolo Goch ac Eraill*, p. 360.

68. *Gwaith Lewis Glyn Cothi*, I, ed. E. D. Jones (Cardiff and Aberystwyth, 1953), no. 77.49-52; *Gwaith Lewis Glyn Cothi* (Oxford, 1837), p. 126.

69. ibid., p. 260.

70. *Cywyddau Iolo Goch ac Eraill*, ed. Lewis et al., p. 158.21.

71. Cf. Andrew Breeze, 'lliw papir', *BBCS*, 30 (1982-83), 277; Bromwich, *Dafydd ap Gwilym: Selected Poems*, p. 162.

72. Patrick Sims-Williams, '*anfab*^{2} "illegitimate child": A Ghost-Word', *BBCS*, 28 (1978-80), 90-93. The word division *(a)an ap* occurs in Lewys's autograph, Peniarth MS 109, ed. Jones, *Gwaith Lewis Glyn Cothi*, I, no. 31.25 and n.

73. Cf. Parry, *Gwaith Dafydd ap Gwilym*, p. 537: '*Nyf*... enw merch, ... ond ni wyddys pwy'.

74. Cf. Sims-Williams, 'Voiced Labiovelars', p. 219; J. Vendryes, *Lexique étymologique de l'irlandais ancien* (Paris and Dublin, 1959-), N-16 and 20.

75. Lewis Morris, *Celtic Remains* (London, 1878), p. 335; *Barddoniaeth Dafydd ab Gwilym*, ed. Owen Jones and William Owen (London, 1789), p. 541; William Owen, *The Cambrian Biography* (London, 1803), p. 267; cf. *Gwaith Lewis Glyn Cothi* (Oxford, 1837), p. 126.

76. *Historia Peredur vab Efrawc*, ed. Glenys Witchard Goetinck (Cardiff, 1976), p. 30.

77. *Cywyddau Dafydd ap Gwilym a'i Gyfoeswyr*, 1st edn (Cardiff, 1914), p. 190.

78. *Detholion o Gywyddau Dafydd ap Gwilym* (Bangor, 1921), p. 133 =

Cywyddau Dafydd ap Gwilym a'i Gyfoeswyr, 2nd edn, p. 187.

79. *Tir* [*sic*] *na n-Óg: Awdl Delynegol at Beroriaeth* (Cardiff, 1916); cf. *Caniadau* (Wrexham, 1934), pp. 60-74. T. Gwynn Jones called his own daughter Nia, and this is still a popular girl's name in Wales. Niamh Chinn Óir was invented in the eighteenth century on the basis of one or more earlier Ossianic beauties called Niamh, according to Dáithí Ó hÓgáin, *Fionn mac Cumhaill: Images of the Gaelic Hero* (Dublin, 1988), p. 254, and Máirtín Ó Briain, 'Some Material on Oisín in the Land of Youth', in *Sages, Saints and Storytellers: Celtic Studies in Honour of Professor James Carney*, ed. Donnchadh Ó Corráin et al. (Maynooth, 1989), pp. 192-3.

80. 'My own debt, at least, to as much as I know about Irish literature is great, and it would be very splendid if this attempt to versify an Irish tale in Welsh served to attract some of my fellow-countrymen to Ireland's marvellous old language and amazing literature.'

81. This paper for Arwyn Watkins, who first introduced me to Modern Welsh at the Dublin Institute for Advanced Studies summer school in 1972, is based on part of lecture on 'Adleisiau Cymraeg o Chwedloniaeth Iwerddon yn yr Oesoedd Canol Diweddar', delivered at the University of Wales Centre for Advanced Welsh and Celtic Studies on 3 March 1988.

The Significance of the 'Cad Goddau' Tree-List in the Book of Taliesin[1]

Marged Haycock
University College of Wales, Aberystwyth

Cad Goddau, usually translated as 'The Battle of the Trees',[2] has excited more attention than any other poem in the fourteenth-century collection of poetry known as the Book of Taliesin.[3] Pierre le Roux summed up the poem as 'a metaphysical text about which there is always something to be said, and in which - as with a Biblical verse - everyone can always find what they want'.[4] This is not surprising given the poem's inordinate length of 250 lines[5] and its rich mix of curiosities. *Cad Goddau* contains some of the legendary Taliesin's most spectacular exploits: his genesis and transformations, his grapplings with hellish monsters and his dealings with the divine family of Dôn, all laced with boastful allusions to his own knowledge and prophetic powers. As with other poems in this manuscript,[6] the figure of Taliesin is a medium for displaying different strands of traditional and exotic learning, primarily, it would seem, for the purpose of entertainment although that function does not preclude others. Such poems were most likely intended for an early medieval audience familiar on the one hand with the content and style of primary heroic poetry, but also able to savour more recondite allusions to received book- or school-learning.

This discussion addresses some of the literary problems raised by the section of the poem (BT 24.15-25.19) in which various trees and shrubs go into battle, not against one another[7] but against a common foe. The context of the battle is not altogether explicit, but 'Taliesin' states early on in the poem (BT 23.20-21) that:

> **Keint yg kat godeu bric**
> I sang in the van of the tree-battalion/in the battle of the branchy trees[8]
> **Rac Prydein wledic**
> Before the lord of Britain.

Although the identity of the *gwledic*[9] is not specified, Arthur would be an illustrious candidate, not only on the grounds that he is mentioned towards the end of the poem,[10] but also because he is associated with Taliesin elsewhere in early verse, notably in the poem *Preiddiau Annwn.*[11] One would like to know what the arch-poet sang on this particular occasion. The line *o Warchan Maelderw* 'because of *Gorchan Maeldderw*' (BT 25.19-20: see text below) may imply that it was the prestigious poem of that name ascribed to Taliesin by Hand A of the Book of Aneirin,[12] and that *Gorchan Maeldderw* was regarded as having exhortatory powers in battle similar to those which the Blegywryd law text imputes to the poem *Unbeiniaeth Prydain*, 'The Monarchy of Britain'.[13]

Another passage in *Cad Goddau* (BT 24.2-3) juxtaposes the activities of poets and warriors:

> **Bum yg Kaer Nefenhir:**
> I was in the fortress of Nefenhir:
> **Yt gryssynt wellt a gwyd;**
> The grass and the trees were on the move;
> **Kenynt gerdoryon,**
> Singers/poets were singing,
> **Kryssynt katuaon.**
> Soldiers were attacking.

These lines appear to connect the arboreal battle with a place called Caer Nefenhir. *Nefenhir* forms a type of 'Irish' rhyme with *gwŷð*. Such an *i/y* correspondence is found elsewhere in early verse. On the other hand, the scribe may have failed to modernise his exemplar where *-ir* represented final *-yr*. The Book of Taliesin reading, *nefenhir naw* with deleting points beneath *naw*, suggests that the scribe was familiar with a cognomen similar to that which occurs in *Culhwch ac Olwen*:[14]

> **Mi a uum gynt yghaer oeth ac anoeth. Ac yghaer neuenhyr naw naut [RB nawd] teyrndynyon tec a welsam ni yno . . ..**
> 'I was formerly in Caer Oeth and Anoeth, and in Caer Nefenhyr *Naw Naut*:[15] we saw fair nobles there . . ..'

In the tale the name occurs towards the end of a list of place-names, some exotic or fabricated, others significant in Welsh story.[16] Caer Nefenhyr may have been imagined here as a paradise (by association with *nef* 'heaven'), contrasting with Caer Oeth and Anoeth which are regarded as places of captivity in the Triads;[17] this would explain the emphasis on the fine appearance of its inhabitants. On the other hand, a form *Newenhyr* (with *w* [w] being a variant of [v], or merely an orthographic slip) occurs in a list of real place-names in 'Y Canu Mawr', an early-thirteenth-century praise-poem to Llywelyn ab Iorwerth by Prydydd y Moch:[18]

> **A Dinbych wrthrych, orthorryant ar uil,**
> And awaiting Denbigh - they hew down a thousand -
> **a'r Uoel Las, a Gronant;**
> And Moel Las, and Gronant;
> **A Dinas Emreis amrygant,**
> And the vicinity of Dinas Emrys,
> **Amrygyr Newenhyr Naw Nant,**
> Tumultuous Newenhyr Naw Nant,
> **A Chaer yn Aruon, a charant yg gnif.**
> And Caernarfon, and kinsmen in battle.

The adjective *amrygyr* 'noisy, restless'[19] is used elsewhere to describe the movement of the waters of the sea (cf. BT 79.18) and this might suggest that *Newenhyr* was, or was identified with a real place on the coast in the north-west near Dinas Emrys and Caernarfon. John Lloyd-Jones implausibly thought that *Newenhyr* was a distinct place-name, which might be derived from **nouantorigs*, whereas the Book of Taliesin form *Nefenhir* (the intervocalic [v] of which is supported by the *Culhwch* form) might come from **nāmantorigs* 'enemy king; king over enemies' via **nămantorigs*.[20] Newenhyr/Nefenhir may have been connected, rightly or wrongly, with Nefyn on the Llŷn coast: certainly this would be a suitable identification, both in Prydydd y Moch's poem, and in the *Cad Goddau* example given that the Dôn family was active in nearby Arfon. In Lloyd-Jones's view, however,

Nefyn is a name of Irish origin.[21]

Our poem continues with a garbled account of how the tree battle came about. The key figure is Gwydion son of Dôn, the well-known enchanter of plant matter who made mushrooms into shields in *Math fab Mathonwy*, and who had a hand in the vegetable cocktails of Blodeuwedd and of Taliesin himself.[22] In extremis, he has implored higher powers for help (BT 24.3-5):

Gelwyssit ar Neifon,[23]
He called on ?God,
Ar Grist o achwysson,
On omnipotent Christ,
Hyt pan y gwarettei,
In order that He should deliver them,
Y ren rwy digonsei.
Their Lord who had made them.

God replies that Gwydion should look to his own magical resources (BT 24.5-7):

As attebwys Dofyd:
God answered him:
'Trwy ieith, *a celuyd*,[24] — **MS ac eluyd**
By means of speech, o magician,
Rithych[25] **riedawc wyd -** — **MS rithwch**
Conjure up lordly trees -
***Gant daw* yn lluyd -** — **MS gantaw**
A hundred soldiers in hosts -
A rwystraw peblic,[26]
And impede the vigorous one/Peblig,
Kat arllaw annefic.'
The battle-giver commanding great resources.'

There may be a further allusion to one of the causes of the battle in the line *Budyant buch Anhun* 'the prize [was] the buck/cow of Antonius'(BT 24.11-12).[27] where the mention of the animal brings to mind the triad of the 'Three Futile Battles' ('Tair Ofergat'): Cad Goddau, Arfderydd and Camlan. The Peniarth 50 text of that triad states that Cad Goddau was fought *o achavs yr Ast [y] ar ivrch fechvys a Chornvgil*, 'because of the bitch and the . . . roebuck and a lapwing'.[28] The cause of the battle of Arfderydd is said to have been 'a lark's nest',[29] while the battle of Camlan supposedly came about because of a quarrel between Gwenhwyfar and Gwenhwyfach. All three battles were regarded as futile either because they had trivial causes, or, as Dr Bromwich suggests, because they were fought amongst the Britons themselves.[30] Four seventeenth-century manuscripts containing the two 'Englynion Cad Goddau'[31] provide the additional information that the battle, also called Cad Achren,[32] was fought *o achos iwrch gwyn a chenau milgi a hanoeddynt o Annwn, ac Amathaon ap Don a'i daliodd*, 'because of a white roebuck and a greyhound whelp which came from Annwn, and Amathaon son of Dôn caught them'. He was helped by his brother Gwydion who triumphed over Arawn king of Annwn by guessing the name of one of his opponents. Dr Bromwich is tempted to connect this allusion with the swine originating from Annwn which Gwydion steals in *Math*.[33] The englynion themselves do not shed further light on the battle.

In our poem, the trees conjured into being bring fresh hope: they fall on the enemy forces and battle continues for thirty grievous days.[34] A woman wails at the touch-line, in keeping with the best heroic traditions: *Dyar gardei bun* (BT 24.10).[35] Another cliché is echoed when Taliesin says that he and the others have blood up to their thighs: *Gwaet gwyr hyt an clun* (BT 24.12-13).[36] The poet is poised to place the momentous battle in a triad of three great clashes of arms (*aryfgryt*), perhaps the very same grouping of Camlan, Arfderydd and Cad Goddau which forms the triad already discussed; instead he veers off to the more weighty Christian schema of upheavals (BT 24.14-15):[37]

Ac vn a deryw
And the first one happened
O ystyr dilyw,
As a result of the story of the Flood,
A Christ y croccaw,
And [the second because of] Christ's crucifixion,
A Dyd Brawt rac llaw.
And [the third is] the forthcoming Judgment-Day.

Then the tree-list proper begins, some seventy-four lines in all, an unusually developed and sustained passage by Book of Taliesin standards. It is the fullest medieval Welsh tree-list extant in legal or literary sources,[38] with approximately 34 named trees, shrubs and flowers, which are of importance to the botanist and the woodland historian.

In addition to the problems of the plant-names and their identification, the passage raises questions of literary interpretation. How are the trees described? What was the poet trying to do, and how would the piece have been received by the audience? Where did he get the idea of an arboreal army from? Should we be looking for any significant order or symbolism in the tree-names: do they, for example, stand for letters of the alphabet, as Robert Graves thought?[39] Is this 'sacred grove' mythology, or is it, as I would prefer to argue, the first Welsh example of mock-heroic parody?

Trees, weedy shrubs and flimsy flowers form the motley battalion, and they are not very well-organized. The Old Irish tree-list from the legal collection, *Bretha Comaithchesa*,[40] has four classes of seven, each class corresponding to a division of society. The list ranges from the nobles of the wood (*airig fedo*) such as the oak, down to the shrubs of the wood (*losa fedo*) such as bracken, broom and heather. The Irish text attempts to arrange the plants according to their usefulness and worth, rather than merely according to size. No such groupings by worth or size are sustained in the *Cad Goddau* list, although the first three trees (alder, willow and mountain-ash, lines 1-4 below) correspond to the same Irish class of 'commoners of the wood' *aithig fedo*,[41] and some medium-sized shrubs (rose, raspberry-cane, privet and honeysuckle) are also found together (lines 9-14), as are the lowlier fern, broom, gorse and heather (lines 45-50). There is no correspondence at all with the order of the Welsh legal tree-tracts[42] nor with the order of plants listed in the early nature poetry.[43]

The trees and shrubs are mostly treated individually with a vignette for each extending over two, three or even four lines, as shown in the arrangement of the text below. They are anthropomorphicised as warriors and the tree-list passage resounds with the hackneyed phrases of heroic poetry. For example the alder was first to the attack: *a want gysseuin* (lines 1-2).[44] The privet is a 'bull of battle': *tarw trin* (line 35).[45] The whitethorn (line 41) dispenses pestilence 'from his hand' (*ech y aghat*) like the Gododdin warriors.[46] Broom (line 45) stands at the forefront of the battalion: *rac bragat*.[47] Elm (lines 30-31) slashes the centre, the wing and the rear of the enemy army.[48]

Many of the plant-names are accompanied by an alliterating

absolute verbal-form which describes their action: *ffawydd ffynyessit*, 'beech flourished' (line 37); *siryan se<i>nyssit*, '*siryan* resounded/clamoured' (line 17). Others are characterised by a ridiculously unsuitable agent noun: vine/woodbine 'the destroyer' (line 42), bracken 'the pillager' (line 44). Some plants exhibit the extreme rashness prized in the heroic ideal: the raspberry-bush (lines 11-13) was so brave that he did not bother to erect the usual wooden palisade to safeguard his life. Others are more naturally fitted for warfare: the plum-tree with his thorns at the ready was only too eager for slaughter (lines 5-6).

The tone is one of play: the over-extended roll-call is even more suspect in this respect than the gratuitously inflated catalogues in *Culhwch ac Olwen*.[49] As the intrepid alder launches first into the fray our expectations are high, but they are dashed immediately by the bathos of the stragglers: willow and mountain-ash. The birch (lines 18-21) has unheroic difficulty in getting his armour on - not out of cowardice, it is stressed, but because of his greatness. And what could be more terrifying than an attack (line 63) by a host of clover?

We are clearly in the realm of parody, a reaction to the pre-existing form and content - and perhaps even the ideology - of heroic poetry. It is well-known that all genres contain their antithesis and the seeds for their parody.[50] The simplest forms of parody use substitution, very often food: 'My heart leaps up when I behold/ A mincepie on the table'. The best-known Celtic example of such 'kitchen humour'[51] is *Aislinge Meic Con Glinne* in which dairy products (the food of the masses) debase various literary conventions.[52] Another kind of substitution might use animals and birds: an example is the Carolingian poet Theodulf's 'Battle of the Birds' where 'wing clashed with wing' and where the slaughtered birds are piled high on waggons.[53]

The tree-list portion of *Cad Goddau* is an even more subtle revelation of the affectations of heroic poetry than it appears at first sight. Certain features of Welsh nomenclature and of the conventional language used in heroic verse have facilitated the particular parodic substitution of trees for warriors. Firstly, there is the fact that real-life personal names could be taken from tree-names: e.g. Celynnin (< *celyn* 'holly'), Ceri (rowan), Gwern (alder), Eithinyn (< *eithin* 'gorse'), or Grugawg, Grugyn and Grugunan (< *grug* 'heather'), with which we may compare such Old Irish personal-names as Eithne and Fróech.[54] In other instances personal names might be interpreted as tree-names: for example, the name Afan, identical with the word for raspberry.[55] It is interesting that the song which Taliesin seems to have sung at the battle should be called *Gorchan Maeldderw*, for its hero's name (Maeldderw) could have been understood either as 'oak prince' or 'princely oak', rather than as a compound of the homophone *derw* 'certain'.

Secondly, Welsh tradition, like others world-wide, was fond of arboreal and architectural metaphors such as tree, column, post, prop, beam, roofbeam, to describe warriors and kings.[56] The basic similarity in shape between trees and humans, with flowing hair and limbs that move, encourages such metaphors. The blind man at Bethsaida whose sight is restored by Christ sees 'men as trees, walking' (Mark 8.24). Gruffudd ab yr Ynad Coch's lament on Llywelyn II's death transfers the human agitation at the outrage to oak trees smiting against one another.[57] Human warriors, like trees, are 'felled' in medieval Welsh battle descriptions.[58] By extension, whole armies are likened to woods: a well-known example in *Canu Heledd* employs both the metaphor of a single tree (= warrior), and a forest (= army).[59] There are copious Irish parallels for such metaphoric usage found in developed form in texts such as *Mesca Ulad* and *Cath Ruis na Rig*;[60] the moving Birnam Wood of *Macbeth* has been traced by August Knoch[61] and others to such sources.

Thirdly, many trees furnish the weapons of war, and in Welsh poetry arms are often referred to simply by the name of their constituent woods: e.g. *onn* 'ash' and *celyn* 'holly'. More general 'wood' terms, such as *gwŷdd*, *pren* and *gwiail*, can also bear the meaning 'weapons' throughout the poetry of the Cynfeirdd and Gogynfeirdd.

A coincidence which may have contributed to the *Cad Goddau* substitution of trees for warriors is that the names of many battles recorded in historical sources, or otherwise known in medieval Wales, tend to contain *coed* 'forest' or a synonym, presumably because wooded areas were often on boundaries between kingdoms or territories, and - like fords and rivers - would have been strategic battle sites. This tendency is reflected in the names of some of the battles mentioned in the Urien poems such as *Gweith Argoet Llwyfein*, *kat ym Prysc Katleu*, *kat yg Coet Beit* and *Gweith Pencoet*,[62] and by other battles such as that fought at Bangor [Is-coed] Orchard (*Gweith Perllan*

Vangor)[63] and the Battle of Celyddon Forest (*Cad Coed Celyddon*),[64] the most famous of the northern battles. Such battle-titles were open to being interpreted facetiously as 'the battle/battalion of the forest of X', thus facilitating the sort of substitution we find in our poem.

To sum up: there are certain native features which, singly or together, could have triggered the central idea of the mock-heroic tree battle. As regards the tree-listing itself, one would assume that there were in Welsh, as in Irish, traditional lists and compendia of tree- and plant-names which were known and schematized in different ways by specialist classes, whether lawyers, physicians, or churchmen,[65] and that the *Cad Goddau* poet is drawing, albeit in a random fashion, on a register of this sort. Such specialized knowledge, shown off in the poem by the Taliesin figure, may be compared with the *materia medica* with which he claims familiarity in another Book of Taliesin poem.[66]

One should bear in mind, however, that tree-catalogues (like other lists) were a commonplace in Classical literature and were widely imitated by medieval authors. One of the earliest of the Classical catalogues which characterize individual trees - as opposed to those give a bald listing of names - is Ennius' emotive account of the felling of the forest for Achilles' funeral pyre.[67] Five kinds of trees are mentioned, and alliteration (for example, *fraxinus frangitur*) conveys the way they crash to the ground. Virgil's *Aeneid* is similar.[68] Statius' inflated list of 13 species in the *Thebaid*[69] was roundly condemned by Gordon Williams as being 'absurdly wide' and 'a still further extreme of nonsense'.[70] Ovid's *Metamorphoses*, where the trees are conjured up by Orpheus's lyre, names 26 species in all.[71] But if any of these texts were a source of inspiration for our poet - as they were to be for Chaucer's *Parlement of Foulyes*[72] and the *Knight's Tale*[73] - one might have expected some borrowing of stock epithets: in the catalogues named above, conventional descriptions are transmitted, albeit with modifications, from author to author, indeed from Ennius right down to Dryden and beyond.[74] In *Cad Goddau* there is no such evidence for direct imitation of this kind, and we can surely credit the Welsh poet either with the nous to list trees for himself, or if that were beyond him, to draw on the contents of a pre-existing native catalogue. But if there was anyone in his audience familiar with the Classical topos of tree-listing, this might have added an extra piquancy to the passage. The ensuing parodic substitution of trees for warriors similarly needs no external literary models if we take into account the factors already discussed.

The reddest of red herrings was served up in Robert Graves' eccentric but highly influential classic, *The White Goddess.*[75] Graves, like earlier scholars from the eighteenth century onwards,[76] was fascinated by the poem, and it was his original intent to name the book *The Roebuck in the Thicket*, a reference to the mysterious *buch Anhun* noted above. The main thrust of Graves' interpretation is that *Cad Goddau* is a mystical alphabet poem in which the names of the trees denote various letters. The eclectic comparative evidence he used to support this theory included Irish ogam-lore, Germanic runes, and the 'alphabet of Nemnivus', three areas in which there has been much speculation about the origin of the letter-names, and the possibility of correspondences or borrowings between Celtic and Germanic.

Damian McManus's work on the Irish ogam-names[77] suggests that previous scholars, such as George Calder,[78] were mistaken in interpreting so many of the difficult ogam letter-names as tree-names. It is true that Irish *fid* 'wood' can also mean letter, but Dr McManus believes that this was because much of the earliest writing was executed on wood.[79] One might expect the Welsh cognate *gwŷdd* to bear the same meaning, but there is no evidence until the time of the notorious forger Iolo Morganwg - who was particularly interested in *Cad Goddau* - that the word was used in this sense.[80]

More significantly, there is no evidence that the medieval Welsh gave tree-names to the letters of the alphabet, nor even to a few of them, as in the case of Germanic runes[81] or the early Irish ogam-names.[82] The list of Welsh letter-names attached to the ninth-century Alphabet of Nemnivus, extant in four manuscripts,[83] does not include a single tree-name, unless the problematic *dexu* were emended to *deru* 'oak'.[84] Some of the names, as René Derolez and others note, seem to mimic the forms or meanings of Germanic names for other letters,[85] just as the bogus Welsh 'alphabet' itself, drawn up to confound an Englishman who had taunted the Welsh with not having an alphabet of their own, is in fact a set of quasi-runes.

Cad Goddau cannot possibly be an acrophonic poem in the sense that the Old English 'Runic Poem'[86] is, for the banal reason that too many of the tree-names would begin with the same 'letter'. The only line in the whole passage which could conceivably suggest that the trees were imagined as letters - with a tortuous double substitution being called for - is line 55: *y enw ym peullawr*, 'his name in a wax tablet'.[87] But this could equally well be taken as a satirical suggestion that this plant's name was indeed worthy to be recorded in writing, but only in the transitory medium of wax.

If, as suggested, the tree-list is to be read primarily as a mock-heroic parody, one might expect not only the content and phraseology of heroic poetry to be fair game - as it clearly is - but also that the poet might have reproduced older forms or quirks of the literary register in order to swell the patent absurdity of the passage. One notes in particular the unusually high frequency of absolute verbal forms: *eithyt*, *gwneithyt*, *seinyssit*, *gwiscyssit*, *bernissit*, *ffynyessit*, *glessyssit*;[88] and also the subject + verb word-order: e.g. *ffuonwyd eithyt*, line 9; *auanwyd gwneithyt*, line 11; *onn goreu ardyrched*, line 26. It would perhaps be a mistake in a passage of this kind to put too much trust in these features as genuine dating criteria since they could be merely dredged up from older poetry, understood by the audience, but included in order to strike a deliberately archaic note, much as does the use of the abnormal sentence in Modern Welsh. Other traditional criteria for dating are shaky, and need to be refined by more detailed attention to the poetry of the 'Bwlch' and the early Gogynfeirdd. 'Irish' rhyme, for instance (as in lines 20-21 below), is often regarded as a litmus test to detect 'early' verse; while it is true that such rhyme is eschewed by the official poets from the twelfth century onwards, we know little of its status outside those circles.[89]

The passage's quasi-learned list is just what we expect of the Taliesin figure, always ready to show off, as he does in the *Vita Merlini* with his Isidorean catalogue of the names of the fishes and fountains of Britain.[90] The unknown poet who composed this piece has combined such a list with a sophisticated parody, which must have been intended for an audience able to feel some distance (whether of time or of milieu) between themselves and the world of primary heroic tradition.

Finally we turn to the words *goddau* and *Goddau*. There is no problem about the existence of the well-attested verb-noun *goddef/goddau*, 'to make for, intend; reach', and the related singular noun *goddef/goddau* (pl. *goddeuon*) 'aim, intent'. The latter is used with *ar*, *yg*, *yr* to mean 'in order to, for the sake of, because of', and has been compared with Old Irish *fo dáig*, 'because'.[91] The rare homophone *goddau*, however, is attested in Medieval Welsh only in the Book of Taliesin, where the contexts suggest a collective or plural noun meaning 'trees', 'shrubs' or 'wood'. The most telling example is in the present poem (BT 25.24) where Taliesin says that he himself has been formed *o vlawt gwyd a godeu*, 'from the blossom of trees and *goddau*'. This seems to be a pair of alliterating synonyms (cf. *llen a llyfreu*, or *syr a sygneu*). The same collocation is found in a list of medical ingredients (BT 32.18): *a blaen gwyd godeu*, 'and the tips of the trees of the *goddau*/and the foremost branches of the *goddau*'. The remaining examples are found in the present poem (e.g. BT 24.8, *pan swynhwyt godeu*, 'when the *goddau* were conjured up').

Although it is reasonable to adduce the meaning 'trees, wood' from these examples, the derivation has never been explained. A tentative suggestion is that it contains the element *-deu* found in *cynneu* 'burning, fire',[92] with the prefix *g(w)o-*, 'beneath', with a development to 'kindling-wood' and thence to 'wood' in general, in which case *goddau* would presumably have been originally a collective noun like *gwŷdd* rather than a plural.

A further complication is that in two of the 'historical' Taliesin poems, *Goddau* appears to be the name of a region in North Britain: PT VI.4, *Godeu a Reget y ymdullu*, and PT VII.44, *Godeu a Reget yn ymdullyaw*, 'Goddau and Rheged mustering'. In these examples, the region seems to be either bordering on Rheged or else under its dominion and providing auxiliary forces for the battle of Argoed Llwyfain. The personal-name *Gurycon Godheu*, given to the daughter of Brachan who married Cadrawd Calchfynydd according to *De Situ Brecheniauc*,[93] may contain a place-name *Goddau*, but is of no help in determining the whereabouts of the region; the name *Gurycon* is similar to the Welsh name for the Wrekin.[94] While the etymology tentatively suggested for the common name *goddau* above does not at first sight appear very suitable as a regional name, one might bear in mind such 'shrub' names as Shrewsbury and Shropshire. On the other hand, the common noun and the regional name may be two separate words.

The fact that the battle of Goddau is listed in the triad of the Three Futile Battles along with Camlan and Arfderydd may indicate that it too was, or came to be regarded as, an historical battle. Ifor Williams suggested,[95] on the basis of the rather vague geographical correspondence, that Cad Goddau, which he understood as the battle in the region of Goddau, might be identified with Cad Coed Celyddon, the seventh of Arthur's battles in the *Historia Brittonum* list. Kenneth Jackson, in discussing the localization of Coed Celyddon,[96] notes the Classical identification with the mountain massif of the Grampians while stressing that Welsh tradition might have localized the battle somewhat differently. If it were possible to identify the *Prydein wledic* mentioned in our poem as Arthur - and that is far from certain - the equation of the battle of Celyddon Wood with the battle in the region of Goddau ('Cad Goddau') would be an attractive suggestion; furthermore, since the common noun *goddau* was understood to mean 'wood', the name of that battle could easily have been interpreted as 'the Battle of the Trees', thus facilitating the central idea of the passage in *Cad Goddau*.

Notes

1. I would like to acknowledge the kindness of the editor and staff of *Geiriadur Prifysgol Cymru*, and the many helpful comments which Jim Davies, William Linnard, and Patrick Sims-Williams made on an earlier draft.

2. The possible meanings are discussed below. The title is presumably abstracted from the poem as were other titles in the collection; the arboreal battle was considered to be the high point of the work. An edition of the complete poem is in preparation. Previous translations include: D. W. Nash, *Taliesin; or the Bards and Druids of Britain* (London, 1858), 224-34; William F. Skene, *The Four Ancient Books of Wales*, 2 vols (Edinburgh, 1868), I 276-84; Christian F. Guyonvarc'h, 'Kat Godeu', *Ogam*, 5, fascicles 5-6 (no. 30, December 1953), 111-20; Pierre le Roux, 'Le *Kat Godeu*', *Ogam*, 11 (1959), 185-205, a continuation of 'Les arbres combattants et la forêt guerrière: le mythe et l'histoire', *Ogam*, 11 (1959), 1-10; *The Mabinogi and Other Medieval Welsh Tales*, translated by Patrick K. Ford (Berkeley, 1977), 184-87 = *Sources and Analogues of Old English Poetry, II*, translated by Daniel G. Calder et al. (Woodbridge, 1983), 101-3.

3. For a description of this manuscript and four others by the same hand, see Haycock, 'Llyfr Taliesin', *National Library of Wales Journal*, 25 (1988), 357-86.

4. Le Roux, 'Kat Godeu', 185.

5. On the autonomy of the short line, see Haycock, 'Metrical models for the poems in the Book of Taliesin', in *Early Welsh Poetry: Studies in the Book of Aneirin*, edited by Brynley F. Roberts (Aberystwyth, 1988), 155-77.

6. Further discussed by Haycock, '"Preiddeu Annwn" and the figure of Taliesin', *SC*, 18/19 (1984/84), 52-78; '"Some talk of Alexander and some of Hercules": three early medieval poems from the Book of Taliesin', *CMCS*, 13 (Summer 1987), 7-38.

7. Rachel Bromwich, TYP 207, maintains that the battle was fought between different kinds of trees, but I would agree with Le Roux, 'Les arbres combattants', 193, that they are all on the same side.

8. See below, p. 308-10.

9. See GPC s.v. *gwledig*; TYP 453-54. On the phrase *udd Prydain*, applied to Urien Rheged, see PT 28. *Lluyddawg Prydain* 'the commander of the troops of Britain' is used of Cadwallon, and it has been suggested by R. Geraint Gruffydd that Cadwallon, and Gwallog before him, may have laid claim to a British overlordship: 'Canu Cadwallon ap Cadfan', in *Astudiaethau ar yr Hengerdd*, edited by Rachel Bromwich and R. Brinley Jones (Caerdydd, 1979), 25-43 at pp. 28-29. A range of terms (e.g. *priodawr*, *priawd*) used with *Prydain* by the *Gogynfeirdd* may reflect the archaic idea of the union of the rightful ruler with the sovereignty of the Island, according to Rhian Andrews, 'Rhai agweddau ar sofraniaeth yng ngherddi'r Gogynfeirdd', *B*, 27 (1976-78), 23-30.

10. BT 27.8-9: *Derwydon doethur/ Darogenwch y Arthur*, 'Druids of the wise one, prophesy |the coming of| Arthur'.

11. Haycock, '"Preiddeu Annwn"', 52-78.

12. CA 55: *Eman weithyon e dechreu gwarchan maelderw. Talyessin ae cant ac a rodes breint idaw. kemeint ac e odleu e gododin oll ae dri gwarchan yng kerd amrysson* 'Here begins Gorchan Maeldderw. Taliesin sang it and gave it status equal to all the awdlau of *Y Gododdin* and its three gorchanau'. For discussion, see GOSP 52; A. O. H. Jarman, *Aneirin: Y Gododdin* (Llandysul, 1988), lxvii-iii; Kathryn A. Klar, 'What

are the Gwarchanau?', in Roberts (ed.), *Early Welsh Poetry*, 97-137.

13. *Cyfreithiau Hywel Dda yn ôl Llyfr Blegywryd*, edited by Stephen J. Williams and J. Enoch Powell (Caerdydd, 1961), 22: *ac or byd darpar ymlad arnunt, canet y canu a elwir 'Vnbeinyaeth Prydein' racdunt*, further discussed *ibid.*, 175-76; Dafydd Jenkins, *Hywel Dda: The Law* (Llandysul, 1986), 227-28, and put in a wider context by J. E. Caerwyn Williams, 'Beirdd y Tywysogion: arolwg', *LlC*, 11 (1970), 33-35.

14. *Llyfr Gwyn Rhydderch: Y Chwedlau a'r Rhamantau*, edited by J. Gwenogvryn Evans (ail argraffiad, Caerdydd, 1973), col. 229; *Culhwch ac Olwen*, edited by Rachel Bromwich and D. Simon Evans (Caerdydd, 1988), line 126: *Neuenhyr Naw Nawt*.

15. The Red Book reads *nawd* 'patronage'. The White Book form, *nawt*, could be a lenited form or a variant of *gnawt*. G lists *gnawt*[1] 'câr, perthynas; ?cydymaith, cyfadnabod'; *gnawt*[2] 'anian, natur; ?dull, modd, arfer', both of which occur in variation with *nawt*. D. Ellis Evans, *Gaulish Personal Names* (Oxford, 1967), 207-9, discusses these homonyms. The Prydydd y Moch example discussed below, in which the name is in rhyme position, suggests that the *Culhwch ac Olwen* form should be emended to *nant* as Lloyd-Jones indicated, followed by Thomas and Gwyn Jones, *The Mabinogion* (London, 1949), 99 and 279. Like Lloyd-Jones, 'Nefenhyr', *B*, 14 (1952), 35-37, at p. 35, they understand the form to be a nasalization of *dant* 'tooth, eminence' ('Caer Nefenhyr Nine-teeth') rather than the radical *nant* ('Nefenhyr of the Nine Streams').

16. Brynley F. Roberts, 'Yr India Fawr a'r India Fechan', *LlC*, 13 (1980-81), 281-83; Haycock, 'Alexander', 12-13.

17. TYP 140-43.

18. H 276, lines 27-31.

19. See Léon Fleuriot, 'Gallois *amrygyr*', *ÉC*, 12 (1968-71), 573-79.

20. Lloyd-Jones, 'Nefenhyr', 35-37. On personal-names in *namo-*, *namanto-*, see Evans, *Gaulish Personal Names*, 234-36; E. P. Hamp, 'On some Gaulish names in *-ant-* and Celtic verbal nouns', *Ériu*, 27 (1976), 1-20, believes that the form would be **nāmant-* (long ā): if so this would not suit *Nefenhyr*, the first vowel of which must be from from ă.

21. John Lloyd-Jones, *Enwau Lleoedd Sir Gaernarfon* (Caerdydd, 1928), 6.

22. PKM 70. Cf. the magic phantom army motif: Andrew Welsh, 'The traditional narrative motifs of *The Four Branches of the Mabinogi*',

CMCS, 15 (Summer 1988), 51-62, at p. 61. On the genesis of Blodeuwedd, see PKM 83, comparing that of Taliesin, BT 25.21-26.6.

23. *Neif[i]on* may be derived either from *naf*, 'lord; Lord' (on which see Evans, *Gaulish Personal Names*, 234 and n.5), or else from *nef* 'heaven'. If the former, it could be the plural form, or else a singular formation from *naf* + *-ion*/*-iawn*. If from *nef* 'heaven' (with pl. adjectival ending), perhaps 'heavenly' as suggested by HGC 291, or 'heavenly being(s)'. The two twelfth-century examples, H 9.21-22 *vndec deir person uch archegylyon/ vn donyon neiuyon nerth heb dreghi* and H 82.28-29 *Can derrwyn can doryf egylyon/Can doruoet niueroet neiuyon*, do not resolve the problem, for either 'Lord' or 'heavenly being(s)' would be suitable. The later usage of *neifion* 'seas, waters' and *Neifion* 'Neptune' seems to have arisen through association with *nawf* and *nofio*.

24. *Ac eluyd*: G follows the manuscript: *eluyd*, 'earth, region'.

25. *Rithwch*: if God were addressing Gwydion alone, one would expect the 2 sg. imperative. I have emended tentatively to *rithych*, 2 sg. jussive subjunctive. But the pl. may be allowed to stand by assuming that his confrère Lleu was present (with other members of the family of Dôn), as another poem suggests: BT 33.23-25 *Bum yg Kat Godeu gan Leu a Gwydyon/ uy a rithwys guyd eluyd ac elestron*, 'I was at Cad Goddau with Lleu and Gwydion; they, Euwydd [emending to *euuyd*] and Elestron, conjured up trees'.

26. Peblig is attested as a personal-name, thought to be a version of the Latin name *Publicius*, but Melville Richards, 'Places and persons of the early Welsh church', *Welsh History Review*, 5 (1970-77), 333-49, at p. 349, suggests that Peblig may be a purely Welsh name which then became equated with the Latin name. Saint Peblig was thought to be a son of Macsen Wledig (see EWGT 63, 70; Molly Miller, *The Saints of Gwynedd* (Woodbridge, 1979), 97), and he is associated particularly with the Caernarfon area. My alternative interpretation derives the adjective (here used substantivally) from the noun *pabl*, 'activity, vigour': this may also be the derivation of the name Peblig if - as Richards suggests - it is native.

27. The letter /u/ does not normally represent [u] in the Book of Taliesin orthography; one would expect /6/ if the word is *bwch* 'buck'. *Buch*, Mod. Welsh *buwch* 'cow', would be perhaps more likely. For the personal name *Annhun* < Latin *Antonius* (or *Antonia*), see LLDC poem 10.28; HGC 111; CA 245-46. EWGT 170 lists references to characters

with this name, including Annhun fab Macsen Wledig, who would be the brother of the Peblig possibly alluded to above. The spelling *anhun* might suggest the adjective 'sleepless' rather than a personal name (although *nh* and *nnh* do alternate), but this does not yield much sense - 'unsleeping buck/cow'.

28. TYP 206-8. *Fechvys* is uncertain: it may mean 'fierce, aroused' if it is to be connected with *ffechyn* ('ardent, fervent', GPC s.v.); cf. perhaps *fechid* LLDC poem 35.17, although that example is usually emended to *techid*: LLDC 116. Tudur Aled draws on the triad, describing Cad Goddau as 'the battle where a lap-dog carried the day' (*Gwaith colwyn yn dwyn y dydd*).

29. Kenneth H. Jackson, 'O achavs nyth yr ychedydd', *YB*, 10 (1977), 45-50, considers Nora Chadwick's suggestion that this phrase is based on an explanation of the northern place-name Caerlaverock.

30. TYP 206.

31. Peniarth 111D (c. 1610 in the hand of John Jones, Gellilyfdy), 353; Peniarth 98B (John Davies, Mallwyd), 81; NLW 253 (Thomas Evans, c. 1621), 451; NLW 20574A (c. 1652), 77. The englynion are attributed to Gwydion (Peniarth 111 text): *Karngraff vy march rhag ottoyw/ bann blaen gwern ar yasoyw/ Brân ith elwir briger loyw. Karngraff dy farch yn y dydd kâd/ bann blaen gwern ar dy angad/ Brn lorgric ai vrig arnad/ Y gorfu Amathaon mad.* See CLIH i-li; TYP 207-8.

32. This is explained as a woman's name in Peniarth 111, 352: *a gwraic oedd yn y gad y tu arall a elwid Achren, ac oni wyppid i henw ni orfyddid arnynt*, on which see John Rhŷs, *Lectures on the Origin and Growth of Religion as Illustrated by Celtic Heathendom*, Hibbert Lectures, 1886 (London, 1898), 244-46.

33. TYP 208 following W. J. Gruffydd, *Math vab Mathonwy* (Cardiff, 1928), 331.

34. BT 24.10: *Trychwn trymdieu.* See Lloyd-Jones, 'Nefenhyr', 36, for *trychwn* meaning '30'. This idea (first put forward by Anwyl) has been revived by Pierre-Yves Lambert, '"Thirty" and "sixty" in Brittonic', *CMCS*, 8 (Winter 1984), 29-44, but is not taken up by Jarman, (*Y Gododdin*, lines 191, 328, 877) who follows CA 125 and 163, where it is understood as a compound of *try-* 'three' + *cwn* 'hounds'. For the pl. noun *trymdieu* following a cardinal number, see GMW 45.

35. Cf. CA lines 672-73; AP line 37: *dec[h]ymyd anaeleu dagreu gwraged.*

36. Cf. CA line 839: *diw llun hyt benn clun gwaetlin gwelet*; R 1042.36: *gwyr yg gryt a gwaet hyt deulin*; R 1313.23: *A gwedy delych gwaet hyt deulin.*

37. Ifor Williams, *Lectures on Early Welsh Poetry* (Dublin, 1944), 57; *Chwedl Taliesin* (Caerdydd, 1957), 22.

38. Native trees and shrubs which are notable absentees include poplar, juniper, elder and yew. Legal lists are disappointing with only 11 varieties (those also in the *Cad Goddau* list are marked with an asterisk): *alder, apple, *ash, *beech, crab-apple, *elm, *hazel, *oak, thorn, *willow and yew. These have been discussed by William Linnard: 'Forests and forestry in the ancient Welsh laws', *Quarterly Journal of Forestry*, 1976, 38-43; *Trees in the Law of Hywel* (Aberystwyth, 1979); *Welsh Woods and Forests: History and Utilization* (Cardiff, 1982), 12-19. There are two other lists in medieval literary sources. The first, in R 1032.13-37 (edited in EWGP 20-21), names only ash, birch, oak, brambles, fern, gorse, cow-parsley and reeds (**onn, *bedw, *derw, dryssi a mwyar erni, *redyn, *eithin, euwr, cawn*). The second, R 1033.1-1034.23 (edited in EWGP 29-32), is a much longer series of tree- and plant-names used (without any attempt at a rational order) usually in the line *Gorwyn blaen . . .* which is repeated at the beginning of each englyn, thus giving unity to the series of verses, as do numbers, days of the week and months of the year: **onn, *helic, (gwrysc man), *eithin, *meillyon, kawn, *derw, euwr, egroes, *banadyl, auall, *coll, (corsyd), elestyr, *gruc, brwyn, *redyn, kadawarth, kyrawal, *dar, kelli, *kelyn, *yspydat, berwr, erwein, ysgaw*. Information about plant-names and the medical properties of plants are contained in several manuscripts. BL Addl. 14912 (second half of 14th century) is discussed by Morfydd E. Owen, 'Meddygon Myddfai: a preliminary survey of some medieval medical writing in Welsh', *SC*, 10/11 (1975-76), 210-33, and the plant-names and their Latin equivelants from that manuscript are printed by Whitley Stokes, 'A List of Welsh plantnames', *Archiv für celtische Lexicographie*, 1 (1898), 37-49. For the material from the Red Book of Hergest (Oxford, Jesus College cxi, *c.* 1400), see *The Physicians of Myddveu*, edited by John Williams (Ab Ithel) (Llandovery and London, 1861), and P. Diverres, *Le plus ancien texte des Myddygon Myddveu* (Paris, 1913). Hafod 16 (Hand A, *c.* 1400) is edited by Ida B. Jones, 'Hafod 16. A medieval Welsh medical treatise', *ÉC*, 7 (1955), 46-75, 270-339; 8 (1958-59), 66-97, 346-93; the work of Hand B is discussed by Melville Richards, 'Havod 16, tt. 101-9', *B*, 14 (1950-52), 186-90. Other manuscripts containing medical material, such as Oxford, Jesus College

xxii, and Bodleian Library, Rawlinson B 467 (both 15th century), are further discussed by Owen, 'Meddygon Myddfai'.

39. Discussed below.

40. Edited and discussed by Fergus Kelly, 'The Old Irish tree list', *Celtica*, 11 (1976), 107-24.

41. Class B in Kelly, 'Tree list'.

42. See note 38.

43. See note 38.

44. Cf. CA lines 418, 873, and note, p. 177. Damian McManus, 'Irish Letter-names and their kennings', *Ériu*, 39 (1988), 127-68, at p. 151, notes the Irish kenning 'vanguard of hunting/warrior bands' for *fern* 'alder', comparing the *Cad Goddau* line.

45. The collocation occurs frequently: e.g. CA lines 427, 433, 587, 921; LIDC poems 18.203, 18.212, 34.1, 40.14; H 100.24; 279.27; see TYP 11-13. Similar phrases include *tarw bydin* CA lines 345, 921; *bydindarw* R 1288.7; *tarw bragad* R 1288.1; *tarw caduc* R 1423.37; *tarv torment* LLDC poem 18.16.

46. Cf. *ech adaf* CA line 948, and note, p. 298; CLlH 60-61: *echadaf torrit aruaeth. Ech* as an independent preposition is attested only in the early verse: GMW 192.

47. Cf. *blaen bragat* CA line 211; *bric bragad* H 94.18 etc.

48. Cf. CA lines 417, 636, 1238, and note CA p. 228; also BT 71.1-2 *a rewinyaw Gwyned/ oe heithaf oe pherued/ oe dechreu oe diwed*, AP xlii.

49. *Culhwch ac Olwen*, e.g. lines 175-374, discussed by Patrick Sims-Williams, 'The significance of the Irish personal names in *Culhwch ac Olwen*', *B*, 29 (1980-82), 600-620, and by Doris Edel, 'The catalogues in *Culhwch ac Olwen* and insular Celtic learning', *B*, 30 (1982-83), 253-67. The problem of detecting parodic and ironic intent in medieval texts is addressed by Joan N. Radner, 'Interpreting irony in medieval Celtic narrative: the case of *Culhwch ac Olwen*', *CMCS*, 16 (Winter 1988), 41-60.

50. Ernst Robert Curtius, *European Literature and the Latin Middle Ages*, translated by W. R. Trask (London, 1953).

51. Curtius, *European Literature*, 431-35; Paul Lehmann, *Die Parodie im*

Mittelalter (München, 1922), 199-208; George Fenwick Jones, 'The function of food in medieval German literature', *Speculum*, 35 (1960), 78-86; P. L. Henry, 'The land of Cockaygne', *Studia Hibernica*, 12 (1972), 120-42.

52. *The Vision of Mac Conglinne*, edited by Kuno Meyer (London, 1892), the comic aspects of which are discussed by Marged Haycock, 'Astudiaeth o *Aislinge Meic Conglinne*' (University of Wales dissertation, 1975).

53. D. Schaller, 'Lateinische Tierdichtung in frühkarolingischer Zeit', in *Das Tier in der Dichtung*, edited by U. Schwab (Heidelberg, 1970), 104-11; partly printed and translated by Peter Godman, *Poetry of the Carolingian Renaissance* (London, 1985), 172-75.

54. Cf. *Celynyn/in*: G 128; *Ceri*: G 136; *Gwern*: G 669; *Eithinyn*, *Eithinyawn*: G 465; *Grugawc*, *Grugyn*, *Grugunawc*: G 594. On Old Irish *Fróech mac Idaith*, see *Táin Bó Fraích*, edited by Wolfgang Meid (Dublin, 1976). Evans, *Gaulish Personal Names*, 291, notes names which may contain tree name-elements.

55. G 14.

56. The metaphorical usage of *colofyn*, *coeden*, *post*, *gwanas*, *coryf*, *nennbren* etc. is a commonplace in the work of medieval Welsh poets, and is discussed in TYP 483, and by T. J. Morgan, 'Trosiad y golofn', *YB*, 10 (1977), 94-105. It is frequent in Irish too, e.g. Cú Chulainn is 'an oak' (*ráil*) in *Cath Ruis na Ríg for Bóinn*, edited by Edmund Hogan, Todd Lecture Series, 4 (Dublin, 1892), 86-87, and warriors are described as 'pillars of strife', 'columns of support', 'a bush of shelter'. References to this usage in other cultures are collected by Patrick Sims-Williams, 'Riddling treatment of the "watchman device" in *Branwen* and *Togail Bruidne Da Derga*', *SC*, 12/13 (1977/78), 112-13, and by Enrico Campanile, 'Aspetti della cultura indoeuropea arcaica: I. La raffigurazione del re e dell'eroe', *Studi e Saggi Linguistici*, 14 (1974), 185-227.

57. Edited by J. E. Caerwyn Williams in *Llywelyn y Beirdd*, edited by Alan Llwyd (Abertawe, 1984), 96-104.

58. E.g. CA line 26; LlDC poem 34.35-36.

59. *Ny elwir coet o vn prenn* CLlH 35; *Vn prenn ygwyduit a gouit arnaw* CLlH 33. Ifor Williams, *B*, 9 (1937-39), 323-24, understood *gwyduit* as 'forest', but this was questioned by Heinrich Wagner, 'Welsh *gwydvit*', *ZcP*, 32 (1972), 81-85, who suggested that the second element was cognate with OI *bith* 'a cutting down, hewing; battle, slaughter'. Further

examples of army as wood include: R 1363.19, R 1431.6.

60. *Mesca Ulad*, edited by J. Carmichael Watson (Dublin, 1941), especially 17-20 (translated *Scottish Gaelic Studies*, 5 (1938-42), 12-14); *Cath Ruis na Ríg*, 40-43, 86-87, 94-95. For further parallels, see works cited in note 56.

61. *Macbeth*, Act V, 5. On Shakespeare's source, Holinshed's *Chronicles*, see Geoffrey Bullough, *Narrative and Dramatic Sources of Shakespeare*, 8 vols (London, 1957-75), vii, 504-5; cf. August Knoch, 'Irische parallelen zum wandernden Wald von Birnam in Shakespeare's *Macbeth*', *ZcP*, 22 (1941), 149-65.

62. PT VI.20, VII.23, XI.24, VII.25, XI.38.

63. TYP 163-65.

64. HB cap. 56. See discussion below.

65. See notes 38 and 40.

66. BT 32.7-19.

67. *Annales*, vi.197-91. Five trees are named; each tree has its own verb to describe its felling, sometimes with alliteration or assonance. On the 'mixed forest' topos, see Curtius, *European Literature*, 194-95.

68. *Aeneid*, vi.179-82; see Curtius, *European Literature*, 193-95.

69. *Thebaid*, vi.98-107.

70. Gordon Williams, *Tradition and Originality in Roman Poetry* (Oxford, 1968), 266, 267. David Vessey, however, regards the description as a legitimate 'mannered aggrandisement': *Statius and the Thebaid* (Cambridge, 1973), 193; cf. his comments on the epic convention of mustering an army, p. 19.

71. *Metamorphoses*, x.90-106; see John Block Friedman, *Orpheus in the Middle Ages* (Cambridge, Mass., 1970), 7, 153.

72. *The Parlement of Foulyes*, edited by D. S. Brewer (London and Edinburgh, 1960), lines 172-82, and note at pp. 105-6; the passage is discussed by J. A. W. Bennett, *The Parlement of Foules: An Interpretation* (Oxford, 1957), 70-73, and F. N. Robinson, *The Works of Geoffrey Chaucer*, second edition (Oxford, 1974), 793-94.

73. Robinson, *Chaucer*, 45, lines 2920-22.

74. See works cited in note 73, and Arthur Johnston, *Enchanted Ground* (London, 1964), 90.

75. Robert Graves, *The White Goddess: A Historical Grammar of Poetic Myth*, amended and enlarged edition (London, 1961).

76. Particularly Iolo Morganwg and his son Taliesin Williams, John Williams (Ab Ithel), and Edward 'Celtic' Davies.

77. Damian McManus: 'Ogam: archaizing, orthography and the authenticity of the manuscript key to the alphabet', *Ériu*, 37 (1986), 1-32; 'Irish letter-names and their kennings', *Ériu*, 39 (1988), 127-68; 'Runic and Ogam letter-names: a parallelism', in *Sages, Saints and Storytellers: Celtic Studies in Honour of Professor James Carney*, edited by Donnchadh Ó Corráin, Liam Breatnach and Kim McCone (Maynooth, 1989), 144-48.

78. George Calder, *Auraicept na n-Éces: The Scholar's Primer* (Edinburgh, 1917); J. Loth, 'L'écriture à l'époque préhistorique chez les Celtes', *RC*, 44 (1927), 1-13; J. Vendryes, 'Notes sur les noms des lettres de l'alphabet irlandais', *RC*, 44 (1927), 317-19; Howard Meroney, 'Early Irish letter-names', *Speculum*, 24 (1949), 19-43.

79. McManus, 'Ogam', 14; Vendryes, 'L'écriture ogamique et ses origines', *ÉC*, 4 (1940-48), 83-116, at p. 100; James Carney, 'The invention of the Ogom cipher', *Ériu*, 26 (1975), 53-65.

80. See GPC s.v.

81. B (birch, OE *beorc*) and Y (yew, OE *ēoh*). A (oak, OE *āc*) and Æ (ash, OE *æsc*) are regarded as later additions in the Anglo-Saxon extension of the *fuþark*: Ralph W. V. Elliott, *Runes* (Manchester, 1959), 48-49.

82. E.g. *beithi*, *fern*, *duir*, *coll*.

83. René Derolez, *Runica Manuscripta* (Brugge, 1954), 157-59; the oldest text is found in the third gathering (Liber Commonei) of Oxford, Bodleian Library, Auct. F 4.32 (early 10th century), f. 20r, described with facsimile by R. W. Hunt, *Saint Dunstan's Classbook from Glastonbury* (Amsterdam, 1961). The Welsh letter-names were discussed by in J. C. Zeuss, *Grammatica Celtica*, edited by H. Ebel (Berlin, 1871), 1059, and by Ifor Williams, 'Notes on Nennius', *B*, 7 (1933-35), 380-89.

84. Derolez, *Runica Manuscripta*, 157-59.

85. E.g. *rat* 'grace' (cf. OE *wynn*, OHG *rat*); *uir* (cf. OE *ur*, *ir*, *uir*, *uyr*): Derolez, *Runica Manuscripta*, 159.

86. *Runic and Heroic Poems of the Old Teutonic Peoples*, edited by Bruce Dickins (Cambridge, 1915), 12-23.

87. *Peullawr* is a borrowing from Latin *puuillǭres* < *pugillāres*: LHEB 442; Henry Lewis and Holger Pedersen, *A Concise Comparative Celtic Grammar* (Göttingen, 1937), 60; WG 109. The *Hisperica Famina* (vol. 1, edited by Michael W. Herren (Toronto, 1974), lines 532-46), describes a *tabula* covered in wax, which was inscribed with a stylus (*graphium*). For archaeological evidence from Britain, see A. K. Bowman and J. D. Thomas, *Vindolanda: the Latin Tablets*, Britannia Monographs, 4 (London, 1984); for Irish evidence, see E. A. Lowe, *Codices Latini Antiquiores: Supplement* (Oxford, 1971), 5. A religious lyric, LlDC poem 10.39, refers to writing on wax: *a wnaeth tuim ac oer./a llythyr yg cuir./a fflam im pabuir* '[God] who created warm and cold, and letters in wax and a flame in a candle'.

88. Recent wide-ranging discussions of word order include T. Arwyn Watkins, 'Constituent order in the Old Welsh verbal sentence', *B*, 34 (1987), 51-60; *id.*, *Constituent Order in the Positive Declarative Sentence in the Medieval Welsh Tale 'Kulhwch ac Olwen'*, Innsbrucker Beiträge zur Sprachwissenschaft: Vorträge und kleinere Schriften 41 (Innsbruck, 1988); John T. Koch, 'Prosody and the old Celtic verbal complex', *Ériu*, 38 (1987), 143-76.

89. See R. M. Jones, *Seiliau Beirniadaeth*, vol. 2 (Aberystwyth, 1986), 211-15.

90. *Life of Merlin: Geoffrey of Monmouth, Vita Merlini*, edited and translated by Basil Clarke (Cardiff, 1973), lines 820-55.

91. J. Loth, 'Irlandais *dáig*; *ar dáig*; *fo-dáig*; gallois *goddeu*', *RC*, 44 (1927), 281-99.

92. See Patrick Sims-Williams, 'The development of the Indo-European voiced labiovelars in Celtic', *B*, 29 (1980-82), 217.

93. EWGT 16.

94. *Gwrygon*: G 722.

95. PT xliv.

96. Kenneth Jackson, 'Once again Arthur's battles', *Modern Philology*, 40 (1945), 44-75, at p. 48. The many Welsh references are collected in G.

Abbreviations

AP	*Armes Prydein*, edited by Ifor Williams. English version by Rachel Bromwich (Dublin, 1972)
B	*Bulletin of the Board of Celtic Studies*
BT	J. Gwenogvryn Evans, *Facsimile and Text of the Book of Taliesin* (Llanbedrog, 1910)
CA	*Canu Aneirin*, edited by Ifor Williams (Caerdydd, 1938)
CLlH	*Canu Llywarch Hen*, edited by Ifor Williams (Caerdydd, 1934)
CMCS	*Cambridge Medieval Celtic Studies*
DD	John Davies, *Dictionarium Duplex* (London, 1632)
ÉC	*Études Celtiques*
EEW	T. H. Parry-Williams, *The English Element in Welsh* (London, 1923)
EWGP	Kenneth Jackson, *Early Welsh Gnomic Poems* (Cardiff, 1935)
EWGT	*Early Welsh Genealogical Tracts*, edited by P. C. Bartrum (Cardiff, 1966)
FBI	A. R. Clapham, T. G. Tutin and E. F. Warburg, *Flora of the British Isles* (Cambridge, 1962)
G	John Lloyd-Jones, *Geirfa Barddoniaeth Gynnar Gymraeg* (Caerdydd, 1931-63)
GMW	D. Simon Evans, *A Grammar of Middle Welsh* (Dublin, 1970)
GOSP	Kenneth Hurlstone Jackson, *The Gododdin: the Oldest Scottish Poem* (Edinburgh, 1969)
GPC	*Geiriadur Prifysgol Cymru* (Caerdydd, 1951-)
H	*Llawysgrif Hendregadredd*, edited by John Morris-Jones and T. H. Parry-Williams (Caerdydd, 1933)
HGC	*Hen Gerddi Crefyddol*, edited by Henry Lewis (Caerdydd, 1931)
LHEB	Kenneth Hurlstone Jackson, *Language and History in Early Britain* (Edinburgh, 1953)
LlC	*Llên Cymru*
LlDC	*Llyfr Du Caerfyrddin*, edited by A. O. H. Jarman (Caerdydd, 1982)
MM	*The Physicians of Myddveu*, edited by John Williams ab Ithel (Llandovery and London, 1861)
PKM	*Pedeir Keinc y Mabinogi*, edited by Ifor Williams (Caerdydd, 1951)
PT	*The Poems of Taliesin*, edited by Ifor Williams and J. E. C. Williams (Dublin, 1968)
R	*Poetry from the Red Book of Hergest*, edited by J. G. Evans (Llanbedrog, 1911)

RC	*Revue Celtique*
SC	*Studia Celtica*
TYP	*Trioedd Ynys Prydein*, edited by Rachel Bromwich (second edition, Cardiff, 1978)
VVB	Joseph Loth, *Vocabulaire vieux-breton* (Paris, 1884)
WB	Hugh Davies, *Welsh Botanology* (London, 1813)
WG	John Morris-Jones, *A Welsh Grammar* (Oxford, 1913)
YB	*Ysgrifau Beirniadol*
ZcP	*Zeitschrift für celtische Philologie*

The Tree-List: BT 24.15 - 25.19
[Emended and punctuated text, with tree- and plant-names capitalized]

1 **GWERN blaen llin**
ALDER at the head of the line
2 **A want gysseuin.**
Pierced first.

3 **HELYC a CHERDIN**
WILLOW and MOUNTAIN-ASH
4 **Buant hwyr y'r vydin.**
Were slow [to join] the army.

5 **EIRINWYD yspin**
Thorny [wild] PLUM-TREES
6 **Anwhant o dynin.**
Eager for slaughter.

7 **KERI kywrenhin:**
The strong SERVICE-TREE:
8 **Gwrthrychyat gwrthrin.**
One who anticipates the battle.

9 **FFUONWYD eithyt**
ROSE-TREES advanced
10 **Erbyn llu o <gywryt>.** **MS gewryt**
Against a wrathful host.

11 **AUANWYD gwneithyt:**
RASPBERRY-BUSH took action:

12 **Ny goreu emwyt**
He did not make a defensive palisade
13 **Yr amgelwch bywyt.**
In order to protect [his] life.

14 **RYSWYD a <GWYDUYT>** **MS gwyduwyt**
?PRIVET-WOOD and HONEYSUCKLE
15 **Ac EIDO, yr y bryt,**
And IVY, despite their appearance,
16 **Mor eithin y'r gryt.**
How fiercely [did they go] into the fray.

17 **SIRYAN se<i>nyssit.** **MS senyssit**
?CHERRY made a commotion.

18 **BEDW, yr y vawr vryt,**
BIRCH, despite his mighty appearance,
19 **Bu hwyr gwiscyssit:**
Was slow in putting on armour:
20 **Nyt yr y lyfyrder,**
Not because of his cowardice,
21 **Namyn yr y vawred.**
Rather because of his greatness.

22 **<AWRON> delis bryt;** **MS anron**
?GOLDEN ROD maintained [his] resolve;
23 **Allmyr uch <allffryt>.** **MS allfryt**
Strangers on the foreign waters.

24 **FFENITWYD yg kynted,**
PINE in the seat of honour,
25 **Kadeir <gywryssed>.** **MS gygwryssed**
Contention in the shape of branches/ contention for a chair.

26 **ONN goreu ardyrched**
ASH wrought magnificence
27 **Rac bron teyrned.**
Before princes.

28 **LLWYF, yr y varanhed,**
ELM, despite his bluster,
29 **Nyt oscoes troetued:**
Did not move a foot:

30 **Ef lladei a pherued**
He slashed the centre [of the army]
31 **Ac eithaf a diwed.**
And the wing and the rear.

32 **COLLWYD bernissit**
HAZEL adjudged
33 **Eiryf dy aryfgryt.**
The weapons for the conflict.

34 **GWYROS gwyn y vyt,**
Blessed/white DOGWOOD,
35 **Tarw trin, teyrn byt.**
The bull of battle, lord of the world.

36 **Morawc a Moryt.**
. . . .

37 **FFAWYD ffynyessit.**
BEECH was successful.

38 **KELYN glessyssit;**
HOLLY grew vigorous/verdant;
39 **Bu ef ygwrhyt.**
He was present in battle.

40 **YSPYDAT amnat:**
WHITETHORN the skilful one
41 **Heint ech y aghat.**
[Dispensing] pestilence from his hand.

42 **GWINWYD gorthorat**
VINE/WOODBINE the destroyer/was destroyed
43 **Gorthoryssit ygat.**
([Yet]) hewed in the fray.

44 **REDYN anreithat.**
BRACKEN the pillager.

45 **BANADYL rac bragat**
BROOM in the forefront of the battalion
46 **Yn rychua briwat.**
Was wounded in the churned-up [battle-ground].

47 **EITHIN ny bu vat;**
GORSE was not worthy;

48 **Yr hynny gwerinat.**
All the same he was brought into line.

49 **GRUC, budyd amnat,**
HEATHER, skilful victor,
50 **Dy werin swynat.**
Was enchanted into the army.

51 **HYDGWYR erlynyat.**
HINDBERRY the pursuer.

52 **DERW buanawr:**
OAK [was] swift his shout:
53 **Racdaw crynei nef a llawr.**
Heaven and earth trembled before him.

54 **<GLESYN> glew drussyawr:** **MS glelyn**
?BUGLE, a brave warrior:
55 **Y enw ym peullawr.**
His name [is kept] on a writing-tablet.

56 **CLAFUSWYD kygres**
The attack of the . . . .
57 **Kymraw a rodes.**
Caused terror.
58 **Gwrthodi, gwrthodes,**
He was repulsing, he repulsed,
59 **Ereill <otylles>.** **MS o tylles**
[And] stabbed others.

60 **PER goreu gormes**
The SWEET FRUIT-TREE [?pear] wrought oppression
61 **Ym plymlwyt maes.**
On the battle-field

62 **<Goruthrawc> kywyd** **MS goruthawc**
A terrifying array
63 **Aches <VEILLONYD>.** **MS veilon. wyd**
[Was] the surging CLOVER/WOOD-SORREL.

64 **KASTAN kewilyd,**
Bashful CHESTNUT,
65 **Gwrthryat <ferwyd>.** **MS fenwyd**
?His strong branches repulsing.

66 **<Handit> du muchyd,** **MS Hantit**
Jet is black,
67 **Handit crwm mynyd;**
Rounded is a mountain;
68 **Handit kyl <coedyd>,** **MS coetdyd**
Spiky are the trees,
69 **Handit kynt myr mawr**
The great seas are swifter
70 **Er pan gigleu yr awr.**
Since I heard the battle-cry.

71 **A'n deilas blaen BEDW,**
The top of the BIRCH put forth leaves for us,
72 **A'n <datwrith> datedw;** **MS datrith**
[Its] vigour reinforced us;
73 **A'n maglas blaen DERW**
The top of the OAK ensnared [the enemy] ?for us
74 **O Warchan Maelderw.**
Because of [the declamation of] Maeldderw's *Gorchan*.

Notes to the Text

2. **A want gysseuin**: see Introduction, note 44.

5. **Eirinwyd yspin**: I take this to be the wild *Prunus spinosa* (*yspin* < L. *spina*) as opposed to the sweet *P. domestica* or *P. institia*; see WB 47. If *yspin* is an independent name, however, cf. OI *spín* 'wild rose' (Kelly, 'Tree List', 122-23) and W. *yspinwydden/yspinys* 'prenmelyn (barberry)': WB 246.

6. **Anwhant o dynin**: cf. CA line 884: *oed mor guanauc idinin. maliuet med neu win*; EWGP 37: *chwannawg drut i chwerthin* where *anwhant* is followed by *i*.

7. **Keri**: possibly *Sorbus terminalis*. A tree-name would be preferable to the common noun 'berries, kernels'. As a personal-name, see Introduction, note 54.

9. **Ffuonwyd**: see G and GPC s.v. *ffion* 'rose; purple foxglove'. Only the former meaning is suitable in this compound; cf. *pren fion*, LlDC poem 16, lines 74 and 81.

9. **eithyt**: on the absolute verb-ending (not always in sentence-initial

position), see GMW 124, 132; Haycock, 'Alexander', 37.

10. **Erbyn llu o gywryt (MS gewryt)**: following G's emendation to *kywryt* 'cynddaredd, llid', and assuming an exemplar in which the schwa vowel was represented by the letter e. Another possibility would be to read *o geuuryt* (*geu* + *bryd*), 'of false intent'.

11. **Auanwyd**: see Introduction, note 55 on the personal name *Auan*. Afan = L. *Rubus* in Hafod 16; see WB 154; FBI 369-70; Ifor Williams, *Enwau Lleoedd* (reprinted Lerpwl, 1962), 68.

12. **emwyt**: CA 231-32; GOSP 30.

14. **Ryswyd**: *Lentiscus*, BL 41912, p. 41, and Hafod 16 where it also translates *Mirtus sydoria* (C, 7 (1955-56), 54. Other sources (MM 18, WB 233, 246, Jesus 10), favour *Ligustrum*. Thomas Wiliems's dictionary (Peniarth 228) has *y rhyswydh, y rheswydh, yr yswydh, prenn a ossotir mewn gardhae a rhotfeydh. Gwyros*, and DD follows this identification with *gwyros*, on which see below on line 34. Compare the first element perhaps with OI *ruis* 'elder'?

14. **gwyduyt (MS gwyduwyt)**: emend with G for the rhyme, yielding what may be, according to G 734, an earlier form of the name *gwyduit*. Alternatively, emend to *gwyduit*, with *i* and *y* rhyming.

15. **eido**: one of the earlier forms; later *eidew*. See further Eric P. Hamp, '"Ivy" in Italic and Celtic', *Journal of Indo-European Studies*, 2 (1974), 87-93.

16. **yr y bryt**: I take this to refer to the frail appearance of the three aforementioned plants; cf. Ford, *Mabinogi*, 184-85 'ivy for its beauty'.

17. **Mor eithin**: 'how fierce', with a play on words since *eithin* is also a plant-name: see below, line 47. On this line, see CA 154 'mor wyllt/danbaid i'r gad'. Ford, *Mabinogi*, 184-85, favours a compound: 'sea-furze'.

17. **Siryan**: *Siryan* is invariably given as the equivelant of *Prunus cerasus* 'cherries' (Jesus 10, 41, 206; DD; WB 235), and literary examples confirm the identification, either with the black or red varieties (e.g. *The Poetical Works of Dafydd Nanmor*, edited by Thomas Roberts and Ifor Williams (Cardiff, 1923), 89.4, 192; *Canu Rhydd Cynnar*, edited by T. H. Parry-Williams (Caerdydd, 1932), 51). Cf. Irish *sirín/silín* 'cherry', *seiríne* 'cherries' from English 'cherry'; the Welsh *siryan*, too, may derive from a form of that word: EEW 143. It is not impossible that there

has been confusion with the plant-name *suryon/suran* which translates *Oxalis acetosella* (MM 214; WB 235); Hafod 16 (*ÉC*, 7 (1955-56), 54), equates *suryon y coet* with *Panis cuculi* (wood-sorrel).

17. **<seinyssit> (MS senyssit)**: from an exemplar where e = ei, rather than a form of the verb *senni* 'to chide': CA 159.

18. **Bedw**: *Betula pubescens* is the variety of birch which grows in the north and west of Britain, as opposed to *B. pendula* in the east.

22. **<Awron> (MS anron)**: the second element would appear to be *ron* 'rod'. There are many plant-names which are compounded with *eur-* 'gold' (e.g. *eurddrain, eurfanadl, eurflawd, eurllys*), and our word may be a compound of *awr*, also meaning 'gold'. If so, *awron* may mean *Solidago virgaurea* (golden rod, common in the west), although this is later known as *eurwialen*. *Euron* 'Laburnum' (WB 183) is a late introduction to Britain.

23. **<Allffryt> (MS allfryt)**: emending with G yields linking alliteration with line 24. The line seems to refer to sea-borne foreign attackers.

24. **Ffenitwyd**: probably *Pinus sylvestris*: FBI 49-51, WB 191. Cf. *pin* 'pine' CA line 233. Linnard, *Trees in the Law of Hywel*, notes that pine is absent from the tree lists in the Welsh laws, and that this 'suggests very strongly that it had become completely extinct in Wales by the time the Laws came to be compiled'.

25. **Kadeir <gywryssed> (MS gygwryssed)**: see GPC s.v. *cadair*, in particular the meanings 'chair' (noting the connection with *kynted* in line 24) and 'cluster, especially of spreading branches or twigs from one stock'. G suggests emending *gygwryssed* to either *cywryssed* (< *cywrys* < *gwrys*) or *cyvryssed* (< *cyf-* + *ryssed*: CA 352-53), both meaning 'battle, contention' and used of bardic (e.g. H 228.12-13) as well as military encounters.

26. **goreu**: this could also be understood as 'best', with lines 26-27 forming a nominal sentence.

28. **varanhed**: I understand this as a lenited form of *baran(h)ed* (< *baran* 'bluster, noise'), rather than *maranned* 'riches', PT 49.

30. **a pherued/ac eithaf a diwed**: see Introduction, note 48.

33. **Eiryf dy aryfgryt**: MS *ac* is deleted and *dy* inserted above the line. This form of the preposition (*ddy*) is still found in early Gogynfeirdd poetry.

34. **Gwyros gwyn y vyt**: this is the only early attestation of *gwyros*, a plant identified with *Ligustrum* in some dictionaries, and with *Cornus sanguinea* 'cornel-tree, dogwood' in others: see GPC s.v. *gwyros*. Both plants have white flowers, giving a double meaning to the description *gwyn y vyt*.

35. **Tarw trin**: see Introduction, note 45.

36. **Morawc a Moryt**: capitals as in MS. *Morawc* occurs as a personal name, but the word here may be a mistake for *morawt* 'a great host': *B*, I (1921-23), 21-22. *Moryt* is attested as a common noun meaning 'river mouth' (*Gwaith Guto'r Glyn*, edited by J. Llywelyn Williams (Caerdydd, 1939), 102; cf. *Gwaith Dafydd ap Gwilym*, edited by Thomas Parry (Caerdydd, 1952), 434); as a place-name near Rhyl (*Gwaith Tudur Aled*, edited by T. Gwynn Jones (Caerdydd, 1926), 638); and as a river-name near Llanwnda: Lloyd-Jones, *Enwau Lleoedd Sir Gaernarfon*, 96. Reading *Morawt am moryt* 'a great host around the inlet' gives tolerable sense, although it cuts across the pattern of plant-names(s) + descriptive vignettes. There may be a line or two missing.

37. **Ffawyd**: beech grows mainly in south and east Wales: William Linnard, 'Ffawydd fel elfen mewn enwau lleoedd', *B*, 28 (1978-80), 83-86; 'Beech and the lawbooks, *B*, 28 (1978-80), 605-7.

38. **Kelyn glessyssit**: cf. BT 21.3-4 *pan yw glas kelyn*. The verb *glasu* can also mean 'to blanch, to grow pale'.

40. **Yspydat**: for the identification with whitethorn, hawthorn, see MM 221-22; WB 246.

40. **amnat**: GPC 'skilful, fine', but cf. CA 290 'enwog' (connecting it with *nad* 'song').

41. **ech y aghat**: see Introduction, note 46.

42. **Gwinwyd gorthorat**: *gwinwyd*, 'vine(s)' (WB 197 *Vitis vinifera*), sometimes used for woodbine, bryony and honeysuckle (see GPC s.v.). On *gorthorat* (which could also be the past impersonal of *gorthorri*), see GPC s.v.; CA 278, 291.

44. **anreithat**: G understands this as the past impersonal of *anreithaw*; GPC favours the nomen agentis with the suffix *-iad*. If the latter, cf. *gorthorat* in line 42: in both cases, the BT orthography fails to show the semi-vowel of the suffix.

45. **rac bragat**: see Introduction, note 47.

46. **briwat**: past impersonal of *briwaw*, following G.

49. **budyd**: G tentatively connects *budyd* (with a medial -ð-) with *buð* 'profit'. GPC adds that it may be connected with the *budd-* in *buddai* or *rhybudd*, and offers 'to strike, beat, push, fight; know, understand, judge; be beneficial or seemly; wizard, diviner'. I understand it here as *budd* 'profit, gain; victory' with agentive ending.

49. **amnat**: see note on line 40.

51. **Hydgwyr**: this is the only early example, and was identified in the 16th cent. with 'hindberries' (i.e. raspberries) on the basis of the similarity of the supposed meanings of the first elements (cf. English *buckthorn*). Lhuyd, *Archaeologia Britannica* (Oxford, 1709), 218, and WB 202, however, identified it with *Prunus cerasus nigra*, 'black cherries'. If the second element is *gwyr* (with our text retaining an older orthography, cf. perhaps *gwyros*, line 34 above.

52. **<bu> buanawr**: G suggests *bu buanawr* (*buan* + *gawr* 'noise, shout'); or *bu anawr*; *anawr* '?might, force; passion, assistance': see GPC and AP 59.

53. **Racdaw crynei nef a llawr**: an unusually long line; perhaps delete *Racdaw*.

54. **<Glesyn> (MS glelyn)**: *glelyn* appears to be a slip. Early examples of *glesyn* (e.g. R 1041.20) are unlikely to refer to *Borago officinalis* since that plant was a later introduction, *pace* CLlH 143-44. Native plants bearing small blue flowers include *Lycopsis arvensis* (bugloss), *Echium vulgare* (viper's bugloss), *E. lycopsis* (purple bugloss), or *Ajuga reptans* (bugle). *Isatis tinctoria* (woad) has yellow flowers but yields blue dye. . See further GPC s.v. and MM 22, note 194.

54. **drussyawr**: a hapax form, but cf. *drusiad* (CA 255-56), *drwssyat* (R 1415.35) and *drussad* (LLDC 78.15). The agent suffix *-awr* added to a nominal base, although fairly common in early sources, is in decline from the 14th cent.

55. **y enw ym peullawr**: see Introduction, note 87.

56. **Clafuswyd kygres**: *clafuswyd* 'elm' according to G, but the identification is not early. It is not certain that this is a plant-name, although the context favours one. A compound either of *claf* 'sick, leprous' and *uswyd* 'pieces of wood' (see CA 162; for a similar phrase, cf. R 1405.2 *klwyf uswyd nyt plyd neut plyc*); or else *clafus* 'sickly' and *gwŷd* 'trees'. On *kygres*, see G: 'ymladd, ymosod, cyrch, cyfarfod; ?llu'.

59. **<otylles> (MS o tylles)**: understanding this as the 3 sg. pret. of *godyllu*; on the absence of the relative pronoun *a* before verbs containing the prefix *go-* , see GMW 61.

60. **Per**: Latin *pira* (Classical *pirus* 'pear tree', *pirum* 'pear fruit') gives W. *per* 'pears'. The form *pyr* also occurs (e.g. *coch blaen pyr* R 1029) and Jackson, EWGP 50, suggests that that form may come from Latin *pyrum, pyrus, pirum, pirus* 'pear tree'. It has also been suggested (EEW 32) that *per* is a loan-word from Old or Middle English. According to Stefan Zimmer, 'Three Welsh etymologies', *CMCS*, 14 (Winter 1987), 61-67, at p. 62, the adjective *per* 'sweet' is probably 'a semantic and syntactic specialization of *pêr* "pear"'. We find both *per* and *peren* meaning 'sweet; domesticated' (e.g. *afallen peren, perwydd*) as opposed to 'sour; wild', and *per(wydd)* may have come to be used to denote any sweet fruit-tree, not just the pear-tree. The latter, *Pyrus pyraster*, is not very common in Wales.

61. **ym plymlwyt maes**: on *plymlwyt*/*plymnwyt*, see CA 123, 337; PT 62. *Maes* is disyllabic: LHEB 460.

62. **<goruthrawc> (MS goruthawc)**: the MS form is a hapax: G 'arswydus, brawychus, rhyfeddol; ofn', followed by GPC. An emendation to *goruthrawc* (*gor-* + *uthr* +*-awc*) would bring the word into line with *goruthrus, goruthre*, but cf. G s.v. *goruthawc*.

63. **<veillonyd> (MS veilon. wyd)**: l has not been modernised to ll; *-wyd* appears to be a mistake for *-yd* which is required for the rhyme, although GPC notes other examples of *meillionwydd*, and gives as its meaning 'trees with a sweet scent like clover' (cf. *meillionwellt* '?kind of grass having a sweet scent like clover'). *Mellhionou* glosses *uiolas*, VVB 184, but *meillion* appears to be used for other plants bearing purple flowers, particularly clover and wood-sorrel: Ifor Williams, *Y Beirniad*, 8, 256-57; EWGP 57: 'small meadow flowers'. I understand *meillonyd* as *meillon*, the collective noun, with plural *-yd*, comparable with the formation of *mellhionou*.

64. **Kastan**: probably from Latin *castanea* if this tree was introduced by the Romans. GPC, however, suggests a derivation from Middle English *castayne* or French *castaine*.

65. **Gwrthryat <ferwyd> (MS fenwyd)**: the hapax *gwrthryat* may be compared, as G notes, with the verb *ethryadu* 'restrain, impede' [< *ethry* + *gadu* according to GPC], and perhaps meaning 'repulser, opposer'. On the other hand, G suggests emending to the attested *gwrthyat* (on which

see CA 184), or to *gwrthrychyat* as in line 8 above. MS *fenwyd* is regarded by both G and GPC as a miscopying of *ffenidwyd*, but that tree has already been mentioned in line 24. My translation relies on a simpler emendation to *ferwyd* |*fer* 'strong' + *gwyd*|, understanding this to be a description of the chestnut tree in line 64.

66. **<Handid> (MS hantit) muchyd**: see GMW 147 on the use of *handid* as copula. *Muchyd* alternates with *muchud*.

68. **kyl**: cf BT 3.4 *Gwydyl kyl diuerogyon* 'armed pillaging Irishmen'.

69. **myr**: most likely in this context is the pl. of *mor* 'sea'. On *myr* as a plant-name, see CLlH 19, 145, 210; *myr(r)* also means 'myrrh', the gum resin itself or a tree or shrub yielding such a substance.

70. **pan gigleu**: either 1 or 3 sg.

71. **A'n deilas**: for the infixed pronoun with dative meaning, as found in lines 71-73, see GMW 57.

72. **<datwrith> (MS datrith)**: G understands the MS *datrith* as 3 sg. present of *datrithaw* 'change form, transform (through magic), turn back into original form'. The problem is that the verbs in lines 71 and 73 are in the past tense. '*Datwrith*, like *gwrith*, is attested (BT 26.18 *ef gwrith ef datwrith ef gwrith ieithoed*), and would provide a past tense. The prefix *dad* often has a privative force, but it may here, as in *datgan* etc., have an emphatic meaning.

74. **O Warchan Maelderw**: see Introduction, note 12.

Notes on *The Gododdin*

Jenny Rowland
University College Dublin

In CA 368 *en ol gwyr pebyr temyr gwinvaeth* Ifor Williams interprets *temyr* as an example of *tymyr* 'land, lands, kingdom'; cf. also CLlH, p. 138, and CA 816, 362, 600. Reading '[grief] ...for the splendid men of the kingdom, feasted on wine' makes perfect sense, and the misplacement of the adjective *gwinvaeth* might easily be ascribed to the exigencies of rhyme were it not for the fact that the overall metrical pattern of the line is awkward and atypical. A more flowing and typical metrical pattern is obtained by placing the pause/comma after *pebyr*, with internal rhyme providing a link between two phrases. Unless *tymyr-winfaeth* is then taken as an inverted noun phrase used as a pl. substantive, as seems rather unlikely and is equally awkward metrically, a different meaning must be sought for *temyr*.

The answer may well lie in the widespread confusion found in romance languages and presumably deriving from Vulgar Latin between *tempus* 'time, season' and *temperies* 'temperature, weather'. This confusion may well have existed in the Vulgar Latin of Britain, and indeed may have been encouraged by the range of meanings of the native *amser* 'time, season, weather'. If *temyr* in CA 368 is identical in meaning to *tymor* the line is regular and sensible: '[grief] ...for splendid men, for a time feasted on wine', comparing other examples of references in the poem to the period of the feast, often underlying the brevity of the warriors' lives, as here. Although most forms in MW show *tymer* from *temperies* the rhyme with *pybyr* is no real objection, since the expected form from *temperies* would be **tymyr* as seems to be found here.[1] This variant does appear the compound *ardymyr* 'weather, temperament', rather dubiously listed separately in GPC from *ardymer* with a similar range of meanings. It suggests that the form *tymer* may be a scholastic correction of an earlier **tymyr*, and that the strict distinction of meaning between *tymer/*tymyr* and *tymor* may also be scholastic in origin.

An alternative solution may be that *tymyr* in CA 368 is an analogous pl. of *tymor* 'for a (few) seasons nurtured on wine', comparing *mor*, *myr* and *cynghor*, *cynghyr*. On the whole the first solution appears more likely. It should be noted, too, that in CA 600-1: *o win bebyll ar lles tymyr/ tymor tymestyl* a play on words could be found on *tymyr* 'country' and *tymyr* if the latter is substituted for *tymor*. The three versions of this *awdl*, although fairly corrupt, are unanimous on the *-or* form, but *tymyr* 'country' is not found in the other two versions, and may indicate that an earlier *tymyr* 'period of time' was corrected to *tymor*.

CA 140-1

Blaen echeching gaer glaer ewgei
gwyr gweiryd gwanar ae dilynei.

Both *echeching* and *ewgei* in 140 are unknown. *Ewgei* is almost certainly a corrupt verbal form, and several possibilities, none terribly obvious are listed in CA 115 and in *Geirfa Barddoniaeth Gynnar Gymraeg*. A more convincing orthographic corruption is offered by John Koch, SC 20/21 (1985-6), p. 54, based on a mismodernization of very archaic **uuce* = *gwgei* 'fought'. However, two further suggestions can be made based on misunderstanding of rather later orthographic systems. GPC takes this as a verb from the noun *ewyg*. This requires only a common misreading of minims <**euigei*. The meaning would be: 'Blaen...inspired the ?faithful men of war who followed him'. On the same lines is a misreading of **elligei* = *ellyngei* as *euigei* > *ewgei*: 'Blaen...sent out/ unleashed the men of war who used to follow him.' This is preferable if the suggestion below for the corruption of the first part of line 140 is accepted.

There are also many suggestions for *echeching*; see CA, p. 113-4; GPC *echyngaf*, Koch, p. 54, but the obvious solution is again misreading, in this case of the preposition *ech* 'out of' and an inversion compound, *Eidyn Gaer* (cf. CA 1385 *eidyn gaer* *gleissyon glaer*, and 115 *ech e dir*, 816 *ech eu tymyr*). The errors can be ascribed to an OW form **ecetincair*. Having recognized *ech* the scribe went on to make the common error of misreading *t* for *c*, seeing a duplicate form. While he did recognize *caer*, the combination *-nc-* may have influenced his modernizing *in* to *ing*, although *in* and *ing* were in variation.[2] The translation would then best be: 'Blaen sent out from the splendid fortress of Eidyn the ?faithful men of war who used to follow him.'

CA 37-8

ny ellir--anet ry vaethpwyt--
rac ergyt catvannan catwyt.

Anet ry vaethpwyt taken as a *sangiad* in this couplet has caused some difficulties of interpretaton. Ifor Williams makes two suggestions: (1) *anet* is an error for OW *anit* '*onid*' or (2) an error for *ar met* '*ar fedd*'. Jackson's translation follows the first: '...unless one had been well-nourished it was not possible to withstand Cadfannan's blow.'[3] This would seem to put a ridiculous and unlikely limitation on the praise of Cadfannan's strength: he could cut down only underfed weaklings. Heroic overstatement is surely much more normal than quibbling on the extent of the hero's powers. The second suggestion, therefore, looks more promising, even if it is somewhat disjointed. 'He was nurtured on mead' could refer to Cadfannan's noble up-bringing or be an indirect reminder of his determination to fulfil the resolutions made at Mynyddog's feast, referred to earlier in the *awdl* (32-3). Along these lines a slightly more extensive emendation can be proposed, but one also more relevant and in keeping with the rest of the stanza: *a[ru]ed ry v[n]aethpwyt* '(his) intention was performed' or 'his promise was fulfilled'. This would also echo the previous use of *cadwyt* in the stanza, reinforcing the word-play: *e amot a vu not a gatwyt/ gwell a wnaeth e aruaeth* 'His promise was a point which was kept; better he fulfilled his intention.'

Also supporting the more extensive emendation is the fact that the ending *-pwyt* attached to the preterite 3rd sg. is very rare in early poetry. The only other occurence in The Gododdin, in the *cymeriad* opening of *awdlau* XXXIV, XXXV, XXXVI, and XXXVII, is of *gwnaethpwyt*.[4] John Morris-Jones states that this form originated in the irregular verbs as a part of the tendency to create forms from the conjugation of *bod*, spreading later to the t-preterite verbs.[5] Therefore, in an early poetic text *gwnaethpwyt* might be the expected genuine form rather than *maethpwyt*.

In CA 906 *Gwrdweryt gwaet am irved* Ifor Williams suggests that *gwrdweryt* is an error for *gwyrdweryt* 'a green sod' under the influence of *gwrduedel* in the previous line. But the translation 'a bloodstained sod around a new grave' requires interpreting *gwaet* as an adjective and for this there is no attestation. *Gwrdweryt* could also be a scribal mismodernization of *gwrdberit* = *gwrthferid*, again under the influence of *gwrduedel*. The meaning of the verb *gwrthferaf:gwrthferu*, *gwrthfryd* is 'restore, give back'; see GPC. The form could be either 3rd sg. pres. indic. absolute, or preterite impersonal. *Irved* is more likely to be a compound of *medd* meaning 'new mead'. This gives yet another example in the poem of the idea of paying for mead: 'Blood was given for fresh mead.' There is perhaps a deliberate wordplay here between *bedd* and *medd*, the drink and its result, in the use of the compound since the lenited second element had a closely similar sound and made good sense for both.

In CA 445/6 *an gelwit e nef bit athledhawr. e myt* Ifor Williams interprets *an gelwit* as either *'fe'n gelwid'*, *'fe'n geilw'* or *'a'n geilw'*. The latter seems the most likely and features in his interpretation of the line: *'Disgrifiad sydd yma o'r ddau lu yn wynebu ei gilydd. Gwrthyd y Brython heddwch. "Yr Un a'n geilw i nef, bit athledhawr (ym myd)."'* The tense of the verb, however, needs to be clarified. If this is the 3rd sg. present absolute in *-id* it is undoubtedly a late and suspect construction after both the relative pronoun and an infixed object pronoun. It is far more likely that the form here is the rare 3rd sg. present relative *gelwydd*, with *t* standing for [ð]. On analogy with Old Irish one would expect this form too to be absolute, but there are numerous examples of the Welsh form after conjunct particles; cf. *ny wneyd*, *na welyd*; see Donald Howells, 'The Nasalizing Relative Clause', SC 1 (1966), p. 47.

Further interpretation of the line depends on the sense of *athledhawr*. From context Ifor Williams suggests *'amddiffynydd'*. G notes possible connections with *achles* or *athreidd*, or, less likely, reading *'a'th leddawr'*. Closer to the text and giving good sense would be a derivative noun from the verb, *adladdaf:*

adladd. GPC lists a variant *adledd*, although no examples are listed. The verb is rare enough for there to be some uncertainty about its meaning, despite the obvious formation. G gives for *adladd '?enllibo, athrodi, difrio'*. GPC suggests 'strike, kill again'. 'One who strikes back, avenger' would make good sense here: 'Let He who calls us to heaven be our avenger in the world'. This would not be a word of challenge to the enemy but a heart-felt aside by the poet who knows that the defeated Gododdin people cannot themselves avenge their fallen.[6]

CA 31 *ruthyr eryr en ebyr pan llithywyt* contains a striking image, but the tense of the verb is a bit surprising. One would expect the swoop of ospreys to be more imperative while actually feeding, rather than after feeding. The passive also suggests that they have not been feeding on their own initiative. Warriors are said to 'feed' birds of prey by leaving numerous fallen on the battlefield, but the context here does not directly relate to the behaviour of birds of prey in war, and the notion of being fed is otherwise nonsensical with wild animals. An absolute form, *lithiyt*, is unlikely in a clause. Possibly the scribe has been misled by the fairly rare ending of the vn, *-wyt* (which occurs in line 38 of this *awdl*). I suggest we have here a misinterpretation of the vn loosely compounded with an adj, *ban llithiwyt*: 'of the rush of an eagle in the estuaries, noisily feeding'. This would give further relevance to the image since the warrior's battle-cry and uproar are often stressed as well as his charge. *Ban* is found elsewhere in the text as a variant of *pan* (CA 1110), so the scribal error is readily understandable, especially since *llithiwyt* is followed by two preterite impersonal forms of verbs in rhyme position.

CA 1316-7 ('Gwarchan Tudfwlch') *Blwydyn hiraeth/ er gwyr gatraeth am maeth ys meu* at first glance may seem to refer to a set period of mourning, a concept found in many cultures and expressed in many ways. But this reference should be compared with others which suggest that a period of a year had a special significance as regards bardic praise poetry. PT VI ends:

> A gwerin a grysswys gan einewyd.
> Armaf y blwydyn nat wy kynnyd

The interpretation that *blwydyn nat* is an inverted phrase, 'a year's song' is convincing, although further references may indicate a more precise meaning than just the victory will provide a year's worth of subject matter. Less directly, the opening of PT V, *Ar vn blyned*, speaks of a year's worth of reward to the poet from his patron. This could suggest a length of a contract for a peripatetic poet, although 'a year' is a very stereotyped expression for a length of time, and perhaps should not be taken too seriously here (any more than the length of the feasting of the Gododdin warriors should be). Two proverbs, variants of each other, in the Red Book, however, would seem to confirm the association of a praise poem with a year's time. These are RB 962 *Ny bu nat namyn un ulwydyn* and RB 1067 *Ny phara kywyd namyn vn vlwydyn*. I have argued elsewhere than the proverb lists and composition were a part of poetic activity and can help illuminate the *hengerdd*.[7] Without the PT reference to *blwydyn nat* it would be tempting to interpret these proverbs, particularly the version with the term *kywyd*, that songs of a popular nature are ephemeral, only so many weeks on the medieval hit parade. If, however, they refer to bardic poetry speculation on their meaning is imperative, particularly since this limited period seems to fly in the face of the often-expressed idea that bardic praise poetry preserves fame *hyt brawt*.

A good starting point is consideration of the 'ownership' of a praise poem in a pre-literate society. A patron paid good money to have his fame sung, but the copyright, as it were, would have stayed with the poet. In the absence of manuscripts and an ability to read, or of a trained memory, the patron was dependent on the will of the poet to recite 'his' poem again. Whether the fame preserved in this particular poem will last till the end of days rested solely with the poet, how often he would recite it, and whether it was good enough to get into the bardic repertoire of memorized poetry. The patrons may have protected their heavy investments by an accepted contractual agreement that the poem would remain 'theirs' for a set length of time. The poet may have been obliged to recite the poem whenever requested by his patron, or at set periods throughout the year such as major feasts. This would give a greater impression that the poem belonged to the patron, and that he had bought the lasting fame promised.

A similar late reference suggests that this idea of a year-long song continued amongst the poets, although it gradually became derogatory. In his debate with Gruffydd Gryg Dafydd ap Gwilym accuses him of being: *Cynnydd cerdd bun o unflwydd* (GDG 148.3). This is only to be expected. Despite all the protestations of lasting fame through poetry, it would be readily apparent to both patrons and poets that the reality was that most poems survived in the repertoire for only a short time, possibly a contractual year. So in the two proverbs cited, and the *cywydd* we may have a decline of the meaning of *blwydyn nat* of ancient practice to 'ephemeral song, one not good enough to become permanently enshrined', hence the disparagement of inferior love *cywyddau* with this old idea.

Returning to *blwydyn hiraeth...ys meu*, I would suggest it is not the period the poet will mourn formally for his companions, but rather that it is a statement that it is his role to provide another sort of *blwydyn nat, blwyddyn farwnad*.

It is a well-known feature of Welsh metrics that end rhyme is only between final syllables. Since in most stress languages rhyme occurs from the accented vowel this feature suggests (a) the practice was enshrined in the early *hengerdd* when the accent in Welsh was on the final syllable or (b) as suggested by Arwyn Watkins, early Welsh did not have a stress accent, and thus metrical principles would not have been greatly affected by the 'accent-shift' which occurred sometime between the 9th and 11th centuries.[8] Celtic metrics, too, have other types of rhyme which warn against extrapolation from other metrical systems. Old Irish, although it conformed generally in rhyming from the accented syllable also had a system of accented-unaccented rhyme found in the important *debide* metres. This type of rhyme at the very least was not avoided in Middle Welsh, and could be found even in the limited cadence patterns offered by Old Welsh accentuation in *llusg* rhymes. Eventually, of course, this type of rhyme became an important requirement of the *cywydd deuair hirion* and the *paladr* of the *englyn unodl union*.

I would like to call attention to certain two syllable rhymes in *The Gododdin*. For the reasons given in the remarks above I do not believe these have any particular relevance to the dating question, either as arguments for early date or late. They do, however, possibly suggest a single author with certain metrical individualisms is responsible for part of the poetry, as in the 'core' theory of Kenneth Jackson.[9] Two syllable rhymes on the whole are fairly rare in early poetry, although they do not seem to have been avoided. Some occur accidentally, when verbal or other endings have two syllables such as *-ator, -assei, -edic.* Others appear primarily in internal rhymes: CLlH III.47 *tawel awel*, CLlH IX.96 *nyt ynat kyn mynat ohonaw*, CLlH VI.26 *crin calaf alaf yn eiliat*, LlDC 30 *Oer guely pisscaud yg kisscaud iaen*, BT 4 *A decuet seint seic seithoed/ gwrhydrych ryfyd ieithoed*, BT 23 *bum aeduedic/ bum llat rac gwledic*, H 189 *Brennhin kywrenhin kywir yny dyt*.

Internal rhyme often provides an opportunity for verbal contrast, pleasingly playing against metrical similarity. This is found in the two syllable rhymes of *The Gododdin*, but in itself is not overly significant. An example is CA 485 *trenghis ny dienghis bratwen*. Cf. also 616 *nyt anghwy a wanwy odiwes*. Two syllable rhyme, like other metrical stresses, is also used to stress the most important adjective in 920, with a typical pun on the hero's name: *savwy cadavwy gwyned*. Word-play is responsible for 267 *[r]ac ysberi [r]y beri creu*. The most impressive example of a two syllable rhyme involves both contrastive stress and punning in the famous line, CA 71 *a gwedy elwch tawelwch vu*. While as noted above simpler types of rhyme can be used for these purposes, this meaningful use of two syllable rhyme is very rare in other examples of two syllable rhymes, and not invariable for all internal rhymes. The handful of examples from *The Gododdin* all make telling points, and suggest deliberate use of a more involved rhyme by a single master.

Abbreviations

BBCS	*Bulletin of the Board of Celtic Studies*
BT	Book of Taliesin
CA	*Canu Aneirin*. Ed. Ifor Williams. Caerdydd: Gwasg Prifysgol Cymru, 1961.
CLlH	*Canu Llywarch Hen*. Ed. Ifor Williams. Caerdydd: Gwasg Prifysgol Cymru, 1953.
GDG	*Gwaith Dafydd ap Gwilym*. Ed. Thomas Parry. Caerdydd: Gwasg Prifysgol Cymru, 1963.
G	*Geirfa Barddoniaeth Gynnar Gymraeg*. J. Lloyd-Jones. Caerdydd: Gwasg Prifysgol Cymru, 1950-63.
GPC	*Geiriadur Prifysgol Cymru*. Caerdydd: Gwasg Prifysgol Cymru, 1950-).

H	*Llawysgrif Hendregadredd.* Ed. Rhiannon Morris-Jones, *et al.*. Caerdydd: Gwasg Prifysgol Cymru, 1971.
LlDC	*Llyfr Du Caerfyrddin.* Ed. A.O.H. Jarman. Caerdydd: Gwasg Prifysgol Cymru, 1982.
MW	Middle Welsh
OW	Old Welsh
PT	*The Poems of Taliesin.* Ed. Ifor Williams, English ed. J.E. Caerwyn Williams. Dublin: Dublin Institute for Advanced Studies, 1968.
RB	Red Book of Hergest
SC	*Studia Celtica*

Notes

1. See Henry Lewis, *Yr Elfen Ladin yn yr Iaith Gymraeg* (Caerdydd: Gwasg Prifysgol Cymru, 1943), p. 47.

2. Cf. Ifor Williams, *Pedeir Keinc y Mabinogi* (Caerdydd: Gwasg Prifysgol Cymru, 1951), pp. 284-5; D. Simon Evans, *A Grammar of Middle Welsh* (Dublin: Dublin Institute for Advanced Studies, 1970), p. 8.

3. *The Gododdin: The Oldest Scottish Poem* (Edinburgh: Edinburgh University Press, 1969), p. 117.

4. Of the well over a hundred examples of other verbs I have found in G only two forms in *-pwyt* from relatively early poetry: *ducpwyt* H 22 and *clywspwyt* RB 1155.31. The form, however, is extremely common in prose.

5. *A Welsh Grammar* (Oxford: Oxford University Press, 1931), p. 338.

6. See also my comments on CLlH I.17 *nyt car ath ladawr* in *Early Welsh Saga Poetry: A Study and Edition of the Englynion* (Boydell and Brewer, forthcoming).

7. See *Early Welsh Saga Poetry*.

8. See T. Arwyn Watkins, 'The Accent in Old Welsh: its Quality and Development', BBCS 25 (1972), pp. 1-11; 'The Accent-Shift in Old Welsh', *Indo-Celtica: Gedächtnisschrift für Alf Sommerfelt* (München: Max Heuber,1972), pp. 399-405; 'Cyfnewidiadau Seinegol sy'n gysylltiedig â'r acen Gymraeg', BBCS 26 (1976), pp. 399-405. For an opposing date see

also Kenneth Jackson, 'The Date of the OW Accent Shift', SC 10/11 (1975-6), pp. 40-53.

9. 'Some Questions in Dispute about Early Welsh Literature and Language', SC 8/9 (1973-4), p. 1.

The Early Insular Elegies: ITEM ALIA

Hildegard L. C. Tristram
Albert-Ludwigs Universität

Much has been written on the early Insular elegies.[1] Some scholars have denied the Insular character of these poems and have preferred to look at them within their Welsh, Irish and English frames of reference.[2] Others, like myself, have in varying degrees affirmed it.[3] Most criticism has been directed either at proposing native origin hypotheses[4] or influence from Celtic or Anglo-Saxon[5], or from (medieval) Latin.[6] I have no doubt that a number of Welsh, Irish, English and Latin lyrics (as well as Latin, Irish and English prose works) of the early Middle Ages feature common strands of elegiac thought and lyrical sensitivity. They give expression to the emotional response of the individual to the vicissitudes of life (*conditio humana*). The question is, are these poems related, and if so, how?

The prevailing mode of explanation of international literary parallels has been along the lines of monocausal hypotheses - only one is maintained to the exclusion of others. With this premise only three basic possibilities can be envisaged:

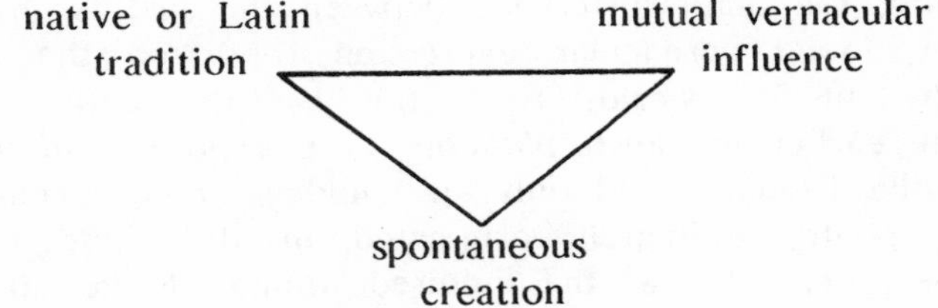

Either the shared features represent a continuous tradition of native origin or a dispersion from a Latin base to the various vernaculars, or there is borrowing between contemporary contact literatures, somewhat on the lines described by Kenneth Jackson and Proinsias Mac Cana for the medieval Welsh tales.[7] The third possibility is that there was spontaneous creation of forms and themes perhaps due to a shared background of ideas. Though there may be some truth in each of the monocausal hypotheses proposed so far,[8] monocausal explanations can, however, be objected to, because they don't do justice to the complexities of historical processes. What we need in order to come closer to the historical truth is polycausal thinking. I am not advocating an easy syncretism, but making a plea for a closer look at the methodology of the various approaches and at what is mutually reconcilable in them. In particular, I wish to plead for a more comprehensive and profound study of the early Middle Ages' *planctus* tradition.[9]

My view is that the (vernacular) Insular "elegy" was an international genre ultimately drawn from Latin sources but acculturated, and thereby transformed, into the specifically Welsh, Irish and English types of *planctus*. It was international in the same sense that later courtly love poetry was. *Amour courtois* originated on the Continent and found its typically French, German, English, Welsh and Irish expression in the respective native cultural sphere with the help of existing native traditions. The "elegies", as a genre, also originated on the Continent. Typologically, the main difference between the two is that courtly love poetry found vernacular expression, both on the Continent and in the Insular world, from the twelfth century onwards, whereas the earlier medieval *planctus* were expressed in vernacular writing in the Insular world only. It could even be speculated that troubadour poetry ultimately originated in the same geographic area as the "elegies", i.e. the cultured milieu of the ancient city of Poitiers.[10] Here again, more research into the nature of early medieval international literary affiliations is needed.

The sixth century seems to have been formative for the "elegies" as a specifically Christian genre, for whatever the cause of the *persona*'s despair, after the *miseria mundi* there is always the prospect of hope in the salvational promise. This may be given verbal expression or may be left unexpressed, but it is always present in the background. I am thinking of three authors in particular, each very different in his personal philosophy of life, who wrote in the sixth century: Boethius (480-524), Venantius Fortunatus (ca 530-610) and Columbanus (ca 543-615). Each contributed in different ways and in addition to the respective native settings, I think, to the formation of the Insular *planctus* tradition.

Boethius was not himself a Christian, but the Middle Ages read his *De consolatione philosophiae* (written in 524) as a Christian book[11] and medieval authors referred to his imprisonment in Pavia as an "exilium". The Psalter and the Old Testament 'Lamentations of Jeremiah' helped to give it a specifically Christian interpretation. Just as Boethius was the philosophical advocate of consolation, Columbanus was the eloquent preacher of the *miseria mundi*. Of his thirteen *instructiones*[12], five harp on the theme of human misery (*O infelicissima miseria! Vae tibi humana miseria! Misera humana vita, humanae vitae miseria, O nos miseri! O me miserum!* etc.) and this somber view of life is also voiced in his poems, most impressively in his 'Mundus iste transibit /Cottidie descrescit /Nemo vivens manebit /Nullus vivus remansit ...'[13] Columbanus had left Ireland for permanent exile and he keeps referring to the need for spiritual exile (*peregrinatio*) in his *instructiones*. He preaches the necessity of journeying to the (heavenly) *patria* and the tribulations (*O dolor incomparabilis!*) man needs to suffer on the way there: *quasi peregrini semper patriam suspiremus, semper patriam desideremus; finis enim viae semper viatoribus optabilis et desiderabilis est, et ideo quia sumus mundi viatores et peregrini de fine viae, id est, vitae nostrae semper cogitemus, viae enim finis nostrae patria nostra est.*[14] For all his spiritual fervour, Columbanus' writing shows very little of his personality and hardly any reference to current events. He lived in the troubled age of Merovingian Gaul and Lombard Northern Italy, the age of the establishment of the semi-barbarian Germanic Kingdoms on former Roman soil, an age of political chaos and brutality.[15] Columbanus does mention wars (*Tempus enim hoc tempus belli est; ideo enim nemo putet securitatem in bello, quia nullus dormit in bello et nullus securus ingreditur aciem*[16]), and this looks like a topical allusion (he himself had been affected by the power politics of Austrasia), but what he is really referring to is the spiritual war of the vices attacking the soul. Columbanus is a fervent ascetic, but his writing is never really personal. He teaches the somber lessons of the tribulations which beset the individual in this world and which he must endure before he reaches the heavenly home.

Venantius Honoris Clementianus Fortunatus, presbyter Italicus, as he calls himself at the beginning of his impressive collection of poems (eleven books and 265 'carmina') comes closest to the Insular "elegies".[17] His poetry is personal, even at times intimately so, and full of exuberant and yet learned imagination. He has a fine feeling for nature and gives expression to a "powerful overflow of emotions recollected in tranquility" (to use Wordsworth's words).

Fortunatus was born in a small village near Treviso, to the north of Venice, and received a classical education (grammar and rhetoric) in Ravenna. In 565 he left Italy, presumably for political reasons, never to return there again. He was an exile like Columbanus and he, too, finally settled in the belligerent new Germanic kingdoms, Fortunatus north of the Alps, and Columbanus south. Fortunatus established himself in Poitiers as the 'spiritual adviser' (cf. Irish *anmcharae*) of the former Neustrian queen Radegunde, founder of the convent of the Holy Cross at Poitiers, and the young abbess Agnes. There he wrote his best poetry, between 567 and 577.

We only need to consider his "elegies"; his other, rather prolific, writing falls outside the scope of the present study. I will first briefly discuss his most important *planctus* relating to the Insular "elegies", and then proceed to single out particularly striking parallels. Two of Fortunatus' "elegies" have been called "true masterpieces of the genre".[18] The first goes by the title of *De excidio Thoringiae.*[19] This is a misnomer, since only the exordium deals with the description of the destruction of the royal hall of the Thuringians by the Frankish king Chlotar I in the year 531.[20] The text is a (first person) verse letter, where the lyrical *persona* 'Radegunde' addresses her cousin Amalafred in Constantinople and implores him to send her a sign of his affection.[21] She and Amalafred were Thuringian royal offspring and had been lovers in their youth. After the destruction of the kingdom of Thuringia they were forever separated. Amalafred eventually made a military career in Constantinople and Radegunde, after a loathsome marriage to Chlotar I, the murderer of her family, led an ascetic life in her convent of the Holy Cross at Poitiers. The poem is a pathetic plea for love and friendship from one who is suffering from mental affliction, because she is all alone, without family and in foreign lands, although she could have all the material goods imaginable, if she only wanted them.

The second "elegy" is another verse epistle 'in persona Radegundis', this time addressed to her nephew, the only male survivor of the royal house of Thuringia: 'Ad Artachin'.[22] After Radegunde learned that Amalafred was dead, she addressed this letter to the son of her brother, who had been killed by her own husband Chlotar I, when he was in his early twenties. She reminds Artachis that he is the last of her kin and asks him to send her messengers frequently with his news.

The third "elegy" is known by the title of 'De virginitate'.[23] It is a fictitious letter by an unnamed nun, addressed to Christ, but it is easy to guess who is meant, since we know that the poem was composed for the ceremony of Agnes' installation as abbess of the Convent of the Holy Cross in 567. The nun professes in the most fervent terms her mystical love for her 'dominus'. She suffers as a result of her separation from him and longs to be united with him (in heaven). This poem is perhaps the least close to the Insular "elegies", but it is important for my argument, as it reveals most clearly the main source of Fortunatus' *planctus* (if we indeed take him to be the author of these first person letters), namely Ovid's *Heroides*. The particular source for 'De virginitate' is the language and the imaginative situation of Ovid's Ariadne abandoned by Theseus. The poem "transposes it, an extended conceit, *a lo divino*".[24]

There are two further letter "elegies": 'De Gelesuintha'[25] and 'Ad Iovinum inlustram ac patricium et rectorem provinciae'.[26] The poem 'Epitaphium Vilithutae'[27] is a dirge rather than a *planctus* in the sense of the Insular "elegies". Here the *persona* laments the death of the newly married Wilithuta, who died in childbirth. Its purpose is to console the mourning husband. These three poems are by Fortunatus, although 'De Gelesuintha' may have been written by him at the request of Radegunde to appease (or console?) the enraged Austrasian queen Brunichilde, a Visigothic princess. Her sister Geleswinda had been married to the Neustrian king Chilperich, but was strangled soon after the wedding at the instigation of Chilperich's mistress Fredegunde. The poem does not focus on the terrible events themselves, but rather on the emotional response of the women connected with Geleswinda's misfortune: The *planctus* of the young princess, when she learns that she has to leave her beloved home (Toledo) forever, the bitter words of her mother who accompanies her daughter a while on the way north (which is presented as an arctic country), the frightful journey through Gaul to Rouen and then the desperate laments of the mother when she learns of her daughter's murder, the outraged laments of Geleswinda's sister Brunichilde and the elemental laments of the nurse, who accuses herself of not having protected her better. Some of the details are quite graphic, as in 'De excidio Thoringiae'. 'Ad Iovinum' sets out to console a friend who has lost his position as governor of Provence and is represented as suffering as a result of his fall from political power to social insignificance - though he was not executed like Boethius, but allowed to retire to his country estates. "Tempora lapsa volant, fugitivis fallimur horis... Time that is fallen is flying, we are fooled by the passing hours..."[28]

Themes of transitoriness and the mutability of *sors* and *fortuna* occur in other poems of Fortunatus' as well, but the combination of first person impersonations, laments on the *miseria mundi*, hints at a specific occasion underlying the events, the tense emotional language of personal suffering and the prospect of Christian salvation for the sufferer (somewhat on the lines of *per aspera ad astra*)[29] is most successful in the elegiac poems mentioned.

I will now give a short list of the most striking themes and motifs shared by these poems and the Insular "elegies". I refrain from giving exact verse identifications of the analogues ("Similienliste"), as this would exceed the scope of this essay, but I hope to publish this elsewhere.

exile[30] - Fortunatus: De excidio, De Gelesuintha; Irish: Caillech Bérri; English: Wulf and Eadwacer, Wife's Lament, Husband's Message, Wanderer, Seafarer, Deor, Eangyth's letter to Boniface and Berhtgyth's letter to her brother Balthard [31]

isolation - Fortunatus: De excidio, Ad Artachin; Welsh: Canu Llywarch Hen, Canu Heledd, the Juvencus englynion; Irish: Caillech Bérri, Líadan ocus Cuirithir; English: Wulf and Eadwacer, Wife's Lament, Husband's Message, Wanderer, Seafarer, Deor, the elegies incorporated in 'Beowulf', Cynewulf's first epilogue to his 'Elene' *separation by sea*[32] - Fortunatus: De excidio; English: Wulf and Eadwacer, Wife's Lament, Husband's Message, Resignation, the Anglo-Saxón women's letters

miseria mundi - Fortunatus: De excidio, De Gelesuintha, (Epitaphium Vilithutae), Ad Iovinum; English: Wanderer, Seafarer, Riming Poem, elegiac passages in Cynewulf and elsewhere

female personae lamenting - Fortunatus: De excidio, Ad Artachin, De Gelesuintha, (De virginitate); Welsh: Canu Heledd; Irish: Caillech Bérri, Liadan ocus Cuirithir, Créide's Lament, Mé Eba; English: Wulf and Eadwacer, Wife's Lament[33] and the vernacular *winileodas*

triangular (love) relationships - Fortunatus: De excidio; Irish: Créide's Lament; English: Wulf and Eadwacer, Wife's Lament, Hildeburh of the Finnsburgepisode in 'Beowulf'

admission of guilt - Fortunatus: De excidio, De Gelesuintha; Welsh: Canu Llywarch Hen I.28: 'Marwnad Gwen': *Drwy vyn tanawt lle<de>ssaint* etc; Canu Heledd: 'Ffreuer' 57c: *O anffawt vyn tauawt yt llessaint*; English: Riming Poem, Resignation

destruction of cities (or royal hall) - Fortunatus: De excidio[34]; Welsh: Canu Llywarch Hen: 'Diffaith Aelwyd Rheged'; Canu Heledd: 'Stafell Gynddylan'; English: Ruin, Riming Poem

parents' lament over loss of children - Fortunatus: De excidio, De Gelesuintha;[35] Welsh: Canu Llywarch Hen; Irish: *Cumhthach labhras an lonsa*[36]

Christian consolation - Fortunatus: De Gelsuintha, (Epitaphium Vilithutae), Ad Iovinum, De virginitate; Irish: Caillech Bérri, *At-lochar duit a mo Ri*;[37] English: Wanderer, Seafarer; Riming Poem, Resignation, (Deor)

Many more analogues could be cited (hostile nature with wind, rain, ice; the island in the sea; old age and sickness; the messenger as only means of contact; eschatological motifs etc.), but this may suffice.

I am tempted to believe that the monologic form of the Insular "elegies" could be indebted to Fortunatus' verse epistles and the Continental tradition underlying them. The epistolary setting got lost, however, in its transfer from the Continent to the Insular world, where verse epistolography had no tradition like that of sixth century Gaul and Italy. When one reads or hears Fortunatus' *planctus*, one is not immediately aware of the epistolary character, unless one knows about their generic background. So it is easy to imagine that when manuscripts containing his poems were read in Wales, Ireland or England, they were adapted to the Insular modes of thinking, that is, in the form of a lonely speaker's sorrowful monologue.

Was Fortunatus known at all in the early medieval Insular world? It seems that he was widely read in the centuries immediately after his death.[38] I have no positive proof for knowledge of his works in Wales and Ireland outside the quotes from Fortunatus' poems in Columbanus' *carmina*[39] and his contacts with Brittany[40], but Aldhelm used him in his writing and Bede frequently quoted 'De virginitate' in his 'De arte metrica' and mentioned his name once in his *Historia ecclesiastica* (I.vii). Alcuin quoted from him even more extensively than Bede and referred to him in his 'Versus de ... sanctis Euboricensis Ecclesiae' (l. 1553)[41]. Fortunatus apparently belonged to a group of late Antique and early Medieval Latin poets who had, by the end of the eighth century, formed a definable "school canon" - Caelius Sedulius, Arator, Juvencus, Paulinus of Nola and Venantius Fortunatus.[42] He is also referred to in an eleventh century vernacular *catena* of traditional learned school matter ('Interrogationes').[43] Two of his hymns, 'Vexilla regis prodeunt' and 'Pange lingua gloriosi' still formed part of the Catholic liturgy until the Second Vaticanum.[44] But although positive proof is lacking, there is no reason to believe that his elegiac verse should not have contributed to the formation of the Insular elegiac tradition.

If we look at the features not shared by the Insular specimens and Fortunatus' *planctus*, it appears that the characteristics of the Welsh elegies lie in the unflinchingly heroic and often gnomic tone, their martial setting and their lack of a verbalized Christian perspective. The Irish elegies are much more personal and religious, but they are also characterized by a mythological component, which removes them from the realities of contemporary life and sets them completely apart from the other Insular *planctus*. The English elegies, like most other Anglo-Saxon writing, are more impersonal than the Irish and less heroic than the Welsh. Their strongly Christian overtones, mingled with the gnomic, reach out in the direction of the *sensus figuralis* or even the *sensus moralis*.[45]

With none of these Insular poems do we know their specific historical background, so that we cannot follow the pattern of fictionalization as with Fortunatus. But it seems to me that in the early centuries of the Christian kingdoms north of the Alps the traditon of elegiac verse expression was a correlate of the heroic panegyric and heroic epic.[46] It gave utterance to the impassioned feelings of the suffering individual, that is, *her or his* emotional response to the calamities of life in the semi-barbarian Christian societies in this world, and to the promise of shelter and salvation in the world to come, while the heroic panegyric and epic reflect the ideals and values of the community as a whole and as such leave no room for 'naked' emotions to be expressed.[47]

Notes

1. The most important studies of the Old English elegies are by L. L. Schücking, 'Das altenglische Totenklagelied', *Englische Studien*, vol. 39 (1908), pp. 1-13; E. Sieper, *Die altenglische Elegie* (Straßburg 1915); R. Imelmann, *Forschungen zur altenglischen Poesie* (Berlin, 1920); Andreas Heusler, *Die altgermanische Dichtung*, 2nd edn (Potsdam, 1941); D. Whitelock, 'Beowulf 2444-2471', *Medium Ævum*, vol. 8 (1939), pp. 198-204; S. B. Greenfield, 'The Formulaic Expression of the Theme of "Exile" in Anglo-Saxon Poetry', *Speculum*, vol. 30 (1955), pp. 200-206; reprinted in J. B. Bessinger and St. J. Kahrl (eds), *Essential Articles for the Study of Old English Poetry* (Hamdon, Conn., 1968), pp. 352-373; Greenfield, 'The Old English Elegies', in E. G. Stanley (ed), *Continuations and Beginnings* (London, 1966), pp. 142-175; Willi Erzgräber, '*Der Wanderer*: Eine Interpretation zu Aufbau und Gehalt', in H. Viebrock und W. Erzgräber (eds), *Festschrift für Theodor Spira* (Heidelberg, 1961), pp. 57-85; Kemp Malone, 'Two English *Frauenlieder*', *Comparative Literature*, vol. 14 (1962), pp. 106-117; L. H. Frey, 'Exile and Elegy in Anglo-Saxon Christian Epic Poetry', *Journal of English and Germanic Philology*, vol. 62 (1962), pp. 293-302; K. H. Göller, 'Die angelsächsischen Elegien', *Germanisch-Romanische Monatsschrift*, vol. 45 (1964), pp. 225-241; Herbert Pilch, 'The Elegiac Genre in Old English and Early Welsh Poetry', *ZCP*, vol. 29 (1964), pp. 209-224; P. L.

Henry, *The Early English and Celtic Lyric* (London, 1967); T. A. Shippey, *Old English Verse* (London, 1972), pp. 53-79; Michael Alexander, *Old English Literature* (London, 1983), pp. 111-131; Martin Green (ed), *The Old English Elegies, New Essays in Criticism and Research*, (London, 1983); Ursula Schaefer, 'The Fictionalized Dilemma: Old English Poems at the Crossroads of Orality and Literacy', in Willi Erzgräber and Sabine Volk (eds), *Mündlichkeit und Schriftlichkeit im englischen Mittelalter*, ScriptOralia, vol. 5 (Tübingen, 1988), pp. 39-51. Important studies of the early Welsh elegiac poetry are Ifor Williams, 'The poems of Llywarch Hen' (1933 Rhŷs lecture), repr. in Rachel Bromwich (ed), *Ifor Williams: The Beginnings of Welsh Poetry* (Cardiff, 1972), pp. 122-154; Williams, *Canu Llywarch Hen* (Cardiff, 1935, repr. 1953), pp. ix-xcii; Williams (ed), *Lectures on Early Welsh Poetry* (Dublin, 1944, repr. 1970); Patrick K. Ford, 'Llywarch, ancestor of Welsh princes', *Speculum*, vol. 45 (1970), pp. 442-450; Ford, *The Poetry of Llywarch Hen* (Berkeley, Cal., 1974); N. J. A. Williams, 'Canu Llywarch Hen and the Finn Cycle', in Rachel Bromwich and R. Brinley Jones (eds), *Astudiaethau ar yr Hengerdd* (Cardiff, 1978), pp. 234-265; A. O. H. Jarman, 'Saga Poetry - The Cycle of Llywarch Hen', in A. O. H. Jarman and Gwilym Rees Hughes (eds), *A Guide to Welsh Literature* (Swansea, 1976), vol. 1, pp. 81-97; Jenny Rowland, 'The Prose Setting of the Early Welsh Englynion Chwedlonol', *Ériu*, vol. 36 (1985), pp. 29-43. In contrast to the English and the Welsh situation, critical studies of the early Irish "elegies" are surprisingly scanty. Myles Dillon (*Early Irish Literature*, Chicago, 1948, pp. 168-171) has little to say and there is next to nothing in James Carney (ed), *Eleonor Knott and Gerard Murphy: Early Irish Literature* (London, 1966), pp. 45f. For criticism of the 'Caillech Bérri' poem see B. K. Martin, 'The Old Woman of Beare: A Critical Evaluation', *MÆ*, vol. 38 (1969), pp. 245-261; Donncha Ó hAodha, 'The Lament of the Old Woman of Beare' in Kim McCone (ed), *Sages, Saints and Storytellers: Celtic Studies in Honour of Professor James Carney* (Maynooth, 1989), pp. 308-331.

2. See for instance Ford, *The Poetry of Llywarch Hen*, p. 54: "Thus it may be seen that the saga theory and the programmatic approach has caused some otherwise serious and well-directed criticism (Henry and Pilch) to miss its mark". Ford (section 2) prefers to read them along nativist lines as "a direct development of earlier Welsh tradition and, ultimately, of Celtic tradition" (p. 55).

3. See for instance Sieper, *Die altenglische Elegie*, pp. 55-77; Nora K. Chadwick, *The Heritage of Early Britain* (London, 1952), p.125; H. Idris

Bell (trans), *Thomas Parry, A History of Welsh Literature* (Oxford, 1955), p. 15; H. Pilch, 'The Elegiac Genre', especially at p. 224; P. L. Henry, *The Early English and Celtic Lyric*; Shippey, *Old English Verse*, p. 69; Alexander, *Old English Literature*, p.121; Daniel F. Melia, 'An Odd but Celtic Way of Looking at Old English Elegy', in P. K. Ford (ed), *Connections Between Old English and Medieval Celtic Literature*, Old English Colloquium Series, vol. 2 (Los Angeles, 1983), pp. 8-30; Sarah L. Higley, 'Lamentable Relationships? Non-Sequitur in Old English and Middle Welsh Elegy', in Ford (ed), *Connections Between Old English and Medieval Celtic Literature*, pp. 45-66; Hildegard L. C. Tristram, 'Early Modes of Insular Expression', in Kim McCone (ed), *Sages, Saints and Storytellers*, pp. 427-448.

4. L. L. Schücking and Ernst Sieper interpreted the Old English "elegies" along the lines of a genre of death laments inherited from pre-Christian Germanic times. A. O. H. Jarman sees the Welsh "elegies" as a further development of the Old Welsh death laments as in Aneirin and Taliesin ('Saga Poetry', p. 86), while P. K. Ford takes them as ninth or tenth century compositions eulogizing the dynastic ancestry of Merfyn Frŷch (d. 844) (*The Poetry of Llywarch Hen*, p. 55). The 'Caillech Bérri' has been related to a lost Munster saga cycle by David Greene and Frank O'Connor (eds and trans), *A Golden Treasury of Irish Poetry, A. D. 600 to 1200* (London, 1967), p. 7ff., and explained as an eleventh century edition of independent saga verse, some of it a lament like Cú Chulainn's lament for Fer Diad. Gerard Murphy, on the other hand, writes that "everything indicates that she was originally a mythological figure ... an ancestress of races, who, like Medb, had husbands in succeeding generations" ('The Lament of the Old Woman of Beare', *PRIA*, vol. 55 (1952-53), p. 84); see also A. H. Krappe, 'La Cailleach Bhéara, Note de mythologie gaélique', *Études Celtiques*, vol. 1 (1936), pp. 292-302; 'The Sovereignty of Erin', *American Journal of Philology*, vol. 63 (1942), pp. 444-454.

5. Pilch, 'The Elegiac Genre'; Henry, 'The Early English and Celtic Lyric', Herbert Pilch and Hildegard Tristram, *Altenglische Literatur* (Heidelberg, 1979), p. 141; compare also Ida L. Gordon (ed), *The Seafarer* (London, 1960), pp. 15-22. S. B. Greenfield, *A Critical History of Old English Literature* (New York, 1965), p. 225 rejects straightforward connections between the Old English *Frauenlieder* and the Old Irish 'Líadan ocus Cuirithir'.

6. Andreas Heusler, following R. Imelmann, links the Old English elegies to

classical Latin models, especially Ovid and Vergil (*Die altgermanische Dichtung*, pp. 145-150). Willi Erzgräber ('*Der Wanderer*') advocates indebtedness of this particular poem to Boethius' *Consolatio philosophiae*, which was known to the Anglo-Saxons especially through Alfred the Great's translation into the vernacular (late ninth century). Erzgräber implicitly suggests that the topic of lament plus consolation may also have had some bearing on the formation of the other Old English consolatory poems. U. Schaefer's 'Two Women in Need of a Friend: A Comparison of *The Wife's Lament* and Eangyth's Letter to Boniface', in Bela Brogyanyi and Thomas Krömmelbein (eds), *Germanic Dialects: Linguistic and Philological Investigations* (Amsterdam, 1986), pp. 491-524, demonstrates the shared intellectual and emotional atmosphere between the Old English *Frauenlieder* and the early English nuns' letters. The parallelism is even closer in Berhtgyth's Latin letters to her brother Balthard, probably written in the 770s, as Peter Dronke points out in his *Women Writers of the Middle Ages* (Cambridge, 1984), pp. 30ff. Dronke notes (p. 30) that they are "near the close of the Boniface collection" and "have no direct link with the saint. Because of this they have not appeared in modern selections of the Boniface letters, and have been neither translated nor discussed. They are related to the vernacular *winileodas* 'songs for a lover', which, according to the famous prohibition of 789, abbesses and the nuns in their charge were forbidden to send from their convents." (p. 31). Peter Dronke ('Poetic Individuality. Questions', in *Poetic Individuality in the Middle Ages, New Departures in Poetry 1000-1150*, 2nd edn (London, 1986), pp. 27-29) sees all the Insular "elegies", including Old Norse poems like Egill Skallagrímssons 'Sonatorrek', as forming part of an international genre of *lyrical planctus*, culminating in Abelard's superb cycle of laments. Within the genre, he distinguishes between five sub-genres: (i) vernacular *planctus* to be sung by women, (ii) dirges, represented in Latin from the eighth century with Paulinus of Aquileia's song on the death of Duke Eric of Friuli, and abundantly from then on, (iii) a Germanic tradition of complaints of exile and voyaging, often enriching the literal sense of these with a wider range of evocative meanings, (iv) fictional narrative *planctus* and (v) lyrical *planctus* with biblical themes (p.27, fn. 1). He quotes examples from Anglo-Saxon, Old Norse, Mozarabic, Irish, Welsh and Latin.

7. Proinsias Mac Cana, *Branwen, Daughter of Llŷr, A Study of the Irish Affinities and the Composition of the Second Branch of the Mabinogi* (Cardiff, 1958); Kenneth Jackson, *International Popular Tales and the*

Early Welsh Tradition (Cardiff, 1961). In both books themes and forms are presented as having travelled between literatures through cultural contact at the oral level. In the domain of the elegies the contact would have to have been of a written quality, as the aesthetics of these lyrics is of an essentially written nature, as I will endeavour to show. In Walther Bulst's words all writing in the early Middle Ages is art: "Auch die 'schlichte' Prosa hat Stil, vielmehr *ist* ein Stil. Der Gebrauch einer in der Schule erlernten Sprache der Literatur, wie das Lateinische in den Jahrhunderten des Mittelalters, bedingte einen literarischen und Kunst-Charakter aller schriftlichen Außerung" ('Radegundis an Amalafred', in Siegfried Joost (ed), *Bibliotheca docet, Festschrift Carl Wehmer* (Amsterdam, 1963), p. 374; repr. in Walter Berschin (ed), *Walther Bulst. Lateinisches Mittelalter. Gesammelte Beiträge* (Heidelberg, 1984), p. 50). What holds for Latin holds for the vernaculars as well, since the proficiency of writing Welsh, Irish or English came after the writing of Latin in the training of the scholar.

8. Therefore we shouldn't perhaps reject too rashly even P. K. Ford's politico-shamanistic reading of the *Canu Llywarch Hen* "as extremely dubious", as Jenny Rowland does in her 'Welsh Englynion Chwedlonol' (p. 37).

9. There is a terminological problem. The term "elegy" is ambiguous and frequently refers to "dirge" and/or "lament". The Latin term *planctus* is equally ambiguous. The dirge for Charlemagne for instance has been called 'Planctus Caroli'. It was composed by a monk of Bobbio, the great Columban foundation, and has the elegiac "heu mihi misero" for its refrain; cf. Karl Langosch (ed and trans), *Lyrische Anthologie des lateinischen Mittelalters* (Darmstadt), 1968, pp. 94-98. Dronke (cf. note 6) seems to take *planctus* as the more general term. Our "elegies" would correspond to his types (ii) and (iii). The "dirge" (Welsh *marwnad*; Irish *marbnad, caíne*) is not meant here and for that reason Irish poems like 'The Lament for Cuimine Fota' (Gearóid Mac Eoin (ed), *Ériu*, vol. 28 (1977), pp. 17-31; cf. Francis J. Byrne, 'The Lament for Cuimmíne Foto', *Ériu*, vol. 31 (1980), pp. 111-121) are excluded from consideration here. Old Germanic dirges have survived in Old Norse literature and two Old English ones are mentioned in 'Beowulf' (Bwf 1118a and 3152), both sung by women. On the traditon of medieval Latin dirges see for instance M. Hereswitha Hengstl, *Totenklage und Nachruf in der mittellateinischen Literatur seit dem Ausgang der Antike* (Diss. Würzburg, 1936).

10. Cf. Reto R. Bezzola, *Les Origines et la Formation de la Littérature Courtoise en Occident* (Paris, 1944), pp. 55f., 75f. The view that Venantius Fortunatus' poetry may "be linked with the conventions of ancient, nor yet, as Bezzola would have it, medieval *courtoisie*" has not met the approval of Peter Dronke, *Medieval Latin and the Rise of European Love-Lyric* (Oxford, 1965), p. 208.

11. On the influence of his treatment of *consolatio* in the Old English "elegies", see Willi Erzgräber, '*Der Wanderer*'; more generally on medieval consolation literature see Peter I. von Moos, *Consolatio. Studien zur mittelalterlichen Trostliteratur über den Tod und zum Problem der christlichen Trauer*, 4 vols. (München, 1971/2). See also Joseph S. Wittig, 'King Alfred's *Boethius* and its Latin sources: a reconsideration', *Anglo-Saxon England*, vol. 11 (1983), pp. 157-198.

12. G. S. M. Walker (ed), *Sancti Columbani Opera* (Dublin, 1970), pp. 60-120.

13. Ibid., p. 182; cf. Michael J. B. Allen and Daniel G. Calder, *Sources and Analogues of Old English Poetry. The Major Latin Texts in Translation* (Cambridge, 1976), pp. 134-136. For the authenticity of 'Mundus iste' as a poem of Columbanus', see Peter Christian Jacobsen, 'Carmina Columbani', in Heinz Löwe (ed), *Die Iren und Europa im frühen Mittelalter* (Stuttgart, 1982), vol. 1, p. 440, and Dieter Schaller, 'Die Siebensilberstrophen "de mundi transitu" - eine Dichtung Columbans?', in ibid., pp. 468-483.

14. *Instructio* VIII (Walker, *Sancti Columbani Opera*, p. 96).

15. Cf. Theodor Schieder (ed), *Handbuch der europäischen Geschichte* (Stuttgart, 1979), vol. 1, pp. 250-296, 372-433; Walker, *Sancti Columbani Opera*, pp. xix-xxxii (France, Switzerland and Italy); Karl Langosch, *Profile des lateinischen Mittelalter. Geschichtliche Bilder aus dem europäischen Geistesleben* (Darmstadt, 1965), pp. 13-26 ("Die politische und kirchliche Lage im frühen Merowingerreich"). What is negatively called "semi-barbarian" and "brutal" (or positively, "semi-civilized") in the historical accounts corresponds to the "heroic age" in literature. The praises of this very same Merovingian Gaul of fraternal strife and murder are still sung of six hundred years later in the (late) heroic Middle High German 'Nibelungenlied'.

16. Walker, *Sancti Columbani Opera*, p. 104.

17. F. Leo (ed), *Venantius Fortunatus, Opera Poetica*, MGH, AA, IV, 1

(Berlin, 1881); Wilhelm Meyer, 'Der Gelegenheitsdichter Venantius Fortunatus', in *Abh. der Götting. Ges. der Wiss., hist. Kl. NF.* 4, 5 (Berlin, 1901), repr. abridged in Karl Langosch (ed), *Mittellateinische Dichtung. Ausgewählte Beiträge zu ihrer Erforschung* (Darmstadt, 1969), pp. 57-90; Richard Koebner, *Venantius Fortunatus* (Leipzig, 1915); René Aigrin, *Sainte Radegonde* (Paris, 1918); F. Brittain, *Saint Radegunde* (Cambridge, 1928); D. Tardi, *Fortunat; Étude sur un dernier représentant de la poésie latine dans la Gaule mérovingienne* (Paris, 1928); R. R. Bezzola, *Les Origines*, pp. 41-76; F. J. E. Raby, *A History of Secular Latin Poetry in the Middle Ages*, 2nd edn (Oxford, 1957), pp. 127-146; Walther Bulst, 'Radegundis an Amalafred'; Peter Dronke, *Medieval Latin and the Rise of European Love Lyric*, pp. 200-209; Karl Langosch, *Profile des lateinischen Mittelalters*, pp. 49-79; Langosch, *Lyrische Anthologie*, pp. 9-63, 331-337; Joseph Szövérffy, 'Venantius Fortunatus and the Earliest Hymns to the Holy Cross', *Classical Folia*, vol. 20 (1966), pp. 107-122; P. I. von Moos, *Consolatio*, vol. 1, pp. 94-97 and *passim*; K. Steinmann, *Die Gelesuintha-Elegie des Venantius Fortunatus (carm. VI, 5)* (Diss, Zürich, 1975); Franz Brunhölzl, *Geschichte der lateinischen Literatur des Mittelalters* (München, 1975), pp. 118-128; Marc Reydellet, 'Fortunat et la vision poétique de la royauté mérovingienne', in *La Royauté dans la littérature latine de Sidoine Apollinaire à Isidore de Séville* (Rome, 1981), pp. 291-344; Leandro Navarra, 'Venanzio Fortunato: Stato degli studi e proposte di ricerca', in *La cultura in Italia fra tardo antico et alto medioevo*, Atti del Convegno tenuto a Roma, Consiglio Nazionale delle Ricerche, dal 12 al 16 Novembre 1979 (Rome, 1981), vol. 2, pp. 605-610.

18. Brunhölzl, *Geschichte der lateinischen Literatur des Mittelalters*, p. 122.

19. Text: MGH, AA, IV, 1, App. 1, pp. 271-275; Langosch, *Lyrische Anthologie*, pp. 20-29. The poem consists of 172 lines of metrical (elegiac) distichs.

20. Stanley B. Greenfield had already pointed out the affinities between the opening of this poem, the 'Stafell Gynddylan' poem in the Heledd Cycle and the Old English 'Ruin' (*A Critical History*, p. 215). His comparison does not go beyond that. Michael J. B. Allen and Daniel G. Calder print an English translation of *De Excidio Thuringiae* in their *Sources and Analogues of Old English Poetry* (Cambridge, 1976), pp. 137-141.

21. There is dissent among scholars as to the authorship of the poem. The older criticisms as well as Walther Bulst ('Radegundis an Amalafred', p.

372), J. Szöverffy, *Weltliche Dichtungen des lateinischen Mittelalters* (Berlin, 1970), vol. 1, p. 281) and Langosch (*Lyrische Anthologie*, p. 334) see the author as Fortunatus writing the letter 'in persona Radegundis'. Brunhölzl (*Geschichte der lateinischen Literatur des Mittelalters*, p. 122, fn. 1), however, admits that Radegunde, too, could have been the author, as she is known to have been highly cultured and to have written poems addressed to Fortunatus, and Peter Dronke, *Women Writers of the Middle Ages* (Cambridge, 1984), p. 28 (cf. p. 298), is convinced, that she, indeed, wrote this verse epistle, "though ... it is hard to rule out some collaboration by Fortunatus in the writing".

22. Text: MGH, AA, IV, 1, App. 3, pp. 278-279; 42 lines of metrical distichs; Langosch, *Lyrische Anthology*, pp. 30-32. The problems of authorship are the same as for 'De excidio Thuringiae'.

23. Text: MGH, AA, IV, 1, pp. 181-191; 400 lines of metrical distichs; cf. M. I. Campanile, 'Il *De verginitate* di Venanzio Fortunato (Carm. 8, 3 Leo): un epitalamio mistico', *Invigilata lucernis*, vol. 2 (Bari, 1980), pp. 75-128.

24. Dronke, *Women Writers*, p. 86; cf. Wolfgang Schmid, 'Ein christlicher Heroidenbrief des sechsten Jahrhunderts', in H. Dahlmann und R. Merkelbach (eds), *Studien zur Textgeschichte und Textkritik, Günther Jachmann z. 50. Wiederkehr seiner Promotion gewidmet* (Köln-Opladen, 1959), pp. 253-263. As Walther Bulst noted ('Radegundis an Amalafred'), Ovid's 'Heroides' also underlie the verse epistles to Amalafred and Artachis. On the one hand, they were true letters and fullfilled a definite political purpose, but on the other hand they are clad in the rhetorical language of high passion and despair. Bulst also mentions that Catullus may have been known among the Poitiers *literati*.

25. Text: MGH, AA, IV, 1, pp. 136-146; 370 lines of metrical distichs; cf. Langosch, *Lyrische Anthologie*, pp. 34-52; K. Steinmann, *Die Gelesuintha-Elegie*.

26. Text: MGH, AA, IV, 1, pp. 165-168 ('Item ad eundem'). This is perhaps a fragment only, as its structure seems to be imbalanced in comparison to Fortunatus' other well-formed poems.

27. Text: MGH, AA, IV, 1, pp. 95-99; 160 lines of metrical distichs; cf. Langosch, *Lyrische Anthologie*, pp. 54-62.

28. Helen Waddell (ed and trans), *Medieval Latin Lyrics* (London, 1929, repr.

1966), pp. 66-67.

29. Cf. Koebner, *Venantius Fortunatus*, p. 117.

30. Fortunatus calls himself "exul" in his prose letters; cf. Meyer, 'Der Gelegenheitsdichter', p. 9.

31. Cf. Dronke, *Women Writers*, p. 31.

32. Peter Dronke ('Dido's Lament: From Medieval Latin Lyric to Chaucer', in Ulrich Justus Stache, Wolfgang Maaz und Fritz Wagner (eds), *Kontinuität und Wandel. Lateinische Poesie von Naevius bis Baudelaire* (Hildesheim, 1986), pp. 364-390 at p. 370) mentions the topicality of sea storms separating Dido and Aeneas since Vergil and Ovid.

33. Kemp Malone ('Two English *Frauenlieder*', p. 117) was, of course, right when he said that they "stand isolated in *our* inherited poetical corpus of Saxon times" (my italics). But they are the "lone survivors" of a well-established early medieval *international* tradition and not only analogues of German and Romance *Frauenlieder* of the high Middle Ages. On the supposedly "universal" character of women's love-laments, see Peter Dronke, 'Dido's Lament', p. 372.

34. The destruction of Troy is referred to in line 19 and some of the images are taken from there; others recall the destruction of Jerusalem in the Old Testament 'Lamentations of Jeremiah'. Cf. also Alcuin's lament on the 'Sack of the Monastery of Lindisfarne' (MGH, Poet. Lat. Aevi Carol., 1, pp. 229-235, translated in Allen and Calder, *Sources and Analogues*, pp. 141-146), and Kathryn Hume, 'The "Ruin" Motif in Old English Poetry', *Anglia*, vol. 94 (1976), pp. 339-360.

35. Cf. also Brunichilde's prose letter to the empress of Constantinople (referred to in P. Dronke, *Women Writers*, p. 27).

36. Greene and O'Connor, *A Golden Treasury*, pp. 154f. Although this is a late poem (twelfth century), the theme recalls Llywarch's lament over the loss of his sons and the elegy of the father, who cannot revenge the death of his only son, because he had been lawfully hanged for an unspecified crime (Bwf 2444-2462 and Egill's Old Norse 'Sonatorrek' where the revenge motif, otherwise absent, is equally present). But *Cumthach labhras an lonsa* is unique in its (Irish) nature setting. It addresses the blackbird, because the lyrical *persona* feels that it has been wronged in the same way as he himself. This is not a regular feature in "elegiac" poetry, but it is well to remember that in his other "occasional" poetry Fortunatus shows a remarkable sensitivity to nature.

In fact, he has as much sensitivity to nature as to the innermost feelings of a troubled soul.

37. Greene and O'Connor, *A Golden Treasury*, pp. 171f. This poem combines the themes of exile (from the north of Ireland in the south), loneliness, sickness, confession of guilt or sin and implied hope for salvation through suffering.

38. Cf. MGH, AA, IV, 1, at the end, pp. 137ff. (M. Manitius) and Langosch, *Profile*, p. 79.

39. See Walker, *Sancti Columbani Opera*, pp. 184, 186. There is no entry on Venantius Fortunatus in Michael Lapidge and Richard Sharpe, *A Bibliography of Celtic-Latin Literature* (Dublin 1985), and he is not mentioned in Michael Herren, 'Classical and Secular Learning among the Irish before the Carolingian Renaissance', *Florilegium*, vol. 3 (1981), pp. 118-159.

40. 'Ad Rucconem diaconam, modo presbyterum' (MGH, AA, IV, 1, pp. 75f.): *nos unda Britannica cingit* (l. 4). Possible connections with early Welsh panegyric are pointed out by Patrick Sims-Williams, 'Gildas and Vernacular Poetry', in M. Lapidge and D. Dumville (eds), *Gildas: New Approaches*, Studies in Celtic History, vol. V (Cambridge, 1984), pp. 180ff.

41. See Peter Goodman (ed), *Alcuin: the Bishops, Kings, and Saints of York* (Oxford, 1982), pp. lxixff and p. 124; Michael Lapidge, 'Knowledge of the Poems in the Earlier Period', Appendix to R. W. Hunt, 'Manuscript Evidence for knowledge of the poems of Venantius Fortunatus in late Anglo-Saxon England', *Anglo-Saxon England*, vol. 8 (1979), p. 294; cf. Rodney Thomson, 'Identifiable books from the pre-Conquest library of Malmesbury Abbey', *Anglo-Saxon England*, vol. 10 (1982), pp. 5 and 14; Michael Lapidge, 'Surviving booklists from Anglo-Saxon England', in Michael Lapidge and Helmut Gneuss (eds), *Learning and Literature in Anglo-Saxon England. Studies presented to Peter Clemoes on the occasion of his sixty-fifth birthday* (Cambridge, 1985), pp. 46ff., 89.

42. Goodman, *Alcuin*, p. lxxi.

43. Patrizia Lendinara, 'Donne bibliche da Venanzio Fortunato ad un ignoto compilatore anglosassone', in *Miscellania in onore del Prof. Giusto Monaco* (Rome, 1988), pp. 3-16.

44. Cf. J. Szövérffy, 'Venantius Fortunatus and the Earliest Hymns to the Holy Cross', p. 109.

45. Cf. Hildegard L. C. Tristram, 'Der insulare Alexander', in Willi Erzgräber (ed), *Akten des zweiten Symposions des Mediävistenverbandes, 16. - 20. März 1987* (Sigmaringen, forthcoming); Tristram, 'Early Modes of Insular Expression', in Kim McCone (ed), *Sages, Saints and Storytellers*, pp. 427-448; Ursula Schaefer, 'A *Song of Myself*: Poetic *I* in Old English Poetry' (Proceedings of the Anglistentag 1988 in Göttingen, forthcoming).

46. For which see for instance Patrick Sims-Williams, 'Is it Fog or Smoke or Warriors Fighting?: Irish and Welsh Parallels to the Finnsburg-Fragment', *BBCS*, vol. 27 (1976-78), pp. 504-514; Nicholas Jacobs, 'Y Traddodiad Arwrol Hen Saesneg o'i gymharu a'r Dystiolaeth Gymraeg', in Rachel Bromwich and R. Brinley Jones (eds), *Astudiathau ar yr Hengerdd* (Cardiff, 1978), pp. 165-178; a revised English version appeared as 'The Old English Heroic Tradition in the Light of Welsh Evidence', *Cambridge Medieval Celtic Studies*, vol. 2 (1981), pp. 9-20.

47. I wish to express my sincere thanks to Prof. Fidel Rädle (Göttingen), who put me on the track of Venantius Fortunatus and helped me with the bibliography. I also wish to thank Richard Matthews, Ph. D. (Freiburg) for reading through the typescript of this paper as well as correcting my English and Jenny Rowland (Dublin) for her very helpful suggestions. Any infelicities or errors are, of course, my responsibility.

The Middle Welsh Text *Ystorya Judas*

J. E. Caerwyn Williams
Centre for Advanced Welsh and Celtic Studies
University College of Wales, Aberystwyth

0. Texts

I. Pen. 3, p.40: ca. 1300 (RWM i.304). Incomplete. *Incipit: Ystorya Judas.*

II. Pen. 5, f.xi r.,v.: 1300-25 (RWM i.308-9). Complete. *Inc.: Llyma mal y treithyr historia Judas.*

III. Pen. 14, pp.161-64: 1325-50 (RWM i.333). Complete. *Inc.: ystoria judas yw hon.*

IV. Pen. 7, col.237a-241a; xiv cent. (RWM i.231). Complete. *Inc.: ystoria judas ysgarioth.*

V. Llan. 117, pp.195-98: 20 August, 1548. (RWM ii.568-79). Scribe: Jeuan ap W. ap D. ap Einws. Complete. *Inc.: Llyma ystoria svddas vyradwr.*

VI. Pen. 118, pp.682-3: 1575-1600 (RWM i.718-25). Excerpts in the hand of Dr Siôn Dafydd Rhys.

VII. Card. 11, Pt.ii, p.111: late xvi cent. (RWM ii.138-45). Incomplete. Scribe: ?John Jones, Gellilyfdy. Part of the end only.

VIII. Llan. 24, f.93r.: late xvi cent. (RWM ii.454). Incomplete. Beginning missing.

IX. Llan. 165, pp.151-2: 'around 1680' (RWM ii.754). Complete. *Inc.: Dyma History Suddas Fradwr.*

X. NLW MS. 6735, pp.72-76: xvii-xviii cent. (*Handlist MSS. NLW*, Pt. x, p.211.) Complete. *Inc.: llyma ystori Suddas Fradwr.*

XI. NLW MS. 2281, pp.6-10: xviii cent. (*Handlist MSS. NLW*, Pt. iv, p.198.) Scribe: Evan Thomas, Cwmhwylfod, near Bala. Complete. *Inc.: Dyma Stori neu hanes suddas Fradwr.*

1. Classification of Texts

Text I consists of one page which apparently at one time was the end page of the manuscript, for as RWM i.304 informs us, it is 'much rubbed and stained', and is very difficult to read. To judge from what remains of it, Text I did not agree closely with any one of the other texts: indeed, it differs from Texts II, III and IV as much as they differ from each other, and there are considerable differences between these as we can see by comparing the following extracts:

> II (E)F a darlle6yt ynebun ystoria bot gur ygkaerussalem aruben oed yeno. ac aeluyt heuyt o lin iren o luyd iudas neu o lin ysachar heruyd ereill. a gureic a oed idau oed y heno cyborea. a nos6eith guedy bot kyt yda6 ae 6reic kyscu a oruc hy a breudwyt a 6elei a deffroi yn dechrynedic a oruc ae datkanu y gur dan vcheneitav a ch6ynvain. ef a welit ym heb hy eskor ohonaf ar vab bonhedic ac avei achaus kyuyrgoll kenedyl ysgymyn. Ae datkannyat a pr*o*ph6ydy di heb y ruben. Ae o duv ae druc yspryt ae o seithuc ydu6yt yn arwein hynny. Os beichiogy a geueis heb y 6reic diamhev nat seith y6 namyn gueledigaeth...

> III Gwr a oed gynt yngkarusalem a elwit ruben ereill ae galwei simeon o lin judas ac o lin isakar herwyd ereill a henw y wreic oed kiborea a nosweith gwedy bot kyt ydaw ae wreic y gweles y wreic breudwyt A phann deffroes y wreic y datkanawd y wreic y breudwyt oe gur drwy gwynvan ac ucheneidieu Myui a welwn hep hi esgor mab bonhedic ohonofi ac ef a uydei achaws y gyuyrgolli kenedyl ohonaw. Ys ysgymun a datkan yw y teu hep y gwr ac nyt o rat duw ydwyt yn hynny namyn o drycysbryt yn arwein dy seuthuc Os beichyogi a geueistitheu nyt seuthuc namyn gweledigaeth...

> IV Gwr a oed gynt yngkaeruselem a rvben oed y henw ereill ay galwei simion o lin judas ac o lin jsacar h*er*wyd ereill. A ciborea oed hy*n*ny (*sic*) y wreic. A nossweith wedy bot kyt idaw ay wreic breudwyt a weles y wreic. A phan diffroes y wreic y datkanawd y breudwyt oy gwr Gan gwynvan ac vcheneidiaw Myvi heb hi a welwn vy mot yn esgor mab bonhedic. Ac ef a vydei achos y gyvyrgolli kenedyl. Ysgymvn a datanyat eb ef yw y tev di Ac nyt o rat duw ydwyt yn arwein dy seithvc os beichiogi a gevis eb hi nyt seithvc namyn gweledigaeth...

It is not usual to find such differences between early Welsh texts of this period. These differences, however, are not such as to warrant the assumption that there were more than one translation from the Latin behind Texts II, III and IV.

Text V is later than the above and differs considerably from them, as the following extract shows:

> llyma ystoria svddas vyradwr y gwr hwnw a vradychodd ac a werthod (*sic*) yn harglwydd ni Jessu grist ir X X X o genhioge avr ir eiddeon hwn sy ysbvs i bawb gida i lyvodreth ai vowyd amherffaith tra vv vo yn y byd hvn gwr oedd gynt yngaer iselem a elwid rrvben ai wraic a elwid tyboria a nosweth gwedi bod achos rryngthvnt yhi a welai trwy i hvn yhi yn cael beichiogi ar vab ysgymvna a gwaetha yn byd ac efo a vydde vradwr yw genedl i hvn a ffan ddoeth yr amser y mab aned ac a henwyd siwdas ai dad ai vam a vv ffiedd yma o achos y brevddwyd a welsai i vam pan i kowsai vo...

It is difficult to take Text V as a late copy of the version behind Texts II, III and V. It contains many English words and this suggests that its exemplar was based on an English rather than a Latin text. The word 'based' is used advisedly. If Text V represents a translation from an English text, that translation was a rather free translation. It should be noted that it is preceded by the text 'Llyma ystoria Peiladvs ap teirvs o ordderch' which ends: 'Ac velly i tervyna ystoria peilat medd llyfr Antwn o Went,' so that V seems to belong to the same group as IX, X and XI; see *infra*.

It is misleading to call VI a text. Pen. 118 is rightly called 'Llyfr Siôn Dafydd Rhys', 'The Book of Dr John David Rhys', author of *Cambrobrytannicae Cymraecaeve Linguae Institutiones et Rudimenta* (1592), as most of it is in his hand. It contains glossaries and extracts of texts. Pp.673-91 contain '*Extracts* from the story of *Adam and Eve*, the *Gospel of Nicodemus*, the *Story* of the *Crucifixion*, of *Pontius Pilate*, of *Judas*, and of the *Blessed Virgin*, etc,; also a brief collection of *Proverbs* (p.684)' (RWM i.723) and are in John David Rhys's hand (RWM i.718). The items referred to, apart from *Adam and Eve* and the *Proverbs*, are to be found in Pen. 5, (some of them are to be found also in Pen. 7 and Pen. 14), and it may be that the ultimate source of these extracts are Pen. 5. My comparison of the extracts from the *Story of Judas* would seem to confirm this, but Pen. 5, 7 and 14 do not have the signature of John David Rhys nor apparently any marginalia in his hand. Richard Langford of Trefalun made a copy of parts of *Llyfr Gwyn Rhydderch* (= Pen. 4 and 5) and John Jones, Gellilyfdy, transcribed his copy (see RWM 1. 664 and 667). Thomas Wiliems and perhaps Jaspar Griffith wrote marginalia on Pen. 4. If John David Rhys did not see *Llyfr Gwyn Rhydderch*, it is not at all improbable that he saw a copy of it or of parts of it.

Text VII is contained in one page of Card. 11 and consists of a summary of the end of the *Ystorya Judas*. The summary is too compressed to allow one to decide definitely its connection with the other texts, but the words it uses suggest that it is related to Texts V and VIII rather than to the earlier texts.

Text VIII cannot be a copy of Text V but it is not unlikely that both go back to the same examplar. It should be noted that both are followed by copies of the text 'Saith Cas Ddyn Duw'.

Texts IX, X and XI are related to each other in one way or another.

Text IX follows the text 'Dyma Histori Pilatus Fab Terus' (Llan. 165, pp.149-50) which ends with the statement: 'medd Llyfur Antwn o Went'. NLW MS. 6735 which contains Text X, also has 'Ystori Pilatvs' (pp.40-45) and the statement: 'medd llyfr antwn o went', and NLW MS. 2281 which contains Text XI has the 'Story of Pilate', again from 'Llyfr Antwn o Went'. In addition to this we are told that NLW MS. 6735 'belonged in 1763 to Evan Thomas "Cwmchwilod" (Cwmhwylfod), parish of Llanfawr near Bala' and that NLW MS. 2281 is in the hand of 'Evan Thomas, Cwmhwylfod, near Bala'. In fact, Text XI has at its end 'Evan Thomas of Cwmchwilod, his book 1762'.

Compare the following extracts:

> IX. Dyma History Suddas Fradwr
> Y Gwr a fradychodd ag a werthodd ein Harglwydd ni Jesu Grist er deg ar hugien a Arian neu Geinioge ir Iddewon, hyn sydd yn hysbys i bawb gida ei lyfodraeth ai fowyd amherffaith tra fu yn y byd, Gwr oedd gynt yn Nghaer Salem a elwyd Reuben ai wraig a elwyd Tibora, a noswaith gwedi bod achos gnowdol rhyngthynt yhi a welai drwy chwsg yhi yn cael beichiogi ar fab ysgymuna a gwaetha yn y byd ag efe a fyddai fradychwr iw Genedl ei hun a ffan ddaeth yr amser y Mab a aned ag a henwyd Judas neu Suddas ai Dad ai Fam a fu ffiedd a drwg ganthynt o achos y breuddwyd a welsai ei fam pan gawse hi ef...

X. llyma ystori Suddas Fradwr
Gwr afradychodd ag awerthodd yn harglwydd ni Jesv grist er deg ar higen o geinioge ir Jddewon syn hysbys i bawb gida ei lyfodreth ai fowyd amherffaith tra fv fo yn y byd: gwr oedd gynt ynghaer Selem aelwid Rvwben ai wraig aelwid tiboria anoswaith wedi bod achos gnowdol rhyngthynt y hi awelai ei hvn drwy ei chwsg y hi yn gael beichiogi ar fab ysgymyna a gwaetha yn y byd ag ef afyddai fradychwr iw genedl ei hvn a pan ddaeth yr amser y mab aned ag a enwed Svddas ai dad ai fam a fv ffiedd a drwg ganthynt o achos y breuddwyd awelsai ei fam pan gowsai hi fo...

XI. Dyma stori neu hanes suddas Fradwr
Gwr a fradychodd ag a werthodd yn Harglwydd ni lesu grist am ddeg ar hugiain o ddarnau arian. Ir Iddewon hyn sydd hyspvs i bawb gida ei lyfodraeth ai fowyd amherffaith tra fu fo yn y Byd, gwr oedd gynt ynghaersalem a elwid Ruwben ai wraig a elwid Tiboria, a noswaith wedi bôd achos cnowdol rhyngthynt, y hi a welai ei hun Drwy i chwsg yn cael beichiogi ar fâb ysgymun ar gwautha yn y byd, ag efe a fydde fradychwr i'w genedl ei hun a phan ddaeth yr amser y mâb a aned ag a enwed Suddas, ei Dad ai fam fy ffiedd a drŵg ganddynt o achos y breuddwyd a welse ei fam pan gowse hi fo...

Text XI is not an exact copy of X, but seeing that we know that the scribe who wrote XI, Evan Thomas, Cwmhwylfod (or Cwmchwilod) near Bala, had the MS. which contained X in his possession, we may safely assume that he copied XI from X, and as IX (Llan. 165), X (NLW MS. 6735), V (Llan. 117) each occur after the 'Story of Pilate' with the references to the 'Book of Antwn (or Anthony) of Gwent', we may, perhaps, assume the ultimate source of V, IX, X, XI, either directly or indirectly, as well as the text 'The Story of Pilatus' common to their manuscripts, was the 'Book of Antwn (or Anthony) of Gwent'. Unfortunately, as far as we know, that book has not survived.

2. Origin

I regret to say that I have not been able to compare the various texts which could have provided the Latin original translated into Welsh and represented in our earlier texts, although there is no lack of candidates. J. Gwenogvryn Evans, RWM ii. 308, refers his readers to MS. Laud Misc. 633, f.97v. *De Juda traditore*. The notes to 'Hanes Pontius Pilatus' in Robert Williams, *Selections from the Hengwrt MSS.* II (London, 1892) 751 informs us that the *Historia Judas* follows (B.L.) Royal 8E xvii. Latin versions are also found in Royal 9A xiv, f.14, St. John's College Cambridge MS. 258. (M. R. James, *Catalogue*), Pembroke College Cambridge MS. 258, i, f.14, and other manuscripts too numerous to list here. See Ulysse Chevalier, *Répertoire des Sources Historiques du Moyen Age*, Vol II (Paris, 1907), col.2669-2671.

3. Edition of Text II

I add an edited version of Text II. Robert Williams, *Selections from the Hengwrt MSS.*, II (London, 1891) 271-74, has printed a transcription. The following is a more accurate copy. The original is almost illegible in parts and seems to be deteriorating with the passage of time. Missing letters have been supplied in parentheses.

Text II

Llyma mal y treithyr *Historia Judas*.

(E)f a darlle6yt y(n) nebun ystoria bot gur yg Kaerussalem a Ruben oed y eno ac a eluyt heuyt o lin Iren o luyd Iudas neu o lin Ysachar heruyd ereill. A gureic a oed idau, oed y heno Cyborea. A nos6eith guedy bot kyt ida6 a'e 6reic, kyscu a oruc hy a breuduyt a 6elei, a deffroi yn dechrynedic a oruc a'e dattkanv y gur dan vcheneitav a ch6ynvan. 'Ef a 6elit ym', heb hy, 'eskor ohonaf ar vab bonhedic ac a vei achaus kyuyrgoll kenedyl ysgymyn'. 'Ae datkannyat a p*ro*ph6ydy di?' heb y Ruben. 'Ae o Du6 ae[1] druc yspryt ae o seithuc ydu6yt yn ar6ein hynny?' 'Os beichogy a geueis', heb y 6reic, 'diamhev nat seith(uc) y6 namyn gueledigaeth'. A phann doeth ydy amsser escor, mab a anet idy. Ac ouvn y bobyl a fu arnunt am hynny, a medylya6 beth a 6neint amdana6. A chyt bei aruthyr gantunt y mab, ny[2] allassant arnuntt y diua. Ac eissoes rac eu dist*ry*6 o'r genedyl y buryassant ef ymy6n boly croen yn y mor. A'r tonneu a'e burryaud odyno (y) ynys a el6it Scarioth. Ac yno y caffat ac y gel6it Iudas Scharioth wedy hynny. Ac yd oed brenhines y lle h6nn6 di6arnaut yn gorymdeith ger lla6 glan y traeth, (ac) yd arganuu llestyr gan y tonnev yn tir. Ac yd erchis y brenhines y agori. A phan agoret nachaf vab gorthedol[3] y bryt, a chan vcheneitau y di6at hy: 'Ia, wir Vab Du6', heb hy, '(...) a allaf vy caffel didanuch pla*n*t (...) hvnn[4] yn etiued ym rac ada6 vy teyrnnas yn dietiued cannyt oes ym etiued'. A pheri a oruc meithrin y mab dan gel a dechymygu y bot yn veichauc. Ac yn yr amsser y diuat geny mab ydy, a honny hynny yn gyhoedauc ar hyt y teyrnnas. A'r ty6yssogyon a ly6enhaud yn vaur y bobyl o vot etiuet y'r vrenhines. A'r mab a berit y veithrin her6yd y (f.xi, *v*) mauredigruyd. Ac ny bu hir wedy hynny y cauas y brenhines veichogi o'r brenhin, ac esgor a oruc ar vab. Ac guedy eu meithrin ell deu ygyt a cytyfuu yn oetrann, kaentach a wnaethant yn vynych. A Iudas a 6nnaei godyant y vab y brenhin, a pheri ida6 wyla6 yn vynych. Ac a(n)niodef vu gan y vrenhines hynny can(n)y pherthynei Iudas ydy, a'e vaedu yn vynych a oruc, ac yr hynny ny pheidey a'r mab. Yn y di6ed y menegit y Iudas nad oed vab ef y'r brenhines namyn y vot yn vab dywan. Ac yna y daeth kewilyd ar Iudas a llad mab y brenhin a 6naeth. Ac odyno y ffoes rac ofyn y dihenyd ygyt a chetemeithon[5] y Gaerusalem. Ac yno yd ym6ascuys a llys pilat*us* a oed raglao yno. Ac ual y kyuuna pob peth a vo vn defua6t a'e gilyd, y kytwedaud yn y lle deuodeu Iudas a rei Pilat*us*. Ac 6rth hynny y bu agar6[6] gantha6 ef, ac vrth hynny y rodes y Iudas medyant yr eidau yn gubyl ac ar un amneyt y llunyeithynt ell deu pob peth. A di6arnaut yd arganuu[7] Pilat*us* o'e lys p*er*llan, ac y damuna6d yr aualev yn gymeint ac na allei bot hebdunt. A'r berllan honno a oed eida6 Ruben tat Iudas. Ac nyt atuaenat Ruben Iudas na Iudas Ruben y tat, achaus daruot y vorv ef yr mor y(n) ne6yd eny hyt na wydat Iudas o ba daer pan hanoed. Pilat*us* a eluys attav Iudas ac y dyuat 6rthau bot yn gymeint y damunet ar yr aualeu ac onys caffei y tebygei y varo. Ac yn y lle y neitaud Iudas y'r berllan ac yn gyflym y kymyrth yr aualeu. Ac yn hynny nachaf Ruben yn dyuot ac yn caffel Iudas yn kynull yr avaleu.[8] Ac odyna ymrysson a 6naethant ac ymgeina6 ac ymlad, ac o'r di6ed y lladaud Iudas benn Ruben. Ac yna y duc ef yr aualeu[9] y Pilat*us* ac y datkgana6yd[10] yda6 y damwein. A phan doeth y dyd a'r nos yn daruot y caffat Ruben yn varo, ac yna y tebyguyt pan y6 dam6ein arall a gyfuaroed ac ef. Ac yna y rodes Pilatus y Iudas holl allu Ruben a Ciborea, gureic Ruben, yn wreic y Iudas. A di6arnaut yd oed Ciborea yn vcheneitav, gouyn a wnaeth Iudas pa daroed ydi. 'Vy mot,' heb hy, 'yn direitaf gureic o'r gwraged oll'. 'My', heb hy, 'a vodes vy mab yn y mor, ac a geueis vy g6r yn varo y'm perllan vy hun, ac whaneccau[11] vyn dolur vy rody o Pilat*us* a my yn truanhaf g6reig y(n) neithoryeu y ty. A guedy daruot idi[12] datkanu y dam6ein y datkanaud Iudas a gyuaroed ac yntev[13] ac yna y caffat pann y6 y vam a dugassei yn

6reic a phan y6 y tat a ladassei. Ac yna o ediuaruch y daeth Cyborea at yn Hargluyd ny Iessu Grist y adol6yn madeueint o'e phechodeu. A'r Argluyd a oruc y mab yn disgybl ida6 ac yn vn o'e ebystyl. A chyn[14] vu ganta6 ef Iudas ac y gunaeth yn vaer ida6. Ac odyno y cauas yn vraudur[15] ac ar6edey y llest*ri* y bydei yndunt yr hynn a rodit y Grist. Ac yn yr amsser y diodefuaud yr Argluyd y bu dolur gan Iudas na werth6yt yr ireit a doeth y yra6 yr Argluyd yr dec ar hugeint o aryant mal y dygey ynteu yn llettrad yr aryant h6nn6. Ac odyna y daeth[16] ynteu ac y guerthaud yr Argluyd yr dec ar hugeint aryant, a phob vn ohonunt a talhei dec keinnavc o'r aryant aruer, ac val hynny y kywerthydyei ef y gollet o trychant keinna6c o[17] g6erth yr ireit, neu val y dy6eit eraill, o bop da a rodet y G*ri*st y llattrataei ef y decuet rann, ac 6rth hynny dros y decuet ran a gollassei o werth yr yreit y guerthuys y Argluyd yr dec ar hugeint. A'r rey hynny o ediuaruch a duc tracheuen. Ac odyna yd ymgroges e hunan, ac ac ef yn dibynn y r6ygaud y berued a gellug y amyscar y'r llaur. Ac yn hynny yd arbetuyd y genev, can(n)yt oed teilug o'e halogy achaus y vot vrth enev yr Argluyd. Teillug hagen oed yr amyscar a vedylyassei y brat, eu ruyga6 ac eu dygv6yda6, a theillug oed heuyt y guduc a doeth y brat ohona6, y dagu o'r magyl ef yn yr a6yr vry. A chånys codyassei ef yr egylyon yn y nef a'r dynyon yn y daear y dieithruyt ynteu o teyrnas yr egylyon a'r dynyon a'e ketemdeithassaud ygyt a'r dieuyl yn a6yr.

Notes on MS. readings

1. MS. has *y* with a (subscript) *punctum delens* preceding *ae*.

2. MS. has *y* with a *punctum delens* preceding *ny*.

3. MS. *gorthedol* seems to be an error for *gordethol*. Robert Williams read: *gorthedod*.

4. MS. seems to have omitted some words. The sense requires the restoration of some words like the following: *gan n*(a allaf vy caffel didanuch plant) kymeraf (hvnn... Robert Williams read 'a allaf vi caffel diddanwch ei plant hwnn yn etiued'. An *i* could be read before *plant*.

5. MS. *chetemeideithon* with *puncta delentia* under *ide*.

6. MS. *agar6* seems to be error for *hygar*.

7. MS. has *adarganuu* with *puncta delentia* under *ad*.

8. MS. has *avaualeu* with *puncta delentia* under *av*.

9. MS. has *araualeu* or *avaualeu* with *puncta delentia* under the first two letters.

10. The scribe seems to have started to write the ending *-a6d* but to have written *-a6yd* with *-6yd* ending.

11. MS. *whaneccau* seems to be the correct reading although one could read *whaneccan* as Robert Williams did.

12. MS. *idi* is preceded by *ida6* with *puncta delentia* under each letter.

13. Robert Williams has 'y datkanawd iudas ... at ynteu'.

14. MS. *chyn*. We should perhaps read *chun* with Robert Williams for the sense. *Cuf* as a variant form of *cu* (<Celt **koimo-*) is not attested in early texts by *Geiriadur Prifysgol Cymru* (University of Wales Dictionary of the Welsh Language).

15. MS. *vraudur* should be read *vradur* for the sense.

16. MS. *daeaeth* with *puncta delentia* under *ea*.

17. Perhaps *a* should be read for *o* for the sense.

PART FOUR

Studies in Historical Linguistics

The Welsh Bahuvrīhis

Stefan Zimmer
Freie Universität Berlin

1. Introduction

Bahuvrīhi[1] is a technical term of Comparative Grammar taken over from the Old Indian grammarian Pāṇini (around 500 BC). He uses this model word to denote a special class of nominal compound: *bahú-vrīhi-* 'characterized by much rice', i.e. 'rich farmer' (vel. sim.): words of this type are always adjectives. The only distinction between this type of nominal compound and ordinary determinative compounds (Karmadhāraya, e.g. English *bluebird*, and Tatpuruṣa, e.g. English *manslaughter*) is the original accent as shown in Vedic Sanskrit and, partially, in Greek: cf. Vedic *rā́ja-putra-* 'whose son is king' or 'whose sons are kings', lit. 'characterized by a son / sons who is / are king(s)' (Bahuvrīhi) vs. *rāja-putrá-* 'son of a king' (Tatpuruṣa). The Indo-European accent being lost elsewhere, only the meaning and function of a given word can decide on its composition type. Therefore, an isolated word as e.g. Old Celtic *seno-condo-* (attested as personal name in Gaulish) can be understood in at least two ways: 'ancient head' (O'Rahilly, see Schmidt 1957: 266 n.2) or 'characterized by an old head'. Some consequences of this situation will be seen later.

The type of Bahuvrīhi-compound is well-known from all older Indo- European languages. The type originated in personal names including surnames and nicknames of all kind. Not all modern Indo-European languages have preserved it, and most have modified the semantic range of possible composition members.

English and German Bahuvrīhi-compounds e.g. must have either a numeral as first member or a part of the body or mind (including weapons and clothes) as second member. In Celtic, no such restriction seems to exist. Whereas the Bahuvrīhis of English and German have been fully treated in monographs by Last (1925) and Fabian (1931), the Celtic equivalents have never been the object of separate investigation. They have of course been discussed in the extant comparative grammars.

In what follows, a complete description of the Bahuvrīhi-type in Welsh and its different sub-types according to the class of words used as first or second members is intended. Unfortunately, this survey could not be based on a personal reading and excerption of all Welsh texts, so that it had to rely on the extant dictionaries with all their known philological shortcomings. As GPC is not yet fully published, an occasional imbalance of attestations may occur, and I can neither claim absolute completeness of categories nor ultimate reliability in details. Nevertheless, I am confident that the general outline of the following classification is sufficiently exact to allow a linguistic consideration of the status of Bahuvrīhi-compounds in Modern Welsh.

2. Adjective + Substantive

The majority of Welsh Bahuvrīhis being compounds of an adjectival first member and a substantival second member is formally identical with determinative compounds of the Karmadhāraya-type. Even the context does not always decide whether a word belongs to one category or the other, because a Bahuvrīhi, like any other adjective, can be used freely as a substantive by dropping or suppressing the substantive it depends upon semantically. On the other hand, there seems to exist a tendency among Welsh substantives to acquire the syntactic qualities of adjectives, a problem widely neglected so far. This might be due to the loss of case categories, especially the genitive. Even an influence from ambiguous Bahuvrīhis cannot be excluded. So, it is the meaning of the compound alone which can give a hint to its true nature.

2.1 Semantically unrestricted composition members

The first sample is given to show the wide semantic range covered by Welsh Bahuvrīhis. Contrary to English and German,

Welsh has no restrictions in the choice of possible first or second members for Bahuvrihi compounds.

brwd-ias 'hot', 18th c., lit. 'characterized by a hot temper'

byr-bwyll 'rash, impulsive', 16th-17th c., 'characterized by a short reason / reflexion' (= Breton *ber-boell*)

byr-fyfyr 'impromptu',19th c., lit. 'characterized by a short memory'

croes-ad m 'crossbreed' (modern formation), lit. 'characterized by crossed seeds'

crom-lech f originally an adjective meaning 'characterized by curved stones'. Today, it is only used for the well-known prehistoric monuments, but from the 16th to 18th c., it meant also 'cavern, fissure or cleft in a rock, cranny': the suppressed substantive was a word for 'spot' or something similar. Common British formation, cf. Cornish *cromlegh*, Breton *kroumlec'h*

cu-fodd 'genial, pleasant', 18th c., lit. 'characterized by kind manners'

glan-wedd 'clean, tidy', 15th c.+ (esp. in South Wales, of women), lit. 'characterized by pure mode'

gwag-law 'with empty hands', 14th c.+ (cf. the reversed counterpart *lla(w)ag*, 'id.', 13th c.+, today mostly in South Wales)

gwag-saw (also *gwyc-saw*) 'frivolous, trivial', 13th c.+, lit. 'characterized by an empty standpoint (**saf*)'

gwall-gof 'insane, mad', 17th c.+, also m 'madness', 17th c.+ (of humans, 19th c.+), lit. 'characterized by wild (in the sense of 'deviating') intellect'

gwan=galon 'faint-hearted', 16th c.+ (formation of W. Salesbury)

gwan-drew 'sneezing feebly', 14th c. once, lit. 'characterized by a feeble sneeze'

gwan-obaith m 'despondency, despair', 17th c.+, lit. '(state) characterized by faint hope (only)'

gwastad-wres 'of continually high temperature', 17th c.dict.,

	also m 'homothermal' (modern re-use)
gwen-dor	'white-breasted' (modern formation?), lit. 'characterized by a white belly(!)'
gwen-fflam	'blazing', 15th c.+ (today mostly in North Wales), lit. 'characterized by white flames'
haner-cof	'half-witted', 18th c.+ (as a term of abuse in shortened form *nerco*!), lit. 'characterized by (only) half (of the normal) intelligence'
hen-draul	'threadbare', 18th c.dict., lit. 'characterized by old usage'
hir-ben	'shrewd', 19th c.+, modern also in lit. meaning 'dolichocephalic'
hir-glust(-iog)	'having long ears', 19th c.+
hir-(i)ell m	'hero' (also as personal name), 12th c.+, lit. 'characterized by long (wide reaching) power'
hoyw-ne	'pretty', 14th c., lit. 'characterized by a vivid complexion'
hoyw-fryd	'gay', 16th c., lit. 'characterized by a vivid mind'
mawr-werth m	'preciousness', lit. '(state) characterized by a big price'
mein-we f	'tissue', lit. 'characterized by very thin spin-fibre'
melys-lais	'sweet-voiced'
per-sain	'euphonious, melodious, sweet', lit. 'characterized by a sweet tone'
rhudd-liw	'reddish, red', lit. 'characterized by red colour'
rhyw-fodd adv	'somehow', lit. 'characterized by any mode'
symud-liw	'of changing colours, opalescent', lit. 'characterized by moving/changing colours'[2]
uchel-drem	'haughty', lit. 'characterized by a high regard'
uchel-fryd	'ambitious', also 'ambition', lit. 'characterized by a high (aiming?) mind'.

2.2 Productive groups

Some minor groups of compounds with the same first member or second member can be regarded as productive groups.

2.2.1 Second member -radd

Adjectives of classification are formed with the appropriate adjective + *gradd* 'grade':

canol-radd(-ol) 'comparative', 16th c. (in grammar)[3]; 'intermedial', 19th c., lit. 'characterized by central = medial grade'

is-radd(-ol) 'subordinate', 17th c.+ (as m 'inferior person' or 'root' [math.]), lit. 'characterized by a lower grade'

isel-radd 'inferior', 16th c.+, lit. 'characterized by a low grade'

uchel-radd 'superior', lit. 'characterized by a high grade'

uwch-radd(-ol) 'superior, secondary', lit. 'characterized by a higher grade'

uchaf-radd 'supernormal', lit. 'characterized by the highest grade'.

For similar formations with a numeral as first member, see § 4.

2.2.2 Second member -ryw

Adjectives denoting qualities are often formed with *rhyw* 'kind, race' as second member:

brith-ryw 'heterogenous', 18th c., lit. 'characterized by speckled kind'

croes-ryw 'hybrid', 19th c., lit. 'characterized by crossed kind/race'

cymysg-ryw 'mongrel, hybrid, heterogenous', 17th c. dicts., lit. 'characterized by mixed race/kind'

uchel-ryw 'superior', lit. 'characterized by a high kind'.

2.2.3 First member all-

The small number of formations with first member *all-* deserve special interest. There are only a few old words of this type, but some modern formations point to continuing productivity. The oldest example is:

all-fro m 'foreigner', 13th c. once, lit. 'characterized by another border region (= homeland?)'.

This is a CC formation, as shown by the Gaulish tribe's name *Allobroges* (latinized form). The simple adjectival meaning is not attested before the 19th c.; one attestation of the 15th c. with the meaning 'foreign land' (according to GPC), if this is correct, reflects the identical Karmadhāraya.

all-tud m 'foreigner, exile' has a similar semantic field. It is, however, a younger formation because it postdates the loss of the original meaning of **teutā-*[4], and the syncope of the thematic vowel[5] as shown by the non-lenition of *-tud*. In Welsh, *tud* acquired the meaning of 'region, country', perhaps influenced by *all-fro*. This may have caused the formation of:

all-wlad m — 'id.', 16th c.+, as a kind of remake of *all-tud*.

It has, together with the corresponding derivations, exactly the same meaning as *all-tud* and its derivations. - All these words are obsolete today.

all-myr c — 'foreigners', 13th - 15th c. thrice (18th c. dict. also 'foreign') is a loan from Old Irish *all-muir* 'foreign land, overseas'.

all-ryw — 'heterogenous; different kind', modern formation of the 18th and 19th century.

In recent times, the first member *all-* has become productive for loan translations of technical terms with *e-*, *ex-*, *extra-* etc.:

all-blyg — 'extrovert'[6]

all-echelin — 'abaxial'

all-ganol — 'excentre', etc.

2.2.4 First member aml–

A fourth group, with first member *aml-*, has only become productive in modern times. The oldest example stems from the 14th c.:

aml-blaid — 'having many followers or supporters', 14th c. once, lit. 'characterized by a numerous party'.

The meaning of *aml* in Welsh has always been, from the beginning of the tradition on, 'numerous, many(fold)'. As the word is a loan from Latin *amplus*, a semantic change from 'wide' (over 'widely found') to 'numerous' must be assumed for the period from British Latin to Mediæval Welsh.

Then there are a number of learned formations (translations of foreign terms with *multi-* or *poly-*) from the 16th c. on, but the majority of them are already obsolete today.

aml-air m — 'verbosity', 17th c., lit. '(state) characterized by many words'

aml-barth — 'having many sides or aspects', 16th c., lit. 'characterized by many regions'

aml-benn-og — 'having many heads', 18th c. dict.

aml-blwyf m — eccesiastical administrative term describing the fact that one parson has several parishes at once, lit. 'characterized by many parishes'[7], 19th c.+

aml-blyg 'multi-plex', 17th c. dict.

aml-briod 'polygamous', 18th c. dict., lit. 'characterized by many weddings'

aml-droed 'poly-pod', 17th and 18th c. dicts.

aml-ddull 'multifarious', 18th c., lit. 'characterized by many forms'

aml-dduw m 'polytheist', 18th c. dict., lit. 'characterized by (the veneration of) many gods'

aml-gainc 'branchy, sympodical' (botan.), 19th c.+, lit. 'characterized by many branches'

aml-gyswllt m 'polyadelphia' (botan. term), 19th c., lit. 'characterized by many connections'

aml=liw 'motley, speckled' 18th c. dict., lit. 'characterized by many colours'[8]

aml-ochr-og 'multangulus', 17th and 18th c. dicts.; 'versatile', 20th c., lit. 'characterized by many sides'

aml-ongl-og 'polygonal', 17th c. dict.

aml-wraig 'polygamous', 18th c. dict., lit. 'characterized by many women'

A number of recent formations speak for lasting productivity of the type. It is, of course, impossible to predict whether these recent formations will gain a firm place in the vocabulary of Modern Welsh.

aml-arfod 'multi-range', lit. 'characterized by many weapons/battles/occasions (?)'

aml-bwrpas 'multi-purpose'

aml-ffurf 'polymorphic'

aml=lawr 'multi-storey' (house).

2.3 Extended Bahuvrīhis

The formal identity of Bahuvrīhi and Karmadhāraya led very early to a differentiation of the two types. One way to achieve this is the addition of an adjective-suffix to the Bahuvrīhi. This has become very popular in Welsh, and some examples have already been cited. Usually, the common suffixes *-ig*, *-og*, *-ol* are used to ensure the correct, viz. adjectival, understanding of the compound. Sometimes, both the basic Bahuvrīhi and its extended form coexist, but a secondary semantic differentiation is only rarely to be observed. As an example, only those with second member *-fryd(-ig)* will be cited here:

brwd-fryd-ig 'enthusiastic', lit. 'characterized by a hot mind', 18th c. dict., besides *bwd-fryd-og* 'zealous, enthusiastic, ardent', 18th c. dict., and *-us* 'id.' and 'fanatic', 19th c. The unextended *brwd-fryd* is not attested.[9]

duwiol-fryd 'godly, pious, devout', 17th and 18th c.; also m (Karmadhāraya) 'godly aspiration or disposition, piety, devotion'. In order to avoid misunderstandings, the Bahuvrīhi has been extended by *-us* and *-ig*, and the Karmadhāraya by *-edd* (all 19th c.). The basic meaning of *duwiol- fryd* is 'characterized by a divine mind'.

eang-fryd-ig is given as 'magnanimous' by GPC with an entry for 1862, the abstract *eang-fryd-edd* 'magnanimity' 1844. But Geiriadur Mawr has both the simple Bahuvrīhi *ehang-fryd* 'magnanimous' and the extended form *eang-fryd-ig* 'broad-minded': if this is a correct description of current usage, it would be a case of secondary semantic differentiation. The basic meaning is, of course, 'characterized by a wide mind'.

hael-fryd-ig 'liberal', lit. 'characterized by a generous mind', is first attested 1815, and then the simple *hael-fryd* 'generous, liberal, free' 1839, whereas the corresponding abstracts are recorded just in reverse order: *hael-fryd-edd* 1815, *hael-fryd-ig-rwydd* 1836.

hwyr-fryd-ig 'reluctant', lit. 'characterized by a slow mind', is attested from the 14th c. on; the unextended *hwyr-fryd* 'slow, slothful, tardy', first in the New Testament of 1567, must be much older, because the abstract *hwyr-fryd-edd* 'gentleness, submission' occurs already in the Black Book of Carmarthen (12/13th c.).

isel-fryd 'humble', lit. 'characterized by a low mind', 17th c.+ (no extended form attested)

mawr-fryd-ig 'magnanimous'
rhydd-fryd-ig 'liberal', lit. 'characterized by free thinking'; cf. *rhydd-fryd-wr* 'Radical, Liberal', (North Wales)
uchel-fryd 'ambitious', lit. 'characterized by a high mind'.

It is remarkable that nearly all formations of this group are recent ones. This is a clear sign of continuing productivity of the Bahuvrihi-type in general, and of the described extension pattern in detail.

3. Substantive + Substantive

The second type of Welsh Bahuvrihis consists of two substantives compounded. Therefore, these compounds are formally identical with the determinative compounds of the Tatpuruṣa-type. Exactly as in Tatpuruṣas, the two substantives can stand in any logical relation to each other. Very often, the dictionaries give two meanings for such compounds: a substantival and an adjectival one corresponding to the Tatparuruṣa and Bahuvrihi respectively.
Two semantic groups deserve special attention: the first is formed by colour terms, the second by compounds with parts of the body.

3.1 Colour terms

The compounds indicate, by a kind of comparison, a special hue of colour. There are two sub-types: the first has a well-known material of typical colour as first member (cf. Greek ῥοδο-δάκτυλος), the second the word *lliw* 'colour' as second member. As a sample of words of the first sub-type, compounds with first member *eur-* 'gold' will be cited here. It should be noted that *eur-* in these words does not denote the metal but its colour[10], and that many other compounds of *eur-* do exist which belong to other composition types or other semantic classes.

Three words are used as adjectives:

eur-frig 'having a golden top, tip or head', 15th c.+
eur-liw 'of yellow hue, gold-coloured', 14th c.+ (also m 'arsenic')
eur-wallt 'golden-haired', 15th c. (later only as Karmadhāraya).

More often, such compounds are names for plants and animals:

eur-asgell f	'goldfinch', 1852, lit. 'characterized by golden wings'
eur-ben m	'gilt-head, goldney, John Dory' (a fish), 17th c.; 'sunflower', 19th c.
eur-ddanadl c	'Yellow Archangel, weasel-snout' (a plant), 1813, lit. 'characterized by golden nettles'
eur-ddrain c	'gooseberries, barberry-bushes', 17th c., lit. 'characterized by golden thorns'
eur-fanadl c	'dyer's greenweed', 16th c., lit. 'characterized by golden brooms(?)'
eur-flodau c	'corn marigold, ox-eye daisy' (a flower), 19th c., lit. 'characterized by golden flowers'
eur-gefn m	'dory, goldfish', 18th c., lit. 'characterized by a golden back'
euros c	'sunflowers', 19th c., lit. 'characterized by golden roses'.

The construction of Bahuvrihis with second member *-liw* is obvious (cf. *eur-liw* just cited):

cig-liw	'flesh-coloured', 18th c. dict., lit. 'characterized by the colour of flesh'
llyg-liw	'grey, mouse-coloured', 14th c.+, lit. 'characterized by the colour of a mouse'
pyg-liw	'dusky, swarty', lit. 'characterized by the colour of pitch' (but the meaning is not 'pitch-black'!)
tan-lli(w)	'flame-coloured'[11].

3.2 Compounds with parts of the body

Designations for parts of the body occur as first member or second member in a number of Welsh Bahuvrihis. They are, however, not typical nicknames or terms of abuse as the (literally) corresponding words in English or German normally are. There are names for plants and diseases, and some characterizing adjectives, but on the whole, this group is far from being so large and prominent as would be expected from a comparative standpoint. The reason for this will be seen further down in the chapter on Reversed Bahuvrihis.

Parts of the body as first member:

bys-wellt m	'cocksfoot' (a flower), 19th c., lit. 'characterized by grass like fingers'
cefn-bant	'saddle-backed' (of cows, etc.), 14th c.+, lit.

'characterized by a cavity in the back'

cefn-rhwd 'gall-backed', 14th c.+, lit. 'characterized by dirt on the back'

ewin-rhew f 'frostbite', 14th c.+, lit. 'characterized by (the effect of) frost at the fingernail'[12]

min-dlws 'fine-mouthed, affected', lit. 'characterized by jewels on the lips' or 'by jewels as lips'

pen-sach f 'mumps' (a disease), lit. 'characterized by sacks at the head'

tin-dro f 'swayback' (disease of sheep and horses), lit. 'characterized by turning to the rear' (= the symptom)

wynep-clawr 'flat-faced', lit. 'characterized by a (flat) cover as face'.

Parts of the body as second member:

blaen-llaw 'prominent, previous, ready, bold, forhead', 17th c.+; as m 'leader' already since the 15/16th c. The basic meaning is 'characterized by one's hand on the front (of the matter)'[13]

cyn-ben 'having a wolf's head' (of men and arms), 12th-13th c., probably a CC formation, cf. the Middle Irish surname *coincheann*

lluos-gell 'multicellular', modern formation, lit. 'characterized by cells in multitude'

llyn-coes m (also *-goes* und *llym-*) 'spavin' (and other diseases of horses), 14th c.+, lit. 'characterized by a leg/foot affected by liquids'.

3.3 Other Bahuvrihis from Substantive + Substantive

In order to illustrate the wide variety of possible formations, some other compounds not belonging to one of the groups mentioned above may be cited:

beis-ton f 'beach, shallows', 14th c.+, lit. 'characterized by waves in the shallows'; in Môn and Arfon, the meaning has further developed to 'land between the flooded shore and the cultivated fields'

ceiniog-werth f 'pennyworth', 14th c.+, lit. 'characterized by the value of a penny' (mostly in North

	Wales)
croes-ffurf(-iog)	'cruci-form', 20th c. (calque)
cun-ffurf	'cunei-form', lit. 'characterized by the form of a wedge' (modern calque)
haf-lug	'abundant', also mf 'abundance', 15th c.+, lit. 'characterized by the splendour of summer'
llor-wedd	'horizontal, flat', 19th c.,lit. 'characterized by the form of the floor', also m 'horizontal', 20th c.
lluos-flwydd	'perennial', 20th c., lit. 'characterized by a multitude of years'
lluosillaf-og	'polysyllabic', 14th c.+, extended form (simple form as pluralic substantive only *lluosillafion* 'polysyllabics', 20th c.), lit. 'characterized by syllables in pluralism' (< *lluos* + *sillaf*)
mel-ged m,c	'sea beet, wild beet', 19th c., lit. 'characterized by the gift of sweetness'[14]
wy-ffurf	'ovoid', recent calque
wy=rith m	'oospore', recent calque (second member *rhith* 'imprecisely visible form'
ysbien-ddrych m	'telescope, binocular', lit. 'characterized by (offering) a view for spying'

4. Numeral + Substantive

The last, but by far not the least important category of ordinary Welsh Bahuvrīhis is the group of compounds using a numeral as first member. This is one of the oldest Indo-European Bahuvrīhi-rypes in regard to attestation, cf. Hittite *dā-i̯uga-* 'two years old', early Indo-Aryan (in the Kikkuli text): *aika-u̯artanna-*, *tiera-u̯artanna*, *panza-u̯artanna-*, *šatta-u̯artanna-*, *na(ua)-u̯artanna-*, lit. 'characterized by one, three, five, seven, nine turns', i.e. distances corresponding to so many rounds on the race course[15], Mycenean Greek *ti-ri-po-de*, and so on. The type is continued in all Indo-European languages, not only in learned formations (like French *unicorne*), but also in popular terms (e.g. French *deux-pièce* 'suit consisting of two parts'[16].

In Welsh, Bahuvrīhi-compounds from numeral + substantive are still a vivid and productive class. It may be sufficient therefore to give a simple list of examples (including words with extension and those which are used as substantives only), arranged according to numerical order.

With 'one':
un-corn 'having one chimney; unicorn' (modern formation); *un-cwrs-aidd* 'unicursal' (recent formation); *un-don* 'monotone'; *un-fryd(-ol)* 'unanimous'; *un-ffon* a kind of fishing-net (Fynes-Clinton 1913), lit. 'characterized by only one stick'; *un-glust* 'having one ear only' (Fynes-Clinton 1913); *un-gor* 'untwisted' (second member *cord* (=English?[17]); *un-hadbig-og* 'mono-cotyledon'; *un-iaith* (*un-ieith-iog*) 'monoglot'; *un-llygeid-iog* 'one-eyed' (modern?); *un-nos* 'of or for one night'; *un-plyg*[18] 'simple, sincere' (Fynes-Clinton 1913); *un-rhyw* 'same, any', lit. 'characterized by one (common) / any(-one) kind'; *un-sill(-af[-og])* 'monosyllabic'.

Also with the ordinal:
cyn-flith f 'young heifer', 13th c.+, lit. 'characterized by the first milk'; *cyn-radd* 'elementary', 20th c., lit. 'characterized by the first degree'[19].

With 'two':
dwy-adein-iog 'dipterous'; *deu-barth-ol* 'dichotomous' (probably a modern formation)[20]; *dwy-big* 'forked', 17th c.+, lit. 'characterized by two tops'; *deu-blyg* 'double, twofold', 15th c.+ (mostly in North Wales)[21]; *dau-dafod-iog* 'double-tongued', 16th c.+; *dwy-ddalen* f 'Twayblade' (a flower), 19th c.; *dau-fin-iog* 'double-edged', 13th-17th c.; *Dwy-for* name of a small brook in Lleyn and of a *dosbarth* (administrative unit) of Gwynedd (= the Lleyn penisula). Difficult to explain as a river name, but as name of a region clearly a Bahuvrihi, lit. 'characterized by two seas'[22]; *deu-ffocal* "bifokal" (modern hybrid formation); *deu-glust* 'biaural', new meaning[23]; *deu-groesryw* 'dihybrid' (recent formation), lit. 'characterized by two (parents) of (already) crossed kind'; *dwy-ieith-iog* 'bilingual'[24]; *deu-lais* 'for two voices' 18th c.+[25]; *deu-lun* 'dimorphous', new meaning[26]; *deu-pen(nog/-iog)* 'with two ends, double', 13th c.+; *dwy-radd* 'quadratic' (in math. sense), lit. 'characterized by two grades'; *dwy-ran(n-ol)* 'bipartite' (also in place names)[27]; *deu-ryw* 'hermaphrodite, bisexual', as m 'epikoinon', 17th c.[28]; *deu-sill(-af-[og])* 'of two syllables', 15th c.+; *dwy-waith* adv 'twice', 13th c.+; *deu-wyneb-og* 'deceitful', 12/13th c.+, lit. 'characterized by two (different) faces'.

With ordinal:
eil-chwyl adv 'again', 13th c.+, lit. 'characterized by a second turn'; *eil-flwydd* 'bi-ennial' (recent formation), lit. 'characterized by (occurence in every) second year'; *eil-radd* 'secondary', 18th

c.+; *eil-waith* adv 'again', 13th c.+, lit. 'characterized by a second work'; *eil-wers* adv 'again, anew', 15th c.+, lit. 'characterized by a second while'.

With 'three':
tri-ban m 'triplet', lit. ' (poem) characterized by three tops'; *tri-daint* 'three-pronged'[29], lit. 'characterized by three teeth'; *tra-dwy* adv 'in three days', lit. 'characterized by (a space of time of) three days'[30]; *teir-ongl* f (also *tri-ongl* mf) 'triangle'; *tri-phlyg* 'triple', lit. 'characterized by three fold(ing)s'; *teiran* 'tripartite', lit. 'characterized by three parts' (< *teir-* + *-ran*)[31]; *trybedd* f 'tripod' is no parallel to the well-known Greek and Latin words, but a loan from Latin *tri-pedem*.

With higher numbers:
pedwar-carn-ol 'four-footed', lit. 'characterized by four hoofs'; *pedry-fan* m 'quarter', lit. 'characterized by the fourth[32] corner'; *pedr-ongl* a 'square', as m 'quadrangle, quadrilateral', lit. 'characterized by four angles'; *pedwar-plyg* 'quarto, quadruple', lit. 'characterized by four fold(ing)s'; *pum-ochr* m and *pum-ongl* m 'pentagon', lit. 'characterized by five corners / angles'; *chwe-ongl* m 'hexagon'[33]; *seith-ochr* m 'heptagon'; *wyth-ban* 'with eight metrical feet or syllables, of eight parts', lit. 'characterized by eight tops'; *wyth-blyg* 'octavo'; *wyth-nos* f 'week', lit. 'characterized by eight nights'[34]; *deg-sill(-af-og)* 'of ten syllables', 19th c.; *deg-tant* m 'ten-stringed instrument'; *pythef-nos* f (also *pythew-nos*) 'fortnight', lit. 'characterized by fifteen nights'[35]; *can-clwm* m 'knot-grass', 16th c.+, lit. 'characterized by hundred knots'; *can-dryll* shattered to fragments', 15/16th c.+, also c 'shattered fragments', 17th c., lit. 'characterized by hundred pieces'; *can-ewin* m 'knot-grass', 14th c.+, lit. 'characterized by hundred claws(?)'; *can-mlwydd* 'one hundred years old', 14th c.+ (today only formulaic)[36]; *can-plyg* 'hundredfold', 17th c.+; *can-radd* a 'centigrade', 19th c., lit. 'characterized by (a scale of) hundred steps' (calque of English *centigrade*); *can-ran* m 'percentage', 18th c., lit. 'characterized by (a calculation base divided in) hundred parts'; *can-tref* m 'hundred' (administration unit), 12th c.+, lit. 'characterized by (one) hundred settlements'; *can-tro* 'centuple' (modern formation), lit. 'characterized by hundred turns'; *can-troed* 'centipede, centipedal', 17th c.+; *can-twll* 'riddled with holes' (South Wales), lit. 'characterized by hundred holes'.

5. Reversed Bahuvrihis

All Bahuvrihis mentioned in the preceding paragraphs showed the composition members in the classical order of Indo-European nominal compounds, viz. determinans + determinatum. There is another type where this order is inverted: in these words, the first member, always a substantive, is determined by the second member which is in most cases an adjective. Following the German term "umgedrehtes Bahuvrihi", I propose to label this type 'reversed Bahuvrihi' in English.

The type is rare outside Celtic and Germanic.[37] In Celtic, the type is already established in Old Celtic personal names like *Pennovindos* (which is the pre-form of modern Welsh *pen-wyn*), and it became quite productive in Gaelic and Welsh during the Middle Ages and the Renaissance period as shown by the lists in Schmidt 1957 (KGP). Nearly all words are part of the poetical language only.

As mentioned, the first member of all reversed Bahuvrihis is a substantive. The definition given by Schmidt (1957: 88 = Pokorny 1958: 172) as denoting "stets einen Körperteil oder einen Begriff, der vom Körper ausgeht oder ihm nahesteht" is not wholly complete: though it covers by far the largest group of Welsh reversed Bahuvrihis, there is at least one other productive class, and some further examples can also not be ranged under its categories.

5.1 First member is a part of the body

ael-gam	'leering', lit. 'characterized by curved eyebrows' (modern formation)
ber-fain	'thin-legged', 18th c.
ber-gam	'bandy-legged', 14th-17th c.
blaen-bwl	'blunt', 16th and 18th c., lit. 'characterized by a blunt forehead'
blaen-fain	'pointed, tapering', 15th c.+, lit. 'characterized by a thin forehead'
boch-goch	'rosy-cheeked' (modern formation)
bol-rwth	'greedy', 17th c., lit. 'characterized by a greedy belly'
bon-drwm	'proper' (of a fraction, math.), lit. 'characterized by a heavy base (= a denominator which is greater than the numerator)' (modern formation)

bon-gam — 'bandy-legged', 14th c.+, lit. 'characterized by a curved base'

bon-llwm — 'nude', 13th c.+, lit. 'characterized by a bare base'

bron-ddu — 'black-breasted, harbouring malice in one's bosom', 18th c.

bron-fraith f — 'song thrush', lit. 'characterized by a speckled breast'; this is the oldest Welsh reversed Bahuvrihi, first attested in the Codex Oxoniensis prior 40 b (9th c., perhaps c. 820): *cecinet bronnbreitet* gl. *cicadae* (the glossator took cicadas as a kind of birds). ²*Cegin* is a bird's name, found only in this word and once c. 1400 meaning 'jay' or 'green woodpecker', cf. Middle Breton *quiguin*, Modern Breton *kégin*, Le Gonidec *gegin* 'jay'.

bron-goch — 'red-breasted, robin redbreast', 17th c.+

bron-losgedig — 'with scorched breast', epithet of Amazones in Llyfr Taliesin (mkymr. *bron loscedigyon*)[38]

bron-rhudd-og m — 'redbreast' (a bird) (modern formation)

bron-rhudd-yn m — 'redbreast, chaffinch', 15th c.+

bron-wen f — 'weasel', lit. 'characterized by a white breast', 14th c.+

bron-wyllt — 'passionate, excited' (modern formation), lit. 'characterized by a wild breast'

calon-galed — 'hard-hearted', 17th c.+[39]

cefn-frwd — 'sore-backed', 17th c. once[40]

cefn-grwm — 'hump-backed', 17th c.+, lit. 'characterized by a curved back'[41]

cefn-ir — 'long-backed', 14th-15th c.

cefn-llwm — 'bare-backed', 16th-17th c.

ceg-rwth — 'gaping, wide-mouthed', 16th c.+

ceg-syth — 'arrogant' (modern formation), lit. 'characterized by a straight / stiff mouth'

cein-faglog — 'hump-backed', 14th c. twice, lit. 'characterized by a bent back (Middle Welsh *cain*, *ceing*)'[42]

cig-noeth — 'raw, painful', 18th c.+, lit. 'characterized by bare flesh'[43]

cil-dyn — 'obstinate', 16th c.+, lit. 'characterized by a

firm neck'

clun-llaes 'limping', 18th c.dicts., lit. 'characterized by a loose leg'

clust-fain 'attentive', lit. 'characterized by thin (= sharp, pointed) ears' (taken over from hunters' language), attested since the 16th c., but certainly older, cf. *clust-fein-ydd* 'attentive listener', 13th c.+[44]

clust-fyddar 'deaf', 18th c.+, lit. 'characterized by deaf ears'

clustrwm 'hard of hearing', 15th c.+, lit. 'characterized by heavy ears' (< *clust* + *trwm*)

cnawd-wyn 'with white flesh', 15th-16th c.

croen-denau 'touchy, sensitive', 18th c.+, lit. 'characterized by a thin skin'

croen-dew 'thick-skinned, callous', 14th c.+, lit. 'characterized by a thick skin'

croen-galed 'id.', 17th c.+, lit. 'characterized by a hard skin'

croen-iach 'unhurt, unharmed', 17th c. dict., lit. 'characterized by a sane skin'

croen-lan 'fair-skinned' (modern formation)

croen-llwm 'nude, bare', 15th c.+, lit. 'characterized by naked skin'

coes-gam 'bandy-legged', 16th c.+

coes-goch 'red-legged', 14th c.+ (also bird's name)

coes-groes 'cross-legged' (modern formation)

dan-wyn 'white-toothed' (modern formation)

drwyn-dwn 'flat-nosed', surname of Llywelyn Fawr's father, 12th c.[45]

dyrn-chwith 'left-handed', 18th c., lit. 'characterized by the left fist'

esgair-hir 'long-legged', surname, 12th c.[46]

ffroen-uchel 'haughty, proud', 18th c., lit. 'characterized by high nostrils'

gar-gam 'knock-kneeed', mf since the 14th c., used as adjective since the 16th c., lit. 'characterized by curved shanks' (cf. Breton *gar-gan* 'lame')

gar-llaes 'limping', 15th c.+, lit. 'characterized by by loose shanks'

gar-syth 'stiff-legged', 14th c.+, lit. 'characterized by

	straight shanks'
glin-gam	'knock-kneed', 16th c.+, lit. 'characterized by curved knees'
gwaed-wyllt	'hot-blooded', 15th c.+, lit. 'characterized by wild blood'
gwallt-laes	'long-haired' (modern formation), lit. 'characterized by loose (hanging) hair'
gwar-syth	'stubborn', 17th c.+, lit. 'characterized by a straight neck'
gylfin-braff m	'crossbeak' (a bird), 19th c., lit. 'characterized by a thick beak'
gylfin-ir m	'curlew' (a bird), 15th c.+, lit. 'characterized by a long beak'
llaw-agor and *llaw-agored*	'generous', both 14th c.+, parallel formations: 'characterized by open hands' / 'characterized by opened hands' (*llaw-agor* also used as plant's name since the 15th c.)
llaw-dde	'skilful, dexterous' (modern formation), lit. 'characterized by the right hand', inversion of *deheu-law* f 'right hand' (Karmadhāraya), 14th c.+, and as a Bahuvrihi 'dexterous, skilful' (South Wales)
llof-rudd m	(also *llaw-*) 'murderer', 13th c.+, lit. 'characterized by red hands (from the blood!)'
llost-lydan m	'beaver', 13th c.+, lit. 'characterized by a broad tail'; also 'broad-tailed', 18th c.
llygad=ddu	(also *llygeitu*, *llygatu*, *llygeid=ddu*) 'black-eyed', 14th c.+
llygat-graff	'sharp-eyed', 18th c., lit. 'characterized by keen eyes'
llygat-groes	'squint-eyed', 19th c., lit. 'characterized by cross(ing) eyes'
llygad-rwth	'staring', 14th c.+, lit. 'characterized by wide eyes'
min-ffug	'lying', lit. 'characterized by a fictitious lip'
min-llym	'sharp-edged, keen'
naws-wyllt	'passionate', lit. 'characterized by wild feelings / temper'
pen-agored	'wide open, undecided', lit. 'characterized by an opened head / end'[47]
pen-boeth	'hot-headed, fanatical'

pen-bwl(-a) 'stupid', as m 'blockhead' and a fish's name
pen-chwiban 'flighty, light-hearted', in North Wales also 'irresolute', lit. 'characterized by a whistling (?) head'
pen-chwidr 'wild, rash, fuzzy', lit. 'characterized by a wild head'
pen-dew 'stupid', lit. 'characterized by a thick head'[48]
pen-drist 'sad', lit. 'characterized by a sad head'
pen-drwm 'drowsy, topheavy, improper', lit. 'characterized by a heavy head'
pen-ddu 'black-haired' (North Wales), lit. 'characterized by a black head'
pen-fas 'stupid', lit. 'characterized by a flat head'
pen-feddw 'dizzy', lit. 'characterized by a drunken head'
pen-felyn 'yellow-headed' (the feminine form *pen-felen* is used as a plant's name in North Wales (Fynes-Clinton 1913)
pen-foel 'bald-headed'
pen-fras m 'cod-fish', lit. 'characterized by a thick head' (cf. *cor-benfras* m 'haddock', lit. 'dwarf-cod')
pen-gadarn 'stubborn, head-strong'
pen-galed 'stubborn' (North Wales), lit. 'characterized by a hard/difficult head' (also a flower's name)
pen-grwm 'round-headed'
pen-grych 'curly-haired'
pen-gryf 'stubborn, head-strong'
pen-isel 'downcast', lit. 'characterized by a low head'
pen-llwyd 'grey-haired'
pen-noeth 'bare-headed'
pen-rhydd 'loose, wild', lit. 'characterized by a free head'
pen-sych 'without wetting one's hair', lit. 'characterized by a dry head' (Fynes-Clinton 1913)
pen-syfrdan 'light-headed, dazed, giddy', lit. 'characterized by a dissaranged head'
pen-wan 'giddy, weak-headed'
pen-wyn 'white-headed', cf. Gaulish ΠΕΝΝΟΟΥΙΝΔΟΥ and archaic Old Irish (in Ogam and Latin letters) QVENVENDANI (CIIC 364), literary Old Irish *cenand* (Thurneysen 1946: 218)

pen-ysgafn	'giddy, dizzy', lit. 'characterized by a light head'
safn-rwth	'gaping', lit. 'characterized by a wide mouth'
tafod=drwg, *tafod=ddrwg*	'dirty, filthy', lit. 'characterized by a bad tongue' (Fynes-Clinton 1913)
tafod-rhydd	'garrulous, flippant', lit. 'characterized by a free tongue'
tal-fyr	'abrupt, short', lit. 'characterized by a short forehead'
tal-grwn	'compact, short', lit. 'characterized by a round forehead'
tal-gron f	'syllable with a rising diphthong' (spezialized usage, the feminine gender pointing to the ellipse of a feminine noun, probably *sillaf*)
tal-grych	'scowling', lit. 'characterized by a frowned / wrinkled forehead'
tal-gryf	'robust, sturdy, impudent', lit. 'characterized by a strong forehead'
tal-syth	'erect', lit. 'characterized by a straight forehead'
tin-chwith	'clumsy', lit. 'characterized by leftish buttocks'
troed-noeth	'barefoot'
wyneb-galed	'barefaced', lit. 'characterized by a hard face'.

5.2 Second member -fawr

The second group of reversed Bahuvrīhis is defined by the common second member *-fawr*.[49] This is the most frequent second member of reversed Bahuvrīhis in Welsh, a situation which may reflect the popularity of corresponding personal names, cf. the long list of Gaulish names given by Schmidt (1957: 238 n.2). Schmidt accepts the theory of Pedersen and Vendryes that Gaulish *-māro-* (together with Irish *-mar* and Welsh *-fawr*) has in most cases the value of a suffix. This is an unnecessary exaggeration, even with regard to the modern formations, because the etymological meaning (which is still the actual meaning!) of *-fawr* is obvious to the present day.[50] Gaulish *nertomaros* or Welsh *nerthfawr* are not simply 'strong, powerful', but 'characterized by great strength'. Note that no part of the body occurs as first member in the following compounds.[51]

bloedd-fawr	'vociferous, noisy', 13th c.+, lit. 'characterized by great (= loud) cries'
bost-fawr	'boastful', 15th c.+
budd-fawr	'advantageous', 13th-17th c., lit. 'characterized by great profit'
cnyd-fawr	'productive, fruitful', 16th c.+, lit. 'characterized by great harvest'
clod-fawr	'famous', 12/13th-17th c., lit. 'characterized by great fame'
cost-fawr	'expensive, costly', 16th-17th c., lit. 'characterized by great costs'
cynhwys-fawr	'capacious, comprehensive', 18th c., lit. 'characterized by (the possibility of) great content'
cynhyr-fawr	'excitable', 16th c. one, lit. 'characterized by great agitation or stir'
enill-fawr	'lucrative', 16th c.+, lit. 'characterized by great gain(s)'
gwerth-fawr	'valuable', 13th c.+, lit. 'characterized by great value'[52]
llafur-fawr	'laborious, elaborate' 1848, lit. 'characterized by great work/trouble/labour'
mas-fawr	'massive' (modern hybrid formation, first member = English *mass*), lit. 'characterized by a great / big mass'
nerth-fawr	'mighty', lit. 'characterized by great strength'[53]
pris-fawr	'precious', lit. 'characterized by a great (= high) price'
pwys-fawr	'heavy, important', lit. 'characterized by great weight'
rhwysg-fawr	'pompous, ostentatious', lit. 'characterized by great pomp'
sein-fawr	'loud', lit. 'characterized by great tones (= loud sound)'
tes-fawr	'hot', lit. 'characterized by great heat'
tryst-fawr	'noisy, sonorous', lit. 'characterized by great noise / din / uproar'

5.3 Other reversed Bahuvrihis

There are some further compounds belonging to the category of reversed Bahuvrīhi which have neither a part of the body as first member nor *-fawr* as second member. Some of their first members might be classified as "Begriff, der vom Körper ausgeht oder ihm nahesteht", but even then other words remain to prove the looseness of any semantic restriction within Welsh reversed Bahuvrīhis.

awch-lym	'sharp-edged, accurate', 14th c.+
brig-laes	'branchy', 14th c. twice, lit. 'characterized by loose tops' (to § 5.1 ?)
brig-lwyd	'hoary-headed', 15th-16th c., lit. 'characterized by grey tops' (perhaps to § 5.1, because *brig* 'top' is a poetical variation for *gwallt* 'hair')
cerdd-ber	'melodious', 14th-18th c., lit. 'characterized by sweet music'
cil-agored	'partly open, ajar', 17th-18th c., lit. 'characterized by an opened corner (only)'
cyr-gam	'with crooked edge', 14th-15th c. twice
gwrit-goch	'ruddy, rosy', 16th c.+, lit. 'characterized by red rosy complexion (?)' (to § 5.1 ?)
lliw-deg	'brightly coloured', 15th c.+, lit. 'characterized by fair colour'[54]
rhin-wyllt	'wild', lit. 'characterized by wild secrets (?)'
sein-fan	'loud', lit. 'characterized by high tones'
synhwyr-gall	'prudent', lit. 'characterized by prudent feeling' (to § 5.1 ?).

6. Bahuvrīhis with particles as first member

Only from the standpoint of Comparative Grammar, words of the structure particle + noun like *an-foes* 'unseemliness, immorality', lit. 'state characterized by the absence of manners', *cyf-eb* 'with foal', lit. 'characterized by the state of being together with a(nother, viz. still unborn) horse', *di-acen* 'unaccented', lit. 'characterized by the state of being separated from the accent', *hy-gar* 'kind', lit. 'characterized by love in good state (vel sim.)', etc. are Bahuvrīhis also. From the standpoint of Welsh grammar, the different particles are nothing more than prefixes used in derivation, not in composition. For the moment, let us follow this custom. Some of these Bahuvrīhi-subtypes will be treated elsewhere.

Notes

1. Revised version of a paper presented to the VIIIth International Congress of Celtic Studies, Swansea/Abertawe 1987, read with Professor T. Arwyn Watkins in the chair. Mae'n pleser gen i gyflwyno'r erthygl hon i'r ysgolhaig o fri gyda'm dymuniadau gorau a chofion caredig: *Ad multos annos!* - The following abbreviations are used: GPC = Geiriadur Prifysgol Cymru; m, f, c = masculine , feminine, collective noun; adv = adverb; c. after number = century/-ies; c.+ after number: century and later; c. before number = circa; dict(s). after number = occurs in dictionary/-ies only, not attested in texts; - is used to indicate composition members and/or suffixes; = is written to separate composition members usually written with a hyphen.

2. Verbal nouns are functionally comparable to participles of other Indo-European languages: here, the verbal noun is used as an adjective.

3. Today, *cymharol* is used for 'comparative'.

4. For this, see my remarks in 'Studien zum indogermanischen Wortschatz' ed. by W. Meid, Innsbruck 1987, p. 326. - Old Irish *túath* 'northern, left, evil' and its congeners, on which Guyonvarc'h bases his reconstruction of Common Celtic **teuto-* 'peuple (venu) du Nord, autrement dit de l'Autre Monde' (Ogam 18.1936.311-323) has nothing to do with the Indo-European word for 'people, mass'.

5. Dated middle of the 6th c. by Jackson (1953: 651).

6. This could be a backformation from *all-blyg-u* or its abstract *all-blygiad* 'extroversion' (no Bahuvrīhi).

7. *plwyf* < Latin *pleb-em.*

8. But the extended form *aml=liw-iog* 'multicoloured' is already attested since the 16th c.

9. But cf. the modern verb *brwd-fryd-af* 'speak or feel with fervour'.

10. Cf. J. Schindler, o-o-pe-ro-si Festschrift E. Risch 1986, p. 394-401. His formulation "gilt bekanntlich die Regel, daβ Stoff- und Zugehörigkeitsadjektiva *nicht* als A |= first member| von Komposita *zulässig* sind, sondern *durch* den Stamm ihres Grundwortes *ersetzt* werden" (394, my italics) seems to imply that all first members of Bahuvrīhis compounded from substantive + substantive are only substitutes for the adjectives used in corresponding syntactic groups of adjective and

substantive. This is to forget about the poetical origin of the Bahuvrīhi type and of the purely formal definition of this class. Bahuvrīhis are not simply transformations of their paraphrases even if such paraphrases can be found in the texts. They denote something which is neither the first nor the second member, but which is characterized by the second member which stands *in any possible logical relation* to the first member. Contrary to what Schindler seems to think, they are not mechanical transformations of syntactic groups consisting of adjective and substantive, but original creations of poetic minds. By the way, the type, as well as the other types of Indo-European nominal compounds, has a good chance to be a remnant of an older, viz. pre-flexion, state of syntax.

11. Cf. Fynes-Clinton 1913: 523 *newydd sbon danlli* 'brandnew'.

12. Common British formation, cf. Cornish *windreaw*, Breton *ivinreo*.

13. The current modern meaning is 'beforehand'.

14. A recent Bahuvrīhi formation, perhaps based on the old Tatpuruṣa *mel-ged* of 'tribute or gift of honey', c.1300+.

15. See A. Kammenhuber, Die Arier im Vorderen Orient, 1968, p. 201 ff.

16. French examples are given, because the Romance languages are notorious for their relative poverty in nominal compounds. The usual French word for 'unicorn' today is *licorne*, a loan from Italian *alicorno* which might be a tabuistic alteration of **unicorno*.

17. This could be an old loan from Latin *corda* 'chord, string', cf. Old Cornish *corden* gl. *fidis*, Breton *korden*. Probably for phonological reasons, GPC thinks of a loan from English *cord*, because Latin *-rd-* usually gives Welsh *-rdd-*. But Jackson (1953: 433) has only one example for Indo-European *rd*, and none for Latin *rd*. However, a different development of the two groups, as in other cases, could be possible. There are furthermore chronological problems in assuming a loan from English: English *cord* is attested only since c. 1300 (Oxford English Dictionary), too late for the Old Cornish and Breton words. Alternatively, the possibility of independent loans (Old Cornish *corden* < Latin *corda*, ecclesiastical or learned loan; Welsh *cord* m, 16th c.+ < English *cord*; Breton *korden* perhaps < French *corde*) cannot be excluded.

18. *p* instead of *b* may be a Northwalian dialectal feature (cf. *tatcu* North Wales vs. *tadgu* South Wales). A semantically parallel formation is Gothic *ain-falþs*.

19. As a Karmadhāraya, the word is already attested in the 18th c.

20. GPC has only the Karmadhāraya *deu-parth* 'two parts (of three)', 13th c.+, which for semantic reasons cannot be the base of the extended Bahuvrīhi given above.

21. Calque (?) of Latin *duplex*, acc. *du-plic-em*; cf. Greek δίπλαξ etc., Umbrian *tu-plak*.

22. Cf. the Old Indian word for 'island', *dv-ī-p-a-*, lit. 'characterized by double (?) water' (< **du̯i-Hp-o-*).

23. According to GPC, the word is a Karmadhāraya only : 'the two ears' (also in the form *dwy-glust*), 14th c.+.

24. GPC cites the form *dwy-ieith-og*, 19th c. - Cf. *un-ieith-iog* above.

25. Earlier as m (Karmadhāraya) 'two voices', 15th and 18th c. once each.

26. Earlier 'a pair' (of letters, horses), probably Karmadhāraya.

27. Since the 13th c. also Karamdhāraya 'two parts'; GPC unfortunately does not separate the attestations of the two types. Probably Bahuvrīhi since 17th c., cf. the causative *dwy-rann-u* 'to bisect'.

28. Karmadhāraya since the 14th c.: 'two kinds, both sexes'; the Bahuvrīhi renewed in the 18th c.: *deu-ryw-iog*.

29. *-d-* instead of *-dd-* through influence by *tri-dànt* m 'trident' which is taken over from English/French *trident*.

30. Cf. the Old Irish compounds of the type *deichthriub* 'the ten tribes', see Thurneysen 1946: 244.

31. Cf. further *traean* m 'one third, legitimate portion' (juridical), probably from *tri-+-ran*. The meaning of these words point ot a basic Bahuvrīhi 'characterized by the third part'. Compounds with first member *trydydd* 'third' are unknown to me.

32. Cf. Gaulish *petru-*.

33. GPC has *chwe-ochr-og* 'hexagonal', 16th-18th c. dicts. and *chwe-ongl-og* 'id.', 16th c. dict., 18th c.

34. Cf. the German and French expressions *acht Tage / huit jours* 'one week' (no Bahuvrīhis!).

35. Cf. French *quinze jours* 'id.'.

36. A parallel **mil-flwydd* 'one thousand years old' underlies the word *mil-flwydd-iant* 'millenium' (cf. *can-mlwydd-iant* 'centenary'.- Very probably, all syntagmata of the type *yn ugain mlwydd oed* 'twenty years old' are formed with Bahuvrīhis (cf. Pedersen's "Biverbierung").

37. On reversed Bahuvrīhis in Indo-European, see my forthcoming article *Die umgekehrten Bahuvrīhi-Komposita im Kymrischen und Indogermanischen*, Akten der 8. Fachtagung der Indogermanischen Gesellschaft Leiden 1987, ed. R.S.P. Beekes, Wiesbaden, Reichert, ca. 1989.

38. Not mentioned in GPC; see M. Haycock in: Cambridge Medieval Celtic Studies 13.1987, 13f.+note 27.

39. First 1630; the derivatives are slightly earlier: *calon-galed-wch* 1620 NT, *calon-galed-u* 1617.

40. According to GPC a variant of *cefn-r(h)wd*.

41. Variants: *-grwba*, *-grwbi*, *-brwb*, *-grwca* (17th-18th c.).

42. Hardly a derivative of *cein-fagl* 'crozier'.

43. The derivative verb *cig-noeth-i* 'to wound, lacerate' already in a 16th c. dictionary.

44. The verb *clust-fein-io* 'to listen attentively' corresponds exactly to the German expression *die Ohren spitzen* 'id.'.

45. Giraldus Cambrensis, Itinerarium Kambriae II 8: *Ierverdum Troyndun, quod Kambrice simus* (Ms. Hc *simum*) *sonat* (James F. Dimock, ed.: Giraldi Cambrensis Opera, vol. VI, London 1968, p. 134).

46. Giraldus Cambrensis, Itinerarium Kambriae II 2: *Seisillus Eskeirhir, id est, Tibia longa* (James F. Dimock, ed.: Giraldi Cambrensis Opera, vol. VI, London 1968, p. 111).

47. For the compounds with first member *pen-* see J. Morris-Jones 1913: 35.

48. The meaning of the Bahuvrīhi is not self-evident, cf. German *Dickkopf* 'a stubborn person'.

49. This is not to deny the possibility of a different interpretation of some of the following compounds, viz. as determinative adjectives (so to say, adjectival Tatpuruṣas). Semantically, the difference between 'great in boast' and 'characterized by great boast' is of course so tiny as to be practically nonexisting. For systematical reasons, I take all adjectives of the type Substantive + *-fawr* as reversed Bahuvrīhis.

50. I propose to speak of a suffix in this context only if an old composition element has lost its old meaning and is used in combination with nouns which could not have been appropriated if the old meaning had persisted, e.g. English *-ly*, German *-lich* < Germanic *-līka-* 'body', used in words like *suddenly*, *plötzlich*. There is, of course, a kind of gradation in the change from 'second member of a nominal compound' to 'suffix of a derivative'. Anyhow, Welsh *-fawr* cannot yet be very advanced in the transition.

51. In personal names, however, such compounds may perhaps occur, cf. Gaelic *Cennmor*, epithet of a Scottish king. Unfortunately, there is no lexicon of Welsh names.

52. The gradation forms *gwerth-fawr-oc-ach*, *gwerth-fawr-oc-af*, the denominal verb *gwerth-fawr-og-i* and the abstract *gwerth-fawr-og-iad* assure the existence of an (unattested) extended form *gwerthfawr-og*.

53. Not recorded in the extant dictionaries (including GPC); given by Thurneysen 1946: 218 as Welsh parallel to Gaulish *nertomaros* and Irish *nertmar* (- a *vox nihili*?).

54. Could be a determinative compound 'pretty by colour'.

References:

Fabian, E. (1931) *Das exozentrische Kompositum im Deutschen* (= Form und Geist, 20). Leipzig: Eichblatt.

Fynes-Clinton, O. H. (1913) *The Welsh Vocabulary of the Bangor District*. London etc.: Humphrey Milford - Oxford University Press

Geiriadur Mawr (1971) H. Meurig Evans & W. O. Thomas. *Y Geiriadur Mawr*. 10th ed. Abertawe: Christopher Davies; Llandysul: Gwasg Gomer.

GPC (1950-) *Geiriadur Prifysgol Cymru*. gol. gan R. J. Thomas [ag wedyn gan] G.A. Bevan. Caerdydd: Gwasg Prifysgol Cymru.

Jackson, K. H. (1953) *Language and History in Early Britain*. Edinburgh: Edinburgh University Press.

Last, W. (1925) *Das Bahuvrīhi-Compositum im Altenglischen, Mittelenglischen und Neuenglischen*. Greifswald: Buchdruckerei Hans Adler.

Morris-Jones, J. (1913) *A Welsh Grammar, Historical and Comparative*. Oxford: Clarendon Press.

Pokorny, J. (1958) Review of Schmidt 1957, *Kratylos*, 3, 170-174

Schmidt, K. H. (1957) Die Komposition in gallischen Personennamen. *Zeitschrift für Celtische Philologie*, 26, 27-301

Thurneysen, R. (1946) *A Grammar of Old Irish*. Dublin: The Dublin Institute of Advanced Studies

Notes on Old Irish and Old Welsh Consonantal Spelling

Anthony Harvey
Royal Irish Academy

1. Vernacular Orthography as Evidence for British-Latin Pronunciation

In a rather intemperate attack on Professor Kenneth Jackson's characterisation of early medieval British Latin as archaic in pronunciation compared with contemporary continental Latin, A. S. Gratwick (1982) concentrates on undermining the thesis that "the loanwords surviving in the British languages show that the Latin spoken by Britons was old-fashioned in its phonology" (1982: 3). He argues with respect to many of the loanwords that they show no such thing and, with respect to those which unquestionably do reflect a Classical or quasi-Classical Latin phonology, that "the reason why the Latin words in question do not show the 'expected' vulgar traits might be that they were borrowed into British *before* these changes in spoken Latin were accomplished, whenever that was" (1982: 9). Gratwick's assumptions, methodology and conclusions have themselves been rigorously assessed (Charles-Edwards, 1984; McManus, 1984; Malkiel, 1984; Russell, 1985) and there is no need to cover the same ground again; suffice it to say that, in general terms, Jackson's original (1953) thesis emerges in rather better shape than does Gratwick's criticism of it, although it seems to me that the latter makes a valid point in the passage just quoted and has, to that extent at least, successfully impugned the testimony of the loanwords.[1]

There is, however, one significant matter, ignored by Gratwick, which is also passed over in the reviews cited above but which would appear germane to the argument. This is the consideration that the individual borrowings provide only a part of the evidence for the resistance of British Latin to phonological change - in my view not the most telling part. More important would seem to be the fact that the whole tradition of representing sounds by means of roman letters was something that was (by definition) borrowed into the vernacular from Latin. Therefore, at the point when this borrowing took place (in other words, at the time when the vernacular began to be written down), the sound in the native language to which each letter was now assigned must have been the same as, or very similar to, the one which that letter already represented in British Latin. What else could have prompted the sound/letter correspondences which in fact were chosen? Jackson himself makes this point with great clarity (1953: Chapter Two; Gratwick's criticisms are actually all applied to arguments in Chapter Three). What it amounts to is this: at the time of the establishment of the spelling system known to us from Old Welsh, Old Cornish and Old Breton, "British-Latin *ratio, Caesar, ancilla, plangere, viverra*" must have been "said as [ra^{i}djō̦, kĕsar, aŋkilla, plaŋgere, wīwerra], and not as [ra^{i}dzo, tsiesar, a^{i}ntsella, plańżere, vivierra]" (or whatever; Jackson (1953: 74) with minor alterations to the phonetic symbols used), *not* because of the evidence of any specific loanwords, but because our vernacular sources show clearly enough that intervocalic *ti* meant /dj/[2] rather than [dz], initial *c* before a front vowel meant /k/[3] rather than [ts], and *ng* before a front vowel (when used) meant /ŋ(g/)[4] rather than [ńż] - and so on - in the orthography being used. We thus have at least approximate information about the pronunciation of British Latin at the time when literacy in the Brittonic dialects began,[5] and the question of whether it was archaic or not will depend on when that was. Unless and until the currently-accepted sixth-century date is shown to be significantly too late for the founding of the *vernacular* written tradition,[6] Jackson's view of British-*Latin* phonology as being in at least some respects old-fashioned must (I would therefore suggest) largely stand, since (for example) the non-assibilation of consonants as described above would surely be agreed by all to be exceptional in the Latin of a period as far-advanced as that.

2. Spelling and the Size of the Sound System

I have argued elsewhere that in both branches of Insular Celtic, gemination as such is best seen as having ceased to be a significant feature of the consonantal system at the point when the sound change of lenition took place (Harvey, 1984). This was because the opposition geminate : single was everywhere replaced by the opposition non-lenited : lenited. It is true that in the case of the lateral, nasal and vibrant resonants (the '*l*s, *n*s and *r*s'), the phonetic nature of the opposition continued in each language to be at least largely one of length; but the same cannot be said, for British anyway, about the original stop consonants. Here, despite some apparent evidence to the contrary from the Modern Breton of le Bourg Blanc (Falc'hun, 1951: 64-65: Jackson, 1967: 85-86), what had been the phonetically single British [p, t, k][7] gave with lenition the same phonemes as did what had been the phonetically geminate [bb, dd, gg],[8] namely simple /b, d, g/ respectively.[9] At the same time [pp, tt, kk][10] became /p, t, k/[11] and [b, d, g][12] became /β, δ, γ/.[13] Restricting ourselves to the dental and velar consonants (in order to facilitate a comparison with Irish, in which the early status of some of the bilabials is disputed) we can thus see that the original British inventory of eight phonemes /t, tt, k, kk, d, dd, g, gg/ was reduced at the time of lenition to six, namely /t, k, d, g, δ, γ/. In Irish, on the other hand, no such impoverishment took place: the prelenition phonetic geminates became the corresponding phonemic singletons, as in British,[14] but the four prelenition singletons [t, k, d, g] yielded the spirants /θ, χ, δ, γ/,[15] keeping the total at eight.

I believe that this difference between the effects of British and Irish lenition on their respective sound systems will have had significant results when the different Insular Celtic languages came to be written down in roman letters. For, taking Old Breton as typical of the early medieval Brythonic tongues, when the scribes wished to spell for example the word they pronounced /adanogjon/, they were obliged to write *atanocion* (Lux.) since (given the effect of British lenition on the pronunciation of postvocalic British-Latin *d* and *g*, and the modelling of the vernacular orthography on that Latin, as described above) *adanogion* would have meant /aδanoγjon/ (compare Jackson, 1953: 70-71). However, in the earliest postlenition Irish spelling one would expect no such enforced consistency, since in no case was the product of the lenition of one consonant the same as the unlenited form of another. This, together with whatever conflict there may have been between an 'indigenous' orthography (that is, one modelled on a Latin that had been conformed to the Irish sound system before lenition, for which see Harvey, 1987, 1989) and a 'standard' Old Irish spelling system based on the British pronunciation of Latin (Carney, 1977/79: 417), may explain the greater variation in the earliest roman-letter Gaelic orthography which Meinir Lewis claims to have detected (1961: 746).

To put effectively the same point another way: in postlenition Irish there was less opportunity than in the corresponding Brythonic sound system for avoiding orthographic ambiguity without adding to the alphabet, since there were two more consonantal phonemes to be coped with. With spirantisation, syncope and provection the British consonantal system was expanded eventually to the same size as the Irish - if one ignores Irish phonemic palatalisation, for the representation of which the vowel symbols were pressed into service - and the result seems indeed to have been confusion in spelling (Jackson, 1953: 572-573). To the extent that Meinir Lewis's allegation of *decreasing* consistency in the earliest *Welsh* spelling is still valid,[16] we may have here a partial explanation of that phenomenon. Furthermore, this observation puts on a more secure footing the reason for believing that the digraphic representation of spirants (principally *th* for /θ/ and *ch* for /χ/) is more likely to have been coined in Ireland than in Britain (Harvey 1989), since in Goidelic phonology there will have been an incentive for it earlier. At all events, the lively discussion of inter-insular influences during the formative years of the earliest Celtic orthography seems certain to continue; and it is perhaps not out of place to remark that, with articles such as Watkins (1964/66), our learned dedicatee will be seen to have played a key role in sustaining it.

Notes

1. Even on Jackson's view, the only word which provides a concrete *terminus post quem* for the sound changes in British Latin is the name *Patricius* (allegedly borrowed into Irish as what became *Cothraige*), and, as I have attempted to show elsewhere (Harvey, 1985), this example is in fact problematical. But in that article I, like Gratwick, overlooked the argument that now follows.

2. As in Old Breton *cospitiot* (Orl.CC.), *cantguoritiat* (Par. 10290), *nouitiou* (Eutych.), Old Welsh *strutiu* (Juvenc.), *Morgetiud Margetiud* (AC. 795, 811), and even thirteenth-century Welsh *llitiawc* (*Ystorya Bown de Hamtwn*: *YBH* 22a; see *GPC* s.v. *llidiog* (a)).

3. As in Old Welsh *cemmein* (Ox. 1), *cephitor* (Comp.), Old Breton *cerpit* (Orl. CC.), *caeninn* (Leid. Leech.).

4. Examples of vernacular *ng* in this environment are admittedly rare, partly because in Breton the sound it would have corresponded to was short-lived (Jackson, 1967: 793-794). It is hard to improve on the "f|orme| v|ieille| g|alloise|" *guorsengir* (Angers 477, Hand B, emended with certainty from *guorsergir* in Evans and Fleuriot, 1985: I, 199), or the Book of Aneirin's Welsh *gangen* (*A* 18.7,9: see *GPC* s.v. *cangen* (1c)).

5. It might of course be argued that in British-Latin pronunciation *ti* had indeed been assibilated to |dz|, but that it was still the most obvious available spelling for vernacular /dj/. The same could not be said, however, in the case of initial *c* before a front vowel, |ts| and vernacular /k/, because if such a *c* did indeed mean |ts| in British Latin one would expect the vernacular sound to be rendered by a choice of *k*, *qu* or even *ch*; and in any case this type of objection assumes that British Latin remained unassimilated to the vernacular sound system, a possibility which is coming to seem less and less likely as scholarship progresses.

6. Even John Koch, whose "fully developed Neo-Britt. writing system" makes a "revolutionary appearance" (1985/86: 44), is not suggesting a date earlier than this. Incidentally, Koch's suggestion of the term 'Common Neo-Brittonic' (1985/86: 53) seems a very good one, particularly in connection with spelling; it might have been an improvement in the title of the present contribution, in which, I admit, 'Old Welsh' must be read as shorthand for 'Old Welsh, Cornish and Breton'. |The texts from Roman Bath now described by Tomlin (1987) can hardly be seen as standing in the same tradition.|

7. Reflecting original postvocalic /p, t, k/.

8. Reflecting original non-postvocalic /b, d, g/ as well as original intervocalic /bb, dd, gg/.

9. Thus |tto:ta:| 'a people' and the root |kkredd-| 'believe' both yielded forms with simple postvocalic /d/ immediately after lenition, namey

/tu:da:/ and /kred-/ respectively (Harvey, 1984: 93, 96).

10. Reflecting original non-postvocalic /p, t, k/ as well as original intervocalic /pp, tt, kk/.

11. Thus |bbrattos| 'cloak' yielded /bratəΣ/ immediately after lenition (Harvey, 1984: 93, 96).

12. Reflecting original postvocalic /b, d, g/.

13. Thus |bbo:dis| 'gain' yielded /bu:δəΣ/ immediately after lenition in Irish (Harvey 1984: 93, 96. The suggestion that in archaic Old Irish the corresponding form was a feminine *a*-stem *bód* (Carney, 1971: 50) would imply that the prelenition form should instead be |bbo:da:|, but that would not affect the present argument).

14. Thus |kkredd-| and |bbrattos| similarly yielded /kred-/ and /bratah/ immediately after lenition (Harvey, 1984: 93, 91).

15. Thus |tto:ta:| gave /to:θa:/, rather than a form with post-vocalic /d/, immediately after lenition (Harvey, 1984: 93, 91).

16. Her classification of the Book of Llandaff spellings simply as eleventh to twelfth century no longer holds (Davies, 1980; Koch, 1985/86). Incidentally, I do not wish to imply by this paragraph that I necessarily envisage the British vernacular as having been written down as such before the expansion of the sound system mentioned (though see the reference to Tomlin, 1987 given above). What I am saying is that a sufficiently strong orthographic tradition seems to have been established before that time - presumably by the rendering of native names in Latin-medium texts - for traces of it to appear in manuscripts which have survived.

References

Brooks, N. (ed.) (1982) *Latin and the vernacular languages in early medieval Britain.* Leicester: Leicester University Press.

Carney, J. (1971) Three Old Irish accentual poems. *Ériu,* **22,** 23-80.

Carney, J. (1977/79) Aspects of archaic Irish. *Éigse,* **17,** 417-435.

Charles-Edwards, T. M. (1984) [review of Brooks (1982)]. *Journal of Roman Studies,* **74,** 252-254.

Davies, W. (1980) The orthography of personal names in the charters of *Liber Landavensis*. *BBCS*, **28**, 553-557.

Evans, C. and Fleuriot, L. (1985) *A dictionary of Old Breton/Dictionnaire du Vieux Breton*, 2 vols. Toronto: Precorp.

Falc'hun, F. (1951) *Le système consonantique du Breton*. Rennes: Plihon.

Gratwick, A. S. (1982) Latinitas Britannica: Was British Latin archaic? In Brooks, N. (ed.) Pp 1-79.

Harvey, A. (1984) Aspects of lenition and spirantization. *CMCS*, **8**, 87-100.

Harvey, A. (1985) The significance of *Cothraige*. *Ériu*, **36**, 1-9.

Harvey, A. (1987) Early literacy in Ireland: The evidence from ogam, *CMCS*, **14**, 1-15.

Harvey, A. (1989) Some significant points of early insular Celtic orthography. In L. Breatnach, K. McCone and D. Ó Corráin (eds.), *Sages, saints and storytellers. Celtic studies in honour of Professor James Carney*. Maynooth: An Sagart. Pp 56-66.

Jackson, K. (1953) *Language and history in early Britain*. Edinburgh: Edinburgh University Press.

Jackson, K. (1967) *A historical phonology of Breton*. Dublin: Dublin Institute for Advanced Studies.

Koch, J. T. (1985/86) When was Welsh literature first written down?, *SC*, **20/21**, 43-66.

Lewis, M. (1961) *Disgrifiad o orgraff Hen Gymraeg gan ei chymharu ag orgraff Hen Wyddeleg*. Unpublished M.A. dissertation, University College, Aberystwyth.

McManus, D. (1984) *Linguarum diversitas*: Latin and the vernaculars in early medieval Britain. *Peritia*, **3**, 151-188.

Malkiel, Y. (1984) [review of Brooks (1982)]. *Language*, **60**, 615-617.

Russell, P. (1985) Recent work in British Latin. *CMCS*, **9**, 19-29.

Tomlin, R. S. O. (1987) Was Ancient British Celtic ever a written language? Two texts from Roman Bath. *BBCS*, **34**, 18-25.

Watkins, T. A. (1964/66) Points of similarity between Old Welsh and Old Irish orthography. *BBCS*, **21**, 135-141.

On the Uses of the Conjunctive Pronouns in Middle Welsh

Proinsias Mac Cana
Dublin Institute for Advanced Studies

This paper is not directly concerned with the history of the morphology of the conjunctive pronouns, a topic which was examined many years ago by Holger Pedersen and John Morris-Jones, and recently by Dr Paul Russell. Both Pedersen (1909: 442, 1913: 173, 184-185) and Morris-Jones (1913: 274; cf. Evans, 1964: 49-53) explain the conjunctive forms by the generalization of the *-teu* of 3 sg. m. *ynteu*, though they differ concerning the origin of this latter form. For Russell (1982/83) the key-form was 3 pl. MW *wynteu*, an unaccented variant of the reduplicated pronoun *wyntwy* "in its early usage as a dependent pronoun"; the *-teu* of this form was generalized to the other weakened reduplicated pronouns, thus creating a new class of conjunctive pronouns. His argument presumes that the primary use of the conjunctive forms was as dependent pronouns and that their familiar role in Middle Welsh as independent pronouns is therefore a secondary development (1982/83: 34, 38).

Morris-Jones has also some brief comments on the syntax of the conjunctive pronouns (1913: 273). He notes that a "pronoun of this series is always set against a noun or pronoun that goes before (or is implied)", but that sometimes the meaning added is so subtle as to be untranslatable: "Thus *chwi a minnau* means literally 'you and I', but generally *minnau* signifies 'I too', 'even I', 'I for my part', 'but I', 'while I', etc." He notes that a conjunctive pronoun often stands in apposition to a noun: *ynteu*

Pwyll 'Pwyll also', that the 3 sg. *ynteu* answers *naill* in the expression *naill ai ... ai ynteu* 'on the one hand either ... or on the other hand', and that from its unaccented use as 'on the other hand' it became a conjunction 'then': *Paham ynteu LlA* 13 'Why, then?'.

In the brief comments which I have here further abbreviated Sir John has adverted to the main semantic and syntactic features involved in the use of the Welsh conjunctive pronouns, and his account underlies the descriptions of this category found in the works of subsequent grammarians. In returning to the subject in the present essay my purpose is not to emend Sir John's treatment, which is hardly necessary, but rather to supplement and perhaps refine it by a detailed examination of the use of the conjunctive pronouns in several representative Middle Welsh texts. I would hope that such an examination would have stylistic as well as syntactic and semantic implications, revealing as it does the rich variety and nuance encompassed in the use of the conjunctive pronouns by Middle Welsh prose writers. (Since completing this essay I note that Joseph Vendryes had many years ago commented briefly on several of the sub-usages discussed here; *RC* 42, 1925, 396-398.)

The texts on which I have principally relied, in other words those from which I have excerpted instances of the conjunctive pronoun exhaustively, are *Branwen* and *Manawydan* from the Four Branches (though I also cite instances from the other two branches), *Kulhwch ac Olwen*, *Owein*, and *Peredur*. For the first two I refer to PKM = *Pedeir Keinc y Mabinogi*, ed. Ifor Williams (Caerdydd 1930), for the third (*KO*) to *WM* = *The White Book Mabinogion* (Pwllheli 1907; repr. Caerdydd 1973) and *RM* = *The Text of the Mabinogion ... from the Red Book of Hergest* (Oxford 1887), both ed. J. Gwenogvryn Evans, for *Owein* to *Owein or Chwedyl Iarlles y Ffynnawn*, ed. R. L. Thomson (Dublin 1968, repr. 1975), and for the last to *Per.* = *Historia Peredur vab Efrawc*, ed. Glenys Witchard Goetinck (Caerdydd 1976).

It is clear that the conjunctive pronoun, independent and dependent, could be used as subject (or auxiliary to subject contained in a verb) or object of a finite verb (or auxiliary of objective infixed pronoun):

Ay dodi a oruc ynteu y mys y uanec ... a chymryt a oruc

hitheu y uodrwy or uanec 'and he placed it in the finger of his glove ... and she took the ring from the glove' *WM* 473.27-31; *amkawd ynteu* 'said he' 477.28; *y tynnei deu uaen ureuan ynteu yr affwys* 'two quernstones pulled him down to the depths' 505.4;

or as an auxiliary to a genitive pronoun with noun or verbal noun:

ac yn y ol ynteu y wreic' and his wife after him' *PKM* 36.21; *yny dyrr y galon ynteu* 'until his heart bursts' 44.19; *Ae dyuot hitheu* 'and she came' *WM* 475.35; *Ny uynhei Gaswallawn y lad ynteu* 'Caswallawn did not wish to kill him' *PKM* 46.7;

or following a preposition or prepositional pronoun:

ac y roes y peir y minheu 'and he gave the cauldron to me' 36.24; *Gwascu o honei hitheu yr eiras* 'She squeezed the stake' *WM* 474.27.

However, as Morris-Jones noted, it has generally an anaphoric reference - at least in the third person - indicating a person or thing previously mentioned. It is this element of retrospection which gives rise to the various subtleties of meaning which Morris-Jones mentions. What I propose here is to comment *seriatim* on the several sub-usages which make up the semantic-syntactic range of the conjunctive pronoun in Middle Welsh, illustrating them by a selection of examples from the cited texts, but always mindful of the fact that with multivalent terms of this sort it is often impossible to distinguish clearly between their several semantic roles.

1. The conjunctive pronoun is often used to indicate a new subject, normally a person or persons mentioned in the preceding text.

Amkawd y mab ... Dywawd hitheu 'The boy said ... She said in reply' 454.15 (the line numbers refer to those lines in which the conjunctive pronoun occurs)

dyro di imi y diot y kellellprenneu o heni a chaffwyf inheu gwneuthur rei newyd idaw 'Give it to me to remove the wooden side-pieces, and let me make new ones for it' 488.28

A gwedy disgynnu Arthur yr tir, dyuot seint Iwerdon attaw y erchi nawd idaw. Ac y rodes ynteu nawd udunt hwy, ac y rodassant *wynteu* *eu bendyth idaw ef* 'And when Arthur came to land, the saints of Ireland came to him to seek his protection, and he granted them protection, and they gave him their blessing' 499.18,20

Kynn kaffel diot y grib, kaffel dayar o honaw *ynteu* *ae draet* 'Before the comb could be removed, he found land with his feet' 504.34 (the v.n. *kaffel* is impersonal)

The new subject may refer back to the object of the preceding sentence,

Duw y vyr nat ymhoylwn hyt pan welhom y uorwyn. A daw *hitheu* *yntheruyn y gweler* 'God knows we will not turn back until we have seen the girl. Will she come to were she can be seen' 475.21

or it may refer to a possessive adjective in the preceding sentence,

ac ny chauas dim hagen namyn un oe wrych. Kyuodi a oruc *ynteu* *yn wychyr da* 'but he got nothing but one of his bristles. Then he [Twrch Trwyth] arose in full fury' 498.5 (*Ynteu* refers to the possessive in *oe*)

or to a personal pronoun,

Ac yd ymordiwedawd Arthur ac ef yno. Rodi kyuarth a wnaeth *ynteu* *yna* 'and Arthur caught up with him there. He stood at bay there' 503.14

Ac yna yd ymordiwedawd Arthur ymPelumyawc ac ef, ac yna y lladawd *ynteu* *Madawc mab Teithyon* 'And then Arthur caught up with him at Peluniawg, and he [Twrch Trwyth] then slew Madawg son of Teithion' 502.9

(This is one of a string of sentences containing the verb *y lladawd (ef)*, but the only one to have *ynteu* after the verb. The function of the conjunctive pronoun is to refer back to Twrch Trwyth (as represented in *ac ef* in the preceding sentence) in the alternation of subjects, but in another sentence in the series with virtually the same structure (501.34-36) *ynteu* is not used. This underlines the fact that the use of the conjunctive pronoun to identify the subject in an alternating series is very much a matter of stylistic choice.)

or to a pluriform antecedent,
Dyuynnu a oruc Arthur Gwyn uab Nud attaw, a gouyn idaw a wydyat ef dim y wrth Twrch Trwyth. Y dywawt ynteu nas gwydyat 'Arthur called Gwyn son of Nudd to him and asked him did he know anything about Twrch Trwyth. He replied that he did not' 502.21

The reference of the anaphoric pronoun as subject may extend beyond the preceding sentence,

Achub a oruc ynteu parth ac yno 'He sprang forward in that direction' 494.10 (*ynteu* refers back to Gwythyr mab Greidawl in l. 6-7)

Kychwynnu a oruc Arthur ac ysgawn niuer ganthaw a mynet ymPrytwen y long a dyuot y Ywerdon a dygyrchu ty Diwrnach Wydel a orugant. Gwelsant niuer Otgar eu meint a gwedy bwyta o nadunt ac yuet eu dogyn erchi y peir a oruc Arthur. Y dywawt ynteu ... 'Arthur set out with a light force and went in Prydwen his ship and came to Ireland, and they made for the house of Diwrnach the Irishman. The retinue of Odgar noted their strength, and after they had eaten and drunk their fill, Arthur asked for the cauldron. He answered ...' 498.24 (*Ynteu* here refers back to Diwrnach)

Ac yna y kychwynnwys ynteu o Lynn Nyuer 'And then he set out from Glyn Nyfer' 501.22 (*Ynteu* refers back to Twrch Trwyth in l. 8, which is an unusually far remove.)

2. It may serve to indicate a given subject, or speaker, where this alternates with another subject or speaker.

Kyrchu a orugant vy porth llys Custenhin heusawr. Clybot o heni hitheu eu trwst yn dyuuot. Redec o heni yn eu herbyn o lywenyd. Goglyt a oruc Kei ymprenn or gludweir, ae dyuot hitheu yn eu herbyn y geissaw mynet dwylaw mynwgyl udunt. Gossot o Gei eiras kyfrwg y dwy law. Gwascu o honei hitheu yr eiras hyt pan yttoed yn vden diednedic 'They came to the entrance of the shepherd Custennin's dwelling. She heard the noise of them approaching. She ran with joy to meet them. Cei seized a log from the wood-pile, and she came to meet them and sought to put her arms about their necks. Cei thrust a stake between her two hands. She squeezed the stake so that it became a twisted

piece of wood' 474.19,23,28
Here we have a short series of sentences in which a 3 sg. f. subject alternates with other subjects, and each time it does so it is represented by or accompanied by the conjunctive pronoun.

This usage is familiar in passages of dialogue. Where, however, there is little danger of confusion, contributions from different speakers may simply be juxtaposed without reference to the speaker, or they may be marked by use of a proper noun or a simple pronoun. This variation is one of the stylistic devices employed to enhance the dramatic effect of dialogue,

'Arglwyd,' heb yr yscolheic, 'dyd da it.' 'Duw a rodo da it, a grayssaw wrthyt,' heb ef. 'Pan doy di, yr yscolheic?' heb ef. 'Pan doaf, Arglwyd, o Loygyr o ganu. A phaham y gouynhy di, Arglwyd?' heb ef. 'Na weleis,' heb ef, 'neut seith mylned, un dyn yma, onyt pedwar dyn diholedic, a thitheu yr awr honn.' 'Ie, Arglwyd, mynet,' heb ef, 'drwy y wlat honn yd wyf inheu yr awr honn, parth a'm gwlat uy hun. A pha ryw weith yd wyte yndaw, Arglwyd?' 'Crogi lleidyr a geueis yn lledratta arnaf,' heb ef. 'Ba ryw leidyr, Arglwyd?' heb ef. 'Pryf a welaf i'th law di ual llygoden. A drwc y gueda y wr kyuurd a thidi, ymodi pryf kyfryw a hwnnw. Gellwg e ymdeith ef.' 'Na ellynghaf, y rof a Duw,' heb ynteu. 'Yn lledratta y keueis ef, a chyfreith lleidyr a wnaf inheu ac ef, y grogi.' 'Arglwyd,' heb ynteu, 'rac guelet gwr kyuurd a thidi yn y gueith hwnnw, punt a geueis i o gardotta, mi a'e rodaf it, a gellwng y pryf hwnnw e ymdeith.' 'Nac ellynghaf, y rof a Duw, nys guerthaf.' 'Gwna di, Arglwyd,' heb ef. 'Ony bei hagyr guelet gwr kyuurd a thidi yn teimlaw y ryw bryf a hwnnw, ny'm torei.' "'Lord,' said the clerk, 'good day to you.' 'God prosper you, and welcome to you,' said he. 'Where are you coming from, clerk?' said he. 'I am coming, lord, from song-making in Lloegyr. And why do you ask, lord?' said he. 'Because for the last seven years,' said he, 'I have seen no one here, except the four of us in isolation, and now you.' 'Well, lord,' he said, 'I am just now passing through this land on the way to my own country. And what kind of work are you engaged in, lord?' 'Hanging a thief I caught stealing from me,' said he. 'What kind of thief, lord?' said he. 'I see a creature in your hand like a mouse, and it ill becomes a man of your dignity to handle a creature like that. Let it go.' 'I will not let it go,' said he, 'between me and God. I caught it thieving, and I shall

execute upon it the judgement for a thief, which is hanging.' 'Lord,' said he, 'rather than see a man of your dignity at that task, I shall give you a pound which I received as alms, and let that creature go.' 'I will not let it go, between me and God, nor will I sell it.' 'Do as you will, lord,' said he, 'if it were not so degrading to see a man of your standing handling such a creature, it would not bother me'" PKM 61.21-62.14

Here we have the sequence *heb yr yscolheic* once ... *heb ef* seven times (once without change of speaker) ... *heb ynteu* twice ... Ø... *heb ef* once. The only reason one can suggest for the two consecutive instances of *ynteu* is that of stylistic variation.

Virtually the whole range of alternatives is brought into play in the dialogue between Pwyll and Arawn at the beginning of Pwyll (PKM 2.8-3.28): *heb ef* ... *heb ef* ... *heb ef* ... *heb ynteu* ... *heb ynteu* ... Ø ... *heb ef* ... *heb ef* ... *heb ef* (the last two instances without change of speaker) ... *heb ef* ... *heb ynteu* ... Ø... Ø ... *heb ynteu* ... *heb ynteu* ... *heb ynteu* ... *heb ynteu* ... *heb ynteu* ... *heb ynteu* ... *heb ef* (without change of speaker) ... *heb ynteu* ... *heb ef* ... *heb ef* (without change of speaker) ... *heb y Pwyll* ... *heb yr Arawn* ... *heb y Pwyll* ... Ø. Here again the mode of reference to the speaker is a matter of stylistic choice, even to the use of the proper names towards the end of the passage. The only 'rule' that one might state in this regard is the fairly obvious one that, when reference is made more than once in sequence to the same speaker within a segment of dialogue, the second and subsequent references may not employ the conjunctive form of the pronoun.

Where there is a regular interchange between more than two speakers the use of the conjunctive pronoun to indicate one or other of them is infrequent, for the simple reason that in such cases proper names are used more often than pronouns to identify the speakers (whereas in two-part dialogues the pronouns predominate). Thus in PKM 17.15-18.15 a dialogue between Gwawl (= *y gwr o'r got*), Heueyd, Pwyll and Rhiannon has the following sequence: *heb y gwr o'r got* ... *heb H.* ... *heb y P.* ... *heb R.* ... *heb hi* (without change of speaker) ... *heb y gwr o'r got* ... *heb y P.* ... *heb wynt* (Heueyd and Rhiannon) ... *heb y P.* ... *heb H.* ... [an intervening narrative sentence] ... *heb yr H.* ... *heb y Gw.* ... *heb y P.* ... *heb y Gw.* ... *heb y P.*, where each speaker is clearly defined by name; and another in PKM 14.1-11 between Pwyll, the stranger (Gwawl) and Rhiannon has: *heb y P.* ... *heb ef* ... *heb y P.* ... *heb ef* ... Ø (Pwyll) ... *heb y R.* ... *heb ef* ... *heb y P.*, where the pronoun *ef* is reserved for the stranger.

In so far as conjunctive pronouns are used to identify the speakers in a two-part dialogue where they are not distinguished by gender (or number), they should not normally be necessary where the speakers are a male and a female. Thus Rhiannon and Pwyll, PKM 14.13-15.5.: *heb y R.* ... *heb ef* ... *heb hi* ... *heb ef* ... *heb hi* ... *heb y P.* ... *heb hi* ... *heb hi* ... *heb hi* ... *heb hi* ... *heb hi* ... *heb hi* (these six instances without a change of speaker). But, as should be clear from the present survey, the function of the conjunctive pronouns is not merely one of identification; it has, for example, very commonly an adversative force (see infra) which explains its occasional use in dialogue between male and female, as in PKM 23.2-13 (one instance, 23.9), 7.13-8.3 (four instances, 7.13,25,28,8.3), 12.13-13.9 (three instances, 12.27, 13.3,8).

3. The switch from simple to conjunctive pronoun may be a stylistic device to mark the end of a given passage of dialogue. For example, the conversation between Matholwch and his swineherds has the following sequence: *heb vy* ... *heb ef* ... *heb wy* ... *heb ef* ... *heb wy* ... *heb ynteu* PKM 39.18-27. The fact that this passage is followed immediately by a single sentence of narrative and then another separate passage of dialogue makes it all the more important to provide it with a stylistic closure.

Another such instance is the opening conversation in the Third Branch between Manawydan and Pryderi, which has the following series: *heb ef* ... *heb y Pryderi* ... *heb ef* (without change of speaker) ... *heb ef* ... *heb y Pryderi* ... *heb ef* ... *heb y Pryderi* ... *heb ef* (without change of speaker) ... *heb ef* ... Ø (Pryderi) ... *heb ef* ... *heb ynteu* 49.6-50.7. One might also compare the exchange between Pwyll and his subjects on his return from Annwfn: *heb wy* ... *heb ynteu* ... *heb wy* ... *heb ynteu Pwyll* 8.7-17, where the incremental form serves as a closure to the dialogue.

4. Where several persons have been mentioned, the conjunctive pronoun may be used to identify which of them, normally the last mentioned, is referred to.

Gyrru a oruc Arthur y wyr yr erhyl, Eli a Thrachmyr, a Drutwyn keneu Greit mab Eri yny law ehun, a Gwarthegyt uab Kaw yghongyl arall a deu gi Glythmyr Letewic yny law ynteu, *a Bedwyr a Chauall ki Arthur yn y law* ynteu 'Arthur sent his men to the hunt, Eli and Trachmyr, and Drudwyn the whelp of Greid son of Eri in his own hand, and Gwarthegydd son of Caw in another quarter with the two hounds of Glythyr Ledewig in *his* hand, and Bedwar with Cafall, Arthur's hound, in *his* hand' *WM* 501.16,17

Here we have the short series *ehun* ... *ynteu* ... *ynteu*, with *ynteu* in each of the second two coordinate phrases performing the same identifying function as *ehun* in the first.

Sef ual yd eistedyssant, brenhin Ynys y Kedeirn, a Manawydan uab Llyr o'r neill parth idaw, a Matholwch o'r parth arall, a Branwen uerch Lyr gyt ac ynteu 'This is how they sat: the king of the Island of the Mighty with Manawydan son of Llŷr on one side of him and Matholwch on the other, and Branwen daughter of Llŷr next to him [Manawydan]' PKM 31.10

5. A conjunctive pronoun may stand in juxtapostion with a proper name (or definite noun), which it may precede or follow.

Ynteu Pwyll a oed yn dyuot o gylchaw Dyuet 'Pwyll himself was returning from a circuit of Dyfed' 25.20; *'Ie,' heb ynteu Pwyll, 'y mae yno ryw ystyr hut'* "'Yes,' said Pwyll, 'there is some magic meaning here'" 10.10; *Pwyll ynteu a doeth y Dyuet* 'Pwyll, however (for his part), came to Dyfed' 15.27 (In this last instance the pronoun has come to function as an adversative adverb; see §14 infra)

Where the pronoun precedes, the initial of the noun is mutated: *ynteu Gei*, *Per*. 22.18, 31.18.

The distribution of this combination is more irregular than the standard accounts would suggest. It is particularly interesting that the earliest of the texts closely surveyed here, *Kulhwch ac Olwen*, has by my reckoning not a single instance. This holds for *Owein* as well. For the Four Branches of the *Mabinogi* the figures are (the first number in brackets indicating the incidence with preposed pronoun, the second with postposed pronoun): *Pwyll* 16 (13 + 3), *Branwen* 1 (1 + 0), *Manawydan* 0, *Math* 11 (11 + 0), and for *Peredur* 14 (13 + 1). This raises the question whether the conjunction of noun and pronoun is an old and well established feature of Welsh discourse and narrative, or whether it is a relatively new development in the early Middle Welsh period, or one which simply becomes more common in the prose of this period.

Personal preference and contemporary fashion may have something to do with the uneven distribution of the syntagm in our core texts. In this regard two points may be mentioned. First, instances with the pronoun following the noun acccount for only a small proportion of the total. My impression is that this proportion increases in some later Middle Welsh prose texts, but this must await more comprehensive scrutiny. Secondly, there is the odd correlation between instances where the syntagm has a purely narrative function and those in which it identifies a speaker in *oratio recta*. In the Four Branches the relevant figures are 20:8, but with one exception in *Branwen*, all of the latter occur in the first two thirds of *Pwyll*. Of the eleven instances of the syntagm in *Math* none is used with *oratio recta*. Similarly, of the eleven instances in *Peredur* none indicates *oratio recta*. This is true also of the three instances with postposed pronoun in *Pwyll* itself.

The figures I have given exclude two examples which look similar to the others but which have in fact a somewhat different structure: *ac irwn y hwyneb hitheu Riannon a'r gwaet* 'and let us smear Rhiannon's face with the blood' PKM 20.18; *a thorri ohonaw ynteu Gradawc y galon o aniuyget* 'and Cradawg broke his heart with dispair' 46.3. In these cases the conjunctive pronoun is auxiliary to the possessive adjective preceding the noun, and syntactically the proper name is in apposition to the possessive adjective and conjunctive pronoun. It might also be noted here that the simple independent pronoun may occur in combination with a proper name: *A dechreu a wnaeth ef Uanawydan llunyaw corueu* 'And Manawydan began to make pommels' 52.22

The function of the collocation of noun and pronoun in narrative is to shift the focus, or the action, from one character to another; in dialogue it usually serves to indicate the transition to a different, named speaker, but it may occasionally refer to the last speaker mentioned where the two utterances are separated by an interval of time and an intervening narrative element:

'Ie,' heb ynteu Pwyll, 'y mae yno ryw ystyr hut. Awn parth a'r llys.' Y'r llys y doethant, a threulau y dyd hwnnw a wnaethant. A thrannoeth, kyuodi e uynyd a wnaethant, a threulaw hwnnw yny oed amser mynet y uwyta. A gwedy y bwyta kyntaf, 'Ie,' heb ynteu Pwyll, 'ni a awn ...' "'Yes,' said Pwyll, 'there is some magic meaning here. Let us go to the court.' They came to the court and passed that day. And on the next day they arose, and that too they passed until it was time to go to eat. And after the first sitting, 'Yes', said Pwyll, 'we will go ...'" 10.10,15

Since the speaker is identified by name, the conjunctive pronoun has no deictic function and consequently tends to assume an adverbial role - conjunctive, adversative, etc - the connotational value of which is largely determined by the context. This is so familiar that one example will suffice. When Teirnon and his wife bring the child Pryderi to court and are made welcome there, the text says *Ynteu Pwyll a oed yn dyuot o gylchaw Dyuet* 25.20, this could be variously translated as 'Pwyll was (just) then returning from a circuit of Dyfed', 'That was the time that Pwyll ...', 'Pwyll himself ...'. Whether this usage may be considered the starting point of the adverbial role of the conjunctive pronoun (see §14 infra) is uncertain.

6. The 2 sg./pl. imperative is frequently augmented by a concordant pronoun, which may have the conjunctive form.

dos ditheu ar Arthur y diwyn dy wallt 'Go to Arthur to have your hair trimmed' *WM* 454.31; *a ffa ueint bynnac a archo ef iti, adef ditheu y gaffel* 'and however much he demands of you, promise to get it' 476.33; *A bydwch gedymdeithon chwitheu a thatmaetheu idaw* 'And be you companions and fosterfathers to him' PKM 27.4; *A gwna ditheu dy ewyllus, Arglwyd* 'But do as you will, lord' 61.9; *a gwylya ditheu beth a wnel* 'and watch what he will do' *Owein* 593

The imperative may of course be unaccompanied, as in the sentences preceding the last example: *'Dos,' heb hi, 'a hwn genhyt, a dwc y march racko a'r dillat genhyt, a dot gyrllaw y dyn gynheu. Ac ir efo a'r ireit hwn ... a gwylya ditheu ... '* "'Go,' said she, 'and this with you, and take that horse and the garments with you, and set them near the man back there. And anoint him with this ointment ... and watch ...'" *Owein* 589-593 (in this instance the use of the conjunctive pronoun in the final clausula may be compared with the examples cited §3 supra). Or it may be followed by the simple affixed pronoun: *O chlywy diaspat dos wrthi ... O gwely tlws tec, kymer ti euo a dyro titheu y arall* 'If you hear an outcry, go towards it ... If you see a fair jewel, take it and give it to another' *Per.* 9.28-10.1 (which has the three variant forms of the imperative); *A chymerwch chwi y penn ... a dygwch hyt y Gwynuryn yn Llundein, a chledwch a'y wyneb ar Freinc ef* 'And take the head and bring it to the White Mount in London, and bury it with its face towards France' PKM 44.z; *Ar ny deryw o'r wled ... treulwch chwi* 'Continue with what is left of the feast' 50.z.

The conjunctive, as well as the simple, pronoun is also found with the semantically related jussive or hortatory future: *A wney ditheu gynghor arall?* 'Then will you follow a different counsel?' 49.15.

7. The conjunctive as well as the simple pronoun occurs after the affective form gwae.

Gwae uinheu uyn dyuot ar anuab 'Woe am I to have come to a childless man' *WM* 453.35 (beside *guae ui uy mot yn achaws y'r wydwic honn o'wyr Ynys y Kedyrn* 'woe am I that I should be the cause of this slaughter of the men of the Island of the Mighty' PKM 44.15; *guae ui o'm ganedigaeth* 'woe am I that ever I was born' 45.17)

8. The conjunctive pronoun has normally a certain adversative element, as for example when it signals a change of subject or speaker, but in some contexts this element is more pronounced.

(a) *deuparth uy oet a dodyw a deuparth y teu ditheu* 'Two thirds of my life are past and two thirds of yours' *WM* 457.26

Kei nyt edewis uynet namyn hyd yd elhut titheu 'Cei, I only promised to go as far as you would go' 472.34

Ny bo berthach byth y boch chwi no minheu 'May you never be more prosperous than me' 473.4

a meglyt a oruc Yspadaden Penkawr yn un or tri llechwayw guenhwynic a oed ac y law, ae odi ar eu hol. Ae aruoll a oruc Bedwyr. Ae odif ynteu 'and Ysbaddaden Pencawr seized one of the three poisoned stone spears which were by his hand and hurled it after them. And Bedwyr caught it and *he* hurled it back' 477.25

pan gaffwyf inheu a nottwyf arnat ti titheu a geffy uy merch 'when I obtain what I stipulate for you, you will then get my daughter' 479.33-34

y hachub a oruc y wrach, ac ymauael yn Hygwyd herwyd gwallt y benn ae daraw yr llawr deni. Ac ymauel o Gacmwri yndi hitheu 'the hag grabbed at them, catching Hywydd by the hair and throwing him to the floor beneath her. Then Cacamwri seized her' 506.2

Ac y dywawt Kulhwch, 'A eillwyt itti wr?' 'Eillwyt,' heb ynteu. 'Ae meu y minneu dy uerch di weithon?' 'Meu' [leg. 'Teu'], heb ynteu "And Culhwch asked, 'Have you been shaved, man?' 'I have,' said he. 'And is your daughter now mine?' 'She is,' he said" 506.35,36,37

The change of speaker (to Ysbaddaden Pencawr) is here marked twice by *ynteu*; *minneu* is more narrowly adversative, stressing the antithesis between the possessive pronoun *meu* and the possessive adjective *dy*. (The responsive *Meu* has usually been taken as an error for *Teu*, but it has been suggested to me that it may be an instance of *meu* having developed the meaning 'possession', like 3 sg. *eiddo*.)

(b) After the particle *neu*:

Neu titheu pwy vyt? 'And who are you?' 473.11

Neu chwitheu pwy ywch? 'And who are you?' 473.15

Neu chiwtheu kwt ymdewch? 'And you, where are you going?' 477:9

(c) To mark the juxtaposition of two contrasting verbs/actions:

Ac yna y lladawd ef Hir Peisawc brenhin Llydaw, a Llygatrud Emys a Gwrbothu ... Ac yna y llas ynteu 'And he then slew Hir Peisawg king of Llydaw, and Llygadrudd Emys and Gwrfoddw ... And then he himself was slain' 503.34

Here, as usual, there is an anaphoric reference, and it is adversative, its function being to mark a change of voice, creating a stylistic antithesis between the earlier active and the present passive verb. Cf.

Kacmwri ual y tynnit ef y uynyd y tynnei deu uaen ureuan ynteu yr affwys. Osla Gyllelluawr yn redec yn ol y Twrch, y dygwydwys y gyllell oe wein ac y kolles, ae wein ynteu gwedy hynny yn llawn or dwfyr, ual y tynnit ef y uynyd y tynnei hitheu ef yr affwys 'As Cacamwri was pulled upwards, two quernstones pulled him down to the depths. While Osla G. was running after the boar, his knife fell out of his sheath and he lost it, so that his sheath was then full of water. As he was pulled upwards, it pulled him back down to the depths' 505.4,7,10

The first *ynteu* points up the antithesis of Cacamwri being hauled up by his companions while at the same time he is being drawn down by the quernstones. The second *ynteu* has no pronominal function as such and is quasi-adverbial, viz, 'and his sheath consequently being full of water'. Like the first *ynteu*, *hitheu* marks the antithesis, and it refers anaphorically to *(g)wein*, but since the subject is a conjunctive pronoun (*hitheu*) in this instance, not a noun as in the first sentence (*deu uaen ureuan*), then the object of *y tynnei* must be simple *ef* (or an infixed pronoun *y* with auxiliary *ef*), not the *ynteu* of the earlier sentence.

One might compare these examples with that from *WM* 506.2. cited above, §8(a), where *hitheu* is used to juxtapose and contrast the maltreatment inflicted and the maltreatment suffered.

9. The conjunctive pronoun occurs as *nominativus pendens* after the conjunction *a*.

A mineu nys kelaf 'I will conceal him no longer' *WM* 454.7

'A oes porthawr?' 'Oes, a titheu ny bo teu dy penn pyr y kyuerchy di?' "'Is there a porter?' 'There is; and as for you - may your head not be yours - why do you ask?'" 456.2 (= 486.24)

a minneu ederyn ieuanc oodwn 'and as for me I was a young bird' 490.10

a minneu neut ydynt yn gynyon boneu vy esgyll 'and as for me, the roots of my wings are mere stumps' 491.15

'Awn,' heb ef, 'y'r orssed y eiste, a <u>*thitheu*</u>*,' heb ef, wrth was y uarch, 'kyfrwya uy march yn da'* "'Let us go to the mound to sit,' said he, 'and you,' he said to his groom, 'saddle my horse well'" *PKM* 11.19

a <u>*thitheu*</u> *... ni'th elwir bellach byth yn uorwyn* 'and you ... shall never henceforth be called maiden' 79.6

10. The conjunctive pronoun occurs with anaphoric reference after the conjunction *a* in the coordinating construction to which J. Gagnepain has assigned the term 'epitaxis' (Fr.*épitaxe*), *La syntaxe du nom verbal dans les langues celtiques. I. Irlandais* (Paris 1963), 119-124.

A phan daw yd oed widon yn ymordiwes a'r gwylwr, ac <u>*ynteu*</u> *yn diaspedein* 'And when he came, there was a witch overtaking the watchman and he shrieking' *Per.* 29.28

Dygaf y Duw uyg kyffes nat archaf i y wyr Gwyned ymlad drossof i, a <u>*minheu*</u> *uy hun yn cael ymlad a Phryderi* 'I confess to God I will not ask the men of Gwynedd to fight on my behalf since I can myself do battle with Pryderi' *PKM* 73.8

11. The conjunctive pronoun may be used as an appended object after the conjunction *a*.

'Na weleis,' heb ef, 'neut seith mlyned, un dyn yma, onyt pedwar dyn diholedic, a <u>*thitheu*</u> *yr awr honn'* "'Because for the last seven years,' said he, 'I have seen no one here except for four people in isolation, and yourself just now'" *PKM* 61.26

In Irish this construction would have the emphatic form of the personal pronoun: Mod Ir. '... *agus anois tusa*'.

12. The conjunctive pronoun may be used to emphasize or reinforce a verbal statement (though it is often difficult to represent this accurately in a written English translation).

(a) In declarative-responsive sentences to place emphasis on the answers:

'Due a wyr,' heb yr Owein, 'nat y gyrchu dy lewenyd y dodwyf i yma.' 'Duw a wyr,' heb <u>*ynteu*</u>*, 'nas keffy* <u>*ditheu*</u>*'* "'God knows,' said Owein, 'that it was not to seek your welcome that I came

here.' 'And God knows,' said the other, 'that you will not get it' *Owein* 802

Here *Ditheu* has the effect of affirming the negative answer. One might compare Irish response-sentences of the type *ni 'bhfuighidh 'tú* 'You will not (get it)', where the pronoun as well as the verb is stressed to emphasize the verbal response.

Meirych a gaffaf inheu a marchogaeth 'Horses I shall get and horsemen' *WM* 485.35 (which is in response to several of Ysbaddaden's assertions)

(b) To express resolve or determination:

Yn lledrata y keueis ef, a chyfreith lleidyr a wnaf inheu ac ef 'I caught it stealing, and I will execute upon it the penalty for stealing' PKM 62.7

lledrata a wnaeth arnaf, a dihenyd lleidyr a wnaf inheu arnaw ef 'It stole from me and I will execute upon it the penalty for stealing' 62.24 (one might take this as a simple adversative use were it not for the preceding example)

ar messur hwnnw yssyd gennyf ettwa. Hwnnw a uynnaf inheu y gaffel yn y tir newyd draw 'and I have that measure still. That I must have in the newly broken ground over there' *WM* 481.12

The conjunctive pronoun here highlights the inflexible, insistent nature of Ysbaddaden's request.

ac os gouut a daw, o gallaf les, mi a'e gwnaf. Afles ny wnaf inheu 'And if trouble comes, if I can do good, I will. Harm, however, I will not do' *Per*. 29.24

The conjunctive pronoun has no defining role here, and serves simply to reinforce the emphatic word-order. For this word-order in negative response-sentences cf. Mac Cana, *Ériu,* **24** (1973), 100-103.

(c) To express an assertion or affirmation:

'Arglwyd Owein,' heb ef, 'darogan oed dy dyuot ti yma y'm darestwng a thitheu a deuthost ac a orugost hynny' "'Lord Owein,' he said, 'there was a prophecy that you would come here to vanquish me, and that you have come and done' *Owein* 807

'Arglwyd,' heb wy, 'ny bu gystal dy wybot; ny buost gyn hygaret

guas ditheu; ny bu gyn hawsset gennyt titheu treulaw dy da' "'Lord,' said they, 'never were you so perceptive, never were you so lovable a man, never were you so free in spending your possessions'" *PKM* 8.9

13. The conjunctive pronoun may convey a sense of reciprocity.

yd yt uo mwyhaf y kyuarws a rothom mwyuwy uyd yn gwrdaaeth ninheu ac an clot 'The greater the bounty we show, the greater will be our own nobility and fame' *WM* 458.29 (where the conjunctive pronoun underlines the reciprocity of benefits involved)

y lledais uygcryuangheu y mywn ehawc ... ac y tynnwys ynteu ui hyt yr affwys 'I sank my claws into a salmon ... and he pulled me down into the depths' 492.3

Here the adversative use of the pronoun expresses a reciprocity of action and effect. For a similar adversative-reciprocal use cf.

Sef a wneuthum inheu, mi am holl garant, mynet yggwryf wrthaw y geissaw y diuetha. Kennadeu a yrrwys ynteu y gymot a mi 'And I went after him with my whole kindred to seek to destroy him; but he sent messengers to make peace with me' 492.5,8

'Ie,' heb wynteu, 'yr atteb goreu a gaffom ninheu, attat ti y down ac ef, ac aro ditheu yn kennadwri ninheu' "'Then,' they replied, 'the best answer we can get, we shall bring it to you, and you await our message'" *PKM* 41.18,19

In this one sentence we have four instances of the conjunctive pronoun. They are not necessary for clarity, but their adversative force serves to point up the reciprocal nature of the negotiations.

14. The conjunctive pronoun may be used adverbially.

As we have noted already, the pronoun is employed as an anaphoric index and may, for example, indicate a change of subject or speaker or select one of several referents. But it is sometimes used where its deictic role is weakened to the point where it becomes merely a vague anaphoric connector:

ny eill neb uynet drwydi, nyt oes bont arnei hitheu 'no one can cross it, for there is no bridge over it' *PKM* 40.26

There is no conjunction at the beginning of the second, semantically subordinate clause; this linking is provided by the conjunctive pronoun *hitheu*.

Mal y kyuyt rodi modrwy eur a oruc Culhuch itaw. Keissaw gwiscaw y uodrwy o honaw ac nyd ai idaw. Ay dodi a oruc ynteu y mys y uanec. ... a chymryt a oruc hitheu y uodrwy or uanec 'As he arose Culhwch gave him a gold ring. He tried to put on the ring, but it would not fit him, and he then put it in the finger of his glove. ... and she took the ring from the glove' *WM* 473.27

Hitheu marks a change of subject and refers to a person mentioned in the preceding sentence. But *ynteu* has no such function, since it indicates the same subject as in the preceding sentence, and its only role is as a linking (adverbial) element with the foregoing action, such as might be expressed as 'then, so'.

y chennatau a orucpwyd ae dyuot hitheu ... 'She was sent for and she came ...' 475.35

Here *hitheu* has no deictic function. It provides an anaphoric allusion which may be left untranslated, or may be rendered as 'and so she came', 'and she *did* come'.

Ac nyt gwr anhygar efo: gwr hagyr yw ynteu 'He is not unfriendly, but/however he is ugly' *Owein* 111

This might be compared with §8 supra.

... ac ymdeith yd aeth ef a'r deu varch ganthaw, a'm hadaw inheu yno. Ny wnaeth y gwr du o vawred ymdanaf i kymeint a'm karcharu inheu; nyt yspeilwys ynteu vi 'and off he went and the two horses with him, and left me there. The black man out of pride did not so much as (/The black man did not accord me so much respect as to) take me prisoner, nor did he even despoil me' 194,195,196

The first *inheu* is clearly adversative, but the second *inheu* and the following *ynteu* are adverbial rather than pronominal.

Nyd eynt wy o'y bod; nit oed reit udunt wynteu oc eu hanuod 'They would not go of their own volition, nor was there any need for them to go against their will' *PKM* 36.6

This quasi-adverbial use of *wynteu* might equally well be included among the examples of antithesis in §8 supra.

... a'r cadwyneu yn kyrchu yr awyr; a diben ny welei arnunt. Gorawenu a wnaeth ynteu wrth decket yr eur, a dahet gueith y cawc 'and the chains going up into the air, and he could see no end to them. He was enraptured with the beauty of the gold and the excellence of the bowl's workmanship' 56.14

There is no change of subject and *ynteu* must be adverbial, with a semantic nuance similar to that of French *alors*.

Y neuad ynteu a gyweirwyt y Pwyll a'e niuer 'The hall was then made ready for Pwyll and his retinue' 18.16

Here the transition from pronoun to adverb is confirmed by the fact that it differs in gender from the preceding noun. We are already very close to the simple adverbial use of *ynteu* in later Middle Welsh in such phrases as *Paham, ynteu* 'why, then?' and *Pwy, ynteu*? 'who, then' quoted by John Morris-Jones from *LlA* (1913: 273) and still current in modern spoken Welsh: *cerwch 'ta* 'go then' (O. H. Fynes-Clinton, *The Welsh Vocabulary of the Bangor District* (Oxford 1913), 520; also 398).

15. The conjunctive pronoun has sometimes an incremental function. Only a slight shift of emphasis is required to move from the adversative to the incremental.

nyt da im yndi ac nyṭ digrif ... kynny cheissych ditheu wneuthur cam im 'I have no comfort or pleasure here, without you too trying to cause me harm' *WM* 489.20

Dos ym erchi ym tat, a ffa ueint bynnac a archo ef iti, adef ditheu y gaffel a minheu a geffy 'Go to ask my father for me. And however much he demands of you, promise to get it and you will get me as well' 476.34

First we have the familiar use of *ditheu* after the imperative 2 sg. and secondly the adversative *minheu* shading off into the sense of 'me also, me then'.

A'r llu a bebyllywys yg kylch y castell, ac yr rodi bywyt y'r iarll y rodes ef y dwy iarllaeth idi trachefyn. Ac yr rydit idaw ynteu y rodes hanher y gyfoeth e hun 'And the army pitched its tents around the castle. And in return for granting his life to the earl he gave back to her the two earldoms, and in return for his freedom as well he gave up half of his own realm' *Owein* 656

Since there is no change of subject, *ynteu* must be used adverbially, and the sense seems to be augmentative or incremental.

Emystynnu idaw ynteu yn y peir, yny dyrr y peir yn pedwar dryll, ac yny dyrr y galon ynteu 'He stretched himself out in the cauldron, so that the cauldron burst in four pieces and so that his heart burst as well' *PKM* 44.19

16. The conjunctive pronoun occurs commonly in the 'either/or' construction.
The combination *ae* ('is it?') ... *ae* (Evans, 1964: 86-87, 174-175), or *ae ... neu* is familiar in Middle and early Modern Welsh. It came to be used so frequently with the conjunctive pronoun as to invest the latter with a new function and meaning. This kind of construction varies greatly in frequency from text to text, and it is not always easy to decide in what measure this disparity is chronological or merely stylistic. The only relevant example I have noted in *KO* is

Hyd pan dywettych ti nat oes hi yny byt neu ninheu ae caffom, nyn hyscarhawr a thi 'Until you say that she does not exist in the world, or until we find her, we will not be parted from you' *WM* 470.35

This does not use *ae/ay ... ae/ay (neu)*, but it poses alternatives with *neu* + the conjunctive pronoun introducing the second of them. In instances such as this the pronoun may be justified as marking a change of subject, but one can see how it gradually came to be considered an essential component of the sign of alternation.

I have noted no example in *Branwen*, *Manawydan* or *Owein*, but the following occurs in *Pwyll*:

kynnedyf yr orssed yw, pa dylyedauc bynnac a eistedo arnei, nat a odyno heb un o'r deupeth, ay kymriw neu archolleu, neu ynteu a welei rywedawt 'It is the peculiarity of the mound that whatever nobleman sits upon it will go from there without one of two things: either wounds or blows, or else he would see a wonder' *PKM* 9.7

Here we have *ay ... neu* and then another *neu* followed

immediately by the conjunctive pronoun, itself the subject of a verbal clause.

The author of *Peredur* seems to have a penchant for the 'either/or' construction. In the first of my examples the alternative is expressed by simple *neu*:

A dyuot y ymgynnic ittitheu, arglwyd, yn y wed y bo hygar genhyt, yr bot yn nerth in y'n dwyn odyma *neu* *y an hamdiffyn* *ninheu* *yma* 'And I have come to offer myself to you, lord, in whatever way you think fit, in return for your support to us to bring us away from here or to defend us where we are' *Per.* 25.23

Although *ninheu* must come after the possessive + verbal noun and is therefore separated from *neu*, its function is essentially the same as in the instances cited above.

Ny dylyei neb kyffro marchawc vrdawl y ar y medwl y bei arnaw yn aghyfartal, kanys atuyd *ae* *collet ar dothoed idaw,* *neu* *ynteu* *yn medylyaw am y wreic uwyhaf a garei* 'No one should disturb an ordained knight discourteously from the meditation in which he is engaged; for it may be that he has suffered loss or else that he is thinking of the woman he loves best' 32.10

Syntactically *ynteu* is still subject of the following progressive verbal noun phrase, but it is also in the process of being functionally attached to *neu*.

Vn o'r ffyrd hyn a a y'm llys i, ac vn o'r deu a gyghoraf i itti, *ae* *mynet y'r llys o'r blaen at vyg gwreic i yssyd yno,* *ae* *titheu* *a arhoych yma* 'One of these roads leads to my court, and one of two things I advise you: either to go on ahead to the court to my wife who is there, or else that you wait here' 48.21

The sense of this statement could be expressed more simply by two coordinate verbal nouns, *ae mynet ... ae arhos*, but there is a tendency in the 'either/or' construction to generalize the use of a conjunctive pronoun followed by a relative clause or a verbal noun.

Mae y neill peth: *ae* *tydi yn wr o bell,* *ae titheu* *yn ynuyt* 'It is one of two things: either you are someone from afar or you are a fool' 53.3

It may be noted that, while the first *ae* is followed by the reduplicated pronoun, the second has the conjunctive form, as has become characteristic of the alternating formula. This sequence occurs also in the next example:

Gwna y neyll peth ... ae tydi a tynho dy penn ymdeith, ae titheu a el y'r twrneimeint 'Do one of two things ... either turn your head away or go to the tournament' 54.3

Dewis ti, vnben, ae ti elych y'r llys, ae titheu dyuot gyt a mi y hela 'Choose, chieftain, whether you will go to the court or come with me to hunt' 62.28

Here the pronominal sequence is simple ... conjunctive, and it is clear that the latter has become the regular sign, with *ae/neu*, of the second phrase of the 'either/or' construction. Eventually this led to the Modern Welsh use of the pronoun alone as the equivalent of *ai/neu* + pronoun: *nyd ydych yn sicr pa un ai cysgu wnewch, ynteu ceisio barddoni* (cf. M. Richards, *Cystrawen y Frawddeg Gymraeg* (Caerdydd 1938), §§ 175 (b), 157). Concurrently with this another change took place which is exemplified in the same Modern Welsh sentence. In the period covered by the texts examined here the person and number of the conjunctive pronoun changed in accord with its referent, but, as with other comparable linguistic features, the 3 sg. masc., *ynteu*, being the most frequent form, gradually became generalized in all contexts.

* * * * * * * * * * * * * *

The foregoing notes are intended as an approximate not an exhaustive syntactic-semantic classification of the uses of the conjunctive pronouns in some of the principal Middle Welsh prose texts. In particular, they do not include some points of special interest raised by several individual instances of the conjunctive pronouns within the texts surveyed. These I hope to discuss on another occasion.

References

Evans, D. S. (1964) *A Grammar of Middle Welsh*. Dublin: Dublin Institute for Advanced Studies.

Morris-Jones, J. (1913) *A Welsh Grammar*. Oxford: Clarendon Press.

Pedersen, H. (1909/1913) *Vergleichende Grammatik der keltischen Sprachen*, 2 vols. Göttingen: Vandenhoeck & Ruprecht (repr. 1976).

Russell, P. (1982/83) The Origin of the Welsh Conjunctive Pronouns. *BBCS,* **30,** 30-38.

Über *Albiōn*, *elfydd*, *Albiorīx* und andere Indikatoren eines keltischen Weltbildes

Wolfgang Meid
Universität Innsbruck

Wie wir wissen, ist der Name *Albiōn* - in dieser seiner ältesten Lautform aus griechisch-lateinischer Überlieferung bekannt, in jüngerer Lautform auch insular bezeugt - einer der ältesten Namen für Britannien, und offenbar älter als letzterer Name selbst, da er in historischer Zeit fast völlig von diesem verdrängt ist. Lediglich im Irischen hat er sich im lebendigen Gebrauch erhalten: in der alt- und mittelirischen Überlieferung ist *Albu* (Genetiv *Alban*) das überseeische Pendant zu *Ériu* (Genetiv *Érenn*), dem Namen der eigenen Insel. In einem engeren Sinn ist *Albu* zwar meist der Name für Schottland, doch ist dies zweifellos eine Einengung der ursprünglich allgemeineren Geltung des Namens, deren sich auch die frühirische Überlieferung noch bewußt ist, auf das Gebiet, wo im frühen Mittelalter die Verwandten der Iren - die Auswanderer aus Irland - sich angesiedelt hatten. Ursprünglich erstreckte sich der Name somit auf die gesamte britische Hauptinsel, wie auch Beda zu Anfang seiner englischen Kirchengeschichte betont (I,1), der den Namen in seiner älteren, aus der Antike bekannten Form zitiert (die Stelle geht wohl auf Plinius zurück): *Britannia Oceani insula cui quondam Albion nomen fuit*. Ein anderer überlieferter Name ist *insula Albionum* (Avienus). Dem Namen *Albiōn* liegt wohl das indogermanische Farbadjektiv **albho-* 'weiß' zugrunde (lat. *albus*), das auch im Namen der Alpen (*Alpēs*) und in zahlreichen Flußnamen (*Albis* 'Elbe') erscheint. Nach einer älteren Theorie wäre die britannische Hauptinsel nach den weißen

Kreidefelsen ihrer Südküste benannt worden, vielleicht von frühen indogermanischen Einwanderern. Daß auch schon vor den eigentlichen Kelten indogermanische Einwanderer nach Britannien gekommen waren, dafür gibt es auch sonst Anhaltspunkte, namentlich in der Gewässernamengebung, die in der älteren Schicht vorkeltisch, aber indogermanisch ist ("alt-europäische" Hydronymie nach H. Krahe).

Mir ist jedoch wahrscheinlicher, daß der Name nicht eine real- topographische, sondern eine mythologische Signifikanz hatte. Im Kymrischen gibt es in poetischen Texten ein Wort *elfydd* m., das 'Welt' bedeutet und aufgrund der kymrischen Lautgesetze auf britannisch **albii̯o*–, indogermanisch folglich **albhii̯o*–, zurückgehen muß. Wenn wir uns erinnern, daß es noch ein anderes Wort für 'Welt', nämlich **dubno*–, *dumno*– (in altirisch *domun*), gab, so haben wir möglicherweise zwei in ihren semantischen Konnotationen verschiedene, ja gleichsam gegensätzliche Wörter, die verschiedene "Welten" in einem kosmologischen System bezeichneten. Denn **dubno*– (*dumno*–) hat Assoziationen zu **dub*– 'tief', 'dunkel, schwarz' und 'Wasser' - Bedeutungen, die wir auf verschiedene Lexeme verteilt im Keltischen und in verwandten Sprachen finden, die sich aber alle unter einer Wurzel, indogermanisch **dheub*–/*dhub*– subsumieren lassen (Pokorny, *Indogermanisches etymologisches Wörterbuch* 267f., 264), während **albio*– Assoziationen zu Licht, Helligkeit und oberen Regionen hat. Auch die germanischen Alben oder Elfen gehören als Lichtwesen in diesen Zusammenhang; nach der nordgermanischen *Snorra Edda* wohnten die Lichtalben im Himmel, die Schwarzalben - ihr negatives Gegenstück - in der Erde. Es scheint also, daß in einem ursprünglichen kosmologischen System **albio*– die lichte Oberwelt und **dubno*– die Erde mit ihren dunklen Tiefen, gelagert in Wasser, bezeichnete. Daß man seinen Lebensraum als "die Welt" bezeichnet, ist verständlich und hat viele Parallelen. Was die Assoziation mit 'Licht' betrifft, sei auf slawisch *svet* 'Welt' = 'Licht' verwiesen. Zur Stütze des Gesagten kann man noch auf die mit diesen Lexemen gebildeten Herrschernamen auf *-rīx* verweisen, wo zu **albio*– ein *Albio-rīx* und zu **dubno*–, *dumno*– ein *Dumno-rīx* gehört. *Albiorīx* ist, identifiziert mit Mars, Genius des hochragenden Berges Ventoux in der Provence, und nicht weit davon ist auch eine Göttin *Albiorīca* bezeugt. Ἀλβιοριξ /Albioriks/ ist ferner der Name eines

Galaterfürsten, und *Dumnorīx* ist aus Caesar als Fürst der Haeduer bekannt. Beide Namen bedeuten, mit ursprünglich gegensätzlichen semantischen Konnotationen, 'Weltkönig' - quasi eine göttergleiche Bezeichnung. Da mit *rīx* 'Herrscher, König' das denominale Suffix *-no-* funktionell gleichwertig sein kann (**Teuto-rīx*, kymrisch *Tud-ri*: gotisch *Þiudans* usw. < **teuto-no-s*), dürfte auch der Stammesname *Dumnonii* im Südwesten Britanniens (der im heutigen *Devon* fortlebt) auf einer semantisch gleichwertigen Herrscherbezeichnung basieren und somit ebenfalls ein Name mit mythologischer Signifikanz sein: die *Dumnonii* sind offenbar 'die Leute des **Dumno-no-s*', des 'Weltherrschers', eines Gottes oder göttergleichen Königs (= *Dumno-rīx*). Man darf hier auch an den Namen des zentralgallischen Stammes der *Bitu-rīges* erinnern, der ebenfalls 'Weltkönige' beziehungsweise 'die Leute des Weltkönigs' (des **Bitu-rīx*) bedeutet. In diesem Zusammenhang verdient ferner Beachtung der britannische Stammesname *Coriono-tōtae*, der im Vorderglied ebenfalls eine *-no-*Bildung enthält, abgeleitet von **kori̯o-* 'Heer'. Wenn man hier dem Suffix *-no-* die gleiche überordnende Funktion zuschreibt, wäre das zugrundeliegende **Kori̯o-no-s* als 'der Heerführer' zu interpretieren und könnte mit altnordisch *Herjann*, Beiname des Gottes Odin (= Wodan), gleichgesetzt werden. Appellativisch liegt die Bezeichnung im homerischen Griechisch vor: κοίρανος (aus *κοιρονος < **kori̯o-no-s* umgebildet). Da im interkulturellen Vergleich der germanische Wodan dem römischen Merkur, und dieser wiederum dem keltischen *Lugus* entspricht, könnte hinter dem britischen **Kori̯onos* ebenfalls ein Gott, und zwar *Lugus*, stehen. Dies ist freilich Spekulation, die sich auf nichts anderes als die Plausibilität des Arguments stützen kann. Sie fügt sich aber in den Gesamtzusammenhang. Das 'Heer' des Kriegergottes Odin ist bekanntlich ein Totenheer: die Krieger, die ihm ihr Leben geweiht haben, sind als gefallene Tote mit ihm vereint.[1]

Die keltischen Bezeichnungen für 'Welt', **albio-* und **dubno-*, in historischer Zeit durch Zerfall des sinngebenden Weltbildes isoliert und zu lexikalischen Varianten geworden, sind ursprünglich komplementäre Begriffe in einem (zumindest) zweiteiligen Weltbild, in welchem **albio-* , als **albhi-i̯o-* 'durch Licht, Helligkeit (**albho-*) charakterisiert', den oberen (lichthaften, 'himmlischen') Teil der Welt, **dubno-*, als **dhub-no-* 'durch

Tiefe, oder Dunkel, (**dhub-*) charakterisiert', den unteren (dunklen, 'chtonischen') Bereich, die 'Gegenwelt' dazu, symbolisieren. Dieses 'Oben' oder 'Unten', 'Hell' oder 'Dunkel' kann auch mit 'Süden' oder 'Norden' assoziiert sein, je nach mythologischer Konnotation (die Totenwelt war im Norden gedacht). In ihrem irdischen Leben fühlten sich die Menschen wohl gruppenweise jeweils dem einen oder anderen mythologischen Bereich zugeordnet.

In der mittelkymrischen Literatur finden sich bekanntlich noch mythologische Erinnerungen an die 'normale', die Oberwelt (welche ursprünglich wohl **albio–* hieß), und ihren Gegenpol, die 'andere', die Unterwelt, welche *annwfn* (das ist **an-dwfn*) heißt.

Anmerkung

1. Früher neigte ich dazu, den Namen *Coriono-tōtae* als 'Volk der Heerleute' zu deuten und in dem Vorderglied eine Bildung mit zuordnender Funktion des Suffixes zu sehen (**korio-no-s* 'Angehöriger des Heeres', Plural kollektiv 'Heerleute'; vergleiche die zuordnende Bedeutung in *Teutonī* 'Volksgenossen' gegenüber der überordnenden in gotisch *þiudans* 'Oberhaupt der *þiuda*'). Heute halte ich es angesichts der Parallele *Dumnonii* doch für nicht unwahrscheinlich, daß in *Coriono-* hier die überordnende Bedeutung vorliegt, der Name somit 'die Scharen des Heerführers' (in einem dem germanischen *Herjann* vergleichbaren Sinne) bedeuten könnte.

   Zum Suffix *-no-* sei hier nur noch soviel bemerkt, daß seine 'überordnende' Funktion (wie sie in gotisch *þiudans*, lateinisch *dominus* und in Götternamen, die das Walten über einen Bereich zum Ausdruck bringen, wie *Bellōna*, vorliegt) im Keltischen zwar ebenfalls belegbar ist, beispielsweise im Namen der Pferdegöttin *Epona* ('Herrin der Pferde'), daß typischer hier aber seine (im Lateinischen durch *patrōnus*, *mātrōna* belegbare) augmentative Funktion ist: *Mātrona* die 'Große Mutter', *Maponos* ihr göttlicher Sohn, kymrisch *gwron* 'Held' (< **u̯iro-no-s* 'Mann par excellence'). Bei diesen augmentativen Bildungen ist die Ableitung wesensgleich mit dem Grundwort, das "endozentrisch" in ihr enthalten ist; bei *Epona*, **Dumno-no-s* usw. liegt dagegen ein "exozentrisches" Verhältnis des Grundwortes zur Ableitung vor, was sich semantisch als Überordnung des abgeleiteten Personenbegriffs über den Bereich des Grundwortes kundtun kann.

W. Meid, "Das Suffix *-no-* in Götternamen", *Beiträge zur Namenforschung,* **8,** (1957), 72-108, 113-126; "Die Königsbezeichnung in den germanischen Sprachen", *Die Sprache,* **12,** (1966), 182-189; *Germanische Sprachwissenschaft III: Wortbildungslehre*, (Berlin 1967), § 94.2b.

Welsh *moes*

Eric P. Hamp
University of Chicago

1. We pose ourselves the problem of explaining the genesis and development of *moes*:

moes fy march 'give me my horse'
moes imi y gorulwch 'give me the goblet'
moesswch attaf i 'give me (pl) <to me>'

2. Let us note the simplex:

Welsh and Med. Bret. *ro*, BD 137.18 *dyro* (≡ *dy-ro*), WM 478.3 *doro* (≡ *dy-ro* or **dā+ro*?) 'give'; Gaul. *da* (*ă*?) (Simon Evans, 1964 155 §175).

These forms show that *moes* is a portmanteau and not a mistranslation. From this point on we label the grammatical criteria for each observation.

3. We note the construction and accentuation of a verbal complex:

OIr. *ticed* < **'t(o)inketV* < **to'enk* (syntax) ∴ **'to-ro-dā̆* > **toroð* (= OIr. *tog*: *do·goa*) → *doro(ð)* → *dyro* (Welsh *dy-* < **to-'*)

4. And with an *enclitic, or infixed, pronoun:

do-m·iced < **to-me'inketV*
du-m·em-se < **di-me'*Vb (syntax)
no-m·ain 'spare me' (Thurneysen, 1946 §588) **nu-me'aness-*
∴ **to-me'V...* > **to'mV...* (phonetic)

5. Observe an infixed object pronoun with dative value (semantax):

Simon Evans, 1964 §175 pres. 3sg. *ryd*, *dyry*, 'gives': §61 *dy-m-ryt*, 'gives me'

**(to-)'ro-d-ī-t* — **to-me'ro-d-ī-t(*-mi/u?)*
y'm oed 'I had (=was to me)'
**i-dhe-me'esāt*

6. In the Indo-European background we find:

Oscan-Umbrian *fust*, 'erit', Umbrian *ferest*, 'feret' (categories); vowel ablaut alternation: (Schmidt, 1966, 23)

πείσομαι	:	ἔπαθον	**bhendh-s-o-*	:	*bhndh-o-*
τεύξομαι	:	ἔτυχον	**teukso-*	:	*tukh-o-*
			(morphology)		
			**dheugh-s-o-*(?)	:	*dhugh-o-* (?)

7. Celtic shows verbal deuterotonesis and Wackernagel's enclisis: *dyret* 'come!': *redec* (verbal noun):
**to'rete* **retikā*
Simon Evans, 1964 136 §143, n7

ryres = OIr. *ress-*, *·ré* : *rethid* 'runs'
**ro'ret-s-ti* 'may run' **ret-s-t* **ret-e-t-i-s*
(Schmidt, 1966, 19, 24)
Simon Evans, 1964 128 §137, n

(lexicon, morphology = §6)

8. On the basis of the above, we choose the desired string and perform the indicated derivation:
**to-me'ret-s-si* (*me* as goal of GO) ≅ OIr. *tair* 'come' < **t(o)'a-erge*[1]: *eirg(g)* 'go!'
→ **to-me'ressi* 'may you come to me' (phonetic) + CAUSATIVE
> **to-me'rossi* (: **ro-dă*, and as with causative *-o-* in root; cf. *hollti*, *torri*, *troi*) (semantics, morphology)
= **to-me'ro-oss-* (*ry phrinom-ne* 'may we deserve'; with pronoun:
o'th ry ledir 'if thou wilt be kiiled',
ry lad v.n. 'having slain',
guedy eu ry lad 'after they had been killed')
(phrasal morphology)

≅ **to–me–oss-* (aspectual *ro–*) (semantics)
→ **to'meoss-* (prevocalic rule; see §4)
→ **(to)meoss-* (= *ro* : *dyro*; see §2) "(a)syndeton" of **to* in old sentence connective value (syntax)
> *moes* (: *oedd*, *Lloegr*; phonetic - Lautgesetz)[2]

9. As a coda, we may attempt to make the best of an earlier proposal. Morris-Jones 1913, 380 would have **moi estō(d)*, which violates IE grammar.

But we may start with impv. 3sg. *caret* **kar–e–tō̆(t)*: Lat. *estō*, Greek ἔστω: *rothid* 'give'.

10. Then we form a string and derive:
**(p)ro–me'es–tō̆(t)* 'let be to me = let me have'
→ **ro'm–essV*
> **(to–)m'ro–ess-* (*ro* moved before *ro'* > *ry*)
= **(to–)m–(y)r–'oess* (by Simon Evans, 1964, §187)
≅ *(to–)'moess* (aspectual *ro-*; semantics)
This derivation requires more unmotivated changes.

11. To do adequate historical reconstruction one cannot keep grammatical or structural levels apart.

Notes

1. See Hamp (1987: 433-35) for an account of *-a-*.
2. See Hamp (1974: 269-70); and Hamp (1982: 83-5).

References

Evans, D. Simon (1964) *A Grammar of Middle Welsh*. Dublin: Institute for Advanced Studies.

Hamp, E. P. (1974) Miscellanea: II some difficult Welsh forms in *oe*. *Studia Celtica*, **8/9**, 269-70.

Hamp, E. P. (1982) *Lloegr*: The Welsh name for England. *Celtic Studies*, **4**, 83-5.

Hamp, E. P. (1987) OIr. *'tab(a)ir* 'brings', *'taít* 'comes'. In G. Cardona and N. Zide (eds.), *Festschrift for Henry Hoenigswald*. Tübingen: Gunter Narr. Pp 433-35.

Morris-Jones, J. (1913) *A Welsh Grammar: Historical and Comparative*. Oxford: Oxford University Press.

Schmidt, K. H. (1966) Konjunktiv und Futurum im Altirischen. *Studia Celtica,* 1, 19-26.

Thurneysen, R. (1946) *A Grammar of Old Irish*. (Translated by D. A. Binchy and O. Bergin). Dublin: Institute for Advanced Studies.

Word-Order Patterns in *Breudwyt Ronabwy*

Erich Poppe
University of Marburg

0. Introduction

The following survey of word-order patterns in the Middle Welsh native tale *Breudwyt Ronabwy* is based on a corpus containing all positive verbal statements of the text, i.e. all positive main clauses with a communicative force other than question, response, wish, and command, with the exception only of copula- sentences. Its aim is to provide the discussion of MW syntax and stylistics with comprehensive statistics of the forms of one sentence-type in one text, and it is thus indebted in its approach to T. Arwyn Watkins's analyses of *Branwen*, *Manawydan*, and *Kulhwch ac Olwen* (Watkins, 1983/84, 1977/78, 1988).

Literary historians generally agree that *Breudwyt Ronabwy* is "the last wholly native tale to be written in the Middle Welsh tradition" (Roberts, 1976: 234). There is also agreement that it is a highly artistic and literary work. But, as P. Mac Cana has pointed out, it is "not a story in the sense that the other texts of the Mabinogi are stories [...] It does not tell a tale, but rather creates a situation comprising several sustained images" (Mac Cana, 1977: 87). He describes it as a "prolonged parody of native genres and styles" (Mac Cana, 1977: 87). Literary critics do not agree whether the tale was intended to be read or to be listened to: P. Mac Cana (1977: 93) calls it a "written text intended to be read", whereas M. Richards stresses:

"mai chwilio am effaith ar glust ac nid ar lygad y byddai'r cyfarwyddiaid [...] Cynulleidfa o wrandawyr oedd ganddynt ac nid darllenwyr" (Richards 1948: xliii)

G. Jones and Th. Jones (1974: xxvi) appear to feel uneasy about a lack of coherence of the text: "In detail *The Dream of Rhonabwy* is impeccable, the portraits shine like jewels, but the whole hardly equals, much less exceeds, the sum of its parts". R. M. Jones, however, has recently stressed that "a medieval audience was more prepared to accept some sort of self-containment in the various units forming the 'flow of events'" (Jones, 1986: 186) and that therefore "the impression left on a medieval reader by the disjointed details of Breuddwyd Rhonabwy would be less incongruous than they are to us" (Jones, 1986: 187).

Breudwyt Ronabwy has been transmitted in only one manuscript, the *Red Book of Hergest* (c. 1375-1425); it may have been contained in the now incomplete *White Book of Rhydderch*. M. Richards (1948: xi) points out that the text must have been known well enough in the 14th century for poets to refer to it.

The date of the text is still under discussion. There are basically three suggestions:
(1) in Madawc uab Maredud's lifetime (Madog ap Maredudd, referred to in the first line of the text) or very shortly after his death in 1160;
(2) in the early 13th century, before the middle of the 13th century;
(3) between 1293 and the death of Gruffydd ap Owein in 1309.

The "succession of illuminated pages" (Jones and Jones, 1974: xxvi) in *Breudwyt Ronabwy* has repercussions for its syntactic structure, since its characteristic feature is the sequence of long descriptive passages of warriors, of their dress, armour and of the trappings of their horses which contain only few verbal sentences. This is also reflected in the colophon which says that no bard or story-teller would know the story without a written text because of these descriptive passages (even if this statement is not to be taken at face-value).

A complete syntactic description of the text would have to include sentences without a finite verb as well as verbal sentences other than positive statements. But perhaps the most controversial issue in MW syntax is the filling of the pre-verbal position in positive statements and the phenomena covered by the terms 'mixed' and 'abnormal' sentences in traditional MW descriptive syntax (see the bibliographical references in Jones (1986: 198, n.124)). T. A. Watkins (1977/78: 376; 1987: 57; 1988: 5) has suggested comprising 'abnormal' and 'mixed' order as '*trefn berthynol*', 'relative' or 'cleft' order.

It is a well-known feature of the syntax of MW prose that the statistically 'normal' word-order in a positive statement is 'abnormal', at least in current grammatical terminology, but also when compared to the dominant verb-initial order VSO in Old and Modern Welsh (for Old Welsh see Watkins (1987)). In its place we find an order in which (at least) one sentence-constituent precedes the verb. This constituent can be the subject or the object or an adverbial expression. We can thus posit the following basic sequence of constituents in a positive statement in MW prose (the position of adverbial expressions within the sentence following the verb is not taken into account):

C_2, C_1 V (S) (O)

C_1 is the position of the fronted constituent which governs the relative pronoun or particle. C_2 is the position of the second fronted constituent (usually an adverbial expression, see the statistics below) in a double-fronting situation. It can be preceded by further fronted constituents. S and O are the unmarked positions of subject and object if not fronted. The rules which underlie the choice of C_1 and C_2 in a sentence are still under discussion. For the purpose of this survey a purely descriptive approach is taken; all positive statements in the relativized order are classified according to the constituent which governs the relative pronoun or particle.

The edition used here is Melville Richards's (1948); references are to the page and the line in which the finite verb of the sentence under discussion occurs.

1. Classification of word-order patterns

1.1 Verb-initial sentences

There are two clear examples of positive statements with the finite verb in initial position, in what T. A. Watkins (1977/78: 376) has called the 'verbal order' ('*trefn uniongyrchol*'):

Ac y doeth Ronabwy ... (2.5), *neur derw llad dy uackwyeit* ... (17.10)

They occur in a narrative passage and in direct speech. The pre-verbal particle *neur* is used with *derw* as auxiliary (Evans,

1964: 170). Not included are the instances of sentences containing the defective verb *heb* 'says, said', which always occurs in clause-initial position.

There is one ambiguous example of a verb-initial positive statement:

Ac odyna Idawc a gymerth Ronabwy is y gil, ac y kychwynnyssont y llu mawr hwnnw bop bydin yn y chyweir parth a Chevyn Digoll. (9.8)

In the preceding sentence, the subject *Idawc* is fronted and governs the relative pronoun *a*, the adverb *odyna* precedes it in C_2. Note the lack of concord between *kychwynnyssont* and *y llu mawr hwnnw* which suggests that the noun-phrase functions as an apposition to the subject contained in the personal ending of the verb (see the corresponding translation by Jones and Jones (1974: 143) and PKM 64.13 for a similar example, also with a collective noun of the *llu* type, namely *teulu*). It is perhaps possible to interpret *y kychwynnyssont* as syntactically dependent on *odyna*, but such a syntactic pattern in co-ordinate sentences (where C_1 governs the choice of relative pronoun in the first clause and C_2 the choice of relative particle in the second) does not appear to be otherwise attested. It seems thus best to classify this sentence as a doubtful example of a verb-initial positive statement.

Sentence 12.3, *yny vyd mackwy [...] yn dyuot*, even if semantically a main clause (see Parry-Williams, 1922: 103), is formally introduced by a conjunction, and the position of the finite verb immediately following *yny* is therefore regular.

1.2 Pronominal subject + a *+ verb*

Chwi a'e keffwch ... (4.20), *Mi a'e dywedaf* ... (4.29), *Y ran a weda ymi y rodi mi a'e rodaf* (5.30), *Mi a'e keueis* (6.24), *wynteu a dylyant* ... (7.15), *Minneu a'e kymeraf* ... (8.12), *Miui a gerdaf* (8.27), *Ef a'e kyfarchwys* ... (12.19), *ti a glywy* ... (12.26)

There are nine instances of this pattern, all in direct speech, which agrees with the findings of Watkins (1977/78: 395). In one instance (5.30) the pronominal subject is preceded by a *nominativus pendens* (left-dislocated phrase) which is taken up in the clause proper by an infixed pronoun. This left-dislocated element is not a constituent of the sentence, but is syntactically independent.

1.3 Noun subject + a *+ verb*

Ac yn yr amser hwnnw brawt a oed idaw (1.4), *A gwr a oed ar y keis hwnnw* (2.4), *A blaenbren oed gan vn onadunt* ... (2.25), *A chyscu a disgynnwys* ... (3.19), *A'r gwyr racko a gaffant* ... *ac a gaffant* ... (7.12,13), *Reit oed itt* ... (8.7), *Ac odyna Idawc a gymerth* ... (9.7), *A'r gwr* ... *a vydei ar eu kanawl* ... (10.9) *A'r hwnn* ... *a vydei ar yr ymyl* (10.10), *A'r gwr* ... *yssyd yn bryssyaw* ... (10.20), *a'r gwr* ... *yssyd yn ffo* ... (10.22), *Y mackwy a dywawt* ... (13.17), *A chynnwryf mawr a uu yn yr awyr* ... (15.4), *Lliw enryued a oed ar y uarch* ... (15.13), *Y mackwy a gyuarchawd* ... *ac a dywawt* ... (16.9,10), *A digawn o lu a deuth* ... (20.5)

There are sixteen instances of this pattern; in two sentences the fronted noun subject is preceded by a scene-setting (1.4) or a connective (9.7) adverb in C_2 (double-fronting).

1.4 Object + a *+ verb*

A hwnnw a gymerth goueileint mawr yndaw ... (1.6), *A chyghor a gymerth Madawc* ... (1.18), *Breckan lwytkoch galetlom toll a dannwyt* ... (3.15), *a'e ohen a'e vryt a debygei* ... (3.28), *A thrugared a gefeis* (5.16), *A hynny a oruc y marchawc* ... (6.2), *Y gwas ieuanc kymhennaf a doethaf a wneir* ... (8.16), *Gwir a dywedy* (8.27), *A phan tynnit y cledyf o'r wein, ual dwy fflam o tan a welit* ... (10.29), *Y gware hwnnw a teruynwyt* ... (13.25), *ac ar ny las onadunt wynt a vrathwyt ac a vriwyt* ... (14.16), *Penneu rei a dygynt* (15.2), *A'r ystorya honn a elwir* ... (21.9)

There are thirteen examples of this pattern; in six instances the verb is in the impersonal form. In one instance the object is preceded by an adverbial clause in C_2 (10.29); here *ual dwy fflam o tan* functions as the object of *gwelit* and *ual* is thus probably not the preposition, but rather the noun 'form, manner'. In another sentence (14.16) the pronominal object *wynt* is preceded by a left-dislocated phrase (demonstrative *ar* specified by relative clause) which is taken up by the pronominal fronted object.

*1.5 Verbal-noun object + a + auxiliary verb (*gwneuthur*)*

Ac ymgeissaw a oruc ... (1.9), *A gwrthot hynny a oruc Iorwoerth* (1.15), *a mynet ar herw hyt yn Lloeger, a llad kalaned a llosgi tei a dala karcharoryon a oruc Iorwoerth* (1.17), *A gwedy eu heisted gofyn a orugant* ... (2.27), *A glasressawu a wnaethant* ... (3.4), *A chynneu tan gwrysc udunt a mynet y pobi a oruc y wreic* (3.5), *Ac rac annesmwythet gantunt eu kerdet dyffygyaw a orugant* (3.10), *A Ronabwy, hyt na allei na chyscu na gorffowys, medylyaw a oruc* ... (3.22), *Ac edrych a oruc* ... (4.1), *A rac druttet y gwelynt y marchawc dala ofyn a wnaethant* (4.14), *Ac eu hymlit a oruc y marchawc* (4.15), *A phan y gordiwedawd erchi nawd a orugant* ... (4.20), *nyt chwerthin a wnaf* (6.28), *A thynnu a oruc y marchawc* ... (8.4), *A gwedy eu dyuot hyt ym perued y Ryt ar Hafren troi a oruc Idawc* ... (9.11), *ac edrych a oruc Ronabwy* ... (9.12), *A disgyn a oruc y gwas* ... (11.13), *A thannu y llen a oruc* ... (11.16), *Ac eisted a oruc Arthur* ... (11.23), *A dechreu gware a wnaethant* (11.29), *A chyuarch gwell a oruc y mackwy* ... (12.13), *A gwybot a wnaeth Arthur* ... (12.16), *Teruynu y gware hwnnw a wnaethant* (13.1), *Dyuot a oruc y mackwy* ... (14.9), *Ac adnabot a orugant* ... (14.13), *A chyuarch gwell eissoes y Owein a oruc ef* (14.14), *A'e kyuodi y'r awyr a wneynt* (15.4), *Dyuot a oruc y marchawc* ... (16.6), *Ac adnabot a orugant* ... (16.8), *Ac edrych a oruc Arthur* ... (16.11), *A gware a wnaethant* (16.14), *Ymchoelut a oruc y marchawc* ... (16.15), *A chyfarch gwell a oruc y mackwy* ... (17.9), *Daruot a wnaeth* ... (17.16), *A dyuot a oruc y marchawc* ... (18.9), *Ac rac meint y kynnwrwf hwnnw deffroi a oruc Ronabwy* (21.5)

There are thirty-six instances of this pattern in the text. In six sentences an adverbial phrase precedes the verbal-noun object in C_2; in one sentence (3.22) a left-dislocated element co-referential with the subject contained in the finite verb and an adverbial clause precede the verbal-noun object. Sentence 6.28 is taken as a positive statement with the fronted verbal-noun negated for (correcting) emphasis, i.e. to correct the supposition contained in the preceding question "*beth a chwerdy di?*" (6.27), in accordance with T. A. Watkins's analysis (1983/84: 147).

1.6 Adverbial phrase + y + verb

A chystal y gwneynt ... (1.21), *A hyt yn Nillystwn Trefan yn y rychtir hwnnw yd ymrannassant* ... (2.3), *A phan doethant y mywn y gwelynt* ... (2.11), *Yn y lle y bei vrynn arnaw abreid y glynei* ... (2.13), *Yn y lle y bei bwll, dros vynwgyl y troet yd aei* ... (2.15), *A phan deuthant y kynted y ty y gwelynt* ... (2.19), *A phan delei annwyt arnei y byryei* ... (2.21), *Ac ar y parth arall y gwelynt* ... (2.24), *Ac y gyscu yd aethant* (3.19), *Ac yno y kysgwys* (3.24), *Ac yn gytneit ac yd aeth hun yn y lygeit y rodet* ... (3.25), *Ac val yd oed yn kerdet y clywei twryf* (3.29), *A phan rynnei y march y anadyl y wrthaw y pellaei* ... (4.16), *A phan y tynnei attaw y nesseynt* ... (4.18), *Ac nyt o'm henw y'm clywir* ... (4.25), *Idawc Cord Prydein y'm gelwir* (4.27), *ac rac vy chwannocket y vrwydyr y tervysgeis* ... (5.2), *pan ym gyrrei i yr amherawdyr* ... *a phan dywettei Arthur* ... *y dywedwn* ... (5.8), *Ac o hynny y gyrrwyt* ... (5.10), *Ac o hynny yd ystovet* ... (5.11), *Ac eissoes teirnos kynn gorffen y Gatgamlan yd ymedeweis* ... *ac y deuthum* ... (5.13), *Ac yno y bum* ... (5.14), *Ar hynny nachaf y clywynt* ... (5.16), *Ac yna y kerdassant* ... (6.6), *A milltir y wrth y Ryt o pob tu y'r fford y gwelynt* ... (6.8), *Ac y lan y Ryt y deuthant* (6.10), *Ac yna y dywawt* ... (7.3), *A gwedy hynny y gwelei* ... (7.9), *Ac ar hynny y gwelynt* ... (7.23), *Ac ual yd oed yn trossi penn y varch y trewis* ... (7.31), *Ac yna y dywawt* ... (8.20), *Ac odyna y gwelei* ... (9.24), *A phan ordiwedassant y llu neur disgynnassei* ... (10.3), *Ar fford y kerdei Arthur y gwelei* ... (10.5), *A gwedy y disgynnv y klywei* ... (10.6), *Ac ar hynny nachaf y gwelei* ... (10.10), *Ac ar hynny y clywynt* ... (11.8), *A phan yttoedynt uelly* ... *nachaf y gwelynt* ... (11.31), *Ac attat titheu y mae y neges ef* (12.20), *Ac yna y dywawt* ... (12.21), *Ac yna yd ymchoeles* ... (12.29), *A drwc yd aeth* ... (13.15), *Ac yna yd ymchoeles* ... (13.24), *Yn dyuot o'r pebyll y gwelynt* ... (13. 30), *Yn llaw y mackwy yd oed* ... (14.7), *Ac yna y dywawt* ... (14. 21), *Ac yna y kerdwys* ... (14.24), *Ac ual y dyrchefit y kyuodant* ... (14.26), *A gwedy kaffel eu hangerd* ..., *yn llidyawc orawenus yn gytneit y gostygassant* ... (14.31), *A phan edrychant y klywynt* ... (15.11), *Ac y wrth y kynnwryf y gwelynt* ... (16.22), *Ar glun y mackwy yd oed gledyf* ... (16.28), *A phan yttoedynt ar diwed y gware hwnnw, nachaf y klywynt* ... (17.18), *Ac yna y gwelynt* ... (17.23), *Yna yd erchis* ... (18.12), *Ac yna y gwasgwys ... ac yd erchis ...* (18.13-4,15), *Ac yna y gostyghwyt ac y tagnouedwyt ...* (18.16,17), *Yna y govynnwys ... ac y dywawt ...* (18.18,20), *Yna yd erchis ...* (20.20), *Ac ar hynny y trigywyt* (20.25), *Ac yna y kyuodes ... ac y dywawt* (21.1), *A phan deffroes yd oed ar groen ...* (21.6)

There are sixty-two instances of this pattern, including one sentence where the fronted constituent functions as predicate to *gelwir*. In sentence 10.3 *neur* is equi-functional with *y* (compare PKM 9.20 and 10.27). All verbal sentences with *nachaf* in the text are of the structure adv + *nachaf* + *y* + verb; *nachaf* is taken here as functioning as a sentence-constituent, thus all these sentences are considered to have double frontings. There are four further examples of double frontings, bringing the total to eight, and one example of triple fronting. In 4.25 the fronted adverbial is negated for contrastive emphasis (being known by name, *enw*, is contrasted with being known by nickname, *llysenw*); the analysis of the sentence as a positive statement is analogical to 6.28 (see above, (5)). In sentence (18.18,20) the punctuation of M. Richards has been changed to avoid a verb- initial reading (note the change of subject in the two co-ordinated clauses, but see 18.13-4, 15 for a parallel); in 5.8 his punctuation has been changed too.

In sentence 10.5 Richards reads *A'r*, conjunction 'and' plus definite article, but the use of the relative particle *y* in front of *kerdei* shows that *fford* is not marked as the direct object of this verb. An example for a transitive use of *kerdet* is found in the following sentence from *Ystorya Bown de Hamtwn*: *ac yskynnu a orugant ar eu meirch ar [= a'r] fford a gerdassant* (YBH, 3409-3411). It is better to read *ar*, the preposition, used with both *y kerdei* and *yn kerdet*. The phrase *Ar fford y kerdei Arthur* is a preposed expression fronted out of a verbal-noun expression * *yn kerdet ar fford y kerdei Arthur*: 'On the road Arthur was going he [Rhonabwy] could see himself and Iddawg going too'. Other examples of a similar use of *kerdet* with prepositional phrases are *ar hyt y fford honno y kerdawd* (YBH 1148-1149) and *yn y llog uawr honno y kerdassant ar y mor* (*Breuddwyd Maxen*, 6. 24-25).

1.7 Other sentence patterns

It is finally necessary to discuss one sentence not included in the survey above: *Madawc uab Maredud a oed idaw Powys yn y theruyneu* (1.1). This is the first sentence of the text. *Madawc uab Maredud* is left-dislocated, and the use of the relative pronoun *a* is ungrammatical here, since the fronted phrase is neither subject nor object of *oed*, but a *nominativus pendens* outside the construction of the sentence - it is taken up by the pronoun in *idaw*: 'Madog son of Maredudd, Powys belonged to him from end to end'. This construction is used here to introduce the name of a well-known person as the starting point of the narrative, and at the same time its historical setting is defined (see also Mac Cana (1973: 106-109) on stylistic properties of first sentences in MW stories).

Verbal sentences containing *sef* are also not included in the above survey; they are classified here according to the categories established by E. Evans (1958/60):

(a) substantival *sef* as predicate of copula:
Sef yw hynny (1.2), *Sef oed hwnnw* (1.5), *sef oed y enw* (2.4);

(b) substantival *sef* plus relative clause:
Sef a gawssant yn eu kyghor (1.11), *Ssef a oruc yr amherawdyr* (6.25), *Sef a wnaeth Arthur* (19.5);

(c) adjectival *sef* plus noun specified by a relative clause:
Sef y ryw teruysc a orugum (5.3) (see below).

In all these instances *sef* refers forward (i.e. cataphorically) to bring into relief some contextually important information.

(d) adverbial *sef y* plus verb:
Sef y kynnigywys ... (1.13), *Sef y kawssant* ... (1.19), *A phan doethant parth a'r ty, sef y gwelynt* ... (2.9), *Sef y gwelei*... (4.2), *Sef y gwelynt* ... (6.10), *Ssef y gwelynt* ... (7.26), *Sef y gwelei* ... (9.13), *Ar hynny sef y clywynt* ... (10.25), *Ac ual yd oedynt yn dechreu y symut kyntaf ar y gware, sef y gwelynt* ... (13.27), *A phan yttoedynt gwedy gware talym, sef y klywynt* ... (16.18), *Sef yd aeth* ... (19.7).

According to Evans (1958/60: 53) *sef y* in such sentences is synonymous with *felly* or *yna* (Engl. 'now, then') and similar expressions.

As can be seen from the examples above, an adverbial expression can precede *sef* only in type (d). This usage may be an indication that in these instances *sef* has not only lost its etymological meaning (< *ys ef*), but perhaps also that it has developed into some kind of preverbal particle (compare the similar sentences 2.9 and 2.11 with and without *sef*).

In the idiom *sef* with *cael yn y gynghor* both the relative pronoun *a* and the relative particle *y* can be used (see 1.11 and 1.19 and Evans (1958/60: 47-49, 54) for further examples).

Sentence 5.3 is not listed by Evans, but it clearly corresponds to his type adjectival *sef* plus noun specified by a relative clause (see Evans (1958/60: 52) for examples, e.g. *Sef attep a rodes Pwyll, "Nyt oed achaws ganthunt wy y erchi y mi yscar am gwreic ..."* (PKM 21.14-16)). The sentence referred to by *sef* consists of two fronted adverbial clauses and the main clause *y dywedwn ...*; this analysis, which is different from Richards's, is also implied in the translation of Jones and Jones (1974: 149):

> "This was the kind of strife I kindled: when the emperor Arthur would send me [...] and when Arthur would speak to me [...] I would speak those words the ugliest way I knew to Medrawd".

Furthermore, this sentence is another example of the sequence *sef* plus article plus noun which is found three times only among Evans's examples (1958/60: 51) and which in P. Mac Coisdealbha's view (1974: 54) contradicts the interpretation of *sef* as adjectival in such instances as proposed by E. Evans.

2. Discussion

The results of the survey of word-order patterns in positive statements in *Breudwyt Ronabwy* are summarized in the following table:

sentence type			
verb-initial	3	=	2,2%
pron. subj. + *a* + vb	9	=	6,5%
noun subj. + *a* + vb	16	=	11,5%
obj. + *a* + vb	13	=	9,3%
VN-obj. + *a* + aux. vb	36	=	25,9%
adv + *y* + vb	62	=	44,6%

The verb-initial type is rare; it was obviously avoided by writers of MW narrative prose, but it was not considered ungrammatical. Sentences with fronted adverbial phrases constitute a very high proportion of the examples, and this sentence type should therefore find more attention in the discussion of MW syntax. It should be noted that from the point of view of the information structure of the sentence the type with a fronted verbal-noun object has the main semantic content of the verbal phrase in sentence-initial position (unless another constituent occurs in C_2) and is thus similar to the verb-initial type (see also Fife (1986) for other features of this construction).

Double-frontings, i.e. sentences with constituents both in C_1 and C_2, are relatively rare in this text.

It is obvious that such statistics cannot yield any information about the function of an individual fronted constituent in its context. Since the approach taken here is descriptive, a functional analysis (e.g. along the lines of Poppe (1987) and Fife (1988)) would fall outside the scope of this contribution.

In the following table, the occurrences of the sentence-patterns in direct speech and in narrative are confronted:

sentence type	*direct speech*			*narrative*		
verb-initial	1	=	3,6%	2	=	1,8%
pron.subj.+*a*+vb	9	=	32,1%	0		
noun subj.+*a*+vb	4	=	14,3%	12	=	10,8%
obj.+*a*+vb	4	=	14,3%	9	=	8,1%
VN-obj.+*a*+aux.vb	1	=	3,6%	35	=	31,5%
adv.+*y*+vb	9	=	32,1%	53	=	47,7%

The differences between the two sets may be significant and require further research from a functional point of view, but also on the basis of statistics from other MW narrative texts.

In this final section sentences expressing the same or a similar information content will be compared with regard to their word-order patterns. The aim is to find out to what degree syntactic structure may be subject to variation. *Breudwyt Ronabwy* is especially suited for such an analysis because of the repetition or near repetition of parallel events in the tale, primarily during the six games of *gwyddbwyll* between Arthur and Owein.

The following sets of sentences express comparable information contents:

(1a) *A phan doethant parth a'r ty, sef y gwelynt hen neuad ...* (2.9)

(1b) *A phan doethant y mywn y gwelynt lawr* ... (2.11)
(1c) *A phan deuthant y kynted y ty y gwelynt partheu* ... (2.19)

The only difference here is the use of adverbial *sef* in (1a), see also sets (3) and (4).

(2a) *A gwedy hynny y gwelei vydin yn dyuot* ... (7.9)
(2b) *Ac ar hynny y gwelynt vydin arall yn dyuot* ... (7.23)

There is no difference with regard to syntactic structure between these two sentences.

(3a) *Ar hynny sef y clywynt galw ar Gadwr* ... (10.25)
(3b) *Ac ar hynny y clywynt galw ar Eiryn Wych Amheibyn* ... (11.8)

The only difference here is the use of adverbial *sef* in (3.a), see also sets (1) and (4).

In the following set of sentences the interruption of the game of *gwyddbwyll* is described:

(4a) *A phan yttoedynt ..., nachaf y gwelynt* ... (11.31)
(4b) *Ac ual yd oedynt ..., sef y gwelynt* ... (13.27)
(4c) *A phan edrychant y klywynt* ... (15.11)
(4d) *A phan yttoedynt ..., sef y klywynt* ... (16.18) continued by: *Ac y wrth y kynnwryf y gwelynt* ... (16.22)
(4e) *A phan yttoedynt ..., nachaf y klywynt* ... (17.18) continued by: *Ac yna y gwelynt* ... (17.23)

These sentences belong to the same type and have the same basic structure, they differ only with regard to the use of adverbial *nachaf* and *sef*, which bring into relief the information following the finite verb. Only in the second round of *gwyddbwyll* is the interruption of the game described in a non-finite sentence: *A phan ..., llyma* ... (13.2-5). The sentences continuing (4d) and (4c) are also of the same basic structure.

In the following set of sentences the approach of the messenger is described:

(5a) *Dyuot a oruc y mackwy yn llidyawc ... tu a'r lle yd oed Arthur* ... (14.9)
(5b) *Dyuot a oruc y marchawc tu a'r lle yd oed Arthur* ... (16.6)

(5c) *A dyuot a oruc y marchawc yn llidiawc y'r lle yd oed Arthur* ... (18.9)

All these sentences represent the same type.

The following identical set of sentences reveals that the messenger's emotions are known to Arthur and Owein:

(6a) *Ac adnabot a orugant y vot yn llidiawc.* (14.13)
(6b) *Ac adnabot a orugant y uot yn lludedic lityawcvlin yn dyuot attunt.* (16.8)

In the following set of sentences the salutation of the messenger is described:

(7a) *A chyuarch gwell a oruc y mackwy y Owein* (12.13)
(7b) *A chyuarch gwell eissoes y Owein a oruc ef* (14.14)
(7c) *Y mackwy a gyuarchawd gwell y Arthur* (16.9)
(7d) *A chyfarch gwell a oruc y mackwy y'r amherawdyr* (17.9)

Only in the second round of *gwyddbyll* is the address of the messenger expressed in a non-finite sentence: *A chyuarch gwell idaw* (13.15). Three sentences are of the same structure, they differ with regard to the position of the directional adjuncts of the fronted verbal noun. In sentence (7b) the fronting of *y Owein* together with the verbal noun may be conditioned by the adversative adverb *eissoes* as part of the verbal phrase. Sentence (7c) differs structurally: here the subject is fronted. The reason for this difference is not immediately clear from a comparison of the contexts. The following set of sentences introduces the address of the messenger:

(8a) *Ac yna y dywawt y mackwy wrth Owein* (12.21)
(8b) *Y mackwy a dywawt wrth Owein* (13.17)

Here the two sentences represent different sentence-types, the immediately preceding contexts are different as well. In the case of (8a), Arthur addresses Owein in direct speech; in the case of (8b), the feelings of Owein are described. This may have influenced to some degree the selection of the fronted constituent as a means to organize the flow of information in the sentence.

The following set of sentences describes the return of the messenger:

(9a) *Ac yna yd ymchoeles y mackwy tu a'e bebyll* (12.29)

(9b) *Ac yna yd ymchoeles y mackwy tu a'e pebyll* (13.24)
(9c) *Ac yna y kerdwys y mackwy racdaw hyt y lle* ... (14.24)
(9d) *Ymchoelut a oruc y marchawc drachefyn tu a'r vrwydyr* (16.15)

The first three sentences have the same structure. Sentence (9d) has a different context: the other sentences immediately follow a direct speech of Arthur or Owein, whereas this sentence follows the statement that they begin another game (see (10d)).

The last set of sentences describes the end of one game of *gwyddbwyll* and the resumption of another:

(10a) *A dechreu gware a wnaethant* (11.29)
(10b) *Teruynu y gware hwnnw a wnaethant a dechreu arall* (13.1)
(10c) *Y gware hwnnw a teruynwyt a dechreu arall* (13.25)
(10d) *A gware a wnaethant* (16.14)
(10e) *Daruot a wnaeth y gware hwnnw a dechreu arall* (17.16)

These sentences are basically of the same structure, the fronted constituent is the object in all cases. In four sentences this object is a verbal noun as object of the auxiliary verb *gwneuthur*, in one sentence it is the direct object of a verb in the impersonal form.

This survey shows that variation in word-order and sentence types is remarkably infrequent in sentences expressing the same or, at least, a very similar information content. This stability of the word-order patterns in comparable sentences may have important consequences for the understanding of the so-called 'abnormal sentence', since it seems to indicate that the selection of the fronted constituent does not depend on a purely stylistic principle of *variatio* (as seems to be implied e.g. in some of T. J. Morgan's remarks (1951: 167-170) about sentence-structure in the *Pedair Keinc*).

References

Breuddwyd Maxen (1927) ed. I. Williams. Bangor: Jarvis a Foster.

Breudwyt Ronabwy (1948) ed. M. Richards. Caerdydd: Gwasg Prifysgol Cymru (repr. 1980).

Evans, E. (1958/60) Cystrawennau 'Sef' mewn Cymraeg Canol. *BBCS,* **18,** 38-54.

Evans, D. S. (1964) *A Grammar of Middle Welsh.* Dublin: Dublin Institute for Advanced Studies (repr. 1976).

Fife, J. (1986) The Semantics of *gwneud* Inversions. *BBCS,* **33,** 133-144.

Fife, J. (1988) *Functional Syntax. A Case Study in Middle Welsh.* Lublin: Redakcja Wydawnictw KUL.

Foster, I. Ll. (1959) Culhwch and Olwen and Rhonabwy's Dream. In R. S. Loomis, (ed.) *Arthurian Literature in the Middle Ages.* Oxford: Clarendon Press. Pp 31-43.

Giffin, M. (1958) The Date of the 'Dream of Rhonabwy'. *Transactions of the Honourable Society of Cymmrodorion,* 33-40.

Jones, G. and Jones, Th. (1974) *The Mabinogi.* London, New York: Dent- Dutton (repr. 1975).

Jones, R. M. (1986) Narrative Structure in Medieval Welsh Prose Tales. In D. E. Evans, J. G. Griffith, and E. M. Jope, (eds.) *Proceedings of the Seventh International Congress of Celtic Studies.* Oxford. Pp 171-198.

Mac Cana, P. (1973) Celtic Word Order and the Welsh 'Abnormal Sentence'. *Ériu,* **24,** 90-120.

Mac Cana, P. (1977) *The Mabinogi.* Cardiff: University of Wales Press.

Mac Cana, P. (1979/80) Notes on the 'Abnormal Sentence'. *SC,* **14/15,** 174-187.

Mac Coisdealbha, P. (1974) *The Syntax of the Sentence in Old Irish.* Diss. phil. Bochum.

Morgan, T. J. (1951) *Ysgrifau Llenyddol.* Llundain: W. Griffiths a'i frodyr.

Parry, Th. (1955) *A History of Welsh Literature.* Oxford: Clarendon Press.

Parry-Williams, T. H. (1922) Yny. *BBCS*, **1**, 103.

Pedeir Keinc y Mabinogi (1930) ed. I. Williams. Caerdydd: Gwasg Prifysgol Cymru (repr. 1978).

Poppe, E. (1987) A Functional Approach to Middle Welsh Word Order. Paper given at the *Eighth International Congress of Celtic Studies*, Swansea.

Richards, M. (1948) Rhagymaddrodd. *Breudwyt Ronabwy*, ix-xlv.

Roberts, B. F. (1976) Tales and Romances. In A. O. H. Jarman and G. R. Hughes, (eds.) *A Guide to Welsh Literature*, vol. 1. Swansea: Christopher Davies. Pp 203-243.

Watkins, T. A. (1977/78) Trefn yn y Frawddeg Gymraeg. *SC*, **12/13**, 367-395.

Watkins, T. A. (1983/84) Trefn y Constitwentau Brawddegol yn Branwen. *SC*, **18/19**, 147-157.

Watkins, T. A. (1987) Constituent Order in the Old Welsh Verbal Sentence. *BBCS*, **34**, 51-60.

Watkins, T. A. (1988) *Constituent Order in the Positive Declarative Sentence in the Medieval Welsh Tale 'Kulhwch ac Olwen'*. Innsbruck: Institut für Sprachwissenschaft (= Innsbrucker Beiträge zur Sprachwissenschaft: Vorträge und kleinere Schriften 41).

Ystorya Bown de Hamtwn (1958) ed. M. Watkin. Caerdydd: Gwasg Prifysgol Cymru.

Author Index

Subject Index

In the CURRENT ISSUES IN LINGUISTIC THEORY (CILT) series (Series Editor: E.F. Konrad Koerner) the following volumes have been published thus far, and will be published during 1990:

1. KOERNER, E.F. Konrad (ed.): *The Transformational-Generative Paradigm and Modern Linguistic Theory*. Amsterdam, 1975.
2. WEIDERT, Alfons: *Componential Analysis of Lushai Phonology*. Amsterdam, 1975.
3. MAHER, J. Peter: *Papers on Language Theory and History I: Creation and Tradition in Language*. Foreword by Raimo Anttila. Amsterdam, 1977.
4. HOPPER, Paul J. (ed.): *Studies in Descriptive and Historical Linguistics: Festschrift for Winfred P. Lehmann*. Amsterdam, 1977. Out of print.
5. ITKONEN, Esa: *Grammatical Theory and Metascience: A critical investigation into the methodological and philosophical foundations of 'autonomous' linguistics*. Amsterdam, 1978.
6. ANTTILA, Raimo: *Historical and Comparative Linguistics*. Amsterdam/Philadelphia, 1989.
7. MEISEL, Jürgen M. & Martin D. PAM (eds): *Linear Order and Generative Theory*. Amsterdam, 1979.
8. WILBUR, Terence H.: *Prolegomena to a Grammar of Basque*. Amsterdam, 1979.
9. HOLLIEN, Harry & Patricia (eds): *Current Issues in the Phonetic Sciences, Proceedings of the IPS-77 Congress, Miami Beach, Fla., 17-19 December 1977*. Amsterdam, 1979. 2 vols.
10. PRIDEAUX, Gary (ed.): *Perspectives in Experimental Linguistics. Papers from the University of Alberta Conference on Experimental Linguistics, Edmonton, 13-14 Oct. 1978*. Amsterdam, 1979.
11. BROGYANYI, Bela (ed.): *Studies in Diachronic, Synchronic, and Typological Linguistics: Festschrift for Oswald Szemerényi on the Occasion of his 65th Birthday*. Amsterdam, 1980.
12. FISIAK, Jacek (ed.): *Theoretical Issues in Contrastive Linguistics*. Amsterdam, 1980.
13. MAHER, J. Peter with coll. of Allan R. Bomhard & E.F. Konrad Koerner (ed.): *Papers from the Third International Conference on Historical Linguistics, Hamburg, August 22-26, 1977*. Amsterdam, 1982.
14. TRAUGOTT, Elizabeth C., Rebecca LaBRUM, Susan SHEPHERD (eds): *Papers from the Fourth International Conference on Historical Linguistics, Stanford, March 26-30, 1980*. Amsterdam, 1980.
15. ANDERSON, John (ed.): *Language Form and Linguistic Variation. Papers dedicated to Angus McIntosh*. Amsterdam, 1982.
16. ARBEITMAN, Yoël & Allan R. BOMHARD (eds): *Bono Homini Donum: Essays in Historical Linguistics, in Memory of J. Alexander Kerns*. Amsterdam, 1981.
17. LIEB, Hans-Heinrich: *Integrational Linguistics*. 6 volumes. Amsterdam, 1984-1986. Vol. I available; Vol. 2-6 n.y.p.
18. IZZO, Herbert J. (ed.): *Italic and Romance. Linguistic Studies in Honor of Ernst Pulgram*. Amsterdam, 1980.
19. RAMAT, Paolo et al. (eds): *Linguistic Reconstruction and Indo-European Syntax. Proceedings of the Coll. of the 'Indogermanische Gesellschaft' Univ. of Pavia, 6-7 Sept. 1979*. Amsterdam, 1980.
20. NORRICK, Neal R.: *Semiotic Principles in Semantic Theory*. Amsterdam, 1981.
21. AHLQVIST, Anders (ed.): *Papers from the Fifth International Conference on Historical Linguistics, Galway, April 6-10, 1981*. Amsterdam, 1982.

22. UNTERMANN, Jürgen & Bela BROGYANYI (eds): *Das Germanische und die Rekonstruktion der Indogermanische Grundsprache.* Akten, Proceedings from the Colloquium of the Indogermanische Gesellschaft, Freiburg, 26-27 February 1981. Amsterdam, 1984.
23. DANIELSEN, Niels: *Papers in Theoretical Linguistics.* Amsterdam, n.y.p.
24. LEHMANN, Winfred P. & Yakov MALKIEL (eds): *Perspectives on Historical Linguistics. Papers from a conference held at the meeting of the Language Theory Division, Modern Language Ass., San Francisco, 27-30 December 1979.* Amsterdam, 1982.
25. ANDERSEN, Paul Kent: *Word Order Typology and Comparative Constructions.* Amsterdam, 1983.
26. BALDI, Philip (ed.) *Papers from the XIIth Linguistic Symposium on Romance Languages, University Park, April 1-3, 1982.* Amsterdam, 1984.
27. BOMHARD, Alan: *Toward Proto-Nostratic.* Amsterdam, 1984.
28. BYNON, James: *Current Progress in Afroasiatic Linguistics: Papers of the Third International Hamito-Semitic Congress, London, 1978.* Amsterdam, 1984.
29. PAPROTTÉ, Wolf & René DIRVEN (eds): *The Ubiquity of Metaphor: Metaphor in Language and Thought.* Amsterdam, 1985.
30. HALL, Robert A., Jr.: *Proto-Romance Morphology*. Amsterdam, 1984.
31. GUILLAUME, Gustave: *Foundations for a Science of Language*. Translated and with an introd. by Walter Hirtle and John Hewson. Amsterdam, 1984.
32. COPELAND, James E. (ed.): *New Directions in Linguistics and Semiotics*. Houston/ Amsterdam, 1984. No rights for US/Can. *Customers from USA and Canada: please order from Rice University*.
33. VERSTEEGH, Kees: *Pidginization and Creolization: The Case of Arabic*. Amsterdam, 1984.
34. FISIAK, Jacek (ed.): *Papers from the VIth International Conference on Historical Linguistics, Poznan, 22-26 August 1983.* Amsterdam, 1985.
35. COLLINGE, N.E.: *The Laws of Indo-European*. Amsterdam, 1985.
36. KING, Larry D. & Catherine A. MALEY (eds): *Selected Papers from the XIIIth Linguistics Symposium on Romance Languages*. Amsterdam, 1985.
37. GRIFFEN, T.D.: *Aspects of Dynamic Phonology*. Amsterdam, 1985.
38. BROGYANYI, Bela & Thomas KRÖMMELBEIN (eds): *Germanic Dialects: Linguistic and Philological Investigations*. Amsterdam, 1986.
39. BENSON, James D., Michael J. CUMMINGS & William S. GREAVES (eds): *Linguistics in a Systemic Perspective*. Amsterdam, 1988.
40. FRIES, Peter Howard and Nancy (eds): *Toward an Understanding of Language: Charles C. Fries in Perspective.* Amsterdam, 1985.
41. EATON, Roger, et al. (eds): *Papers from the 4th International Conference on English Historical Linguistics*. Amsterdam, 1985.
42. MAKKAI, Adam & Alan K. MELBY (eds): *Linguistics and Philosophy. Essays in honor of Rulon S. Wells.* Amsterdam, 1985.
43. AKAMATSU, Tsutomu: *The Theory of Neutralization and the Archiphoneme in Functional Phonology*. Amsterdam, 1988.
44. JUNGRAITHMAYR, Herrmann & Walter W. MUELLER (eds): *Proceedings of the 4th International Hamito-Semitic Congress*. Amsterdam, 1987.
45. KOOPMAN, W.F., F.C. VAN DER LEEK, O. FISCHER & R. EATON (eds): *Explanation and Linguistic Change*. Amsterdam, 1987.

46. PRIDEAUX, Gary D., and William J. BAKER: *Strategies and Structures: The Processing of Relative Clauses*. Amsterdam, 1986.
47. LEHMANN, Winfred P.: *Language Typology 1985. Papers from the Linguistic Typology Symposium, Moscow, 9-13 Dec. 1985*. Amsterdam, 1986.
48. RAMAT, Anna Giacalone (ed.): *Proceedings of the VII International Conference on Historical Linguistics, Pavia 9-13 September 1985*. Amsterdam, 1987.
49. WAUGH, Linda R. & Stephen RUDY (eds): *New Vistas in Grammar: Invariance and Variation*. Amsterdam/Philadelphia, 1990. n.y.p.
50. RUDZKA-OSTYN, Brygida (ed.): *Topics in Cognitive Linguistics*. Amsterdam/Philadelphia, 1988.
51. CHATTERJEE, Ranjit: *Aspect and Meaning in Slavic and Indic*. Amsterdam/Philadelphia, 1988.
52. FASOLD, Ralph & Deborah SCHIFFRIN (eds): *Language Change and Variation*. Amsterdam/Philadelphia, 1989.
53. SANKOFF, David (ed.): *Diversity and Diachrony*. Amsterdam, 1986.
54. WEIDERT, Alfons: *Tibeto-Burman Tonology. A Comparative Analysis*. Amsterdam, 1987.
55. HALL, Robert A. Jr.: *Linguistics and Pseudo-Linguistics*. Amsterdam, 1987.
56. HOCKETT, Charles F.: *Refurbishing our Foundations. Elementary Linguistics from an Advanced Point of View*. Amsterdam, 1987.
57. BUBENIK, Vít: *Hellenistic and Roman Greece as a Sociolinguistic Area*. Amsterdam/Philadelphia, 1989.
58. ARBEITMAN, Yoël L.: *FUCUS. A Semitic/Afrasian Gathering in Remembrance of Albert Ehrman*. Amsterdam/Philadelphia, 1988.
59. VOORST, Jan van: *Event Structure*. Amsterdam/Philadelphia, 1988.
60. KIRSCHNER, Carl and Janet DECESARIS (eds): *Studies in Romance Linguistics*. Amsterdam/Philadelphia, 1989.
61. CORRIGAN, Roberta, Fred ECKMAN and Michael NOONAN (eds): *Linguistic Categorization*. Amsterdam/Philadelphia, 1989.
62. FRAJZYNGIER, Zygmunt (ed.): *Current Progress in Chadic Linguistics*. Amsterdam/Philadelphia, 1989.
63. EID, Mushira (ed.): *Perspectives on Arabic Linguistics I. Papers from the First Annual Symposium on Arabic Linguistics*. Amsterdam/Philadelphia, 1990.
64. BROGYANYI, Bela and Reiner LIPP (eds): *Essays in Linguistics. Offered in honor of Oswald Szemerényi on the occasion of his 75th birthday*. Amsterdam/Philadelphia, n.y.p. 1990.
65. ADAMSON, Sylvia, Vivien A. LAW, Nigel VINCENT and Susan WRIGHT (eds): *Papers from the 5th International Conference of English Historical Linguistics*. Amsterdam/Philadelphia, 1990.
66. ANDERSEN, Henning and Konrad KOERNER (eds): *Historical Linguistics 1987. Papers from the 8th International Conference on Historical Linguistics, Lille, August 30-September 4, 1987*. Amsterdam/Philadelphia, 1990.
67. LEHMANN, Winfred (ed.): *Language Typology 1987. Systematic Balance in Language. Papers from the Linguistic Typology Symposium, Berkeley, 1-3 December 1987*. Amsterdam/Philadelphia, 1990.
68. BALL, Martin, James FIFE, Erich POPPE and Jenny ROWLAND (eds): *Celtic Linguistics / Ieithyddiaeth Geltaidd. Readings in the Brythonic Languages. Festschrift for T. Arwyn Watkins*. Amsterdam/Philadelphia, 1990.

69. WANNER, Dieter and Douglas A. KIBBEE (eds): *New Analyses in Romance Linguistics. Papers from the XVIII Linguistic Symposium on Romance Languages, Urbana-Champaign, April 7-9, 1988*. Amsterdam/Philadelphia, n.y.p.
70. JENSEN, John T.: *Morphology. Word Structure in Generative Grammar*. Amsterdam/Philadelphia, 1990.
71. O'GRADY, WILLIAM: *Categories and Case. The sentence structure of Korean.* Amsterdam/Philadelphia, n.y.p.
72. EID, Mushira and John McCARTHY (eds): *Perspectives on Arabic Linguistics II Papers from the Second Annual Symposium on Arabic Linguistics*. Amsterdam/ Philadelphia, 1990.